The Philosophy
of (Erotic) Love

The Philosophy of (Erotic) Love

Edited by
Robert C. Solomon and
Kathleen M. Higgins

Foreword by Arthur C. Danto

University Press
of Kansas

For Our Friends

For source notes and additional copyright
information see page 519

Published by the University Press of Kansas (Lawrence, Kansas
66049), which was organized by the Kansas Board of Regents and is
operated and funded by Emporia State University, Fort Hays State
University, Kansas State University, Pittsburg State University, the
University of Kansas, and Wichita State University

Library of Congress Cataloging-in-Publication Data
The Philosophy of (erotic) love / edited by Robert C. Solomon and
Kathleen M. Higgins : foreword by Arthur C. Danto.
p. cm.
Includes bibliographical references.
ISBN 0-7006-0479-0 (alk. paper). – ISBN 0-7006-0480-4
(pbk. : alk. paper)
1. Love 2. Sex I. Solomon, Robert C. II. Higgins, Kathleen Marie.
BD436.P45 1991   90–19340
128'.4–dc20

British Library Cataloguing in Publication Data is available.

Printed in the United States of America
10 9 8 7 6 5
The paper used in this publication meets the
minimum requirements of the American National Standard
for Permanence of Paper for Printed Library Materials
Z39.48-1984.

i

ii

iii

iv

Arthur C. Danto

Foreword

Stand still, and I will read to thee
A lecture, Love, in love's philosophy.
John Donne, A Lecture upon the Shadow

Ironically diffident on behalf of his cognitive powers, famously disposed to
say he at best knows that he knows nothing, Socrates makes a suspicious
and uncharacteristic exception in his discourse on love — the only subject, I
think him sincere in claiming, about which he understands anything at all.
What he understands is that the object of love is Beauty, but "in its essence
and unalloyed . . . instead of a beauty tainted by human flesh and color
and a perishable mass of rubbish"— by "this muddy vesture of decay," as
Shakespeare speaks of it in a platonic moment. Socrates' effort is to connect
love with philosophy in such a way that they come out one — "Love must be
a lover of Wisdom," he contends at one point, and as we know, "lover of
wisdom" is what "philosopher" etymologically breaks down into. Both
theses are so out of phase with anything I would recognize as love — which
is achingly of enfleshed humans by enfleshed humans in all our perish-
ability — that I early concluded that philosophy could address the vivid subject of love only by changing it.

Such is the will-to-power of philosophers that they will set up some
ghostly effigy of an important subject and then use all their logical muscle,
as in the example of Socrates, to wrestle their readers into believing they
have gotten to the heart of things. In truth, one can talk about love as love,
one feels, only in some other mode — like that of Alcibiades, for example,
who stumbles drunk into the *Symposium* just after Socrates has completed
his preposterous panegyric, and improvises a love poem on the subject of
Socrates, that paradigmatically ugly comedian, a poem so particular, so totally a portrait, that we ourselves become in reading it lovers of Socrates,
despite his touching windiness and his sham argumentative shrewdness. It
is as if Plato were intent on demonstrating that Love lies outside the philosophical repertoire, if Socrates is the exemplary philosopher doing his best,
and at the same time demonstrating, *against* Socrates, that love, even of

beings as worthy as Socrates, goes no distance whatever toward making the lover a good person, Alcibiades being the worst sort of person since the perversion of one who could have been morally great. The *Symposium* is one of the most mysterious and self-deconstructing exercises in the history of literature, but it at least shows what typically happens when we try philosophically to talk about love. We turn it into philosophy, and in so doing lose touch with the reality everyone cherishes. In the great, witty preface to *Beyond Good and Evil*, Nietzsche exploits the fact that Truth takes the feminine gender in German, in order to question "the terrible seriousness and clumsy importunity" with which philosophers have addressed Truth — *Die Wahrheit* — as "unskilled and unseemly methods for winning a woman." As grammar would have it, Love is a woman as well — *Die Liebe* — and if philosophical overtures to Truth, about which philosophers ought to have something natural to say, are oblique and maladroit, what hope for a philosophy of love when Love, to Plato's chagrin, has only ears for poetry?

Socrates addresses love as he elsewhere addresses the philosophically more tractable subject of belief, noting that both are transitive. In the *Theatetus*, he argues that to believe is to believe *something*, which is unexceptionable, but then goes on, especially in the *Republic*, to seek for the defining traits of the *objects* of belief which, on his view, had to differ from the objects of knowledge. In the *Symposium* he similarly argues that to love is to love *something*, and he then presses on to identify the objects of love — and in particular what makes them lovable, the answer being Beauty. This gets things absolutely backwards, as the poet Sappho recognizes, getting it right. It is not Beauty that makes things objects of love but love that makes its objects beautiful. *Whatever* one loves is the finest sight on earth — even, improbably, a snub-nosed, pot-bellied logic chopper when the object of Alcibiades' passion. It is characteristic of platonic metaphysics to have sought the one common feature in all cases of love, whereas it is the fine and funny truth that there are as many lovable things as there are loves. It is Sappho's truth that accounts for the comedy of love — the wild implausibility that queens as radiant as dewdrops should go mad for love of donkey-headed louts, when it is a standing question, for her to be sure, but for all the shes and hes of history, of what does she see in him or he in her? Socrates perhaps was looking for what perhaps *deserves* to be loved. But it is part of the actual truth of love that the cracked hearts that deserve but do not receive the love they merit vastly outnumber those that receive the love they merit, but ordinarily not because they merit it. Love is a philosophically unruly being, and the despair of moral epistemologists.

Philosophers should be more astute than even the Greek poets were in handling today the inference that, since to love is to love something, there must in every case *be* something that is the object of love. If the parallel with belief holds, then "loves" is an *intentional* state, the object of which is the content of that state. My own view of belief is that it is a relationship between an individual and a representation the believer holds true, and the "something" that is believed is just that representation. By parity, I should think, the object of love is the content of the love-state, or the *representation* of someone as the lover's beloved. It is always legitimate for that person to ask what it is that the lover loves her or him *for*, what in her or him the lover finds lovable. And the answer will refer to the components of the representation, providing the lover is able to state what they are. The advantage to the beloved is that the representation can survive all sorts of changes in the beloved, so that the lover can truthfully say such things as that, for him, she will always be the lithe dancer, the slender flower, the shy and tender flaxen-haired wraith that promised paradise, whatever time has wrought. And representations are selective, so that the beloved's faults need not figure in the object of the love state. Intentionality also, of course, makes it possible to love what might not or does not exist, or to fall in love with fictional beings like the Duchesse de Guermantes or Socrates.

There are some further parallels. To believe that *p* is to believe that *p* is true, not because one believes it, but because of the way things are. And that means that believers cannot believe that they hold their beliefs only because they want to, or that they can change them when they care to change them. We are just as little capable of loving at will, and certainly explain our love with reference to those properties in the beloved for which we love her or him. We fall in love, but it is not too much to say that we equally fall into belief. And though beliefs change, they do not change easily or rapidly, so we do not expect people to fall in and out of love easily or rapidly. Someone may change sexual partners with some frequency and rapidity, but love partnership is a more enduring thing.

Unlike sex, in fact, love is not really a relationship, at least not directly, between individuals, any more than belief is a direct relationship between the believer and the world. It is rather a relationship between individuals and representations. Thus the lover loves the beloved only as he or she represents the latter. The beloved is then the individual represented — or misrepresented — by the lover. And as a belief is not an inert furnishing of the mind, but disposes the believer to behave in certain ways, neither is love a mere state of the soul: it too disposes the lover to behave, in extreme cases, as foolishly as Alcibiades at the dinner table, in his cups. And this will be extremely oppressive to the beloved unless there is an answering representation. Knowing one is loved gives one a reason to return love, but no more in the beloved than in the lover is love something over which the will holds any dominion. We prefer to think of love in terms of two hearts that beat as one, but the truth of love again is more raucous and farcical or — as Socrates seems to be saying at the end of the *Symposium* — more tragic, which comes to the same thing.

But I am here not to read to thee a lecture, but to introduce an anthology. But I took the opportunity to demonstrate how incorrigibly stiff philosophy is when it undertakes to lay its icy fingers on the frilled and beating wings of the butterfly of love. Or this philosopher is, as was Socrates, who of course belongs in the anthology anyway. Perhaps there is something a bit absurd in the very idea of a philosophy of love, as comic as the yoked crazy representations of Titania and Bottom. What exactly will Philosophy and Love have to say to one another across the breakfast table?

Philosophy: $\ulcorner(x)(y)[x \text{ love } y \supset (\Sigma w)$ w is a representation such that........)))))]$\urcorner$

Love: $\heartsuit$ How I do dote upon thee . . . . $\heartsuit$

Well, Robert Solomon and Kathleen Higgins, experts on both, have brought together the classic texts with an assembly of classy amorologists in an effort to make harmony out of mismatched personae. It may sound like braying to the lute, but who knows, dear reader, what sweet resolutions may not echo in the heart when you are done, and what clarity not find room in mind and heart?

Robert C. Solomon and Kathleen M. Higgins

Introduction

Love has always been one of the favorite themes of philosophy, even if it has only rarely emerged as a minor theme in most philosophers. Romantic love, in our time, has achieved something of the status of a global obsession. Deep philosophical questions infiltrate even our least thoughtful popular magazines: What is the essential nature of love? How does one know when one comes across the "real thing"? What is the meaning of love? Is it first of all a feeling or is it primarily a mode of behavior? Is it basic biology or is it the product of culture and cultivation? How can sexual desire turn into such a noble emotion, or must "true love," as many authors have argued, put sex in second place if not leave it behind? Is it possible to love more than one person? Why is love so good, so important, so necessary? Or is it so good? Is it necessary at all? Isn't it possible that love could be a disruptive force in human society, an idle entertainment appropriate only to idle aristocrats, a neurotic obsession that impedes healthy self-realization, or even a conspiracy by men to keep women in subservient roles? The philosophy of love is as filled with suspicion as it is with praise. But many philosophers have themselves been suspiciously silent on love, as if it were overly sexual or "too subjective" to be worthy of serious theoretical attention.

One of the first great works of philosophy, however, was Plato's *Symposium*. That dialogue is wholly devoted to the praise and analysis of love. Two of the greatest philosophers of our time, Bertrand Russell and Jean-Paul Sartre, devoted considerable energy to the subject. Indeed, if one looks through the millions of pages concerning the conditions of knowledge and the references of signs, one can find some substantial philosophical literature on the topic of love. Nevertheless, if it now seems odd to us that one of Plato's characters (Pausanias) complains (at the beginning of the *Symposium*) that the poets have had virtually nothing to say about love, so too it should strike us as extremely odd how little so many great philosophers have had to say on the subject of erotic love.

Perhaps some partial explanation is to be found in the fact that so many of the definitive figures of the Western philosophical tradition were male bachelors. And then, of course, erotic love as such—as opposed to more spiritual versions of love—has been in ill repute throughout most of the Christian Era. Some of the greatest writing about it has, accordingly, taken the form of a warning or a diagnosis. Moreover, writing about love— as opposed to speculating about the mathematical talents of the human mind or the ontological status of numbers—carries with it the very real danger of unintended self-betrayal, even for the most cautious thinker. What seems at first to be an obvious point about sexual desire turns out to be an embarrassing confession of eccentricity; what is argued to be a general feature of love turns out to be no more than a prominent feature of the author's last failed marriage. Thus we look in vain for some deep or sensitive insight into erotic love, even in passing, in the supposedly most encyclopedic thinkers—in Immanuel Kant, for example, or even in Aristotle, who does talk at considerable length about friendship but says little about eros. Philosophy, the discipline whose very name includes reference to love (though "phil-" rather than "eros"), has offered us less than it should by way of insight into what is often taken (even by philosophers) to be our most profound emotion.

And yet philosophy begins with love; it is Socrates' theme as well as the subject matter of the *Symposium*. The erotic longing for another beautiful human being is the first step on a ladder that elevates us to an appreciation of beauty as such and so to philosophical wisdom as well. Perhaps no one else in the Western tradition would tie eros and wisdom so tightly together, but whether or not that tradition is nothing but "a series of footnotes to Plato" (as Whitehead once wrote in a fit of enthusiasm) we should expect that the issues surrounding the nature and stature of love discussed in the *Symposium* will in one form or another turn out to be basic to those questions that have more obviously defined philosophy. Indeed, many of the seminal discussions of faith and love as well as broader questions of metaphysics and the nature of God in the Christian tradition return again and again to the Socratic analysis of eros in the *Symposium*, even while rejecting eros as such. Modern questions about the relationship between the mind and the body raise just those issues in which the nature of erotic love is or ought to be central, and at least some of the greatest modern philosophers—Spinoza, Schopenhauer and Sartre, for example—have considered the nature of erotic desire and love to lie at the very heart of ethics.

Of course, no one with any historical sense would restrict the history of philosophy to that limited list of authors traditionally designated "philosophers" by philosophy professors, and the history of work on the philosophy of love would be impoverished indeed if we did not allow ourselves to look to poets, novelists, and other students of human nature for philosophical insights, so long as we keep in mind that our goal is insight and understanding rather than mere romantic expression and edification. The philosophy of love consists of ideas about love, what it is, what purpose (if any) it serves in the well-lived human life. Not surprisingly, we can expect to find the best answers not always in those who have thought the "deepest" but in those who have lived the fullest, those who have lived thoughtfully through love rather than just thought abstractly about it.

The overriding question in the philosophy of love, a nagging doubt that will not go away, is *whose* concept of love is at issue. The fact that most of those philosophers who wrote at length about love were male is not to be taken lightly. Is our understanding of love a peculiarly male understanding, yet another aspect of some more or less universal masculine outlook on the world, on human relationships, on our relation to our own and others' bodies? Simone de Beauvoir famously wrote that "men and women understand love quite differently. That is why they do not understand one another." Would a fair representation by female authors (which we have tried to provide here) give us a very different account of love, a different perspective, a different philosophy? Or would the differences be wholly explicable in terms of other social role and status differences, differences in power? To put the questions differently, do men and women have different *concepts* of love — that is, the word "love" actually has different meanings for them — or is it rather that their different and sometimes antagonistic perspectives on the pragmatics of love provide them with different *conceptions* of love, alternative understandings of the same phenomenon?

Yet this question, this doubt, is not limited to the much-touted conceptual "battle between the sexes." Plato's participants in the *Symposium* were not only all males; they were describing (and practicing) a form of eros that was predominantly homoerotic. Indeed, erotic relations between men and women are degraded throughout the dialogue as "vulgar" and certainly far less than the ideal. How much of the philosophy of love and thinking about love that we have inherited from Plato is similarly if subtly biased against women, even if it is not at all homoerotic and even homophobic in turn? On the other hand, to what extent is our current conception of "romantic" love overly wedded to the limited form of marriage-oriented heterosexual couples? Does this discriminate against same-sex couples and mathematically more complex erotic arrangements? Does our conception of love represent an overly institutionalized and rather overbearing promotion of "traditional" (i.e., very modern) marriage rather than erotic love? It is worth noting even here that the linkage between love and marriage has been at best tenuous; indeed, the two have been openly antagonistic throughout most of the history of the subject. Even Abelard and Heloise, two of the most famous (married) lovers in history, express their contempt for marriage in contrast to the freedom of a secret and passionate love affair. Marriage appears as the culmination of love (as opposed to a primarily economic and social institution) only in the sixteenth century or so, for example, in many of Shakespeare's plays.

Moreover, the form of eros which is described in considerable detail in the *Symposium* was not at all a symmetrical relationship between equals. The proper relationship was between a man (the lover) and a "youth" (the beloved), and while the youth was expected to respond to the man (after a proper period of resistance) with gratitude and respect, he was not expected (indeed, was forbidden) to respond with love in return. Again, we have to ask how much of this asymmetrical dichotomy between lover and beloved—which continues in Western literature well into this century—is essential to the philosophy of love. (Talk in terms of "love objects" is one of its more vulgar manifestations.) And even if we insist that love must be reciprocal, is there not the very real danger that our model of love may have built into it a ferocious form of competition, summarized in the almost always destructive comparison: "Do I love you more than you love me?" A great many modern social scientists have written without embarrassment or hesitation about love and relationships as manifestations of a psychological "market," defined by supply and demand, in which all of us seek to "sell ourselves" and get "the best bargain" available. How much must any such conception of love be antithetical to and destructive of love? Is such competition or some other form of antagonism, perhaps domination and submission, built into love as we know it?

Our point here is not just to raise the inevitable question, whether the philosophy of love as it has evolved over the past 2500 years of Western thought is male-biased or, worse, some sort of male conspiracy, nor is it just to raise the equally important question whether our concept of love has built into it a tacit homoerotic or dogmatic heteroerotic paradigm, or whether inequality of competition or some form of domination and submission are built into love as we understand it, although all of these questions will be addressed at some length in the readings to follow. The question is a more general one, which we might call the "historicist" question, and it is the question whether there is any single phenomenon called "love" ("amour," "eros," or whatever) that can be found even in those various cultures, networks of shared feelings and affections and social practices that we call "Western." Or are there many different phenomena, linked by a discontinuous evolution perhaps but serving very different social and psychological functions and only misleadingly collected together under the same glamorous label, already grown trite with abuse and overuse?

Even within Plato's *Symposium*, it is obvious that there is serious disagreement among the various speakers about what love is. But is one speaker right and the others wrong? Or have various speakers given us rightly differing descriptions of different aspects of a multifaceted phenomenon? Is it not a single phenomenon at all, but a grab bag of affections loosely united by their underlying passion? Consider how we clumsily try to distinguish today between "loving and being in love" and between love and infatuation, thus displaying both the obsessiveness of our concern and the poverty of our language at one and the same time. Is the philosophically abstract conception of eros defended by Socrates (which is clearly at odds with the standard Athenian conceptions of the time) anything more than tangentially connected to the metaphysical coupling depicted by Aristophanes or the passionate affection expressed (unrequited) by Alcibiades? And once we move beyond the *Symposium* what reason — apart from a handful of footnotes — do we have for supposing that the love so praised by the neo-Platonists and early Christians has anything to do with the love practiced and praised by the Greeks, or that the aristocratic, adulterous love that was called "courtly" in twentieth-century France was anything like the middle-class marriage so celebrated by popular novels in eighteenth-century England?

Moreover, the word "love" refers not just to erotic love but to all sorts of loves that are not sexual at all, notably religious love and that universal love for humanity that is sometimes called "agape." Should these obviously very different phenomena be considered together at all, much less referred to indiscriminately? It has been argued that Platonic love, for example, is eros without the sex and without the emphasis on the particular beloved. But is there anything left of the erotic once we subtract sex and the person loved? Is there anything left of love once we take away all of the social and psychological contingencies that define it at any given time? Does it make sense for us to try to understand what we now call "love" in terms of a Greek paradigm that denigrates women, presumes inequality and asymmetry between lover and beloved, and has virtually no connection to marriage? Is the phi-

losophy of love a single subject matter or a confusion of a number of subject matters, most of them peculiar to a time and a place and culture if not
also a particular social class? There have been many different ideas about
love. The question is whether there is anything that underlies all of those
ideas which singularly can be called "love" and, if so, what it is and how it
manifests itself under these or those social conditions.

In the selections that follow, we have tried to present a broad spectrum
of classic and contemporary philosophical perspectives on love. Although
we have included many more women than are usually represented in such a
collection, the overall voice of the book is nevertheless male-dominated,
and it will be one of the critical tasks of the reader to discern how much this
does or does not define or distort the subject matter itself. The readings are
from different ages and different societies with different moral and religious ideas and prohibitions. How much of what one author says can be
translated into the language of a different time and place will also be a
challenge for the reader; indeed, even the contemporary essays in the final
half of the book should provoke this challenge. Almost all of them were
written within the past year or so in the United States and Canada, and yet
the differences in perspective and opinion are enormous.

We have not tried to homogenize our selections or squeeze very different
authors into a single format. Some of our classical selections are substantial
and suitable for detailed study; others provide a mere taste of an author or
a period. Some of the authors will be clearly concerned with very personal
experiences; others go out of their way to disguise any personal involvement. Some of the authors are highly theoretical; others recognize the in-
eliminably practical nature of any writing about love. Accordingly, one of
the features of the philosophy of love is that it typically emerges as "advice"
(which is why many serious philosophers assiduously avoid it). Thus the
classic work of ancient Rome on love is Ovid's often-banned but much-read
instructional poem on the art of having love affairs. Andreas Capellanus's
discourse on "courtly" love follows Ovid in its instructional tone. In the seventeenth and eighteenth centuries, love is conceived as a kind of interpersonal glue, bringing people together in an increasingly complex and fragmented world. Accordingly, a great thinker like Shakespeare (no less so
because he failed to write in the jargon of metaphysics) became fascinated
with the process of "falling in love" and the dialectic followed by love
through its early vicissitudes (ideally culminating in marriage). Jean-
Jacques Rousseau similarly tried to understand love as a "natural" phenomenon, binding us to each other while leaving us essentially ourselves. In-

deed, this tension between being bound or "merging" and remaining independent and free becomes one of the dominant themes of modern discussions of love, in D. H. Lawrence and Jean-Paul Sartre, for example, and in the work of many feminists, including Emma Goldman, Simone de Beauvoir and Shulamith Firestone. As love becomes more "romantic" in recent modern times, it becomes intimately bound up with the cosmic-minded romantic philosophy with which it shares its name, and the analysis of love is intermingled with an abstract metaphysics that has far more in mind than the mere emotions of two particular human beings. Thus the great German Idealist G. W. F. Hegel employs the concept of love to summarize his cosmic conception of a unified, all-encompassing worldview, while his pessimistic rival Arthur Schopenhauer takes erotic love to be the most obvious manifestation of an all-pervasive cosmic Will, which he takes to be the unifying principle of philosophy.

This long, speculative phase of the philosophy of love comes to an end just about the beginning of this century, in particular with the work of Sigmund Freud. Freud did not disparage love; indeed, he often insisted that love was the foundation of any decent life as well as one of the most basic impulses of human nature. But for Freud love became something of a mystery, not in the theological sense in which love in the middle ages had often been proclaimed a "mystery" but according to that peculiarly twentieth-century attitude of unrelenting *suspicion*, the refusal to take any human phenomenon at face value and an aptitude for unearthing dirty little secrets beneath even the most spiritual or aesthetic aspirations. Of course, Freud had an illustrious predecessor in Friedrich Nietzsche, who had laid bare much of what was called "love" as nothing but the two-faced viciousness of *ressentiment* (unacknowledged, unconscious, seething hate and envy). But what impressed Freud far more than the virtues of love were its various pathologies, and, consequently the language in which we now talk and think about love is riddled with the language of the psycho-neuroses. "Narcissism" is offered up as the paradigm of love, and the infamous "Oedipal complex" becomes a source of constant suspicion. Love becomes a *problem*, rather than the celebrated answer to our problems.

Thus, as the century proceeds, we are accused of making "a mess of love" by D. H. Lawrence, an early Freud enthusiast, by overintellectualizing it into pure ego. We are told by Jean-Paul Sartre that all love is an attempt (necessarily unsuccessful) at domination of the other. (Superficially, Sartre was one of Freud's great antagonists, but in fact he was much in sympathy with Freud's psychoanalytic perspective—from his own "existential" point of view.) We are accused of turning love into a "commodity" and, in effect, making it into a merchandising campaign, recently by Philip Slater but before him by Marx and Engels, who identified romantic love as nothing but a self-deceptive form of prostitution. But the most dramatic development in the philosophy of love in this (and the end of the last) century has been, without a doubt, the evolution of contemporary feminism. Feminism shares with Freud and most Marxists an attitude of suspicion toward love, the suspicion that it is not at all what it seems and, far from being the highest ideal, it is in fact an invitation to self-degradation. Emma Goldman, a Marxist sympathizer, a devoted anarchist and feminist, raises some of these now familiar accusations. Shulamith Firestone more recently suggests in no uncertain language that romantic love is nothing other than a male conspiracy to "keep women in their place" and ought to be done away with. Similar sentiments will be expressed in some of the contemporary essays in the final section of the book. The literature on love, particularly in this century, is by no means dominated by traditional Platonic praise. Much of the recent debate about love—while always remaining tied to the basic question "what it love?"—questions whether love should be praised or encouraged at all. Whatever else it may be, accordingly, *The Philosophy of (Erotic) Love* is not another encomium, one more symposium filled with unmixed praise of love.

We have divided *The Philosophy of (Erotic) Love* into four parts. The first two comprise established writings on love, from Plato and Sappho to some modern feminists and critics of love. The last two contain a collection of new essays by some leading contemporary philosophers.

The first part includes some of the "classic" writings on love, beginning with substantial excerpts from Plato's *Symposium* (in a new and much improved translation), poetry from Sappho, recommendations on seduction from Ovid and Andreas Capellanus and the passionate letters between Heloise and Abelard. We have also included Augustine, Shakespeare, Rousseau, Hegel, Schopenhauer and some bits from Nietzsche. The second part begins with the turn into the twentieth century and includes excerpts from Freud, Jung, Karen Horney, Emma Goldman, Jean-Paul Sartre and Simone de Beauvoir, Philip Slater, and Shulamith Firestone.

The third and fourth parts of the book consist of contemporary essays, many of them solicited especially for this volume and almost all of them written within the past year or so. The third part offers a half-dozen essays about some of the texts in the first half of the book but which go beyond those texts to contemplate the nature of contemporary love as well. The fourth part of the book is more theoretical and includes a number of new attempts to define and understand love, inevitably with passing reference to the great texts of the past. We want to thank Robert Nozick, Martha Nussbaum, Elizabeth Rapaport, Louis Mackey, William Gass, Irving Singer, Annette Baier, Amelie Rorty, Jerome Neu, Ronald de Sousa, Kathryn Morgan, and Larry Thomas for their cooperation and contributions to the ongoing development of the philosophy of love. (Source notes for previously published selections appear on p. 519.)

i

Plato

from Symposium

Plato's Symposium *is perhaps the greatest and best-known work on love in the Western tradition. The dialogue is one of Plato's earliest (probably written about 380 B.C.). It at least appears to be a report of conversations that might actually have taken place, though it is evident that much of the dialogue was created by Plato even if all of the characters were genuine (except for the muse Diotima, who is most likely an invention). A symposium is an after-dinner drinking party, and this world-famous conversation about love was initiated, quite unphilosophically, as a device to keep the participants from overindulging (as most of them had the evening before). The* Symposium *consists for the most part of a dramatic series of speeches in praise of love, in which a good many of the prevailing customs and the ethos of Athenian erotic love are spelled out, for example, the asymmetry of love (between an older man and a youth) and the precise requirements of age and decorum (the youth should not be too young or too yielding). There is much said about the linkage between love and virtue, the insistence (culminating in Socrates' speech) that true love must be love of the good; and far from being the case that "love is good in itself," it is made very clear in virtually all of the speeches that love misplaced can be degrading and humiliating.*

We have included a half-dozen or so speeches of the dialogue, three of which deserve special note. In his tragi-comic speech, the comic playwright Aristophanes explains the power of love by suggesting that human beings as we know them are in fact semihumans, split in two by Zeus long ago, who are now and forever running around the world "looking for our other halves." In the most famous and by far the longest speech of the dialogue, Socrates (through the voice of Diotima, who has supposedly instructed him) argues that love must be understood ultimately not in terms of the longing for a particular human being but in terms of a "higher" longing for the Eternal Good itself. Finally Alcibiades, a notorious rascal in ancient Athens, breaks the increasingly abstract mood of the symposium to declare his own very particular, frustrated love for Socrates. The three speeches rub against and contradict one another, providing very different conceptions of love. In the excerpt that

14 *follows, taken from the new Nehamas-Woodruff translation, we have in-cluded virtually all of Aristophanes's speech, most of Diotima's speech (as "re-ported" by Socrates), and a good deal of the quasi speech of Alcibiades, which ends the dialogue. We have also tried to include sufficient connecting mate-rial to provide some sense of the dramatic and often humorous form of Plato's writing. (For detailed analysis and commentary of the* Symposium, *see the se-lections by Martha Nussbaum and Jerome Neu in Part III.)*

Symposium

"Well, gentlemen, how can we arrange to drink less tonight? To be honest, I still have a terrible hangover from yesterday, and I could really use a break."

"Let us instead spend our evening in conversation. If you are so minded, I would like to propose a subject."

They all said they were quite willing, and urged him to make his pro-posal. So Eryximachus said:

"Let me begin by citing Euripides' *Melanippe*: 'Not mine the tale.' What I am about to tell belongs to Phaedrus here, who is deeply indignant on this issue, and often complains to me about it:

" 'Eryximachus,' he says, 'isn't it an awful thing! Our poets have com-posed hymns in honor of just about any god you can think of; but has a sin-gle one of them given one moment's thought to the god of love, ancient and powerful as he is? As for our fancy intellectuals, they have written volumes praising Heracles and other heroes (as did the distinguished Prodicus). Well, perhaps *that's* not surprising, but I've actually read a book by an ac-complished author who saw fit to extol the usefulness of salt! How *could* people pay attention to such trifles and never, not even once, write a proper hymn to Love? How could anyone ignore so great a god?"

"Now, Phaedrus, in my judgment, is quite right. I would like, therefore, to take up a contribution, as it were, on his behalf, and gratify his wish. Be-sides, I think this a splendid time for all of us here to honor the god. If you agree, we can spend the whole evening in discussion, because I propose that each of us give as good a speech in praise of Love as he is capable of giving, in proper order from left to right. And let us begin with Phaedrus, who is at the head of the table and is, in addition, the father of our subject."

The Speech of Phaedrus

All sides agree, then, that Love is one of the most ancient gods. As such, he gives to us the greatest goods. I cannot say what greater good there is for a young boy than a gentle lover, or for a lover than a boy to love. There is a certain guidance each person needs for his whole life, if he is to live well; and nothing imparts this guidance—not high kinship, not public honor, not wealth—nothing imparts this guidance as well as Love. What guidance do I mean? I Mean a sense of shame at acting shamefully, and a sense of pride in acting well. Without these, nothing fine or great can be accomplished, in public or in private.

What I say is this: if a man in love is found doing something shameful, or accepting shameful treatment because he is a coward and makes no defense, then nothing would give him more pain than being seen by the boy he loves—not even being seen by his father or his comrades. We see the same thing also in the boy he loves, that he is especially ashamed before his lover when he is caught in something shameful. If only there were a way to start a city or an army made up of lovers and the boys they love! Theirs would be the best possible system of society, for they would hold back from all that is shameful, and seek honor in each other's eyes. Even a few of them, in battle side by side, would conquer all the world, I'd say. For a man in love would never allow his loved one, of all people, to see him leaving ranks or dropping weapons. He'd rather die a thousand deaths! And as for leaving the boy behind, or not coming to his aid in danger—why, no one is so base that true Love could not inspire him with courage, and make him as brave as if he'd been born a hero. When Homer says a god "breathes might" into some of the heroes, this is really Love's gift to every lover.

The Speech of Pausanias

Phaedrus, I'm not quite sure our subject has been well defined. Our charge has been simple—to speak in praise of Love. This would have been fine if Love himself were simple, too, but as a matter of fact, there are two kinds of Love. In view of this, it might be better to begin by making clear which kind of Love we are to praise. Let me therefore try to put our discussion back on the right track and explain which kind of Love ought to be praised. Then I shall give him the praise he deserves, as the god he is.

It is a well-known fact that Love and Aphrodite are inseparable. If, therefore, Aphrodite were a single goddess, there could also be a single Love; but, since there are actually two goddesses of that name, there also are two kinds of Love. I don't expect you'll disagree with me about the two goddesses, will you? One is an older deity, the motherless daughter of Uranus, the god of heaven: she is known as Urania, or Heavenly Aphrodite. The other goddess is younger, the daughter of Zeus and Dione: her name is Pandemos, or Common Aphrodite. It follows, therefore, that there is a

16   Common as well as a Heavenly Love, depending on which goddess is Love's partner. And although, of course, all the gods must be praised, we must still make an effort to keep these two gods apart.

The reason for this applies in the same way to every type of action: considered in itself, no action is either good or bad, honorable or shameful. Take, for example, our own case. We had a choice between drinking, singing, or having a conversation. Now, in itself none of these is better than any other: how it comes out depends entirely on how it is performed. If it is done honorably and properly, it turns out to be honorable; if it is done improperly, it is disgraceful. And my point is that exactly this principle applies to being in love: Love is not in himself noble and worthy of praise; that depends on whether the sentiments he produces in us are themselves noble.

Now the Common Aphrodite's Love is himself truly common. As such, he strikes wherever he gets a chance. This, of course, is the love felt by the vulgar, who are attached to women no less than to boys, to the body more than to the soul, and to the least intelligent partners, since all they care about is completing the sexual act. Whether they do it honorably or not is of no concern. That is why they do whatever comes their way, sometimes good, sometimes bad; and which one it is is incidental to their purpose. For the Love who moves them belongs to a much younger goddess, who, through her parentage, partakes of the nature both of the female and the male.

Contrast this with the Love of Heavenly Aphrodite. This goddess, whose descent is purely male (hence this love is for boys), is considerably older and therefore free from the lewdness of youth. That's why those who are inspired by her Love are attracted to the male: they find pleasure in what is by nature stronger and more intelligent. But, even within the group that is attracted to handsome boys, some are not moved purely by this Heavenly Love; those who are do not fall in love with little boys; they prefer older ones whose cheeks are showing the first traces of a beard—a sign that they have begun to form minds of their own. I am convinced that a man who falls in love with a young man of this age is generally prepared to share everything with the one he loves—he is eager, in fact, to spend the rest of his own life with him. He certainly does not aim to deceive him—to take advantage of him while he is still young and inexperienced and then, after exposing him to ridicule, to move quickly on to someone else.

We can now see the point of our customs: they are designed to separate the wheat from the chaff, the proper love from the vile. That's why we do everything we can to make it as easy as possible for lovers to press their suits and as difficult as possible for young men to comply; it is like a competition, a kind of test to determine to which sort each belongs. This explains two further facts: First, why we consider it shameful to yield too quickly: the passage of time in itself provides a good test in these matters. Second, why we also consider it shameful for a man to be seduced by money or political power . . . .

Our customs, then, provide for only one honorable way of taking a man as a lover. In addition to recognizing that the lover's total and willing subjugation to his beloved's wishes is neither servile nor reprehensible, we allow that there is one—and only one—further reason for willingly subjecting oneself to another which is equally above reproach: that is subjection for the sake of virtue. If someone decides to put himself at another's disposal because he thinks that this will make him better in wisdom or in any other part of virtue, we approve of his voluntary subjection: we consider it neither shameful nor servile. Both these principles—that is, both the principle governing the proper attitude toward the lover of young men and the principle governing the love of wisdom and of virtue in general—must be combined if a young man is to accept a lover in an honorable way. When an older lover and a young man come together and each obeys the principle appropriate to him—when the lover realizes that he is justified in doing anything for a loved one who grants him favors, and when the young man understands that he is justified in performing any service for a lover who can make him wise and virtuous—and when the lover *is* able to help the young man become wiser and better, and the young man *is* eager to be taught and improved by his lover—then, and only then, when these two principles coincide absolutely, is it ever honorable for a young man to accept a lover.

When Pausanias finally came to a pause (I've learned this sort of fine figure from our clever rhetoricians), it was Aristophanes' turn, according to Aristodemus. But he had such a bad case of the hiccups—he'd probably stuffed himself again, though, of course, it could have been anything—that making a speech was totally out of the question. So he turned to the doctor, Eryximachus, who was next in line, and said to him:

"Eryximachus, it's up to you—as well it should be. Cure me or take my turn."

The Speech of Aristophanes
First you must learn what Human Nature was in the beginning and what has happened to it since, because long ago our nature was not what it is

18   now, but very different. There were three kinds of human beings, that's my first point — not two as there are now, male and female. In addition to these, there was a third, a combination of those two; its name survives, though the kind itself has vanished. At that time, you see, the word "androgynous" really meant something: a form made up of male and female elements, though now there's nothing but the word, and that's used as an insult. My second point is that the shape of each human being was completely round, with back and sides in a circle; they had four hands each, as many legs as hands, and two faces, exactly alike, on a rounded neck. Between the two faces, which were on opposite sides, was one head with four ears. There were two sets of sexual organs, and everything else was the way you'd imagine it from what I've told you. They walked upright, as we do now, whatever direction they wanted. And whenever they set out to run fast, they thrust out all their eight limbs, the ones they had then, and spun rapidly, the way gymnasts do cartwheels, by bringing their legs around straight.

In strength and power, therefore, they were terrible, and they had great ambitions. They made an attempt on the gods, and Homer's story about Ephialtes and Otos was originally about them: how they tried to make an ascent to heaven so as to attack the gods. Then Zeus and the other gods met in council to discuss what to do, and they were sore perplexed. They couldn't wipe out the human race with thunderbolts and kill them all off, as they had the giants, because that would wipe out the worship they receive, along with the sacrifices we humans give them. On the other hand, they couldn't let them run riot. At last, after great effort, Zeus had an idea.

"I think I have a plan," he said, "that would allow human beings to exist and stop their misbehaving: they will give up being wicked when they lose their strength. So I shall now cut each of them in two. At one stroke they will lose their strength and also become more profitable to us, owing to the increase in their number. They shall walk upright on two legs. But if I find they still run riot and do not keep the peace," he said, "I will cut them in two again, and they'll have to make their way on one leg, hopping."

So saying, he cut those human beings in two, the way people cut sorb-apples before they dry them or the way they cut eggs with hairs. As he cut each one, he commanded Apollo to turn its face and half its neck towards the wound, so that each person would see that he'd been cut and keep better order. Then Zeus commanded Apollo to heal the rest of the wound, and Apollo did turn the face around, and he drew skin from all sides over what is now called the stomach, and there he made one mouth, as in a pouch with a drawstring, and fastened it at the center of the stomach. This is now called the navel. Then he smoothed out the other wrinkles, of which there were many, and he shaped the breasts, using some such tool as shoemakers have for smoothing wrinkles out of leather on the form. But he left a few wrinkles around the stomach and the navel, to be a reminder of what happened long ago.

Now, since their natural form had been cut in two, each one longed for its own other half, and so they would throw their arms about each other, weaving themselves together, wanting to grow together. In that condition they would die from hunger and general idleness, because they would not do anything apart from each other. Whenever one of the halves died and one was left, the one that was left still sought another and wove itself together with that. Sometimes the half he met came from a woman, as we'd call her now, sometimes it came from a man; either way, they kept on dying.

Then, however, Zeus took pity on them, and came up with another plan: he moved their genitals around to the front! Before then, you see, they used to have their genitals outside, like their faces, and they cast seed and made children, not in one another, but in the ground, like cicadas. So Zeus brought about this relocation of genitals, and in doing so he invented interior reproduction, *by* the man *in* the woman. The purpose of this was so that, when a man embraced a woman, he would cast his seed and they would have children; but when male embraced male, they would at least have the satisfaction of intercourse, after which they could stop embracing, return to their jobs, and look after their other needs in life. This, then, is the source of our desire to love each other. Love is born into every human being; it calls back the halves of our original nature together; it tries to make one out of two and heal the wound of human nature.

Each of us, then, is a "matching half" of a human whole, because each was sliced like a flatfish, two out of one, and each of us is always seeking the half that matches him. That's why a man who is split from the double sort (which used to be called "androgynous") runs after women. Many lecherous men have come from this class, and so do the lecherous women who run after men. Women who are split from a woman, however, pay no attention at all to men; they are oriented more towards women, and lesbians come from this class. People who are split from a male are male-oriented. While they are boys, because they are chips off the male block, they love men and enjoy lying with men and being embraced by men; those are the best of boys and lads, because they are the most manly in their nature. Of course, some say such boys are shameless, but they're lying. It's not because they have no shame that such boys do this, you see, but because they are bold and brave and masculine, and they tend to cherish what is like themselves. Do you want me to prove it? Look, these are the only kind of boys who grow up to be politicians. When they're grown men, they are lovers of young men, and they naturally pay no attention to marriage or to making babies, except insofar as they are required by local custom. They, however, are quite satisfied to live their lives with one another unmarried. In every way, then, this sort of man grows up as a lover of young men and a lover of Love, always rejoicing in his own kind.

And so, when a person meets the half that is his very own, whatever his orientation, whether it's to young men or not, then something wonderful happens: the two are struck from their senses by love, by a sense of belonging to one another, and by desire, and they don't want to be separated from one another, not even for a moment.

These are the people who finish out their lives together and still cannot say what it is they want from one another. No one would think it is the intimacy of sex—that mere sex is the reason each lover takes so great and deep a joy in being with the other. It's obvious that the soul of every lover longs for something else; his soul cannot say what it is, but like an oracle it has a sense of what it wants, and like an oracle it hides behind a riddle. Suppose two lovers are lying together and Hephaestus stands over them with his mending tools, asking, "What is it you human beings really want from each other?" And suppose they're perplexed, and he asks them again: "Is this your heart's desire, then—for the two of you to become parts of the same whole, as near as can be, and never to separate, day or night? Because if that's your desire, I'd like to weld you together and join you into something that is naturally whole, so that the two of you are made into one. Then the two of you would share one life, as long as you lived, because you would be one being, and by the same token, when you died, you would be one and not two in Hades, having died a single death. Look at your love, and see if this is what you desire: wouldn't this be all the good fortune you could want?"

Surely you can see that no one who received such an offer would turn it down; no one would find anything else that he wanted. Instead, everyone would think he'd found out at last what he had always wanted: to come together and melt together with the one he loves, so that one person emerged from two. Why should this be so? It's because, as I said, we used to be complete wholes in our original nature, and now "Love" is the name for our pursuit of wholeness, for our desire to be complete.

The Speech of Agathon

. . . I maintain, then, that while all the gods are happy, Love—if I may say so without giving offence—is the happiest of them all, for he is the most beautiful and the best. His great beauty lies in this: First, Phaedrus, he is the youngest of the gods. He proves my point himself by fleeing old age in headlong flight, fast-moving, though it is (that's obvious—it comes after us faster than it should). Love was born to hate old age and will come nowhere near it. Love always lives with young people and is one of them: the old story holds good that like is always drawn to like. And though on many other points I agree with Phaedrus, I do not agree with this: that Love is more ancient than Kronos and Iapetos. No, I say that he is the youngest of the gods and stays young forever.

· · ·

And the exquisite coloring of his skin! The way the god consorts with flowers shows that. For he never settles in anything, be it a body or a soul, that cannot flower or has lost its bloom. His place is wherever it is flowery and fragrant; there he settles, there he stays.

Enough for now about the beauty of the god, though much remains still to be said. After this, we should speak of Love's moral character. The main point is that Love is neither the cause nor the victim of any injustice; he does no wrong to gods or men, nor they to him. If anything has an effect on him, it is never by violence, for violence never touches Love. And the effects he has on others are not forced, for every service we give to love we give willingly. And whatever one person agrees on with another, when both are willing, that is right and just; so say "the laws that are kings of society."

· · ·

That too is how the gods' quarrels were settled, once Love came to be among them—love of beauty, obviously, because love is not drawn to ugliness. Before that, as I said in the beginning, and as the poets say, many dreadful things happened among the gods, because Necessity was king. But once this god was born, all goods came to gods and men alike through love of beauty.

The Speech of Socrates

"Come, then," said Socrates. "Let us review the points on which we've agreed. Aren't they, first, that Love is the love of something, and, second, that he loves things of which he has a present need?"

"Yes," he said.

"Now, remember, in addition to these points, what you said in your speech about what it is that Love loves. If you like, I'll remind you. I think you said something like this: that the gods' quarrels were settled by love of beautiful things, for there is no love of ugly ones. Didn't you say something like that?"

"I did," said Agathon.

"And that's a suitable thing to say, my friend," said Socrates. "But if this is so, wouldn't Love have to be a desire for beauty, and never for ugliness?"

He agreed.

"And we also agreed that he loves just what he needs and does not have."

"Yes," he said.

"So Love needs beauty, then, and does not have it."

"Necessarily," he said.

"So! If something needs beauty and has got no beauty at all, would you still say that it is beautiful?"

"Certainly not."

"Then do you still agree that Love is beautiful, if those things are so?"

Then Agathon said, "It turns out, Socrates, I didn't know what I was talking about in that speech."

"It was a beautiful speech, anyway, Agathon," said Socrates.

• • •

Now I'll let you go. I shall try to go through for you the speech about Love I once heard from a woman of Mantinea, Diotima—a woman who was wise about many things besides this: once she even put off the plague for ten years by telling the Athenians what sacrifices to make. She is the one who taught me the art of love. . . .

She used the very same arguments against me that I used against Agathon; she showed how, according to my very own speech, Love is neither beautiful nor good.

So I said, "What do you mean, Diotima? Is Love ugly, then, and bad?"

But she said, "Watch your tongue! Do you really think that, if a thing is not beautiful, it has to be ugly?"

"I certainly do."

"And if a thing's not wise, it's ignorant? Or haven't you found out yet that there's something in between wisdom and ignorance?"

"What's that?"

"It's judging things correctly without being able to give a reason. Surely you see that this is not the same as knowing—for how could knowledge be unreasoning? And it's not ignorance either—for how could what hits the truth be ignorance? Correct judgment, of course, has this character: it is *in between* understanding and ignorance."

"True," said I, "as you say."

"Then don't force whatever is not beautiful to be ugly, or whatever is not good to be bad. It's the same with Love: when you agree he is neither good nor beautiful, you need not think he is ugly and bad; he could be something in between," she said.

"Yet everyone agrees he's a great god," I said.

"Only those who don't know."

• • •

"Then, what is he?" I asked.

"He's like what we mentioned before," she said. "He is in between mortal and immortal."

"What do you mean, Diotima?"

"He's a great spirit, Socrates. Every spiritual being, you see, is in between god and mortal."

"What is their function?" I asked.

"They are messengers who shuttle back and forth between the two, conveying prayer and sacrifice from men to gods, while to men they bring commands from the gods and gifts in return for sacrifices. Being in the middle of the two, they round out the whole and bind fast the all to all.

• • •

"[Love] is by nature neither immortal nor mortal. But now he springs to life when he gets his way; now he dies—all in the very same day. . . .

"He is in between wisdom and ignorance as well. In fact, you see, none of the gods loves wisdom or wants to become wise—for they are wise—and no one else who is wise already loves wisdom; on the other hand, no one who is ignorant will love wisdom either or want to become wise. For what's especially difficult about being ignorant is that you are content with yourself, even though you're neither beautiful and good nor intelligent. If you don't think you need anything, of course you won't want what you don't think you need."

"In that case, Diotima, who *are* the people who love wisdom, if they are neither wise nor ignorant?"

"That's obvious," she said. "A child could tell you. Those who love wisdom fall in between those two extremes. And Love is one of them, because

24   he is in love with what is beautiful, and wisdom is extremely beautiful. It follows that Love *must* be a lover of wisdom and, as such, is in between being wise and being ignorant.

So I said, "All right then, my friend. What you say about Love is beautiful, but if you're right, what use is Love to human beings?"

"Well, I'll tell you," she said. "It is giving birth in beauty, whether in body or in soul."

"It would take divination to figure out what you mean. I can't."

"Well, I'll tell you more clearly," she said. "All of us are pregnant, Socrates, both in body and in soul, and, as soon as we come to a certain age, we naturally desire to give birth. Now no one can possibly give birth in anything ugly; only in something beautiful."

"This is the source of the great excitement about beauty that comes to anyone who is pregnant and already teeming with life: beauty releases them from their great pain. You see, Socrates," she said, "what Love wants is not beauty, as you think it is."

"Well, what is it, then?"

"Reproduction and birth in beauty."

"Maybe," I said.

"Certainly," she said. "Now, why reproduction? It's because reproduction goes on forever; it is what mortals have in place of immortality. A lover must desire immortality along with the good, if what we agreed earlier was right, that Love wants to possess the good forever. It follows from our argument that Love must desire immortality. . . .

"Now, some people are pregnant in body, and for this reason turn more to women and pursue love in that way, providing themselves through childbirth with immortality and remembrance and happiness, as they think, for all time to come; while others are pregnant in soul because there surely *are* those who are even more pregnant in their souls that in their bodies, and these are pregnant with what is fitting for a soul to bear and bring to birth. And what is fitting? Wisdom and the rest of virtue, which all poets beget, as well as all the craftsmen who are said to be creative. But by far the greatest and most beautiful part of wisdom deals with the proper ordering of cities and households, and that is called moderation and justice. When someone has been pregnant with these in his soul from early youth, while he is still a virgin, and, having arrived at the proper age, desires to beget and give birth, he too will certainly go about seeking the beauty in which he would beget; for he will never beget in anything ugly. Since he is pregnant, then, he is much more drawn to bodies that are beautiful than to those that

are ugly; and if he also has the luck to find a soul that is beautiful and noble and well-formed, he is even more drawn to this combination; such a
man makes him instantly teem with ideas and arguments about virtue—
the qualities a virtuous man should have and the customary activities in
which he should engage; and so he tries to educate him. In my view, you
see, when he makes contact with someone beautiful and keeps company
with him, he conceives and gives birth to what he has been carrying inside
him for ages. And whether they are together or apart, he remembers that
beauty. And in common with him he nurtures the newborn; such people,
therefore, have much more to share than do the parents of human children, and have a firmer bond of friendship, because the children in whom
they have a share are more beautiful and more immortal.

"Even you, Socrates, could probably come to be initiated into these rites
of love. But as for the purpose of these rites when they are done correctly—
that is the final and highest mystery, and I don't know if you are capable of
it. I myself will tell you," she said, "and I won't stint any effort. And you
must try to follow if you can.

"A lover who goes about this matter correctly must begin in his youth to
devote himself to beautiful bodies. First, if the leader leads aright, he
should love one body and beget beautiful ideas there; then he should realize that the beauty of any one body is brother to the beauty of any other
and that if he is to pursue beauty of form he'd be very foolish not to think
that the beauty of all bodies is one and the same. When he grasps this, he
must become a lover of all beautiful bodies, and he must think that this
wild gaping after just one body is a small thing and despise it.

"After this he must think that the beauty of people's souls is more valuable than the beauty of their bodies, so that if someone is decent in his soul,
even though he is scarcely blooming in his body, our lover must be content
to love and care for him and to seek to give birth to such ideas as will make
young men better. The result is that our love will be forced to gaze at the
beauty of activities and laws and to see that all this is akin to itself, with the
result that he will think that the beauty of bodies is a thing of no importance. After customs he must move on to various kinds of knowledge. The
result is that he will see the beauty of knowledge and be looking mainly not
at beauty in a single example—as a servant would who favored the beauty
of a little boy or a man or a single custom (being a slave, or course, he's low
and small-minded)—but the lover is turned to the great sea of beauty, and,
gazing upon this, he gives birth to many gloriously beautiful ideas and the-

ories, in unstinting love of wisdom, until, having grown and been strengthened there, he catches sight of such knowledge, and it is the knowledge of such beauty. . . .

"Try to pay attention to me," she said, "as best you can. You see, the man who has been thus far educated in matters of Love, who has beheld beautiful things in the right order and correctly, is coming now to the goal of Loving: all of a sudden he will catch sight of something wonderfully beautiful in its nature; that, Socrates, is the reason for all his earlier labors:

"First, it always *is* and neither comes to be nor passes away, neither waxes nor wanes. Second, it is not beautiful this way and ugly that way, nor beautiful at one time and ugly at another, nor beautiful in relation to one thing and ugly in relation to another; nor is it beautiful here but ugly there, as it would be if it were beautiful for some people and ugly for others. Nor will the beautiful appear to him in the guise of a face or hands or anything else that belongs to the body. It will not appear to him as one idea or one kind of knowledge. It is not anywhere in another thing, as in an animal, or in earth, or in heaven, or in anything else, but itself by itself with itself, it is always one in form; and all the other beautiful things share in that, in such a way that when those others come to be or pass away, this does not become the least bit smaller or greater nor suffer any change. So when someone rises by these stages, through loving boys correctly, and begins to see this beauty, he has almost grasped his goal. This is what it is to go aright, or be led by another, into the mystery of Love; one goes always upwards for the sake of this Beauty, starting out from beautiful things and using them like rising stairs: from one body to two and from two to all beautiful bodies, then from beautiful bodies to beautiful customs, and from customs to learning beautiful things, and from these lessons he arrives in the end at this lesson, which is learning of this very Beauty, so that in the end he comes to know just what it is to be beautiful.

"And there in life, Socrates, my friend," said the woman from Mantinea, "there if anywhere should a person live his life, beholding that Beauty. If you once see that, it won't occur to you to measure beauty by gold or clothing or beautiful boys and youths. . . .

"If someone got to see the Beautiful itself, absolute, pure, unmixed, not polluted by human flesh or colors or any other great nonsense of mortality, if he could see the divine Beauty itself in its one form do you think it would be a poor life for a human being to look there and to behold it and to be with it? Or haven't you remembered," she said, "that in that life alone, when he looks at Beauty in the only way that Beauty can be seen—only then will it become possible for him to give birth not to images of virtue (because he's in touch with no images), but to true virtue (because he is in touch with the true Beauty). The love of the gods belongs to anyone who has given birth to true virtue and nourished it, and if any human being could become immortal, it would be he."

The Speech of Alcibiades

Socrates' speech finished to loud applause. Meanwhile, Aristophanes was trying to make himself heard over their cheers in order to make a response to something Socrates had said about his own speech. Then, all of a sudden, there was even more noise. A large drunken party had arrived at the courtyard door and they were rattling it loudly, accompanied by the shrieks of some flute-girls they had brought along.

A moment later they heard Alcibiades shouting in the courtyard, very drunk and very loud. He wanted to know where Agathon was, he demanded to see Agathon at once. Actually, he was half-carried into the house by the flute-girl and by some other companions of his, but, at the door, he managed to stand by himself, crowned with a beautiful wreath of violets and ivy and ribbons in his hair.

"Good evening, gentlemen. I'm plastered," he announced. "May I join your party? Or should I crown Agathon with this wreath—which is all I came to do, anyway—and make myself scarce? I really couldn't make it yesterday," he continued, "but nothing could stop me tonight! See, I'm wearing the garland myself. I want this crown to come directly from my head to the head that belongs, I don't mind saying, to the cleverest and best looking man in town. Ah, you laugh; you think I'm drunk! Fine, go ahead—I know I'm right anyway. Well, what do you say? May I join you on these terms? Will you have a drink with me or not?"

"Listen to me," Eryximachus said. "Earlier this evening we decided to use this occasion to offer a series of encomia of Love. We all took our turn—in good order, from left to right—and gave our speeches, each according to his ability. You are the only one not to have spoken yet, though, if I may say so, you have certainly drunk your share. It's only proper, therefore, that you take your turn now. After you have spoken, you can decide on a topic for Socrates on your right; he can then do the same for the man to his right, and we can go around the table once again."

"Well said, O Eryximachus," Alcibiades replied. "But do you really think it's fair to put my drunken ramblings next to your sober orations?

28 And anyway, my dear fellow, I hope you didn't believe a single word Socrates said: the truth is just the opposite! He's the one who will most surely beat me up if I dare praise anyone else in his presence—even a god!"

"Hold your tongue!" Socrates said.

"By god, don't you dare deny it!" Alcibiades shouted. "I would never—*never*—praise anyone else with you around."

"Well, why not just do that, if you want?" Eryximachus suggested. "Why don't you offer an encomium to Socrates?"

"What do you mean?" asked Alcibiades. "Do you really think so, Eryximachus? Should I unleash myself upon him? Should I give him his punishment in front of all of you?"

"Now, wait a minute," Socrates said. "What do you have in mind? Are you going to praise me only in order to mock me? Is that it?"

"I'll only tell the truth—please, let me!"

"I would certainly like to hear the truth from you. By all means, go ahead," Socrates replied.

•   •   •

I'll try to praise Socrates, my friends, but I'll have to use an image. And though he may think I'm trying to make fun of him, I assure you my image is no joke: it aims at the truth. Look at him! Isn't he just like a statue of Silenus? You know the kind of statue I mean; you'll find them in any shop in town. It's a Silenus sitting, his flute or his pipes in his hands, and it's hollow. It's split right down the middle, and inside it's full of tiny statues of the gods. Now look at him again! Isn't he also just like the satyr Marsyas?

Nobody, not even you, Socrates, can deny that you *look* like them. But the resemblance goes beyond appearance, as you're about to hear.

You are impudent, contemptuous, and vile! No? If you won't admit it, I'll bring witnesses. And you're quite a flute-player, aren't you? In fact, you're much more marvelous than Marsyas, who needed instruments to cast his spells on people. And so does anyone who plays his tunes today—for even the tunes Olympos played are Marsyas' work, since Olympos learned everything from him. Whether they are played by the greatest flautist or the meanest flute-girl, his melodies have in themselves the power to possess and so reveal those people who are ready for the god and his mysteries. That's because his melodies are themselves divine. The only difference between you and Marsyas is that you need no instruments; you do exactly what he does, but with words alone. You know, people hardly ever take a speaker seriously, even if he's the greatest orator; but let anyone—

man, woman, or child—listen to you or even to a poor account of what you say—and we are all transported, completely possessed.

If I were to describe for you what an extraordinary effect his words have always had on me (I can feel it this moment even as I'm speaking), you might actually suspect that I'm drunk! Still, I swear to you, the moment he starts to speak, I am beside myself: my heart starts leaping in my chest, the tears come streaming down my face, even the frenzied Corybantes seem sane compared to me—and, let me tell you, I am not alone. I have heard Pericles and many other great orators, and I have admired their speeches. But nothing like this ever happened to me: they never upset me so deeply that my very own soul started protesting that my life—*my* life!—was no better than the most miserable slave's. And yet that is exactly how this Marsyas here at my side makes me feel all the time: he makes it seem that my life isn't worth living! You can't say that isn't true, Socrates. I know very well that you could make me feel that way this very moment if I gave you half a chance. He always traps me, you see, and he makes me admit that my political career is a waste of time, while all that matters is just what I most neglect: my personal shortcomings, which cry out for the closest attention. So I refuse to listen to him; I stop my ears and tear myself away from him, for, like the sirens, he could make me stay by his side till I die.

Socrates is the only man in the world who has made me feel shame—ah, you didn't think I had it in me, did you? Yes, he makes me feel ashamed: I know perfectly well that I can't prove he's wrong when he tells me what I should do; yet, the moment I leave his side, I go back to my old ways: I cave in to my desire to please the crowd. My whole life has become one constant effort to escape from him and keep away, but when I see him, I feel deeply ashamed, because I'm doing nothing about my way of life, though I have already agreed with him that I should. Sometimes, believe me, I think I would be happier if he were dead. And yet I now that if he dies I'll be even more miserable. I can't live with him, and I can't live without him! What *can* I do about him? . . .

But I once caught him when he was open like Silenus' statues, and I had a glimpse of the figures he keeps hidden within: they were so godlike—so bright and beautiful, so utterly amazing—that I no longer had a choice—I just had to do whatever he told me.

What I thought at the time was that what he really wanted was *me*, and that seemed to me the luckiest coincidence: all I had to do was to let him have his way with me, and he would teach me everything he knew—believe me, I had a lot of confidence in my looks. Naturally, up to that time we'd never been alone together; one of my attendants had always been present. But with this in mind, I sent the attendant away, and met Socrates alone. (You see, in this company I must tell the whole truth: so pay attention. And, Socrates, if I say anything untrue, I want you to correct me.)

So there I was, my friends, alone with him at last. My idea, naturally, was that he'd take advantage of the opportunity to tell me whatever it is that lovers say when they find themselves alone; I relished the moment. But no such luck! Nothing of the sort occurred. Socrates had his usual sort of conversation with me, and at the end of the day he went off.

· · ·

All I did was to invite him to dinner, as if *I* were his lover and he my young prey! To tell the truth, it took him quite a while to accept my invitation, but one day he finally arrived. That first time he left right after dinner: I was too shy to try to stop him. But on my next attempt, I started some discussion just as we were finishing our meal and kept him talking late into the night. When he said he should be going, I used the lateness of the hour as an excuse and managed to persuade him to spend the night at my house. He had had his meal on the couch next to mine, so he just made himself comfortable and lay down on it. No one else was there.

Now you must admit that my story so far has been perfectly decent; I could have told it in any company. But you'd never have heard me tell the rest of it, as you're about to do, if it weren't that, as the saying goes, 'there's truth in wine when the slaves have left'—and when they're present, too.

· · ·

To get back to the story. The lights were out; the slaves had left; the time was right, I thought, to come to the point and tell him freely what I had in mind. So I shook him and whispered:

"Socrates, are you asleep?"

"No, no, not at all," he replied.

"You know what I've been thinking?"

"Well, no, not really."

"I think," I said, "you're the only worthy lover I have ever had—and yet, look how shy you are with me! Well, here's how I look at it. It would be really stupid not to give you anything you want: you can have me, my belongings, anything my friends might have. Nothing is more important to me than becoming the best man I can be, and no one can help me more than you to reach that aim. With a man like you, in fact, I'd be much more ashamed of what wise people would say if I did *not* take you as my lover, than I would of what all the others, in their foolishness, would say if I did."

He heard me out, and then he said in that absolutely inimitable ironic manner of his:

"Dear Alcibiades, if you are right in what you say about me, you are already more accomplished than you think. If I really have in me the power to make you a better man, then you can see in me a beauty that is really beyond description and makes your own remarkable good looks pale in comparison. But, then, is this a fair exchange that you propose? You seem to me to want more than your proper share: you offer me the merest appearance of beauty, and in return you want the thing itself, 'gold in exchange for bronze.'

"Still, my dear boy, you should think twice, because you could be wrong, and I may be of no use to you. The mind's sight becomes sharp only when the body's eyes go past their prime—and you are still a good long time away from that."

When I heard this I replied:

"I really have nothing more to say. I've told you exactly what I think. Now it's your turn to consider what you think best for you and me."

"You're right about that," he answered. "In the future, let's consider things together. We'll always do what seems the best to the two of us."

His words made me think that my own had finally hit their mark, that he was smitten by my arrows. I didn't give him a chance to say another word. I stood up immediately and placed my mantle over the light cloak which, though it was the middle of winter, was his only clothing. I slipped underneath the cloak and put my arms around this man—this utterly unnatural, this truly extraordinary man—and spent the whole night next to him. Socrates, you can't deny a word of it. But in spite of all my efforts, this hopelessly arrogant, this unbelievably insolent man—he turned me down! He spurned my beauty, of which I was so proud, members of the jury—for this is really what you are: you're here to sit in judgment of Socrates' amazing arrogance and pride. Be sure of it, I swear to you by all the gods and goddesses together, my night with Socrates went no further than if I had spent it with my own father or older brother!

How do you think I felt after that? Of course, I was deeply humiliated, but also I couldn't help admiring his natural character, his moderation, his fortitude—here was a man whose strength and wisdom went beyond my wildest dreams! How could I bring myself to hate him? I couldn't bear to lose his friendship. But how could I possibly win him over? I knew very well that money meant much less to him than enemy weapons ever meant to Ajax, and the only trap by means of which I had thought I might capture him had already proved a dismal failure. I had no idea what to do, no purpose in life; ah, no one else has ever known the real meaning of slavery!

You could say many other marvelous things in praise of Socrates. Perhaps he shares some of his specific accomplishments with others. But, as a whole, he is unique; he is like no one else in the past and no one in the present—this is by far the most amazing thing about him. For we might be able to form an idea of what Achilles was like by comparing him to Brasidas or some other great warrior, or we might compare Pericles with Nestor or Antenor or one of the other great orators. There is a parallel for everyone—everyone else, that is. But this man here is so bizarre, his ways and his ideas are so unusual, that, search as you might, you'll never find anyone else, alive or dead, who's even remotely like him. The best you can do is not to compare him to anything human, but to liken him, as I do, to Silenus and the satyrs, and the same goes for his ideas and arguments. . . .

Well, this is my praise of Socrates, though I haven't spared him my reproach, either; I told you how horribly he treated me—and not only me but also Charmides, Euthydemus, and many others. He has deceived us all: he presents himself as your lover, and, before you know it, you're in love with him yourself! I warn you, Agathon, don't let him fool you! Remember our torments; be on your guard: don't wait, like the fool in the proverb, to learn your lesson from your own misfortune.

Final Dialogue

Alcibiades' frankness provoked a lot of laughter, especially since it was obvious that he was still in love with Socrates, who immediately said to him:

"You're perfectly sober after all, Alcibiades. Otherwise you could never have concealed your motive so gracefully: how casually you let it drop, almost like an afterthought, at the very end of your speech! As if the real point of all this has not been simply to make trouble between Agathon and me! You think that I should be in love with you and no one else, while you, and no one else, should be in love with Agathon—well, we were *not* deceived; we've seen through your little satyr play. Agathon, my friend, don't let him get away with it: let no one come between us!"

And then, all of a sudden, while Agathon was changing places, a large drunken group, finding the gates open because someone was just leaving, walked into the room and joined the party. There was noise everywhere, and everyone was made to start drinking again in no particular order.

Sappho
Poems

Sappho (c. 620-550 B.C.) was a Greek lyric poet who lived on the island of Lesbos, in the Aegean Sea off the coast of Asia Minor. A member of the aristocracy, Sappho devoted much of her poetry to the expression of erotic sentiments toward (and rivalries with) other young women of her class. The homoerotic vision of these poems has led to the use of the term "lesbian" ("of Lesbos") to connote female homosexuality.

Sappho's vision of love was unique for its time not only because it focused on love between women but also because she rejected the conventional wisdom of her era that love was a dangerous mental disorder and held that it was the great fulfillment available in life, even a criterion of value unto itself. Her poetic portrayals of love range from relatively public "wedding poems" to intimate statements of personal ardor. The poems reprinted here reveal her interest in the many aspects of romantic love and desire, which span the emotional gamut from bitter jealousy to ecstasy. Translations are by Jon Solomon.

To Anaktoria

Some speak of cavalry, others infantry,
And some a fleet of ships as most beautiful
On this dark earth. Not I. It is the one
One loves.

Here is a sure and easy demonstration
Known to everyone: Helen, far
surpassing all in beauty,
her excellent husband

Abandoned, sailing to Troy
Neither of her child nor of her dear parents
At all mindful. He led her away

       • • •

This reminds me now of Anaktoria
Far away.

34   To gaze at her lovely gait and the dazzling
Brightness of her face I would love,
More than at Lydian chariots and marching,
Armored soldiers.

The Blast of Love

                          Love shook
My heart, like mountain winds descending upon oaks.

To Aphrodite

On your exquisite throne, immortal Aphrodite,
Child of Zeus, weaver of wiles, I pray you
Not overwhelm me with grief and pain,
Mistress, in my heart.

But come to me, if you have ever before
Listened from afar to my voice and
Heard me: leaving your father's home
Golden you came

Yoking your chariot. Fine and swift sparrows brought you.
Whipping their wings above the dark earth,
Whirling from the heavens through
The middle air,

Arriving quickly. Then you, blessed one,
With smiling, immortal countenance, asked
What I suffered this time, and whom
I called this time.

And what special thing my disturbed heart
desired. "Whom should I recapture for
your love this time? Who does you
Disservice, Sappho?

Even if she flees now, she will soon pursue.
If she rejects your gifts now, she will give them.
If she does not love you, she soon will,
Albeit reluctantly."

Come to me again. Now. Free me from my
impossible worries. Wherever our heart

Wishes to succeed, make it succeed. Be
My ally.

Loss

Q: Virginity, virginity. You have left me and gone . . . where?
A: I will never return to you. I will never return!

Remorse

Do I even now long for my virginity?

Homecoming

You came! You have done well. I wanted
You. You fired up my heart burning
With desire. Hail!

Hail for all the time we did not have each other
Three times over.

Andromeda, What Now?

Some peasant girl beguiles you.
She wears her peasant dress
And doesn't even know to pull it above her ankles.

Ungiven Love

I crave and I also desire . . .

Out of All People

Do you love some other man more than me?

To a Friend

I see you there across from me.
You are like Hermione.
You are like blond Helen.

Bittersweet Love

Paingiving.

Mythweaving.

Theano

Letter on Marriage and Fidelity

The following letter is attributed to a woman named Theano, a Pythago-rean who seems to have lived somewhat before the Christian Era, several centuries later than Pythagoras himself. Theano's letters are not devoted to the topic of love in an abstract, theoretical sense. Instead, they discuss cer-tain practical problems of love, those that women face in married life: for example, what is appropriate behavior for a woman whose husband is un-faithful to her? In such circumstances Theano advises the wife to adhere to woman's unique virtue. The woman's role is to create harmony in the home. Accordingly, women should treat their profligate husbands with justice and moderation, even when they themselves are treated unfairly.

The ideas that the sexes have distinct virtues and that it is the woman's responsibility to maintain domestic tranquility may strike most of us as out-moded and sexist in their implication. It should be noted, however, that Theano's perspective is not one of passive acquiescence to mistreatment. Her admonition to women to be fair and moderate is coupled in the letter with the emphatic point that this is good strategy. A woman, she argues, stands the best chance of getting repentance from an errant husband if she consistently inspires admiration, not resentment.

Theano II

Theano to Nikostrate: Greetings. I hear repeatedly about your husband's madness: he has a courtesan; also that you are jealous of him. My dear, I have known many men with the same malady. It is as if they are hunted down by these women and held fast; as if they have lost their minds. But you are dispirited by night and by day, you are sorely troubled and con-trive things against him. Don't *you*, at least, be that way, my dear. For the moral excellence of a wife is not surveillance of her husband but compan-ionable accommodation; it is in the spirit of accommodation to bear his folly.

If he associates with the courtesan with a view towards pleasure, he asso-ciates with his wife with a view towards the beneficial. It is beneficial not to compound evils with evils and not to augment folly with folly. Some faults, dear, are stirred up all the more when they are condemned, but cease when they are passed over in silence, much as they say fire quenches itself if left alone. Besides, though it seems that you wish to escape notice yourself, by condemning him you will take away the veil that covers your own condition.

Then you will manifestly err: You are not convinced that love of one's husband resides in conduct that is noble and good. For this *is* the grace of marital association. Recognize the fact that he goes to the courtesan in order to be frivolous but that he abides with you in order to live a common life; that he loves you on the basis of good judgment, but her on the basis of passion. The moment for this is brief; it almost coincides with its own satisfaction. In a trice it both arises and ceases. The time for a courtesan is of brief duration for any man who is not excessively corrupt. For what is emptier than desire whose benefit of enjoyment is unrighteousness? Eventually he will perceive that he is diminishing his life and slandering his good character.

No one who understands persists in self-chosen harm. Thus, being summoned by his just obligation towards you and perceiving the diminution of his livelihood [he will take notice of you,] unable to bear the outrage of moral condemnation, he will soon repent. My dear, this is how you must live: not defending yourself against courtesans but distinguishing yourself from them by your orderly conduct towards your husband, by your careful attention to the house, by the calm way in which you deal with the servants, and by your tender love for your children. You must not be jealous of that woman (for it is good to extend your emulation only to women who are virtuous); rather, you must make yourself fit for reconciliation. Good character brings regard even from enemies, dear, and esteem is the product of nobility and goodness alone. In this way it is even possible for the power of a woman to surpass that of a man. It is possible for her to grow in his esteem instead of having to serve one who is hostile towards her.

If he has been properly prepared for it by you, he will be all the more ashamed; he will wish to be reconciled sooner and, because he is more warmly attached to you, he will love you more tenderly. Conscious of his injustice towards you, he will perceive your attention to his livelihood and make trial of your affection towards himself. Just as bodily illnesses make their cessations sweeter, so also do differences between friends make their reconciliations more intimate. As for you, do resist the passionate resolutions of your suffering. Because he is not well, he excites you to share in his plight; because he himself misses the mark of decency, he invites you to fail in decorum; having damaged his own life, he invites you to harm what is beneficial to you. Consequently you will seem to have conspired against him and, in reproving him will appear to reprove yourself.

If you divorce yourself from him and move on, you will change your first husband only to try another and, if he has the same failings, you will resort to yet another (for the lack of a husband is not bearable for young women); or else you will abide alone without any husband like a spinster. Do you intend to be negligent of the house and to destroy your husband? Then you will share the spoils of an anguished life. Do you intend to avenge yourself upon the courtesan? Being on her guard, she will circumvent you; but, if she actively wards you off, a woman who has no tendency to blush is formidable in battle. Is it good to fight with your husband day after day? To what advantage? The battles and reproaches will not stop his licentious behavior, but they will increase the dissension between you by their escalations. What, then? Are you plotting something against him? Don't do it, my dear. Tragedy teaches us to conquer jealousy, encompassing a systematic treatise on the actions by which Medea was led to the commission of outrage. Just as it is necessary to keep one's hands away from a disease of the eyes, so must you separate your pretension from your pain. By patiently enduring you will quench your suffering sooner.

Ovid

from The Art of Love

Ovid (43 B.C.–17 A.D.) lived and wrote in Rome during the reign of Augustus. He was married several times and had a number of serious love affairs, one of which, with a woman named Corinna, he celebrates in his Loves. *The tone of his writing is sensuous, playful, even naughty, reflecting the rather unrestrained spirit of a powerful society intent most of all on amusing itself. But following a scandal at the turn of the millennium (2 B.C.) in which the emperor's daughter was caught in an extremely dangerous liaison with the son of Mark Antony (Augustus's old rival), the moral mood of the country changed abruptly. It was at this inopportune moment that Ovid published his* Art of Love, *a brilliant but intentionally scandalous work which deeply offended the new morality. The book shocked the emperor, and several years later the book was banned and its author exiled. Ovid's continuing fame and importance rests mainly on his vivid bringing to life of the imaginative world of the Greeks, particularly in his* Metamorphoses, *which had enormous influence not just on subsequent Roman poets and thinkers but on most of the great minds of the Renaissance and the greatest writers of English literature, such as Marlowe, Shakespeare, Milton, and Pope. But* The Art of Love *too has endured through the ages, perhaps as an exemplar of the quality to which pornography and willful perversion can aspire. Ovid's sense of humor and his keen practical understanding of all too human vanities and temptations has kept him a beacon for writers on love—at least those who also have a sense of humor and a concern for practical as opposed to merely ethereal matters. The following brief excerpt—just a "taste"—is from* The Art of Love, *Books II and III.*

Love is a kind of war, and no assignment for cowards.

Where those banners fly, heroes are always on guard.
Soft, those barracks? They know long marches, terrible weather,
Night and winter and storm, grief and excessive fatigue.
Often the rain pelts down from the drenching cloudbursts of heaven,
Often you lie on the ground, wrapped in a mantle of cold.
Did not Apollo once, in bondage to King Admetus,

40   Care for the heifers, and find sleep on a pallet of straw?
    What Apollo could stand is not disgraceful for mortals;
       Put off your pride, young man; enter the bondage of love.
    If you are given no path where the journey is level and easy,
       If in your way you find barricade, padlock on door,
    Use your inventive wits, come slipping down through a skylight,
       Clamber, hand over hand, where a high window swings wide.
    She will be happy to know that she was the cause of your danger;
       More than anything else, that will be proof of your love.
    Think of Leander, who could, no doubt, get along without Hero,
       Yet he would swim the straits, so his beloved might know.

    Do not feel ashamed to win her serving-maids over,
       Take them according to rank; also, win over her slaves.
    Greet each one by name—the courtesy can't be expensive—
       Show them your *Noblesse oblige*, clasping their hands in your own.
    If, on the Day of Good Luck, some slave should ask for a present,
       Give him some little gift; this should cost nothing at all.
    On the Handmaidens' Day, recalling the Gauls and the fig tree,
       Think of the girls in the house, try to remember each one.
    Take my advice: it is worth your while to be good to the lowly,
       Even the guard at her gate, even the slave at her door.
    I do not say you should spend great sums on gifts for the lady:
       Let them, however small, seem to be chosen with care.
    While the fields are rich, and the boughs droop under their burden,
       Have a boy come to the door, bringing her baskets of fruit.
    Tell her they came from your farm, your little place in the country:
       She would not know, nor suspect fruit stands are easy to find.
    Have the boy bring her grapes, or the nuts Amaryllis was fond of,
       Send her a thrush or a dove, proof of your passionate love.
    But, don't send souvenirs suggestive of anything morbid,
       Death, or a childless old age, anything hinting of guilt.

    What about sending her poems? A very difficult question.
       Poems, I am sorry to say, aren't worth so much in this town.
    Oh, they are praised, to be sure; but the girls want something more costly.
       Even illiterates please, if they have money to burn.
    Ours is a Golden Age, and gold can purchase you honors,
       All the "Golden Mean" means is, gold is the end.
    Homer himself, if he came attended by all of the Muses,

With no scrip in his purse, would be kicked out of the house.
There are a few, very few, bright girls with a real education,
    Some (perhaps) here and there, willing to give it a try.
So, go ahead, praise both: the worth of the song matters little
    Just so you make it sound lovely while reading aloud.
Whether or not she can tell one kind of verse from another,
    If there's a line in her praise she will assume, "It's a gift!"

                        • • •

If you are ever caught, no matter how well you've concealed it,
    Though it is clear as the day, swear up and down it's a lie.
Don't be too abject, and don't be too unduly attentive,
    That would establish your guilt far beyond anything else.
Wear yourself out if you must, and prove, in her bed, that you could not
    Possibly be that good, coming from some other girl.
Some recommend Spanish Fly as useful on such an occasion:
    This I do not endorse; I think it poison or worse.
Others say pepper is good, compounded with seeds of the nettle,
    Or try a camomile brew, steeping pyrethrum in wine,
But I very much doubt whether these can be very effective:
    Venus will hardly respond, called to the usual joys.
Scallions might work, if you get the kind that are shipped from Megara;
    Rocket and basil are good, culled from the gardens of home.
Also, eat plenty of eggs, and the honey that comes from Hymettus,
    Nuts from the long-leaved pine, oysters (in months with an R).

Why fool around with all this medicinal magic and nostrums?
    There is a better way; turn your direction, and heed.
Not long ago I said it was wise to dissemble your cheating,
    Now I reverse myself — let it be openly told.
Inconsistent? Of course, but is that any reason to scold me?
    Winds do not always blow from the same reach of the sky.
East, West, North, or South — and we plan our course in accordance.
    Drivers can hold the reins easy or tight at their will.
There are some girls who are bored with over-devoted indulgence:
    Given no rival, their love languishes, fades, dies away.
Spirit can grow too rank, when matters are going too smoothly,
    Nor is it easy to bear Fortune's continual smile.
Just as a fire dies down, and weakens, little by little,
    While the embers lie hid under the gray of the ash,

42 But if you rouse the flame, half-dead, by throwing on sulphur,
  Then it flares up again, brighter in light than before.
So, when hearts grow dull with too much freedom from worry,
  They must be given the spur, given incentive to love.
Heat her cooling mind, and let her grow anxious about you:
  Let her grow pale when she hears evidence you are untrue.
Lucky beyond all count is the man whom a woman grieves over,
  Pales at the word of his wrong, falls in a faint to the ground.
I would not mind, in that case, if she tried to snatch me bald-headed,
  Tore at my cheeks with her nails, frantic and weeping with rage,
Gave me her angriest looks, and wanted to do what she could not, . . .

      • • •

I was about to omit the art of deceiving a husband,
  Fooling a vigilant guard, crafty though either might be.
Let the bride honor, obey, pay proper respect to her husband,
  That is only correct; decency says so, and law.
But why should you, set free, and not too long ago, either,
  By the decree of the court, have to be kept like a bride?
Listen to me, and learn; though your watchers are there by the hundred,
  If you will take my advice, you can get rid of them all.
How can they interfere or stop you from writing a letter?
  What is a bathroom for? Tell them you have to go there.
Haven't you any close friend who knows how to carry a tablet
  Under her arm, or perhaps tucked in the fold of a gown?
Isn't she able to hide a note in the top of her stocking,
  Or, if that's apt to be found, in the instep of a shoe?
Is her guardian on to such tricks? — let her offer herself as a tablet,
  Carry, in code, on her back, letters in lipstick of red.
For your invisible ink, use milk: it will show when you heat it;
  Write with a stem of wet flax — no one will ever suspect.
Danae's father supposed he was careful in guarding his daughter;
  He was a grandfather soon, proving his vigilance vain.
What can a guardian do, with theaters all through the city?
  What can a guardian do when a girl goes to the track?
What can he do when she kneels to offer her homage to Isis?
  That is a place where no man ever has freedom to go.
There are more temples than one from which male eyes are forbidden,
  Where the Good Goddess allows only her servants to come.
What can a guardian do but sit and look at her clothing

When a girl goes to the baths, finding her games and her fun?
What is the use? She must go to take care of a friend, in a sickroom;
    Then her friend's perfectly well, leaving her half of the bed.
What can be done when the town is full of experienced locksmiths,
    When it's not only the door letting you enter at will?
Even the cheapest wine from Spain will befuddle a guardian;
    Drugs are effective as well, working with opiate spell.
He can be put to sleep if you send your maid to seduce him,
    Keeping him by her side, joined in delightful delay.
Why do I waste so much time with all this instruction in detail?
    There is an easier way; it won't take much of a bribe.
Take my word for it, bribes can buy both men and immortals;
    Jupiter, even, is won if you bring gifts to his shrine.
Fools will brag about bribes, but what can be done with a wise man?
    Bribe him. He'll take the bribe; furthermore, he will keep still.

Augustine
from The City of God

Augustine (354–430) became the leading theologian and spokesman for Christianity, which had been made the official religion of the Roman Empire only a half century before by Constantine. The first part of his life, much of which he spent in Rome, was devoted to eros and the pleasures of life. But after his conversion to Christianity in 386, he recast his views of erotic love through the harsh eyes of the Christian condemnation of the flesh. In the following passage from The City of God, *Augustine traces the origins of erotic lust back to the Fall, Adam and Eve's disobedience to God's commands. Procreation, he argues, was part of God's divine plan, but lust and eroticism, which blindly drive us to have intercourse, were rather the consequences of our own disobedience. In Paradise, he argues, we would have been fruitful and multiplied, but the procreative act would have been strictly a matter of will, not of the indecent and shameful desires of the flesh. True love is the spiritual love of God to which eros can only serve as an impediment. Much of the subsequent history of love and its spiritualization as well as our still ambivalent attitudes toward sex and love can be traced to these early Christian teachings.*

On the justice of the retribution that was meted out to the first human beings for their disobedience.

Man, as we know, scorned the bidding of God who had created him, who had made him in his own image, who had placed him above the other animals, who had established him in paradise, who had provided him with an abundance of all things and of security, and who had not laden him with commands that were numerous or onerous or difficult but had propped him up for wholesome obedience with one very brief and easy command, whereby he sought to impress upon this creature, for whom free service was expedient, that he was the Lord. Therefore, as a consequence, just condemnation followed, and this condemnation was such that man, who would have been spiritual even in flesh if he had observed the order, became carnal in mind as well. Moreover, this man who had pleased himself in his pride was then granted to himself by God's justice; yet this was not done in such a way that he was completely in his own power, but that he disagreed with himself and so led, under the rule of the one with whom he agreed when he sinned, a life of cruel and wretched slavery in place of the freedom for which he had conceived a desire. He was willingly dead in spirit and unwillingly destined to die in body; a deserter of the eternal life, he was doomed also to eternal death, unless he were freed by grace. Whoever thinks that condemnation of this sort is either excessive or unjust surely does not know how to gauge the magnitude of wickedness in sinning when the opportunity for not sinning was so ample. . . .

When we say that the flesh feels desire or pain, we mean that it is either man himself, as I have argued, or some part of the soul affected by what the flesh experiences, whether it be harsh and painful or gentle and pleasant. Pain of the flesh is only a vexation of the soul arising from the flesh and a sort of disagreement with what is done to the flesh, just as the pain of the mind that we call grief is a disagreement with the things that have happened to us against our will. But grief is generally preceded by fear, which is also something in the soul and not in the flesh. Pain of the flesh, on the other hand, is not preceded by anything like fear on the part of the flesh that is felt in the flesh before the pain. Pleasure, however, is preceded by a certain craving that is felt in the flesh as its own desire, such as hunger, thirst and the desire that is mostly called lust when it affects the sex organs, though this is a general term applicable to any kind of desire.

• • •

Therefore, although there are lusts for many things, yet when the term lust is employed without the mention of any object, nothing comes to mind usually but the lust that excites the shameful parts of the body. Moreover, this lust asserts its power not only over the entire body, nor only externally, but also from within. It convulses all of a man when the emotion in his mind combines and mingles with the carnal drive to produce a pleasure unsurpassed among those of the body. The effect of this is that at the very moment of its climax there is an almost total eclipse of acumen and, as it were, sentinel alertness. But surely any friend of wisdom and holy joys, who lives in wedlock but knows, as the Apostle admonished, "how to possess his bodily vessel in holiness and honor, not in the disease of lust like the gentiles who do not know God," would prefer, if he could, to beget children without this kind of lust. For he would want his mind to be served, even in this function of engendering offspring, by the parts created for this kind of work, just as it is served by the other members, each assigned to its own kind of

46 work. They would be set in motion when the will urged, not stirred to action when hot lust surged.

But not even those who are enamoured of this pleasure are aroused whether to marital intercourse or to the uncleanness of outrageous vice just when it is their will. At times the urge intrudes uninvited; at other times it deserts the panting lover, and although desire is ablaze in the mind, the body is frigid. In this strange fashion lust refuses service not only to the will to procreate but also to the lust for wantonness; and though for the most part it solidly opposes the mind's restraint, there are times when it is divided even against itself and, having aroused the mind, inconsistently fails to arouse the body.

• • •

It is reasonable then that we should feel very much ashamed of such lust, and reasonable too that those members which it moves or does not move by its own right, so to speak, and not in full subjection to our will, should be called pudenda or shameful parts as they were not before man sinned; for we read in Scripture: "They were naked, and not embarrassed." And the reason for this is not that they were unaware of their nakedness, but that their nakedness was not yet base because lust did not yet arouse those members apart from their will, and the flesh did not yet bear witness, so to speak, through its own disobedience against the disobedience of man. . . .

Let us consider the act itself that is accomplished by such lust, not only in every kind of licentious intercourse, for which hiding-places are prerequisite to avoid judgment before human tribunals, but also in the practice of harlotry, a base vice that has been legalized by the earthly city. Although in the latter case the practice is not under the ban of any law of this city, nevertheless even the lust that is allowed and free of penalty shuns the public gaze. Because of an innate sense of shame even brothels have made provision for privacy, and unchastity found it easier to do without the fetters of legal prohibition than shamelessness did to eliminate the secret nooks of that foul business.

But this harlotry is called a base matter even by those who are base themselves, and although they are enamored of it, they dare not make public display of it. What of marital intercourse, which has for its purpose, according to the terms of the marriage contract, the procreation of children? Lawful and respectable though it is, does it not seek a chamber secluded from witnesses? Before the bridegroom beings even to caress his bride, does he not first send outside all servants and even his own groomsmen as well as any who had been permitted to enter for kinship's sake, whatever the tie? And since, as a certain "supreme master of Roman eloquence" also maintains, all right actions wish to be placed in the light of day, that is, are eager to become known, this right action also desires to become known, though it still blushes to be seen. For who does not know what goes on between husband and wife for the procreation of children? Indeed, it is for the achievement of this purpose that wives are married with such ceremony. And yet, when the act for the birth of children is being consummated, not even the children that may already have been born from the union are allowed to witness it. For this right action does indeed seek mental light for recognition of it, but it shrinks from visual light. What is the reason for this if not that something by nature fitting and proper is carried out in such a way as to be accompanied also by something of shame as punishment?

Human nature then doubtless feels shame at this lust, and rightly so. For its disobedience, which subjected the sexual organs to its impulses exclusively and wrested them from control by the will, is a sufficient demonstration of the punishment that was meted out to man for that first disobedience. And it was fitting that this punishment should show itself particularly in that part of the body which engenders the very creature that was changed for the worse through that first great sin. No one can be delivered from the meshes of that sin unless the offence that was committed to the common disaster of all and punished by the justice of God when all men existed in but one, is expiated in each man singly by the grace of God.

• • •

When anyone says that there would have been no copulation or generation if the first human beings had not sinned, does he not imply that man's sin was required to complete the number of saints? For if by not sinning they would have continued to be solitary because, so some think, they could not have produced offspring if they had not sinned, then surely sin was required before there could not be just two but many righteous persons. But if that is too absurd to believe, we must rather believe that even if no one had sinned, a sufficiently large number of saints would have come into existence to populate that supremely happy city—as large a number, that is, as are now being gathered through the grace of God from the multitude of sinners, and as will be, so long as "the children of this world" beget and are begotten.

This leads to the conclusion that if no sin had been committed, that marriage, being worthy of the happiness of paradise, would have produced

48   offspring to be loved, yet no lust to cause shame. But there is now no example with which to illustrate how this could have been effected. Nevertheless,
that is no reason why it should seem incredible that the will, which is now
obeyed by so many members, might also have been obeyed in the absence
of this lust by that one part as well. Consider how, when we choose, we set
our hands and feet in motion to do the things that are theirs to do, how we
manage this without any conflict and with all the facility that we see both
in our own case and in that of others, especially among workers in all kinds
of physical tasks, where a natural capacity that is too weak and slow is fitted
for its employment by the application of greater dexterity and effort. May
we not similarly believe that those organs of procreation could, like the others, have served mankind by obedience to the decision of the will for the
generation of children even if there had been no lust inflicted as punishment for the sin of disobedience?

Certain human beings too, as we know, have natural endowments that
are quite different from those of others and remarkable for their very rarity. They can at will do with their bodies some things that others find utterly impossible to imitate and scarcely credible to hear. For some people
can actually move their ears, either one at a time or both together. Other
people, without moving their head, can bring all the scalp that is covered
with hair to the forefront and then draw it back again at will. . . . From
my own experience I know of a man who used to perspire at will. Certain
people are known to weep at will and to shed a flood of tears.

The body then, as we have seen, even now remarkably serves certain
people beyond the ordinary limits of nature in many kinds of movement
and feeling although they are living our present wretched life in perishable
flesh. That being so, what is there to keep us from believing that human
members may have served the human will without lust for the procreation
of offspring before the sin of disobedience and the consequent punishment
of deterioration? Man therefore was handed over to himself because he for-
sook God in his self-satisfaction, and since he did not obey God, he could
not obey even himself. From this springs the more obvious wretchedness
whereby man does not live as he chooses. For if he lived as he chose, he
would deem himself happy; but yet he would not be happy even so if he
lived an indecent life.

Heloise and Abelard

Letters

Heloise (whose parentage still remains disputed) was the abbess of the convent at Paraclete and one of the most learned persons of the twelfth-century Renaissance. Her husband, Peter Abelard, was born into a minor aristocratic family but renounced his noble rights and became the keenest and most influential scholar-theologian of his day. He was already renowned as a brilliant thinker and lecturer in Paris when he was brought into the house of Heloise's "uncle," Fulbert (surmised by some to be her father), to be the young girl's tutor. The relationship soon grew beyond its pedagogical bounds, and Heloise and Abelard became lovers, indeed, two of the most famous lovers in the Western tradition. But their love became famous first of all through a brutal tragedy. Fulbert would not tolerate the dangerous liaison between his ward and her tutor—even their secret marriage and their baby would not stem his jealousy—and he had Abelard attacked and emasculated. Heloise went off to the convent, and Abelard retreated to the Abbey of St. Denis, where he continued his theological disputations and wrote a history of their calamitous affair.

For the remainder of their lives, they kept up a passionate correspondence in which they explored, as deeply and with as much pathos as any lovers in history, the meaning of love and its place in life. In their letters, the split between sexual eros and philosophy implicit in Socrates and manifest in the Christian teachings of Saint Paul and Augustine turns into moral turmoil. In most of her letters, Heloise adopts a classical rather than a Christian perspective on love, but it is a Socratic perspective in which "disinterested" (sublimated) friendship is the ideal, "virtue joined to love, disengaged from the senses." To such a love, warmed by the memories of their passionate physical union, Heloise devotes her life. Abelard, on the other hand, seems to have a harder time with his passion and his humiliation. He sees both his love and his physical condition as antithetical to his philosophy; whereas Heloise sees her love as freedom, Abelard seems to feel his idealized philosophical freedom compromised by his. It is worth noting that, despite their marriage, both Heloise and Abelard praise love and dis-

play contempt for marriage, which they describe as the mere legalization of the weakness of the flesh. True love is essentially secret rather than public, and Heloise famously insists that she would rather be Abelard's mistress, even in such frustrating circumstances, than an empress. Through their tragedy, their celebration of secret love outside marriage, and their enduring love through letters, they become a prototype of the emerging institution of "courtly love." From their letters, we can sense that they managed to keep alive lifelong the lost joy of their brief but tragic affair. The following is a brief selection from those letters.

Letter II. Heloise to Abelard.

Let me always meditate on your calamities; let me publish them through all the world, if possible, to shame an age that has not known how to value you. I will spare no one, since no one would interest himself to protect you, and your enemies are never weary of oppressing your innocence. Alas; my memory is perpetually filled with bitter remembrances of past evils, and there more to be feared still? Shall my Abelard never be mentioned without tears? Shall the dear name be never mentioned without sighs? Observe, I beseech you, to what a wretched condition you have reduced me; sad, afflicted, without any possible comfort, unless it proceed from you. Be not, then unkind, nor deny me, I beg of you, that little relief which you only can give. Let me have a faithful account of all that concerns you. I would know everything, be it ever so unfortunate. Perhaps, by mingling my sighs with yours, I make your sufferings less; if that observation be true, that all sorrows divided are made lighter.

Tell me not, by way of excuse, you will spare our tears; the tears of women shut up in a melancholy place, and devoted to penitence, are not to be spared and if you wait for an opportunity to write pleasant and agreeable things to us, you will delay writing too long: Prosperity seldom chooses the side of the virtuous; and Fortune is so blind, that in a crowd, in which there is perhaps but one wise and brave man, it is not to be expected she should single him out. Write to me, then immediately, and wait not for miracles. . . . By a peculiar power, love can make [your picture] seem life itself, which, as soon as the loved object returns, is nothing but a little canvas and dead colours. I have your picture in my room. I never pass by it without stopping to look at it; and yet when you were present with me, I scarce ever cast my eyes upon it. If a picture which is but a mute representation of an object, can give such pleasure, what cannot letters inspire? They have souls, they can speak, they have in them all that force which expresses the transports of the heart; they have all the fire of our passions, they can raise them as much as if the persons themselves were present; they have all the softness and delicacy of speech, and sometimes a boldness of expression even beyond it.

We may write to each other, so innocent a pleasure is not forbidden us. Let us not lose, through negligence, the only happiness which is left us, and the only one perhaps which the malice of our enemies can never ravish from us. I shall read that you are my husband, and you shall see me address you as a wife. In spite of all your misfortunes, you may be what you please in your letters. Letters were first invented for comforting such solitary wretches as myself. Having lost the substantial pleasures of seeing and possessing you, I shall in some measure compensate this loss by the satisfaction I shall find in your writing. There I shall read your most secret thoughts; I shall carry them always about me. I shall kiss them every moment; if you can be capable of any jealousy, let it be for the fond caresses I shall bestow on your letters, and envy only the happiness of those rivals. That writing may be no trouble to you, write always to me carelessly, and without study: I had rather read the dictates of the heart than of the brain. I cannot live, if you do not tell me you always love me: but that language ought to be so natural to you, that I believe you cannot speak otherwise to me without great violence to yourself; and since by that melancholy relation to your friend you have awakened all my sorrows, it is but reasonable you should allay them by some marks of an inviolable love. . . .

You cannot but remember (for what do not lovers remember?) with what pleasure I have passed whole days in hearing your discourse. How when you were absent I shut myself from every one to write to you; how uneasy I was till my letter had come into your hands; what artful management it required to engage confidants: this detail perhaps surprises you and you are in pain for what will follow. But I am no longer ashamed that my passion has had no bounds for you, for I have done more than all this. I have hated myself that I might love you; I came hither to ruin myself in a perpetual imprisonment, that I might make you live quiet and easy. Nothing but virtue, joined to a love perfectly disengaged from the commerce of the senses, could have produced such effects. Vice never inspires any thing like this, it is too much enslaven to the body. . . . If formerly my affection for you was not so pure, if in those days the mind and the body shared in the pleasure of loving you, I often told you even then, that I was more pleased with possessing your heart, than with any other happiness, and the man was the thing I least valued in you.

You cannot but be entirely persuaded of this by the extreme unwillingness I showed to marry you; though I knew that the name of wife was honourable in the world, and holy in religion, yet the name of your mistress
had greater charms, because it was more free. The bonds of matrimony,
however honourable, still bear with them a necessary engagement, and I
was very unwilling to be necessitated to love always a man who perhaps
would not always love me. I despised the name of wife that I might live
happy with that of mistress. . . . Riches and pomp are not the charms of
love. True tenderness makes us separate the lover from all that is external to
him; and setting aside his quality, fortune, and employments, consider him
singly by himself.

It is not love, but the desire of riches and honour which makes women
run into the embraces of an indolent husband. Ambition, not affection,
forms such marriages. I believe, indeed, they may be followed by some honours and advantages, but I can never think that this is the way to enjoy the
pleasures of an affectionate union, nor to feel those secret and charming
emotions of hearts that have long strove to be united. . . . Their interested
vows occasion regret, and regret produces hatred. They soon part, or always desire it. This restless and tormenting passion punishes them for aim-
ing at other advantages by love than love itself.

If there be any thing which may properly be called happiness here below, I am persuaded it is in the union of two persons who love each other
with perfect liberty, who are united by a secret inclination, and satisfied
with each other's merit: their hearts are full, and leave no vacancy for any
other passion; they enjoy perpetual tranquility, because they enjoy content.

If I could believe you as truly persuaded of my merit as I am of yours, I
might say there has been a time when we were such a pair. Alas! how was it
possible I should not be certain of your merit? If I could ever have doubted
it, the universal esteem would have made me determine in your favour.
What country, what city has not desired your presence? Could you ever re-
tire, but you drew the eyes and hearts of all after you? . . .

But tell me whence proceeds your neglect of me since my being pro-
fessed? You know nothing moved me to it but your disgrace, nor did I give
any consent but yours. Let me hear what is the occasion of your coldness,
or give me leave to tell you now my opinion. Was it not the sole view of pleasure which engaged you to me? and has not my tenderness, by leaving you
nothing to wish for, extinguished your desires? Wretched Heloise! you could
please when you wished to avoid it: you merited incense when you could remove to a distance the hand that offered it. But since your heart has been

softened and has yielded; since you have devoted and sacrificed yourself you are deserted and forgotten, I am convinced, by a sad experience, that it is natural to avoid those to whom we have been too much obliged; and that uncommon generosity produces neglect rather than acknowledgment. My heart surrendered too soon to gain the esteem of the conqueror; you took it without difficulty, and gave it up as easily. But ungrateful as you are, I will never consent to it. And though in this place I ought not to retain a wish of my own, yet I have ever secretly preserved the desire of being beloved by you. When I pronounced my sad vow, I then had about me your last letters, in which you protested you would be wholly mine, and would never live but to love me. It is to you, therefore, I have offered myself; you had my heart; and I had yours; do not demand any thing back; you must bear with my passion as a thing which of right belongs to you, and from which you can no way be disengaged. . . .

Since you have forsaken me I glory in being wedded to Heaven. My heart adores that title, and disdains any other. Tell me how this divine love is nourished, how it operates, and purifies itself. When we were tossed in the ocean of the world we could hear of nothing but your verses, which published every where our joys and our pleasures. Now we are in the haven of grace, is it not fit you should discourse to me of this happiness, and teach me every thing which might improve and heighten it? Shew me the same complaisance in my present condition as you did when we were in the world. Without changing the ardour of our affections, let us change their object; let us leave our songs, and sing hymns; let us lift up our hearts to God, and have no transports but for his glory.

I expect this from you as a thing you cannot refuse me. God has a peculiar right over hearts of great men, which he has created. When he pleases to touch them, he ravishes, and suffers them not to speak or breathe but for his glory. Till that moment of grace arrives, oh! think of me; do not forget me; remember my love, my fidelity, my constancy; love me as your mistress, cherish me as your child, your sister, your wife. Consider that I still love you, and yet strive to avoid loving you. What a word, what a design is this! I shake with horror, and my heart revolts against what I say. I shall blot all my paper with tears. I end my long letter, wishing you, if you can desire it (would to Heaven I could), for ever adieu.

Letter II. Abelard to Heloise.

Could I have imagined that a letter not written to yourself could have fallen into your hands, I had been more cautious not to have inserted any thing in it which might awaken the memory of our past misfortunes. I described with boldness the series of my disgraces to a friend, in order to make him less sensible of a loss he had sustained. If by this well-meaning artifice I have disturbed you, I purpose here to dry up those tears which the sad description occasioned you to shed: I intended to mix my grief with yours, and pour out my heart before you; in short, to lay open before your eyes all my trouble, and the secret of my soul, which my vanity has hitherto made me conceal from the rest of the world, and which you now force from me, in spite of my resolutions to the contrary.

It is true, that in a sense of the afflictions which had befallen us, and observing that no change of our condition was to be expected; that those prosperous days which had seduced us were now past, and there remained nothing but to erase out of our minds, by painful endeavours, all marks and remembrance of them. I had wished to find in philosophy and religion a remedy for my disgrace; I searched out an asylum to secure me from love. I was come to the sad experiment of making vows to harden my heart. But what have I gained by this? If my passion has been put under a restraint, my ideas yet remain. I promise myself that I will forget you, and yet cannot think of it without loving you; and am pleased with that thought. My love is not at all weakened by those reflections I make in order to free myself. The silence I am surrounded with makes me more sensible to its impressions; and while I am unemployed with any other things; this makes itself the business of my whole vocation; till, after a multitude of useless endeavours, I begin to persuade myself that it is a superfluous trouble to strive to free myself, and that it is wisdom sufficient if I can conceal from every one but you my confusion and weakness.

I remove to a distance from your person, with an intention of avoiding you as an enemy; and yet I incessantly seek for you in my mind; I recall your image in my memory, and in such different disquietudes I betray and contradict myself. I hate you; I love you; shame presses me on all sides; I am at this moment afraid lest I should seem more indifferent than you are, and yet I am ashamed to discover my trouble. How weak are we in ourselves, if we do not support ourselves on the cross of Christ. Shall we have so little courage, and shall that uncertainty your heart labours with, of serving two masters, affect mine too? You see the confusion I am in, what I blame myself for, and what I suffer. Religion commands me to pursue virtue since I have nothing to hope for from love; but love still preserves its dominion in my fancy, and entertains itself with past pleasures. Memory supplies the place of a mistress. Piety and duty are not always the fruits of retirement; even in deserts, when the dew of Heaven falls not on us, we love what we ought no longer to love. The passions, stirred up by solitude, fill those regions of death and silence; and it is very seldom that what ought to be is followed there, and that God only is loved and served. Had I always had such notions as these, I had instructed you better. . . .

I find myself much more guilty in my thoughts of you, even amidst my tears, than in possessing yourself when I was in full liberty. I continually think of you, I continually call to mind that day when you bestowed on me the first marks of your tenderness. In this condition, O Lord, if I run to prostrate myself before thy altars, if I beseech thee to pity me, why does not the pure flame of thy spirit consume the sacrifice that is offered to thee? Cannot this habit of penitence which I wear interest Heaven to treat me more favourably? But that is still inexorable because my passion still lives in me; the fire is only covered with deceitful ashes, and cannot be extinguished but by extraordinary grace. We deceive men, but nothing is hid from God. . . .

What a troublesome employment is love! and how valuable is virtue even upon consideration of our own case! Recollect your extravagancies of passion, guess at my distractions; number up our cares, if possible, our griefs, and our inquietudes; throw these things out of the account, and let love have all its remaining softness and pleasure. Are we so weak our whole lives that we cannot now help writing to each other, covered as we are with sackcloth and ashes: how much happier should we be, if by our humiliation and tears we could make our repentance sure. The love of pleasure is not eradicated out of the soul but by extraordinary efforts; it has so powerful a party in our breasts that we find it difficult to condemn it ourselves. What abhorrence can I be said to have of my sins, if the objects of them are always amiable to me? How can I separate from the person I love, the passion I must detest? Will the tears I shed be sufficient to render it odious to me? I know not how it happens, there is always a pleasure in weeping for a beloved object. It is difficult in our sorrow to distinguish penitence from love. The memory of the crime, and the memory of the object which has charmed us, are too nearly related to be immediately separated. And the love of God in its beginning does not wholly annihilate the love of the creature.

Andreas Capellanus

from On Love

Andreas Capellanus (Andrew the Chaplain) studied and consolidated the developing rules and customs of courtship that defined the practice of what later came to be called "courtly love." Courtly love was an aristocratic practice, and though it focused on the charms and virtues of the individual it was always tightly framed by a strict social hierarchy in which differences in status were never out of mind. Courtly love was opposed to marriage and typically adulterous, which has led some authors (e.g. C. S. Lewis and Denis de Rougemont) to conclude that amorous love is as such illicit and opposed to marriage and that it is the danger of love that explains much of its excitement.

The truth about courtly love is somewhat less dramatic. Twelfth-century love was already varied and served several social purposes, licit as well as illicit, and among its virtues were a heightened sense of individual worth and, in particular, a new sense of the individual charms (as opposed to the economic utility) of women. In place of the quite uncharming economic negotiations that usually preceded a marriage-match, courtly love played wholly on the whims and desires of the potential lovers themselves. Courtship became a form of seduction rather than an affirmation of social status, and the practice thus placed great emphasis on individual elegance and eloquence. Accordingly, courtship became an arena for poetry and music, the rich, sensuous world of the troubadours. The emphasis in courting was placed on the process of wooing, not the winning. Our contemporary sexual impatience and forwardness, by contrast, would have been dismissed as entirely vulgar and virtueless. It is sometimes said, by way of lampoon, that courtly love was wholly based on sexual frustration, but while sexual culmination or consummation was by no means the "end" of the practice, it was by no means forbidden or assiduously avoided. True, most of the participants in the practice were already married to someone else, and sexual consummation often brought dangers which mere flirtation did not. But courtly love offered important new emotional freedoms to a feudal world on the verge of collapse, and it opened the way to what we call romantic love, with which it is mistakenly identified. The latter is a far more all-embracing conception which typically includes rather than opposes marriage within its scope and which is at least thought to be available to everyone, not just a small number of privileged aristocrats.

Capellanus himself, as well as his work, is something of an enigma. On Love is presented very much in the style of Ovid, as a guidebook for the potentially amorous, and most of the text consists of practical suggestions for seduction, even sample dialogues and rules for the pursuit of a courtly love affair. But at the end of the book, Capellanus reverses himself and makes clear that all of this is to be avoided at all costs, that courtly love is sinful and his entire treatise has in fact been not a guidebook but a warning. Equally enigmatic is the status of the person to whom the book is addressed, "Walter." Was he a student, a disciple, a lover? (For an analysis of and commentary on courtly love and Capellanus's presentation of it, see the selection by Louis Mackey in Part III.)

Book One. Introduction to the Treatise on Love

We must first consider what love is, whence it gets its name, what the effect of love is, between what persons love may exist, how it may be acquired, retained, increased, decreased, and ended, what are the signs that one's love is returned, and what one of the lovers ought to do if the other is unfaithful.

Chapter I. What Love Is

Love is a certain inborn suffering derived from the sight of and excessive meditation upon the beauty of the opposite sex, which causes each one to wish above all things the embraces of the other and by common desire to carry out all of love's precepts in the other's embrace.

That love is suffering is easy to see, for before the love becomes equally balanced on both sides there is no torment greater, since the lover is always in fear that his love may not gain its desire and that he is wasting his efforts. He fears, too, that rumors of it may get abroad, and he fears everything that might harm it in any way, for before things are perfected a slight disturbance often spoils them. If he is a poor man, he also fears that the woman may scorn his poverty; if he is ugly, he fears that she may despise his lack of beauty or may give her love to a more handsome man; if he is rich, he fears that his parsimony in the past may stand in his way. To tell the truth, no one can number the fears of one single lover [cf. Ovid]. This kind of love, then, is a suffering which is felt by only one of the persons and may

58 be called "single love." But even after both are in love the fears that arise are just as great, for each of the lovers fears that what he has acquired with so much effort may be lost through the effort of someone else, which is certainly much worse for a man than if, having no hope, he sees that his efforts are accomplishing nothing, for it is worse to lose the things you are seeking than to be deprived of a gain you merely hope for. The lover fears, too, that he may offend his loved one in some way; indeed he fears so many things that it would be difficult to tell them.

That this suffering is inborn I shall show you clearly, because if you will look at the truth and distinguish carefully you will see that it does not arise out of any action; only from the reflection of the mind upon what it sees does this suffering come. For when a man sees some woman fit for love and shaped according to his taste, he begins at once to lust after her in his heart; then the more he thinks about her the more he burns with love, until he comes to a fuller meditation. Presently he begins to think about the fashioning of the woman and to differentiate her limbs, to think about what she does, and to pry into the secrets of her body, and he desires to put each part of it to the fullest use [cf. Ovid]. Then after he has come to this complete meditation, love cannot hold the reins, but he proceeds at once to action; straightway he strives to get a helper and to find an intermediary. He begins to plan how he may find favor with her, and he begins to seek a place and a time opportune for talking; he looks upon a brief hour as a very long year, because he cannot do anything fast enough to suit his eager mind. It is well known that many things happen to him in this manner. This inborn suffering comes, therefore, from seeing and meditating. Not every kind of meditation can be the cause of love, an excessive one is required; for a restrained thought does not, as a rule, return to the mind, and so love cannot arise from it.

Chapter II. Between What Persons Love May Exist

Now, in love you should note first of all that love cannot exist except between persons of opposite sexes. Between two men or two women love can find no place, for we see that two persons of the same sex are not at all fitted for giving each other the exchanges of love or for practicing the acts natural to it. Whatever nature forbids, love is ashamed to accept.

Every attempt of a lover tends toward the enjoyment of the embraces of her whom he loves; he thinks about it continually, for he hopes that with her he may fulfill all the mandates of love — that is, those things which we find in treatises on the subject. Therefore in the sight of a lover nothing can be compared to the act of love, and a true lover would rather be deprived of all his money and of everything that the human mind can imagine as indispensable to life rather than be without love, either hoped for or attained. For what under heaven can a man possess or own for which he would undergo so many perils as we continually see lovers submit to of their own free will? We see them despise death and fear no threats, scatter their wealth abroad and come to great poverty. Yet a wise lover does not throw away wealth as a prodigal spender usually does, but he plans his expenditures from the beginning in accordance with the size of his patrimony; for when a man comes to poverty and want he begins to go along with his face downcast and to be tortured by many thoughts, and all joyousness leaves him. And when that goes, melancholy comes straightway to take its place, and wrath claims a place in him; so he begins to act in a changed manner toward his beloved and to appear frightful to her, and the things that cause love to increase begin to fail. Therefore love begins to grow less, for love is always either decreasing or increasing. I know from my own experience that when poverty comes in, the things that nourished love begin to leave, because "poverty has nothing with which to feed its love" [cf. Ovid].

But I do not tell you this, my friend, with the idea of indicating by what I say that you should follow avarice, which, as all agree, cannot remain in the same dwelling with love, but to show you that you should by all means avoid prodigality and should embrace generosity with both arms. Note, too, that nothing which a lover gets from his beloved is pleasing unless she gives it of her own free will.

Chapter III. Where Love Gets Its Name

Love gets its name (*amor*) from the word for hook (*amus*), which means "to capture" or "to be captured," for he who is in love is captured in the chains of desire and wishes to capture someone else with his hook. Just as a skillful fisherman tries to attract fishes by his bait and to capture them on his crooked hook, so the man who is a captive of love tries to attract another person by his allurements and exerts all his efforts to unite two different hearts with an intangible bond, or if they are already united he tries to keep them so forever.

Chapter IV. What the Effect of Love is

Now it is the effect of love that a true lover cannot be degraded with any avarice. Love causes a rough and uncouth man to be distinguished for his handsomeness; it can endow a man even of the humblest birth with nobility of character; it blesses the proud with humility; and the man in love becomes accustomed to performing many services gracefully for everyone. O what a wonderful thing is love, which makes a man shine with so many virtues and teaches everyone, no matter who he is, so many good traits of character! There is another thing about love that we should not praise in few words: it adorns a man, so to speak, with the virtue of chastity, because he who shines with the light of one love can hardly think of embracing another woman, even a beautiful one. For when he thinks deeply of his beloved the sight of any other woman seems to his mind rough and rude.

I wish you therefore to keep always in mind, Walter my friend, that if love were so fair as always to bring his sailors into the quiet port after they had been soaked by many tempests, I would bind myself to serve him forever. But because he is in the habit of carrying an unjust weight in his hand, I do not have full confidence in him any more than I do in a judge whom men suspect. And so for the present I refuse to submit to his judgment, because "he often leaves his sailors in the mighty waves." But why love, at times, does not use fair weights I shall show you more fully elsewhere in this treatise.

Chapter V. What Persons Are Fit for Love

We must now see what persons are fit to bear the arms of love. You should know that everyone of sound mind who is capable of doing the work of Venus may be wounded by one of Love's arrows unless prevented by age, or blindness, or excess of passion. Age is a bar, because after the sixtieth year in a man and the fiftieth in a woman, although one may have intercourse his passion cannot develop into love; because at that age the natural heat begins to lose its force, and the natural moisture is greatly increased, which leads a man into various difficulties and troubles him with various ailments, and there are no consolations in the world for him except food and drink. Similarly, a girl under the age of twelve and a boy before the fourteenth year do not serve in love's army. However, I say and insist that before his eighteenth year a man cannot be a true lover, because up to that age he is overcome with embarrassment over any little thing, which not only interferes with the perfecting of love, but even destroys it if it is well perfected. But we find another even more powerful reason, which is that before this age a man has no constancy, but is changeable in every way, for such a tender age cannot think about the mysteries of love's realm. Why love should kindle in a woman at an earlier age than in a man I shall perhaps show you elsewhere.

Blindness is a bar to love, because a blind man cannot see anything upon which his mind can reflect immoderately, and so love cannot arise in him, as I have already fully shown. But I admit that this is true only of the acquiring of love, for I do not deny that a love which a man acquires before his blindness may last after he becomes blind.

An excess of passion is a bar to love, because there are men who are slaves to such passionate desire that they cannot be held in the bonds of love—men who, after they have thought long about some woman or even enjoyed her, when they see another woman straightway desire her embraces, and they forget about the services they have received from their first love and they feel no gratitude for them. Men of this kind lust after every woman they see; their love is like that of a shameless dog. They should rather, I believe, be compared to asses, for they are moved only by that low nature which shows that men are on the level of the other animals rather than by that true nature which sets us apart from all the other animals by the difference of reason. Of such lovers I shall speak elsewhere.

Chapter VI. *In What Manner Love May Be Acquired, and in How Many Ways*

It remains next to be seen in what ways love may be acquired. The teaching of some people is said to be that there are five means by which it may be acquired: a beautiful figure, excellence of character, extreme readiness of speech, great wealth, and the readiness with which one grants that which is sought. But we hold that love may be acquired only by the first three, and we think that the last two ought to be banished completely from Love's court, as I shall show you when I come to the proper place in my system.

A beautiful figure wins love with very little effort, especially when the lover who is sought is simple, for a simple lover thinks that there is nothing to look for in one's beloved besides a beautiful figure and face and a body well cared for. I do not particularly blame the love of such people, but neither do I have much approval for it, because love between uncautious and unskilled lovers cannot long be concealed, and so from the first it fails to increase. For when love is revealed, it does not help the lover's worth, but brands his reputation with evil rumors and often causes him grief. Love between such lovers seldom lasts; but if sometimes it should endure it cannot indulge in its former solaces, because when the girl's chaperone hears the rumors, she becomes suspicious and watches her more carefully and gives her no opportunities to talk, and it makes the man's relatives more careful and watchful, and so serious unfriendliness arises. In such cases, when love cannot have its solaces, it increases beyond all measure and drives the lovers to lamenting their terrible torments, because "we strive for what is forbidden and always want what is denied us" [cf. Ovid].

A wise women will therefore seek as a lover a man of praiseworthy character — not one who anoints himself all over like a woman or makes a rite of the care of the body, for it does not go with a masculine figure to adorn oneself in womanly fashion or to be devoted to the care of the body. It was people like this the admirable Ovid meant when he said,

Let young men who are decked out like women stay far away from me,
    A manly form wants to be cared for within moderate limits.

Likewise, if you see a woman too heavily rouged you will not be taken in by her beauty unless you have already discovered that she is good company besides, since a woman who puts all her reliance on her rouge usually doesn't have any particular gifts of character. As I said about men, so with women — I believe you should not seek for beauty so much as for excellence of character. Be careful therefore, Walter, not to be taken in by the empty beauty of women, because a woman is apt to be so clever and such a ready talker that after you have begun to enjoy the gifts you get from her you will not find it easy to escape loving her. A person of good character draws the love of another person of the same kind, for a well-instructed lover, man or woman, does not reject an ugly lover if the character within is good. A man who proves to be honorable and prudent cannot easily go astray in love's path or cause distress to his beloved. If a wise woman selects as her lover a wise man, she can very easily keep her love hidden forever; she can teach a wise lover to be even wiser, and if he isn't so wise she can restrain him and make him careful. A woman, like a man, should not seek for beauty or care of the person or high birth, for "beauty never pleases if it lacks goodness," and it is excellence of character alone which blesses a man with true nobility and makes him flourish in ruddy beauty. For since all of us human beings are derived originally from the same stock and all naturally claim the same ancestor, it was not beauty or care of the body or even abundance of possession, but excellence of character alone which first made a distinction of nobility among men and led to the difference of class. Many there are, however, who trace their descent from these same first nobles, but have degenerated and gone in the other direction. The converse of this proposition is likewise true. ·

Character alone, then, is worthy of the crown of love. Many times fluency of speech will incline to love the hearts of those who do not love, for an elaborate line of talk on the part of the lover usually sets love's arrows a-flying and creates a presumption in favor of the excellent character of the speaker. How this may be I shall try to show you as briefly as I can.

To this end I shall first explain to you that one woman belongs to the middle class, a second to the simple nobility, and a third to the higher nobility. So it is with men; one is of the middle class, another of the nobility, a third of the higher nobility, and a fourth of the very highest nobility. What I mean by a woman of the middle class is clear enough to you; a noblewoman is one descended from a vavasor or a lord, or is the wife of one of these, while a woman of the higher nobility is descended from great lords. The same rules apply to men, except that a man married to a woman of higher or lower rank than himself does not change his rank. A married woman changes her status to match that of her husband, but a man can never change his nobility by marriage. In addition, among men we find one rank more than among women, since there is a man more noble than any of these, that is, the clerk.

· · ·

Book Two. How Love May Be Retained

Chapter I. How Love, When It Has Been Acquired, May Be Kept
Now since we have already said enough about acquiring love, it is not unfitting that we should next see and describe how this love may be retained after it has once been acquired. The man who wants to keep his love affair for a long time untroubled should above all things be careful not to let it be known to any outsider, but should keep it hidden from everybody; because when a number of people begin to get wind of such an affair, it ceases to develop naturally and even loses what progress it has already made. Furthermore a lover ought to appear to his beloved wise in every respect and restrained in his conduct, and he should do nothing disagreeable that might annoy her. Moreover every man is bound, in time of need, to come to the aid of his beloved, both by sympathizing with her in all her troubles and by acceding to all her reasonable desires. Even if he knows sometimes that what she wants is not so reasonable, he should be prepared to agree to it after he has asked her to reconsider. And if inadvertently he should do something improper that offends her, let him straightway confess with downcast face that he has done wrong, and let him give the excuse that he lost his temper or make some other suitable explanation that will fit the

case. And every man ought to be sparing of praise of his beloved when he is among other men; he should not talk about her often or at great length, and he should not spend a great deal of time in places where she is. When he is with other men, if he meets her in a group of women, he should not try to communicate with her by signs, but should treat her almost like a stranger, lest some person spying on their love might have opportunity to spread malicious gossip. Lovers should not even nod to each other unless they are sure that nobody is watching them. Every man should also wear things that his beloved likes and pay a reasonable amount of attention to his appearance—not too much because excessive care for one's looks is distasteful to everybody and leads people to despise the good looks that one has. If the lover is lavish in giving, that helps him retain a love he has acquired, for all lovers ought to despise all worldly riches and should give alms to those who have need of them. Nothing is considered more praiseworthy in a lover than to be known to be generous, and no matter how worthy a man may be otherwise, avarice degrades him, while many faults are excused if one has the virtue of liberality. Also, if the lover is one who is fitted to be a warrior, he should see to it that his courage is apparent to everybody, for it detracts very much from the good character of a man if he is timid in a fight. A lover should always offer his services and obedience freely to every lady, and he ought to root out all his pride and be very humble. He ought to give a good deal of attention to acting toward all in such fashion that no one may be sorry to call to mind his good deeds or have reason to censure anything he has done. Then, too, he must keep in mind the general rule that lovers must not neglect anything that good manners demand or good breeding suggests, but they should be very careful to do everything of this sort. Love may also be retained by indulging in the sweet and delightful solaces of the flesh, but only in such manner and in such number that they may never seem wearisome to the loved one. Let the lover strive to practice gracefully and manfully any act or mannerism which he has noticed is pleasing to his beloved. A clerk should not, of course, affect the manners or the dress of the laity, for no one is likely to please his beloved, if she is a wise woman, by wearing strange clothing or by practicing manners that do not suit his status. Furthermore a lover should make every attempt to be constantly in the company of good men and to avoid completely the society of the wicked. For association with the vulgar makes a lover who joins them a thing of contempt to his beloved.

What we have said about retaining love you should understand as referring to a lover of either sex. There are doubtless many other things which may be useful in retaining love that a wide-awake diligent lover may discover for himself.

Chapter II. How a Love,
Once Consummated, May Be Increased

We shall attempt to show you in a few words how love may be increased after it has been consummated. Now in the first place it is said to increase if the lovers see each other rarely and with difficulty; for the greater the difficulty of exchanging solaces, the more do the desire for them and the feeling of love increase. Love increases, too, if one of the lovers shows that he is angry at the other; for the lover falls at once into a great fear that this feeling which has arisen in his beloved may last forever. Love increases, likewise, if one of the lovers feels real jealousy, which is called, in fact, the nurse of love. Even if he does not suffer from real jealousy, but from a shameful suspicion, still by virtue of this his love always increases and grows more powerful. What constitutes real jealousy and what shameful suspicion you can easily see in the discussion between the man of the higher nobility and the noblewoman. Love increases, too, if it happens to last after it has been made public; ordinarily it does not last, but begins to fail just as soon as it is revealed. Again, if one of the lovers dreams about the other, that gives rise to love, or if love already exists it increases it. So, too, if you know that someone is trying to win your beloved away from you, that will no doubt increase your love and you will begin to feel more affection for her. I will go further and say that even though you know perfectly well that some other man is enjoying the embraces of your beloved, this will make you begin to value her solaces all the more, unless your greatness of soul and nobility of mind keep you from such wickedness. When you have gone to some other place or are about to go away—that increases your love, and so do the scoldings and beatings that lovers suffer from their parents, for not only does a scolding lecture cause love to increase after it is perfected, but it even gives a perfect reason for beginning a love affair that has not yet started. Frequent dwelling with delight on the thought of the beloved is of value in increasing love; so is the sight of her eyes when you are by yourselves and fearful, and her eager acceptance of a demand for the acts of love. Love is greatly intensified by a carriage and a way of walking that please the beloved, by a readiness to say pretty things, by a pleasant manner of speaking, and by hearing men sing the praises of the loved one. There are doubtless still other things by which love is increased which you can find out for yourself if you will study the matter attentively and if you have paid careful attention to those things that we have set down. For all the other things that are effective in such an affair seem to be dependent upon those which we have mentioned and to grow out of them.

Chapter III. In What Ways Love May Be Decreased

Now let us see in what ways love may be decreased. Too many opportunities for exchanging solaces, too many opportunities of seeing the loved one, too much chance to talk to each other all decrease love, and so does an uncultured appearance or manner of walking on the part of the lover or the sudden loss of his property. For a lover who suffers from great poverty is so tormented by the thought of household affairs and his urgent necessities that he can give no heed to the impulses of love and cannot allow it to increase as it should; as a result everybody tires to find fault with his character and his life, and he is despised and hated by all, and no one will look upon him as a friend because

> While you are fortunate you will number many friends,
> When the skies grow dark you will be alone.

Because of all these things a man's face and figure begin to change, and restful sleep deserts him, and so he can hardly escape becoming contemptible in the eyes of his beloved. It also decreases love if one discovers any infamy in the lover or hears of any avarice, bad character, or any kind of unworthiness; so it does for him to have an affair with another woman, even if he is not in love with her. Love decreases, too, if the woman finds that her lover is foolish and indiscreet, or if he seems to go beyond reasonable bounds in his demands for love, or if she sees that he has no regard for her modesty and will not forgive her bashfulness. For a faithful lover ought to prefer love's greatest pains to making demands which deprive his beloved of her modesty or taking pleasure in making fun of her blushes; he is not called a lover, but a betrayer, who would consider only his own passions and who would be unmindful of the good of his beloved. Love decreases, too, if the woman considers that her lover is cowardly in battle, or sees that he is unrestrained in his speech or spoiled by the vice of arrogance. For nothing appears more seemly in the character of any lover at all than that he should be clad in the garment of humility and wholly lack the nakedness of pride. The utterance of silly and foolish words frequently decreases love. Many men, when with a woman, think that they will please her if they utter the first silly words that come into their heads, which is really a great mistake. The man who thinks he can please a wise woman by doing something foolish shows a great lack of sense.

Other things which weaken love are blasphemy against God or His saints, mockery of the ceremonies of the Church, and a deliberate withholding of charity from the poor. We find that love decreases very sharply if one is unfaithful to his friend, or if he brazenly says one thing while he deceitfully conceals a different idea in his heart. Love decreases, too, if the lover piles up more wealth than is proper, or if he is too ready to go to law over trifles. We could tell you many more things about the weakening of love, but we leave you to find these out for yourself, for we see that you are so devoted to the practice of love as to neglect all other business and so determined to love that nothing in the art of love can escape you, since there is not a thing in it that you leave undiscussed. But we do not want you to overlook the fact that when love has definitely begun to decline, it quickly comes to an end unless something comes to save it.

The Rules of Love

I. Marriage is no real excuse for not loving.

II. He who is not jealous cannot love.

III. No one can be bound by a double love.

IV. It is well known that love is always increasing or decreasing.

V. That which a lover takes against the will of his beloved has no relish.

VI. Boys do not love until they arrive at the age of maturity.

VII. When one lover dies, a widowhood of two years is required of the survivor.

VIII. No one should be deprived of love without the very best of reasons.

IX. No one can love unless he is impelled by the persuasion of love.

X. Love is always a stranger in the home of avarice.

XI. It is not proper to love any woman whom one would be ashamed to seek to marry.

XII. A true lover does not desire to embrace in love anyone except his beloved.

XIII. When made public love rarely endures.

XIV. The easy attainment of love makes it of little value; difficulty of attainment makes it prized.

XV. Every lover regularly turns pale in the presence of his beloved.

XVI. When a lover suddenly catches sight of his beloved his heart palpitates.

XVII. A new love puts to flight an old one.

XVIII. Good character alone makes any man worthy of love.

XIX. If love diminishes, it quickly fails and rarely revives.

XX. A man in love is always apprehensive.

XXI. Real jealousy always increases the feeling of love.

XXII. Jealousy, and therefore love, are increased when one suspects his beloved.

XXIII. He whom the thought of love vexes eats and sleeps very little.

XXIV. Every act of a lover ends in the thought of his beloved.

XXV. A true lover considers nothing good except what he thinks will please his beloved.

XXVI. Love can deny nothing to love.

XXVII. A lover can never have enough of the solaces of his beloved.

XXVIII. A slight presumption causes a lover to suspect his beloved.

XXIX. A man who is vexed by too much passion usually does not love.

XXX. A true lover is constantly and without intermission possessed by the thought of his beloved.

XXXI. Nothing forbids one woman being loved by two men or one man by two women.

• • •

Book Three. The Rejection of Love

Now, friend Walter, if you will lend attentive ears to those things which after careful consideration we wrote down for you because you urged us so strongly, you can lack nothing in the art of love, since in this little book we gave you the theory of the subject, fully and completely, being willing to accede to your requests because of the great love we have for you. You should know that we did not do this because we consider it advisable for you or any other man to fall in love, but for fear lest you might think us stupid; we believe, though, that any man who devotes his efforts to love loses all his usefulness. Read this little book, then, not as one seeking to take up the life of a lover, but that, invigorated by the theory and trained to excite the minds

of women to love, you may, by refraining from so doing, win an eternal recompense and thereby deserve a greater reward from God. For God is more
pleased with a man who is able to sin and does not, than with a man who
has no opportunity to sin.

Now for many reasons any wise man is bound to avoid all the deeds of
love and to oppose all its mandates. The first of these reasons is one which it
is not right for anyone to oppose, for no man, so long as he devotes himself
to the service of love, can please God by any other works, even if they are
good ones. For God hates, and in both testaments commands the punishment of, those whom he sees engaged in the works of Venus outside the
bonds of wedlock or caught in the toils of any sort of passion. What good
therefore can be found in a thing in which nothing is done except what is
contrary to the will of God? . . .

We all know, moreover, that there is a second argument against love, for
by it we injure our neighbor whom, according to the divine mandate, every
man is bidden to love as himself. But even without the divine mandate and
considering only worldly convenience, we are bound to love our neighbors,
for no one can get along without neighbors even for a short time.

There is still a third thing which persuades everybody to avoid love: by
it one friend is estranged from another and serious unfriendlinesses grow
up between men, and these even lead to homicide or many other evils. No
one is so bound to another by the bonds of affection or friendship that if he
finds out that the other man is suing urgently for the love of his wife or his
daughter or some near relative he will not at once be filled with a spiteful
hatred toward him or conceive a venomous anger. . . .

Still another argument forbids us to indulge in the crime of love. Although all sins, by their very nature, stain the soul, this is the only one that
defiles both body and soul, and therefore it is more to be avoided than any
of the others; clearly, then, it is not without reason that the divine authority
declares there is no sin more serious than fornication.

But it seems that there is still another reason why we should avoid love.
The man who is in love is bound in a hard kind of slavery and fears that almost anything will injure this love of his, and his soul is very much upset by
a slight suspicion, and his heart is greatly troubled within him. Because of
love's jealousy he is afraid every time his beloved talks with any other man,
or goes walking with one, or stays out of sight longer than usual, because
"Love is a thing full of anxious fear" [Ovid]. He does not dare to do or to
think anything that is in the least contrary to what his beloved wants, because a lover is always afraid that his beloved may change her desire for

him, or her faithfulness, and whether waking or sleeping a lover can never get rid of this thought. He whom the sword of Love has really wounded is shaken all the time by the constant thought of his beloved, and he cannot be happy over wealth, or any honor in the world, or any dignity, so much as he is if he really enjoys his love just as his soul desires it. For even if a lover should gain the whole world, but suffer some detriment or hindrance in his love, he would look upon all the rest as the deepest poverty, but he would think that no penury could harm him so long as his love was as he wished it to be. A lover is afraid to do or to say anything which might for any reason make his beloved angry or give her a grievance against him. Who, then, is so foolish and mad as to try to get that which forces a man into such cruel servitude to another person and submits him to her will in everything? Besides, even if your friend happens not to be offended by your love because it is directed toward some person in whom he is not interested, still he can never feel real friendship for you until true love dominates him too. For he whom Love's darts hit thinks about nothing else, and he does not think that anything is of any use to him except to please his beloved and be always devoted to her service, and he renders a poor return to his friend whom, in his love, he neglects or loses. That wretch is considered to live only for himself and his beloved who neglects being useful or friendly to everyone else and puts all his reliance on the love of one woman; so with good reason he should be dropped by all his friends, and all men should avoid him.

There is yet another argument that seems hostile to the lover. From love comes hateful poverty, and one comes to the prison of penury. For love inevitably forces a man to give without regard to what he should give and what he should not; and this is not generosity, but what ancient common sense calls prodigality, a vice which sacred Scripture teaches us is a mortal one — one for which no abundance of goods can suffice — and thus it brings every man, regardless of who he is, to the depths of poverty. Thus it forces a man to pile up wealth, honestly or dishonestly, so that his poverty may have something on which to feed his love and something to keep his honor unharmed in the world. . . . Be careful, therefore, not to seek such an antecedent cause, the consequences of which you cannot easily avoid.

You can see now what people will think of a man after he has committed robberies and thefts and other furtive and wicked acts and with what a face a man can mingle with men after he has been found guilty of any of these crimes. Besides, what renders a man more contemptible to other men than for him to be compelled to suffer the obscurities of poverty for the love of a woman?

There is another argument, weighty enough, which stands in the way of every lover, and this is that love brings intolerable torments to all men during their lifetimes, and after they are dead it makes them suffer infinitely greater ones. O what a marvellously good thing should everybody consider that which promises to the living unremitting pain and threatens the dying with everlasting torment, and provides for all lovers that heritage which the Holy Scripture shows us is situated in outer darkness where there shall be weeping and gnashing of teeth! If you will take my advice, Walter, you will leave good things like that for someone else. But although I have said a great deal about the pains that lovers suffer while still alive, I do not think that anybody can fully appreciate them unless he has been taught by experience.

William Shakespeare

Thirteen Sonnets

The plays of William Shakespeare (1564–1616), both tragedies and comedies, abound with images of love and lovers. Some of our most deeply imbedded cultural images associated with romantic love stem from his plays. Consider, for instance, Romeo and Juliet, A Midsummer Night's Dream, *or* Othello. *Shakespeare's plays treat the range of human experience, but love emerges as perhaps the dominant theme in his works.*

Shakespeare's identity has long been a matter of controversy, and his private life is not well documented. He was married to Anne Hathaway when he was eighteen years old, and they subsequently had three children. Other details of the early decades of his life are matters of speculation.

The sonnets, like much of Shakespeare's life, are shrouded in mystery. Although he is said to have written "sugared sonnets" in his thirties that were known among his friends, his public literary output was largely confined to the theater. When an edition of his sonnets was first published in 1609, it was apparently produced without his permission. Thus, while the sonnets may have been intended to constitute a sequence (as was typical for Elizabethan sonnets), the order in which we know them may not have been the sequence that Shakespeare had in mind. The dominant view in contemporary scholarship is that Shakespeare wrote the sonnets we possess many years before they were published, during the era in which he wrote Romeo and Juliet.

Other debates concern the thematic content of the poems and its relationship to Shakespeare's own experiences. Many of the sonnets concern a handsome young man who is variously adulated by the poet and encouraged to marry and have children or berated for inspiring jealousy and for stealing the poet's woman (a situation which the poet ultimately seems to accept). Others concern a "dark lady" with whom the poet is entranced. The suggestion that these characters and the situations described reflect Shakespeare's own relationships and circumstances is supported by the relative obscurity of many of the sonnets. (One often gets the impression that Shakespeare did not want to be too obvious.) On the other hand, the iden-

tity of the real-life counterparts to the sonnets' characters, if indeed they ex-
ist, remains uncertain.

    Although some of the sonnets deal with other themes, the most famous
among them are love poems. These run the gamut of emotions associated
with romantic love: exultation, fervent devotion, jealousy, annoyance, des-
peration, a sense of betrayal, fear that love will wane, and peaceful happi-
ness. Taken together as a collection, however, Shakespeare's sonnets seem to
emphasize the tragic aspects of love over the joyous. The inevitability of
death and the frequency of disenchantment in love are recurrent themes;
and while the sonnets acknowledge the fleeting joys of love, they most often
reflect what may have been Shakespeare's own belief that the sole compen-
sation for the pains of love and death is the immortality of poetry.

XXIII.

As an unperfect actor on the stage
Who with his fear is put besides his part,
Or some fierce thing replete with too much rage,
Whose strength's abundance weakens his own heart,
So I, for fear of trust, forget to say
The perfect ceremony of love's rite,
And in mine own love's strength seem to decay,
O'ercharged with burden of mine own love's might,
O, let my books be then the eloquence
And dumb presagers of my speaking breast,
Who plead for love and look for recompense
More than that tongue that more hath more express'd.
    O, learn to read what silent love hath writ:
    To hear with eyes belongs to love's fine wit.

XXXI.

Thy bosom is endeared with all hearts,
Which I by lacking have supposed dead,
And there reigns love and all love's loving parts,
And all those friends which I thought buried.
How many a holy and obsequious tear
Hath dear religious love stol'n from mine eye
As interest of the dead, which now appear
But things removed that hidden in thee lie!
Thou art the grave where buried love doth live,

74   Hung with the trophies of my lovers gone,
    Who all their parts of me to thee did give;
    That due of many now is thine alone:
        Their images I loved I view in thee,
        And thou, all they, hast all the all of me.

XL.

Take all my loves, my love, yea, take them all;
What hast thou then more than thou hadst before?
No love, my love, that thou mayst true love call;
All mine was thine before thou hadst this more.
Then if for my love thou my love receivest,
I cannot blame thee for my love thou usest;
But yet be blamed, if thou thyself deceivest
By wilful taste of what thyself refusest.
I do forgive thy robbery, gentle thief,
Although thou steal thee all my poverty;
And yet, love knows, it is a greater grief
To bear love's wrong than hate's known injury.
        Lascivious grace, in whom all ill well shows,
        Kill me with spites; yet we must not be foes.

LVI.

Sweet love, renew thy force; be it not said
Thy edge should blunter be than appetite,
Which but to-day by feeding is allay'd,
To-morrow sharpen'd in his former might:
So, love, be thou; although to-day thou fill
Thy hungry eyes even till they wink with fullness,
To-morrow see again, and do not kill
The spirit of love with a perpetual dullness.
Let this sad interim like the ocean be
Which parts the shore, where two contracted new
Come daily to the banks, that, when they see
Return of love, more blest may be the view;
        Else call it winter, which being full of care
        Makes summer's welcome thrice more wish'd, more rare.

LXI.

Is it thy will thy image should keep open
My heavy eyelids to the weary night?
Dost thou desire my slumbers should be broken,
While shadows like to thee do mock my sight?
Is it thy spirit that thou send'st from thee
So far from home into my deeds to pry,
To find out shames and idle hours in me,
The scope and tenor of thy jealousy?
O, no! thy love, though much, is not so great:
It is my love that keeps mine eye awake;
Mine own true love that doth my rest defeat,
To play the watchman ever for thy sake:
      For thee watch I whilst thou dost wake elsewhere,
      From me far off, with others all too near.

LXXIII.

That time of year thou mayst in me behold
When yellow leaves, or none, or few, do hang
Upon those boughs which shake against the cold,
Bare ruin'd choirs, where late the sweet birds sang.
In me thou see'st the twilight of such day
As after sunset fadeth in the west,
Which by and by black night doth take away,
Death's second self, that seals up all in rest.
In me thou see'st the glowing of such fire
That on the ashes of his youth doth lie,
As the death-bed whereon it must expire
Consumed with that which it was nourish'd by.
      This thou perceivest, which makes thy love more strong,
      To love that well which thou must leave ere long.

LXXXVIII.

When thou shalt be disposed to set me light,
And place my merit in the eye of scorn,
Upon thy side against myself I'll fight,
And prove thee virtuous, though thou art forsworn.
With mine own weakness being best acquainted,
Upon thy part I can set down a story

76 Of faults conceal'd, wherein I am attainted,
  That thou in losing me shalt win much glory:
  And I by this will be a gainer too;
  For bending all my loving thoughts on thee,
  The injuries that to myself I do,
  Doing thee vantage, double-vantage me.
    Such is my love, to thee I so belong,
    That for thy right myself will bear all wrong.

XCII.

  But do thy worst to steal thyself away,
  For term of life thou art assured mine,
  And life no longer than thy love will stay,
  For it depends upon that love of thine.
  Then need I not to fear the worst of wrongs,
  When in the least of them my life hath end.
  I see a better state to me belongs
  Than that which on thy humor doth depend;
  Thou canst not vex me with inconstant mind,
  Since that my life on thy revolt doth lie.
  O, what a happy title do I find,
  Happy to have thy love, happy to die!
    But what's so blessed-fair that fears no blot?
    Thou mayst be false, and yet I know it not.

CII.

  My love is strengthen'd, though more weak in seeming;
  I love not less, though less the show appear:
  That love is merchandized whose rich esteeming
  The owner's tongue doth publish every where.
  Our love was new and then but in the spring
  When I was wont to greet it with my lays,
  As Philomel in summer's front doth sing
  And stops her pipe in growth of riper days:
  Not that the summer is less pleasant now
  Than when her mournful hymns did hush the night,
  But that wild music burthens every bough
  And sweets grown common lose their dear delight.

Therefore like her I sometime hold my tongue,
Because I would not dull you with my song.

CIX.

O, never say that I was false of heart,
Though absence seem'd my flame to qualify.
As easy might I from myself depart
As from my soul, which in thy breast doth lie:
That is my home of love: if I have ranged,
Like him that travels I return again,
Just to the time, not with the time exchanged,
So that myself bring water for my stain.
Never believe, though in my nature reign'd
All frailties that besiege all kinds of blood,
That it could so presposterously be stain'd,
To leave for nothing all thy sum of good;
    For nothing this wide universe I call,
    Save thou, my rose; in it thou art my all.

CXVI.

Let me not to the marriage of true minds
Admit impediments. Love is not love
Which alters when it alteration finds,
Or bends with the remover to remove:
O, no! it is an ever-fixed mark
That looks on tempests and is never shaken;
It is the star to every wandering bark,
Whose worth's unknown, although his height be taken.
Love's not Time's fool, though rosy lips and cheeks
Within his bending sickle's compass come:
Love alters not with his brief hours and weeks,
But bears it out even to the edge of doom.
    If this be error and upon me proved,
    I never writ, nor no man ever loved.

CXXX.

My mistress' eyes are nothing like the sun;
Coral is far more red than her lips' red;
If snow be white, why then her breasts are dun;

78   If hairs be wires, black wires grow on her head.
I have seen roses damask'd, red and white,
But no such roses see I in her cheeks;
And in some perfumes is there more delight
Than in the breath that from my mistress reeks.
I love to hear her speak, yet well I know
That music hath a far more pleasing sound;
I grant I never saw a goddess go;
My mistress, when she walks, treads on the ground;
    And yet, by heaven, I think my love as rare
    As any she belied with false compare.

CXXXVIII.

When my love swears that she is made of truth
I do believe her, though I know she lies,
That she might think me some untutor'd youth,
Unlearned in the world's false subtleties.
Thus vainly thinking that she thinks me young,
Although she knows my days are past the best,
Simply I credit her false speaking tongue:
On both sides thus is simple truth suppress'd.
But wherefore says she not she is unjust?
And wherefore say not I that I am old?
O, love's best habit is in seeming trust,
And age in love loves not to have years told:
    Therefore I lie with her and she with me,
    And in our faults by lies we flatter'd be.

John Milton

On Marriage and Divorce

John Milton (1608–1674) is known to us as one of the greatest canonical po-
ets of the English language, but in his own time he was considered a rather
dangerous man. Of the three periods into which biographers divide his life,
the middle period is marked by his engagement in "the pamphlet wars."
After a youth which involved an excellent education and considerable tra-
vel, Milton refused to enter the ministry, which would have been expected
after his extensive studies. Instead, he began a personal era of controversy
by publishing pamphlets on the clergy, on the Cromwell regime, and on di-
vorce. The pamphlets on the clergy attacked the government of the Church
of England by bishops. The pamphlets on the Cromwell regime defended
Parliament's decision to execute Charles I. In both of these pamphlets,
Milton took positions which, while controversial, had significant following
at the time.

Milton's series of pamphlets on divorce, however, were another matter.
His own personal interest in the subject stemmed from his unsuccessful
marriage to Mary Powell in 1624. She left him to return to her parents
within six weeks of their marriage. Milton responded to this experience by
publishing tracts that advocated divorce on the grounds of incompatibility.
Although he appealed to Scripture in his arguments and advanced a num-
ber of religious considerations in support of his position, Milton's pam-
phlets on divorce earned him the reputation of a radical whose views ap-
proached anarchy. In fact, Milton and his wife never were divorced. Mary
Powell returned to him, and they had three children. After her death, he
remarried but his second wife died in childbirth. He married his third wife
in 1663, after having been imprisoned at the fall of the Cromwell regime
and having lost most of his property. It was during this third marriage that
he wrote the great epics Paradise Lost *and* Paradise Regained, *which make*
use of his extensive experience with love and marriage, for example, in
their depiction of Adam and Eve.

The reading below comes from one of Milton's tracts on divorce. Al-
though his primary concern is divorce, Milton's discussion develops an im-

age of a desirable kind of marriage. Milton holds that the good marriage endures, in part, because the partners share a conversational life together. Milton thus defends what Shakespeare describes as "the marriage of true minds." In opposition to the reigning view of marriage as an economic arrangement between families, Milton defends the more modern idea that marriages should be based upon individual compatibility and personal preference.

. . . This therefore shall be the task and period of this discourse to prove, first that other reasons of divorce besides adultery, were by the Law of *Moses*, and are yet to be allow'd by the Christian Magistrate as a peece of justice, and that the words of Christ are not hereby contraried. Next, that to prohibit absolutely any divorce whatsoever except those which *Moses* excepted, is against the reason of Law, as in due place I shall shew out of *Fagius* with many additions. He therefore who by adventuring shall be so happy as with successe to light the way of such an expedient liberty and truth as this, shall restore the much wrong'd and over-sorrow'd state of matrimony, not onely to those mercifull and life-giving remedies of *Moses*, but, as much as may be, to that serene and blisfull condition it was in at the beginning; and shall deserv of all apprehensive men (considering the troubles and distempers which for want of this insight have bin so oft in Kingdomes, in States and Families) shall deserve to be reckon'd among the publick benefactors of civill and humane life; above the inventors of wine and oyle; for this is a far dearer, far nobler, and more desireable cherishing to mans life, unworthily expos'd to sadness and mistake, which he shall vindicate. Not that licence and levety and unconsented breach of faith should herein be contenanc't, but that some conscionable and tender pitty might be had of those who have unwarily in a thing they never practiz'd before, made themselves the bondmen of a luckles and helples matrimony. In which Argument he whose courage can serve him to give the first on-set, must look for two severall oppositions: the one from them who having sworn themselves to long customs and the letter of the Text, will not out of the road: the other from those whose grosse and vulgar apprehensions conceit but low of matrimoniall purposes, and in the work of male and female think they have all. Neverthelesse, it shall be here sought by due wayes to be made appeare, that those words of God in the institution, promising a meet help against lonelines; and those words of Christ, *That his yoke is easie and his burden light*, were not spoken in vain. . . .

To remove therefore if it be possible, this great and sad oppression

which through the strictnes of a literall interpreting hath invaded and disturb'd the dearest and most peaceable estate of houshould society. to the
over-burdening, if not the over-whelming of many Christians better worth
then to be so deserted of the Churches considerate care, this position shall
be laid down, first proving, then answering what may be objected either
from Scripture or light of reason.

*That indisposition, unfitnes, or contrariety of mind, arising from a
cause in nature unchangeable, hindring and ever likely to hinder the main
benefits of conjugall society, which are solace and peace, is a greater reason
of divorce then naturall frigidity, especially if there be no children, and
that there be mutuall consent. . . .*

. . . For all sence and equity reclaims that any Law or Cov'nant how
solemne or strait soever, either between God and man, or man and man,
though of Gods joyning, should bind against a prime and principal scope
of its own institution, and of both or either party cov'nanting; neither can
it be of force to ingage a blameles creature to his owne perpetuall sorrow,
mistak'n for his expected solace, without suffering charity to step in and
doe a confest good work of parting those whom nothing holds together, but
this of Gods joyning, falsly suppos'd against the expresse end of his own ordinance. And what his chiefe end was of creating woman to be joyn'd with
man, his own instituting words declare, and are infallible to informe us
what is mariage and what is no mariage: unlesse we can think them set
there to no purpose: *It is not good,* saith he, *that man should be alone; I
will make him a help meet for him.* From which words so plain, lesse cannot be concluded, nor is by any learned Interpreter, then that in Gods intention a meet and happy conversation is the chiefest and the noblest end
of mariage: for we find here no expression so necessarily implying carnall
knowledge, as this prevention of lonelines to the mind and spirit of man. To
this, *Fagius, Calvin, Pareus, Rivetus,* as willingly and largely assent as can
be wisht. And indeed it is a greater blessing from God, more worthy so excellent a creature as man is, and a higher end to honour and sanctifie the
league of marriage, whenas the solace and satisfaction of the mind is regarded and provided for before the sensitive pleasing of the body. And with
all generous persons maried thus it is; that where the mind and person
pleases aptly, there some unaccomplishment of the bodies delight may be
better born with, then when the mind hangs off in an unclosing dispropor-
tion, though the body be as it ought; for there all corporall delight will
soone become unsavoury and contemptible. And the solitarines of man,
which God had namely and principally order'd to prevent by mariage, hath

no remedy, but lies under a worse condition then the loneliest single life; for in single life the absence and remotenes of a helper might inure him to expect his own comforts out of himselfe, or to seek with hope; but here the continuall sight of his deluded thoughts without cure, must needs be to him, if especially his complexion incline him to melancholy, a daily trouble and pain of losse in som degree like that which Reprobats feele. Lest therefore so noble a creature as man should be shut up incurably under a worse evill by an easie mistake in that ordinance which God gave him to remedy a lesse evill, reaping to himselfe sorrow while he went to rid away solitarines, it cannot avoid to be concluded, that if the woman be naturally so of disposition, as will not help to remove, but help to increase that same God forbidd'n lonelines which will in time draw on with it a generall discomfort and dejection of mind, not beseeming either Christian profession or morall conversation, unprofitable and dangerous to the Common-wealth, when the houshold estate, out of which must flourish forth the vigor and spirit of all publick enterprizes is so ill contented and procur'd at home, and cannot be supported; such a mariage can be no mariage whereto the most honest end is wanting. . . .

. . . How vaine therefore is it, and how preposterous in the Canon Law to have made such carefull provision against the impediment of carnall performance, and to have had no care about the unconversing inability of mind, so defective to the purest and most sacred end of matrimony: and that the vessell of voluptuous enjoyment must be made good on him that has taken it upon trust without any caution, when as the mind from whence must flow the acts of peace and love, a farre more pretious mixture then the quintessence of an excrement, though it be found never so deficient and unable to performe the best duty of mariage in a cheerfull and agreeable conversation, shall be thought good anough, however flat and melancholious it be, and must serve, though to the eternall disturbance and languishing of him that complains him. Yet wisdom and charity waighing Gods owne institution, would think that the pining of a sad spirit wedded to lonelines should deserv to be free'd, as well as the impatience of a sensuall desire so providently reliev'd. Tis read to us in the Liturgy, that *we must not marry to satisfie the fleshly appetite, like brute beasts that have no understanding*; but the Canon so runs, as if it dreamt of no other matter then such an appetite to be satisfy'd; for if it happen that nature hath stopt or extinguisht the veins of sensuality, that mariage is annull'd. But though all the faculties of the understanding and conversing part after triall appeare to be so ill and so aversly met through natures unalterable working, as that neither peace, nor any sociable contentment can follow, 'tis as nothing, the contract shall stand as firme as ever, betide what will. What is this, but secretly to instruct us, that however many grave reasons are pretended to the maried life, yet that nothing indeed is thought worth regard therein, but the prescrib'd satisfaction of an irrationall heat; which cannot be but ignominious to the state of mariage, dishonourable to the undervalu'd soule of man, and even to Christian Doctrine it selfe. . . .

But some are ready to object, that the disposition ought seriously to be consider'd before. But let them know again, that for all the warinesse can be us'd, it may yet befall a discreet man to be mistak'n in his choice, and we have plenty of examples. The sobrest and best govern'd men are least practiz'd in these affairs; and who knowes not that the bashfull muteness of a virgin may oft-times hide all the unliveliness and naturall sloth which is really unfit for conversation; nor is there that freedom of acccesse granted or presum'd, as may suffice to a perfect discerning till too late: and where any disposition is suspected, what more usuall then the perswasion of friends, that acquaintance, as it increases, will amend all. And lastly, it is not strange though many who have spent their youth chastly, are in some things not so quick-sighted, while they hast so eagerly to light the nuptiall torch; nor is it therefore that for a modest error a man should forfeit so great a happines, and no charritable means to release him. Since they who have liv'd most loosely by reason of their bold accustoming, prove most successfull in their matches, because their wild affections unsetling at will, have been as so many divorces to teach them experience. When as the sober man honouring the appearance of modesty, and hoping well of every sociall vertue under that veile, may easily chance to meet, if not with a body impenetrable; yet often with a mind to all other due conversation inaccessible, and to all the more estimable and superior purposes of matrimony uselesse and almost liveles: and what a solace, what a fit helpe such a consort would be through the whole life of a man, is lesse pain to conjecture then to have experience. . . .

. . . This pure and more inbred desire of joyning to it selfe in conjugall fellowship a fit conversing soul (which desire is properly call'd love) *is stronger then death*, as the spouse of Christ thought, *many waters cannot quench it, neither can the floods drown it*. This is that rationall burning that mariage is to remedy, not to be allay'd with fasting, nor with any penance to be subdu'd, which how can he asswage who by mishap hath met the most unmeetest and unsutable mind? Who hath the power to struggle with an intelligible flame, not in paradice to be resisted, become now more ardent by being fail'd of what in reason it lookt for; and even then most unquencht, when the importunity of a provender burning is well anough appeas'd; and yet the soule hath obtained nothing of what it justly desires. Certainly such a one forbidd'n to divorce, is in effect forbidd'n to marry, and compell'd to greater difficulties then in a single life; for if there be not a more human burning which mariage must satisfie, or els may be dissolv'd, then that of copulation, mariage cannot be honourable for the meet reducing and terminating lust between two: seeing many beasts in voluntary and chosen couples, live together as unadulterously, and are as truly maried in that respect. But all ingenuous men will see that the dignity and blessing of mariage is plac't rather in the mutuall enjoyment of that which the wanting soul needfully seeks, then of that which the plenteous body would joyfully give away. . . .

. . . He therefore who lacking of his due in the most native and humane end of mariage, thinks it better to part then to live sadly and injuriously to that cheerfull covnant (for not to be belov'd and yet retain'd is the greatest injury to a gentle spirit) he I say who therefore seeks to part, is one who highly honours the maried life and would not stain it: and the reasons which now move him to divorce, are equall to the best of those that could first warrant him to marry; for, as was plainly shewn, both the hate which now diverts him and the lonelinesse which leads him still powerfully to seeke a fit help, hath not the least grain of a sin in it, if he be worthy to understand himselfe.

Baruch Spinoza
from Ethics

Baruch Spinoza (1632–1677) was a Jewish Dutch philosopher and one of the great thinkers of early modern times. His book Ethics *is a sweeping cosmic panorama concerning the nature of the universe, the place of human beings within it, and the nature of God (who is and must be identical to the universe as a whole). The style of the book is mathematical (definitions, axioms, postulates, and proofs), and the subject matter is metaphysics. It is, nevertheless, first of all an ethics, a thoughtful account of the proper way to live in a world filled with suffering, in which our sense of freedom and control is an illusion and in which our celebrated rationality is buffeted and weakened by the continuing onslaught of our passions.*

Spinoza's Ethics, *therefore, is a book that is very much concerned with human emotions. Much like the ancient Stoics (to whom he is kin in many ways), Spinoza teaches a doctrine of the emotions as essentially "thoughts" which can be well- or ill-considered, correct or incorrect, conducive to personal growth or self-destructive. Emotions like anger that presume control of the world and emotions such as envy and resentment that wish that the world were other than it is are dangerous, ultimately destructive, while love, which is above all else a blissful acceptance of the world, turns out to be the most positive emotion of all. Of course, Spinoza is primarily concerned with a much more general form of love than the erotic, but his discussion makes clear that the erotic too must be taken seriously as love, particularly because of all its attendant dangers. The language is extremely formal, but Spinoza's sensitivity, we hope, will be obvious. (For a sympathetic study of Spinoza's view of love, see Amelie Rorty's selection in Part III.)*

Part III. On the Origin and Nature of the Emotions
• • •

I do not forget, that the illustrious Descartes, though he believed, that the mind has absolute power over its actions, strove to explain human emotions by their primary causes, and, at the same time, to point out a way, by which the mind might attain to absolute dominion over them. However, in my opinion, he accomplishes nothing beyond a display of the acuteness of his own great intellect, as I will show in the proper place. For the present I wish to revert to those, who would rather abuse or deride human emotions than understand them. Such persons will, doubtless think it strange that I should attempt to treat of human vice and folly geometrically, and should wish to set forth with rigid reasoning those matters which they cry out against as repugnant to reason, frivolous, absurd, and dreadful.

· · ·

Prop. XIII . . . *Love* is nothing else but *pleasure accompanied by the idea of an external cause: Hate* is nothing else but *pain accompanied by the idea of an external cause.* We further see, that he who loves necessarily endeavours to have, and to keep present to him, the object of his love; while he who hates endeavours to remove and destroy the object of his hatred.

· · ·

Prop. XIV. *If the mind has once been affected by two emotions at the same time, it will, whenever it is afterwards affected by one of the two, be also affected by the other.*

· · ·

Prop. XV. *Anything can, accidentally, be the cause of pleasure, pain, or desire.*

· · ·

Corollary. —Simply from the fact that we have regarded a thing with the emotion of pleasure or pain, though that thing be not the efficient cause of the emotion, we can either love or hate it.

· · ·

Prop. XIX. *He who conceives that the object of his love is destroyed will feel pain; if he conceives that it is preserved, he will feel pleasure.*

Proof. —The mind, as far as possible, endeavours to conceive those things which increase or help the body's power of activity (III. xii); in other words (III. xii. note), those things which it loves. But conception is helped by those things which postulate the existence of a thing, and contrariwise is hindered by those which exclude the existence of a thing (II. xvii.); therefore the images of things, which postulate the existence of an object of love, help the mind's endeavour to conceive the object of love, in other words (III. xi. note), affect the mind pleasurably; contrariwise those things, which exclude the existence of an object of love, hinder the aforesaid mental endeavour; in other words, affect the mind painfully. He, therefore,

who conceives that the object of his love is destroyed will feel pain, &c.
Q.E.D.

. . .

Prop. XXI. *He who conceives, that the object of his love is affected plea-*
surably or painfully, will himself be affected pleasurably or painfully; and
the one or the other emotion will be greater or less in the lover according as
it is greater or less in the thing loved.

Proof. — The images of things (as we showed in III. xix.) which postulate the existence of the object of love, help the mind's endeavour to conceive the said object. But pleasure postulates the existence of something
feeling pleasure, so much the more in proportion as the emotion of pleasure is greater; for it is (III. xi. note) a transition to a greater perfection;
therefore the image of pleasure in the object of love helps the mental endeavour of the lover; that is, it affects the lover pleasurably, and so much
the more, in proportion as this emotion may have been greater in the object
of love. This was our first point. Further, in so far as a thing is affected with
pain, it is to that extent destroyed, the extent being in proportion to the
amount of pain (III. xi. note); therefore (III. xix.) he who conceives, that
the object of his love is affected painfully, will himself be affected painfully,
in proportion as the said emotion is greater or less in the object of love.
Q.E.D.

Prop. XXII. *If we conceive that anything pleasurably affects some object*
of our love, we shall be affected with love towards that thing. Contrariwise,
if we conceive that it affects an object of our love painfully, we shall be af-
fected with hatred towards it.

Proof. — He, who affects pleasurably or painfully the object of our love,
affects us also pleasurably or painfully — that is, if we conceive the loved object as affected with the said pleasure or pain (III. xxi.). But this pleasure
or pain is postulated to come to us accompanied by the idea of an external
cause; therefore (III. xiii. note), if we conceive that anyone affects an object of our love pleasurably or painfully, we shall be affected with love or
hatred towards him. Q.E.D.

Note. — Prop. xxi. explains to us the nature of *Pity*, which we may define as *pain arising from another's hurt.* What term we can use for pleasure
arising from another's gain, I know not.

We will call the *love towards him who confers a benefit on another*, *Ap-*
proval; and the *hatred towards him who injures another*, we will call *Indig-*
nation. We must further remark, that we not only feel pity for a thing
which we have loved (as shown in III. xxi.), but also for a thing which we

88   have hitherto regarded without emotion, provided that we deem that it resembles ourselves (as I will show presently). Thus, we bestow approval on one who has benefited anything resembling ourselves, and, contrariwise, are indignant with him who has done it an injury.

. . .

Prop. XXV. *We endeavour to affirm, concerning ourselves and concerning what we love, everything that we conceive to affect pleasurably ourselves, or the loved object. Contrariwise, we endeavour to negative everything, which we conceive to affect painfully ourselves or the loved object.*

Proof.—That, which we conceive to affect an object of our love pleasurably or painfully, affects us also pleasurably or painfully (III. xxi.). But the mind (III. xii.) endeavours, as ar as possible, to conceive those things which affect us pleasurably; in other words (II. xvii. and Coroll.), it endeavours to regard them as present. And, contrariwise (III. xiii.), it endeavours to exclude the existence of such things as affect us painfully; therefore, we endeavour to affirm concerning ourselves, and concerning the loved object, whatever we conceive to affect ourselves, or the loved object pleasurably. *Q.E.D.*

. . .

Prop. XXX. . . . *Note.*—As love (III. xiii.) is pleasure accompanied by the idea of an external cause, and hatred is pain accompanied by the idea of an external cause; the pleasure and pain in question will be a species of love and hatred. But, as the terms love and hatred are used in reference to external objects, we will employ other names for the emotions now under discussion: pleasure accompanied by the idea of an external cause we will style *Honour*, and the emotion contrary thereto we will style *Shame*: I mean in such cases as where pleasure or pain arises from a man's belief, that he is being praised or blamed: otherwise pleasure accompanied by the idea of an external cause is called *self-complacency*, and its contrary pain is called *repentance*. Again, as it may happen (II. xvii. Coroll.) that the pleasure, wherewith a man conceives that he affects others, may exist solely in his own imagination, and as (III. xxv.) everyone endeavours to conceive concerning himself that which he conceives will affect him with pleasure, it may easily come to pass that a vain man may be proud and may imagine that he is pleasing to all, when in reality he may be an annoyance to all.

Prop. XXXI. *If we conceive that anyone loves, desires, or hates anything which we ourselves love, desire, or hate, we shall thereupon regard the thing in question with more steadfast love, &c. On the contrary, if we think that anyone shrinks from something that we love, we shall undergo vacillation of soul.*

Proof.—From the mere fact of conceiving that anyone loves anything we shall ourselves love that thing (III. xxvii.): but we are assumed to love it already; there is, therefore, a new cause of love, whereby our former emotion is fostered; hence we shall thereupon love it more steadfastly. Again, from the mere fact of conceiving that anyone shrinks from anything, we shall ourselves shrink from that thing (III. xxvii). If we assume that we at the same time love it, we shall then simultaneously love it and shrink from it; in other words, we shall be subject to vacillation. . . . *Q.E.D.*

Corollary.—From the foregoing, and also from III. xxviii. it follows that everyone endeavours, as far as possible, to cause others to love what he himself loves, and to hate what he himself hates: as the poet says: "As lovers let us share every hope and every fear: ironhearted were he who should love what the other leaves."

Note.—This endeavour to bring it about, that our own likes and dislikes should meet with universal approval, is really ambition . . . ; wherefore we see that everyone by nature desires . . . , that the rest of mankind should live according to his own individual disposition: when such a desire is equally present in all, everyone stands in everyone else's way, and in wishing to be loved or praised by all, all become mutually hateful.

Prop. XXXII. *If we conceive that anyone takes delight in something which only one person can possess we shall endeavour to bring it about that the man in question shall not gain possession thereof.*

Proof.—From the mere fact of our conceiving that another person takes delight in a thing (III. xxvii. and Coroll.) we shall ourselves love that thing and desire to take delight therein. But we assumed that the pleasure in question would be prevented by another's delight in its object; we shall, therefore, endeavour to prevent his possession thereof (III. xxviii.). *Q.E.D.*

Note.—We thus see that man's nature is generally so constituted, that he takes pity on those who fare ill, and envies those who fare well with an amount of hatred proportioned to his own love for the goods in their possession. Further, we see that from the same property of human nature, whence it follows that men are merciful, it follows also that they are envious and ambitious. Lastly, if we make appeal to Experience, we shall find that she entirely confirms what we have said; more especially if we turn our attention to the first years of our life. We find that children, whose body is continually, as it were, in equilibrium, laugh or cry simply because they see others laughing or crying; moreover, they desire forthwith to imitate whatever they see others doing, and to possess themselves whatever they conceive as delighting others: inasmuch as the images of things are, as we have said, modifications of the human body, or modes wherein the human body is affected and disposed by external causes to act in this or that manner.

Prop. XXXIII. *When we love a thing similar to ourselves, we endeavour, as far as we can, to bring it about that it should love us in return.*

Proof. —That which we love we endeavour, as far as we can, to conceive in preference to anything else (III. xii.). If the thing be similar to ourselves, we shall endeavour to affect it pleasurably in preference to anything else (III. xxix.). In other words, we shall endeavour, as far as we can, to bring it about, that the thing should be affected with pleasure accompanied by the idea of ourselves, that is (III. xiii. note), that it should love us in return. *Q.E.D.*

Prop. XXXIV. *The greater the emotion with which we conceive a loved object to be affected towards us, the greater will be our complacency.*

Proof. —We endeavour (III. xxxiii.), as far as we can, to bring about, that what we love should love us in return: in other words, that what we love should be affected with pleasure accompanied by the idea of ourself as cause. Therefore, in proportion as the loved object is more pleasurably affected because of us, our endeavour will be assisted . . . —that is (III. xi. and note) the greater will be our pleasure. But when we take pleasure in the fact, that we pleasurably affect something similar to ourselves, we regard ourselves with pleasure (III. xxx.); therefore the greater the emotion with which we conceive a loved object to be affected, &c. *Q.E.D.*

Prop. XXXV. *If anyone conceives, that an object of his love joins itself to another with closer bonds of friendship than he himself has attained to, he will be affected with hatred towards the loved object and with envy towards his rival.*

Proof. —In proportion as a man thinks, that a loved object is well affected towards him, will be the strength of his self-approval (by the last Prop.), that is (III. xxx. note), of his pleasure; he will, therefore (III. xxviii.), endeavour, as far as he can, to imagine the loved object as most closely bound to him: this endeavour or desire will be increased, if he thinks that someone else has a similar desire (III. xiii.). But this endeavour or desire is assumed to be checked by the image of the loved object in conjunction with the image of him whom the loved object has joined to itself; therefore (III. xi. note) he will for that reason be affected with pain, accompanied by the idea of the loved object as a cause in conjunction with the image of his rival; that is, he will be (III. xiii.) affected with hatred towards the loved object and also towards his rival (III. xv. Coroll.), which latter he will envy as enjoying the beloved object. *Q.E.D.*

Note. — This hatred towards an object of love joined with envy is called *Jealousy*, which accordingly is nothing else but a wavering of the disposition arising from combined love and hatred, accompanied by the idea of some rival who is envied. Further, this hatred towards the object of love will be greater, in proportion to the pleasure which the jealous man had been wont to derive from the reciprocated love of the said object; and also in proportion to the feelings he had previously entertained towards his rival. If he had hated him, he will forthwith hate the object of his love, because he conceives it is pleasurably affected by one whom he himself hates: and also because he is compelled to associate the image of his loved one with the image of him whom he hates. This condition generally comes into play in the case of love for a woman: for he who thinks, that a woman whom he loves prostitutes herself to another, will feel pain, not only because his own desire is restrained, but also because, being compelled to associate the image of her he loves with the parts of shame and the excreta of another, he therefore shrinks from her.

We must add, that a jealous man is not greeted by his beloved with the same joyful countenance as before, and this also gives him pain as a lover, as I will now show.

Prop. XXXVI. *He who remembers a thing, in which he has once taken delight, desires to possess it under the same circumstances as when he first took delight therein.*

Proof. — Everything, which a man has seen in conjunction with the object of his love, will be to him accidentally a cause of pleasure (III. xv.); he will, therefore, desire to possess it, in conjunction with that wherein he has taken delight; in other words, he will desire to possess the object of his love under the same circumstances as when he first took delight therein. *Q.E.D.*

Corollary. — A lover will, therefore, feel pain if one of the aforesaid attendant circumstances be missing.

Proof. — For, in so far as he finds some circumstance to be missing, he conceives something which excludes its existence. As he is assumed to be desirous for love's sake of that thing or circumstance (by the last Prop.), he will, in so far as he conceives it to be missing, feel pain (III. xix.). *Q.E.D.*

Note. — This pain, in so far as it has reference to the absence of the object of love, is called *Regret*.

Prop. XXXVII. *Desire arising through pain or pleasure, hatred or love, is greater in proportion as the emotion is greater.*

Proof. — Pain diminishes or constrains man's power of activity (III. xi. note), in other words (III. vii.), diminishes or constrains the effort, wherewith he endeavours to persist in his own being; therefore (III. v.) it is contrary to the said endeavour: thus all the endeavours of a man affected by pain are directed to removing that pain. But (by the definition of pain), in proportion as the pain is greater, so also is it necessarily opposed to a greater part of man's power of activity; therefore the greater the pain, the greater the power of activity employed to remove it; that is, the greater will be the desire or appetite in endeavouring to remove it. Again, since pleasure (III. xi. note) increases or aids a man's power of activity, it may easily be shown in like manner, that a man affected by pleasure has no desire further than to preserve it, and his desire will be in proportion to the magnitude of the pleasure.

Lastly, since hatred and love are themselves emotions of pain and pleasure, it follows in like manner that the endeavour, appetite, or desire, which arises through hatred or love, will be greater in proportion to the hatred or love. *Q.E.D.*

Prop. XXXVIII. *If a man has begun to hate an object of his love, so that love is thoroughly destroyed, he will, causes being equal, regard it with more hatred than if he had never loved it, and his hatred will be in proportion to the strength of his former love.*

Proof. — If a man begins to hate that which he had loved, more of his appetites are put under restraint than if he had never loved it. For love is a pleasure (III. xiii. note) which a man endeavours as far as he can to render permanent (III. xxviii.); he does so by regarding the object of his love as present, and by affecting it as far as he can pleasurably; this endeavour is greater in proportion as the love is greater, and so also is the endeavour to bring about that the beloved should return his affection (III. xxxiii.). Now these endeavours are constrained by hatred towards the object of love (III. xiii. Coroll. and III. xxiii.); wherefore the lover (III. xi. note) will for this cause also be affected with pain, the more so in proportion as his love has been greater; that is, in addition to the pain caused by hatred, there is a pain caused by the fact that he has loved the object; wherefore the lover will regard the beloved with greater pain, or in other words, will hate it more than if he had never loved it, and with the more intensity in proportion as his former love was greater. *Q.E.D.*

· · ·

Prop. XLI. *If anyone conceives that he is loved by another, and believes that he has given no cause for such love, he will love that other in return.* (Cf. III. xv. Coroll., and III. xvi.)

· · ·

Note. — If he believes that he has given just cause for the love, he will take pride therein (III. xxx. and note); this is what most often happens (III. xxv.), and we said that its contrary took place whenever a man conceives himself to be hated by another. (See note to preceding proposition.) This reciprocal love, and consequently the desire of benefiting him who loves us (III. xxxix.), and who endeavours to benefit us, is called *gratitude* or *thankfulness*. It thus appears that men are much more prone to take vengeance than to return benefits.

Corollary. — He who imagines, that he is loved by one whom he hates, will be a prey to conflicting hatred and love. This is proved in the same way as the first corollary of the preceding proposition.

Note. — If hatred be the prevailing emotion, he will endeavour to injure him who loves him; this emotion is called cruelty, especially if the victim be believed to have given no ordinary cause for hatred.

Prop. XLII. *He who has conferred a benefit on anyone from motives of love or honour will feel pain, if he sees that the benefit is received without gratitude.*

Proof. — When a man loves something similar to himself, he endeavours, as far as he can, to bring it about that he should be loved thereby in return (III. xxxiii.). Therefore he who has conferred a benefit confers it in obedience to the desire, which he feels of being loved in return; that is (III. xxxiv.) from the hope of honour, or (III. xxx. note.) pleasure; hence he will endeavour, as far as he can, to conceive this cause of honour, or to regard it as actually existing. But, by the hypothesis, he conceives something else, which excludes the existence of the said cause of honour: wherefore he will thereat feel pain (III. xix.). *Q.E.D.*

Prop. XLIII. *Hatred is increased by being reciprocated, and can on the other hand be destroyed by love.*

Proof. — He who conceives, that an object of his hate hates him in return, will thereupon feel a new hatred, while the former hatred (by hypothesis) still remains (III. xl.). But if, on the other hand, he conceives that the object of hate loves him, he will to this extent (III. xxxviii.) regard himself with pleasure, and (III. xxix.) will endeavour to please the cause of his emotion. In other words, he will endeavour not to hate him (III. xli.), and not to affect him painfully; this endeavour (III. xxxvii.) will be greater or less in proportion to the emotion from which it arises. Therefore, if it be greater than that which arises from hatred, and through which the man endeavours to affect painfully the thing which he hates, it will get the better of it and banish the hatred from his mind. *Q.E.D.*

Prop. XLIV. *Hatred which is completely vanquished by love passes into love: and love is thereupon greater than if hatred had not preceded it.*

Proof. — The proof proceeds in the same way as Prop. xxxviii. of this Part: for he who begins to love a thing, which he was wont to hate or regard with pain, from the very fact of loving feels pleasure. To this pleasure involved in love is added the pleasure arising from aid given to the endeavour to remove the pain involved in hatred (III. xxxvii.), accompanied by the idea of the former object of hatred as cause.

Note. — Though this be so, no one will endeavour to hate anything, or to be affected with pain, for the sake of enjoying this greater pleasure; that is, no one will desire that he should be injured, in the hope of recovering from the injury, nor long to be ill for the sake of getting well. For everyone will always endeavour to persist in his being, and to ward off pain as far as he can. If the contrary is conceivable, namely, that a man should desire to hate someone, in order that he might love him the more thereafter, he will always desire to hate him. For the strength of the love is in proportion to the strength of the hatred, wherefore the man would desire, that the hatred be continually increased more and more, and, for a similar reason, he would desire to become more and more ill, in order that he might take a greater pleasure in being restored to health: in such a case he would always endeavour to be ill, which (III. vi.) is absurd.

. . .

Prop. XLIX. *Love or hatred towards a thing which we conceive to be free must, other conditions being similar, be greater than if it were felt towards a thing acting by necessity.*

Proof. — A thing which we conceive as free must (I. Def. vii.) be perceived through itself without anything else. If, therefore, we conceive it as the cause of pleasure or pain, we shall therefore (III. xiii. note) love it or hate it, and shall do so with the utmost love or hatred that can arise from the given emotion. But if the thing which causes the emotion be conceived as acting by necessity, we shall then (by the same Def. vii. Part I.) conceive it not as the sole cause, but as one of the causes of the emotion, and therefore our love or hatred towards it will be less. *Q.E.D.*

Note. — Hence it follows, that men, thinking themselves to be free, feel more love or hatred towards one another than towards anything else: to this

consideration we must add the imitation of emotions treated of in III. xxvii. xxxiv. xl. and xliii.

. . .

Prop. LVI. *There are as many kinds of pleasure, of pain, of desire, and of
every emotion compounded of these, such as vacillations of spirit, or derived from these, such as love, hatred, hope, fear, &c., as there are kinds of
objects whereby we are affected.*

Proof. — Pleasure and pain, and consequently the emotions compounded thereof, or derived therefrom, are passions, or passive states (III.
xi. note); now we are necessarily passive (III. i.), in so far as we have inadequate ideas; and only in so far as we have such ideas are we passive (III.
iii.); that is, we are only necessarily passive (II. xl. note), in so far as we conceive, or (II. xvii. and note) in so far as we are affected by an emotion,
which involves the nature of our own body, and the nature of an external
body. Wherefore the nature of every passive state must necessarily be so explained, that the nature of the object whereby we are affected be expressed. Namely, the pleasure, which arises from, say, the object A, involves the nature of that object A, and the pleasure, which arises from the
object B, involves the nature of the object B; wherefore these two pleasur-
able emotions are by nature different, inasmuch as the causes whence they
arise are by nature different. So again the emotion of pain, which arises
from one object, is by nature different from the pain arising from another
object, and, similarly, in the case of love, hatred, hope, fear, vacillation,
&c.

Thus, there are necessarily as many kinds of pleasure, pain, love, hatred, &c., as there are kinds of objects whereby we are affected. Now desire
is each man's essence or nature, in so far as it is conceived as determined to
a particular action by any given modification of itself (III. ix. note); therefore, according as a man is affected through external causes by this or that
kind of pleasure, pain, love, hatred, &c., in other words, according as his
nature is disposed in this or that manner, so will his desire be of one kind or
another, and the nature of one desire must necessarily differ, wherefrom
each desire arose. Thus there are as many kinds of desire, as there are kinds
of pleasure, pain, love, &c., consequently (by what has been shown) there
are as many kinds of desire, as there are kinds of objects whereby we are affected. *Q.E.D.*

Note. — Among the kinds of emotions, which, by the last proposition,
must be very numerous, the chief are *luxury, drunkenness, lust, avarice,*
and *ambition,* being merely species of love or desire, displaying the nature

of those emotions in a manner varying according to the object, with which they are concerned. For by luxury, drunkenness, lust, avarice, ambition, &c., we simply mean the immoderate love of feasting, drinking, venery, riches, and fame. Furthermore, these emotions, in so far as we distinguish them from others merely by the objects wherewith they are concerned, have no contraries. For *temperance*, *sobriety*, and *chastity*, which we are wont to oppose to luxury, drunkenness, and lust, are not emotions or passive states, but indicate a power of the mind which moderates the last-named emotions. However, I cannot here explain the remaining kinds of emotions (seeing that they are as numerous as the kinds of objects), nor, if I could, would it be necessary. It is sufficient for our purpose, namely, to determine the strength of the emotions, and the mind's power over them, to have a general definition of each emotion. It is sufficient, I repeat, to understand the general properties of the emotions and the mind, to enable us to determine the quality and extent of the mind's power in moderating and checking the emotions. Thus, though there is a great difference between various emotions of love, hatred, or desire, for instance between love felt towards children, and love felt towards a wife, there is no need for us to take cognizance of such differences, or to track out further the nature and origin of the emotions.

· · ·

Definitions of the Emotions

I. *Desire* is the actual essence of man, in so far as it is conceived, as determined to a particular activity by some given modification of itself.

Explanation. — We have said above, in the note to Prop. ix. of this part, that desire is appetite, with consciousness thereof; further, that appetite is the essence of man, in so far as it is determined to act in a way tending to promote its own persistence. But, in the same note, I also remarked that, strictly speaking, I recognize no distinction between appetite and desire. For whether a man be conscious of his appetite or not, it remains one and the same appetite. Thus, in order to avoid the appearance of tautology, I have refrained from explaining desire by appetite; but I have taken care to define it in such a manner, as to comprehend, under one head, all those endeavours of human nature, which we distinguish by the terms appetite, will, desire, or impulse. I might, indeed, have said, that desire is the essence of man, in so far as it is conceived as determined to a particular activity; but from such a definition (cf. II. xxiii.) it would not follow that the mind can be conscious of its desire or appetite. Therefore, in order to imply the cause of such consciousness, it was necessary to add, *in so far as it is determined by some given modification*, &c. For, by a modification of man's essence, we understand every disposition of the said essence, whether such disposition be innate, or whether it be conceived solely under the attribute of thought, or solely under the attribute of extension, or whether, lastly, it be referred simultaneously to both these attributes. By the term desire, then, I here mean all man's endeavours, impulses, appetites, and volitions, which vary according to each man's disposition, and are, therefore, not seldom opposed one to another, according as a man is drawn in different directions, and knows not where to turn.

II. *Pleasure* is the transition of a man from a less to a greater perfection.

III. *Pain* is the transition of a man from a greater to a less perfection.

Explanation. — I say transition: for pleasure is not perfection itself. For, if man were born with the perfection to which he passes, he would possess the same, without the emotion of pleasure. This appears more clearly from the consideration of the contrary emotion, pain. No one can deny, that pain consists in the transition to a less perfection, and not in the less perfection itself: for a man cannot be pained, in so far as he partakes of perfection of any degree. Neither can we say, that pain consists in the absence of a greater perfection. For absence is nothing, whereas the emotion of pain is an activity; wherefore this activity can only be the activity of transition from a greater to a less perfection — in other words, it is an activity whereby a man's power of action is lessened or constrained (cf. III. xi. note). I pass over the definitions of merriment, stimulation, melancholy, and grief, because these terms are generally used in reference to the body, and are merely kinds of pleasure or pain.

• • •

I, therefore, recognize only three primitive or primary emotions (as I said in the note to III. xi.), namely, pleasure, pain, and desire.

• • •

VI. *Love* is pleasure accompanied by the idea of an external cause.

Explanation. — This definition explains sufficiently clearly the essence of love; the definition given by those authors who say that love is *the lover's wish to unite himself to the loved object* expresses a property, but not the essence of love; and, as such authors have not sufficiently discerned love's essence, they have been unable to acquire a true conception of its properties, accordingly their definition is on all hands admitted to be very obscure. It must, however, be noted, that when I say that it is a property of love, that the lover should wish to unite himself to the beloved object, I do not here mean by *wish* consent, or conclusion, or a free decision of the mind (for I have shown such, in II. xlviii., to be fictitious); neither do I mean a desire of being united to the loved object when it is absent, or of continuing in its presence when it is at hand; for love can be conceived without either of these desires; but by *wish* I mean the contentment, which is in the lover, on account of the presence of the beloved object, whereby the pleasure of the lover is strengthened, or at least maintained.

• • •

XLVIII. *Lust* is desire and love in the matter of sexual intercourse.

Explanation. — Whether this desire be excessive or not, it is still called lust.

• • •

General Definition of the Emotions

Emotion, which is called a passivity of the soul, is a confused idea, whereby the mind affirms concerning its body, or any part thereof, a force for exist-ence (*existendi vis*) greater or less than before, and by the presence of which the mind is determined to think of one thing rather than another.

• • •

Part IV. Of Human Bondage
or the Strength of the Emotions

Preface

Human infirmity in moderating and checking the emotions I name bond-age: for, when a man is a prey to his emotions, he is not his own master, but lies at the mercy of fortune: so much so, that he is often compelled, while seeing that which is better for him, to follow that which is worse.

• • •

Prop. XXXII. *In so far as men are a prey to passion, they cannot, in that respect, be said to be naturally in harmony.*

Proof. — Things, which are said to be in harmony naturally, are under-stood to agree in power (III. vii.), not in want of power or negation, and consequently not in passion (III. iii. note); wherefore men, in so far as they are a prey to their passions, cannot be said to be naturally in harmony. Q.E.D.

Note. — This is also self-evident; for, if we say that white and black only agree in the fact that neither is red, we absolutely affirm that they do not agree in any respect. So, if we say that a man and a stone only agree in the fact that both are finite — wanting in power, not existing by the necessity of their own nature, or, lastly, indefinitely surpassed by the power of external causes — we should certainly affirm that a man and a stone are in no respect alike; therefore, things which agree only in negation, or in qualities which neither possess, really agree in no respect.

• • •

Prop. XXXIV. *In so far as men are assailed by emotions which are passions, they can be contrary one to another.*

Proof. — A man, for instance Peter, can be the cause of Paul's feeling pain, because he (Peter) possesses something similar to that which Paul hates (III. xvi.), or because Peter has sole possession of a thing which Paul also loves (III. xxxii. and note), or for other causes (of which the chief are enumerated in III. lv. note); it may therefore happen that Paul should hate Peter (Def. of Emotions, vii.), consequently it may easily happen also, that Peter should hate Paul in return, and that each should endeavour to do the other an injury (III. xxxix.), that is (IV. xxx.), that they should be contrary one to another. But the emotion of pain is always a passion or passive state (III. lix.); hence men, in so far as they are assailed by emotions which are passions, can be contrary one to another. *Q.E.D.*

Note. — I said that Paul may hate Peter, because he conceives that Peter possesses something which he (Paul) also loves; from this it seems, at first sight, to follow, that these two men, through both loving the same thing, and, consequently, through agreement of their respective natures, stand in one another's way; if this were so, Props. xxx. and xxxi. of this Part would be untrue. But if we give the matter our unbiassed attention, we shall see that the discrepancy vanishes. For the two men are not in one another's way in virtue of the agreement of their natures, that is, through both loving the same thing, but in virtue of one differing from the other. For, in so far as each loves the same thing, the love of each is fostered thereby (III. xxxi.), that is (Def. of the Emotions, vi.) the pleasure of each is fostered thereby. Wherefore it is far from being the case, that they are at variance through both loving the same thing, and through the agreement in their natures. The cause for their opposition lies, as I have said, solely in the fact that they are assumed to differ. For we assume that Peter has the idea of the loved object as already in his possession, while Paul has the idea of the loved object as lost. Hence the one man will be affected with pleasure, the other will be affected with pain, and thus they will be at variance one with another. We can easily show in like manner, that all other causes of hatred depend solely on differences, and not on the agreement between men's natures.

. . .

Prop. XLIV. *Love and desire may be excessive.*

Proof. — Love is pleasure, accompanied by the idea of an external cause (Def. of Emotions, vi.); therefore stimulation, accompanied by the idea of an external cause is love (III. xi. note); hence love may be excessive. Again, the strength of desire varies in proportion to the emotion from which it arises (III. xxxvii.). Now emotion may overcome all the rest of men's actions (IV. vi.); so, therefore, can desire, which arises from the same emotion, overcome all other desires, and become excessive, as we showed in the last proposition concerning stimulation.

Note. — Mirth, which I have stated to be good, can be conceived more easily than it can be observed. For the emotions, whereby we are daily assailed, are generally referred to some part of the body which is affected more than the rest; hence the emotions are generally excessive, and so fix the mind in the contemplation of one object, that it is unable to think of others; and although men, as a rule, are a prey to many emotions — and very few are found who are always assailed by one and the same — yet there are cases, where one and the same emotion remains obstinately fixed. We sometimes see men so absorbed in one object, that, although it be not present, they think they have it before them; when this is the case with a man who is not asleep, we say he is delirious or mad; nor are those persons who are inflamed with love, and who dream all night and all day about nothing but their mistress, or some woman, considered as less mad, for they are made objects of ridicule. But when a miser thinks of nothing but gain or money, or when an ambitious man thinks of nothing but glory, they are not reckoned to be mad, because they are generally harmful, and are thought worthy of being hated. But, in reality, Avarice, Ambition, Lust, &c., are species of madness, though they may not be reckoned among diseases.

. . .

Appendix

What I have said in this Part concerning the right way of life has not been arranged, so as to admit of being seen at one view, but has been set forth piece-meal, according as I thought each Proposition could most readily be

deduced from what preceded it. I propose, therefore, to rearrange my remarks and to bring them under leading heads.

I. All our endeavours or desires so follow from the necessity of our nature, that they can be understood either through it alone, as their proxi-
mate cause, or by virtue of our being a part of nature, which cannot be adequately conceived through itself without other individuals.

II. Desires, which follow from our nature in such a manner, that they
can be understood through it alone, are those which are referred to the
mind, in so far as the latter is conceived to consist of adequate ideas: the remaining desires are only referred to the mind, in so far as it conceives
things inadequately, and their force and increase are generally defined not
by the power of man, but by the power of things external to us: wherefore
the former are rightly called actions, the latter passions, for the former always indicate our power, the latter, on the other hand, show our infirmity
and fragmentary knowledge.

III. Our actions, that is, those desires which are defined by man's
power or reason, are always good. The rest may be either good or bad.

IV. Thus in life it is before all things useful to perfect the understanding, or reason, as far as we can, and in this alone man's highest happiness
or blessedness consists, indeed blessedness is nothing else but the contentment of spirit, which arises from the intuitive knowledge of God: now, to
perfect the understanding is nothing else but to understand God, God's attributes, and the actions which follow from the necessity of his nature.
Wherefore of a man, who is led by reason, the ultimate aim or highest desire, whereby he seeks to govern all his fellows, is that whereby he is brought
to the adequate conception of himself and of all things within the scope of
his intelligence.

V. Therefore, without intelligence there is not rational life: and things
are only good, in so far as they aid man in his enjoyment of the intellectual
life, which is defined by intelligence. Contrariwise, whatsoever things hinder man's perfecting of his reason, and capability to enjoy the rational life,
are alone called evil.

VI. As all things whereof man is the efficient cause are necessarily
good, no evil can befall man except through external causes; namely, by
virtue of man being a part of universal nature, whose laws human nature is
compelled to obey, and to conform to in almost infinite ways.

VII. It is impossible, that man should not be a part of nature, or that
he should not follow her general order; but if he be thrown among individ-

uals whose nature is in harmony with his own, his power of action will thereby be aided and fostered, whereas, if he be thrown among such as are but very little in harmony with his nature, he will hardly be able to accommodate himself to them without undergoing a great change himself.

VIII. Whatsoever in nature we deem to be evil, or to be capable of injuring our faculty for existing and enjoying the rational life, we may endeavour to remove in whatever way seems safest to us; on the other hand, whatsoever we deem to be good or useful for preserving our being, and enabling us to enjoy the rational life, we may appropriate to our use and employ as we think best. Everyone without exception may, by sovereign right of nature, do whatsoever he thinks will advance his own interest.

IX. Nothing can be in more harmony with the nature of any given thing than other individuals of the same species; therefore (cf. vii.) for man in the preservation of his being and the enjoyment of the rational life there is nothing more useful than his fellow-man who is led by reason. Further, as we know not anything among individual things which is more excellent than a man led by reason, no man can better display the power of his skill and disposition, than in so training men, that they come at last to live under the dominion of their own reason.

X. In so far as men are influenced by envy or any kind of hatred, one towards another, they are at variance, and are therefore to be feared in proportion, as they are more powerful than their fellows.

XI. Yet minds are not conquered by force, but by love and high-mindedness.

XII. It is before all things useful to men to associate their ways of life, to bind themselves together with such bonds as they think most fitted to gather them all into unity, and generally to do whatsoever serves to strengthen friendship.

XIII. But for this there is need of skill and watchfulness. For men are diverse (seeing that those who live under the guidance of reason are few), yet are they generally envious and more prone to revenge than to sympathy.

· · ·

XIX. Again, meretricious love, that is, the lust of generation arising from bodily beauty, and generally every sort of love, which owns anything save freedom of soul as its cause, readily passes into hate; unless indeed, what is worse, it is a species of madness; and then it promotes discord rather than harmony (cf. III. xxxi. Coroll.).

XX. As concerning marriage, it is certain that this is in harmony with reason, if the desire for physical union be not engendered solely by bodily beauty, but also by the desire to beget children and to train them up wisely; and moreover, if the love of both, to wit, of the man and of the woman, is not caused by bodily beauty only, but also by freedom of the soul.

• • •

XXV. Correctness of conduct (*modestia*), that is, the desire of pleasing men which is determined by reason, is attributable to piety (as we said in IV. xxxvii. note i.). But, if it spring from emotion, it is ambition, or the desire whereby men, under the false cloak of piety, generally stir up discords and seditions. For he who desires to aid his fellows either in word or in deed, so that they may together enjoy the highest good, he, I say, will before all things strive to win them over with love: not to draw them into admiration, so that a system may be called after his name, not to give any cause for envy. Further, in his conversation he will shrink from talking of men's faults, and will be careful to speak but sparingly of human infirmity: but he will dwell at length on human virtue or power, and the way whereby it may be perfected. Thus will men be stirred not by fear, nor by aversion, but only by the emotion of joy, to endeavour, so far as in them lies, to live in obedience to reason.

Jean-Jacques Rousseau
from the Second Discourse, Emile *and* New Heloise

The life of Jean-Jacques Rousseau (1712–1778), writer and political philos-opher from Geneva, suggests an unusual perspective on love, to say the least. In his Confessions, *which were unique in their day for their frankness about sexuality, he claims that his greatest sexual satisfaction came from the moment of kneeling before a mistress and begging her pardon. He "married" only in his forties, and then under odd circumstances. After liv-ing with illiterate, possibly retarded Thérèse Lavasseur for twelve years, he declared her his wife in a ceremony before two civilians. At the time, Rous-seau was using an assumed name to avoid arrest for having written the banned* Emile. *The only practical benefit of his marriage seems to be that Rousseau would now allow his friends who wrote him in code to refer to Thérèse in their letters explicitly as his "wife." (Previously, Thérèse had been referred to as his "governess" or "sister.")*

In his writings on love and sex, Rousseau reveals predictably mixed feel-ings. On the one hand, he romanticizes love, extolling the transcendence of sexual gratification in favor of more ephemeral or imaginary joys. He also insists on love without mercenary motive, for his age still associated mar-riage with economic gains and losses. At the same time, however, he is sus-picious of love's power over the individual will, and his vision of utopian ex-istence is a vision in which love plays no part.

The romantic side of Rousseau's thought is apparent in the excerpts be-low taken from his La Nouvelle Heloise, *a novel written in the form of a se-ries of letters. The book itself is a testimony to Rousseau's autobiographic ability to substitute imaginary for actual gratification. He wrote the novel in the (apparently successful) effort to sublimate his sexual passion for a Madame D'Houdetot, the lover of a friend. In the novel, the heroine (Julie) does eventually succumb to her passion for her tutor, Saint-Preux, and thus enters her later marriage in a "deflowered" state. The letters included here record the growth of both parties' ardor—and also their rather idealistic views of love as an ennobling force. But the novel ultimately celebrates Ju-lie's marital fidelity despite the proximity of Saint-Preux, whom her hus-*

band (rather perversely) hires as a tutor to his and Julie's children. Lest we believe that her fidelity results from lack of passion and not its transcendence, the resolution of the novel occurs with Julie's death and her declaration that Saint-Preux was the only man she had ever loved. The novel may have been a substitute for physical love; but as its era's best seller, it achieved for Rousseau considerable monetary reward. Although he abhorred fiscal gain as a motive in love affairs, Rousseau apparently found it not incompatible with his imaginary love life. Perhaps this partially explains his preference for imaginary thrills over real ones.

Rousseau had other reasons, however, for suspecting love. He argues in his "Letter to d'Alembert" (a diatribe against the theater) that love is woman's empire. Nature gave the male superior physical strength, but it compensated the female through the existence of love. Love makes woman ascendent over man. Love therefore poses a threat to men, a threat that is heightened by theatrical portrayals of love stories, which render the innocent male viewer vulnerable to the wiles of almost any woman. The excerpt below from Emile *elaborates this same point. The narrator, who is the tutor of the novel's hero, Emile, advises Emile's wife (Sophie) to use her power in the bedroom to ensure that Emile will continually cherish her. Sophie takes the tutor's words to heart, so much so that he later feels compelled to urge her not to withhold her favors with too much tenacity. Our opening passages from Rousseau's* Discourse on the Origins of Inequality *also reflect his dubious attitude toward romantic love. In the* Discourse, *Rousseau contrasts an ideal state of nature with the corruption of civilization, in which love defined by possessiveness and jealousy emerges. (For further analysis of Rousseau's views on love, see Elizabeth Rapaport's "On the Future of Love: Rousseau and the Radical Feminists," in Part III.)*

From *Second Discourse*

[In the State of Nature]

. . . in the primitive state, having neither houses, nor huts, nor property of any kind, everyone took up his lodging by chance and often for only one night. Males and females united fortuitously, depending on encounter, occasion, and desire, without speech being a very necessary interpreter of the things they had to say to each other; they left each other with the same ease. The mother nursed her children at first for her own need; then, habit having endeared them to her, she nourished them afterward for their need. As soon as they had the strength to seek their food, they did not delay in leaving the mother herself; and as there was practically no other way to find one another again than not to lose sight of each other, they were soon at a point of not even recognizing one another.

[In Society]

Everything begins to change its appearance. Men who until this time wandered in the woods, having adopted a more fixed settlement, slowly come together, unite into different bands, and finally form in each country a particular nation, unified by customs and character, not by regulations and laws but by the same kind of life and foods and by the common influence of climate. A permanent proximity cannot fail to engender at length some contact between different families. Young people of different sexes live in neighboring huts; the passing intercourse demanded by nature soon leads to another kind no less sweet and more permanent through mutual frequentation. People grow accustomed to consider different objects and to make comparisons; imperceptibly they acquire ideas of merit and beauty which produce sentiments of preference. By dint of seeing one another, they can no longer do without seeing one another again. A tender and gentle sentiment is gradually introduced into the soul and at the least obstacle becomes an impetuous fury. Jealousy awakens with love; discord triumphs, and the gentlest of the passions receives sacrifices of human blood.

In proportion as ideas and sentiments follow upon one another and as mind and heart are trained, the human race continues to be tamed, contacts spread, and bonds are tightened. People grew accustomed to assembling in front of the huts or around a large tree; song and dance, true children of love and leisure, became the amusement or rather the occupation of idle and assembled men and women. Each one began to look at the others and to want to be looked at himself, and public esteem had a value. The one who sang or danced the best, the handsomest, the strongest, the most adroit, or the most eloquent became the most highly considered; and that was the first step toward inequality and, at the same time, toward vice. From these first preferences were born on one hand vanity and contempt, on the other shame and envy; and the fermentation caused by these new leavens eventually produced compounds fatal to happiness and innocence.

From *Emile* (Book V)

"If it is true, then, dear Emile, that you want to be your wife's lover, let her always be your mistress and her own. Be a fulfilled but respectful lover. Obtain everything from love without demanding anything from duty, and always regard Sophie's least favors not as your right but as acts of grace. I know that modesty flees formal confessions and asks to be conquered. But does the lover who has delicacy and true love make mistakes about his beloved's secret will? Is he unaware when her heart and her eyes accord what her mouth feigns to refuse? Let each of you always remain master of his own person and his caresses and have the right to dispense them to the other only at his own will. Always remember that even in marriage pleasure is legitimate only when desire is shared. Do not fear, my children, that this law will keep you at a distance. On the contrary, it will make both of you more attentive to pleasing each other, and it will prevent satiety. Since you are limited solely to each other, nature and love will bring you sufficiently close together."

Upon hearing these remarks and others of the kind, Emile becomes irritated and protests. Sophie is ashamed; she holds her fan over her eyes and says nothing. The most discontented of the two is perhaps not the one who complains the most. I insist pitilessly. I make Emile blush at his lack of delicacy. I stand as guarantor for Sophie's accepting the treaty on her side. I provoke her to speak. One can easily guess that she does not dare to give me the lie. Emile uneasily consults the eyes of his young wife. He sees that beneath their embarrassment they are full of a voluptuous agitation which reassures him about the risk he takes in trusting her. He throws himself at her feet, ecstatically kisses the hand she extends to him, and swears that, with the exception of the promised fidelity, he renounces every other right over her. "Dear wife," he says to her, "be the arbiter of my pleasures as you are of my life and my destiny. Were your cruelty to cost me my life, I would nonetheless give to you my dearest rights. I want to owe nothing to your compliance. I want to get everything from your heart."

Good Emile, reassure yourself: Sophie is too generous herself to let you die a victim of your generosity.

That evening, when I am ready to leave them, I say to them in the gravest tone possible for me, "Remember, both of you, that you are free, and that the question here is not one of marital duties. Believe me, let there be no false deference. Emile, do you want to come with me? Sophie gives you permission." Emile is in a fury and would like to hit me." "And you, Sophie, what do you say about it? Should I take him away?" The liar, blushing, says yes. How charming and sweet a lie, worth more than the truth!

The next day . . . The image of felicity no longer attracts men. The corruption of vice has depraved their taste as much as it has depraved their hearts. They no longer know how to sense what is touching nor how to see what is lovable. You who wish to paint voluptuousness and can only imagine satisfied lovers swimming in the bosom of delights, how imperfect your paintings still are! You have captured only the coarsest half of it. The sweetest attractions of voluptuousness are not there. O who among you has never seen a young couple, united under happy auspices, leaving the nuptial bed? Their languid and chaste glances express all at once the intoxication of the sweet pleasures they have just tasted, the lovable assurance of innocence, and the certitude — then so charming — of spending the rest of their days together. This is the most ravishing object which can be presented to man's heart. This is the true painting of voluptuousness! You have seen it a hundred times without recognizing it. Your hardened hearts are no longer capable of loving it. Sophie is happy and peaceful, and she passes the day in the arms of her tender mother. This is a very sweet rest to take after having passed the night in the arms of a husband.

On the day after that, I already perceive some change of scene. Emile wants to appear a bit discontented. But beneath this affectation I note such tender eagerness and even such submissiveness that I augur nothing very distressing. As for Sophie, she is gayer than the day before. I see satisfaction gleaming in her eyes. She is charming with Emile. She is almost flirtatious with him, which only vexes him more.

These changes are hardly noticeable, but they do not escape me. I am uneasy about them. I question Emile in private. I learn that, to his great regret and in spite of all his appeals, he had had to sleep in a separate bed the previous night. The imperious girl had hastened to make use of her right. Explanations are given. Emile complains bitterly, and Sophie responds with jests. But finally, seeing him about to get really angry, she gives him a glance full of sweetness and love; and, squeezing my hand, she utters only these two words, but in a tone which goes straight to the soul: "The ingrate!" Emile is so dumb that he understands none of this. I understand it. I send Emile away, and now I speak to Sophie in private.

"I see the reason for this caprice," I say to her. "One could not have greater delicacy nor make a more inappropriate use of it. Dear Sophie, reassure yourself. I have given you a man. Do not fear to take him for a man. You have had the first fruits of his youth. He has not squandered it on anyone. He will preserve it for you for a long time.

"My dear child, I must explain to you what my intentions were in the conversation all three of us had the day before yesterday. You perhaps perceived in my advice only an art of managing your pleasures in order to make them durable. O Sophie, it had another object more worthy of my efforts. In becoming your husband, Emile has become the head of the house. It is for you to obey, just as nature wanted it. However, when the woman resembles Sophie, it is good that the man be guided by her. This is yet another law of nature. And it is in order to give you as much authority over his heart as his sex gives him over your person that I have made you the arbiter of his pleasures. It will cost you some painful privations, but you will reign over him if you know how to reign over yourself; what has happened already shows me that this difficult art is not beyond your courage. You will reign by means of love for a long time if you make your favors rare and precious, if you know how to make them valued. Do you want to see your husband constantly at your feet? Then keep him always at some distance from your person. But put modesty, and not capriciousness, in your severity. Let him view you as reserved, not whimsical. Take care that in managing his love you do not make him doubt your own. Make yourself cherished by your favors and respected by your refusals. Let him honor his wife's chastity without having to complain of her coldness.

"It is by this means, my child, that he will give you his confidence, listen to your opinions, consult you about his business, and decide nothing without deliberating with you about it. It is by this means that you can bring him back to wisdom when he goes astray; lead him by a gentle persuasion; make yourself lovable in order to make yourself useful; and use coquetry in the interests of virtue and love to the benefit of reason.

"Nevertheless, do not believe that even this art can serve you forever. Whatever precautions anyone may take, enjoyment wears out pleasures, and love is worn out before all others. But when love has lasted a long time, a sweet habit fills the void it leaves behind, and the attraction of mutual confidence succeeds the transports of passion. Children form a relationship between those who have given them life that is no less sweet and is often stronger than love itself. When you stop being Emile's beloved, you will be his wife and his friend. You will be the mother of his children. Then, in place of your former reserve, establish between yourselves the greatest intimacy. No more separate beds, no more refusals, no more caprices. Become his other half to such an extent that he can no longer do without you, and that as soon as he leaves you, he feels he is far from himself. You were so good at making the charms of domestic life reign in your paternal household; now make them reign in your own. Every man who is pleased in his home loves his wife. Remember that if your husband lives happily at home, you will be a happy woman.

"As for the present, do not be so severe with your love. He has merited more obligingness. He would be offended by your fears. No longer be so careful about his health at the expense of his happiness, and enjoy your own happiness. You must not expect disgust, nor rebuff desire. You must refuse not for refusing's sake but to give value to what is granted."

From *New Heloise*

To Julie

I can immediately answer the article in your letter which regards payment, for I have no need, thank God, to reflect on it. These, my Julie, are my sentiments on this point.

In what people call honor, I distinguish between that which is founded on public opinion and that which is derived from self-esteem. The first consists in vain prejudices no more stable than a ruffled wave, but the second has its basis in the eternal truths of morality. The honor of public opinion can be advantageous with regard to fortune, but it does not reach the soul and thus has no influence on real happiness. True honor, on the contrary, is the essence of happiness, because it alone inspires that permanent feeling of interior satisfaction which constitutes the happiness of a rational being. Let us, my Julie, apply these principles to your question and the answer will soon be decided.

To set myself up as a teacher of philosophy and, like the fool in the fable, take money for teaching wisdom will seem base in the eyes of the world, and I confess that there is something ridiculous in it. However, since no man can subsist merely of himself, and since he almost always can manage only by his work, we shall put this scornful opinion in the class of the most dangerous prejudices. We shall not be so foolish as to sacrifice our happiness to this senseless idea. You will not esteem me less on this account, nor shall I deserve any more pity for living by the talents I have cultivated.

But here, my Julie, we have other considerations. Let us leave the multitude and look into ourselves. What would I really be to your father by taking a salary from him for the lessons I give you and thus selling him part of my time, that is to say, part of my person? A mercenary, his hireling, a kind of servant. And as a guarantee of his confidence and of the safety of his possessions, he will have my tacit faith, the same as from the meanest of his domestics.

Now, what more precious possession can a father have than his only daughter, even were it another than Julie? What then will he do who sold that father his services? Will he stifle his feelings for the daughter? Ah! You know that is impossible! Or else, unscrupulously giving in to his heart's inclination, will he wound in the most tender place the man to whom he has pledged his faith? In this case I see such a teacher only as a perfidious man who tramples underfoot the most sacred trust,* a traitor, a seducer-servant whom the law very justly condemns to death. I hope that she to whom I am speaking understands me; it is not death that I fear, but the ignominy of deserving it and my own self-contempt.

When the letters of Eloise and Abelard fell into your hands, you remember what I said to you about reading them and about the conduct of that priest. I have always pitied Eloise. She had a heart made for love, but Abelard has ever seemed to me only a miserable creature who deserved his fate and who was a stranger as much to love as to virtue. After having passed this judgment on him, ought I to imitate him? What wretch dares preach a morality which he will not practice! Whoever is blinded by his passion to that point is soon punished and loses the power to enjoy the sensations to which he has sacrificed his honor. Love is deprived of its greatest charm when honesty abandons it. To feel its whole value, the heart must delight in it, and it must ennoble us by ennobling the one we love. Take away the idea of perfection, and you take away enthusiasm; take away esteem, and love is nothing. How could a woman honor a man who dishonors himself? How could he adore a woman who has no fear of abandoning herself to a vile seducer? This way, mutual contempt soon results, love is nothing for them but a shameful relationship, and they lose honor without finding happiness.

It is different, my Julie, with two lovers of the same age, both seized with the same passion, united by a mutual attachment, under no particular engagements, both enjoying their original liberty, and forbidden by no law to pledge themselves to each other. The most severe laws can impose upon them no other hardship than the natural consequence of their love. Their only punishment for their love is the obligation to love one another forever; and if there is some unhappy region in the world where a cruel authority may break these innocent bonds, it is punished, no doubt, by the crimes that this coercion engenders.

---

*Unfortunate young man! He does not see that in allowing himself to be paid in gratitude what he refuses in money, he is violating a still more sacred trust. Instead of teaching Julie he corrupts her; instead of nourishing her he poisons her. He is thanked by a deceived mother for the ruin of her child. One feels, however, that he has a sincere love of virtue, but his passion leads him astray; and if his extreme youth did not excuse him, with all his fine speeches he would be only a scoundrel. The two lovers are to be pitied; only the mother is inexcusable. [*Rousseau*]

These are my reasons, wise and virtuous Julie. This is only a cold commentary on those which you urged with so much energy and spirit in one of your letters, but it is enough to show you how much I am of your opinion. You remember that I did not insist on refusing your gifts, and that, in spite of my prejudiced aversion, I accepted them in silence, indeed not finding in true honor any substantial reason for refusing them. But in this case, duty, reason, even love, all speak too plainly to be disregarded. If I must choose between honor and you, my heart is prepared to lose you. It loves you too much, oh Julie, to keep you at that price.

· · ·

No, Julie, it is not possible for me to see you each day only as I saw you yesterday. My love must augment and increase forever with the discovery of your charms, and you are an inexhaustible source of new sentiments which I had not even imagined. What a wonderful evening! What unknown delights my heart experienced because of you! Oh enchanting melancholy! Oh the languor of a tender soul! How these surpass turbulent pleasures, wanton gaiety, extravagant joy, and all the ecstasies that a boundless passion offers to the unbridled desires of lovers! Never, never will the impressive memory of that peaceable and pure bliss which has nothing to equal it in the voluptuousness of the senses be erased from my heart. Gods! What a ravishing sight, or rather, what ecstasy to see two such touching beauties tenderly embracing, your head reclining on Claire's bosom, your sweet tears mingling with hers and bathing that charming bosom just as the dew from Heaven moistens a freshly opened lily! I was jealous of so tender a friendship. I found in it something indefinably more interesting than in love itself, and I wished to be somehow punished for not being able to offer you such tender consolations without disturbing them by the violence of my passion. No, nothing, nothing on earth is capable of exciting so voluptuous a tenderness as your mutual caresses, and in my eyes, the sight of two lovers might have offered a less delightful sensation.

Ah, in that moment I might have been in love with that adorable cousin, if Julie had not existed. But no, it was Julie herself who spread her irresistible charm over everything which surrounded her. Your dress, your finery, your gloves, your fan, your work—everything I saw around you enchanted my heart, and you yourself were responsible for the whole enchantment. Stop, oh my sweet friend! By increasing my intoxication, you would deprive me of the pleasure of feeling it. What you make me experience approaches a true delirium, and I am fearful of finally losing my reason in it. Let me at least know a frenzy which constitutes my happiness; let me enjoy this new rapture, more sublime, more penetrating than all my former ideas of love. What, you can believe yourself abased! What, does passion take away your reason also? I find you too perfect for a mere mortal. I should believe you to be a purer species, if this devouring fire which pierces my being did not unite me to yours and did not make me feel that they are one and the same. No, no one in the world knows you. You do not know yourself. My heart alone knows you, feels you, knows what place you are to occupy in it. My Julie! Ah, if you were only adored, what homage would be robbed from you! Ah! If you were only an angel, how much of your value would you lose!

Tell me how it can be that a passion such as mine can increase? I do not know how, but I feel it. However much you are with me at all times, there are some days above all that your image, more beautiful than ever, pursues me and torments me with an assiduousness from which neither space nor time protects me, and I think you left that image with me in the chalet which you mentioned in the conclusion of your last letter. Since there has been talk of this rustic rendezvous, I have left town three times. Each time my feet have carried me to the same slopes, and each time the prospect of so desirable a visit there has seemed to me more pleasant.

> Non vide il mondo si leggiadri rami,
> Ne mosse 'l vento mai si verdi frondi.
> *Petrarch*

> Never did the world see branches so beautiful,
> Nor ever did the wind stir such green leaves.

I find the country more gay, the green more fresh and vivid, the air more pure, the sky more serene. The song of the birds seems to be more tender and voluptuous; the murmur of the brooks evokes a more amorous languor; from afar the blooming vine exudes the sweetest perfumes; a secret charm either embellishes everything or fascinates my senses. One would say that the earth adorns itself to make for your happy lover a nuptial bed worthy of the beauty he adores and of the passion which consumes him. Oh Julie! Oh dear and precious half of my soul, let us hurry to add the presence of two faithful lovers to these ornaments of spring. Let us carry the sentiment of pleasure into the places which afford only an empty idea of it. Let us animate all nature; it is dead without the warmth of love. What! Three days of waiting? Still three days? Drunk with love, greedy for ecstasies, I wait for this delayed moment with a painful impatience. Ah! How fortunate we would be if Heaven removed from life all the tedious intervals which separate such moments!

From Julie

As I left you yesterday, I refused to explain the cause of the sadness for which you reproached me because you were in no state to listen to me. But I owe you this explanation, in spite of my aversions to them, for I have made a promise and will hold to it.

I do not know if you remember the strange conversation you held with me yesterday evening and the manners with which you accompanied it. As for me, I shall not forget them soon enough for your honor and for my repose, and unfortunately I am to shocked to be able to forget them easily. Similar expressions have sometimes struck my ear as I passed near the harbor, but I did not think that they might ever issue from the mouth of an honorable man. I am quite sure at least that they never entered the vocabulary of lovers, and I was quite far from thinking that they might pass between us. Good Heavens! What kind of love is yours, thus to season its pleasures! It is true, you had just come from a prolonged dinner, and I am aware that in this country one must pardon the excesses people may be guilty of at such affairs. It is also for this reason that I speak to you. Be assured that if you had treated me that way when you were sober, the interview would have been the last one of our lives.

But what alarms me with regard to you is that often the conduct of a man inflamed with wine is only the effect of what takes place in his inmost heart at other times. Shall I believe that in a condition where nothing is disguised you showed yourself such as you are? What would become of me if you soberly believed what you said last evening? Rather than bear such contempt, I should prefer to extinguish such a gross passion and lose a lover who, knowing how to respect his mistress so poorly, deserves so little esteem. Tell me, you who cherish honest sentiments, have you succumbed to that cruel, mistaken idea that a lover once made happy need no longer be discreet in regard to modesty and that he owes no more respect to the woman whose severity is no longer to be feared? Ah! If you had always thought so, you would have been less to be feared and I should not be so unfortunate! Do not deceive yourself, my friend; nothing is so dangerous to true lovers as the prejudices of the world. So many people speak of love, and so few know how to love, that for its pure and gentle laws most mistake the vile maxims of an abject commerce which, soon satiated, has recourse to the monsters of the imagination and becomes depraved in order to support itself.

I am possibly mistaken, but it seems to me that true love is the most chaste of all bonds. It is true love, it is its divine fire which can purify our natural inclinations by concentrating them in a single object. It is true love which shelters us from temptations and which makes the opposite sex no longer important, except for the beloved one. For an ordinary woman, every man is always the same, but for her whose heart is in love, there is no man but her lover. What do I say? Is a lover no more than a man? Ah, let him be a much more sublime being! There is no man at all for her who is in love: her lover is more, all the others are less, and she and he are the only of their kind. They have no desires; they are in love. The heart does not follow but guides the senses. It throws a delightful veil over their frenzies. No, in true love, there is nothing of the obscene as in debauchery and its coarse language. True love, always modest, does not wrest its favors audaciously; it steals them timidly. Secrecy, silence, and fearful bashfulness sharpen and conceal its sweet ecstasies; its flame honors and purifies all its caresses; decency and chastity accompany it even into the midst of voluptuousness; and it alone knows how to gratify all the desires without trespassing against modesty. Ah! Tell me, you who once knew true pleasures, how could cynical effrontery be joined to them? How could it not fail to banish their delirium and all their charm? How could it not fail to soil that image of perfection in which one likes to contemplate his beloved? Believe me, my friend, debauchery and love could not live together and cannot even be set against each other. The heart creates true happiness when two people are in love, and nothing can take the place of it when they are no longer so.

But if you were unfortunate enough to take pleasure in this immodest language, how could you have prevailed on yourself to use it so indiscreetly and, toward her who is dear to you, to take on a tone and manners which a man of honor must not even know? Since when has it been pleasant to mortify a loved one, and what is this barbarous voluptuousness which delights in enjoying the torment of others? I have not forgotten that I have lost the right to be respected, but if ever I do forget, is it for you to remind me? Is it for the author of my fault to aggravate its punishment? Rather, he should console me. Everyone except you has the right to scorn me. You owe me the price of the humiliation to which you have reduced me, and so many tears poured out over my weakness ought to make you try to alleviate my sorrow. I am neither prudish nor precious in this. Alas, how far I am from it, I who have not even known how to be discreet! You know too well, ingrate, whether this tender heart can refuse anything to love. But at least what it yields, it wishes to yield only to love, and you have taught me its langauge too well to be able to substitute such a different one in its place. Insults, blows would offend me less than such caresses. Either renounce Julie, or merit her esteem. I have already told you that I do not acknowledge a love without modesty, and whatever it may cost me to lose yours, it would cost me still more to conserve it at that price.

I have many more things left to say on this subject, but I must finish this letter, and I defer them to another time. Meanwhile, you may notice one result of your false precepts on the immoderate use of wine. Your heart is not guilty, I am sure. However, you have wounded mine, and without knowing what you were doing, as if designedly you afflicted this heart, too quick to take fright and indifferent to nothing which comes from you.

G.W. F. Hegel

A Fragment on Love

G. W. F. Hegel (1770–1831) was one of the great philosophers of that rich tradition called German idealism. As a movement, German idealism coincided with the French Revolution and the Napoleonic invasion of Europe, and it shared the same sense of upheaval and rebirth. Hegel's philosophy, in particular, was a philosophy of grand synthesis, of the breaking down of boundaries, of the dynamic movement of world forces and thought. This synthetic vision culminated in this 1807 philosophical masterwork, The Phenomenology of Spirit, *but before writing that work—at the height of the Napoleonic expansion—he attempted a draft of his system in which cosmic love played the central, synthesizing role. Love, he argued, was precisely that union, the breaking down of the false boundaries of individuality, that the new philosophy—and the new world—was trying to express. Soon after, Hegel's language changes and love is no longer the central concept of his philosophy. But the overall vision does not change. The following fragment comes from one of several unpublished manuscripts that preceded the mature work of the* Phenomenology.

True union, or love proper, exists only between living beings who are alike in power and thus in one another's eyes living beings from every point of view; in no respect is either dead for the other. This genuine love excludes all oppositions. It is not the understanding, whose relations always leave the manifold of related terms as a manifold and whose unity is always a unity of opposites [left as opposites]. It is not reason either, because reason sharply opposes its determining power to what is determined. Love neither restricts nor is restricted; it is not finite at all. It is a feeling, yet not a single feeling [among other single feelings]. A single feeling is only a part and not the whole of life; the life present in a single feeling dissolves its barriers and drives on till it disperses itself in the manifold of feelings with a view to finding itself in the entirety of this manifold. This whole life is not contained in love in the same way as it is in this sum of many particular and isolated feelings; in love, life is present as a duplicate of itself and as a single and unified self. Here life has run through the circle of development from an immature to a completely mature unity: when the unity was immature, there still stood over against it the world and the possibility of a cleavage between itself and the world; as development proceeded, reflection produced more and more oppositions (unified by satisfied impulses) until it set the whole of man's life in opposition [to objectivity]; finally, love completely destroys objectivity and thereby annuls and transcends reflection, deprives man's opposite of all foreign character, and discovers life itself without any further defect. In love the separate does still remain, but as something united and no longer as something separate; life [in the subject] senses life [in the object].

Since love is a sensing of something living, lovers can be distinct only in so far as they are mortal and do not look upon this possibility of separation as if there were really a separation or as if reality were a sort of conjunction between possibility and existence. In the lovers there is no matter; they are a living whole. To say that the lovers have an independence and a living principle peculiar to each of themselves means only that they may die [and may be separated by death]. To say that salt and other minerals are part of the makeup of a plant and that these carry in themselves their own laws governing their operation is the judgment of external reflection and means no more than that the plant may rot. But love strives to annul even this distinction [between the lover as lover and the lover as physical organism], to annul this possibility [of separation] as a mere abstract possibility, to unite [with itself] even the mortal element [within the lover] and to make it immortal.

If the separable element persists in either of the lovers as something peculiarly his own before their union is complete, it creates a difficulty for them. There is a sort of antagonism between complete surrender or the only possible cancellation of opposition (i.e., its cancellation in complete union) and a still subsisting independence. Union feels the latter as a hindrance; love is indignant if part of the individual is severed and held back as a private property. This raging of love against [exclusive] individuality is shame. Shame is not a reaction of the mortal body, not an expression of the freedom to maintain one's life, to subsist. The hostility in a loveless assault does injury to the loving heart itself, and the shame of this now injured heart becomes the rage which defends only its right, its property. If shame, instead of being an effect of love, an effect which only takes an indignant form after encountering something hostile, were something itself by nature hostile which wanted to defend an assailable property of its own, then we would have to say that shame is most of all characteristic of tyrants, or of girls who will not yield their charms except for money, or of vain women who want to fascinate. None of these love; their defense of their mortal body is the opposite of indignation about it; they ascribe an intrinsic worth to it and are shameless.

A pure heart is not ashamed of love; but it is ashamed if its love is incomplete; it upbraids itself if there is some hostile power which hinders love's culmination. Shame enters only through the recollection of the body, through the presence of an [exclusive] personality or the sensing of an [exclusive] individuality. It is not a fear *for* what is mortal, for what is merely one's own, but rather a fear *of* it, a fear which vanishes as the separable element in the lover is diminished by his love. Love is stronger than fear. It has no fear of its fear, but, led by its fear, it cancels separation, apprehensive as it is of finding opposition which may resist it or be a fixed barrier against it. It is a mutual giving and taking; through shyness its gifts may be disdained; through shyness an opponent may not yield to its receiving; but it still tries whether hope has not deceived it, whether it still finds itself everywhere. The lover who takes is not thereby made richer than the other; he is enriched indeed, but only so much as the other is. So too the giver does not make himself poorer; by giving to the other he has at the same time and to the same extent enhanced his own treasure (compare Juliet in *Romeo and Juliet* [ii. 1. 175-77: "My bounty is as boundless as the sea, My love as deep;] the more I give to thee, The more I have"). This wealth of life love acquires in the exchange of every thought, every variety of inner experience, for it seeks out differences and devises unifications ad infinitum; it turns to the whole manifold of nature in order to drink love out of every life. What in the first instance is most the individual's own is united into the whole in the lovers' touch and contact; consciousness of a separate self disappears, and all distinction between the lovers is annulled. The mortal element, the body, has lost the character of separability, and a living child, a seed of immortality, of the eternally self-developing and self-generating [race], has come into existence. What has been united [in the child] is not divided again; [in love and through love] God has acted and created.

This unity [the child], however, is only a point, [an undifferentiated unity,] a seed; the lovers cannot so contribute to it as to give it a manifold in itself at the start. Their union is free from all inner division; in it there is no working on an opposite. Everything which gives the newly begotten child a manifold life and a specific existence, it must draw into itself, set over against itself, and unify with itself. The seed breaks free from its original unity, turns ever more and more to opposition, and begins to develop. Each stage of its development is a separation, and its aim in each is to regain for itself the full riches of life [enjoyed by the parents]. Thus the process is: unity, separated opposites, reunion. After their union the lovers separate again, but in the child their union has become unseparated.

This union in love is complete; but it can remain so only as long as the separate lovers are opposed solely in the sense that the one loves and the other is loved, i.e., that each separate lover is one organ in a living whole. Yet the lovers are in connection with much that is dead; external objects belong to each of them. This means that a lover stands in relation to things opposed to him in his own eyes as objects and opposites; this is why lovers are capable of a multiplex opposition in the course of their multiplex acquisition and possession of property and rights. The dead object in the power of one of the lovers is opposed to both of them, and a union in respect of it seems to be possible only if it comes under the dominion of both. The one who sees the other in possession of a property must sense in the other the separate individuality which has willed this possession. He cannot himself annul the exclusive dominion of the other, for this once again would be an opposition to the other's power, since no relation to an object is possible except mastery over it; he would be opposing a mastery to the other's dominion and would be canceling one of the other's relationships, namely, his exclusion of others from his property. Since possession and property make up such an important part of men's life, cares, and thoughts, even lovers cannot refrain from reflection on this aspect of their relations. Even if the use of the property is common to both, the right to its possession would remain undecided, and the thought of this right would never be forgotten, because everything which men possess has the legal form of property. But if the possessor gives the other the same right of possession as he has himself, community of goods is still only the right of one or other of the two to the thing.

Arthur Schopenhauer
from World as Will and Idea

Arthur Schopenhauer (1788–1860) is the best-known pessimist of Western philosophy. And yet he is an idealist. According to Schopenhauer, the world of our experience is but an illusion. The reality concealed by our everyday world is that the world is ultimately a single, turbulent Will, manifesting itself in every conflict and struggle. Human experience is but one tension-filled aspect of the Will. Although individuals are manifestations of the same Will, and thus part of the same ultimate reality, the Will manifests itself in each of us as an individual will, which believes itself to be in competition with all others. Human experience, consequently, is essentially suffering, conflict, dissatisfaction, and enmity with others. Aesthetic experience—a beautiful piece of music or a lovely sunset—can occasionally lift us out of our usual absorption in our personal hankerings and frustrations, but for the most part our lives consist of "the penal servitude of willing." The only way out of this situation is the radical route of sanctity, in which one renounces one's will and resigns oneself to whatever occurs. Schopenhauer borrows rather freely from Eastern religious traditions (particularly that of Buddhism) and suggests that we will suffer unless and until we experience toward every being we encounter the unifying insight, "That art thou"—the recognition that all beings share the same life—and then organize our lives according to this recognition of unity.

Romantic love, according to Schopenhauer's scheme, is one of the clearest cases of human beings causing themselves and others tremendous suffering. Love is competitive. It is the illusion that we can individually gain at the expense of others. Schopenhauer takes the relative rarity of happy marriages as clear evidence that love does not promote the individual's happiness, but is usually itself an obstacle to it. Schopenhauer's own relationships with women presumably did not dissuade him from the view that love does not further individual happiness. Bertrand Russell observes that Schopenhauer had many love affairs that were "sensual but not passionate." And in The World as Will and Idea, *Schopenhauer describes the genitals as the "objectification" of will, the source of all our sufferings. (Augus-*

tine makes a similar complaint, but insists that the genitals cause us trouble because they are not controlled by the will.) Nor did Schopenhauer particularly like or respect women. Besides his mother, with whom he did not get on particularly well, the woman most often mentioned in biographical sketches of Schopenhauer was the neighbor he pushed down the stairs as a result of an altercation. The woman sued him and won, so that he had to pay her a certain amount per month for the rest of her life. Russell observes that Schopenhauer's compassionate spirit is exemplified in the latter's diary entry upon hearing of her death: "The old woman dies, the burden departs."

The reading below comes from Schopenhauer's The World as Will and Idea, *the two-volume work that contains the core of his philosophy. In it he argues that romantic love is the result of a natural delusion that our species-nature foists upon us—the delusion that the object of our sexual desire can make us happy as individuals. In fact, the species alone, not the individual, stands to gain through romantic love. Love, as Schopenhauer sees it, is the delusion that our species-nature inspires in order to ensure that sexual intercourse occurs between individuals with the appropriate traits to produce normal, healthy offspring. Here again, Schopenhauer's pessimism is evident. The love-stricken individual plays the fool in the service of the species. But in a sense, Schopenhauer concludes, the suffering of lovers is deserved. The real aim of love is the birth of another generation, and lovers are therefore guilty of beginning anew the whole drama of human suffering and spiritual blindness.*

The Metaphysics of the Love of the Sexes

. . . all love, however ethereally it may bear itself, is rooted in the sexual impulse alone, nay, it absolutely is only a more definitely determined, specialised, and indeed in the strictest sense individualised sexual impulse. If now, keeping this in view, one considers the important part which the sexual impulse in all its degrees and nuances plays not only on the stage and in novels, but also in the real world, where, next to the love of life, it shows itself the strongest and most powerful of motives, constantly lays claim to half the powers and thoughts of the younger portion of mankind, is the ultimate goal of almost all human effort, exerts an adverse influence on the most important events, interrupts the most serious occupations every hour, sometimes embarrasses for a while even the greatest minds, does not hesitate to intrude with its trash interfering with the negotiations of statesmen and the investigations of men of learning, knows how to slip its love letters

and locks of hair even into ministerial portfolios and philosophical manuscripts, and no less devises daily the most entangled and the worst actions,
destroys the most valuable relationships, breaks the firmest bonds, demands the sacrifice sometimes of life or health, sometimes of wealth, rank,
and happiness, nay, robs those who are otherwise honest of all conscience,
makes those who have hitherto been faithful, traitors; accordingly, on the
whole, appears as a malevolent demon that strives to pervert, confuse, and
overthrow everything; — then one will be forced to cry, Wherefore all this
noise? Wherefore the straining and storming, the anxiety and want? It is
merely a question of every Hans finding his Grethe. (I have not ventured to
express myself distinctly here: the courteous reader must therefore translate
the phrase into Aristophanic language.) Why should such a trifle play so
important a part, and constantly introduce disturbance and confusion into
the well-regulated life of man? But to the earnest investigator the spirit of
truth gradually reveals the answer. It is no trifle that is in question here; on
the contrary, the importance of the matter is quite proportionate to the seriousness and ardour of the effort. The ultimate end of all love affairs,
whether they are played in sock or cothurnus, is really more important
than all other ends of human life, and is therefore quite worthy of the profound seriousness with which every one pursues it. That which is decided by
it is nothing less than *the composition of the next generation*. The *dramatis
personae* who shall appear when we are withdrawn are here determined,
both as regards their existence and their nature, by these frivolous love affairs. As the being, the *existentia*, of these future persons is absolutely conditioned by our sexual impulse generally, so their nature, *essentia*, is determined by the individual selection in its satisfaction, *i.e.*, by sexual love, and
is in every respect irrevocably fixed by this. This is the key of the problem:
we shall arrive at a more accurate knowledge of it in its application if we go
through the degrees of love, from the passing inclination to the vehement
passion, when we shall also recognise that the difference of these grades
arises from the degree of the individualisation of the choice.

The collective love affairs of the present generation taken together are
accordingly, of the whole human race, the serious *meditatio compositionis
generationis futurae, a qua iterum pendent innumerae generationes*. This
high importance of the matter, in which it is not a question of individual
weal or woe, as in all other matters, but of the existence and special nature
of the human race in future times, and therefore the will of the individual
appears at a higher power as the will of the species; — this it is on which the
pathetic and sublime elements in affairs of love depend, which for thou-

sands of years poets have never wearied of representing in innumerable examples; because no theme can equal in interest this one, which stands to all others which only concern the welfare of individuals as the solid body to the surface, because it concerns the weal and woe of the species. Just on this account, then, is it so difficult to impart interest to a drama without the element of love, and, on the other hand, this theme is never worn out even by daily use.

That which presents itself in the individual consciousness as sexual impulse in general, without being directed towards a definite individual of the other sex, is in itself, and apart from the phenomenon, simply the will to live. But what appears in consciousness as a sexual impulse directed to a definite individual is in itself the will to live as a definitely determined individual. Now in this case the sexual impulse, although in itself a subjective need, knows how to assume very skilfully the mask of an objective admiration, and thus to deceive our consciousness; for nature requires this stratagem to attain its ends. But yet that in every case of falling in love, however objective and sublime this admiration may appear, what alone is looked to is the production of an individual of a definite nature is primarily confirmed by the fact that the essential matter is not the reciprocation of love, but possession, *i.e.*, the physical enjoyment. The certainty of the former can therefore by no means console us for the want of the latter; on the contrary, in such a situation many a man has shot himself. On the other hand, persons who are deeply in love, and can obtain no return of it, are contented with possession, *i.e.*, with the physical enjoyment. This is proved by all forced marriages, and also by the frequent purchase of the favour of a woman, in spite of her dislike, by large presents or other sacrifices, nay, even by cases of rape. That this particular child shall be begotten is, although unknown to the parties concerned, the true end of the whole love story; the manner in which it is attained is a secondary consideration. Now, however loudly persons of lofty and sentimental soul, and especially those who are in love, may cry out here about the gross realism of my view, they are yet in error. For is not the definite determination of the individualities of the next generation a much higher and more worthy end than those exuberant feelings and supersensible soap bubbles of theirs? Nay, among earthly aims, can there be one which is greater or more important? It alone corresponds to the profoundness with which passionate love is felt, to the seriousness with which it appears, and the importance which it attributes even to the trifling details of its sphere and occasion. Only so far as this end is assumed as the true one do the difficulties encountered, the infinite exertions and annoyances made and endured for the attainment of the loved object, appear proportionate to the matter. For it is the future generation, in its whole individual determinateness, that presses into existence by means of those efforts and toils. Nay, it is itself already active in that careful, definite, and arbitrary choice for the satisfaction of the sexual impulse which we call love. The growing inclination of two lovers is really already the will to live of the new individual which they can and desire to produce; nay, even in the meeting of their longing glances its new life breaks out, and announces itself as a future individuality harmoniously and well composed. They feel the longing for an actual union and fusing together into a single being, in order to live on only as this; and this longing receives its fulfilment in the child which is produced by them, as that in which the qualities transmitted by them both, fused and united in one being, live on. Conversely, the mutual, decided and persistent aversion between a man and a maid is a sign that what they could produce would only be a badly organised, in itself inharmonious and unhappy being. . . .

But, finally, what draws two individuals of different sex exclusively to each other with such power is the will to live, which exhibits itself in the whole species, and which here anticipates in the individual which these two can produce an objectification of its nature answering to its aims. This individual will have the will, or character, from the father, the intellect from the mother, and the corporisation from both; yet, for the most part, the figure will take more after the father, the size after the mother, — according to the law which comes out in the breeding of hybrids among the brutes, and principally depends upon the fact that the size of the foetus must conform to the size of the uterus. Just as inexplicable as the quite special individuality of any man, which is exclusively peculiar to him, is also the quite special and individual passion of two lovers; indeed at bottom the two are one and the same: the former is *explicite* what the latter was *implicite*. The moment at which the parents begin to love each other—to fancy each other, as the very happy English expression has it—is really to be regarded as the first appearance of a new individual and the true *punctum saliens* of its life, and, as has been said, in the meeting and fixing of their longing glances there appears the first germ of the new being, which certainly, like all germs, is generally crushed out. This new individual is to a certain extent a new (Platonic) Idea; and now, as all Ideas strive with the greatest vehemence to enter the phenomenal world, eagerly seizing for this end upon the matter which the law of causality divides among them all, so also does this particular Idea of a human individuality strive with the greatest eagerness and vehemence towards its realisation in the phenomenon. This eagerness and vehemence is just the passion of the two future parents for each other. . . . It will be in degree so much the more powerful the more *individualised* it is; that is, the more the loved individual is exclusively suited, by virtue of all his or her parts and qualities, to satisfy the desire of the lover and the need established by his or her own individuality. What is really in question here will become clear in the further course of our exposition. Primarily and essentially the inclination of love is directed to health, strength, and beauty, consequently also to youth; because the will first of all seeks to exhibit the specific character of the human species as the basis of all individuality: ordinary amorousness (Αφροδιτη πανδημος) does not go much further. To these, then, more special claims link themselves on, which we shall investigate in detail further on, and with which, when they see satisfaction before them, the passion increases. But the highest degrees of this passion spring from that suitableness of two individualities to each other on account of which the will, *i.e.*, the character, of the father and the intellect of the mother, in their connection, make up precisely that individual towards which the will to live in general which exhibits itself in the whole species feels a longing proportionate to this its magnitude, and which therefore exceeds the measure of a mortal heart, and the motives of which, in the same way, lie beyond the sphere of the individual intellect. This is thus the soul of a true and great passion. . . . Since there do not exist two individuals exactly alike, there must be for each particular man a particular woman—always with reference to what is to be produced—who corresponds most perfectly. A really passionate love is as rare as the accident of these two meeting. Since, however, the possibility of such a love is present in every one, the representations of it in the works of the poets are comprehensible to us. . . .

Let us now set about the more thorough investigation of the matter. Egoism is so deeply rooted a quality of all individuals in general, that in order to rouse the activity of an individual being egoistical ends are the only ones upon which we can count with certainty. Certainly the species has an earlier, closer, and greater claim upon the individual than the perishable individuality itself. Yet when the individual has to act, and even make sacrifices for the continuance and quality of the species, the importance of the matter cannot be made so comprehensible to his intellect, which is calculated merely with regard to individual ends, as to have its proportionate effect. Therefore in such a case nature can only attain its ends by implanting a certain illusion in the individual, on account of which that which is only a good for the species appears to him as a good for himself, so that when he serves the species he imagines he is serving himself; in which process a mere chimera, which vanishes immediately afterwards, floats before him, and takes the place of a real thing as a motive. This illusion is instinct. In the great majority of cases this is to be regarded as the sense of the species, which presents what is of benefit to *it* to the will. Since, however, the will has here become individual, it must be so deluded that it apprehends through the sense of the individual what the sense of the species presents to it, thus imagines it is following individual ends while in truth it is pursuing ends which are merely general (taking this word in its strictest sense). The external phenomenon of instinct we can best observe in the brutes where its rôle is most important; but it is in ourselves alone that we arrive at a knowledge of its internal process, as of everything internal. Now it is certainly supposed that man has almost no instinct; at any rate only this, that the new-born babe seeks for and seizes the breast of its mother. But, in fact, we have a very definite, distinct, and complicated instinct, that of the selection of another individual for the satisfaction of the sexual impulse, a selection which is so fine, so serious, and so arbitrary. With this satisfaction in itself, *i.e.*, so far as it is a sensual pleasure resting upon a pressing want of the individual, the beauty or ugliness of the other individual has nothing to do. Thus the regard for this which is yet pursued with such ardour, together with the careful selection which springs from it, is evidently connected, not with the chooser himself — although he imagines it is so — but with the true end, that which is to be produced, which is to receive the type of the species as purely and correctly as possible. Through a thousand physical accidents and moral aberrations there arise a great variety of deteriorations of the human form; yet its true type, in all its parts, is always again established: and this takes place under the guidance of the sense of beauty, which always directs the sexual impulse, and without which this sinks to the level of a disgusting necessity. Accordingly, in the first place, everyone will decidedly prefer and eagerly desire the most beautiful individuals, *i.e.*, those in whom the character of the species is most purely impressed; but, secondly, each one will specially regard as beautiful in another individual those perfections which he himself lacks, nay even those imperfections which are the opposite of his own. . . . Upon this decided inclination to beauty depends the maintenance of the type of the species: hence it acts with such great power. . . . Thus what guides man here is really an instinct which is directed to doing the best for the species, while the man himself imagines that he only seeks the heightening of his own pleasure. In fact, we have in this an instructive

lesson concerning the inner nature of all instinct, which as here, almost always sets the individual in motion for the good of the species. For clearly the
pains with which an insect seeks out a particular flower, or fruit, or dung, or
flesh, or, as in the case of the ichneumonidae, the larva of another insect, in
order to deposit its eggs there only, and to attain this end shrinks neither
from trouble nor danger, is thoroughly analogous to the pains with which
for his sexual satisfaction a man carefully chooses a woman with definite
qualities which appeal to him individually, and strives so eagerly after her
that in order to attain this end he often sacrifices his own happiness in life,
contrary to all reason, by a foolish marriage, by love affairs which cost him
wealth, honour, and life, even by crimes such as adultery or rape, all merely
in order to serve the species in the most efficient way, although at the cost of
the individual, in accordance with the will of nature which is everywhere
sovereign. Instinct, in fact, is always an act which seems to be in accordance
with the conception of an end, and yet is entirely without such a conception. . . . Thus here, as in the case of all instinct, the truth assumes the
form of an illusion, in order to act upon the will. It is a voluptuous illusion
which leads the man to believe he will find a greater pleasure in the arms of
a woman whose beauty appeals to him than in those of any other; or which
indeed, exclusively directed to a single individual, firmly convinces him
that the possession of her will ensure him excessive happiness. Therefore he
imagines he is taking trouble and making sacrifices for his own pleasure,
while he does so merely for the maintenance of the regular type of the species, or else a quite special individuality, which can only come from these
parents, is to attain to existence. The character of instinct is here so perfectly present, thus an action which seems to be in accordance with the conception of an end, and yet is entirely without such a conception, that he
who is drawn by that illusion often abhors the end which alone guides it,
procreation, and would like to hinder it; thus it is in the case of almost all
illicit love affairs. In accordance with the character of the matter which has
been explained, every lover will experience a marvellous disillusion after the
pleasure he has at last attained, and will wonder that what was so longingly
desired accomplishes nothing more than every other sexual satisfaction; so
that he does not see himself much benefited by it. That wish was related to
all his other wishes as the species is related to the individual, thus as the infinite to the finite. The satisfaction, on the other hand, is really only for the
benefit of the species, and thus does not come within the consciousness of
the individual, who, inspired by the will of the species, here served an end
with every kind of sacrifice, which was not his own end at all.

. . . we have to remark here that by nature man is inclined to inconstancy in love, woman to constancy. The love of the man sinks perceptibly from the moment it has obtained satisfaction; almost every other woman charms him more than the one he already possesses; he longs for variety. The love of the woman, on the other hand, increases just from that moment. This is a consequence of the aim of nature which is directed to the maintenance, and therefore to the greatest possible increase, of the species. The man can easily beget over a hundred children a year; the woman, on the contrary, with however many men, can yet only bring one child a year into the world (leaving twin births out of account). Therefore the man always looks about after other women; the woman, again, sticks firmly to the one man; for nature moves her, instinctively and without reflection, to retain the nourisher and protector of the future offspring. Accordingly faithfulness in marriage is with the man artificial, with the woman it is natural, and thus adultery on the part of the woman is much less pardonable than on the part of the man, both objectively on account of the consequences and also subjectively on account of its unnaturalness. . . .

The unconscious considerations which, . . . the inclination of women follows naturally cannot be so exactly assigned [as those of men]. In general the following may be asserted: They give the preference to the age from thirty to thirty-five years, especially over that of youths who yet really present the height of human beauty. The reason is that they are not guided by taste but by instinct, which recognises in the age named the acme of reproductive power. In general they look less to beauty, especially of the face. It is as if they took it upon themselves alone to impart this to the child. They are principally won by the strength of the man, and the courage which is connected with this; for these promise the production of stronger children, and also a brave protector for them. Every physical defect of the man, every divergence from the type, may with regard to the child be removed by the woman in reproduction, through the fact that she herself is blameless in these respects, or even exceeds in the opposite direction. Only those qualities of the man have to be excepted which are peculiar to his sex, and which therefore the mother cannot give to the child: such are the manly structure of the skeleton, broad shoulders, slender hips, straight bones, muscular power, courage, beard, &c. Hence it arises that women often love ugly men, but never an unmanly man, because they cannot neutralise his defects.

The second class of the considerations which lie at the foundation of sexual love are those which regard psychical qualities. Here we shall find that the woman is throughout attracted by the qualities of the heart or character in the man, as those which are inherited from the father. The woman is won especially by firmness of will, decision, and courage, and perhaps also by honesty and goodheartedness. On the other hand, intellectual gifts exercise no direct and instinctive power over her, just because they are not inherited from the father. Want of understanding does a man no harm with women; indeed extraordinary mental endowment, or even genius, might sooner influence them unfavourably as an abnormity. . . .

The reason is, that here quite other considerations than the intellectual predominate, — those of instinct. In marriage what is looked to is not intellectual entertainment, but the production of children: it is a bond of the heart, not of the head, It is a vain and absurd pretence when women assert that they have fallen in love with the mind of a man, or else it is the overstraining of a degenerate nature. Men, on the other hand, are not determined in their instinctive love by the qualities of character of the woman. . . . The intellectual qualities, however, certainly influence here, because they are inherited from the mother. Yet their influence is easily outweighed by that of physical beauty, which acts directly, as concerning a more essential point. . . .

Hitherto I have only taken account of the *absolute* considerations, *i.e.*; those which hold good for every one: I come now to the *relative* considerations, which are individual, because in their case what is looked to is the rectification of the type of the species, which is already defectively presented, the correction of the divergences from it which the chooser's own person already bears in itself, and thus the return to the pure presentation of the type. Here, then, each one loves what he lacks. Starting from the individual constitution, and directed to the individual constitution, the choice which rests upon such relative considerations is much more definite, decided, and exclusive than that which proceeds merely from the absolute considerations; therefore the source of really passionate love will lie, as a rule, in these relative considerations, and only that of the ordinary and slighter inclination in the absolute considerations. Accordingly it is not generally precisely correct and perfect beauties that kindle great passions. For such a truly passionate inclination to arise something is required which can only be expressed by a chemical metaphor: two persons must neutralise each other, like acid and alkali, to a neutral salt.

• • •

We have seen that the careful selection for the satisfaction of the sexual impulse, a selection which rises through innumerable degrees up to that of passionate love, depends upon the highly serious interest which man takes in the special personal constitution of the next generation. Now this exceedingly remarkable interest confirms two truths which have been set forth in the preceding chapters. (I.) The indestructibility of the true nature of man, which lives on in that coming generation. For that interest which is so lively and eager, and does not spring from reflection and intention, but from the inmost characteristics and tendencies of our nature, could not be so indelibly present and exercise such great power over man if he were absolutely perishable, and were merely followed in time by a race actually and entirely different from him. (2.) That his true nature lies more in the species than in the individual. For that interest in the special nature of the species, which is the root of all love from the passing inclination to the serious passion, is for everyone really the highest concern, the success or failure of which touches him most sensibly; therefore it is called *par excellence* the affair of the heart. Moreover, when this interest has expressed itself strongly and decidedly, everything which merely concerns one's own person is postponed and necessarily sacrificed to it. Through this, then, man shows that the species lies closer to him than the individual, and he lives more immediately in the former than in the latter. Why does the lover hang with complete abandonment on the eyes of his chosen one, and is ready to make every sacrifice for her? Because it is his immortal part that longs after her; while it is only his mortal part that desires everything else. . . .

If now, from the standpoint of this last consideration, we contemplate the turmoil of life, we behold all occupied with its want and misery, straining all their powers to satisfy its infinite needs and to ward off its multifarious sorrows, yet without daring to hope anything else than simply the preservation of this tormented existence for a short span of time. In between, however, in the midst of the tumult, we see the glances of two lovers meet longingly: yet why so secretly, fearfully, and stealthily? Because these lovers are the traitors who seek to perpetuate the whole want and drudgery, which would otherwise speedily reach an end; this they wish to frustrate, as others like them have frustrated it before.

Stendhal (Henri Beyle)

from On Love

Stendhal (1783–1842) was the pen name of Henri Beyle, a French romantic writer who spent much of his adult life in the intrigue-filled villas of Rome. On Love *was, by his own account, his favorite of his books, though it is neither so passionate as some of his greatest novels and stories nor as personal as many of his writings. In fact,* On Love *resembles nothing so much as an eighteenth-century travelogue—a genre in which Stendhal was also one of the most accomplished authors in Europe—a running account of thoughts, anecdotes and occasions stimulated by love. Stendhal's stereotypic generalizations about the differences between French women and Mediterranean women, for example, may make us uncomfortable today, but one gets the clear sense that for Stendhal, whatever else it might be, love was no ethereal abstraction but an urgent practical necessity for which good advice and preparation were essential. In this, of course, his work resembles that of Ovid, but Stendhal also brings in a number of more theoretical observations—the most famous of which are his notes on "crystallization"— in which the dynamics of love as an emotion and not just the exigencies of courtship are brought clearly into focus. Crystallization is a clever and convenient metaphor for the accumulation of perceived charms and virtues that the lover comes to see in his or her beloved. The metaphor refers to the encrustation of salt crystals on a twig or bough in certain caves. The image is particularly illuminating for Stendhal's theory of love, in which it is the beauty of love and its feelings, rather than any actual relationship between two people, that is celebrated. And if that beauty is largely based on imagination and illusion, so much the better for love—and so much the worse for truthful or realistic relationships. "Passion-love"—or what we would call "romantic love"—is not in the business of such mundane matters. The following is from the opening sections of* On Love.

Chapter I: On Love

I want to try and establish exactly what this passion is, whose every genuine manifestation is characterized by beauty.

There are four different kinds of love:

1. Passionate Love. This was the love of the Portuguese nun, that of Heloïse for Abelard, of the captain of Vésel, and of the gendarme of Cento.

2. Mannered Love, which flourished in Paris about 1760, and which is to be found in the memoirs and novels of the period; for example those of Crébillon, Lauzun, Duclos, Marmontel, Chamfort, and Mme d'Epinay. . . .

A stylized painting, this, where the rosy hues extend into the shadows, where there is no place for anything at all unpleasant — for that would be a breach of etiquette, of good taste, of delicacy, and so forth. A man of breeding will know in advance all the rituals he must meet and observe in the various stages of this kind of love, which often achieves greater refinement than real love, since there is nothing passionate or unpredictable about it, and it is always witty. It is a cold, pretty miniature as against an oil painting by one of the Carrachi; and while passionate love carries us away against our real interests mannered love as invariably respects those interests. Admittedly, if you take away vanity, there is very little left of mannered love, and the poor weakened invalid can hardly drag itself along.

3. Physical Love. You are hunting; you come across a handsome young peasant girl who takes to her heels through the woods. Everyone knows the love that springs from this kind of pleasure, and however desiccated and miserable you may be, this is where your love-life begins at sixteen.

4. Vanity-Love. The great majority of men, especially in France, both desire and possess a fashionable woman, much in the way one might own a fine horse — as a luxury befitting a young man. Vanity, a little flattered and a little piqued, leads to enthusiasm. Sometimes there is physical love, but not always; often even physical pleasure is lacking. "A duchess is never more than thirty in the eyes of a bourgeois," said the Duchesse de Chaulnes, and the courtiers of that just king Louis of Holland cheerfully recall even now a pretty woman from The Hague who was quite unable to resist the charms of anyone who happened to be a duke or a prince. But true to hierarchial principles, as soon as a prince came to court she would send her duke packing. She was rather like an emblem of seniority in the diplomatic corps!

The happiest version of this insipid relationship is where physical pleasure grows with habit. Then memories produce a semblance of love; there is the pricking at your pride and the sadness in satisfaction; the atmosphere of romantic fiction catches you by the throat, and you believe yourself love-sick and melancholy, for vanity will always pretend to be grand passion. One thing is certain though: whichever kind of love produces the pleasures, they only become vivid, and their recollection compelling, from the moment of inspiration. In love, unlike most other passions, the recollection of what you have had and lost is always better than what you can hope for in the future.

Occasionally in vanity-love, habit, or despair of finding something better, results in a friendship of the least attractive sort, which will even boast of its *stability*, and so on.

Although physical pleasure, being natural, is known to all, it is only of secondary importance to sensitive, passionate people. If such people are derided in drawing rooms or made unhappy by the intrigues of the worldly, they possess in compensation a knowledge of pleasures utterly inaccessible to those moved only by vanity or money.

Some virtuous and sensitive women are almost unaware of the idea of physical pleasure; they have so rarely, if I may hazard an expression, exposed themselves to it, and in fact the raptures of passionate love have practically effaced the memory of bodily delights.

There are some men who are the victims and instruments of a hellish pride, a pride like that of Alfieri. These men, who are cruel perhaps because like Nero they are always afraid, judge everyone after their own pattern, and can achieve physical pleasure only when they indulge their pride by practising cruelties upon the companion of their pleasures. Hence the horrors of *Justine*. Only in this way can they find a sense of security.

Instead of defining four kinds of love, one might well admit eight or ten distinctions. There are perhaps as many different ways of feeling as there are of seeing, but differences of terminology do not affect the arguments which follow. Every variety of love mentioned henceforth is born, lives, dies, or attains immortality in accordance with the same laws.

Chapter 2: Concerning the Birth of Love

Here is what happens in the soul:

1. Admiration.

2. You think, "How delightful it would be to kiss her, to be kissed by her," and so on. . . .

3. Hope. You observe her perfections, and it is at this moment that a woman really ought to surrender, for the utmost physical pleasure. Even the most reserved women blush to the whites of their eyes at this moment of hope. The passion is so strong, and the pleasure so sharp, that they betray themselves unmistakably.

4. Love is born. To love is to enjoy seeing, touching, and sensing with all the senses, as closely as possible, a lovable object which loves in return.

5. The first crystallization begins. If you are sure that a woman loves you, it is a pleasure to endow her with a thousand perfections and to count your blessings with infinite satisfaction. In the end you overrate wildly, and regard her as something fallen from Heaven, unknown as yet, but certain to be yours.

Leave a lover with his thoughts for twenty-four hours, and this is what will happen:

At the salt mines of Salzburg, they throw a leafless wintry bough into one of the abandoned workings. Two or three months later they haul it out covered with a shining deposit of crystals. The smallest twig, no bigger than a tom-tit's claw, is studded with a galaxy of scintillating diamonds. The original branch is no longer recognizable.

What I have called crystallization is a mental process which draws from everything that happens new proofs of the perfection of the loved one.

You hear a traveller speaking of the cool orange groves beside the sea at Genoa in the summer heat; Oh, if you could only share that coolness with *her*!

One of your friends goes hunting, and breaks his arm: wouldn't it be wonderful to be looked after by the woman you love! To be with her all the time and to see her loving you. . . . In short, no sooner do you think of a virtue than you detect it in your beloved.

The phenomenon that I have called crystallization springs from Nature, which ordains that we shall feel pleasure and sends the blood to our heads. It also evolves from the feeling that the degree of pleasure is related to the perfections of the loved one, and from the idea that 'She is mine.' The savage has no time to go beyond the first step. He feels pleasure, but his brain is fully occupied in chasing deer through the forest, so that he can eat, keep up his strength, and avoid his enemy's axe.

At the other end of the scale of civilization, I have no doubt that a sensitive woman can feel physical pleasure only with the man she loves. This is the direct opposite of the savage's condition. But then, in civilized countries, the woman has leisure, while the savage is so taken up with his occupation that he cannot help treating his female as a beast of burden. If the mates of many animals are happier, it is only because the male has less difficulty in obtaining his food.

But let us leave the forest and return to Paris. A man in love sees every perfection in the object of his love, but his attention is still liable to wander after a time because one gets tired of anything uniform, even perfect happiness.

This is what happens next to fix the attention:

6. Doubt creeps in. First a dozen or so glances, or some other sequence of actions, raise and confirm the lover's hopes. Then, as he recovers from the initial shock, he grows accustomed to his good fortune, or acts on a theory drawn from the common multitude of easily-won women. He asks for more positive proofs of affection and tries to press his suit further.

He is met with indifference, coldness, or even anger if he appears too confident. In France there is even a shade of irony which seems to say 'You think you're farther ahead than you really are.' A woman may behave like this either because she is recovering from a moment of intoxication and obeying the dictates of modesty, which she may fear she has offended; or simply for the sake of prudence or coquetry.

The lover begins to be less sure of the good fortune he was anticipating and subjects his grounds for hope to a critical examination.

He tries to recoup by indulging in other pleasures but finds them inane. He is seized by the dread of a frightful calamity and now concentrates fully. Thus begins:

7. The second crystallization, which deposits diamond layers of proof that 'she loves me.'

Every few minutes throughout the night which follows the birth of doubt, the lover has a moment of dreadful misgiving, and then reassures himself, 'she loves me'; and crystallization begins to reveal new charms. Then once again the haggard eye of doubt pierces him and he stops transfixed. He forgets to draw breath and mutters, 'But does she love me?' Torn between doubt and delight, the poor lover convinces himself that she could give him such pleasure as he could find nowhere else on earth.

It is the pre-eminence of this truth, and the road to it, with a fearsome precipice on one hand and a view of perfect happiness on the other, which set the second crystallization so far about the first.

The lover's mind vacillates between three ideas:

1. She is perfect.

2. She loves me.

3. How can I get the strongest possible proofs of her love?

The most heartrending moment of love in its infancy is the realization that you have been mistaken about something, and that a whole framework of crystals has to be destroyed. You begin to feel doubtful about the entire process of crystallization.

Chapter 6: The Salzburg Bough

Crystallization goes on throughout love almost without a break. The process is something like this: whenever all is not well between you and your beloved, you crystallize out an *imaginary solution*. Only through imagination can you be sure that your beloved is perfect in any given way. After intimacy, ever-resurgent fears are lulled by more real solutions. Thus happiness never stays the same, except in its origin; every day brings forth a new blossom.

If your beloved gives way to her passion and commits the cardinal error of removing your fear by the intensity of her response, then crystallization stops for a moment, but what love loses in intensity—its fears, that is—it makes up for by the charm of complete abandon and infinite trust, becoming a gentle habit which softens the hardships of life and gives a new interest to its enjoyment.

If she leaves you, crystallization begins again, and every act of admiration, the sight of every happiness she could give you, and whose existence you had forgotten, ends in the searing reflection: "I shall never know that joy again, and it is through my fault that I have lost it!" It is no use seeking consolation in pleasures of another sort; they turn to dust and ashes. Your imagination can paint a physical picture for you, and take you a-hunting on a swift horse through Devon woods, but you are aware at the same time that you could find no pleasure in it. This is the optical illusion which leads to the fatal pistol shot. . . .

Hatred, too, has it crystallization; as soon as you see a hope of revenge, your hatred breaks out afresh.

If belief in the absurd or unproven tends to bring the most incongruous people to the top, that is another effect of crystallization. It even exists in mathematics (see the Newtonians in 1740), in minds which could not at any given moment grasp simultaneously all the stages of proof in evidence of their beliefs.

Think of the fate of the great German philosophers, whose immortality, so widely proclaimed, never managed to last more than thirty or forty years.

It is because we can never understand the whys and wherefores of our feelings that even the wisest men are fanatical about such things as music.

It is impossible to justify oneself at will against someone who holds an opposite view.

Chapter 7: Concerning the Different Beginnings of Love for the Two Sexes

A woman establishes her position by granting favours. Ninety-five per cent of her daydreams are about love, and from the moment of intimacy they revolve about one single theme: she endeavours to justify the extraordinary and decisive step she has taken in defiance of all her habits of modesty. A man has no such concern, but a woman's imagination dwells reminiscently on every enchanting detail.

Since love casts doubt upon what seemed proven before, the woman who was so certain, before intimacy, that her lover was entirely above vulgar promiscuity, no sooner remembers that she has nothing left to refuse him than she trembles lest he has merely been adding another conquest to his list.

Only at this point does the second crystallization begin, and much more strongly, since it is now accompanied by fear. (This second crystallization does not occur in women of easy virtue, who are far removed from such romantic ideas.)

The woman feels she has demeaned herself from queen to slave, and matters are aggravated by the dizzy intoxication which results from pleasures as keen as they are rare. And then again, a woman at her embroidery—an insipid pastime that occupies only her hands—thinks of nothing but her lover; while he; galloping across the plains with his squadron, would be placed under arrest if he muffed a manoeuvre.

I should imagine, therefore, that the second crystallization is a good deal stronger in women, because fear is more acute; vanity and honour are in pawn and distractions are certainly not so easy.

A woman cannot fall back on the habit of rational thinking that a man like myself is bound to acquire, working six hours a day at a desk on cold rational matters. Women are inclined, and not only in love, to give way to their imaginations, and to become ecstatic; so their lovers' faults are quickly effaced.

Women prefer emotion to reason. It's quite simple: since in our dull way we never give them any business responsibility in the family *they never have occasion to use reason*, and so never regard it as of any use.

Indeed they find reason a positive nuisance, since it descends upon them only to chide them for their enjoyment of yesterday, or to forbid them the enjoyment of tomorrow.

If you were to hand over the administration of two of your estates to your wife, I wager the accounts would be better kept than by yourself; and then . . . well, you would of course have the *right* to feel sorry for yourself, you pitiable despot, since you lack even the talent to excite love.

As soon as women begin to generalize they are making love without knowing it. They pride themselves on being more meticulous in detail than men, and half the trade across counters is carried on by women, who do better at it than their husbands. It is a commonplace that when you talk about business with them, you must always adopt a very serious tone.

The thing is that they are hungry for emotion, anywhere and at any time: think of the pleasures of a Scottish funeral.

• • •

Chapter 9

I am trying extremely hard to be *dry*. My heart thinks it has so much to say, but I try to keep it quiet. I am continually beset by the fear that I may have expressed only a sigh when I thought I was stating a truth.

• • •

Chapter 11

Once crystallization has begun, you delight in each new beauty that you discover in your beloved.

But what is beauty? It is a new potentiality for pleasure.

Each person's pleasures are different, and often radically so, which explains quite clearly why something that is beautiful to one man is ugly to another. (See the conclusive example of Del Rosso and Lisio on 1st January 1820.)

To determine the nature of beauty, we must investigate each individual's idea of pleasure. For instance, Del Rosso insists upon a woman who allows him to risk a gesture or two, and smilingly licenses the most delightful liberties, a woman who keeps him continually aware of physical pleasure and at the same time gives him the opportunity and incentive to display his particular brand of charm.

Apparently for Del Rosso "love" means physical love, and for Lisio it means passionate love. It is clearly improbable that they will agree about the meaning of the word "beauty."

Since the beauty a man discovers is a new capacity for arousing his pleasure, and since pleasures vary with the individual, each man's crystallization will be tinged with the colour of his pleasures.

The crystallization about your mistress, that is to say her *beauty*, is nothing but the sum of the fulfilment of all the desires you have been able to formulate about her.

Friedrich Nietzsche

Selections

If one considers his biography, the German philosopher Friedrich Nietzsche (1844–1900) appears an even odder authority on romantic love than Rousseau. His most rapturous love affair was his unconsummated ardor for Lou Salomé, who was startled by his belief that she had encouraged him; she preferred the company of one of Nietzsche's (hitherto) closest friends, Paul Rée. Aside from a brief period at the age of thirty-eight when he proposed to several women who were barely acquaintances (and who declined), Nietzsche's life appears almost barren of romantic involvement of any sort. When he went mad at the beginning of 1889, however, he wrote a number of wild notes to friends, some of which confess his love for Cosima, the wife of Richard Wagner, who had been a close friend in the early years of Nietzsche's adult life. Scholars are divided on whether Nietzsche was unusually disinclined to sexual involvements (with women, or men, or either) or merely discreet. If the latter, his sexual policy diverges sharply from his literary voice, which is often unrestrained and outrageous, even (as Freud would put it) "polymorphously perverse."

Nietzsche's philosophical views on romantic love do not fall into a neat, easily classifiable theory. Instead, he comes at the subject from a wide variety of angles, seemingly with diverse purposes in mind. In some of his discussions, Nietzsche reflects his background as student and professor of classical philology, portraying love on the model of the Platonic homoerotic ideal of two men whose mutual admiration motivates each to the pursuit of virtue. In this vein, Nietzsche describes friendship as the highest development of romantic love and diagnoses the contemporary romantic love relationships of his era as "brief follies" made a way of life.

Nietzsche is often portrayed as a misogynist whose diatribes against women were extreme even by nineteenth-century standards. This view is supported by his praise of the Athenian model of love at the expense of modern heterosexual love and marriage. Nonetheless, another facet of Nietzsche's treatment of love is a series of psychological descriptions, many of which cast his alleged misogyny in a somewhat different light. These dis-

cussions usually attempt to explain the psychological motivations behind the details of human romantic behavior in a relatively nonjudgmental fashion. Among the phenomena that Nietzsche sets out to explain are the differences between male and female approaches to love. While his male bias is evident, he is frequently sympathetic toward women and urges his readers to appreciate the tensions inherent in what modern culture expects of women.

A third tendency evident in Nietzsche's discussions of love is a product of his general project of demythologizing the moral ideals of his tradition, in particular those of Christianity. Thus, despite his admiration for the Platonic model of mutual idealization and inspiration in love, Nietzsche frequently assumes the role of romantic debunker. He thus portrays romantic love as the antithesis of Christian virtue and as based on such motives as lust, selfishness, desire for possession, and will to power. But in emphasizing the role of such raw human motives, Nietzsche's aim is to undermine Christianity, not to dethrone eros. It was Christianity, he insists, that uglified and demeaned the passions that are the presupposition of life. In place of Christian standards, Nietzsche advocates a return to those that the Greeks idealized and deified in the figure of Dionysus: delight in the life of the body and worship of the procreative forces that renew that life. And at least in his writing, he was the most erotic and passionate of major philosophers.

From *Daybreak: Thoughts on the Prejudices of Morality*

The value of belief in suprahuman passions. — The institution of marriage obstinately maintains the belief that love, though a passion, is yet capable of endurance; indeed, that enduring, lifelong love can be established as the rule. Through tenaciously adhering to a noble belief, despite the fact that it is very often and almost as a general rule refuted and thus constitutes a *pia fraus*, marriage has bestowed upon love a higher nobility. All institutions which accord to a passion *belief in its endurance* and responsibility for its endurance, contrary to the nature of passion, have raised it to a new rank: and thereafter he who is assailed by such a passion no longer believes himself debased or endangered by it, as he formerly did, but enhanced in his own eyes and those of his equals. Think of institutions and customs which have created out of the fiery abandonment of the moment perpetual fidelity, out of the enjoyment of anger perpetual vengeance, out of despair perpetual mourning, out of a single and unpremeditated word perpetual obligation. This transformation has each time introduced a very great deal of hypocrisy and lying into the world: but each time too, and at this cost, it has introduced a new *suprahuman* concept which elevates mankind.

· · ·

Probable and improbable. — A woman was secretly in love with a man, raised him high above her, and said a hundred times in the most secret recesses of her heart: "if such a man loved me, it would be something I so little deserve I would have to humble myself in the dust!" — And the man felt in the same way, and in regard to the same woman, and he said the same thing in the most secret recesses of his heart. When at last their tongues were loosed and they told one another everything they had kept hidden, there followed a silence; then, after she had been sunk in thought for a time, the woman said in a cold voice: "but everything is now clear! neither of us is what we have loved! If you are that which you say, and no more, I have debased myself and loved you in vain; the demon seduced me, as he did you." — This story, which is not at all an improbable one, never happens — why not?

· · ·

Sample of reflection before marriage. — Supposing she loves me, how burdensome she would become to me in the long run! And supposing she does not love me, how really burdensome she would become to me in the long run! — It is only a question of two different kinds of burdensomeness — therefore let us get married!

· · ·

The most dangerous kind of unlearning. — One begins by unlearning how to love others and ends by no longer finding anything lovable in oneself.

· · ·

"Love makes the same." — Love wants to spare the person to whom it dedicates itself every feeling of *being other*, and consequently it is full of dissimulation and pretence of similarity, it is constantly deceiving and feigning a sameness which in reality does not exist. And this happens so instinctively that women in love deny this dissimulation and continual tender deceit and boldly assert that love *makes the same* (that is to say, that it performs a miracle!). — This process is simple when one party *lets himself be loved* and does not find it necessary to dissimulate but leaves that to the other, loving party; but there is no more confused or impenetrable spectacle than that which arises when both parties are passionately in love with one another and both consequently abandon themselves and want to be the same as one another: in the end neither knows what he is supposed to be imitating,

what dissimulating, what pretending to be. The beautiful madness of this spectacle is too good for this world and too subtle for human eyes.

From *The Joyful Wisdom*

What is called Love. — The lust of property and love: what different associations each of these ideas evoke! — and yet it might be the same impulse twice named: on the one occasion disparaged from the standpoint of those already possessing (in whom the impulse has attained something of repose, and who are now apprehensive for the safety of their "possession"); on the other occasion viewed from the standpoint of the unsatisfied and thirsty, and therefore glorified as "good." Our love of our neighbour, — is it not a striving after new *property?* And similarly our love of knowledge, of truth; and in general all the striving after novelties? We gradually become satiated with the old, the securely possessed, and again stretch out our hands; even the finest landscape in which we live for three months is no longer certain of our love, and any kind of more distant coast excites our covetousness: the possession for the most part becomes smaller through possessing. Our pleasure in ourselves seeks to maintain itself, by always transforming something new *into ourselves,* — that is just possessing. To become satiated with a possession, that is to become satiated with ourselves. (One can also suffer from excess, — even the desire to cast away, to share out, can assume the honourable name of "love.") When we see any one suffering, we willingly utilise the opportunity then afforded to take possession of him; the beneficent and sympathetic man, for example, does this; he also calls the desire for new possession awakened in him, by the name of "love," and has enjoyment in it, as in a new acquisition suggesting itself to him. The love of the sexes, however, betrays itself most plainly as the striving after possession: the lover wants the unconditioned, sole possession of the person longed for by him; he wants just as absolute power over her soul as over her body; he wants to be loved solely, and to dwell and rule in the other soul as what is highest and most to be desired. When one considers that this means precisely to *exclude* all the world from a precious possession, a happiness, and an enjoyment; when one considers that the lover has in view the impoverishment and privation of all other rivals, and would like to become the dragon of his golden hoard, as the most inconsiderate and selfish of all "conquerors" and exploiters; when one considers finally that to the lover himself, the whole world besides appears indifferent, colourless, and worthless, and that he is ready to make every sacrifice, disturb every arrangement, and put every other interest behind his own, — one is verily sur-

144 prised that this ferocious lust of property and injustice of sexual love should have been glorified and deified to such an extent at all times; yea, that out of this love the conception of love as the antithesis of egoism should have been derived, when it is perhaps precisely the most unqualified expression of egoism. Here, evidently, the non-possessors and desirers have determined the usage of language, — there were, of course, always too many of them. Those who have been favoured with much possession and satiety, have, to be sure, dropped a word now and then about the "raging demon," as, for instance, the most lovable and most beloved of all the Athenians— Sophocles; but Eros always laughed at such revilers, — they were always his greatest favourites. — There is, of course, here and there on this terrestrial sphere a kind of sequel to love, in which that covetous longing of two persons for one another has yielded to a new desire and covetousness, to a *common*, higher thirst for a superior ideal standing above them: but who knows this love? Who has experienced it? Its right name is *friendship*.

Women and their Effect in the Distance. —Have I still ears? Am I only ear, and nothing else besides? Here I stand in the midst of the surging of the breakers, whose white flames fork up to my feet; — from all sides there is howling, threatening, crying, and screaming at me, while in the lowest depths the old earth-shaker sings his aria, hollow like a roaring bull; he beats such an earthshaker's measure thereto, that even the hearts of these weathered rock-monsters tremble at the sound. Then, suddenly, as if born out of nothingness, there appears before the portal of this hellish labyrinth, only a few fathoms distant, — a great sailing-ship gliding silently along like a ghost. Oh, this ghostly beauty! With what enchantment it seizes me! What? Has all the repose and silence in the world embarked here? Does my happiness itself sit in this quiet place, my happier ego, my second immortalised self? Still not dead, yet also no longer living? As a ghost-like, calm, gazing, gliding, sweeping, neutral being? Similar to the ship, which, with its white sails, like an immense butterfly, passes over the dark sea! Yes! Passing *over* existence! That is it! That would be it! — —It seems that the noise here has made me a visionary? All great noise causes one to place happiness in the calm and the distance. When a man is in the midst of *his* hubbub, in the midst of the breakers of his plots and plans, he there sees perhaps calm, enchanting beings glide past him, for whose happiness and retirement he longs— *they are women*. He almost thinks that there with the women dwells his better self; that in these calm places even the loudest breakers become still as death, and life itself a dream of life. But still! But still! My noble enthusiast, there is also in the most beautiful sailing-ship so much noise and bustling, and alas, so much petty, pitiable bustling! The enchantment and the most powerful effect of women is, to use the language of philosophers, an effect at a distance, an *actio in distans;* there belongs thereto, however, primarily and above all, — *distance!*

Love. — Love pardons even the lust of the beloved.

Self-dissembling. — She loves him now and has since been looking forth with as quiet confidence as a cow; but alas! It was precisely his delight that she seemed so fitful and absolutely incomprehensible! He had rather too much steady weather in himself already! Would she not do well to feign her old character? to feign indifference? Does not — love itself advise her *to do so? Vivat comœdia!*

On Female Chastity. — There is something quite astonishing and extraordinary in the education of women of the higher class; indeed, there is perhaps nothing more paradoxical. All the world is agreed to educate them with as much ignorance as possible *in eroticis,* and to inspire their soul with a profound shame of such things, and the extremest impatience and horror at the suggestion of them. It is really here only that all the "honour" of woman is at stake; what would one not forgive them in other respects! But here they are intended to remain ignorant to the very backbone: — they are intended to have neither eyes, ears, words, nor thoughts for this, their "wickedness"; indeed knowledge here is already evil. And then! To be hurled as with an awful thunderbolt into reality and knowledge with marriage — and indeed by him whom they most love and esteem: to have to encounter love and shame in contradiction, yea, to have to feel rapture, abandonment, duty, sympathy, and fright at the unexpected proximity of God and animal, and whatever else besides! all at once! — There, in fact, a psychic entanglement has been effected which is quite unequalled! Even the sympathetic curiosity of the wisest discerner of men does not suffice to divine how this or that woman gets along with the solution of this enigma and the enigma of this solution; what dreadful, far-reaching suspicions must awaken thereby in the poor unhinged soul; and forsooth, how the ultimate philosophy and scepticism of the woman casts anchor at this point! — Afterwards the same profound silence as before: and often even a silence to herself, a shutting of her eyes to herself. — Young wives on that account make great efforts to appear superficial and thoughtless; the most ingenious of them simulate a kind of impudence. — Wives easily feel their husbands as a question-mark to their honour, and their children as an apology or atonement, — they require children, and wish for them in quite another spirit than a husband wishes for them. — In short, one cannot be gentle enough towards women!

One must Learn to Love. — This is our experience in music: we must first *learn* in general *to hear*, to hear fully, and to distinguish a theme for a melody, we have to isolate and limit it as a life by itself; then we need to exercise effort and good-will in order *to endure* it in spite of its strangeness, we need patience towards its aspect and expression, and indulgence towards what is odd in it: — in the end there comes a moment when we are *accustomed* to it, when we expect it, when it dawns upon us that we should miss it if it were lacking; and then it goes on to exercise its spell and charm more and more, and does not cease until we have become its humble and enraptured lovers, who want it, and want it again, and ask for nothing better from the world. — It is thus with us, however, not only in music: it is precisely thus that we have *learned to love* all things that we now love. We are always finally recompensed for our good-will, our patience, reasonableness and gentleness towards what is unfamiliar, by the unfamiliar slowly throwing off its veil and presenting itself to us as a new, ineffable beauty: — that is its *thanks* for our hospitality. He also who loves himself must have learned it in this way: there is no other way. Love also has to be learned.

How each Sex has its Prejudice about Love. — Notwithstanding all the concessions which I am inclined to make to the monogamic prejudice, I will never admit that we should speak of *equal* rights in the love of man and woman: there are no such equal rights. The reason is that man and woman understand something different by the term love, — and it belongs to the conditions of love in both sexes that the one sex does *not* presuppose the same feeling, the same conception of "love," in the other sex. What woman understands by love is clear enough: complete surrender (not merely devotion) of soul and body, without any motive, without any reservation, rather with shame and terror at the thought of a devotion restricted by clauses or associated with conditions. In this absence of conditions her love is precisely a *faith*: woman has no other. — Man, when he loves a woman, *wants* precisely this love from her; he is consequently, as regards himself, furthest removed from the prerequisites of feminine love; granted, however, that there should also be men to whom on their side the demand for complete devotion is not unfamiliar, — well, they are really — not men. A man who loves like a woman becomes thereby a slave; a woman, however, who loves like a woman becomes thereby a *more perfect* woman. . . . The passion of woman in its unconditional renunciation of its own rights presupposes in fact that there does *not* exist on the other side an equal *pathos*, an equal desire for renunciation: for if both renounced themselves out of love, there would result—well, I don't know what, perhaps a *horror vacui?* Woman wants to be taken and accepted as a possession, she wishes to be merged in the conceptions of "possession" and "possessed"; consequently she wants one who *takes*, who does not offer and give himself away, but who reversely is rather to be made richer in "himself"—by the increase of power, happiness and faith which the woman herself gives to him. Woman gives herself, man takes her. —I do not think one will get over this natural contrast by any social contract, or with the very best will to do justice, however desirable it may be to avoid bringing the severe, frightful, enigmatical, and unmoral elements of this antagonism constantly before our eyes. For love, regarded as complete, great, and full, is nature, and as nature, is to all eternity something "unmoral."—*Fidelity* is accordingly included in woman's love, it follows from the definition thereof; with man fidelity *may* readily result in consequence of his love, perhaps as gratitude or idiosyncrasy of taste, and so-called elective affinity, but it does not belong to the *essence* of his love—and indeed so little, that one might almost be entitled to speak of a natural opposition between love and fidelity in man, whose love is just a desire to possess, and *not* a renunciation and giving away; the desire to possess, however, comes to an end every time with the possession. . . . As a matter of fact it is the more subtle and jealous thirst for possession in the man (who is rarely and tardily convinced of having this "possession"), which makes his love continue; in that case it is even possible that the love may increase after the surrender, —he does not readily own that a woman has nothing more to "surrender" to him. —

• • •

From *Thus Spake Zarathustra*

I have a question for you alone, my brother: like a sounding lead, I cast this question into your soul that I might know how deep it is.

You are young and wish for a child and marriage. But I ask you: Are you a man *entitled* to wish for a child? Are you the victorious one, the self-conqueror, the commander of your senses, the master of your virtues? This I ask you. Or is it the animal and need that speak out of your wish? Or loneliness? Or lack of peace with yourself?

Let your victory and your freedom long for a child. You shall build living monuments to your victory and your liberation. You shall build over and beyond yourself, but first you must be built yourself, perpendicular in body and soul. You shall not only reproduce yourself, but produce something higher. May the garden of marriage help you in that!

You shall create a higher body, a first movement, a self-propelled wheel—you shall create a creator.

Marriage: thus I name the will of two to create the one that is more than those who created it. Reverence for each other, as for those willing with such a will, is what I name marriage. Let this be the meaning and truth of your marriage. But that which the all-too-many, the superfluous, call marriage—alas, what shall I name that? Alas, this poverty of the soul in pair! Alas, this filth of the soul in pair! Alas, this wretched contentment in pair! Marriage they call this; and they say that their marriages are made in heaven. Well, I do not like it, this heaven of the superfluous. No, I do not like them—these animals entangled in the heavenly net. And let the god who limps near to bless what he never joined keep his distance from me! Do not laugh at such marriages! What child would not have cause to weep over its parents?

Worthy I deemed this man, and ripe for the sense of the earth; but when I saw his wife, the earth seemed to me a house for the senseless. Indeed, I wished that the earth might tremble in convulsions when a saint mates with a goose.

This one went out like a hero in quest of truths, and eventually he conquered a little dressed-up lie. His marriage he calls it.

That one was reserved and chose choosily. But all at once he spoiled his company forever: his marriage he calls it.

That one sought a maid with the virtues of an angel. But all at once he became the maid of a woman; and now he must turn himself into an angel.

Careful I have found all buyers now, and all of them have cunning eyes. But even the most cunning still buys his wife in a poke.

Many brief follies—that is what you call love. And your marriage concludes many brief follies, as a long stupidity. Your love of woman, and woman's love of man—oh, that it were compassion for suffering and shrouded gods! But, for the most part, two beasts find each other.

But even your best love is merely an ecstatic parable and a painful ardor. It is a torch that should light up higher paths for you. Over and beyond yourselves you shall love one day. Thus *learn* first to love. And for that you had to drain the bitter cup of your love. Bitterness lies in the cup of even the best love: thus it arouses longing for the overman; thus it arouses your thirst, creator. Thirst for the creator, an arrow and longing for the overman: tell me, my brother, is this your will to marriage? Holy I call such a will and such a marriage.

Thus spoke Zarathustra.

From *Beyond Good & Evil*

The degree and nature of a man's sensuality extends to the highest altitudes of his spirit.

. . .

The same emotions are in man and woman, but in diferent *tempo*; on that account man and woman never cease to misunderstand each other.

. . .

The immense expectation with regard to sexual love, and the coyness in this expectation, spoils all the perspectives of women at the outset.

. . .

Sensuality often forces the growth of love too much, so that its root remains weak, and is easily torn up.

. . .

Even concubinage has been corrupted — by marriage.

. . .

The sexes deceive themselves about ach other: the reason is that in reality they honour and love only themselves (or their own ideal, to express it more agreeably). Thus man wishes woman to be peaceable: but in fact woman is *essentially* unpeaceable, like the cat, however well she may have assumed the peaceable demeanour.

. . .

In revenge and in love woman is more barbarous than man.

. . .

The chastest utterance I ever heard: *"Dans le véritable amour c'est l'âme qui enveloppe le corps."* [In true love, it is the soul that envelops the body.]

. . .

Comparing man and woman generally, one may say that woman would not have the genius for adornment, if she had not the instinct for the *secondary* role.

. . .

What is done out of love always takes place beyond good and evil.

. . .

Love brings to light the noble and hidden qualities of a lover — his rare and exceptional traits: it is thus liable to be deceptive as to his normal character.

• • •

Christianity gave Eros poison to drink; he did not die of it, certainly, but degenerated to Vice.

• • •

One loves ultimately one's desires, not the thing desired.

From *Twilight of the Idols*

Witness *modern marriage*. All rationality has clearly vanished from modern marriage; yet that is no objection to marriage, but to modernity. The rationality of marriage—that lay in the husband's sole juridical responsibility, which gave marriage a center of gravity, while today it limps on both legs. The rationality of marriage—that lay in its indissolubility in principle, which lent it an accent that could be heard above the accident of feeling, passion, and what is merely momentary. It also lay in the family's responsibility for the choice of a spouse. With the growing indulgence of love matches, the very foundation of marriage has been eliminated, that which alone makes an institution of it. Never, absolutely never, can an institution be founded on an idiosyncrasy; one cannot, as I have said, found marriage on "love"—it can be founded on the sex drive, on the property drive (wife and child as property), on the drive to dominate, which continually organizes for itself the smallest structure of domination, the family, and which needs children and heirs to hold fast—physiologically too—to an attained measure of power, influence, and wealth, in order to prepare for long-range tasks, for a solidarity of instinct between the centuries. Marriage as an institution involves the affirmation of the largest and most enduring form of organization: when society cannot affirm itself as a whole, down to the most distant generations, then marriage has altogether no meaning. Modern marriage has lost its meaning—consequently one abolishes it.

From *Ecce Homo*

Has my definition of love been heard? It is the only one worthy of a philosopher. Love—in its means, war; at bottom, the deadly hatred of the sexes.

ii

Sigmund Freud

*On the Universal Tendency to Debasement in the
Sphere of Love, On Narcissism: An Introduction, and "Civilized"
Sexual Morality and Modern Nervous Illness*

*Sigmund Freud (1856–1939) was the founder of psychoanalysis and a per-
spective on mental life that has come to dominate the Western world in the
twentieth century. Building on his early work with hysterics, whose physical
symptoms were alleviated when unconscious memories were brought to
light, Freud postulated an unconscious region of the mind in which seemingly forgotten ideas continued to have an active effect on conscious life.
Such ideas are not relegated to unconsciousness because they are weaker
than conscious thoughts, but because they are strong and unacceptable to
the conscious mind. These thoughts are "repressed," and continual pressure is exerted in order to hold them in the unconscious mind. Many such
ideas are repressed because of their sexual content. It may be that civilized
life depends on the repression of many sexual desires, but the human cost
in terms of happiness and mental health is considerable, as Freud argues in
" 'Civilized' Sexual Morality and Modern Nervous Illness."*

*Freud also elaborates a theory of instinctual life that stresses the impor-
tance of sexual instincts from the time of infancy and explains many adult
neuroses in terms of aberrant development of these instincts. One of Freud's
most notorious ideas is that normal development requires that the child
overcome its natural libidinal (sexual) attachment to its mother, an attachment which, in the case of the male child, ensures the development of antagonism toward the father (whom the child considers a rival for the mother's attention). Freud considers the resolution of this "Oedipal complex" to
be the crucial psychological task of childhood. The way in which this complex is resolved has tremendous impact on the individual's ability to develop and sustain love relationships as an adult. In his essay "On the Universal Tendency to Debasement in the Sphere of Love," Freud indicates the
difficulty of this achievement. The main psychological task after puberty is
to get the currents of one's sexual desire and one's feelings of affection directed toward the same object. Although both sexual and affectionate feel-*

ings have their prototype in one's infantile relationship toward parents, the child, in surmounting the Oedipal complex, learns to dissociate the two. Because the complex poses a conflict between sensuality and authority, it is only successfully resolved when sensuality gives way to the demands of authority. The psychological price of this essential step in development is that one learns to connect sexual feelings with the model of dominance and submission. Unless this association is overcome, the adult tends to impose the model of domination on the love object. Freud's ideal of a balanced sensual life involves sexual and affectionate feelings exchanged between equal partners, but he considers success in this effort to be far from commonplace.

In certain respects, Freud's conception of optimum development endorses contemporary societal demands, such as insistence on heterosexual orientation and the repression of many of one's sexual desires. But at the same time, he legitimates the range of psychosexual possibilities by contending that these are genuine possibilities for everyone, and that we are all naturally "polymorphously perverse." Moreover, Freud emphasizes the high price of "normal" adjustment and deromanticizes the erotic ideals of our society. In "On Narcissism: An Introduction," Freud argues that romantic love is an outgrowth of our primary state of narcissism. Mental health requires the individual to move beyond narcissism and direct libido toward some external object. Thus love has a functional role in the mechanisms of mental hygiene: "We must begin to love in order that we may not fall ill." Freud's analysis of romantic love as based upon redirected narcissism provides another explanation for the dissatisfaction that many experience in their love lives. One trades a certain amount of narcissism in order to love another. This is reflected in the fact that to be in love is to render oneself vulnerable to the beloved. But Freud also suggests that the cost of being in love is a reduction in self-esteem. He assumes that the individual has a finite amount of libido to direct and that the less one directs libido outward, the more it is directed inward. Losing the ability to love, however, is no recipe for an "ego-boost." The person who directs all or most libido inward becomes incurably psychotic. Love, for Freud, is the lesser of two evils.

On the Universal Tendency to Debasement in the Sphere of Love

If the practising psycho-analyst asks himself on account of what disorder people most often come to him for help, he is bound to reply—disregarding the many forms of anxiety—that it is psychical impotence. This singular disturbance affects men of strongly libidinous natures, and manifests itself in a refusal by the executive organs of sexuality to carry out the sexual act, although before and after they may show themselves to be intact and capable of performing the act, and although a strong psychical inclination to carry it out is present. The first clue to understanding his condition is obtained by the sufferer himself on making the discovery that a failure of this kind only arises when the attempt is made with certain individuals; whereas with others there is never any question of such a failure. He now becomes aware that it is some feature of the sexual object which gives rise to the inhibition of his male potency, and sometimes he reports that he has a feeling of an obstacle inside him, the sensation of a counter-will which successfully interferes with his conscious intention. However, he is unable to guess what this internal obstacle is and what feature of the sexual object brings it into operation. If he has had repeated experience of a failure of this kind, he is likely, by the familiar process of "erroneous connection," to decide that the recollection of the first occasion evoked the disturbing anxiety-idea and so caused the failure to be repeated each time; while he derives the first occasion itself from some "accidental" impression.

Psycho-analytic studies of psychical impotence have already been carried out and published by several writers. Every analyst can confirm the explanations provided by them from his own clinical experience. It is in fact a question of the inhibitory influence of certain psychical complexes which are withdrawn from the subject's knowledge. An incestuous fixation on mother or sister, which has never been surmounted, plays a prominent part in this pathogenic material and is its most universal content. In addition there is the influence to be considered of accidental distressing impressions connected with infantile sexual activity, and also those factors which in a general way reduce the libido that is to be directed on to the female sexual object.

When striking cases of psychical impotence are exhaustively investigated by means of psycho-analysis, the following information is obtained about the psychosexual processes at work in them. Here again—as very probably in all neurotic disturbances—the foundation of the disorder is provided by an inhibition in the developmental history of the libido before it assumes the form which we take to be its normal termination. Two currents whose union is necessary to ensure a completely normal attitude in love have, in the cases we are considering, failed to combine. These two may be distinguished as the *affectionate* and the *sensual* current.

The affectionate current is the older of the two. It springs from the earliest years of childhood; it is formed on the basis of the interests of the self-preservative instinct and is directed to the members of the family and those who look after the child. From the very beginning it carries along with it contributions from the sexual instincts — components of erotic interest — which can already be seen more or less clearly even in childhood and in any event are uncovered in neurotics by psycho-analysis later on. It corresponds to *the child's primary object-choice*. We learn in this way that the sexual instincts find their first objects by attaching themselves to the valuations made by the ego-instincts, precisely in the way in which the first sexual satisfactions are experienced in attachment to the bodily functions necessary for the preservation of life. The "affection" shown by the child's parents and those who look after him, which seldom fails to betray its erotic nature ("the child is an erotic plaything"), does a very great deal to raise the contributions made by erotism to the cathexes of his ego-instincts, and to increase them to an amount which is bound to play a part in his later development, especially when certain other circumstances lend their support.

These affectionate fixations of the child persist throughout childhood, and continually carry along with them erotism, which is consequently diverted from its sexual aims. Then at the age of puberty they are joined by the power "sensual" current which no longer mistakes its aims. It never fails, apparently, to follow the earlier paths and to cathect the objects of the primary infantile choice with quotas of libido that are now far stronger. Here, however, it runs up against the obstacles that have been erected in the meantime by the barrier against incest; consequently it will make efforts to pass on from these objects which are unsuitable in reality, and find a way as soon as possible to other, extraneous objects with which a real sexual life may be carried on. These new objects will still be chosen on the model (imago) of the infantile ones, but in the course of time they will attract to themselves the affection that was tied to the earlier ones. A man shall leave his father and his mother — according to the biblical command — and shall cleave unto his wife; affection and sensuality are then united. The greatest intensity of sensual passion will bring with it the highest psychical valuation of the object — this being the normal overvaluation of the sexual object on the part of a man.

Two factors will decide whether this advance in the developmental path of the libido is to fail. First, there is the amount of *frustration in reality* which opposes the new object-choice and reduces its value for the person concerned. There is after all no point in embarking upon an object-choice if no choice is to be allowed at all or if there is no prospect of being able to choose anything suitable. Secondly, there is the amount of *attraction* which the infantile objects that have to be relinquished are able to exercise, and which is in proportion to the erotic cathexis attaching to them in childhood. If these two factors are sufficiently strong, the general mechanism by which the neuroses are formed comes into operation. The libido turns away from reality, is taken over by imaginative activity (the process of introversion), strengthens the images of the first sexual objects and becomes fixated to them. The obstacle raised against incest, however, compels the libido that has turned to these objects to remain in the unconscious. The masturbatory activity carried out by the sensual current, which is now part of the unconscious, makes its own contribution in strengthening this fixation. Nothing is altered in this state of affairs if the advance which has miscarried in reality is now completed in phantasy, and if in the phantasy-situations that lead to masturbatory satisfaction the original sexual objects are replaced by different ones. As a result of this substitution the phantasies become admissible to consciousness, but no progress is made in the allocation of the libido in reality. In this way it can happen that the whole of a young man's sensuality becomes tied to incestuous objects in the unconscious, or to put it another way, becomes fixated to unconscious incestuous phantasies. The result is then total impotence, which is perhaps further ensured by the simultaneous onset of an actual weakening of the organs that perform the sexual act.

Less severe conditions are required to bring about the state known specifically as psychical impotence. Here the fate of the sensual current must not be that its whole charge has to conceal itself behind the affectionate current; it must have remained sufficiently strong or uninhibited to secure a partial outlet into reality. The sexual activity of such people shows the clearest signs, however, that it has not the whole psychical driving force of the instinct behind it. It is capricious, easily disturbed, often not properly carried out, and not accompanied by much pleasure. But above all it is forced to avoid the affectionate current. A restriction has thus been placed on object-choice. The sensual current that has remained active seeks only objects which do not recall the incestuous figures forbidden to it; if someone makes an impression that might lead to a high psychical estimation of her, this impression does not find an issue in any sensual excitation but in affection which has no erotic effect. The whole sphere of love in such people remains divided in the two directions personified in art as sacred and profane (or animal) love. Where they love they do not desire and where they desire they cannot love. They seek objects which they do not need to love, in order to keep their sensuality away from the objects they love; and, in accordance with the laws of "complexive sensitiveness" and of the return of the repressed, the strange failure shown in psychical impotence makes its appearance whenever an object which has been chosen with the aim of avoiding incest recalls the prohibited object through some feature, often an inconspicuous one.

The main protective measure against such a disturbance which men have recourse to in this split in their love consists in a psychical *debasement* of the sexual object, the overvaluation that normally attaches to the sexual object being reserved for the incestuous object and its representatives. As soon as the condition of debasement is fulfilled, sensuality can be freely expressed, and important sexual capacities and a high degree of pleasure can develop. There is a further factor which contributes to this result. People in whom there has not been a proper confluence of the affectionate and the sensual currents do not usually show much refinement in their modes of behavior in love; they have retained perverse sexual aims whose nonfulfilment is felt as a serious loss of pleasure, and whose fulfilment on the other hand seems possible only with a debased and despised sexual object.

· · ·

We have reduced psychical impotence to the failure of the affectionate and the sensual currents in love to combine, and this developmental inhibition has in turn been explained as being due to the influences of strong childhood fixations and of later frustration in reality through the intervention of the barrier against incest. There is one principal objection to the theory we advance; it does too much. It explains why certain people suffer from psychical impotence, but it leaves us with the apparent mystery of how others have been able to escape this disorder. Since we must recognize that all the relevant factors known to us—the strong childhood fixation, the incest-barrier and the frustration in the years of development after puberty—are to be found in practically all civilized human beings, we should be justified in expecting psychical impotence to be a universal affliction under civilization and not a disorder confined to some individuals.

It would be easy to escape from this conclusion by pointing to the quantitative factor in the causation of illness—to the greater or lesser extent of the contribution made by the various elements which determine whether a recognizable illness results or not. But although I accept this answer as correct, it is not my intention to make it a reason for rejecting the conclusion itself. On the contrary, I shall put forward the view that psychical impotence is much more widespread than is supposed, and that a certain amount of this behavior does in fact characterize the love of civilized man.

If the concept of psychical impotence is broadened and is not restricted to failure to perform the act of coitus in circumstances where a desire to obtain pleasure is present and the genital apparatus is intact, we may in the first place add all those men who are described as psychanaesthetic: men who never fail in the act but who carry it out without getting any particular pleasure from it—a state of affairs that is more common than one would think. Psycho-analytic examination of such cases discloses the same aetiological factors as we found in psychical impotence in the narrower sense, without at first arriving at any explanation of the difference between their symptoms. An easily justifiable analogy takes one from these anaesthetic men to the immense number of frigid women; and there is no better way to describe or understand their behavior in love than by comparing it with the more conspicuous disorder of psychical impotence in men.

If however we turn our attention not to an extension of the concept of psychical impotence, but to the gradations in its symptomatology, we cannot escape the conclusion that the behaviour in love of men in the civilized world to-day bears the stamp altogether of psychical impotence. There are only a very few educated people in whom the two currents of affection and sensuality have become properly fused; the man almost always feels his respect for the woman acting as a restriction on his sexual activity, and only develops full potency when he is with a debased sexual object; and this in its turn is partly caused by the entrance of perverse components into his sexual aims, which he does not venture to satisfy with a woman he respects. He is assured of complete sexual pleasure only when he can devote himself unreservedly to obtaining satisfaction, which with his well-brought-up wife, for instance, he does not dare to do. This is the source of his need for a debased sexual object, a woman who is ethically inferior, to whom he need attribute no aesthetic scruples, who does not know him in his other social relations and cannot judge him in them. It is to such a woman that he prefers to devote his sexual potency, even when the whole of his affection belongs to a woman of a higher kind. It is possible, too, that the tendency so often observed in men of the highest classes of society to choose a woman of a lower class as a permanent mistress or even as a wife is nothing but a consequence of their need for a debased sexual object, to whom, psychologically, the possibility of complete satisfaction is linked.

I do not hesitate to make the two factors at work in psychical impotence in the strict sense—the factors of intense incestuous fixation in childhood and the frustration by reality in adolescence — responsible, too, for this extremely common characteristic of the love of civilized men. It sounds not only disagreeable but also paradoxical, yet it must nevertheless be said that anyone who is to be really free and happy in love must have surmounted his respect for women and have come to terms with the idea of incest with his mother or sister. Anyone who subjects himself to a serious self-examination on the subject of this requirement will be sure to find that he regards the sexual act basically as something degrading, which defiles and pollutes not only the body. The origin of this low opinion, which he will certainly not willingly acknowledge, must be looked for in the period of his youth in which the sensual current in him was already strongly developed but its satisfaction with an object outside the family was almost as completely prohibited as it was with an incestuous one.

In our civilized world women are under the influence of a similar after-effect of their upbringing, and, in addition, of their reaction to men's behaviour. It is naturally just as unfavorable for a woman if a man approaches her without his full potency as it is if his initial overvaluation of her when he is in love gives place to undervaluation after he has possessed her. In the case of women there is little sign of a need to debase their sexual object. This is no doubt connected with the absence in them as a rule of anything similar to the sexual overvaluation found in men. But their long holding back from sexuality and the lingering of their sensuality in phantasy has another important consequence for them. They are subsequently often unable to undo the connection between sensual activity and the prohibition, and prove to be psychically impotent, that is, frigid, when such activity is at last allowed them. This is the origin of the endeavour made by many women to keep even legitimate relations secret for a while; and of the capacity of other women for normal sensation as soon as the condition of prohibition is re-established by a secret love affair: unfaithful to their husband, they are able to keep a second order of faith with their lover.

The condition of forbiddenness in the erotic life of women is, I think, comparable to the need on the part of men to debase their sexual object. Both are consequences of the long period of delay, which is demanded by education for cultural reasons, between sexual maturity and sexual activity. Both aim at abolishing the psychical impotence that results from the failure of affectionate and sensual impulses to coalesce. That the effect of the same causes should be so different in men and in women may perhaps be traced to another difference in the behaviour of the two sexes. Civilized women do not usually transgress the prohibition on sexual activity in the period during which they have to wait, and thus they acquire the intimate connection between prohibition and sexuality. Men usually break through this prohibition if they can satisfy the condition of debasing the object, and so they carry on this condition into their love in later life.

· · ·

The fact that the curb put upon love by civilization involves a universal tendency to debase sexual objects will perhaps lead us to turn our attention from the object to the instincts themselves. The damage caused by the initial frustration of sexual pleasure is seen in the fact that the freedom later given to that pleasure in marriage does not bring full satisfaction. But at the same time, if sexual freedom is unrestricted from the outset the result is no better. It can easily be shown that the psychical value of erotic needs is reduced as soon as their satisfaction becomes easy. An obstacle is required in order to heighten libido; and where natural resistances to satisfaction have not been sufficient men have at all times erected conventional ones so as to be able to enjoy love. This is true both of individuals and of nations. In times in which there were no difficulties standing in the way of sexual satisfaction, such as perhaps during the decline of the ancient civilizations, love became worthless and life empty, and strong reaction-formations were required to restore indispensable affective values. In this connection it may be claimed that the ascetic current in Christianity created psychical values for love which pagan antiquity was never able to confer on it. This current assumed its greatest importance with the ascetic monks, whose lives were almost entirely occupied with the struggle against libidinal temptation.

· · ·

It is my belief that, however strange it may sound, we must reckon with the possibility that something in the nature of the sexual instinct itself is unfavorable to the realization of complete satisfaction. If we consider the long and difficult developmental history of the instinct, two factors immediately spring to mind which might be made responsible for this difficulty. Firstly, as a result of the diphasic onset of object-choice, and the interposition of the barrier against incest, the final object of the sexual instinct is never any longer the original object but only a surrogate for it. Psychoanalysis has shown us that when the original object of a wishful impulse has been lost as a result of repression, it is frequently represented by an endless series of substitutive objects none of which, however, brings full satisfaction. This may explain the inconstancy in object-choice, the "craving for stimulation" which is so often a feature of the love of adults.

Secondly, we know that the sexual instinct is originally divided into a

162 great number of components—or rather, it develops out of them—some of which cannot be taken up into the instinct in its later form, but have at an earlier stage to be suppressed or put to other uses. These are above all the coprophilic instinctual components, which have proved incompatible with our aesthetic standards of culture, probably since, as a result of our adopting an erect gait, we raised our organ of smell from the ground. The same is true of a large portion of the sadistic urges which are a part of erotic life. But all such developmental processes affect only the upper layers of the complex structure. The fundamental processes which produce erotic excitation remain unaltered. The excremental is all too intimately and inseparably bound up with the sexual; the position of the genitals—*inter urinas et faeces*—remains the decisive and unchangeable factor. One might say here, varying a well-known saying of the great Napoleon: "Anatomy is destiny." The genitals themselves have not taken part in the development of the human body in the direction of beauty: they have remained animal, and thus love, too, has remained in essence just as animal as it ever was. The instincts of love are hard to educate; education of them achieves now too much, now too little. What civilization aims at making out of them seems unattainable except at the price of a sensible loss of pleasure; the persistence of the impulses that could not be made use of can be detected in sexual activity in the form of non-satisfaction.

Thus we may perhaps be forced to become reconciled to the idea that it is quite impossible to adjust the claims of the sexual instinct to the demands of civilization; that in consequence of its cultural development renunciation and suffering, as well as the danger of extinction in the remotest future, cannot be avoided by the human race. This gloomy prognosis rests, it is true, on the single conjecture that the non-satisfaction that goes with civilization is the necessary consequence of certain peculiarities which the sexual instinct has assumed under the pressure of culture. The very incapacity of the sexual instinct to yield complete satisfaction as soon as it submits to the first demands of civilization becomes the source, however, of the noblest cultural achievements which are brought into being by ever more extensive sublimation of its instinctual components. For what motive would men have for putting sexual instinctual forces to other uses if, by any distribution of those forces, they could obtain fully satisfying pleasure? They would never abandon that pleasure and they would never make any further progress. It seems, therefore, that the irreconcilable difference between the demands of the two instincts—the sexual and the egoistic—has made men capable of ever higher achievements, though subject, it is true,

to a constant danger, to which, in the form of neurosis, the weaker are suc-
cumbing to-day.

It is not the aim of science either to frighten or to console. But I myself
am quite ready to admit that such far-reaching conclusions as those I have
drawn should be built on a broader foundation, and that perhaps developments in other directions may enable mankind to correct the results of the
developments I have here been considering in isolation.

On Narcissism: An Introduction

. . . It is universally known, and we take it as a matter of course, that a person who is tormented by organic pain and discomfort gives up his interest
in the things of the external world, in so far as they do not concern his suffering. Closer observation teaches us that he also withdraws *libidinal* interest from his love-objects: so long as he suffers, he ceases to love. The commonplace nature of this fact is no reason why we should be deterred from
translating it into terms of the libido theory. We should then say: the sick
man withdraws his libidinal cathexes back upon his own ego, and sends
them out again when he recovers. "Concentrated in his soul," says Wilhelm
Busch of the poet suffering from toothache, "in his molar's narrow hole."
Here libido and ego-interest share the same fate and are once more indistinguishable from each other. The familiar egoism of the sick person covers
both. We find it so natural because we are certain that in the same situation we should behave in just the same way. The way in which a lover's feelings, however strong, are banished by bodily ailments, and suddenly replaced by complete indifference, is a theme which has been exploited by
comic writers to an appropriate extent.

The condition of sleep, too, resembles illness in implying a narcissistic
withdrawal of the positions of the libido on to the subject's own self, or,
more precisely, on to the single wish to sleep. The egoism of dreams fits very
well into this context. In both states we have, if nothing else, examples of
changes in the distribution of libido that are consequent upon a change in
the ego.

• • •

At this point, our curiosity will of course raise the question why this
damming-up of libido in the ego should have to be experienced as unplea-
surable. I shall content myself with the answer that unpleasure is always the
expression of a higher degree of tension, and that therefore what is happening is that a quantity in the field of material events is being transformed
here as elsewhere into the psychical quality of unpleasure. Nevertheless it

may be that what is decisive for the generation of unpleasure is not the absolute magnitude of the material event, but rather some particular function of that absolute magnitude. Here we may even venture to touch on the question of what makes it necessary at all for our mental life to pass beyond the limits of narcissism and to attach the libido to objects. The answer which would follow from our line of thought would once more be that this necessity arises when the cathexis of the ego with libido exceeds a certain amount. A strong egoism is a protection against falling ill, but in the last resort we must begin to love in order not to fall ill, and we are bound to fall ill if, in consequence of frustration, we are unable to love.

· · ·

A . . . way in which we may approach the study of narcissism is by observing the erotic life of human beings, with its many kinds of differentiation in man and woman. Just as object-libido at first concealed ego-libido from our observation, so too in connection with the object-choice of infants (and of growing children) what we first noticed was that they derived their sexual objects from their experiences of satisfaction. The first auto-erotic sexual satisfactions are experienced in connection with vital functions which serve the purpose of self-preservation. The sexual instincts are at the outset attached to the satisfaction of the ego-instincts; only later do they become independent of these, and even then we have an indication of that original attachment in the fact that the persons who are concerned with a child's feeding, care, and protection become his earliest sexual objects: that is to say, in the first instance his mother or a substitute for her. Side by side, however, with this type and source of object-choice, which may be called the "anaclitic" or "attachment" type, psycho-analytic research has revealed a second type, which we were not prepared for finding. We have discovered, especially clearly in people whose libidinal development has suffered some disturbance, such as perverts and homosexuals, that in their later choice of love-objects they have taken as a model not their mother but their own selves. They are plainly seeking *themselves* as a love-object, and are exhibiting a type of object-choice which must be termed "narcissistic." In this observation we have the strongest of the reasons which have led us to adopt the hypothesis of narcissism.

We have, however, not concluded that human beings are divided into two sharply differentiated groups, according as their object-choice conforms to the anaclitic or to the narcissistic type; we assume rather that both kinds of object-choice are open to each individual, though he may show a preference for one or the other. We say that a human being has originally two sexual objects — himself and the woman who nurses him — and in doing so we are postulating a primary narcissism in everyone, which may in some cases manifest itself in a dominating fashion in his object-choice.

A comparison of the male and female sexes then shows that there are fundamental differences between them in respect of their type of object-choice, although these differences are of course not universal. Complete object-love of the attachment type is, properly speaking, characteristic of the male. It displays the marked sexual overvaluation which is doubtless derived from the child's original narcissism and thus corresponds to a transference of that narcissism to the sexual object. This sexual overvaluation is the origin of the peculiar state of being in love, a state suggestive of a neurotic compulsion, which is thus traceable to an impoverishment of the ego as regards libido in favor of the love-object. A different course is followed in the type of female most frequently met with, which is probably the purest and truest one. With the onset of puberty the maturing of the female sexual organs, which up till then have been in a condition of latency, seems to bring about an intensification of the original narcissism, and this is unfavorable to the development of a true object-choice with its accompanying sexual overvaluation. Women, especially if they grow up with good looks, develop a certain self-contentment which compensates them for the social restrictions that are imposed upon them in their choice of object. Strictly speaking, it is only themselves that such women love with an intensity comparable to that of the man's love for them. Nor does their need lie in the direction of loving, but of being loved; and the man who fulfills this condition is the one who finds favour with them. The importance of this type of woman for the erotic life of mankind is to be rated very high. Such women have the greatest fascination for men, not only for aesthetic reasons, since as a rule they are the most beautiful, but also because of a combination of interesting psychological factors. For it seems very evident that another person's narcissism has a great attraction for those who have renounced part of their own narcissism and are in search of object-love. The charm of a child lies to a great extent in his narcissism, his self-contentment and inaccessibility, just as does the charm of certain animals which seem not to concern themselves about us, such as cats and the large beasts of prey. Indeed, even great criminals and humorists, as they are represented in literature, compel our interest by the narcissistic consistency with which they manage to keep away from their ego anything that would diminish it. It is as if we envied them for maintaining a blissful state of mind — an unassailable libidinal position which we ourselves have since abandoned. The great charm of narcissistic women has, however, its reverse side; a large part of the lover's dissatisfaction, of his doubts of the woman's love, of his complaints of her enigmatic nature, has its root in this incongruity between the types of object-choice.

Perhaps it is not out of place here to give an assurance that this description of the feminine form of erotic life is not due to any tendentious desire on my part to depreciate women. Apart from the fact that tendentiousness is quite alien to me, I know that these different lines of development correspond to the differentiation of functions in a highly complicated biological whole; further, I am ready to admit that there are quite a number of women who love according to the masculine type and who also develop the sexual overvaluation proper to that type.

Even for narcissistic women, whose attitude towards men remains cool, there is a road which leads to complete object-love. In the child which they bear, a part of their own body confronts them like an extraneous object, to which, starting out from their narcissism, they can then give complete object-love. There are other women, again, who do not have to wait for a child in order to take the step in development from (secondary) narcissism to object-love. Before puberty they feel masculine and develop some way along masculine lines; after this trend has been cut short on their reaching female maturity, they still retain the capacity of longing for a masculine ideal — an ideal which is in fact a survival of the boyish nature that they themselves once possessed.

• • •

The primary narcissism of children which we have assumed and which forms one of the postulates of our theories of the libido, is less easy to grasp by direct observation than to confirm by inference from elsewhere. If we look at the attitude of affectionate parents towards their children, we have recognize that it is a revival and reproduction of their own narcissism, which they have long since abandoned. The trustworthy pointer constituted by overvaluation, which we have already recognized as a narcissistic stigma in the case of object-choice, dominates, as we all know, their emotional attitude. Thus they are under a compulsion to ascribe every perfection to the child — which sober observation would find no occasion to do — and to conceal and forget all his shortcomings. (Incidentally, the denial of sexuality in children is connected with this.) Moreover, they are inclined to suspend in the child's favour the operation of all the cultural acquisitions which their own narcissism has been forced to respect, and to renew on his behalf the claims to privileges which were long ago given up by themselves.

The child shall have a better time than his parents; he shall not be subject to the necessities which they have recognized as paramount in life. Illness, death, renunciation of enjoyment, restrictions on his own will, shall not touch him; the laws of nature and of society shall be abrogated in his favour; he shall once more really be the centre and core of creation—"His Majesty the Baby," as we once fancied ourselves. The child shall fulfil those wishful dreams of the parents which they never carried out—the boy shall become a great man and a hero in his father's place, and the girl shall marry a prince as a tardy compensation for her mother. At the most touchy point in the narcissistic system, the immortality of the ego, which is so hard pressed by reality, security is achieved by taking refuge in the child. Parental love, which is so moving and at bottom so childish, is nothing but the parents' narcissism born again, which, transformed into object-love, unmistakably reveals its former nature.

"Civilized" Sexual Morality and Nervous Illness

Generally speaking, our civilization is built up on the suppression of instincts. Each individual has surrendered some part of his possessions— some part of the sense of omnipotence or of the aggressive or vindictive inclinations in his personality. From these contributions has grown civilization's common possession of material and ideal property. Besides the exigencies of life, no doubt it has been family feelings, derived from erotism, that have induced the separate individuals to make this renunciation. The renunciation has been a progressive one in the course of evolution of civilization. The single steps in it were sanctioned by religion; the piece of instinctual satisfaction which each person had renounced was offered to the Deity as a sacrifice, and the communal property thus acquired was declared "sacred." The many who, in consequence of his unyielding constitution, cannot fall in with this suppression of instinct, becomes a "criminal," an "outlaw," in the face of society—unless his social position or his exceptional capacities enable him to impose himself upon it as a great man, a "hero."

The sexual instinct—or, more correctly, the sexual instincts, for analytic investigation teaches us that the sexual instinct is made up of many separate constituents or component instincts—is probably more strongly developed in man than in most of the higher animals; it is certainly more constant, since it has almost entirely overcome the periodicity to which it is tied in animals. It places extraordinarily large amounts of force at the disposal of civilized activity, and it does this in virtue of its especially marked characteristic of being able to displace its aim without materially diminishing in intensity. This capacity to exchange its originally sexual aim for another one, which is no longer sexual but which is psychically related to the first aim, is called the capacity for *sublimation*. In contrast to this displaceability, in which its value for civilization lies, the sexual instinct may also exhibit a particularly obstinate fixation which renders it unserviceable and which sometimes causes it to degenerate into what are described as abnormalities. The original strength of the sexual instinct probably varies in each individual; certainly the proportion of it which is suitable for sublimation varies. It seems to us that it is the innate constitution of each individual which decides in the first instance how large a part of his sexual instinct it will be possible to sublimate and make use of. In addition to this, the effects of experience and the intellectual influences upon his mental apparatus succeed in bringing about the sublimation of a further portion of it. To extend this process of displacement indefinitely is, however, certainly not possible, any more than is the case with the transformation of heat into mechanical energy in our machines. A certain amount of direct sexual satisfaction seems to be indispensable for most organizations, and a deficiency in this amount, which varies from individual to individual, is visited by phenomena which, on account of their detrimental effects on functioning and their subjective quality of unpleasure, must be regarded as an illness.

Further prospects are opened up when we take into consideration the fact that in man the sexual instinct does not originally serve the purposes of reproduction at all, but has as its aim the gaining of particular kinds of pleasure. It manifests itself in this way in human infancy, during which it attains its aim of gaining pleasure not only from the genitals but from other parts of the body (the erotogenic zones), and can therefore disregard any objects other than these convenient ones. We call this stage the stage of *auto-erotism*, and the child's upbringing has, in our view, the task of restricting it, because to linger in it would make the sexual instinct uncontrollable and unserviceable later on. The development of the sexual instinct then proceeds from the auto-erotism to object-love and from the autonomy of the erotogenic zones to their subordination under the primacy of the genitals, which are put at the service of reproduction. During this development a part of the sexual excitation which is provided by the subject's own body is inhibited as being unserviceable for the reproductive function and in favorable cases is brought to sublimation. The forces that can be employed for cultural activities are thus to a great extent obtained through the suppression of what are known as the *perverse* elements of sexual excitation.

If this evolution of the sexual instinct is borne in mind, three stages of civilization can be distinguished: a first one, in which the sexual instinct may be freely exercised without regard to the aims of reproduction; a second, in which all of the sexual instinct is suppressed except what serves the aims of reproduction; and a third, in which only *legitimate* reproduction is allowed as a sexual aim. This third stage is reflected in our present-day "civilized" sexual morality.

If we take the second of these stages as an average, we must point out that a number of people are, on account of their organization, not equal to meeting its demands. In whole classes of individuals the development of the sexual instinct, as we have described it above, from auto-erotism to object-love with its aim of uniting the genitals, has not been carried out correctly and sufficiently fully. As a result of these disturbances of development two kinds of harmful deviation from normal sexuality—that is, sexuality which is serviceable to civilization—come about; and the relation between these two is almost that of positive and negative.

In the first place (disregarding people whose sexual instinct is altogether excessive and uninhibitable) there are the different varieties of *perverts*, in whom an infantile fixation to a preliminary sexual aim has prevented the primacy of the reproductive function from being established, and the *homosexuals* or *inverts*, in whom, in a manner that is not yet quite understood, the sexual aim has been deflected away from the opposite sex. If the injurious effects of these two kinds of developmental disturbance are less than might be expected, this mitigation can be ascribed precisely to the complex way in which the sexual instinct is put together, which makes it possible for a person's sexual life to reach a serviceable final form even if one or more components of the instinct have been shut off from development. The constitution of people suffering from inversion—the homosexuals—is, indeed, often distinguished by their sexual instinct's possessing a special aptitude for cultural sublimation.

More pronounced forms of the perversions and of homosexuality, especially if they are exclusive, do, it is true, make those subject to them socially useless and unhappy, so that it must be recognized that the cultural requirements even of the second stage are a source of suffering for a certain proportion of mankind. The fate of these people who differ constitutionally from the rest varies, and depends on whether they have been born with a sexual instinct which by absolute standards is strong or comparatively weak. In the latter case — where the sexual instinct is in general weak — perverts succeed in totally suppressing the inclinations which bring them into conflict with the moral demands of their stage of civilization. But this, from the ideal point of view, is also the only thing they succeed in achieving; for, in order to effect this suppression of their sexual instinct, they use up the forces which they would otherwise employ in cultural activities. They are, as it were, inwardly inhibited and outwardly paralyzed. What we shall be saying again later on about the abstinence demanded of men and women in the third stage of civilization applies to them too.

Where the sexual instinct is fairly intense, but perverse, there are two possible outcomes. The first, which we shall not discuss further, is that the person affected remains a pervert and has to put up with the consequences of his deviation from the standard of civilization. The second is far more interesting. It is that, under the influence of education and social demands, a suppression of the perverse instincts is indeed achieved, but it is a kind of suppression which is really no suppression at all. It can better be described as a suppression that has failed. The inhibited sexual instincts are, it is true, no longer expressed as such — and this constitutes the success of the process — but they find expression in other ways, which are quite as injurious to the subject and make him quite as useless for society as satisfaction of the suppressed instincts in an unmodified form would have done. This constitutes the failure of the process, which in the long run more than counterbalances its success. The substitutive phenomena which emerge in consequence of the suppression of the instinct amount to what we call nervous illness, or, more precisely, the psychoneuroses. Neurotics are the class of people who, since they possess a recalcitrant organization, only succeed, under the influence of cultural requirements, in achieving a suppression of their instincts which is *apparent* and which becomes increasingly unsuccessful. They therefore only carry on their collaboration with cultural activities by a great expenditure of force and at the cost of an internal impoverishment, or are obliged at times to interrupt it and fall ill. I have described the neuroses as the "negative" of the perversions because in the neuroses the perverse impulses, after being repressed, manifest themselves from the unconscious part of the mind — because the neuroses contain the same tendencies, though in a state of "repression," as do the positive perversions.

Experience teaches us that for most people there is a limit beyond which their constitution cannot comply with the demands of civilization.

All who wish to be more noble-minded than their constitution allows fall victims to neurosis; they would have been more healthy if it could have been possible for them to be less good. The discovery that perversions and neuroses stand in the relation of positive and negative is often unmistakably confirmed by observations made on the members of one generation of a family. Quite frequently a brother is a sexual pervert, while his sister, who, being a woman, possesses a weaker sexual instinct, is a neurotic whose symptoms express the same inclinations as the perversions of her sexually more active brother. And correspondingly, in many families the men are healthy, but from a social point of view immoral to an undesirable degree, while the women are high-minded and over-refined, but severely neurotic.

It is one of the obvious social injustices that the standard of civilization should demand from everyone the same conduct of sexual life — conduct which can be followed without any difficulty by some people, thanks to their organization, but which imposes the heaviest psychical sacrifices on others; though, indeed, the injustice is as a rule wiped out by disobedience to the injunctions of morality.

These considerations have been based so far on the requirement laid down by the second of the stages of civilization which we have postulated, the requirement that every sexual activity of the kind described as perverse is prohibited, while what is called normal sexual intercourse is freely permitted. We have found that even when the line between sexual freedom and restriction is drawn at this point, a number of individuals are ruled out as perverts, and a number of others, who make efforts not to be perverts whilst constitutionally they should be so, are forced into nervous illness. It is easy to predict the result that will follow if sexual freedom is still further circumscribed and the requirements of civilization are raised to the level of the third stage, which bans all sexual activity outside legal marriage. The number of strong natures who openly oppose the demands of civilization will increase enormously, and so will the number of weaker ones who, faced with the conflict between the pressure of cultural influences and the resistance of their constitution, take flight into neurotic illness.

Let us now try to answer three questions that arise here:

1. What is the task that is set to the individual by the requirements of the third stage of civilization?

2. Can the legitimate sexual satisfaction that is permissible offer acceptable compensation for the renunciation of all other satisfactions?

3. In what relation do the possible injurious effects of this renunciation stand to its exploitation in the cultural field?

172   The answer to the first question touches on a problem which has often been discussed and cannot be exhaustively treated here — that of sexual abstinence. Our third stage of civilization demands of individuals of both sexes that they shall practice abstinence until they are married and that all who do not contract a legal marriage shall remain abstinent throughout their lives. The position, agreeable to all the authorities, that sexual abstinence is not harmful and not difficult to maintain, has also been widely supported by the medical profession. It may be asserted, however, that the task of mastering such a powerful impulse as that of the sexual instinct by any other means than satisfying it is one which can call for the whole of man's forces. Mastering it by sublimation, by deflecting the sexual instinctual forces away from their sexual aim to higher cultural aims, can be achieved by a minority and then only intermittently, and least easily during the period of ardent and vigorous youth. Most of the rest become neurotic or are harmed in one way or another. Experience shows that the majority of the people who make up our society are constitutionally unfit to face the task of abstinence. Those who would have fallen ill under milder sexual restrictions fall ill all the more readily and more severely before the demands of our cultural sexual morality of today; for we know no better safeguard against the threat to normal sexual life offered by defective innate dispositions or disturbances of development than sexual satisfaction itself. The more a person is disposed to neurosis, the less can he tolerate abstinence; instincts which have been withdrawn from normal development, in the sense in which it has been described above, become at the same time all the more uninhibitable. But even those people who would have retained their health under the requirements of the second stage of civilization will now succumb to neurosis in great numbers. For the psychical value of sexual satisfaction increases with its frustration. The dammed-up libido is now put in a position to detect one or other of the weaker spots which are seldom absent in the structure of sexual life, and there to break through and obtain substitutive satisfaction of a neurotic kind in the form of pathological symptoms. Anyone who is able to penetrate the determinants of nervous illness will soon become convinced that its increase in our society arises from the intensification of sexual restrictions.

This brings us to the question whether sexual intercourse in legal marriage can offer full compensation for the restrictions imposed before marriage. There is such an abundance of material supporting a reply in the negative that we can give only the briefest summary of it. It must above all be borne in mind that our cultural sexual morality restricts sexual intercourse even in marriage itself, since it imposes on married couples the necessity of contenting themselves, as a rule, with a very few procreative acts. As a consequence of this consideration, satisfying sexual intercourse in marriage takes place only for a few years; and we must subtract from this, of course, the intervals of abstention necessitated by regard for the wife's health. After these three, four or five years, the marriage becomes a failure in so far as it has promised the satisfaction of sexual needs. For all the devices hitherto invented for preventing conception impair sexual enjoyment, hurt the fine susceptibilities of both partners and even actually cause illness. Fear of the consequences of sexual intercourse first brings the married couple's physical affection to an end; and then, as a remoter result, it usually puts a stop as well to the mental sympathy between them, which should have been the successor to their original passionate love. The spiritual disillusionment and bodily deprivation to which most marriages are thus doomed puts both partners back in the state they were in before their marriage, except for being the poorer by the loss of an illusion, and they must once more have recourse to their fortitude in mastering and deflecting their sexual instinct. We need not inquire how far men, by then in their maturer years, succeed in this task. Experience shows that they very frequently avail themselves of the degree of sexual freedom which is allowed them — although only with reluctance and under a veil of silence — by even the strictest sexual code. The "double" sexual morality which is valid for men in our society is the plainest admission that society itself does not believe in the possibility of enforcing the precepts which it itself has laid down. But experience shows as well that women, who, as being the actual vehicle of the sexual interests of mankind, are only endowed in a small measure with the gift of sublimating their instincts, and who, though they may find a sufficient substitute for the sexual object in an infant at the breast, do not find one in a growing child — experience shows, I repeat, that women, when they are subjected to the disillusionments of marriage, fall ill of severe neuroses which permanently darken their lives. Under the cultural conditions of today, marriage has long ceased to be a panacea for the nervous troubles of women; and if we doctors still advise marriage in such cases, we are nevertheless aware that, on the contrary, a girl must be very healthy if she is to be able to tolerate it, and we urgently advise our male patients not to marry any girl who has had nervous trouble before marriage. On the contrary, the cure for nervous illness arising from marriage would be marital unfaithfulness. But the more strictly a woman has been brought up and the more sternly she has submitted to the demands of civilization, the more she is afraid of taking this way out; and in the conflict between her desires and her sense of duty, she once more seeks refuge in her neurosis. Nothing protects her virtue as securely as an illness. Thus the married state, which is held out as a consolation to the sexual instinct of the civilized person in his youth, proves to be inadequate even to the demands of the actual period of life covered by it. There is no question of its being able to compensate for the deprivation which precedes it.

But even if the damage done by civilized sexual morality is admitted, it may be argued in reply to our third question that the cultural gain derived from such an extensive restriction of sexuality probably more than balances these sufferings, which after all, only affect a minority in any severe form. I myself confess that I am unable to balance gain against loss correctly on this point, but I could advance a great many more considerations on the side of the loss. Going back to the subject of abstinence, which I have already touched on, I must insist that it brings in its train other noxae besides those involved in the neuroses and that the importance of the neuroses has for the most part not been fully appreciated.

· · ·

The fact that the sexual instinct behaves in general in a self-willed and inflexible fashion is also seen in the results produced by efforts at abstinence. Civilized education may only attempt to suppress the instinct temporarily, till marriage, intending to give it free rein afterwards with the idea of then making use of it. But extreme measures are more successful against it than attempts at moderating it; thus the suppression often goes too far, with the unwished-for result that when the instinct is set free it turns out to be permanently impaired. For this reason complete abstinence in youth is often not the best preparation for marriage for a young man. Women sense this, and prefer among their suitors those who have already proved their masculinity with other women. The harmful results which the strict demand for abstinence before marriage produces in women's natures are quite especially apparent. It is clear that education is far from underestimating the task of suppressing a girl's sensuality till her marriage, for it makes use of the most drastic measures. Not only does it forbid sexual intercourse and set a high premium on the preservation of female chastity, but it also protects the young woman from temptation as she grows up, by keeping her ignorant of all the facts of the part she is to play and by not tolerating any impulse of love in her which cannot lead to marriage. The result is that when the girl's parental authorities suddenly allow her to fall in love, she is unequal to this psychical achievement and enters marriage uncertain of her own feelings. In consequence of this artificial retardation in her function of love, she has nothing but disappointments to offer the man who has saved up all his desire for her. In her mental feelings she is still attached to her parents, whose authority has brought about the suppression of her sexuality; and in her physical behavior she shows herself frigid, which deprives the man of any high degree of sexual enjoyment. I do not know whether the anesthetic type of woman exists apart from civilized education, though I consider it probable. But in any case such education actually breeds it, and these women who conceive without pleasure show little willingness afterwards to face the pains of frequent childbirth. In this way, the preparation for marriage frustrates the aims of marriage itself. When later on the retardation in the wife's development has been overcome and her capacity to love is awakened at the climax of her life as a woman, her relations to her husband have long since been ruined; and, as a reward for her previous docility, she is left with the choice between unappeased desire, unfaithfulness or a neurosis.

· · ·

When society pays for obedience to its far-reaching regulations by an increase in nervous illness, it cannot claim to have purchased a gain at the price of sacrifices; it cannot claim a gain at all. Let us, for instance, consider the very common case of a woman who does not love her husband, because, owing to the conditions under which she entered marriage, she has no reason to love him, but who very much wants to love him, because that alone corresponds to the ideal of marriage to which she has been brought up. She will in that case suppress every impulse which would express the truth and contradict her endeavors to fulfill her ideal, and she will make special efforts to play the part of a loving, affectionate and attentive wife. The outcome of this self-suppression will be a neurotic illness; and this neurosis will in a short time have taken revenge on the unloved husband and have caused him just as much lack of satisfaction and worry as would have resulted from an acknowledgement of the true state of affairs. This example is completely typical of what a neurosis achieves. A similar failure to obtain compensation is to be seen after the suppression of impulses inimical to civilization which are not directly sexual. If a man, for example, has become over-kind as a result of a violent suppression of a constitutional inclination to harshness and cruelty, he often loses so much energy in doing this that he fails to carry out all that his compensatory impulses require, and he may, after all, do less good on the whole than he would have done without the suppression.

Let us add that a restriction of sexual activity in a community is quite generally accompanied by an increase of anxiety about life and of fear of death which interferes with the individual's capacity for enjoyment and does away with his readiness to face death for any purpose. A diminished inclination to beget children is the result, and the community or group of people in question is thus excluded from any share in the future. In view of this, we may well raise the question whether our "civilized" sexual morality is worth the sacrifice which it imposes on us, especially if we are still so much enslaved to hedonism, as to include among the aims of our cultural development a certain amount of satisfaction of individual happiness. It is certainly not a physician's business to come forward with proposals for reform; but it seemed to me that I might support the urgency of such proposals if I were to amplify Von Ehrenfels's description of the injurious effects of our "civilized" sexual morality by pointing to the important bearing of that morality upon the spread of modern nervous illness.

Carl Jung   — How does he explain this?
Marriage as a Psychological Relationship

Jung (1875-1961) began work in the area of psychoanalysis as a disciple of Freud. But Jung initiated a major apostasy from his mentor/teacher, and he developed a branch of psychoanalysis that builds from distinctly non-Freudian premises. Jung rejected, first of all, Freud's reductivist notion that the sexual instincts provide the fundamental explanation for virtually all of mental life. Jung observed that Freud smuggled a wide variety of content into his notion of sexuality, which sometimes referred to a kind of all-creating reproductive force ("Eros") and at other times meant something virtually equivalent to love. Jung's model of psychic life, by contrast, involves a rich texture of dynamic forces, only some of which relate directly to sexuality. Jung also rejected the retrospective orientation of Freud's theory, which explained adult psychology exclusively in terms of previous psychological development and gave no account of how the adult might desirably develop further. Jung, by contrast, developed a forward-looking psychoanalytic perspective that focuses on the adult's developmental goal, which Jung termed "individuation." Individuation involves the creation of unity in the psyche in such a way that all of one's contradictions are embraced and accepted.

Moreover, Jung denied that the psyche was as radically individual as Freud thought. In contrast to Freud's view of the entirely personal unconscious, Jung postulated that the unconscious holds contents that are collective, shared by the entire human species. These collective contents are handed down through heredity. Also in contrast to Freud's theory of unconscious contents, which might have been conscious had they not undergone repression, Jung argues that the collective contents have never been conscious and therefore represent a second unconscious system in addition to that analyzed by Freud. Jung calls these collective contents "archetypes," and he describes them as deeply rooted, nearly automatic patterns of instinctual behavior that appear to consciousness as images of the instincts themselves. For example, "the old wise man" and "the great mother" are archetypal personifications, respectively, of the wise insights of the uncon-

178 *scious and of a complex of ideas about loving, understanding, and helping. Archetypes are genetically encoded psychic traces that developed as a result of human beings' repetition of typical life situation through the generations. In a sense they are forms without content, but they become activated when a typical situation occurs, and they have tremendous impact on the details of individual behavior. Coming to grips with these archetypes is a vital part of psychic development.*

Both archetypes and the goal of individuation figure prominently in Jung's analysis of romantic love. As he suggests in the essay that follows, "Marriage as a Psychological Relationship," both love and marriage involve a complex interaction of both parties' conscious and unconscious minds, with both personal and collective contents. The typical situations that arise in connection with one's lover and/or spouse activate archetypal patterns in both partners, and these must be recognized if one is to avoid distortion in one's awareness of one's partner and of the relationship. In particular, the archetypal image of the opposite sex, the anima or animus, threatens to obstruct genuine relationships between men and women by inciting the individual to compulsively project archetypally generated ideas onto one's lover. This is a common cause of disaster in heterosexual love.

A further cause of marital problems is the natural discrepancy between the individual's goals in early adulthood and those that arise in mid-life. Although mid-life transformation is healthy and crucial to development toward individuation, its onset usually arises at different times for husband and wife, or man and woman, with the result that mutual adjustment is particularly difficult during this period. Although many marriages succumb in the ensuing confusion, the partners who endure through this stage are afterwards able to interact on a new and much improved basis. Neither is any longer motivated to force the other to complement himself or herself in every way, for both have finally discovered psychic integration within themselves.

Regarded as a psychological relationship, marriage is a highly complex structure made up of a whole series of subjective and objective factors, mostly of a very heterogeneous nature. As I wish to confine myself here to the purely psychological problems of marriage, I must disregard in the main the objective factors of a legal and social nature, although these cannot fail to have a pronounced influence on the psychological relationship between the marriage partners.

Whenever we speak of a "psychological relationship" we presuppose one that is *conscious*, for there is no such thing as a psychological relationship between two people who are in a state of unconsciousness. From the psychological point of view they would be wholly without relationship. From any other point of view, the physiological for example, they could be regarded as related, but one could not call their relationship psychological. It must be admitted that though such total unconsciousness as I have assumed does not occur, there is nevertheless a not inconsiderable degree of partial unconsciousness, and the psychological relationship is limited in the degree to which that unconsciousness exists.

In the child, consciousness rises out of the depths of unconscious psychic life, at first like separate islands, which gradually unite to form a "continent," a continuous land-mass of consciousness. Progressive mental development means, in effect, extension of consciousness. With the rise of a continuous consciousness, and not before, psychological relationship becomes possible. So far as we know, consciousness is always ego-consciousness. In order to be conscious of myself, I must be able to distinguish myself from others. Relationship can only take place where this distinction exists. But although the distinction may be made in a general way, normally it is incomplete, because large areas of psychic life still remain unconscious. As no distinction can be made with regard to unconscious contents, on this terrain no relationship can be established; here there still reigns the original unconscious condition of the ego's primitive identity with others, in other words a complete absence of relationship.

The young person of marriageable age does, of course, possess an ego-consciousness (girls more than men, as a rule), but, since he has only recently emerged from the mists of original unconsciousness, he is certain to have wide areas which still lie in the shadow and which preclude to that extent the formation of psychological relationship. This means, in practice, that the young man (or woman) can have only an incomplete understanding of himself and others, and is therefore imperfectly informed as to his, and their, motives. As a rule the motives he acts from are largely unconscious. Subjectively, of course, he thinks himself very conscious and knowing, for we constantly overestimate the existing content of consciousness, and it is a great and surprising discovery when we find that what we had supposed to be the final peak is nothing but the first step in a very long climb. The greater the area of unconsciousness, the less is marriage a matter of free choice, as is shown subjectively in the fatal compulsion one feels so acutely when one is in love. The compulsion can exist even when one is not in love, though in less agreeable form.

180   Unconscious motivations are of a personal and of a general nature. First of all, there are the motives deriving from parental influence. The relationship of the young man to his mother, and of the girl to her father, is the determining factor in this respect. It is the strength of the bond to the parents that unconsciously influences the choice of husband or wife, either positively or negatively. Conscious love for either parent favours the choice of a like mate, while an unconscious tie (which need not by any means express itself consciously as love) makes the choice difficult and imposes characteristic modifications. In order to understand them, one must know first of all the cause of the unconscious tie to the parents, and under what conditions it forcibly modifies, or even prevents, the conscious choice. Generally speaking, all the life which the parents could have lived, but of which they thwarted themselves for artificial motives, is passed on to the children in substitute form. That is to say, the children are driven unconsciously in a direction that is intended to compensate for everything that was left unfulfilled in the lives of their parents. Hence it is that excessively moral-minded parents have what are called "unmoral" children, or an irresponsible wastrel of a father has a son with a positively morbid amount of ambition, and so on. The worst results flow from parents who have kept themselves artificially unconscious. Take the case of a mother who deliberately keeps herself unconscious so as not to disturb the pretence of a "satisfactory" marriage. Unconsciously she will bind her son to her, more or less as a substitute for a husband. The son, if not forced directly into homosexuality, is compelled to modify his choice in a way that is contrary to his true nature. He may, for instance, marry a girl who is obviously inferior to his mother and therefore unable to compete with her; or he will fall for a woman of a tyrannical and overbearing disposition, who may perhaps succeed in tearing him away from his mother. The choice of a mate, if the instincts have not been vitiated, may remain free from these influences, but sooner or later they will make themselves felt as obstacles. A more or less instinctive choice might be considered the best from the point of view of maintaining the species, but it is not always fortunate psychologically, because there is often an uncommonly large difference between the purely instinctive personality and one that is individually differentiated. And though in such cases the race might be improved and invigorated by a purely instinctive choice, individual happiness would be bound to suffer. (The idea of "instinct" is of course nothing more than a collective term for all kinds of organic and psychic factors whose nature is for the most part unknown.)

If the individual is to be regarded solely as an instrument for maintaining the species, then the purely instinctive choice of a mate is by far the best. But since the foundations of such a choice are unconscious, only a kind of impersonal liaison can be built upon them, such as can be observed to perfection among primitives. If we can speak here of a "relationship" at all, it is, at best, only a pale reflection of what we mean, a very distant state of affairs with a decidedly impersonal character, wholly regulated by traditional customs and prejudices, the prototype of every conventional marriage.

So far as reason or calculation or the so-called loving care of the parents does not arrange the marriage, and the pristine instincts of the children are not vitiated either by false education or by the hidden influence of accumulated and neglected parental complexes, the marriage choice will normally follow the unconscious motivations of instinct. Unconsciousness results in non-differentiation, or unconscious identity. The practical consequence of this is that one person presupposes in the other a psychological structure similar to his own. Normal sex life, as a shared experience with apparently similar aims, further strengthens the feeling of unity and identity. This state is described as one of complete harmony, and is extolled as a great happiness ("one heart and one soul")—not without good reason, since the return to that original condition of unconscious oneness is like a return to childhood. Hence the childish gestures of all lovers. Even more is it a return to the mother's womb, into the teeming depths of an as yet unconscious creativity. It is, in truth, a genuine and incontestable experience of the Divine, whose transcendent force obliterates and consumes everything individual; a real communion with life and the impersonal power of fate. The individual will for self-possession is broken: the woman becomes the mother, the man the father, and thus both are robbed of their freedom and made instruments of the life urge.

Here the relationship remains within the bounds of the biological instinctive goal, the preservation of the species. Since this goal is of a collective nature, the psychological link between husband and wife will also be essentially collective, and cannot be regarded as an individual relationship in the psychological sense. We can only speak of this when the nature of the unconscious motivations has been recognized and the original identity broken down. Seldom or never does a marriage develop into an individual relationship smoothly and without crises. There is no birth of consciousness without pain.

The ways that lead to conscious realization are many, but they follow definite laws. In general, the change begins with the onset of the second

182   half of life. The middle period of life is a time of enormous psychological importance. The child begins its psychological life within very narrow limits, inside the magic circle of the mother and the family. With progressive maturation it widens its horizon and its own sphere of influence; its hopes and intentions are directed to extending the scope of personal power and possessions; desire reaches out to the world in ever-widening range; the will of the individual becomes more and more identical with the natural goals pursued by unconscious motivations. Thus man breathes his own life into things, until finally they begin to live of themselves and to multiply; and imperceptibly he is overgrown by them. Mothers are overtaken by their children, men by their own creations, and what was originally brought into being only with labour and the greatest effort can no longer be held in check. First it was passion, then it became duty, and finally an intolerable burden, a vampire that battens on the life of its creator. Middle life is the moment of greatest unfolding, when a man still gives himself to his work with his whole strength and his whole will. But in this very moment evening is born, and the second half of life begins. Passion now changes her face and is called duty; "I want" becomes the inexorable "I must," and the turnings of the pathway that once brought surprise and discovery become dulled by custom. The wine has fermented and begins to settle and clear. Conservative tendencies develop if all goes well; instead of looking forward one looks backward, most of the time involuntarily, and one begins to take stock, to see how one's life has developed up to this point. The real motivations are sought and real discoveries are made. The critical survey of himself and his fate enables a man to recognize his peculiarities. But these insights do not come to him easily; they are gained only through the severest shocks.

Since the aims of the second half of life are different from those of the first, to linger too long in the youthful attitude produces a division of the will. Consciousness still presses forward, in obedience, as it were, to its own inertia, but the unconscious lags behind, because the strength and inner resolve needed for further expansion have been sapped. This disunity with oneself begets discontent, and since one is not conscious of the real state of things one generally projects the reasons for it upon one's partner. A critical atmosphere thus develops, the necessary prelude to conscious realization. Usually this state does not begin simultaneously for both partners. Even the best of marriages cannot expunge individual differences so completely that the state of mind of the partners is absolutely identical. In most cases one of them will adapt to marriage more quickly than the other. The one who is

grounded on a positive relationship to the parents will find little or no difficulty in adjusting to his or her partner, while the other may be hindered by
a deep-seated unconscious tie to the parents. He will therefore achieve
complete adaptation only later, and, because it is won with greater difficulty, it may even prove the more durable.

These differences in tempo, and in the degree of spiritual development,
are the chief causes of a typical difficulty which makes its appearance at
critical moments. In speaking of "the degree of spiritual development" of a
personality, I do not wish to imply an especially rich or magnanimous nature. Such is not the case at all. I mean, rather, a certain complexity of
mind or nature, comparable to a gem with many facets as opposed to the
simple cube. There are many-sided and rather problematical natures bur-
dened with hereditary traits that are sometimes very difficult to reconcile.
Adaptation to such natures, or their adaptation to simpler personalities, is
always a problem. These people, having a certain tendency to dissociation,
generally have the capacity to split off irreconcilable traits of character for
considerable periods, thus passing themselves off as much simpler than
they are; or it may happen that their many-sidedness, their very versatility,
lends them a peculiar charm. Their partners can easily lose themselves in
such a labyrinthine nature, finding in it such an abundance of possible experiences that their personal interests are completely absorbed, sometimes
in a not very agreeable way, since their sole occupation then consists in
tracking the other through all the twists and turns of his character. There is
always so much experience available that the simpler personality is surrounded, if not actually swamped, by it; he is swallowed up in his more
complex partner and cannot see his way out. It is an almost regular occurrence for a woman to be wholly contained, spiritually, in her husband, and
for a husband to be wholly contained, emotionally, in his wife. One could
describe this as the problem of the "contained" and the "container."

The one who is contained feels himself to be living entirely within the
confines of his marriage; his attitude to the marriage partner is undivided;
outside the marriage there exist no essential obligations and no binding interests. The unpleasant side of this otherwise ideal partnership is the disquieting dependence upon a personality that can never be seen in its entirety, and is therefore not altogether credible or dependable. The great
advantage lies in his own undividedness, and this is a factor not to be un-
derrated in the psychic economy.

The container, on the other hand, who in accordance with his tendency
to dissociation has an especial need to unify himself in undivided love for

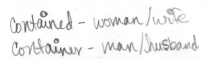

184   another, will be left far behind in this effort, which is naturally very difficult for him, by the simpler personality. While he is seeking in the latter all
the subtleties and complexities that would complement and correspond to
his own facets, he is disturbing the other's simplicity. Since in normal circumstances simplicity always has the advantage over complexity, he will
very soon be obliged to abandon his efforts to arouse subtle and intricate
reactions in a simpler nature. And soon enough his partner, who in accordance with her simpler nature expects simple answers from him, will give
him plenty to do by constellating his complexities with her everlasting insistence on simple answers. Willynilly, he must withdraw into himself before
the suasions of simplicity. Any mental effort, like the conscious process itself, is so much of a strain for the ordinary man that he invariably prefers
the simple, even when it does not happen to be the truth. And when it represents at least a half-truth, then it is all up with him. The simpler nature
works on the more complicated like a room that is too small, that does not
allow him enough space. The complicated nature, on the other hand, gives
the simpler one too many rooms with too much space, so that she never
knows where she really belongs. So it comes about quite naturally that the
more complicated contains the simpler. The former cannot be absorbed in
the latter, but encompasses it without being itself contained. Yet, since the
more complicated has perhaps a greater need of being contained than the
other, he feels himself outside the marriage and accordingly always plays
the problematical role. The more the contained clings, the more the container feels shut out of the relationship. The contained pushes into it by her
clinging, and the more she pushes, the less the container is able to respond.
He therefore tends to spy out of the window, no doubt unconsciously at
first; but with the onset of middle age there awakens in him a more insistent longing for that unity and undividedness which is especially necessary
to him on account of his dissociated nature. At this juncture things are apt
to occur that bring the conflict to a head. He becomes conscious of the fact
that he is seeking completion, seeking the contentedness and undividedness
that have always been lacking. For the contained this is only a confirmation
of the insecurity she has always felt so painfully; she discovers that in the
rooms which apparently belonged to her there dwell other, unwished-for
guests. The hope of security vanishes, and this disappointment drives her in
on herself, unless by desperate and violent efforts she can succeed in forcing her partner to capitulate, and in extorting a confession that his longing
for unity was nothing but a childish or morbid fantasy. If these tactics do
not succeed, her acceptance of failure may do her a real good, by forcing

her to recognize that the security she was so desperately seeking in the other is to be found in herself. In this way she finds herself and discovers in her own simpler nature all those complexities which the container had sought for in vain.

If the container does not break down in face of what we are wont to call "unfaithfulness," but goes on believing in the inner justification of his longing for unity, he will have to put up with his self-division for the time being. A dissociation is not healed by being split off, but by more complete disintegration. All the powers that strive for unity, all healthy desire for selfhood, will resist the disintegration, and in this way he will become conscious of the possibility of an inner integration, which before he had always sought outside himself. He will then find his reward in an undivided self.

This is what happens very frequently about the midday of life, and in this wise our miraculous human nature enforces the transition that leads from the first half of life to the second. It is a metamorphosis from a state in which man is only a tool of instinctive nature, to another in which he is no longer a tool, but himself: a transformation of nature into culture, of instinct into spirit.

One should take great care not to interrupt this necessary development by acts of moral violence, for any attempt to create a spiritual attitude by splitting off and suppressing the instincts is a falsification. Nothing is more repulsive than a furtively prurient spirituality; it is just as unsavoury as gross sensuality. But the transition takes a long time, and the great majority of people get stuck in the first stages. If only we could, like the primitives, leave the unconscious to look after this whole psychological development which marriage entails, these transformations could be worked out more completely and without too much friction. So often among so-called "primitives" one comes across spiritual personalities who immediately inspire respect, as though they were the fully matured products of an undisturbed fate. I speak here from personal experience. But where among present-day Europeans can one find people not deformed by acts of moral violence? We are still barbarous enough to believe both in asceticism and its opposite. But the wheel of history cannot be put back; we can only strive towards an attitude that will allow us to live out our fate as undisturbedly as the primitive pagan in us really wants. Only on this condition can we be sure of not perverting spirituality into sensuality, and vice versa; for both must live, each drawing life from the other.

The transformation I have briefly described above is the very essence of the psychological marriage relationship. Much could be said about the illusions that serve the ends of nature and bring about the transformations that are characteristic of middle life. The peculiar harmony that characterizes marriage during the first half of life — provided the adjustment is successful — is largely based on the projection of certain archetypal images, as the critical phase makes clear.

Every man carries within him the eternal image of woman, not the image of this or that particular woman, but a definite feminine image. This image is fundamentally unconscious, an hereditary factor of primordial origin engraved in the living organic system of the man, an imprint or "archetype" of all the ancestral experiences of the female, a deposit, as it were, of all the impressions ever made by woman — in short, an inherited system of psychic adaptation. Even if no women existed, it would still be possible, at any given time, to deduce from this unconscious image exactly how a woman would have to be constituted psychically. The same is true of the woman: she too has her inborn image of man. Actually, we know from experience that it would be more accurate to describe it as an image of *men*, whereas in the case of the man it is rather the image of *woman*. Since this image is unconscious, it is always unconsciously projected upon the person of the beloved, and is one of the chief reasons for passionate attraction or aversion. I have called this image the "anima," and I find the scholastic question *Habet mulier animam?* especially interesting, since in my view it is an intelligent one inasmuch as the doubt seems justified. Woman has no anima, no soul, but she has an *animus*. The anima has an erotic, emotional character, the animus a rationalizing one. Hence most of what men say about feminine eroticism, and particularly about the emotional life of women, is derived from their own anima projections and distorted accordingly. On the other hand, the astonishing assumptions and fantasies that women make about men come from the activity of the animus, who produces an inexhaustible supply of illogical arguments and false explanations.

Anima and animus are both characterized by an extraordinary manysidedness. In a marriage it is always the contained who projects this image upon the container, while the latter is only partially able to project his unconscious image upon his partner. The more unified and simple this partner is, the less complete the projection. In which case, this highly fascinating image hangs as it were in mid air, as though waiting to be filled out by a living person. There are certain types of women who seem to be made by nature to attract anima projections; indeed one could almost speak of a definite "anima type." The so-called "sphinx-like" character is an indispensable part of their equipment, also an equivocalness, an intriguing elusiveness — not an indefinite blur that offers nothing, but an indefiniteness that seems full of promises, like the speaking silence of a Mona Lisa. A woman of this kind is both old and young, mother and daughter, of more than doubtful chastity, childlike, and yet endowed with a naive cunning that is extremely disarming to men. Not every man of real intellectual power can be an animus, for the animus must be a master not so much of fine ideas as of fine words — words seemingly full of meaning which purport to leave a great deal unsaid. He must also belong to the "misunderstood" class, or be in some way at odds with his environment, so that the idea of self-sacrifice can insinuate itself. He must be a rather questionable hero, a man with possibilities, which is not to say that an animus projection may not discover a real hero long before he has become perceptible to the sluggish wits of the man of "average intelligence."

For man as well as for woman, in so far as they are "containers," the filling out of this image is an experience fraught with consequences, for it holds the possibility of finding one's own complexities answered by a corresponding diversity. Wide vistas seem to open up in which one feels oneself embraced and contained. I say "seem" advisedly, because the experience may be two-faced. Just as the animus projection of a woman can often pick on a man of real significance who is not recognized by the mass, and can actually help him to achieve his true destiny with her moral support, so a man can create for himself a *femme inspiratrice* by his anima projection. But more often it turns out to be an illusion with destructive consequences, a failure because his faith was not sufficiently strong. To the pessimists I would say that these primordial psychic images have an extraordinarily positive value, but I must warn the optimists against blinding fantasies and the likelihood of the most absurd aberrations.

One should on no account take this projection for an individual and conscious relationship. In its first stages it is far from that, for it creates a compulsive dependence based on unconscious motives other than the biological ones. Rider Haggard's *She* gives some indication of the curious world of ideas that underlies the anima projection. They are in essence spiritual contents, often in erotic disguise, obvious fragments of a primitive mythological mentality that consists of archetypes, and whose totality constitutes the collective unconscious. Accordingly, such a relationship is at bottom collective and not individual. (Benoît, who created in *L'Atlantide* a fantasy figure similar even in details to "She," denies having plagiarized Rider Haggard.)

188   ⚹ If such a projection fastens on to one of the marriage partners, a collective spiritual relationship conflicts with the collective biological one and produces in the container the division or disintegration I have described above. If he is able to hold his head above water, he will find himself through this very conflict. In that case the projection, though dangerous in itself, will have helped him to pass from a collective to an individual relationship. This amounts to full conscious realization of the relationship that marriage brings. Since the aim of this paper is a discussion of the psychology of marriage, the psychology of projection cannot concern us here. It is sufficient to mention it as a fact.

One can hardly deal with the psychological marriage relationship without mentioning, even at the risk of misunderstanding, the nature of its critical transitions. As is well known, one understands nothing psychological unless one has experienced it oneself. Not that this ever prevents anyone from feeling convinced that his own judgment is the only true and competent one. This disconcerting fact comes from the necessary overvaluation of the momentary content of consciousness, for without this concentration of attention one could not be conscious at all. Thus it is that every period of life has its own psychological truth, and the same applies to every stage of psychological development. There are even stages which only the few can reach, it being a question of race, family, education, talent, and passion. Nature is aristocratic. The normal man is a fiction, although certain generally valid laws do exist. Psychic life is a development that can easily be arrested on the lowest levels. It is as though every individual had a specific gravity, in accordance with which he either rises, or sinks down, to the level where he reaches his limit. His views and convictions will be determined accordingly. No wonder, then, that by far the greater number of marriages reach their upper psychological limit in fulfillment of the biological aim, without injury to spiritual or moral health. Relatively few people fall into deeper disharmony with themselves. Where there is a great deal of pressure from outside, the conflict is unable to develop much dramatic tension for sheer lack of energy. Psychological insecurity, however, increases in proportion to social security, unconsciously at first, causing neuroses, then consciously, bringing with it separations, discord, divorces, and other marital disorders. On still higher levels, new possibilities of psychological development are discerned, touching on the sphere of religion where critical judgment comes to a halt.

Progress may be permanently arrested on any of these levels, with complete unconsciousness of what might have followed at the next stage of development. As a rule graduation to the next stage is barred by violent prejudices and superstitious fears. This, however, serves a most useful purpose, since a man who is compelled by accident to live at a level too high for him becomes a fool and a menace.

Nature is not only aristocratic, she is also esoteric. Yet no man of understanding will thereby be induced to make a secret of what he knows, for he realizes only too well that the secret of psychic development can never be betrayed, simply because that development is a question of individual capacity.

Karen Horney
Love and Marriage

Karen Horney (1885–1952) was a distinguished psychoanalytic therapist and theorist who, although trained under Freudian auspices (by Freud's close associate Karl Abraham), broke with Freud's doctrines. Horney, like Jung, thought that Freud placed too much emphasis on the sexual instincts in his psychological explanations and too little on environmental and social factors. In her own psychoanalytic papers, Horney developed an account of the development of neuroses from the anxiety the infant experiences upon discovering itself to be helpless in an environment that is potentially hostile. The infant's strategies for coping may develop into habitual irrational behaviors and needs which in turn cause neuroses to develop. While neurotics are frequently afflicted with sexual problems, these problems are the outcome of neurotic development, not the cause of neurosis.

Horney also objected to Freud's analysis of femininity, which he had treated as a variant of "normal" (male) development. In particular, Horney disagreed with Freud's insistence that the female is motivated to self-contempt as a consequence of childhood envy of the male penis. According to Freud, little girls believe themselves damaged (in fact, castrated) because they lack the male organ and come to desire a child as a substitute for the penis which they lack. Horney contended that this "penis envy" theory reflected not what little girls think, but what little boys would like to think little girls think. Many of Horney's own writings develop an alternative view of female psychology, which stresses the social pressures placed on women to develop the passive traits that Freud takes as symptoms of a biologically inherent feminine masochism.

Throughout her writings, Horney emphasized the possibility of healthy psychological development. The concern with romantic love in her writings tends to focus on the possibility that the desire for love can itself preclude self-realization and obstruct the formulation of satisfying relationships with others. In the essay that follows, Horney considers a situation common among modern, talented women: the self-destructive desire for a love relationship that is so obsessional that it ensures the woman's failure both in love and in the work she chooses for herself.

Woman's efforts to achieve independence and an enlargement of her field of interests and activities are continually met with a skepticism which insists that such efforts should be made only in the face of economic necessity, and that they run counter to her inherent character and her natural tendencies. Accordingly, all efforts of this sort are said to be without any vital significance for woman, whose every thought, in point of fact, should center exclusively upon the male or upon motherhood, in much the manner expressed in Marlene Dietrich's famous song, "I know only love, and nothing else."

Various sociological considerations immediately suggest themselves in this connection; they are, however, of too familiar and obvious a character to require discussion. This attitude toward woman, whatever its basis and however it may be assessed, represents the patriarchal ideal of womanhood, of woman as one whose only longing is to love a man and be loved by him, to admire him and serve him, and even to pattern herself after him. Those who maintain this point of view mistakenly infer from external behavior the existence of an innate instinctual disposition thereto; whereas, in reality, the latter cannot be recognized as such, for the reason that biological factors never manifest themselves in pure and undisguised form, but always as modified by tradition and environment. As Briffault has recently pointed out in some detail in *The Mothers*, the modifying influence of "inherited tradition," not only upon ideals and beliefs but also upon emotional attitudes and so-called instincts, cannot possibly be overestimated. Inherited tradition means for women, however, a compressing of her participation (which originally was probably very considerable) in general tasks into the narrower sphere of eroticism and motherhood. The adherence to inherited tradition fulfills certain day-to-day functions for both society and the individual; of their social aspect we shall not speak here. Considered from the standpoint of the psychology of the individual, it need only be mentioned that this mental construction is for the male at times a matter of great inconvenience, yet on the other hand constitutes for him a source from which his self-esteem can always derive support. For woman, conversely, with her lowered self-esteem of centuries' duration, it constitutes a haven of peace in which she is spared the exertions and anxieties associated with the cultivation of other abilities and of self-assertion in the face of criticism and rivalry. It is comprehensible, therefore — speaking solely from the sociological standpoint—that women who nowadays obey the impulse to the independent development of their abilities are able to do so only at the cost of a struggle against both external opposition and such resistances within themselves as are created by an intensification of the traditional ideal of the exclusively sexual function of woman.

It would not be going too far to assert that at the present time this conflict confronts every woman who ventures upon a career of her own and who is at the same time unwilling to pay for her daring with the renunciation of her femininity. The conflict in question is therefore one that is conditioned by the altered position of woman and confined to those women who enter upon or follow a vocation, who pursue special interests, or who aspire in general to an independent development of their personality.

Sociological insight makes one fully cognizant of the existence of conflicts of this kind, of their inevitability, and in broad outline, of many of the forms in which they are manifested and of their more remote effects. It enables one—to give but a single instance—to understand how there result attitudes that vary from the extreme of complete repudiation of femininity on the one hand to the opposite extreme of total rejection of intellectual or vocational activities on the other. . . .

It was only after somewhat prolonged analytic work that I recognized in certain gross examples that the central problem here consisted not in any love-inhibition, but in an entirely too exclusive concentration upon men. These women were as though possessed by a single thought, "I must have a man"—obsessed with an idea overvalued to the point of absorbing every other thought, so that by comparison all the rest of life seemed stale, flat, and unprofitable. The capabilities and interests that most of them possessed either had no meaning at all for them or had lost what meaning they had once had. In other words, conflicts affecting their relations to men were present and could be to a considerable extent relieved, but the actual problem lay not in too little but in too much emphasis on their love life. . . .

Seen from this standpoint, these patients present a discrepancy of a double sort. Their feeling for a man is in reality so complicated—I should like to say descriptively, so loose—that their estimate of a heterosexual relationship as the only valuable thing in life is undoubtedly a compulsive overvaluation. On the other hand, their gifts, abilities, and interests, and their ambition and the corresponding possibilities of achievement and satisfaction, are very much greater than they assume. We are dealing, therefore, with a displacement of emphasis from attainment or the struggle for achievement, to sex; indeed, so far as one may speak of objective facts in the field of values, what we have here is an objective falsification of values. For although in the last analysis sex is a tremendously important, perhaps the most important, source of satisfaction, it is certainly not the only one, nor the most trustworthy. . . .

Thus all these girls experienced throughout their childhood an intensified rivalry for the attention of a man, which either was hopeless from the beginning or resulted ultimately in defeat. This defeat in relation to the father is, of course, the typical fate of the little girl in the family situation. But in these cases it produces specific and typical consequences because of the intensification of the rivalry brought about by the presence of a mother or a sister who absolutely dominates the situation erotically or by the awakening of specific illusions on the part of the father or brother. There is also operative an additional factor, to the significance of which I shall return in another connection. In the majority of these cases, sexual development has received an impulse more precipitate and intensified than in the average case, by reason of exaggerated early experience of sexual excitation called forth by other persons and occurrences. This premature experience of a genital excitation much greater and more intense than the physical pleasure derivable from other sources (oral, anal, and muscle erotism) not only results in bringing the genital sphere into much greater prominence but also lays the foundation for instinctively appreciating earlier and more fully the importance of the struggle for the possession of a man.

In the fact that such a struggle brings in its train a permanent and destructive attitude of rivalry with women, the same psychology is evident as holds true of every competitive situation—the vanquished feels lasting anger toward the victor, suffers injury to his self-esteem, will consequently be in a less favorable psychological position in subsequent competitive situations, and will ultimately feel either consciously or unconsciously that his only chance of success lies in the death of his opponent. Exactly the same consequences can be traced in the cases under discussion: a feeling of being downtrodden, a permanent feeling of insecurity with regard to feminine self-esteem, and a profound anger with their more fortunate rivals. There takes place in all cases, as a result of these, a partial or complete avoidance or inhibition in regard to rivalry with women, or on the other hand, a compulsive rivalry of exaggerated proportions—and the greater the feeling of being worsted, the more intent will the victim be upon the death of the rival, as though to say: Only when you are dead can I be free.

This hatred of the victorious rival may eventuate in either of two ways.

If it remains in large measure preconscious, the blame for the erotic failure is placed upon other women. If it is more deeply repressed, the reason for lack of success is sought in the patient's own personality; the self-tormenting complaints that arise combine with the sense of guilt that originates in the repressed hatred. . . .

In the attempt to get the best of these tormenting ideas, dress plays a very important part, and yet without any permanent success, since doubts invade this sphere as well and make it a perpetual affliction. It becomes unendurable not to have articles of dress match perfectly, and the same if a dress makes the wearer look stout, or if it seems too long or too short, too plain or too elegant, too conspicuous, too youthful, or not modern enough. Granting that the matter of clothes is of importance to a woman, there can be no question but that quite inappropriate affects here come into play—affects of shame, insecurity, and even anger. One patient, for example, was in the habit of tearing up a dress if she thought that it made her appear stout; in others the anger was directed at the dressmaker.

Another attempt at defense is the wish to be a man. "As a woman I am nothing," said one of these patients; "I should be much better off to be a man," and accompanied this remark with markedly masculine gestures. The third and most important means of defense consists in the patient's proving nevertheless that she can attract a man. Here again we encounter the same gamut of emotions. To be without a man, never to have had anything to do with one, to have remained a virgin, to be unmarried—all these things are a disgrace and cause people to look down upon one. Having a man—whether he be admirer, friend, lover, or husband—is the proof that one is "normal." Hence the frantic pursuit of a man. *Au fond*, he need fulfill only the single requirement of being a man. If he has other qualities that enhance the woman's narcissistic satisfaction, so much the better. Otherwise a striking degree of unselectivity on her part may be exhibited, which is in conspicuous contrast to her level in other respects.

But this attempt too, like that in regard to dress, remains unsuccessful—unsuccessful, at any rate, so far as proving anything is concerned. For even when these women succeed in getting one man after another to fall in love with them, they are able to conjure up reasons for depreciating their success—reasons such as the following: There was no other woman about for the man to fall in love with; or, he does not amount to much; or, "I forced him into the situation anyway"; or, "He loves me because I am intelligent, or because I can be useful to him in this or that way." . . .

In brief, one quite evidently finds still operative in the unconscious, in unchanged form and undiminished strength, ⸤the destructive impulses directed against the mother or sister in early childhood;⸥ Melanie Klein has laid much emphasis on the significance of these impulses. By way of accounting for this, it is easy to believe that it is augmented and embittered rivalry, which has not permitted them to become quiescent. The original impulses against the mother have the meaning: You must not have intercourse with my father; you must not have children by him; if you do, you will be so damaged that you cannot do so again and will be rendered harmless forever; or — as further elaborated — you will appear hideous and repulsive to all men. But this, according to the inexorable law of talion that prevails in the unconscious, brings in its train fears of exactly the same kind. Thus if I wish this injury to befall you and inflict it upon you in my masturbation fantasies, I have to fear that the same thing will happen to me; not only this, but I have to feat that the same thing will happen to me when I am in the same situation as that in which I have wished pain and injury upon my mother. . . .

Originally I supposed that the adherence to the idea of not being normal was determined by the illusion of masculinity, the concomitant sense of shame by the idea of having forfeited the penis, or the possibility of its growing, through masturbation; I regarded the pursuit of a man as determined in part by a secondary overemphasis of femininity and in part by a wish to be supplemented by a man if one cannot be a man oneself. But from the dynamics of the course of events, such as I have described above, I have come to the conviction that the fantasies of masculinity do not represent the *dynamically effective agency*, but are merely an *expression of secondary tendencies* that have their root in the rivalry with women described above, being at the same time an accusation against unjust fate or against the mother, rationalized in this way or that, for not having been born a man, or an expression of the need to create in dreams or fantasies a means of escape from the torment of feminine conflicts.

There are, of course, cases in which adherence to the illusion of being a man does play a dynamic part, but these cases seem to be of quite a different structure, since in them a conspicuous degree of identification with a specific man — generally the father or the brother — has taken place, on the basis of which development in a homosexual direction or the formation of a narcissistic attitude and orientation occurs.

The overvaluation of relationships with men has its sources, so far as we have up to this point discussed them, not in any unusual strength of sexual impulse, but in factors lying outside the male-female relationship, namely, restoration of wounded self-esteem and defiance of the victorious (female) rival. And so it becomes needful to inquire whether, and to what extent, the desire for sexual gratification plays an essential part in the pursuit of the male. That consciously it is striven for is certain, but is this also true from an instinctual standpoint? . . .

I believe that the following three factors contribute to this overvaluation of sexuality:

(1) From the economic standpoint there is much in the typical psychological configuration of these women to force them into the sphere of sexuality, because the path to other kinds of possibilities of satisfaction has been made extremely difficult. Homosexual impulses are rejected because they are coupled with destructive impulses and because of the attitude of rivalry toward other women. Masturbation is unsatisfactory, if it has not been, as is true in most cases, completely suppressed. But in large measure all other forms of autoerotic gratification in the broader sense, both of a direct and a sublimated sort, everything that one does or enjoys "only by oneself," such as the enjoyment of eating, of earning money, of art or nature, are inhibited, and this in chief measure because these women, like all people who feel themselves at a decided disadvantage in life, harbor a tremendously strong wish to have everything for themselves alone, not to allow anybody else to enjoy the slightest thing, to take everything away from everybody else—a wish that is repressed because of the reactive anxiety it gives rise to and because of its incompatibility with the individual's standards of behavior in other respects. In addition to this there is the inhibition present in all spheres of activity, which when coupled with ambition, results in great inward dissatisfaction.

(2) This first factor might explain an actual intensification of sexual need; but a further factor might constitute a root of this increased valuation—one based upon the individual's original defeat in the sphere of feminine rivalry, and resulting in a deep-seated fear lest other women should constantly be a disturbing element in heterosexual activities, as indeed is manifested clearly enough in the transference situation. This is in fact something like the "aphanisis" described by Ernest Jones, except that here it is not a question of anxiety regarding the loss of one's own capacity for sexual experience, but rather the fear of being balked of it for all time by an external agency. This anxiety is warded off by the attempts to gain security mentioned above, and contributes to the overestimation of sexuality

insofar as any purpose that becomes an object of controversy is always over-rated.

(3) The third source seems to me the least well-established since I could not detect its presence in all cases and therefore cannot vouch for its relevance in every instance. Some of these women, as has already been mentioned, recall experiencing in early childhood sexual excitation similar to orgasm. In still others one may infer with some justification the occurrence of such an experience, this on the grounds of subsequent phenomena such as the fear of orgasm coupled through this with knowledge of it as betrayed in dreams. The excitation experienced in early life was terrifying either because of the specific conditions under which it was experienced or simply on account of its overwhelming strength relative to the subject's immaturity, so that it was repressed. The experience left certain traces in its wake, however—of a pleasure far in excess of that from any other source, and of something strangely vitalizing to the whole organism. I am inclined to think that these traces cause these particular women—to a greater extent than in the average instance—to conceive of sexual gratification as a kind of elixir of life that only men are able to provide and without which one must dry up and waste away, while the lack of it makes achievement in any other direction impossible. This point, however, must be further corroborated.

Despite this multiple determination of the intensive pursuit of men, and despite the strenuous efforts indulged in for the attainment of this goal, all these attempts are doomed to failure. The reasons for this failure are to be found in part in what has already been said. They have their root in the same soil as engendered defeat in the competition for the male, yet which at the same time gives rise to the very special efforts made to win him.

The embittered attitude of rivalry with women forces them, of course, constantly to demonstrate afresh their erotic superiority, but at the same time their destructive impulses toward women cause any rivalry over a man to be inevitably bound up with deep anxiety. In accordance with the strength of this anxiety, and perhaps even more in accordance with the subjective realization of defeat and the consequent lowering of self-esteem, the conflict between an increased urge to engage in rivalry with other women and the increased anxiety engendered thereby, results outwardly either in an avoidance of such rivalry or in increased efforts in that direction. The manifest picture may therefore run the gamut from women who are extremely inhibited in making any advances in establishing relationships with men, though craving for them to the exclusion of any other wish, to women of a veritable Don Juan type. The justification for including all these women within a single category, despite their outward dissimilarities, lies not only in the similarity of their fundamental conflicts, but also in the similarity of their emotional orientation, in spite of the extreme difference in their outward careers—this, more accurately, with special reference to their attitude regarding the sphere of the erotic. The factor already mentioned, that "success" with men is not emotionally esteemed as such, contributes to an important extent to this similarity. Furthermore, no relationship with a man that is satisfactory either mentally or physically is achieved in any instance.

The insult to their femininity drives these women, both directly and *via* the fear of not being normal, to prove their feminine potency to themselves; but since this goal is never reached on account of the self-depreciation that instantly occurs, such a technique leads of necessity to a rapid change from one relationship to another. Their interest in a man, such as may even amount to an illusion of being tremendously in love with him, vanishes as a rule as soon as he is "conquered"—that is, as soon as he has become emotionally dependent on them.

This tendency to make a person dependent through love, as I have already described as being characteristic of the transference, has still another determinant. It is determined by an anxiety which says that dependence is a danger to be avoided at all costs, that therefore, since love or any emotional bond is that which creates the greatest degree of dependence, these latter constitute the very evil to be avoided. The fear of dependence is, in other words, a profound fear of the disappointments and humiliations that they expect to result from falling in love, humiliations that they have themselves experienced in childhood and would like subsequently to pass on to others. The original experience that has thus left behind it such a strong feeling of vulnerability was presumably caused by a man, but the resultant behavior is directed almost equally toward men and women. The patient, for example, who wanted to make me dependent upon her by means of presents expressed regret on one occasion that she had not gone to a male analyst, for one can more easily make a man fall in love with one and then the game is won.

Protection of oneself against emotional dependence thus corresponds to the desire to be invulnerable, much as Siegfried in the German saga bathed in the dragon's blood for that purpose.

In still other instances, the mechanism of defense manifests itself in a tendency toward despotism as well as in vigilance to make sure that the partner will remain more dependent upon her than she upon him, and this is accompanied, of course, by correspondingly violent overt or repressed reactions of rage whenever the partner gives any sign of independence.

The doubly determined inconstancy toward men serves further to gratify a deep-seated desire for revenge, a desire which likewise has developed on the basis of her original defeat; the desire is to get the better of a man, to cast him aside, to reject him just as she herself once felt cast aside and rejected. From what has already been said, it is evident that the chances of a suitable object choice are very slight, indeed are nonexistent; for reasons having to do in part with their relations to other women and in part with their own self-esteem, these women snatch blindly at a man. These chances, moreover, in two-thirds of the cases dealt with here, were still further reduced by a fixation on the father, who was the person about whom the struggle in childhood primarily centered. These cases at first gave the impression that as a matter of fact they were seeking the father or a father image, and that later on they dropped men very quickly because the latter did not correspond to this ideal or also because they became the recipient of the repetitive revenge originally intended for the father; or in other words, that the fixation on the father constituted the nucleus of these women's neurotic difficulties. Although as a matter of fact this fixation intensifies the difficulties in many of these women, it is nevertheless certain that it is not a specific factor in the genesis of this type. At any rate, it does not constitute the dynamic kernel of the specific problem with which we are here concerned, for in about one-third of these cases nothing was found in this respect that transcended the ordinary in intensity or in any particular characteristic. I mention the matter here only for technical reasons. For one learns by experience that when one follows through these early fixations without having first worked through the entire problem involved, one readily reaches an impasse.

For the patient there is but one way out of a situation so totally unsatisfactory, namely, by means of achievement, of esteem, of ambition. These women without exception seek this way out, in that they all develop tremendous ambition. They are motivated by powerful impulses emanating from wounded feminine self-esteem and from an exaggerated sense of rivalry. One can build up one's self-esteem by achievement and success, if not in the erotic sphere, then in any other field of endeavor, the choice of which is determined by the individual's particular abilities, and thus triumph over all rivals.

However, they are foredoomed to failure along this path as well as in the erotic sphere. . . .

There occurs in all these cases a further difficulty of prime importance, which arises from the striking discrepancy between their increased ambition and their weakened self-confidence. All these women would be capable of productive work, in accordance with their individual endowments, as writers, as scientists, as painters, as physicians, as organizers. It is perfectly self-evident that in every productive activity a certain amount of self-confidence is a prerequisite, and a noticeable lack of it has a paralyzing effect. This holds true, of course, equally here. Hand in hand with their excessive ambition, there is from the very outset a lack of courage resulting from their broken morale. At the same time the majority of these patients are unaware of the tremendous tension under which they labor, due to their ambition.

This discrepancy has a further practical result. For they expect, without being aware of it, to achieve distinction from the very outset — to master the piano, for example, without practice, or to paint brilliantly without technique, to achieve scientific success without hard labor, or to diagnose correctly heart murmurs and pulmonary sounds without training. Their inevitable failure they do not ascribe to their unreal and excessive expectations, but regard it as due to their general lack of ability. They then are inclined to drop whatever work they are doing at the time; they thus fail to attain that knowledge and skill, through patient labor, which is indispensable to success; and thereby they bring about a further and permanent increase in the discrepancy between increased ambition and weakened self-confidence. . . .

What is it that maintains these tendencies? On the one hand, the conviction of one's own incapacity affords an excellent protection against achieving anything worthwhile, and thus insures one against the dangers of successful competition. Adherence to the incapacity to do things subserves this defense far less than it does the positive striving that dominates the entire picture, namely, that of obtaining a man, or rather of extorting from fate a man in spite of all the powers that be — and of doing so by giving proof of one's own weakness, dependence, and helplessness. This "scheme" is always entirely unconscious, but is pursued all the more obstinately for that reason; and that which is seemingly meaningless betrays itself as a planned and purposeful striving toward a definite end, when regarded from the standpoint of this unconscious expectation. . . .

The difficulties naturally become more pronounced with increasing age. A young person is easily consoled in the face of erotic failures and hopes for a better "fate." Economic independence is, at least in the middle classes, not as yet a pressing problem. And the narrowing down of the spheres of interest does not as yet make itself very severely felt. With increasing years, say in about the thirties, continued failure in love comes to be regarded as a fatality, while gradually at the same time the possibilities of a satisfactory relationship become more hopeless, chiefly for internal reasons: increasing insecurity, retardation of general development, and therefore failure to develop the charms characteristic of mature years. Furthermore, the lack of economic independence gradually becomes more of a burden. And finally, the emptiness that comes to pervade the sphere of work and achievement is felt in increasing degree as increased emphasis is, with increasing age, placed by the subject or by the environment upon achievement. Life seems increasingly to lack meaning, and gradually bitterness develops because these persons necessarily lose themselves more and more in their twofold self-deception. They think that they can be happy only through love, whereas, constituted as they are, they can never be, while on the other hand they have an ever-diminishing faith in the worth of their abilities. . . .

This description might give the impression that the two sets of forces, social and individual, are separated from each other. This is certainly not the case. I believe that I can show in each instance that the type of woman described can only result in this form on the basis of individual factors, and I assume that the *frequency* of the type is explained by the fact that, given the social factors, relatively slight difficulties in personal development suffice to drive women in the direction of this type of womanhood.

Rainer Maria Rilke

Poems

Rainer Maria Rilke (1875–1926) was born in Prague but spent most of his life in Germany, Austria, and Switzerland. He is best known for his lyrical, very personal, and sometimes mystical writing, including his Duino Elegies *and his prose masterpiece,* The Notebook of Malte Laurids Brigge. *His love life was notorious and has become even more so since his death. He insisted on being a "poet," superior to the demands of everyday intimacy and commitment. His tenuous relationships with their paradoxical emphasis on solitude and freedom, possessiveness, love, and death are the subject of many of his poems and letters and no doubt a "rationalization and excuse for his own conduct" (William Gass, in his selection in part IV). The poems that follow are from* Duino Elegies *and* New Poems (1907); *translations are by William Gass.*

The Second Elegy

Lovers, satisfied by one another, I am asking you
about us. You embrace, but where's your proof?
Look, sometimes it happens that my hands grow to know
one another, or that my heavy head seeks their shelter.
That yields me a slender sensation. But who wants to live just for that?
You though, who, in one another's passion,
grow until, near bursting, plead: "No more. . ."
you, who, beneath one another's groping, swell
with juice like the grapes of a vintage year;
you, who may go like a bud into another's blossoming:
I am asking you about us. I know
you touch so blissfully because your touch survives such bliss,
because the flesh you caress so tenderly stays flesh;
because just below your fingertip you feel the tip of pure duration.
So you expect eternity to entwine itself in your embrace.
And yet, when you have endured the fear of that first look,
the longing, later, at the window, and your first turn
about the garden together: lovers, are you any longer what you were?

When you lift yourselves up to one another's lips,
and slip wine into wine like an added flavor: oh, how strangely
soon is each drinker's disappearance from the ceremony.

Parting

How I have felt it, that nameless state called parting,
and how I feel it still: a dark, sharp, heartless
Something that displays, holds out with unapparent hands,
a perfect union to us, while tearing it in two.

With what wide-open eyes I've watched whatever
was, while calling to me, loosening its hold,
remaining in the road behind as though all womankind,
yet small and white and nothing more than this:

a waving which has blown the hair beyond its brow,
a slight, continuous flutter — scarcely now
explicable: perhaps the tremor of a plum-tree
and the bough a startled cuckoo has set free.

Emma Goldman

On the Tragedy of Woman's Emancipation, and Marriage and Love

Emma Goldman (1869–1940) was a feminist and radical activist who had a vivid sense of her buoyant individuality. Her perspective is neatly summarized in her comment, "I want no part of any revolution in which I can't dance." An immigrant to the United States from Russia who was later deported back to Russia for her political views, she spent much of her life, in her own words, "in revolt." An anarchist, she became actively political while still in her teens. Although associated with radical causes—Marxist revolution, civil libertarianism, atheism, free love, and birth control— Goldman was no ideologue who advanced views just because her revolutionary cohorts believed them politically correct. She was dubious about the women's suffrage movement, not because she did not believe that women should have the right to vote, but because she was skeptical of the ballot's power. She was similarly disenchanted with feminists whose primary aspiration was to assume roles that had been previously reserved for men. As the selection below from her essay "On the Tragedy of Women's Emancipation" reveals, Goldman deplored the tendency of some feminists to adopt traditional masculine goals and shun the joys of love and motherhood.

Love, for Emma Goldman, is "life's greatest treasure." The emancipated woman is the woman who can respond to the call of love, in defiance of all moralists, whether traditionalists or revolutionaries. Goldman contrasts love and marriage, however, for reasons discussed in her essay "Love and Marriage." Marriage, in her view, is an economic institution that keeps women in servitude to men and discourages their development as individuals. The contemporary economic situation, however, encourages women to marry because they are not given equal education and are denied employment opportunities available to men. Thus, the entire economic structure needs to be changed in order for women to be really emancipated. The first step in emancipation is the liberation of women's own souls from the ideas that love involves conquest, that marriage is desirable, that subordi-

nation to men is tolerable. Only when the inner tyranny of these ideas is destroyed can women—and men—discover genuine fulfillment in love.

The Tragedy of Woman's Emancipation
• • •

The narrowness of the existing conception of woman's independence and emancipation; the dread of love for a man who is not her social equal; the fear that love will rob her of her freedom and independence; the horror that love or the joy of motherhood will only hinder her in the full exercise of her profession—all these together make of the emancipated modern woman a compulsory vestal, before whom life, with its great clarifying sorrows and its deep, entrancing joys, rolls on without touching or gripping her soul.

Emancipation, as understood by the majority of its adherents and exponents, is of too narrow a scope to permit the boundless love and ecstasy contained in the deep emotion of the true woman, sweetheart, mother, in freedom.

The tragedy of the self-supporting or economically free woman does not lie in too many, but in too few experiences. True, she surpasses her sister of past generations in knowledge of the world and human nature; it is just because of this that she feels deeply the lack of life's essence, which alone can enrich the human soul, and without which the majority of women have become mere professional automatons.

That such a state of affairs was bound to come was foreseen by those who realized that, in the domain of ethics, there still remained many decaying ruins of the time of the undisputed superiority of man; ruins that are still considered useful. And, what is more important, a goodly number of the emancipated are unable to get along without them. Every movement that aims at the destruction of existing institutions and the replacement thereof with something more advanced, more perfect, has followers who in theory stand for the most radical ideas, but who, nevertheless, in their every-day practice, are like the average Philistine, feigning respectability and clamoring for the good opinion of their opponents. There are, for example, Socialists, and even Anarchists, who stand for the idea that property is robbery, yet who will grow indignant if anyone owe them the value of a half-dozen pins.

The same Philistine can be found in the movement for woman's emancipation. Yellow journalists and milk-and-water littérateurs have painted pictures of the emancipated woman that make the hair of the good citizen

206   and his dull companion stand up on end. Every member of the woman's rights movement was pictured as a George Sand in her absolute disregard of morality. Nothing was sacred to her. She had no respect for the ideal relation between man and woman. In short, emancipation stood only for a reckless life of lust and sin, regardless of society, religion, and morality. The exponents of woman's rights were highly indignant at such misrepresentation, and, lacking humor, they exerted all their energy to prove that they were not at all as bad as they were painted, but the very reverse. Of course, as long as woman was the slave of man, she could not be good and pure, but now that she was free and independent she would prove how good she could be and that her influence would have a purifying effect on all institutions in society. True, the movement for woman's rights has broken many old fetters, but it has also forged new ones. The great movement of *true* emancipation has not met with a great race of women who could look liberty in the face. Their narrow, puritanical vision banished man, as a disturber and doubtful character, out of their emotional life. Man was not to be tolerated at any price, except perhaps as the father of a child, since a child could not very well come to life without a father. Fortunately, the most rigid Puritans never will be strong enough to kill the innate craving for motherhood. But woman's freedom is closely allied with man's freedom, and many of my so-called emancipated sisters seem to overlook the fact that a child born in freedom needs the love and devotion of each human being about him, man as well as woman. Unfortunately, it is this narrow conception of human relations that has brought about a great tragedy in the lives of the modern man and woman.

· · ·

The average man with his self-sufficiency, his ridiculously superior airs of patronage towards the female sex, is an impossibility for woman. . . . Equally impossible for her is the man who can see in her nothing more than her mentality and her genius, and who fails to awaken her woman nature.

A rich intellect and a fine soul are usually considered necessary attributes of a deep and beautiful personality. In the case of the modern woman, these attributes serve as a hindrance to the complete assertion of her being. For over a hundred years the old form of marriage, based on the Bible, "Till death doth part," has been denounced as an institution that stands for the sovereignty of the man over the woman, of her complete submission to his whims and commands, and absolute dependence on his name and support. Time and again it has been conclusively proved that the old matrimonial relation restricted woman to the function of man's servant and the bearer of his children. And yet we find many emancipated women who prefer marriage, with all its deficiencies, to the narrowness of an unmarried life: narrow and unendurable because of the chains of moral and social prejudice that cramp and bind her nature.

The explanation of such inconsistency on the part of many advanced women is to be found in the fact that they never truly understood the meaning of emancipation. They thought that all that was needed was independence from external tyrannies; the internal tyrants, far more harmful to life and growth—ethical and social conventions—were left to take care of themselves; and they have taken care of themselves. They seem to get along as beautifully in the heads and hearts of the most active exponents of woman's emancipation, as in the heads and hearts of our grandmothers.

· · ·

The greatest shortcoming of the emancipation of the present day lies in its artificial stiffness and its narrow respectabilities, which produce an emptiness in woman's soul that will not let her drink from the fountain of life. I once remarked that there seemed to be a deeper relationship between the old-fashioned mother and hostess, ever on the alert for the happiness of her little ones and the comfort of those she loves, and the truly new woman, than between the later and her average emancipated sister. The disciples of emancipation pure and simple declared me a heathen, fit only for the stake. Their blind zeal did not let them see that my comparison between the old and the new was merely to prove that a goodly number of our grandmothers had more blood in their veins, far more humor and wit, and certainly a greater amount of naturalness, kind-heartedness, and simplicity, than the majority of our emancipated professional women who fill the colleges, halls of learning and various offices. This does not mean a wish to return to the past, nor does it condemn woman to her old sphere, the kitchen and the nursery.

Salvation lies in an energetic march onward towards a brighter and clearer future. We are in need of unhampered growth out of old traditions and habits. The movement for woman's emancipation has so far made but the first step in that direction. It is to be hoped that it will gather strength to make another. The right to vote, or equal civil rights, may be good demands, but true emancipation begins neither at the polls nor in courts. It begins in woman's soul. History tells us that every oppressed class gained true liberation from its masters through its own efforts. It is necessary that woman learn that lesson, that she realize that her freedom will reach as far as her power to achieve her freedom reaches. It is, therefore, far more important for her to begin with her inner regeneration, to cut loose from the weight of prejudices, traditions, and customs. The demand for equal rights in every vocation of life is just and fair; but, after all, the most vital right is the right to love and be loved. Indeed, if partial emancipation is to become a complete and true emancipation of woman, it will have to do away with the ridiculous notion that to be loved, to be sweetheart and mother, is synonymous with being slave or subordinate. It will have to do away with the absurd notion of the dualism of the sexes, or that man and woman represent two antagonistic worlds.

Pettiness separates; breadth unites. Let us be broad and big. Let us not overlook vital things because of the bulk of trifles confronting us. A true conception of the relation of the sexes will not admit of conqueror and conquered; it knows of but one great thing: to give of one's self boundlessly, in order to find one's self richer, deeper, better. That alone can fill the emptiness, and transform the tragedy of woman's emancipation into joy, limitless joy.

Marriage and Love

The popular notion about marriage and love is that they are synonymous, that they spring from the same motives, and cover the same human needs. Like most popular notions this also rests not on actual facts, but on superstition.

Marriage and love have nothing in common; they are as far apart as the poles; are, in fact, antagonistic to each other. No doubt some marriages have been the result of love. Not, however, because love could assert itself only in marriage; much rather is it because few people can completely outgrow a convention. There are to-day large numbers of men and women to whom marriage is naught but a farce, but who submit to it for the sake of public opinion. At any rate, while it is true that some marriages are based on love, and while it is equally true that in some cases love continues in married life, I maintain that it does so regardless of marriage, and not because of it.

On the other hand, it is utterly false that love results from marriage. On rare occasions one does hear of a miraculous case of a married couple falling in love after marriage, but on close examination it will be found that it is a mere adjustment to the inevitable. Certainly the growing-used to each other is far away from the spontaneity, the intensity, and beauty of love, without which the intimacy of marriage must prove degrading to both the woman and the man.

Marriage is primarily an economic arrangement, an insurance pact. It differs from the ordinary life insurance agreement only in that it is more binding, more exacting. Its returns are insignificantly small compared with the investments. In taking out an insurance policy one pays for it in dollars and cents, always at liberty to discontinue payments. If, however, woman's premium is a husband, she pays for it with her name, her privacy, her self-respect, her very life, "until death doth part." Moreover, the marriage insurance condemns her to life-long dependency, to parasitism, to complete uselessness, individual as well as social. Man, too, pays his toll, but as his sphere is wider, marriage does not limit him as much as woman. He feels his chains more in an economic sense.

Thus Dante's motto over Inferno applies with equal force to marriage: "Ye who enter here leave all hope behind."

That marriage is a failure none but the very stupid will deny. One has but to glance over the statistics of divorce to realize how bitter a failure marriage really is. Nor will the stereotyped Philistine argument that the laxity of divorce laws and the growing looseness of woman account for the fact that: first, every twelfth marriage ends in divorce; second, that since 1870 divorces have increased from 28 to 73 for every hundred thousand population; third, that adultery, since 1867, as ground for divorce, has increased 270.8 per cent; fourth, that desertion increased 369.8 per cent.

·   ·   ·

The thoughtful social student will not content himself with the popular superficial excuse for this phenomenon. He will have to dig down deeper into the very life of the sexes to know why marriage proves so disastrous.

Edward Carpenter says that behind every marriage stands the life-long environment of the two sexes; an environment so different from each other that man and woman must remain strangers. Separated by an insurmountable wall of superstition, custom, and habit, marriage has not the potentiality of developing knowledge of, and respect for, each other, without which every union is doomed to failure.

Henrik Ibsen, the hater of all social shams, was probably the first to realize this great truth. Nora leaves her husband, not — as the stupid critic would have it — because she is tired of her responsibilities or feels the need of woman's rights, but because she has come to know that for eight years she had lived with a stranger and borne him children. Can there be anything more humiliating, more degrading than a lifelong proximity between two strangers? No need for the woman to know anything of the man, save his income. As to the knowledge of the woman — what is there to know ex-

cept that she has a pleasing appearance? We have not yet outgrown the
theologic myth that woman has no soul, that she is a mere appendix to
man, made out of his rib just for the convenience of the gentleman who
was so strong that he was afraid of his own shadow.

Perchance the poor quality of the material whence woman comes is responsible for her inferiority. At any rate, woman has no soul — what is there
to know about her? Besides, the less soul a woman has the greater her asset
as a wife, the more readily will she absorb herself in her husband. It is this
slavish acquiescence to man's superiority that has kept the marriage institution seemingly intact for so long a period. Now that woman is coming into
her own, now that she is actually growing aware of herself as a being outside of the master's grace, the sacred institution of marriage is gradually being undermined, and no amount of sentimental lamentation can stay it.

From infancy, almost, the average girl is told that marriage is her ultimate goal; therefore her training and education must be directed towards
that end. Like the mute beast fattened for slaughter, she is prepared for
that. Yet, strange to say, she is allowed to know much less about her function as wife and mother than the ordinary artisan of his trade. It is indecent and filthy for a respectable girl to know anything of the marital relation. Oh, for the inconsistency of respectability, that needs the marriage
vow to turn something which is filthy into the purest and most sacred arrangement that none dare question or criticize. Yet that is exactly the attitude of the average upholder of marriage. The prospective wife and
mother is kept in complete ignorance of her only asset in the competitive
field — sex. Thus she enters into life-long relations with a man only to find
herself shocked, repelled, outraged beyond measure by the most natural
and healthy instinct, sex. It is safe to say that a large percentage of the unhappiness, misery, distress, and physical suffering of matrimony is due to
the criminal ignorance in sex matters that is being extolled as a great virtue. Nor is it at all an exaggeration which I say that more than one home
has been broken up because of this deplorable fact.

If, however, woman is free and big enough to learn the mystery of sex
without the sanction of State or Church, she will stand condemned as utterly unfit to become the wife of a "good" man, his goodness consisting of
an empty head and plenty of money. Can there be anything more outrageous than the idea that a healthy, grown woman, full of life and passion,
must deny nature's demand, must subdue her most intense craving, undermine her health and break her spirit, must stunt her vision, abstain from
the depth and glory of sex experience until a "good" man comes along to

take her unto himself as a wife? That is precisely what marriage means. How can such an arrangement end except in failure? This is one, though not the least important, factor of marriage, which differentiates it from love.

Ours is a practical age. The time when Romeo and Juliet risked the wrath of their fathers for love, when Gretchen exposed herself to the gossip of her neighbors for love, is no more. If, on rare occasions, young people allow themselves the luxury of romance, they are taken in care by the elders, drilled and pounded until they become "sensible."

The moral lesson instilled in the girl is not whether the man has aroused her love, but rather is it, "How much?" The important and only God of practical American life: Can the man make a living? Can he support a wife? That is the only thing that justifies marriage. Gradually this saturates every thought of the girl; her dreams are not of moonlight and kisses, of laughter and tears; she dreams of shopping tours and bargain counters. This soul-poverty and sordidness are the elements inherent in the marriage institution. The State and the Church approve of no other ideal, simply because it is the one that necessitates the State and Church control of men and women.

· · ·

But the child, how is it to be protected, if not for marriage? After all, is not that the most important consideration? The sham, the hypocrisy of it! Marriage protecting the child, yet thousands of children destitute and homeless. Marriage protecting the child, yet orphan asylums and reformatories overcrowded, the Society for the Prevention of Cruelty to Children keeping busy in rescuing the little victims from "loving" parents, to place them under more loving care, the Gerry Society. Oh, the mockery of it!

Marriage may have the power to "bring the horse to water," but has it ever made him drink? The law will place the father under arrest, and put him in convict's clothes; but has that ever stilled the hunger of the child? If the parent has no work, of if he hides his identity, what does marriage do then? It invokes the law to bring the man to "justice," to put him safely behind closed doors; his labor, however, goes not to the child, but to the State. The child receives but a blighted memory of its father's stripes.

As to the protection of the woman—therein lies the curse of marriage. Not that it really protects her, but the very idea is so revolting, such an outrage and insult on life, so degrading to human dignity, as to forever condemn this parasitic institution.

It is like that other paternal arrangement—capitalism. It robs man of his birthright, stunts his growth, poisons his body, keeps him in ignorance, in poverty and dependence, and then institutes charities that thrive on the last vestige of man's self-respect.

The institution of marriage makes a parasite of woman, an absolute dependent. It incapacitates her for life's struggle, annihilates her social consciousness, paralyzes her imagination, and then imposes its gracious protection, which is in reality a snare, a travesty on human character.

If motherhood is the highest fulfillment of woman's nature, what other protection does it need save love and freedom? Marriage but defiles, outrages, and corrupts her fulfillment. Does it not say to woman, Only when you follow me shall you bring forth life? Does it not condemn her to the block, does it not degrade and shame her if she refuses to buy her right to motherhood by selling herself? Does not marriage only sanction motherhood, even though conceived in hatred, in compulsion? Yet, if motherhood be of free choice, of love, of ecstasy, of defiant passion, does it not place a crown of thorns upon an innocent head and carve in letters of blood the hideous epithet, Bastard? Were marriage to contain all the virtues claimed for it, its crimes against motherhood would exclude it forever from the realm of love.

Love, the strongest and deepest element in all life, the harbinger of hope, of joy, of ecstasy; love, the defier of all laws, of all conventions; love, the freest, the most powerful moulder of human destiny; how can such an all-compelling force be synonymous with that poor little State- and Church-begotten weed, marriage?

Free love? As if love is anything but free! Man has bought brains, but all the millions in the world have failed to buy love. Man has subdued bodies, but all the power on earth has been unable to subdue love. Man has conquered whole nations, but all his armies could not conquer love. Man has chained and fettered the spirit, but he has been utterly helpless before love. High on a throne, with all the splendor and pomp his gold can command, man is yet poor and desolate, if love passes him by. And if it stays, the poorest hovel is radiant with warmth, with life and color. Thus love has the magic power to make of a beggar a king. Yes, love is free; it can dwell in no other atmosphere. In freedom it gives itself unreservedly, abundantly, completely. All the laws on the statutes, all the courts in the universe, cannot tear it from the soil, once love has taken root. If, however, the soil is sterile, how can marriage make it bear fruit? It is like the last desperate struggle of fleeting life against death.

Love needs no protection; it is its own protection. So long as love begets life no child is deserted, or hungary, or famished for the want of affection. I know this to be true. I know women who became mothers in freedom by the men they loved. Few children in wedlock enjoy the care, the protection, the devotion free motherhood is capable of bestowing.

• • •

In our present pygmy state love is indeed a stranger to most people. Misunderstood and shunned, it rarely takes root; or if it does, it soon withers and dies. Its delicate fiber can not endure the stress and strain of the daily grind. Its soul is too complex to adjust itself to the slimy woof of our social fabric. It weeps and moans and suffers with those who have need of it, yet lack the capacity to rise to love's summit.

Some day, some day men and women will rise, they will reach the mountain peak, they will meet big and strong and free, ready to receive, to partake, and to bask in the golden rays of love. What fancy, what imagination, what poetic genius can foresee even approximately the potentialities of such a force in the life of men and women. If the world is ever to give birth to true companionship and oneness, not marriage, but love will be the parent.

"Emancipated" women do not exist yet. Women who think they are are miserable because they deny themselves the things women are hardwired to desire

Marriage is a filthy mockery of an institution and should be completely wiped from the face of the earth. Love is what makes things work and once we are free to not have to be married, all will be well.
(yeah right)

Denis de Rougemont

from Love in the Western World

Denis de Rougemont's book Love in the Western World *created a fury when it was published in France just before World War II and has been creating a fury ever since. His central thesis, supported by many pages of still debated scholarly and literary researches, was that what we call romantic love (Stendhal's "passion-love") is a kind of pathology, quite contrary to happiness and nothing less, according to one of the book's less modest formulations, than the will to death and self-destruction. Returning to an ancient distinction, de Rougemont contrasts eros or erotic love with agape or divinely inspired conjugal love, and his book is both an intermittent celebration of the latter and a relentless attack on the former, notwithstanding the invaluable role of eros as a source of great literary inspiration.*

The Love of Love

• • •

It is only "silly" questions that can enlighten us; for behind whatever seems obvious lurks something that is not. Let us then boldly ask: Does Tristan care for Iseult, and she for him? The lovers do not seem to be brought together in any normal *human* way. On the contrary, at their first encounter they confine themselves to having ordinary polite relations; and later, when Tristan returns to Ireland to fetch Iseult, the politeness, it will be remembered, gives place to open hostility. Everything goes to show that they would never have chosen one another were they acting *freely*. But no sooner have they drunk the love-potion than passion flares between them. Yet that any fondness supervenes to unite them as a result of the magic spell I have found, among the thousands of lines of the Romance, only a single indication.

• • •

If it should be imagined that poets in the Middle Ages were less emotional than we have grown to be and felt no need to insist on what goes without saying, let the account of the three years in the forest be read attentively. Its two finest passages—which are no doubt also the most profound passages in the whole legend—describe the lovers' two visits to the hermit Ogrin. The first time they go to see him, it is in order to make confession. But instead of confessing their sin and asking for absolution, they do their best to convince him that they are not to blame for what has befallen, since after all *they do not care for one another!*

. . .

They are thus in a thrillingly contradictory position. They love, but not one another. They have sinned, but cannot repent; for they are not to blame. They make confession, but wish neither to reform nor even to beg forgiveness. Actually, then, like all other great lovers, they imagine that they have been ravished "beyond good and evil" into a kind of transcendental state outside ordinary human experience, into an ineffable absolute irreconcilable with the world, but that they feel to be *more real than the world*. Their oppressive fate, even though they yield to it with wailings, obliterates the antithesis of good and evil, and carries them away beyond the source of moral values, beyond pleasure and pain, beyond the realm of distinctions—into a realm where opposites cancel out.

. . .

Tristan and Iseult do not love one another. They say they don't, and everything goes to prove it. *What they love is love and being in love.* They behave as if aware that whatever obstructs love must ensure and consolidate it in the heart of each and intensify it infinitely in the moment they reach the absolute obstacle, which is death. Tristan loves the awareness that he is loving far more than he loves Iseult the Fair. And Iseult does nothing to hold Tristan. All she needs is her passionate dream. Their need of one another is in order to be aflame, and they do not need one another as they are. What they need is not one another's presence, but one another's absence. *Thus the partings of the lovers are dictated by their passion itself*, and by the love they bestow on their passion rather than on its satisfaction or on its living object. That is why the Romance abounds in obstructions, why when mutually encouraging their joint dream in which each remains solitary they show such astounding indifference, and why events work up in a romantic climax to a fatal apotheosis.

. . .

Now, Eros, it will be recalled, requires union—that is, the complete absorption of the essence of individuals into the god. The existence of distinct individuals is considered to be a grievous error, and their part is to rise progressively till they are dissolved in the divine perfection. Let not a man attach himself to his fellow-creatures, for they are devoid of all excellence, and in so far as they are particular individuals they merely represent so many deficiencies of Being. There is no such thing as our neighbour. And the intensification of love must be at the same time a lover's *askesis*, whereby he will eventually escape out of life.

Agape, on the contrary, is not directed to a union that can only occur after life is over. "God is in heaven, and thou art on earth." And thy fate is being decided here below. Sin consists not in having been born, but in having lost God by becoming independent. And God is not to be found again by means of a limitless *elevation* of desire. However much our eros may be sublimated, it can never cease to be self. Orthodox Christianity allows no room either to illusion or to human optimism. But that does not mean that it condemns us to despair.

For we have had the Good Tidings—the tidings that God is seeking us. And He finds us whenever we hearken to His voice, and answer by obeying Him. God seeks us, and He has found us, thanks to His Son Who came *down* as far as us. The Incarnation is the historic sign of a renewed creation, wherein a believer is reinstated thanks to his very act of faith. Thereupon, forgiven and hallowed—that is to say, reconciled—he is still a man; there has been no divinization—but he no longer lives for himself alone. "Thou shalt love the Lord thy God, and thy neighbour as thyself." It is in loving his neighbour that a Christian is fulfilled and truly loves himself.

Agape brings no fusion or ecstatic dissolving of the self in God. The divine love is the *beginning* of a new life, a life created by the act of communion. And for a real communion there are certainly required two participants, each present to the other. It is thus that each is the other's neighbour. And since *agape* is alone in recognizing the existence of our neighbour—*Eros* failing to do so—and is the love of this neighbour, not as an excuse for self-exaltation, but as an acceptance of him or her in the whole concrete reality of his or her affliction and hope, it seems legitimate to infer that the kind of love called *passion* must have arisen usually among peoples who adored Eros, and that, on the contrary, Christian peoples—historically speaking, the inhabitants of the Western Continent of Europe—must have remained strangers to passion, or at least must have found it incredible. But history compels us to acknowledge that exactly the opposite has happened.

In the East, and also in the Greece of Plato, human love has usually been regarded as mere pleasure and physical enjoyment. Not only has passion—in the tragic and painful sense of the word—seldom been met with there, but also and especially it has been despised in the eyes of current morals and treated as a sickness or frenzy. "Some think it is a madness," Plutarch says. In the West, on the contrary, it was marriage which in the twelfth century became an object of contempt, and passion that was glorified precisely because it is preposterous, inflicts suffering upon its victims, and wreaks havoc alike in the world and in the self.

As a result of identifying the religious components whose presence we had detected in the myth, we find ourselves confronted by a flagrant contradiction between doctrine and manners. Perhaps it is this very contradiction that can account for the myth.

. . .

Assuming that we have now distinguished the causes of the curious contradiction between teaching and manners that grows visible in the twelfth century, it becomes possible to formulate a preliminary inference. *The cultivation of passionate love began in Europe as a reaction to Christianity (and in particular to its doctrine of marriage) by people whose spirit, whether naturally or by inheritance, was still pagan.*

D. H. Lawrence

The Mess of Love, and from Women in Love

D. H. Lawrence was obsessed with the subject of love, and his many novels portray a lifelong struggle to come to terms with the deep issues of sexuality, marriage, romantic attraction, and attachment. Although he has often been accused by feminists (e.g., Kate Millett in her best-seller Sexual Politics*) of being the quintessential male-chauvinist writer and having an unhealthy admiration for the wonders of his own sex, Lawrence expressed many of his concerns for the traps and intrigues of love by writing about women. An early novel,* The Rainbow, *traces the liberation of Ursula, a young farm girl, from her traditional Victorian inhibitions and her development into an independent, amorous young woman.* Women in Love *follows Ursula in this pursuit, and much of the book is a wordy dialogue between her and her new lover Birkin, whose ideas often (but not always) reflect the changing and often convoluted ideas of Lawrence himself.*

The ideal of Lawrence's vision of love can be summarized in the two words, independence ("single in himself") and attachment, and in the image of two pole stars, one not the satellite of the other but both equal, inseparable yet separate, moving together through space. At times an extreme primitivist, Lawrence, like Socrates, can idealize love as an unattainable "beyond." Indeed, he (inconsistently) rejects the word "love" as too ordinary, too routine, too familiar. Throughout Women in Love, *Birkin, a wholly cerebral character, ferociously attacks what he calls "sex in the head" and celebrates the almost mystical reverie of the instincts, love without ego, a pure bodily love, love as animal attraction. (What other author would celebrate the behavior of his cat as a model for human love?) This ironic clash—between cultivated intelligence and uninhibited animal instincts—pervades Lawrence's poetry and prose. All in all, we make "a mess of love" as in the title and theme of the poem which introduces the following passages from Lawrence's* Women in Love.

The Mess of Love

We've made a great mess of love
since we made an ideal of it.

The moment I swear to love a woman, a certain woman,
    all my life
that moment I begin to hate her.

The moment I even say to a woman: I love you! —
my love dies down considerably.

The moment love is an understood thing between us,
    we are sure of it,
it's a cold egg, it isn't love any more.

Love is like a flower, it must flower and fade;
if it doesn't fade, it is not a flower,
it's either an artificial rag blossom, or an immortelle,
    for the cemetery.

The moment the mind interferes with love, or the will
    fixes on it,
or the personality assumes it as an attribute, or the ego
    takes possession of it,
it is not love any more, it's just a mess.
And we've made a great mess of love, mind-perverted,
    will-perverted, ego-perverted love.

From *Women in Love*

• • •

"You are merely making words," he said; "knowledge means everything
to you. Even your animalism, you want it in your head. You don't want to
be an animal, you want to observe your own animal functions, to get a
mental thrill out of them. It is all purely secondary—and more decadent
than the most hide-bound intellectualism. What is it but the worst and last
form of intellectualism, this love of yours for passion and the animal instincts? Passion and the instincts—you want them hard enough, but
through your head, in your consciousness. It all takes place in your head,
under that skull of yours. Only you won't be conscious of what *actually* is:
you want the lie that will match the rest of your furniture."

Hermione set hard and poisonous against this attack. Ursula stood covered with wonder and shame. It frightened her, to see how they hated each
other.

"It's all that Lady of Shalott business," he said, in his strong abstract
voice. He seemed to be charging her before the unseeing air. "You've got
that mirror, your own fixed will, your immortal understanding, your own

tight conscious world, and there is nothing beyond it. There, in the mirror, you must have everything. But now you have come to all your conclusions, you want to go back and be like a savage, without knowledge. You want a life of pure sensation and 'passion.'"

He quoted the last word satirically against her. She sat convulsed with fury and violation, speechless, like a stricken pythoness of the Greek oracle.

"But your passion is a lie," he went on violently. "It isn't passion at all, it is your *will*. It's your bullying will. You want to clutch things and have them in your power. You want to have things in your power. And why? Because you haven't got any real body, any dark sensual body of life. You have no sensuality. You have only your will and your conceit of consciousness, and your lust for power, to *know*."

He looked at her in mingled hate and contempt, also in pain because she suffered, and in shame because he knew he tortured her. He had an impulse to kneel and plead for forgiveness. But a bitterer red anger burned up to fury in him. He became unconscious of her, he was only a passionate voice speaking.

"Spontaneous!" he cried. "You and spontaneity! You, the most deliberate thing that ever walked or crawled! You'd be verily deliberately spontaneous—that's you. Because you want to have everything in your own volition, your deliberate voluntary consciousness. You want it all in that loathsome little skull of yours, that ought to be cracked like a nut. For you'll be the same till it *is* cracked, like an insect in its skin. If one cracked your skull perhaps one might get a spontaneous, passionate woman out of you, with real sensuality. As it is, what you want is pornography—looking at yourself in mirrors, watching your naked animal actions in mirrors, so that you can have it all in your consciousness, make it all mental."

There was a sense of violation in the air, as if too much was said, the unforgivable. Yet Ursula was concerned now only with solving her own problems, in the light of his words. She was pale and abstracted.

"But do you really *want* sensuality?" she asked puzzled.

Birkin looked at her, and became intent in his explanation.

"Yes," he said, "that and nothing else, at this point. It is a fulfilment—the great dark knowledge you can't have in your head—the dark involuntary being. It is death to one's self—but it is the coming into being of another."

· · ·

"But we are sensual enough, without making ourselves so, aren't we?" she asked, turning to him with a certain golden laughter flickering under her greenish eyes, like a challenge. And immediately the queer, careless, terribly attractive smile came over his eyes and brows, though his mouth did not relax.

"No," he said, "we aren't. We're too full of ourselves."

"Surely it isn't a matter of conceit," she cried.

"That and nothing else."

She was frankly puzzled.

"Don't you think that people are most conceited of all about their sensual powers?" she asked.

"That's why they aren't sensual — only sensuous — which is another matter. They're *always* aware of themselves — and they're so conceited, that rather than release themselves, and live in another world, from another centre, they'd — "

.   .   .

"I can't say it is love I have to offer — and it isn't love I want. It is something much more impersonal and harder — and rarer."

There was a silence, out of which she said:

"You mean you don't love me?"

She suffered furiously, saying that.

"Yes, if you like to put it like that. Though perhaps that isn't true. I don't know. At any rate, I don't feel the emotion of love for you — no, and I don't want to. Because it gives out in the last issues."

"Love gives out in the last issues?" she asked, feeling numb to the lips.

"Yes, it does. At the very last, one is alone, beyond the influence of love. There is a real impersonal me, that is beyond love, beyond any emotional relationship. So it is with you. But we want to delude ourselves that love is the root. It isn't. It is only the branches. The root is beyond love, a naked kind of isolation, an isolated me, that does *not* meet and mingle, and never can."

She watched him with wide, troubled eyes. His face was incandescent in its abstract earnestness.

"And you mean you can't love?" she asked, in trepidation.

"Yes, if you like. I have loved. But there is a beyond, where there is not love."

She could not submit to this. She felt it swooning over her. But she could not submit.

"But how do you know — if you have never *really* loved?" she asked.

"It is true what I say; there is a beyond, in you, in me, which is further

222than love, beyond the scope, as stars are beyond the scope of vision, some of them."

"Then there is no love," cried Ursula.

"Ultimately, no, there is something else. But, ultimately, there *is* no love."

Ursula was given over to this statement for some moments. Then she half rose from her chair, saying, in a final, repellent voice:

"Then let me go home—what am I doing here?"

"There is the door, " he said. "You are a free agent."

He was suspended finely and perfectly in this extremity. She hung motionless for some seconds, then she sat down again.

"If there is no love, what is there?" she cried, almost jeering.

"Something," he said, looking at her, battling with his soul, with all his might.

"What?"

He was silent for a long time, unable to be in communication with her while she was in this state of opposition.

"There is," he said, in a voice of pure abstraction, "a final me which is stark and impersonal and beyond responsibility. So there is a final you. And it is there I would want to meet you—not in the emotional, loving plane—but there beyond, where there is no speech and no terms of agreement. There we are two stark, unknown beings, two utterly strange creatures, I would want to approach you, and you me. And there could be no obligation, because there is no standard for action there, because no understanding has been reaped from that plane. It is quite inhuman—so there can be no calling to book, in any form whatsoever—because one is outside the pale of all that is accepted, and nothing known applies. One can only follow the impulse, taking that which lies in front, and responsible for nothing, asked for nothing, giving nothing, only each taking according to the primal desire."

Ursula listened to this speech, her mind dumb and almost senseless, what he said was so unexpected and so untoward.

"It is just purely selfish," she said.

"If it is pure, yes. But it isn't selfish at all. Because I don't *know* what I want of you. I deliver *myself* over to the unknown, in coming to you. I am without reserves or defenses, stripped entirely, into the unknown. Only there needs the pledge between us, that we will both cast off everything, cast off ourselves even, and cease to be, so that that which is perfectly ourselves can take place in us."

She pondered along her own line of thought.

"But it is because you love me, that you want me?" she persisted.

"No it isn't. It is because I believe in you—if I *do* believe in you."

"Aren't you sure?" she laughed, suddenly hurt.

He was looking at her steadfastly, scarcely heeding what she said.

"Yes, I must believe in you, or else I shouldn't be here saying this," he replied. "But that is all the proof I have. I don't feel any very strong belief at this particular moment."

She disliked him for this sudden relapse into weariness and faithlessness.

· · ·

He knew that Ursula was referred back to him. He knew his life rested with her. But he would rather not live than accept the love she proffered. The old way of love seemed a dreadful bondage, a sort of conscription. What it was in him he did not know, but the thought of love, marriage, and children, and a life lived together, in the horrible privacy of domestic and connubial satisfaction, was repulsive. He wanted something clearer, more open, cooler, as it were. The hot narrow intimacy between man and wife was abhorrent. The way they shut their doors, these married people, and shut themselves into their own exclusive alliance with each other, even in love, disgusted him. It was a whole community of mistrustful couples insulated in private houses or private rooms, always in couples, and no further life, no further immediate, no disinterested relationship admitted: a kaleidoscope of couples, disjoined, separatist, meaningless entities of married couples. True, he hated promiscuity even worse than marriage, and a liaison was only another kind of coupling, reactionary from the legal marriage. Reaction was a greater bore than action.

On the whole, he hated sex, it was such a limitation. It was sex that turned a man into a broken half of a couple, the woman into the other broken half. And he wanted to be single in himself, the woman single in herself. He wanted sex to revert to the level of the other appetites, to be regarded as a functional process, not as a fulfilment. He believed in sex marriage. But beyond this, he wanted a further conjunction, where man had being and woman had being, two pure beings, each constituting the freedom of the other, balancing each other like two poles of one force, like two angels, or two demons.

· · ·

And why? Why should we consider ourselves, men and women, as broken fragments of one whole? It is not true. We are not broken fragments of one whole. Rather we are the singling away into purity and clear being, of things that were mixed. Rather the sex is that which remains in us of the mixed, the unresolved. And passion is the further separating of this mixture, that which is manly being taken into the being of the man, that which is womanly passing to the woman, till the two are clear and whole as angels, the admixture of sex in the highest sense surpassed, leaving two single beings constellated together like two stars.

In the old age, before sex was, we were mixed, each one a mixture. The process of singling into individuality resulted into the great polarisation of sex. The womanly drew to one side, the manly to the other. But the separation was imperfect even then. And so our world-cycle passes. There is now to come the new day, when we are beings each of us, fulfilled in difference. The man is pure man, the woman pure woman, they are perfectly polarised. But there is no longer any of the horrible merging, mingling self-abnegation of love. There is only the pure duality of polarisation, each one free from any contamination of the other. In each, the individual is primal, sex is subordinate, but perfectly polarised. Each has a single, separate being, with its own laws. The man has his pure freedom, the woman hers. Each acknowledges the perfection of the polarised sex-circuit. Each admits the different nature in the other.

• • •

So she withdrew away from Gudrun and from that which she stood for, she turned in spirit towards Birkin again. She had not seen him since the fiasco of his proposal. She did not want to, because she did not want the question of her acceptance thrust upon her. She knew what Birkin meant when he asked her to marry him; vaguely, without putting it into speech, she knew. She knew what kind of love, what kind of surrender he wanted. And she was not at all sure that this was the kind of love that she herself wanted. She was not at all sure that it was this mutual unison in separateness that she wanted. She wanted unspeakable intimacies. She wanted to have him, utterly, finally to have him as her own, oh, so unspeakably, in intimacy. To drink him down—ah, like a life-draught. She made great professions, to herself, of her willingness to warm his foot-soles between her breasts, after the fashion of the nauseous Meredith poem. But only on condition that he, her lover, loved her absolutely, with complete self-abandon. And subtly enough, she knew he would never abandon himself *finally* to her. He did not believe in final self-abandonment. He said it openly. It was his challenge. She was prepared to fight him for it. For she believed in an absolute surrender to love. She believed that love far surpassed the individual. He said the individual was *more* than love, or than any relationship.

• • •

Fusion, fusion, this horrible fusion of two beings, which every woman and most men insisted on, was it not nauseous and horrible anyhow, whether it was a fusion of the spirit or of the emotional body? Hermione saw herself as the perfect Idea, to which all men must come: and Ursula was the perfect Womb, the bath of birth, to which all men must come! And both were horrible. Why could they not remain individuals, limited by their own limits? Why this dreadful all-comprehensiveness, this hateful tyranny? Why not leave the other being free, why try to absorb, or melt, or merge? One might abandon oneself utterly to the *moments*, but not to any other being.

He could not bear to see the rings lying in the pale mud of the road. He picked them up and wiped them unconsciously on his hands. They were the little tokens of the reality of beauty, the reality of happiness in warm creation. But he had made his hands all dirty and gritty.

There was a darkness over his mind. The terrible knot of consciousness that had persisted there like an obsession was broken, gone, his life was dissolved in darkness over his limbs and his body. But there was a point of anxiety in his heart now. He wanted her to come back. He breathed lightly and regularly like an infant, that breathes innocently, beyond the touch of responsibility.

She was coming back. He saw her drifting desultorily under the high hedge, advancing towards him slowly. He did not move, he did not look again. He was as if asleep, at peace, slumbering and utterly relaxed.

She came up and stood before him, hanging her head.

"See what a flower I found you," she said, wistfully holding a piece of purple-red bell-heather under his face. He saw the clump of coloured bells, and the tree-like, tiny branch: also her hands, with their over-fine, over-sensitive skin.

'Pretty!" he said, looking up at her with a smile, taking the flower. Everything had become simple again, quite simple, the complexity gone into nowhere. But he badly wanted to cry: except that he was weary and bored by emotion.

Then a hot passion of tenderness for her filled his heart. He stood up and looked into her face. It was new, and oh, so delicate in its luminous wonder and fear. He put his arms round her, and she hid her face on his shoulder.

226   It was peace, just simple peace, as he stood folding her quietly there on the open lane. It was peace at last. The old, detestable world of tension had passed away at last, his soul was strong and at ease.

Jean-Paul Sartre

from Being and Nothingness

Jean-Paul Sartre (1905–1980) was the main figure in the philosophical and literary movement called Existentialism, which excited all of Europe and then America in the years immediately following World War II. His main philosophical work, a weighty tome forbiddingly entitled Being and Nothingness, *attempted nothing less than a thorough reexamination of the very nature of human nature and the "lived experience" through which we define our lives. Sartre's conclusion is that there is no such thing as "human nature," for what defines us above all is our freedom, the fact that we are not determined by nature to be a definitive sort of being. Much of the book is concerned with the tension between our inalienable sense of freedom ("transcendence") and the extent to which we find and feel ourselves caught in the contingencies of our lives, brute facts (our "facticity") over which we may have had no control. The struggle of human existence, Sartre tells us, is largely defined by that tension between what we seem to be and what we want to think of ourselves; there is no escaping the twin pitfalls of "bad faith"—concluding erroneously that one indeed* is *what one seems to be or fantasizing a freedom unrestrained by the facts of our daily existence.*

It is in the context of this struggle that love appears in our lives. Accordingly, Sartre's vision of love is anything but blissful. In an early essay, The Emotions, *Sartre briefly argues that emotions in general and love in particular were forms of "escape behavior" in which we try (unsuccessfully) to deny an intolerable reality. In* Being and Nothingness, *he argues that love is one device among others to overcome the intolerable reality of another person! In ourselves, we struggle with the tension between what we are and what we would like to be, but when other people enter the picture this tension becomes complicated by the fact that other people, too, would like us to be a certain way, subservient to and safe for them. This "being-for-others" introduces a new arena of conflict, a battle between one's sense of one's own freedom and the determination of one's being by another person. In one of his most famous plays,* No Exit, *Sartre sums it up in a much-quoted phrase, "Hell is other people." Sexual desire and activity, under-*

*stood in this context, are neither physiological urgency nor mere recrea-
tion. The body becomes an instrument of battle, and sex is nothing less
than the strategic attempt to undermine the other's freedom by "turning
the other into flesh." Love, in turn, is a strategy, an ongoing struggle for
self-identity and not a blissful "merging." It is a strategy that cannot be
successful, however, for lovers like everyone else exist as irreducible tensions
of facticity, free consciousness, and "being-for-others." Love is bound to fail
and, sooner or later, turns into hatred, indifference, or even sadomaso-
chism.*

*And yet, Sartre maintained a lifelong love relationship with Simone de
Beauvoir. To be sure, Sartre's personality was difficult and often perverse;
he seemed to have no sense of fidelity, and in his self-absorbed insensitivity
he could be cruel. But his enduring love of Simone seems at odds with his
theory of love, as striking and as powerful as that may be.*

I. First Attitude Toward Others: Love,
Language, Masochism

Everything which may be said of me in my relations with the Other applies
to him as well. While I attempt to free myself from the hold of the Other,
the Other is trying to free himself from mine; while I seek to enslave the
Other, the Other seeks to enslave me. We are by no means dealing with unilateral relations with an object-in-itself, but with reciprocal and moving relations. The following descriptions of concrete behavior must therefore be
envisaged within the perspective of *conflict*. Conflict is the original meaning of being-for-others.

• • •

These projects put me in direct connection with the Other's freedom. It
is in this sense that love is a conflict. We have observed that the Other's
freedom is the foundation of my being. But precisely because I exist by
means of the Other's freedom, I have no security; I am in danger in this
freedom. It moulds my being and *makes me be*, it confers values upon me
and removes them from me; and my being receives from it a perpetual passive escape from self. Irresponsible and beyond reach, this protean freedom
in which I have engaged myself can in turn engage me in a thousand different ways of being. My project of recovering my being can be realized only if
I get hold of this freedom and reduce it to being a freedom subject to my
freedom. At the same time it is the only way in which I can act on the free
negation of interiority by which the Other constitutes me as an Other; that
is the only way in which I can prepare the way for a future identification of

the Other with me. This will be clearer perhaps if we study the problem from a purely psychological aspect. Why does the lover want to be *loved?* If Love were in fact a pure desire for physical possession, it could in many cases be easily satisfied. Proust's hero, for example, who installs his mistress in his home, who can see her and possess her at any hour of the day, who has been able to make her completely dependent on him economically, ought to be free from worry. Yet we know that he is, on the contrary, continually gnawed by anxiety. Through her consciousness Albertine escapes Marcel even when he is at her side, and that is why he knows relief only when he gazes on her while she sleeps. It is certain then that the lover wishes to capture a "consciousness." But why does he wish it? And how?

The notion of "ownership," by which love is so often explained, is not actually primary. Why should I want to appropriate the Other if it were not precisely that the Other makes me be? But this implies precisely a certain mode of appropriation; it is the Other's freedom as such that we want to get hold of. Not because of a desire for power. The tyrant scorns love, he is content with fear. If he seeks to win the love of his subjects, it is for political reasons; and if he finds a more economical way to enslave them, he adopts it immediately. On the other hand, the man who wants to be loved does not desire the enslavement of the beloved. He is not bent on becoming the object of passion which flows forth mechanically. He does not want to possess an automaton, and if we want to humiliate him, we need only try to persuade him that the beloved's passion is the result of a psychological determinism. The lover will then feel that both his love and his being are cheapened. If Tristan and Isolde fall madly in love because of a love potion, they are less interesting. The total enslavement of the beloved kills the love of the lover. The end is surpassed; if the beloved is transformed into an automaton, the lover finds himself alone. Thus the lover does not desire to possess the beloved as one possesses a thing; he demands a special type of appropriation. He wants to possess a freedom as freedom.

On the other hand, the lover can not be satisfied with that superior form of freedom which is a free and voluntary engagement. Who would be content with a love given as pure loyalty to a sworn oath? Who would be satisfied with the words, "I love you because I have freely engaged myself to love you and because I do not wish to go back on my word." Thus the lover demands a pledge, yet is irritated by a pledge. He wants to be loved by a freedom but demands that this freedom as freedom should no longer be free. He wishes that the Other's freedom should determine itself to become love—and this not only at the beginning of the affair but at each instant—

and at the same time he wants this freedom to be captured *by itself*, to turn back upon itself, as in madness, as in a dream, so as to will its own captivity. This captivity must be a resignation that is both free and yet chained in our hands. In love it is not a determinism of the passions which we desire in the Other nor a freedom beyond reach; it is a freedom which *plays the role of* a determinism of the passions and which is caught in its own role. For himself the lover does not demand that he be the *cause* of this radical modification of freedom but that he be the unique and privileged occasion of it. In fact he could not want to be the cause of it without immediately submerging the beloved in the midst of the world as a tool which can be transcended. That is not the essence of love. On the contrary, in love the Lover wants to be "the whole World" for the beloved. This means that he puts himself on the side of the world; he is the one who assumes and symbolizes the world; he is a *this* which includes all other *thises*. He is and consents to be an *object*. But on the other hand, he wants to be the object in which the Other's freedom consents to lose itself, the object in which the Other consents to find his being and his *raison d'être* as his second facticity—the object-limit of transcendence, that toward which the Other's transcendence transcends all other objects but which it can in no way transcend. And everywhere he desires the circle of the Other's freedom; that is, at each instant as the Other's freedom accepts this limit to his transcendence, this acceptance is *already* present as the motivation of the acceptance considered. It is in the capacity of an end already chosen that the lover wishes to be chosen as an end. This allows us to grasp what basically the lover demands of the beloved; he does not want to *act* on the Other's freedom but to exist *a priori* as the objective limit of this freedom; that is, to be given at one stroke along with it and in its very upsurge as the limit which the freedom must accept in order to be free. By this very fact, what he demands is a limiting, a gluing down of the Other's freedom by itself; this limit of structure is in fact a *given*, and the very appearance of the given as the limit of freedom means that the freedom *makes itself exist* within the given by being its own prohibition against surpassing it. This prohibition is envisaged by the lover *simultaneously* as something lived—that is, something suffered (in a word, as a facticity) and as something freely consented to. It must be freely consented to since it must be effected only with the upsurge of a freedom which chooses itself as freedom. But it must be only what is lived since it must be an impossibility always present, a facticity which surges back to the heart of the Other's freedom. This is expressed psychologically by the demand that the free decision to love me, which the beloved formerly has taken, must slip in as a magically determining motivation *within* his present free engagement.

. . .

My original attempt to get hold of the Other's free subjectivity through his objectivity-for-me is *sexual desire*. Perhaps it will come as a surprise to see a phenomenon which is usually classified among "psycho-physiological reactions" now mentioned on the level of primary attitudes which manifest our original mode of realizing Being-for-Others. For the majority of psychologists indeed, desire, as a fact of consciousness, is in strict correlation with the nature of our sexual organs, and it is only in connection with an elaborate study of these that sexual desire can be understood. But since the differentiated structure of the body (mammalian, viviparous, *etc.*) and consequently the particular sexual structure (uterus, Fallopian tubes, ovaries, *etc.*) are in the domain of absolute contingency and in no way derive from the ontology of "consciousness" or of the *Dasein*, it seems that the same must be true for sexual desire. Just as the sex organs are a contingent and particular formation of our body, so the desire which corresponds to them would be a contingent modality of our psychic life; that is, it would be described only on the level of an empirical psychology based on biology. This is indicated sufficiently by the term *sex instinct*, which is reserved for desire and all the psychic structures which refer to it. The term "instinct" always in fact qualifies contingent formations of psychic life which have the double character of being co-extensive with all the duration of this life — or in any case of not deriving from our "history" — and of nevertheless not being such that they can not be deduced as belonging to the very essence of the psychic. This is why existential philosophies have not believed it necessary to concern themselves with sexuality. Heidegger, in particular, does not make the slightest allusion to it in his existential analytic with the result that his *Dasein* appears to us as asexual. Of course one may consider that it is contingent for "human reality" to be specified as "masculine" or "feminine"; of course one may say that the problem of sexual differentiation has nothing to do with that of *Existence* (*Existenz*) since man and woman equally exist.

These reasons are not wholly convincing. That sexual differentiation lies within the domain of facticity we accept without reservation. But does this mean that the For-itself is sexual "accidentally," by the pure contingency of having this particular body? Can we admit that this tremendous matter of the sexual life comes as a kind of addition to the human condition? Yet it appears at first glance that desire and its opposite, sexual repulsion, are fundamental structures of being-for-others. It is evident that if sexuality derives its origin from sex as a physiological and contingent determination of man, it can not be indispensable to the being of the For-Others. But do we not have the right to ask whether the problem is not perchance of the same order as that which we encountered apropos of sensations and sense organs? Man, it is said, is a sexual being because he possesses a sex. And if the reverse were true? If sex were only the instrument and, so to speak, the *image* of a fundamental sexuality? If man possessed a sex only because he is originally and fundamentally a sexual being as a being who exists in the world in relation with other men? Infantile sexuality precedes the physiological maturation of the sex organs. Men who have become eunuchs do not thereby cease to feel desire. Nor do many old men. The fact of being able to *make use of* a sex organ fit to fertilize and to procure enjoyment represents only one phase and one aspect of our sexual life. There is one mode of sexuality "with the possibility of satisfaction," and the developed sex represents and makes concrete this possibility. But there are other modes of sexuality of the type which can not get satisfaction, and if we take these modes into account we are forced to recognize that sexuality appears with birth and disappears only with death. Moreover neither the tumescence of the penis nor any other physiological phenomenon can ever explain or provoke sexual desire—no more than the vaso-constriction or the dilation of the pupils (or the simple consciousness of these physiological modifications) will be able to explain or to provoke fear. In one case as in the other although the body plays an important role, we must—in order to understand it—refer to being-in-the-world and to being-for-others. I desire a human being, not an insect or a mollusk, and I desire him (or her) as he is and as I am in situation in the world and as he is an Other for me and as I am an Other for him.

Simone de Beauvoir

from The Second Sex

Simone de Beauvoir (1908–1986) is the author of controversial books about feminism, death, and aging as well as books on moral philosophy, many novels, and a multivolume autobiography in which she provides a rich narrative of her rich and tumultuous literary, personal, and political life in Paris. She is perhaps most famous for her book The Second Sex *(1949), an attack on the notion of "the eternal feminine" which is often and rightly credited as the beginning of contemporary feminism. In that book, she both extends and challenges the philosophy of her lifelong companion, Jean-Paul Sartre, who had developed a philosophical portrait of human nature as both essentially free and inescapably "situated," subject to (but never wholly determined by) the force of circumstances and unavoidably vulnerable to other people.*

She begins the selection here by declaring that "the word love *has by no means the same sense for both sexes," and much of her discussion concerns the faulty projections that male philosophers (and males in general) have foisted onto women and which women, much to their disadvantage, have accepted for themselves. Like Sartre, she insists from the very beginning that love is a matter of culture and interpersonal dynamics, not "nature." A woman "chooses to desire her enslavement," and she can choose not to. But it does not follow that a woman can easily refuse love; it remains, for most women, "irresistible." The problem is that happiness in love for a woman is to be recognized as part of a man, or rather, a god, and she is forever resigned to second place. Furthermore, the gods are inevitably flawed, and when gods fall, she tells us, they become frauds. Thus her disillusion, her sense of wasted sacrifice. The alternative she suggests, "genuine love," is "the mutual recognition of two liberties." Neither would give up freedom and independence, and neither would be mutilated by love. (Kathryn Pauly Morgan gives a sympathetic account of de Beauvoir's argument and applies it to our own society.)*

The Woman in Love

The word *love* has by no means the same sense for both sexes, and this is one cause of the serious misunderstandings that divide them. Byron well said: "Man's love is of man's life a thing apart; 'Tis woman's whole exist-ence." Nietzsche expresses the same idea in *The Gay Science*:

The single word love in fact signifies two different things for man and woman. What woman understands by love is clear enough: it is not only devotion, it is a total gift of body and soul, without reservation, without re-gard for anything whatever. This unconditional nature of her love is what makes it a *faith*, the only one she has. As for man, if he loves a woman, what he *wants* is that love from her; he is in consequence far from postulat-ing the same sentiment for himself as for woman; if there should be men who also felt that desire for complete abandonment, upon my word, they would not be men.

Men have found it possible to be passionate lovers at certain times in their lives, but there is not one of them who could be called "a great lover"; in their most violent transports, they never abdicate completely; even on their knees before a mistress, what they still want is to take possession of her; at the very heart of their lives they remain sovereign subjects; the be-loved woman is only one value among others; they wish to integrate her into their existence and not to squander it entirely on her. For woman, on the contrary, to love is to relinquish everything for the benefit of a master. As Cécile Sauvage puts it: "Woman must forget her own personality when she is in love. It is a law of nature. A woman is nonexistent without a master. Without a master, she is a scattered bouquet."

The fact is that we have nothing to do here with laws of nature. It is the difference in their situations that is reflected in the difference men and women show in their conceptions of love. The individual who is a subject, who is himself, if he has the courageous inclination toward transcendence, endeavors to extend his grasp on the world; he is ambitious, he acts. But an inessential creature is incapable of sensing the absolute at the heart of her subjectivity; a being doomed to immanence cannot find self-realization in acts. Shut up in the sphere of the relative, destined to the male from child-hood, habituated to seeing in him a superb being whom she cannot possi-bly equal, the woman who has not repressed her claim to humanity will dream of transcending her being toward one of these superior beings, of amalgamating herself with the sovereign subject. There is no other way out for her than to lose herself, body and soul, in him who is represented to her as the absolute, as the essential. Since she is anyway doomed to depen-dence, she will prefer to serve a god rather than obey tyrants—parents, hus-band, or protector. She chooses to desire her enslavement so ardently that it will seem to her the expression of her liberty; she will try to rise above her situation as inessential object by fully accepting it; through her flesh, her feelings, her behavior, she will enthrone him as supreme value and reality: she will humble herself to nothingness before him. Love becomes for her a religion.

As we have seen, the adolescent girl wishes at first to identify herself with males; when she gives that up, she then seeks to share in their masculinity by having one of them in love with her; it is not the individuality of this one or that one which attracts her; she is in love with man in general. "And you, the men I shall love, how I await you!" writes Irène Reweliotty. "How I rejoice to think I shall know you soon: especially You, the first." Of course the male is to belong to the same class and race as hers, for sexual privilege is in play only within this frame. If man is to be a demigod, he must first of all be a human being, and to the colonial officer's daughter the native is not a man. If the young girl gives herself to an "inferior," it is for the reason that she wishes to degrade herself because she believes she is unworthy of love; but normally she is looking for a man who represents male superiority. She is soon to ascertain that many individuals of the favored sex are sadly contingent and earthbound, but at first her presumption is favorable to them; they are called on less to prove their worth than to avoid too gross a disproof of it—which accounts for many mistakes, some of them serious. A naive young girl is caught by the gleam of virility, and in her eyes male worth is shown, according to circumstances, by physical strength, distinction of manner, wealth, cultivation, intelligence, authority, social status, a military uniform; but what she always wants is for her lover to represent the essence of manhood.

Familiarity is often sufficient to destroy his prestige; it may collapse at the first kiss, or in daily association, or during the wedding night. Love at a distance, however, is only a fantasy, not a real experience. The desire for love becomes a passionate love only when it is carnally realized. Inversely, love can arise as a result of physical intercourse; in this case the sexually dominated woman acquires an exalted view of a man who at first seemed to her quite insignificant.

But it often happens that a woman succeeds in deifying none of the men she knows. Love has a smaller place in woman's life than has often been supposed. Husband, children, home, amusements, social duties, vanity, sexuality, career, are much more important. Most women dream of a *grand amour*, a soul-searing love. They have known substitutes, they have been close to it; it has come to them in partial, bruised, ridiculous, imperfect, mendacious forms; but very few have truly dedicated their lives to it.

236   The *grandes amoureuses* are most often women who have not frittered
themselves away in juvenile affairs; they have first accepted the traditional
feminine destiny: husband, home, children; or they have known pitiless solitude; or they have banked on some enterprise that has been more or less of
a failure. And when they glimpse the opportunity to salvage a disappoint-
ing life by dedicating it to some superior person, they desperately give
themselves up to this hope. Mlle Aïssé, Juliette Drouet, and Mme d'Agoult
were almost thirty when their love-life began, Julie de Lespinasse not far
from forty. No other aim in life which seemed worth while was open to
them, love was their only way out.

Even if they can choose independence, this road seems the most attractive to a majority of women: it is agonizing for a woman to assume responsibility for her life. Even the male, when adolescent, is quite willing to turn
to older women for guidance, education, mothering; but customary attitudes, the boy's training, and his own inner imperatives forbid him to content himself in the end with the easy solution of abdication; to him such affairs with older women are only a stage through which he passes. It is man's
good fortune—in adulthood as in early childhood—to be obliged to take
the most arduous roads, but the surest; it is woman's misfortune to be surrounded by almost irresistible temptations; everything incites her to follow
the easy slopes; instead of being invited to fight her own way up, she is told
that she has only to let herself slide and she will attain paradises of enchantment. When she perceives that she has been duped by a mirage, it is
too late; her strength has been exhausted in a losing venture.

•   •   •

The supreme goal of human love, as of mystical love, is identification
with the loved one. The measure of values, the truth of the world, are in his
consciousness; hence it is not enough to serve him. The woman in love tries
to see with his eyes; she reads the books he reads, prefers the pictures and
the music he prefers; she is interested only in the landscapes she sees with
him, in the ideas that come from him; she adopts his friendships, his enmities, his opinions; when she questions herself, it is his reply she tries to hear;
she wants to have in her lungs the air he has already breathed; the fruits
and flowers that do not come from his hands have no taste and no fra-
grance. Her idea of location in space, even, is upset: the center of the world
is no longer the place where she is, but that occupied by her lover; all roads
lead to his home, and from it. She uses his words, mimics his gestures, acquires his eccentricities and his tics. "I am Heathcliffe," says Catherine in
Wuthering Heights; that is the cry of every woman in love; she is another

is another incarnation of her loved one, his reflection, his double: she is *he*. She lets her own world collapse in contingence, for she really lives in his.

The supreme happiness of the woman in love is to be recognized by the loved man as a part of himself; when he says "we," she is associated and identified with him, she shares his prestige and reigns with him over the rest of the world; she never tires of repeating — even to excess — this delectable "we." As one necessary to a being who is absolute necessity, who stands forth in the world seeking necessary goals and who gives her back the world in necessary form, the woman in love acquires in her submission that magnificent possession, the absolute. It is this certitude that gives her lofty joys; she feels exalted to a place at the right hand of God. Small matter to her to have only second place if she has *her* place, forever, in a most wonderfully ordered world. So long as she is in love and is loved by and necessary to her loved one, she feels herself wholly justified: she knows peace and happiness. Such was perhaps the lot of Mlle Aïsse with the Chevalier d'Aydie before religious scruples troubled his soul, or that of Juliette Drouet in the mighty shadow of Victor Hugo.

But this glorious felicity rarely lasts. No man really is God. The relations sustained by the mystic with the divine Absence depend on her fervor alone; but the deified man, who is not God, is present. And from this fact are to come the torments of the woman in love. Her most common fate is summed up in the famous words of Julie de Lespinasse: "Always, my dear friend, I love you, I suffer and I await you." To be sure, suffering is linked with love for men also; but their pangs are either of short duration or not overly severe. Benjamin Constant wanted to die on account of Mme Récamier: he was cured in a twelvemonth. Stendhal regretted Métilde for years, but it was a regret that perfumed his life without destroying it. Whereas woman, in assuming her role as the inessential, accepting a total dependence, creates a hell for herself. Every woman in love recognizes herself in Hans Andersen's little mermaid who exchanged her fishtail for feminine legs through love and then found herself walking on needles and live coals. It is not true that the loved man is absolutely necessary, above chance and circumstance, and the woman is not necessary to him; he is not really in a position to justify the feminine being who is consecrated to his worship, and he does not permit himself to be possessed by her.

An authentic love should assume the contingence of the other; that is to say, his lacks, his limitations, and his basic gratuitousness. It would not pretend to be a mode of salvation, but a human inter-relation. Idolatrous love attributes an absolute value to the loved one, a first falsity that is brilliantly apparent to all outsiders. "*He* isn't worth all that love," is whispered around the woman in love, and posterity wears a pitying smile at the thought of certain pallid heroes, like Count Guibert. It is a searing disappointment to the woman to discover the faults, the mediocrity of her idol. Novelists, like Colette, have often depicted this bitter anguish. The disillusion is still more cruel than that of the child who sees the father's prestige crumble, because the woman has herself selected the one to whom she has given over her entire being.

Even if the chosen one is worthy of the profoundest affection, his truth is of the earth, earthy, and it is no longer this mere man whom the woman loves as she kneels before a supreme being; she is duped by that spirit of seriousness which declines to take values as incidental—that is to say, declines to recognize that they have their source in human existence. Her bad faith raises barriers between her and the man she adores. She offers him incense, she bows down, but she is not a friend to him since she does not realize that he is in danger in the world, that his projects and his aims are as fragile as he is; regarding him as the Faith, the Truth, she misunderstands his freedom—his hesitancy and anguish of spirit. This refusal to apply a human measuring scale to the lover explains many feminine paradoxes. The woman asks a favor from her lover. Is it granted? Then he is generous, rich, magnificent; he is kingly, he is divine. Is it refused? Then he is avaricious, mean, cruel; he is a devilish or a bestial creature. One might be tempted to object: if a "yes" is such an astounding and superb extravagance, should one be surprised at a "no"? If the "no" discloses such abject selfishness, why wonder so much at the "yes"? Between the superhuman and the inhuman is there no place for the human?

A fallen god is not a man: he is a fraud; the lover has no other alternative than to prove that he really is this king accepting adulation—or to confess himself a usurper. If he is no longer adored, he must be trampled on. In virtue of that glory with which she has haloed the brow of her beloved, the woman in love forbids him any weakness; she is disappointed and vexed if he does not live up to the image she has put in his place. If he gets tired or careless, if he gets hungry or thirsty at the wrong time, if he makes a mistake or contradicts himself, she asserts that he is "not himself" and she makes a grievance of it. In this indirect way she will go so far as to take him to task for any of his ventures that she disapproves; she judges her judge, and she denies him his liberty so that he may deserve to remain her master. Her worship sometimes finds better satisfaction in his absence than in his presence; as we have seen, there are women who devote themselves to dead or otherwise inaccessible heroes, so that they may never have to face them in person, for beings of flesh and blood would be fatally contrary to their dreams. Hence such disillusioned sayings as: "One must not believe in Prince Charming. Men are only poor creatures," and the like. They would not seem to be dwarfs if they had not been asked to be giants.

Genuine love ought to be founded on the mutual recognition of two liberties; the lovers would then experience themselves both as self and as other: neither would give up transcendence, neither would be mutilated; together they would manifest values and aims in the world. For the one and the other, love would be revelation of self by the gift of self and enrichment of the world.

. . .

But most often woman knows herself only as different, relative; her *pour-autrui*, relation to others, is confused with her very being; for her, love is not an intermediary "between herself and herself" because she does not attain her subjective existence; she remains engulfed in this loving woman whom man has not only revealed, but created. Her salvation depends on this despotic free being that has made her and can instantly destroy her. She lives in fear and trembling before this man who holds her destiny in his hands without quite knowing it, without quite wishing to. She is in danger through an other, an anguished and powerless onlooker at her own fate. Involuntary tyrant, involuntary executioner, this other wears a hostile visage in spite of her and of himself. And so, instead of the union sought for, the woman in love knows the most bitter solitude there is; instead of co-operation, she knows struggle and not seldom hate. For woman, love is a supreme effort to survive by accepting the dependence to which she is condemned; but even with consent a life of dependency can be lived only in fear and servility.

Men have vied with one another in proclaiming that love is woman's supreme accomplishment. "A woman who loves as a woman becomes only the more feminine," says Nietzsche; and Balzac: "Among the first-rate, man's life is fame, woman's life is love. Woman is man's equal only when she makes her life a perpetual offering, as that of man is perpetual action." But therein, again, is a cruel deception, since what she offers, men are in no wise anxious to accept. Man has no need of the unconditional devotion he claims, nor of the idolatrous love that flatters his vanity; he accepts them only on condition that he need not satisfy the reciprocal demands these attitudes imply. He preaches to woman that she should give—and her gifts bore him to distraction; she is left in embarrassment with her useless offer-

240   ings, her empty life. On the day when it will be possible for woman to love not in her weakness but in her strength, not to escape herself but to find herself, not to abase herself but to assert herself—on that day love will become for her, as for man, a source of life and not of mortal danger. In the meantime, love represents in its most touching form the curse that lies heavily upon woman confined in the feminine universe, woman mutilated, insufficient unto herself. The innumerable martyrs to love bear witness against the injustice of a fate that offers a sterile hell as ultimate salvation.

Philip Slater

from The Pursuit of Loneliness

*Philip Slater was deeply influenced by Freud and Marx. He first became known in the sixties with his scholarly work in classics (*The Glory of Hera*) in which he demythologizes the whitewashed vision we have of Greek mythology. Ancient Greece was a cruel and brutal tribal society which included human sacrifice and mayhem, not just Socratic wisdom. In* The Pursuit of Loneliness *he similarly demythologizes some of our own favorite "myths," including American individualism and the supposed rarity of romantic love. Romantic love, he argues, is the result of contrived deprivation, turning what is and should be plentiful and readily available (sexual satisfaction) into a rare commodity.*

Putting Pleasure to Work

A recent study by an English psychologist found that neurotic anxiety was a very good predictor of success and achievement, both at the individual and at the national level, confirming a long-felt suspicion that something sick forms the driving force for our civilization. Freud argued that "culture . . . obtains a great part of the mental energy it needs by subtracting it from sexuality," and saw civilization as an exchange of happiness for security. He felt this process was probably necessary and possibly desirable, but was troubled by it: "One is bound to conclude that the whole thing is not worth the effort and that in the end it can only produce a state of things which no individual will be able to bear."

The urgency of this prophecy grows with the level of anxious and irritable desperation in our society. To assess the validity of Freud's argument that civilization is a parasite on man's eroticism becomes an increasingly pressing task, particularly since the few empirical studies available to us all tend to confirm his hypothesis.

There is one aspect of Freud's theory which is contradicted by the existing evidence. Freud argued that society "borrows" from sexuality in order to neutralize human aggressiveness, although the mechanism through which this was supposed to occur was not described. What evidence there is, however, suggests that restrictions on sexual expression, far from neutralizing aggression, tend to arouse it, just as the frustration–aggression hypothesis would lead us to expect. Apparently sexual restrictions have some more direct relation to civilization: a relationship so powerful that increases in aggressiveness can be tolerated as an unfortunate side effect—or at least have been so tolerated until now.

The nature of the relationship seems to have something to do with energy: "civilized" people are usually described as more energetic or restless than their nonliterate counterparts. This does not mean that they *possess* more energy: even given the same diet the correlation will appear. The difference we are concerned with here lies in the *utilization* of energy. There appears to be, in other words, some difference in motivation.

Konrad Lorenz once remarked that in all organisms locomotion is increased by a bad environment. We might then say that sexual restrictions are a way of artificially creating a bad environment, and hence increasing locomotion. Unfortunately we do not know what constitutes a "bad environment" in this sense, nor why it increases locomotion. Presumably a bad environment is one that is not gratifying, and the locomotion is simply a quest for more adequate or complete gratification. This equation between locomotion and lack of gratification makes us think of holding a carrot in front of a donkey, or an animal on a treadmill. In both cases the constant output of energy by the animal depends upon the sought gratification being withheld. Once gratified, the animal would come to a halt, and further locomotion would have to wait upon adequate deprivation

. . .

But there is a dilemma here. If the donkey never eats he will die, but if he does eat he will stop. How can we get a man to work endlessly for a reward which never comes? Obviously we can never avoid intermittency so long as we are dealing with simple bodily satisfactions, which are easily extinguished. It is clear that a man will work hard for food so long as it is scarce. But what about when he has a full belly? In order to ensure a steady output of energy we must create some sort of artificial scarcity, for it is, paradoxically, only through such scarcity that an abiding surplus of energy can be assured.

Sexual desire provides far better raw material for such an enterprise, since it is an impulse that is both powerful and plastic. Its importance in this respect becomes immediately apparent when we realize that in some hypothetical state of nature it is the only form of gratification that is *not* scarce. In fact, it is infinite. This is what people have in mind when they say that sex is the recreation of the poor.

Yet there is no society that does not put restrictions on this resource. Out of an infinite plenty is created a host of artificial scarcities. It would obviously repay us to look into this matter, since we have already observed that although we live in the most affluent society ever known, the sense of deprivation and discomfort that pervades it is also unparalleled.

The idea of placing restrictions on sexuality was a stunning cultural invention, more important than the acquisition of fire. In it man found a source of energy which was limitless and unflagging—one which enabled him to build his empires on earth. By the weird device of making his most plentiful resource scarce he managed, after many millennia, to make most of his scarce ones plentiful. On the negative side, however, men have achieved this miracle by making themselves into donkeys, pursuing an inaccessible carrot. We are very elegantly liveried donkeys, it is true, but donkeys all the same. The popular use of the term "treadmill" to note the institutions through which men make their living expresses our dim awareness of this metamorphosis.

This raises three questions: (1) how did man happen to transform himself into a donkey? (2) what were the mechanisms through which it was achieved? (3) what are the present consequences of his success?

Trying to find historical beginnings is a trivial as well as futile enterprise. Men are always inventing new follies, most of which are luckily stillborn. What we need to explain is why the invention of sexual scarcity was successful, and not only survived but grew. Most likely it began with the imposition of restrictions on one group by another: women by men, or losers by conquerors. Perhaps temporary restrictions in the service of birth control began it, or perhaps it began with the capacity to symbolize. In any case, once begun, it has always had a tendency to ramify, to diffuse itself, for scarcity breeds scarcity just as anger breeds anger. Once the concept exists that there is not enough, people will begin to deprive each other of what there is.

What sustained this folly was natural selection. Restless, deprived-feeling tribes had a tendency either to conquer their more contented neighbors or more fully to exploit the resources around them, or both. This cultural superiority was by no means automatic, of course, Without the right kind of environment this restlessness was merely destructive, and many of the institutions that have evolved from various scarcity mechanisms are so cumbersome and costly that they absorb more energy than the scarcity mechanism makes available. The ethnographic literature contains as many societies of this type as it does societies that are simply culturally marginal.

• • •

The mechanisms through which sexual scarcity is created are many and complex, and it should be emphasized strongly that we are not discussing anything as simple as frequency of sexual intercourse or orgasm (although there is growing evidence that these, too, are negatively related to civilization). A man may have intercourse as often as he wishes and still feel deprived, because his desire has attached itself to someone or something unattainable. The root of sexual dissatisfaction is the capacity of man to generate symbols which can attract and trap portions of his libido. Restrictions as to time, place, mode, and partner do not simply postpone release but create an absolute deprivation, because man has the capacity to construct a memory, a concept, a fantasy. Thus while increases in the number, variety, and severity of sexual restrictions may intensify the subjective experience of sexual scarcity, a subsequent trend toward sexual "permissiveness" need not produce a corresponding decrease in scarcity. Once you have trained your dog to prefer cooked meat you can let him run about the stockyard without any qualms. The fundamental mechanism for generating sexual scarcity is to attach sexual interest to inaccessible, nonexistent, or irrelevant objects; and for this purpose man's capacity to symbolize is perfectly designed.

• • •

Romantic love is one scarcity mechanism that deserves special comment. Indeed, its only function and meaning is to transmute that which is plentiful into that which is in short supply. This is done in two ways: first, by inculcating the belief that only one object can satisfy a person's erotic and affectional desires; and second, by fostering a preference for unconsummated, unrequited, interrupted, or otherwise tragic relationships. Although romantic love always verges on the ridiculous (we would find it comic if a man died of starvation because he could not obtain any brussels sprouts) Western peoples generally and Americans in particular have shown an impressive tendency to take it seriously. Why is this so? Why is love made into an artificially scarce commodity, like diamonds, or "genuine" pearls (cf. "true" love)?

To ask such a question is to answer it. We make things scarce in order to increase their value, which in turn makes people work harder for them. Who would spend their lives working for pleasures that could be obtained any time? Who would work for love, when people give it away? But if we were to make some form of it somehow rare, unattainable, and elusive, and to devalue all other forms, we might conceivably inveigle a few rubes to chase after it.

This does not in itself, however, account for the wide diffusion of romantic love. To see its function is not to explain its existence. We can only assume that it derives its strength from some intense emotional experience. Few primitive peoples are familiar with it, and in general it seems to be most highly developed in those cultures in which the parent-child relationship is most exclusive (as opposed to those in which the child-rearing role is diffused among so many people as to approach the communal).

Since romantic love thrives on the absence of prolonged contact with its object one is forced to conclude that it is fundamentally unrelated to the character of the love object, but derives its meaning from prior experience. "Love at first sight" can only be transference, in the psychoanalytic sense, since there is nothing else on which it can be based. Romantic love, in other words, is Oedipal love. It looks backwards, hence its preoccupation with themes of nostalgia and loss. It is fundamentally incestuous, hence its emphasis on obstacles and nonfulfillment, on tragedy and trespass. Its real object is not the actual parent, however, but a fantasy image of that parent which has been retained, ageless and unchanging, in the unconscious.

Romantic love is rare in primitive communities simply because the bond between child and parent is more casual. The child tends to have many caretakers and be sensitive to the fact that there exist many alternative suppliers of love. The modern Western child, brought up in a small detached household does not share this sense of substitutability. His emotional life is heavily bound up in a single person, and the process of spreading this involvement over other people as he grows up is more problematic. Americans must make a life task out of what happens effortlessly (insofar as it need happen at all) in many societies. Most Western children succeed in drawing enough money out of their emotional bank to live on, but some always remain tied up in Oedipal fantasy. Most of us learn early that there is one relationship that is more vital than all the others put together, and we tend both to reproduce this framework in later life and to retain, in fantasy, the original loyalty.

The underlying scarcity mechanism on which romantic love is based is thus the intensification of the parent-child relationship. It creates scarcity by a) inculcating a pattern of concentrating one's search for love onto a single object, and b) focusing one's erotic interest on an object with whom consummation is forbidden. The magnification of the emotionality and

246   exclusiveness of the parent-child bond, combined with the incest taboo, is the prototypical scarcity mechanism.

We can think of this process as a kind of forced savings (indeed, emotional banking was probably the unconscious model for the monetary form). The more we can bind up an individual's erotic involvement in a restricted relationship the less he will seek pleasure in those forms that are readily available. He will consume little and produce much. Savings will increase, profits will be reinvested. So long as he is pursuing what cannot be captured we can relax in the assurance that he will work without cessation into the grave. We have found our donkey.

Shulamith Firestone
from The Dialectic of Sex

Shulamith Firestone is the author of The Dialectic of Sex *(1970) and a founder of Redstockings, a radical feminist group in New York. Her book was quickly recognized as one of the most provocative theoretical statements of the then-fledgling feminist revolution in America. She argues that the inequality of men and women in contemporary society is a product of politics and culture, not of nature, and she rejects traditional sex roles as oppressive and inhuman. Against romantic love, in particular, she raises the charge that this celebrated emotion is in fact something of a conspiracy, a device to "keep women in their place." At the same time, she makes a case against men, who are incapable of love, and for love, not romantic and not between man and woman but, as in classical times, for love as friendship. Ideally, love is a mutual exchange of selves. Yet romantic love as it has developed since the industrial revolution has become the unrewarded sacrifice of women only, defined by an all-consuming need that makes life "hell" and a "holocaust."*

Love

A book on radical feminism that did not deal with love would be a political failure. For love, perhaps even more than childbearing, is the pivot of women's oppression today. I realize this has frightening implications: Do we want to get rid of love?

The panic felt at any threat to love is a good clue to its political significance. Another sign that love is central to any analysis of women or sex psychology is its omission from culture itself, its relegation to "personal life." (And whoever heard of logic in the bedroom?) Yes, it is portrayed in novels, even metaphysics, but in them it is described, or better, recreated, not analyzed. Love has never been *understood*, though it may have been fully *experienced*, and that experience communicated.

There is reason for this absence of analysis: *Women and Love are underpinnings. Examine them and you threaten the very structure of culture.*

The tired question "What were women doing while men created masterpieces?" deserves more than the obvious reply: Women were barred from

248   culture, exploited in their role of mother. Or its reverse: Women had no need for paintings since they created children. Love is tied to culture in much deeper ways than that. Men were thinking, writing, and creating, because women were pouring their energy into those men; women are not creating culture because they are preoccupied with love.

That women live for love and men for work is a truism. Freud was the first to attempt to ground this dichotomy in the individual psyche: the male child, sexually rejected by the first person in his attention, his mother, "sublimates" his "libido"—his reservoir of sexual (life) energies—into long term projects, in the hope of gaining love in a more generalized form; thus he displaces his need for love into a need for recognition. This process does not occur as much in the female: most women never stop seeking direct warmth and approval.

There is also much truth in the clichés that "behind every man there is a woman," and that "women are the power behind [read: voltage in] the throne." (Male) culture was built on the love of women, and at their expense. Women provided the substance of those male masterpieces; and for millennia they have done the work, and suffered the costs, of one-way emotional relationships the benefits of which went to men and to the work of men. So if women are a parasitical class living off, and at the margins of, the male economy, the reverse too is true: *(Male) culture was (and is) parasitical, feeding on the emotional strength of women without reciprocity.*

Moreover, we tend to forget that this culture is not universal, but rather sectarian, presenting only half the spectrum. The very structure of culture itself, as we shall see, is saturated with the sexual polarity, as well as being in every degree run by, for, and in the interests of male society. But while the male half is termed all of culture, men have not forgotten there is a female "emotional" half: They live it on the sly. As the result of their battle to reject the female in themselves (the Oedipus Complex as we have explained it) they are unable to take love seriously as a cultural matter; but they can't do without it altogether. Love is the underbelly of (male) culture just as love is the weak spot of every man, bent on proving his virility in that large male world of "travel and adventure." Women have always known how men need love, and how they deny this need. Perhaps this explains the peculiar contempt women so universally feel for men ("men are so dumb"), for they can see their men are posturing in the outside world.

I

How does this phenomenon "love" operate? Contrary to popular opinion, love is not altruistic. The initial attraction is based on curious admiration (more often today, envy and resentment) for the self-possession, the integrated unity, of the other and a wish to become part of this Self in some way (today, read: intrude or take over), to become important to that psychic balance. The self-containment of the other creates desire (read: a challenge); admiration (envy) of the other becomes a wish to incorporate (possess) its qualities. A clash of selves follows in which the individual attempts to fight off the growing hold over him of the other. Love is the final opening up to (or, surrender to the dominion of) the other. The lover demonstrates to the beloved how he himself would like to be treated. ("I tried so hard to make him fall in love with me that I fell in love with him myself.") Thus love is the height of selfishness: the self attempts to enrich itself through the absorption of another being. Love is being psychically wideopen to another. It is a situation of total emotional vulnerability. Therefore it must be not only the incorporation of the other, but an *exchange* of selves. Anything short of a mutual exchange will hurt one or the other party.

There is nothing inherently destructive about this process. A little healthy selfishness would be a refreshing change. Love between two equals would be an enrichment, each enlarging himself through the other: instead of being one, locked in the cell of himself with only his own experience and view, he could participate in the existence of another—an extra window on the world. This accounts for the bliss that successful lovers experience: Lovers are temporarily freed from the burden of isolation that every individual bears.

But bliss in love is seldom the case: For every successful contemporary love experience, for every short period of enrichment, there are ten destructive love experiences, post-love "downs" of much longer duration—often resulting in the destruction of the individual, or at least an emotional cynicism that makes it difficult or impossible ever to love again. Why should this be so, if it is not actually inherent in the love process itself?

Let's talk about love in its destructive guise—and why it gets that way, referring once more to the work of Theodor Reik. Reik's concrete observation brings him closer than many better minds to understanding the *process* of "falling in love," but he is off insofar as he confuses love as it exists in our present society with love itself. He notes that love is a reaction formation, a cycle of envy, hostility, and possessiveness: He sees that it is preceded by dissatisfaction with oneself, a yearning for something better, created by a discrepancy between the ego and the ego-ideal; That the bliss love produces is due to the resolution of this tension by the substitution, in place of one's own ego-ideal, of the other; And finally that love fades "because the other can't live up to your high ego-ideal any more than you could, and the judgment will be the harsher the higher are the claims on oneself." Thus in Reik's view love wears down just as it is wound up: Dissatisfaction with oneself (whoever heard of falling in love the week one is leaving for Europe?) leads to astonishment at the other person's self-containment; to envy; to hostility; to possessive love; and back again through exactly the same process. This is the love process *today*. But why must it be this way?

Many, for example, Denis de Rougemont in *Love in the Western World*, have tried to draw a distinction between romantic "falling in love" with its "false reciprocity which disguises a twin narcissism" (the Pagan Eros) and an unselfish love for the other person as that person really is (the Christian Agape). De Rougemont attributes the morbid passion of Tristan and Iseult (romantic love) to a vulgarization of specific mystical and religious currents in Western civilization.

I submit that love is essentially a much simpler phenomenon—it becomes complicated, corrupted, or obstructed by *an unequal balance of power*. We have seen that love demands a mutual vulnerability or it turns destructive: the destructive effects of love occur only in a context of inequality. But because sexual inequality has remained a constant—however its *degree* may have varied—the corruption "romantic" love became characteristic of love between the sexes. (It remains for us only to explain why it has steadily increased in Western countries since the medieval period, which we shall attempt to do in the following chapter.)

How does the sex class system based on the unequal power distribution of the biological family affect love between the sexes? In discussing Freudianism, we have gone into the psychic structuring of the individual within the family and how this organization of personality must be different for the male and the female because of their very different relationships to the mother. At present the insular interdependency of the mother/child relationship forces both male and female children into anxiety about losing the mother's love, on which they depend for physical survival. When later (Erich Fromm notwithstanding) the child learns that the mother's love is conditional, to be rewarded the child in return for approved behavior (that is, behavior in line with the mother's own values and personal ego gratification—for she is free to mold the child's "creatively," however she happens to define that), the child's anxiety turns into desperation. This, coinciding with the sexual rejection of the male child by the mother, causes, as we have seen, a schizophrenia in the boy between the emotional and the physical, and in the girl, the mother's rejection, occurring for different reasons, produces an insecurity about her identity in general, creating a lifelong need for approval. (Later her lover replaces her father as a grantor of the necessary surrogate identity—she sees everything through his eyes.) Here originates the hunger for love that later sends both sexes searching in one person after the other for a state of ego security. But because of the early rejection, to the degree that it occurred, the male will be terrified of committing himself, of "opening up" and then being smashed. How this affects his sexuality we have seen: To the degree that a woman is like his mother, the incest taboo operates to restrain his total sexual/emotional commitment; for him to feel safely the kind of total response he first felt for his mother, which was rejected, he must degrade this woman so as to distinguish her from the mother. This behavior reproduced on a larger scale explains many cultural phenomena, including perhaps the ideal love-worship of chivalric times, the forerunner of modern romanticism.

Romantic idealization is partially responsible, at least on the part of men, for a peculiar characteristic of "falling" in love: the change takes place in the lover almost independently of the character of the love object. Occasionally the lover, though beside himself, sees with another rational part of his faculties that, objectively speaking, the one he loves isn't worth all this blind devotion; but he is helpless to act on this, "a slave to love." More often he fools himself entirely. But others can see what is happening ("How on earth he could love her is beyond me!"). This idealization occurs much less frequently on the part of women, as is borne out by Reik's clinical studies. A man must idealize one woman over the rest in order to justify his descent to a lower caste. Woman have no such reason to idealize men— in fact, when one's life depends on one's ability to "psych" men out, such idealization may actually be dangerous—though a fear of male power in general may carry over into relationships with individual men, appearing to be the same phenomenon. But though women know to be inauthentic this male "falling in love," all women, in one way or another, require proof of it from men before they can allow themselves to love (genuinely, in their case) in return. For this idealization process acts to artificially equalize the two parties, a minimum precondition for the development of an uncorrupted love—we have seen that love requires a mutual vulnerability that is impossible to achieve in an unequal power situation. *Thus "falling in love" is no more than the process of alteration of male vision—through idealization, mystification, glorification—that renders void the woman's class inferiority.*

252 However, the woman knows that this idealization, which she works so hard to produce, is a lie, and that it is only a matter of time before he "sees through her." Her life is a hell, vacillating between an all–consuming need for male love and approval to raise her from her class subjection, to persistent feelings of inauthenticity when she does achieve his love. Thus her whole identity hangs in the balance of her love life. She is allowed to love herself only if a man finds her worthy of love.

But if we could eliminate the political context of love between the sexes, would we not have some degree of idealization remaining in the love process itself? I think so. For the process occurs in the same manner whoever the love choice: the lover "opens up" to the other. Because of this fusion of egos, in which each sees and cares about the other as a new self, the beauty/character of the beloved, perhaps hidden to outsiders under layers of defenses, is revealed. "I wonder what she sees in him," then, means not only, "She is a fool, blinded with romanticism," but, "Her love has lent her x–ray vision. Perhaps we are missing something." (Note that this phrase is most commonly used about women. The equivalent phrase about *men's* slavery to love is more often something like, "She has him wrapped around her finger," she has him so "snowed" that he is the last one to see through her.) Increased sensitivity to the real, if hidden, values in the other, however, is not "blindness" or "idealization" but is, in fact, deeper vision. It is only the *false* idealization we have described above that is responsible for the destruction. Thus it is not the process of love itself that is at fault, but its *political*, i.e., unequal *power* context: the who, why, when and where of it is what makes it now such a holocaust.

II
. . .

Simone de Beauvoir said it: "The word love has by no means the same sense for both sexes, and this is one cause of the serious misunderstandings which divide them." Above I have illustrated some of the traditional differences between men and women in love that come up so frequently in parlor discussions of the "double standard," where it is generally agreed: That women are monogamous, better at loving, possessive, "clinging," more interested in (highly involved) "relationships" than in sex per se, and they confuse affection with sexual desire. That men are interested in nothing but a screw (Wham, bam, thank you M'am!), or else romanticize the woman ridiculously; that once sure of her, they become notorious philanderers, never satisfied; that they mistake sex for emotion. All this bears out what we have discussed — the difference in the psychosexual organizations of the two sexes, determined by the first relationship to the mother.

I draw three conclusions based on these differences:

1) That men can't love. (Male hormones?? Women traditionally expect and accept an emotional invalidism in men that they would find intolerable in a woman.)

2) That women's "clinging" behavior is necessitated by their objective social situation.

3) That this situation has not changed significantly from what it ever was.

Men can't love. We have seen why it is that men have difficulty loving and that while men may love, they usually "fall in love"— with their own projected image. Most often they are pounding down a woman's door one day, and thoroughly disillusioned with her the next; but it is rare for women to leave men, and then it is usually for more than ample reason.

It is dangerous to feel sorry for one's oppressor — women are especially prone to this failing — but I am tempted to do it in this case. Being unable to love is hell. This is the way it proceeds: as soon as the man feels any pressure from the other partner to commit himself, he panics and may react in one of several ways:

1) He may rush out and screw ten other women to prove that the first woman has no hold over him. If she accepts this, he may continue to see her on this basis. The other women verify his (false) freedom; periodic arguments about them keep his panic at bay. But the women are a paper tiger, for nothing very deep could be happening with them anyway: he is balancing them against each other so that none of them can get much of him. Many smart women, recognizing this to be only a safety valve on their man's anxiety, give him "a long leash." For the real issue under all the fights about other women is that the man is unable to commit himself.

2) He may consistently exhibit unpredictable behavior, standing her up frequently, being indefinite about the next date, telling her that "my work comes first," or offering a variety of other excuses. That is, though he senses her anxiety, he refuses to reassure her in any way, or even to recognize her anxiety as legitimate. For he *needs* her anxiety as a steady reminder that he is still free, that the door is not entirely closed.

3) When he *is* forced into (an uneasy) commitment, he makes her pay for it: by ogling other women in her presence, by comparing her unfavorably to past girlfriends or movie stars, by snide reminders in front of friends

that she is his "ball and chain," by calling her a "nag," a "bitch," "a shrew," or by suggesting that if he were only a bachelor he would be a lot better off. His ambivalence about women's "inferiority" comes out: by being committed to one, he has somehow made the hated female identification, which he now must repeatedly deny if he is to maintain his self-respect in the (male) community. This steady derogation is not entirely put on: for in fact every other girl suddenly does look a lot better, he can't help feeling he has missed something — and, naturally, his woman is to blame. For he has never given up on the search for the ideal; she has forced him to resign from it. Probably he will go to his grave feeling cheated, never realizing that there isn't much difference between one woman and the other, that it is the loving that *creates* the difference.

There are many variations of straining at the bit. Many men go from one casual thing to another, getting out every time it begins to get hot. And yet to live without love in the end proves intolerable to men just as it does to women. The question that remains for every normal male is, then, *how do I get someone to love me without her demanding an equal commitment in return?*

Women's "clinging" behavior is required by the objective social situation. The female *response* to such a situation of male hysteria at any prospect of mutual commitment was the development of subtle methods of manipulation, to force as much commitment as *could* be forced from men. Over the centuries strategies have been devised, tested, and passed on from mother to daughter in secret tête-à-têtes, passed around at "kaffee-klatsches" ("I never understand what it is women spend so much time talking about!"), or, in recent times, via the telephone. These are not trivial gossip sessions at all (as women prefer men to believe), but desperate strategies for survival. More real brilliance goes into one one-hour coed telephone dialogue about men than into that same coed's four years of college study, or for that matter, than into most male political maneuvers. It is no wonder, then, that even the few women without "family obligations" always arrive exhausted at the starting line of any serious endeavor. It takes one's major energy for the best portion of one's creative years to "make a good catch," and a good part of the rest of one's life to "hold" that catch. ("To be in love can be a full-time job for a woman, like that of a profession for a man.") Women who choose to drop out of this race are choosing a life without love, something that, as we have seen, most *men* don't have the courage to do.

But unfortunately The Manhunt is characterized by an emotional urgency beyond this simple desire for return commitment. It is compounded by the very class reality that produced the male inability to love in the first place. In a male-run society that defines women as an inferior and parasitical class, a woman who does not achieve male approval in some form is doomed. To legitimate her existence, a woman must be *more* than woman, she must continually search for an out from her inferior definition; and men are the only ones in a position to bestow on her this state of grace. But because the woman is rarely allowed to realize herself through activity in the larger (male) society—and when she is, she is seldom granted the recognition she deserves—it becomes easier to try for the recognition of one man than of many; and in fact this is exactly the choice most women make. Thus once more the phenomenon of love, good in itself, is corrupted by its class context: women must have love not only for healthy reasons but actually to validate their existence.

In addition, the continued *economic* dependence of women makes a situation of health love between equals impossible. Women today still live under a system of patronage: With few exceptions, they have the choice, not between either freedom or marriage, but between being either public or private property. Women who merge with a member of the ruling class can at least hope that some of his privilege will, so to speak, rub off. But women without men are in the same situation as orphans: they are a helpless sub-class lacking the protection of the powerful. This is the antithesis of freedom when they are still (negatively) defined by a class situation: for now they are in a situation of *magnified* vulnerability. To participate in one's subjection by choosing one's master often gives the illusion of free choice; but in reality a woman is never free to choose love without external motivations. For her at the present time, the two things, love and status, must remain inextricably intertwined.

Women of high ideals who believed emancipation possible, women who tried desperately to rid themselves of feminine "hangups," to cultivate what they believed to be the greater directness, honesty, and generosity of men, were badly fooled. They found that no one appreciated their intelligent conversation, their high aspirations, their great sacrifices to avoid developing the personalities of their mothers. For much as men were glad to enjoy their wit, their style, their sex, and their candlelight suppers, they always ended up marrying The Bitch, and then, to top it all off, came back to complain of what a horror she was. "Emancipated" women found out that the honesty, generosity, and camaraderie of men was a lie: men were all too glad to use them and then sell them out, in the name of *true* friendship. ("I respect and like you a great deal, but let's be reasonable. . . ." And then there are the men who take her out to discuss Simone de Beauvoir, leaving their wives at home with the diapers.) "Emancipated" women found out that men were far from "good guys" to be emulated; they found out that by imitating male sexual patterns (the roving eye, the search for the ideal, the emphasis on physical attraction, etc.), they were not only not achieving liberation, they were falling into something much worse than what they had given up. They were *imitating*. And they had inoculated themselves with a sickness that had not even sprung from their own psyches. They found that their new "cool" was shallow and meaningless, that their emotions were drying up behind it, that they were aging and becoming decadent: they feared they were losing their ability to love. They had gained nothing by imitating men: shallowness and callowness, and they were not so good at it either, because somewhere inside it still went against the grain.

Thus women who had decided not to marry because they were wise enough to look around and see where it led found that it was marry or nothing. Men gave their commitment only for a price: share (shoulder) his life, stand on his pedestal, become his appendage, or else. Or else—be consigned forever to that limbo of "chicks" who mean nothing or at least not what mother meant. Be the "other woman" for the rest of one's life, used to provoke his wife, prove his virility and/or his independence, discussed by his friends as his latest "interesting" conquest. (For even if she had given up those terms and what they stood for, no male had.) Yes, love means an entirely different thing to men than to women: it means ownership and control; it means jealousy, where he never exhibited it before—when she might have wanted him to (who cares if she is broke or raped until she officially belongs to him: then he is a raging dynamo, a veritable cyclone, because his property, his ego extension have been threatened); it means a growing lack of interest, coupled with a roving eye. Who needs it?

iii

Irving Singer
from The Nature of Love

Irving Singer is professor of philosophy at Massachusetts Institute of Technology and the author of the already classic three-volume study The Nature of Love.

Concepts of Love in the West

There are historians who say that love between men and women, what we would ordinarily think of as sexual love, came into existence only after Western civilization achieved a particular stage of development in the early Middle Ages. Those who have held this view often claim that love was virtually unknown in the ancient world and only a rare occurrence among non-Western societies. Anthropologists, for instance Malinowski in his research with Trobriand Islanders, have documented the fact that Western ideas about love seem to be meaningless in many other cultures, some of them quite advanced; and orientalists have often remarked that before the intrusion of European mores, Eastern thinking about relations between men and women contained little of the West's attempt either to purify sex through love or to make erotic passion into an ideal on its own. This effort, which dominates so much of life in the modern world, is said to have arisen in a particular place—Southern France, or Spain, or Northern Africa—at a particular time in the eleventh or twelfth century, and to have evolved in an uninterrupted manner from then until the twentieth century.

Through this way of thinking about the history of love has often engendered useful scholarship, it is confused in several respects. For one thing, is the view I have been summarizing a theory about behavior or about the history of ideas? Is it claimed that non-Westerners or Europeans in the ancient world did not experience with one another the intimacy, longing, and interpersonal oneness that we associate with sexual love? Even Malinowski notes that while the young Trobrianders defined their relation to one another in terms of sexual interest, easily gratified and generally hedonistic in character, they too experienced strong attachments, emotional dependency, and even occasional jealousy. Surely it is reasonable to assume that people in other lands and in earlier times were not so different from ourselves as to have lived without sexual love until a handful of poets in Provence, or elsewhere, discovered or invented it. It seems much more plausible to think that love, in all its varieties, exists as a complex but common occurrence within human nature as a whole. William James is very persuasive when he says of romantic adoration: "So powerful and instinctive an emotion can never have been recently evolved. But our ideas *about* our emotions, and the esteem in which we hold them, differ very much from one generation to another; and literature . . . is a record of ideas far more than of primordial psychological facts."

In saying this, James correctly implies that the *concept* of sexual love has not existed uniformly and fully developed in all cultures and at all times. There is as little reason to assume a unitary structure in this respect as there would be to think that science or technology has been identical throughout the growth of mankind. What happened in the Middle Ages is important as one among other developments in man's thinking about moral goals, about human possibilities, about sexual ideals that influence his conception of himself whether or not they govern his behavior. Great changes in thought did occur in a particular place, Northern Africa and Southern Europe, at a particular time, around the twelfth century, and very dramatically; and these changes did contribute to a massive flowering that continues into modern consciousness. But the principal events occurred in the history of philosophy and the literary arts. By lending dignity and the sense of rectitude that always comes from conformity to social expectations, ideas about love have also had an effect, sometimes an enormous effect, upon Western behavior. Concepts and, above all, ideals mold and subtly modify our experience of the world. The given is never wholly distinguishable from its interpretation. And though men and women may feign to feel whatever kind of love is approved in their society while really having other interests, the feigning becomes a type of behavior that contributes its own reality. Human nature is itself an interaction between mental constructs acquired through patterns of accumulated experience, individual or communal, and biological mechanisms genetically programmed.

To study the history of love completely, we would have to investigate the ways in which developments of mind—developments in ideation and idealization—are capable of altering behavior while also following a course of evolution within their own domain. That is a task for philosophy and the life sciences, but one in which very little progress has been made as yet. And though I hope my work may be of help in this enterprise, I do not address myself to it in the present book. I wish instead to analyze and clarify the concepts themselves. They diverge considerably, so much so that one may wonder whether there is in the West a common culture or a system of common ideals at any time. The diversities can, however, be systematized to a considerable degree; and I begin by suggesting that Western thinking about sexual love may be categorized in terms of two basic approaches. On the one hand, there is the idealist tradition that Plato codifies for the first time, that Christianity amalgamates with Judaic thought, that courtly love humanizes, and that romanticism redefines in the nineteenth century. On the other hand, there is what I shall call, for want of a better term, the realist tradition that from the very beginnings has rejected the pretensions of idealism as unverifiable, contrary to science, and generally false to what appears in ordinary experience.

In the history of thinking about love, the idealist tradition has always been dominant in the sense that its theories were the most interesting and the most fruitful for later speculation. Early in the development of idealism the concept of love became attached to religious and metaphysical doctrines that sought to penetrate nature's secret mysteries. The realist response took the form of critical disbelief, encouraging reliance upon the verities of sensory experience. Whether as an ideal for changing the world or as a psychological state that mattered to many people, love was to be analyzed in terms of what man could learn about himself through empirical observation. The realist tradition usually turns to the latest science in the hope of attaining accurate insights into nature, including human nature; but only in the twentieth century has science provided the knowledge that realism needed to articulate a vision of its own. In studying realism's past responsiveness to concepts generated by various types of idealism, we can see what realists may finally achieve in the present. We may also find that they can accept more of the idealistic attitude than has often been supposed. Particularly in those areas where idealism furthered humanistic perspectives, an accommodation between the two traditions may now be feasible as never before.

There is one point on which realist and idealist accounts of love tend to agree. They usually begin with the loneliness of man. All animals are aware of otherness; they recognize the possible threat in things that are not themselves. Human beings are especially sensitive to the dangers of isolation. The feeling of separateness is distinctly human. Not that men and women have it on all occasions, but they have it sufficiently often to make the phenomenon a central fact in their experience. Its importance is symbolized in the Book of Genesis by the intimation that only man comes into being without a mate. Only after God realizes that it is not good for Adam to be alone does he create Eve. In Plato's *Symposium* the gods are described as being complete within themselves, self-sufficient, autonomous by virtue of their absolute perfection. But for that reason, Plato insists, it would be absurd to think that the gods love anything but themselves. That is the great difference between the gods and human beings. Ideas about the desirability of loveless self-sufficiency recur throughout Western thought, for instance in Rousseau's belief (renewed in different ways by Thoreau, Ibsen, and others) that man is often happiest when he lives in isolation, freed from the shackles of interpersonal dependency. But more characteristic is that passage in Milton's *Paradise Lost* where Adam, reminding God that a mortal such as himself cannot hope to attain the blessedness of divine solitude, requests the making of a fellow creature with whom he may communicate. Adam suffers through the love which then ensues, but he successfully eliminates the sense of loneliness that belonged to his original condition.

In the tradition of idealistic love, man's primordial loneliness and felt separation provide the impetus to his erotic adventures. The lovers are frequently orphans, like Tristan, or persons cut off from home, like Iseult. When we first meet Romeo, he is out of favor with his lady Rosaline and isolated in his sadness, though surrounded by jovial, admiring friends. The realist tradition recognizes something similar. In Proust, who aspires to a realism relevant to the twentieth century, the long first section of *Remembrance of Things Past* begins with the solitary anguish of the child waiting for his mother's goodnight kiss. The entire work consists of a series of attempts to overcome separateness from other people, and from ideals (such as artistic creativity) that matter to the narrator. In psychoanalytic theorists like Fromm and Reik, love is seen not only as the striving to regain oneness with the mother, which Freud emphasized, but also as a healthy means of coping with the necessary separation from her.

Despite the importance it accords the state of isolation, idealist thinking generally considers it surmountable. For the lovers are one, and in some sense always have been. Throughout all possible separations, and despite the blind interference of external forces, they are really indissoluble. How are we to understand the word "really" here? I think it refers to the nature of the oneness itself, the lovers' union, which the idealist refuses to treat as merely a psychobiological fact about man's existence. According to the realist, people come together for the sake of individual benefit: men and women live with one another as a convenient way of satisfying their needs. This kind of community, whether in society or in the love of man and woman, the realist interprets as an overlapping or wedding of interests rather than a merging of personalities. Yet it is merging through love that the idealist tradition often seeks to glorify. For things only conjoined can be readily separated; they may fit together but they cannot become an essential part of one another, and to that extent the overcoming of separateness remains incomplete. What is merged, on the other hand, contains a common element, an identity that defines the nature of both participants equally well. In finding the beloved, each lover discovers the hidden reality which is himself. In this sense, the lovers have always been united, despite their physical separation, for they have always shared the same self-definition. Just as two heaps of salt may be referred to by the same word because there is some property that both possess, so too — the idealist insists — are lovers jointed by a single oneness that is their merged condition.

Though it has always posed difficulties for theologians, the possibility of merging between man and God was affirmed by mystics in the Christian tradition. The idea of merging between human beings in love with one another develops throughout the Middle Ages as a humanization of the mystical approach. It reaches a peak in Renaissance descriptions, such as John Donne's, of intermingled souls and eye-beams twisted upon one double string, the two lovers being one. In the Romantic era the unity that comes from indissoluble merging is often named as the sole defining attribute of an authentic love between man and woman. A great deal of the idealist tradition could be explicated in terms of the concept of merging along.

The notion that people can merge with one another is, however, a strange idea, elusive, baffling. In everyday life, we realize that one person's experience may have something in common with another's. We see the same bear and it frightens us in the same way. In our joint fright, a sense of kinship may develop. But we would not ordinarily speak of merging in our personalities, of being or becoming one another. We are distinct individuals, each living his own life, each responsible for what he does. In the idealist conception, however, people lose their individuality, or revert to a profounder oneness that preceded it. They are caught up by, immersed in, something bigger and grander than themselves as separate entities, something that negates and even destroys the boundaries of routine existence. Nor should we dismiss such ideas, however fanciful they may sound. Emotion is always volatile; when sufficiently torrid, it can melt our sense of individuality and possibly wash it away. The idealist lover no longer feels that he belongs to the world of separate selves, and that is why he often loses all concern for former responsibilities. He may lie, he may steal, he may kill—there is nothing a Tristan or Iseult will not do in order to preserve their sense of oneness. In merging with the beloved, lovers in the idealist tradition believe that they have transcended the restraints of ordinary life, even though they cannot escape them entirely.

Let us assume that the concept of merging makes sense. But how could merging possibly occur in the world as we know it? By means of magic. At least, whatever provides the love for which an idealist yearns will seem magical to everyone else. It is magic that violates empirical laws of nature, thereby creating that which cannot be obtained by ordinary means. Magic violates by its very being: it destroys the orderliness and comfortable routine that characterize everyday existence. To merge in the manner of idealistic love is to obliterate the old reality, one's former way of life. Magic tries to accomplish this, and it may well symbolize radical transformations that love can actually institute.

The techniques of magic are familiar to everyone who has studied the concept of love in the Western world. There is the love philter that Tristan and Iseult drink, believing it is cooling wine—in other words, a good that belongs to their normal, civilized world, whereas instead it destroys their capacity to benefit from civilization. There are the arrows of Cupid that rain down upon Dido and Aeneas, arrows being instruments of war that represent the suffering unto death that soon follows. There are more subtle means as well: the sudden exchange of glances that signifies the meeting and mingling of souls, in *Romeo and Juliet* as in hundreds of courtly romances that preceded it; the delicate touching of fingers that communicates the electric charge which is life called forth by love, in Michelangelo's version of God creating Adam as well as in *La Bohème* when Mimi and Rodolfo grope for her key under the table; the ritualistic kiss with which the prince awakens Sleeping Beauty to heightened consciousness through love, and which Leontes in Shakespeare's romance *The Winter's Tale* wishes to bestow upon what he presumes to be the statue of his dead wife.

The Winter's Tale ends with Leontes' realization that love can be a socially acceptable and wholesome magic. For the statue—his wife in her frozen and withdrawn condition, a state of alienation parallel to the former madness of Leontes alienated from himself—comes alive now that he loves her again. As in Greek mythology the statue of Galatea becomes a living woman for Pygmalion thanks to the magical powers of Aphrodite the goddess of love, Leontes feels his wife respond to his embrace. "If this be magic," he says, "let it be an art/Lawful as eating." If it were lawful, however, love would no longer be magic. And if, like eating, it were a commonplace occurrence in ordinary life, it would not interest the idealist. For him, love is always an *extra*ordinary event, an epiphany of the mystical oneness which is the merging with another person. That, as we shall see, is why the mature Shakespeare can never align himself entirely with the idealists.

The idea of love as merging through magic receives one of its earliest expressions in the speech that Plato gives Aristophanes in the *Symposium*. After explaining how present-day men and women are only half of the totalities they originally were, and which the gods bisected, Aristophanes describes love as a yearning for the other half from whom one has been severed, the person who belongs to us "in the strictest sense." He has Hephaestus, the wonder-worker, ask two lovers: "Is the object of your desire to be always together as much as possible, and never to be separated from one another day or night? If that is what you want, I am ready to melt and weld you together, so that, instead of two, you shall be one flesh; as long as you live you shall live a common life, and when you die, you shall suffer a common death, and be still one, not two, even in the next world."

Aristophanes is not Plato's spokesman, of course, and when Socrates delivers the final speech, he says nothing about melting or welding. Instead he depicts true love as the knowing of absolute beauty provided by a special faculty of reason. Absolute beauty, the form or defining principle of beauty (and goodness), is a metaphysical entity the lover contemplates. In the *Symposium* Socrates does not say that men can merge with it, though in the *Republic* he does mention this is a possibility. Nevertheless, his speech at the end of the *Symposium* is basic to all idealistic thinking about love as merging. Where Aristophanes had spoken mainly of unifying bodies, making the lovers into one flesh, Socrates insists that the object of love is not a specific instance of beauty, certainly not this or that beautiful body, but rather *absolute* beauty—the idea, the essence, the formal character, of beauty wherever it occurs. Since everything is beautiful sub specie aeternitatis, Socrates concludes that absolute beauty is the ground of all being. Aristophanes called love "the pursuit of the whole," meaning the primordial spherical body of man that the gods bisected. For Socrates too, love is the pursuit of the whole—the whole universe seen as a totality and understood by reference to its ideal form, its eternal value.

Plato left the matter there; but Christianity did not. It combined the eroticism of Aristophanes' myth with the spirituality of Plato's conception of an ideal good. The Hebraic God became the object of love, displacing absolute goodness, which served as one of his major attributes. Throughout a long tradition in the West, religious love was defined as a search for union with the supreme reality which was God. For many mystics God was a person with whom one merged as one might with a human lover. It is this strand of mysticism, bristling with physical imagery, that led some realist critics to consider religious love a sublimation of sex. In the religious love of other mystics, however, the independent personality of God—and everything else that might enable one to treat divinity anthropomorphically—vanishes to a point where supreme reality becomes the mystical experience itself. For these mystics, the sense of oneness, the act of merging with all being, contained within itself the religious import that was formerly accorded to an encounter with a separately existent deity.

The differences between these two religious attitudes contribute to the differences between medieval and Romantic mysticism. Both were attacked by Christian orthodoxy, which maintained that man could not merge with God though they might be wedded to one another in a union that retained their ultimate diversity. To the extent that Christian dogma denied the possibility of merging, it has always incorporated some of the realist approach to love. It was mystical beliefs about oneness, however, that enabled concepts of religious and human love to influence each other reciprocally throughout the history if idealistic theorizing. Not only was there a similar emphasis upon indissoluble merging, but also a comparable belief in what is, in effect, magic as a means of initiating it. As the erotic lover is suddenly and madly overcome by love, so too does the religious lover undergo miraculous, usually spontaneous, conversion and revelation. The avowals, commitments, I-love-you's of the one are duplicated by the ritual phrases, prayers, and cabalistic utterances of the other. Even in orthodox religions that deny the possibility of merging with the godhead, elements of magic insinuate themselves in various ways. Thus communion occurs when the believer eats bread that is the body of Christ and drinks wine that is his blood. Christ, himself the merging of man and god, undergoes the Passion—a love that magically enables the world to transcend itself, i.e., to merge with the world beyond. The mystic abstracts this aspect of established doctrine and singlemindedly makes it the principle of his loving aspiration.

Mysticism is not limited to Christianity. But it is largely through the Christian reinterpretation of Greek philosophy that the tradition of idealistic love developed. Aristophanes' myth was probably taken from the Orphic mysteries, and even in Genesis we find the notion of a primordial human whole, Eve having been created from one of Adam's ribs. But only

Christian mysticism (abetted by related developments in Judaism and Islam) was able to synthesize ideas about love-as-merging with the cosmic metaphysics of Plato and Aristotle. Though concepts of idealistic love between men and women may have had forerunners in the ancient world, their most inventive expressions occur after Christianity entrenched itself throughout the West. The two major approaches to ideal erotic love — medieval courtliness and modern romanticism — both consist of attempts to humanize the love that Christian mystics had generally reserved for man in relation to God. Whether or not its object is suprahuman, the idealist tradition seeks ultimate oneness through the magic of merging with another person.

Appraisal and Bestowal

I start with the idea that love is a way of valuing something. It is a positive response *toward* the "object of love"—which is to say, anyone or anything that is loved. In a manner quite special to itself, love affirms the goodness of this object. Some philosophers say that love *searches* for what is valuable in the beloved; others say that love *creates* value in the sense that it makes the beloved objectively valuable in some respect. Both assertions are often true, but sometimes false; and, therefore, neither explains the type of valuing which is love.

In studying the relationship between love and valuation, let us avoid merely semantical difficulties. The word "love" sometimes means liking very much, as when a man speaks of loving the food he is eating. It sometimes means desiring obsessively, as when a neurotic reports that he cannot control his feelings about a woman. In these and similar instances the word does not affirm goodness. Liking something very much is not the same as considering it good; and the object of an obsessive desire may attract precisely because it is felt to be bad. These uses of the word are only peripheral to the concept of love as a positive response toward a valued object. As we generally use the term, we imply an act of prizing, cherishing, caring about — all of which constitutes a mode of valuation.

But what is it to value or evaluate? Think of what a man does when he sets a price upon a house. He establishes various facts — the size of the building, its physical condition, the cost of repairs, the proximity to schools. He then weights these facts in accordance with their importance to a hypothetical society of likely buyers. Experts in this activity are called appraisers; the activity itself is appraisal or appraising. It seeks to find an objective value that things have in relation to one or another community of human interests. I call this value "objective" because, although it exists only insofar as there are people who want the house, the estimate is open to public verification. As long as they agree about the circumstances—what the house is like and what a relevant group of buyers prefer—all fair-minded appraisers should reach a similar appraisal, regardless of their own feelings about this particular house. In other words, appraising is a branch of empirical science, specifically directed toward the determining of value.

But now imagine that the man setting the price is not an appraiser, but a prospective buyer. The price that he sets need not agree with the appraiser's. For he does more than estimate objective value; he decides what the house is worth to *him*. To the extent that his preferences differ from other people's, the house will have a different value for him. By introducing such considerations, we relate the object to the particular and possibly idiosyncratic interests of a single person, his likings, his needs, his wants, his desires. Ultimately, all objective value depends upon interests of this sort. The community of buyers whose inclinations the appraiser must gauge is itself just a class of individuals. The appraiser merely predicts what each of them would be likely to pay for the house. At the same time, each buyer must be something of an appraiser himself; for he must have at least a rough idea of the price that other buyers will set. Furthermore, each person has to weigh, and so appraise, the relative importance of his own particular interests; and he must estimate whether the house can satisfy them. In principle these judgments are verifiable. They are also liable to mistake: for instance, when a man thinks that certain desires matter more to him than they really do, or when he expects greater benefits from an object than it can provide. Deciding what something is worth to *oneself* we may call an "individual appraisal." It differs from what the appraiser does; it determines a purely individual value, as opposed to any objective value.

Now, with this in mind, I suggest that love creates a new value, one that is not reducible to the individual or objective value that something may also have. This further type of valuing I call bestowal. Individual and objective value depend upon an object's ability to satisfy prior interests—the needs, the desires, the wants, or whatever it is that motivates us toward one object and not another. Bestowed value is different. It is created by the affirmative relationship *itself*, by the very act of responding favorably, giving an object emotional and pervasive importance regardless of its capacity to satisfy interests. Here it makes no sense to speak of verifiability; and though bestowing may often be injurious, unwise, even immoral, it cannot be erroneous in the way that an appraisal might be. For now it is the valuing alone that *makes* the value.

Think of what happens when a man comes to love the house he has bought. In addition to being something of use, something that gratifies antecedent desires, it takes on special value for him. It is not *his* house, not merely as a possession or a means of shelter but also as something he *cares about*, a part of his affective life. Of course, we also care about objects of mere utility. We need them for the benefits they provide. But in the process of loving, the man establishes another kind of relationship. He gives the house an importance beyond its individual or objective value. It becomes a focus of attention and possibly an object of personal commitment. Merely by engaging himself in this manner, the man bestows a value the house could not have had otherwise.

We might also say that the homeowner acts as if his house were valuable "for its own sake." And in a sense it is. For the value that he bestows does not depend upon the house's capacity to satisfy. Not that love need diminish that capacity. On the contrary, it often increases it by affording opportunities for enjoyment that would have been impossible without the peculiar attachment in which bestowal consists. Caring about the house, the man may find new and more satisfying ways of living in it. At the same time, the object achieves a kind of autonomy. The house assumes a presence and attains a dignity. It makes demands and may even seem to have a personality, to have needs of its own. In yielding to these "needs"—restoring the house to an earlier condition, perhaps, or completing its inherent design—the homeowner may not be guided by any other considerations.

In love between human beings something similar happens. For people, too, may be appraised; and they may be valued beyond one's appraisal. In saying that a woman is beautiful or that a man is handsome, or that a man or woman is good in any other respect, we ascribe objective value. This will always be a function of *some* community of human interests, though we may have difficulty specifying which one. And in all communities people have individual value for one another. We are means to each other's satisfactions, and we constantly evaluate one another on the basis of our individual interests. However subtly, we are always setting prices on other people, and on ourselves. But we also bestow value in the manner of love. We then respond to another as something that cannot be reduced to *any* system of appraisal. The lover takes an interest in the beloved as a *person*, and not merely as a commodity—which she may also be. (The lover may be female, of course, and the beloved may be male; but for the sake of brevity and grammatical simplicity I shall generally retain the old convention of referring to lovers as "he" and beloveds as "she.") He bestows importance upon *her* needs and *her* desires, even when they do not further the satisfaction of his own. Whatever her personality, he gives it a value it would not have apart from his loving attitude. In relation to the lover, the beloved has become valuable for her own sake.

In the love of persons, then, people bestow value upon one another over and above their individual or objective value. The reciprocity of love occurs when each participant receives bestowed value while also bestowing it upon the other. Reciprocity has always been recognized as a desired outcome of love. Since it need not occur, however, I define the lover as one who bestows value, and the beloved as one who receives it. The lover makes the beloved valuable merely by attaching and committing himself to her. Though she may satisfy his needs, he refuses to use her just as an instrument. To love a woman as a person is to desire her for the sake of values that appraisal might discover, and yet to place one's desire within a context that affirms her importance regardless of these values. Eventually the beloved may no longer matter to us as one who is useful. Treating her as an end, we may think only of how we can be useful to *her*. But still it is we who think and act and make this affirmative response. Only in relation to *our* bestowal does another person enjoy the kind of value that love creates.

In saying that love bestows value, I am not referring to the fact that lovers shower good things upon those they love. Gifts may sometimes symbolize love, but they never prove its existence. Loving is not synonymous with giving. We do speak of one person "giving love" to another, but what is given hardly resembles what we usually mean by a gift. Even to say that the lover gives himself is somewhat misleading. Love need not be self-sacrificial. In responding affirmatively to another person, the lover creates something and need lose nothing in himself. To bestow value is to augment one's own being as well as the beloved's. Bestowal generates a new society by the sheer force of emotional attachment, a society that enables the lovers to discard many of the conventions that would ordinarily have separated them. But such intimacy is only one of the criteria by which bestowal may be identified.

The bestowing of value shows itself in many different ways, not all of which need ever occur at the same time or in equal strength: by caring about the needs and interests of the beloved, by wishing to benefit or protect her, by delighting in her achievements, by encouraging her independence while also accepting and sustaining her dependency, by respecting her individuality, by giving her pleasure, by taking pleasures with her, by feeling glad when she is present and sad when she is not, by sharing ideas and emotions with her, by sympathizing with her weaknesses and depending upon her strength, by developing common pursuits, by allowing her to become second nature to him—"her smiles, her frowns, her ups, her downs"—by having a need to increase their society with other human beings upon whom they can jointly bestow value, by wanting children who may perpetuate their love. These are not necessary and sufficient conditions; but their occurrence would give us reason to think that an act of bestowal has taken place.

Through bestowal lovers have "a life" together. The lover accords the beloved the tribute of expressing *his* feelings by responding to *hers*. If he sends her valuable presents, they will signify that he too appreciates what she esteems; if he makes sacrifices on her behalf, he indicates how greatly her welfare matters to him. It is as if he were announcing that what is real for her is real for him also. Upon the sheer personality of the beloved he bestows a framework of value, emanating from himself but focused on her. Lovers linger over attributes that might well have been ignored. Whether sensuous or polite, passionate or serene, brusque or tender, the lover's response is variably fervent but constantly gratuitous. It dignifies the beloved by treating her as *someone*, with all the emphasis the italics imply. Though independent of our needs, she is also the significant object of our attention. We show ourselves receptive to her peculiarities in the sense that we readily respond to them. Response is itself a kind of affirmation, even when it issues into unpleasant emotions such as anger and jealousy. These need not be antithetical to love; they may even be signs of it. Under many circumstances one cannot respond to another person without the unpleasant emotions, as a parent cannot stay in touch with a wayward child unless he occasionally punishes him. It is when we reject the other person, reducing him to a nothing or expressing our indifference, that love disappears. For then instead of bestowing value, we have withdrawn it.

In general, every emotion or desire contributes to love once it serves as a positive response to an independent being. If a woman is *simply* a means to sexual satisfaction, a man may be said to want her, but not to love her. For his sexual desire to become a part of love, it must function as a way of responding to the character and special properties of this particular woman. Desire wants what it wants for the sake of some private gratification, whereas love demands an interest in that vague complexity we call another person. No wonder lovers sound like metaphysicians, and scientists are more comfortable in the study of desire. For love is an attitude with no clear objective. Through it one human being affirms the significance of another, much as a painter highlights a figure by defining it in a sharpened outline. But the beloved is not a painted figure. She is not static: she is fluid, changing, indefinable—*alive*. The lover is attending to a *person*. And who can say what that is?

In the history of philosophy, bestowal and appraisal have often been confused with one another, perhaps because they are both types of valuation. Love is related to both; they interweave in it. Unless we appraised we could not bestow a value that goes beyond appraisal; and without bestowal there would be no love. We may speak of lovers accepting one another, or even taking each other as is. But this need not mean a blind submission to some unknown being. In love we *attend* to the beloved, in the sense that we respond to what *she* is. For the effort to succeed, it must be accompanied by justifiable appraisals, objective as well as individual. The objective beauty and goodness of his beloved will delight the lover, just as her deficiencies will distress him. In her, as in every other human being, these are important properties. How is the lover to know what they are without a system of appraisals? Or how to help her realize her potentialities—assuming that is what she wants? Of course, in bestowing value upon this woman, the lover will "accentuate the positive" and undergo a kind of personal involvement that no disinterested spectator would. He will feel an intimate concern about the continuance of good properties in the beloved and the diminishing of bad ones. But none of this would be possible without objective appraisals.

Even more important is the role of individual appraisal. The person we love is generally one who satisfies our needs and desires. She may do so without either of us realizing the full extent of these satisfactions; and possibly all individual value is somehow based upon unconscious effects. Be this as it may, our experience of another person includes a large network of individual evaluations continually in progress and available to consciousness. At each moment our interests are being gratified or frustrated, fulfilled or thwarted, strengthened or weakened in relation to the other person. Individual value is rarely stable. It changes in accordance with our success or failure in getting what we want. And as this happens, our perception of the beloved also changes. Though the lover bestows value upon the woman as a separate and autonomous person, she will always be a person in *his* experience, a person whom he needs and who may need him, a person whose very nature may eventually conform to his inclinations, as well as vice versa. The attitude of love probably includes more, not fewer, individual appraisals than any other. How else could a lover, who must respond from his own point of view, really care about the beloved?

Love would not be love unless appraising were accompanied by the bestowing of value. But where this conjunction exists, *every* appraisal may lead on to a further bestowal. By disclosing an excellence in the beloved, appraisal (whether individual or objective) makes it easier for us to appreciate her. By revealing her faults and imperfections, it increases the importance of acting on her behalf. Love may thus encompass all possible appraisals. Once bestowal has occurred, a man may hardly care that his beloved is not deemed desirable by other men. Given a choice, he may prefer her to women who are sexually more attractive. His love is a way of compensating for and even overcoming negative appraisals. If it were a means of repaying the object for value received, love would turn into gratitude; if it were an attempt to give more than the object has provided, it would be generosity or condescension. These are related attitudes, but love differs from them in bestowing value without calculation. It confers importance no matter *what* the object is worth.

When appraisal occurs alone, our attitude develops in the direction of science, ambition, or morality. To do "the right thing" we need not bestow value upon another person; we need only recognize the truth about his character and act appropriately. Admiring a woman's superiority, we may delight in her as an evidence of the good life. We feel toward her what Hume calls "the sense of approbation." We find her socially useful or morally commendable, which is not to say that she excites our love. If she has faults, they offend our moral sensibility or else elicit our benevolence. In short, we respond to this woman as an abstraction, as a something that may be better or worse, an opportunity for judgment or for action, but not a person whom we love. Appraisal without bestowal may lead us to change other people regardless of what they want. As moralists or legislators, or as dutiful parents, we may even think that this is how we *ought* to behave. The magistrate will then enforce a distance between himself and the criminal, whose welfare he is quite prepared to sacrifice for the greater good of society. The parent will discipline his child in the hopes of molding him "in the most beneficial manner." On this moral attitude great institutions are often built. But it is not a loving attitude. We are not responding affirmatively toward others. We are only doing what is (we hope) in their best interests, or else society's.

When love intervenes, morality becomes more personal but also more erratic. It is almost impossible to imagine someone bestowing value without caring about the other person's welfare. To that extent, love implies benevolence. And yet the lover does not act benevolently for the sake of doing the right thing. In loving another person, we respect *his* desire to improve himself. If we offer to help, we do so because *he* wants to be better than he is, not because *we* think he ought to be. Love and morality need not diverge, but they often do. For love is not *inherently* moral. There is no guarantee that it will bestow value properly, at the right time, in the right way. Through love we enjoy another person as he is, including his moral condition; yet this enjoyment may itself violate the demands of morality. Ethical attitudes must always be governed by appraisal rather than bestowal. They must consider the individual in his relations to other people, as one among many who have equal claims. Faced with the being of a particular person, morality tells us to pick and choose those attributes that are most desirable. It is like a chef who makes an excellent stew by bring out one flavor and muffling another. The chef does not care about the ingredients as unique or terminal entities, but only as things that are good to eat. In loving another person, however, we enact a nonmoral *loyalty*—like the mother who stands by her criminal son even though she knows he is guilty. Her loyalty need not be *im*moral; and though she loves her son, she may realize that he must be punished. But what if the value she has bestowed upon her child blinds her to the harm he has done, deters her from handing him over to the police, leads her to encourage him as a criminal? Her love may increase through such devotion, but it will be based on faulty appraisals and will not be a moral love.

Possibly the confusion between appraisal and bestowal results from the way that lovers talk. To love another person is to *treat* him with great regard, to confer a new and personal value upon him. But when lovers describe their beloved, they sometimes sound as if she were perfect just in being herself. In caring about someone, attending to her, affirming the importance of her being what she is, the lover resembles a man who has appraised an object and found it very valuable. Though he is bestowing value, the lover *seems* to be declaring the objective goodness of the beloved. It is *as if* he were predicting the outcome of all possible appraisals and insisting that they would always be favorable.

As a matter of fact, the lover is doing nothing of the sort. His superlatives are expressive and metaphoric. Far from being terms of literal praise, they betoken the magnitude of his attachment and say little about the lady's beauty or goodness. They may even be accompanied by remarks that diminish the beloved in some respect—as when a man lovingly describes a woman's funny face or inability to do mathematics. If he says she is "perfect" in that way, he chooses this ambiguous word because it is used for things we refuse to relinquish. As in appraisal we may wish to accept nothing less than perfection, so too the lover calls perfect whatever he accepts despite its appraisal. The lover may borrow appraisive terminology, but he uses it with a special intent. His language signifies that love alone has bestowed incalculable worth upon this particular person. Such newly given value is not a good of the sort that appraisal seeks: it is not an attribute that supplements her other virtues, like a dimple wrought by some magician to make a pretty woman prettier. For it is nothing but the importance that one person assigns to another; and in part at least, it is created by the language. The valuative terms that lovers use—"wonderful," "marvelous," "glorious," "grand," "terrific"—bestow value in themselves. They are scarcely capable of describing excellence or reporting on appraisals.

If we have any doubts about the lover's use of language, we should listen to the personal appendages he usually adds. He will not say "That woman is perfect," but rather "To *me* she is perfect" or "*I* think she is wonderful." In talking this way, he reveals that objective appraisal does not determine his attitude. For objective appraisal puts the object in relation to a community of valuers, whereas love creates its own community. The men in some society may all admire an "official beauty"—as Ortega calls her. Every male may do homage to her exceptional qualities, as if the lady were a great work of art; and some will want to possess her, as they would want to steal the crown jewels. But this is not the same as love, since that involves a different kind of response, more intimate, more personal, and more creative.

For similar reasons it would be a mistake to think that the lover's language articulates an individual appraisal. If he says that to him the woman is perfect, the lover does not mean that she is perfect *for* him. Unless the beloved satisfied in some respect, no man might be able to love her. For *she* must find a place in *his* experience; she must come alive for him, stimulate new and expansive interests; and none of this is likely to happen unless she has individual value for him. But though the beloved satisfies the lover, she need not satisfy perfectly. Nor does the lover expect her to. In saying that to him she is perfect, he merely reiterates the fact that he loves this woman. Her perfection is an honorific title which he, and only he, bestows. The lover is like a child who makes a scribble and then announces "This is a tree." The child could just as easily have said "This is a barn." Until he tells us, the scribble represents nothing. Once he tells us, it represents whatever he says—as long as his attitude remains consistent.

In being primarily bestowal and only secondarily appraisal, love is never elicited by the object in the sense that desire or approbation is. We desire things or people for the sake of what will satisfy us. We approve of someone for his commendable properties. These are causal conditions for love: as when a man loves a woman *because* she is beautiful, or *because* she satisfies his sexual, domestic, and social needs, or *because* she resembles his childhood memory of mother. Such facts indicate the circumstances under which people love one another; they explain why this particular man loves this particular woman; and if the life sciences were sufficiently developed, the facts could help us to predict who among human beings would be likely to love whom. But explaining the occurrence of love is not the same as explicating the concept. The conditions for love are not the same as love itself. In some circumstances the bestowing of value will happen more easily than in others; but *whenever* it happens, it happens as a new creation of value and exceeds all attributes of the object that might be thought to elicit it. Even if a man loves only a woman who is beautiful and looks like his mother, he does not *love* her for these properties in the same sense in which he might *admire* her for being objectively valuable or *desire* her for satisfying his needs.

For what then does a man love a woman? For being the person she is, for being herself? But that is to say that he loves her for nothing at all. Everyone is himself. Having a beloved who is what she is does not reveal the nature of love. Neither does it help us to understand the saint's desire to love all people. They are what they are. Why should they be loved for it? Why not pitied or despised, ignored or simply put to use? Love supplements the human search for value with a capacity for bestowing it gratuitously. To one who has succeeded in cultivating this attitude, *anything* may become an object of love. The saint is a man whose earthly needs and desires are extraordinarily modest; in principle, every human being can satisfy them. That being so, the saint creates a value-system in which all persons fit equally well. This disposition, this freely given response, cannot be elicited from him: it bestows itself and happens to be indiscriminate.

To the man of common sense it is very upsetting that love does not limit itself to some prior value in the object. The idea goes against our purposive ways of thinking. If I wish to drink the best wine, I have reason to prefer

French champagne over American. My choice is dictated by an objective
goodness in the French champagne. If instead I wish to economize, I act
sensibly in choosing a wine I value less highly. We act this way whenever we
use purposive means of attaining the good life, which covers a major part of
our existence. But love, unlike desire, is not wholly purposive. Within the
total structure of a human life it may serve as a lubricant to purposive attitudes, furthering their aims through new interests that promise new satisfactions; but in creating value, bestowing it freely, love introduces an element of risk into the economy. Purposive attitudes are safe, secure, like
money in the bank; the loving attitude is speculative and always dangerous.
Love is not *practical*, and sometimes borders on madness. We take our life
in our hands when we allow love to tamper with our purposive habits.
Without love, life might not be worth living; but without purposiveness,
there would be no life.

No wonder, then, that the *fear* of love is one of the great facts of human
nature. In all men and women there lurks an atavistic dread of insolvency
whenever we generate more emotion than something has a right to demand
of us. In everyone there is the country bumpkin who giggles nervously at an
abstract painting because it looks like nothing on earth. Man finds the
mere possibility of invention and spontaneous originality disquieting, even
ominous. We are threatened by any new bestowal. Particularly when it
means the origination of feelings, we are afraid to run the usual risks of
failure and frustration, to expose ourselves in a positive response that can so
easily be thwarted. As a character in D. H. Lawrence says of love: "I am almost more afraid of this touch than I was of death. For I am more nakedly
exposed to it." Even Pascal, who spoke of the heart's having reasons
whereof reason does not know, seemed to think that love adheres to a secret, mysterious quality within the object that only feeling can discern. But
Pascal was wrong. Love is sheer gratuity. It issues from the lover like hairs
on his head. It can be stimulated and developed, but it cannot be derived
from outside.

Love is like awakened genius that chooses its materials in accordance
with its own creative requirements. Love does not create its object; it merely
responds to it creatively. That is why one can rarely convince a man that his
beloved is unworthy of him. For his love is a creative means of *making* her
more worthy—in the sense that he invests her with greater value, not in
making her a better human being. That may also happen. But more significantly, the lover changes *himself*. By subordinating his purposive attitudes, he transforms himself into a being who enjoys the act of bestowing.

There is something magical about this, as we know from legends in which the transformations of love are effected by a philter or a wand. In making another person valuable by developing a certain disposition within oneself, the lover performs in the world of feeling something comparable to what the alchemist does in the world of matter.

Martha Nussbaum
The Speech of Alcibiades: A Reading of
Plato's Symposium

Martha Nussbaum is professor of philosophy and classics at Brown University and, most recently, the author of The Fragility of Goodness *and* Love Matters.

> He had a golden shield made for himself, which was emblazoned not with any ancestral device, but with the figure of Eros armed with a thunderbolt.
> *Plutarch,* Alcibiades, *16.*

> Alcibiades: I'm going to tell the truth. Do you think you'll allow that?

He was, to begin with, beautiful. He was endowed with a physical grace and splendor that captivated the entire city. It did not decline as he grew, but flourished at each stage with new authority and power. He was always highly conscious of his body, vain about its influence. He would speak of his beauty as his "amazing good-fortune," and his "windfall from the gods." But this was not the limit of his natural gifts. Energy and intellectual power had made him one of the best commanders and strategists Athens had known, one of the most skillful orators ever to enchant her. In both careers his genius was his keen eye for the situation—the way he could discern the salient features of the particular case and boldly select appropriate action. About all these gifts he was no less vain—vain, and yet also almost morbidly concerned with criticism and gossip. He loved to be loved. He hated to be observed, skinned, discovered. His heart, generous and volatile, was rapidly moved to both love and anger, at once changeable and tenacious. He was, then, a man of great resources who made deep demands on the world, both emotional and intellectual; and he did what resource and courage could to guarantee success.

What else? He hated flute-playing, and the flute-playing satyr Marsyas. . . . He laughed, he staged jokes—at the expense of enemies, of lovers, at his own. He once arranged for a suitor of his, a resident alien, to

win the bid for the local tax receipts, to the great discomfiture of local suitors and tax-farmers. . . . When he wanted to win something, he took no
chances. He entered seven chariots at Olympia and walked off with first,
second, and fourth prizes. But that third prize, elusive, bothered him intensely. . . . He once sliced off the tail of his own dog, saying, "I am quite
content for the whole of Athens to chatter about this. It will stop them from
saying anything worse about me." . . . He financed extravagant spectacles.
The people never had enough of him; he was their darling, their young
"lion." The haters of democratic disorder hated him as its inspiration. . . .
Once he invited a philosopher to dinner and told him the truth before bed-
time. . . . He betrayed two cities. He said, "Love of country is what I do
not feel when I am wronged." He crowned with garlands the empty head of
a beauty who wrote tragedies without having a soul. . . . One dark night
he went for a walk through the streets of Athens and defaced the statues of
the gods, smashing genitals and faces. . . . The man he loved looked like a
snub-nosed Silenus, as he turned over on the bed to sleep—like one of those
toy Sileni you open up to see the shining statues of the gods inside. . . . All
these things.[1]

His story is, in the end, a story of waste and loss, of the failure of practical reason to shape a life. Both the extraordinary man and the stages of his
careening course were legendary at Athens; they cried out for interpretation, and for healing. The *Symposium* situates itself in the midst of this life
and confronts the questions it raises for our thought about love and reason.
Alcibiades is, of course, a major character in the dialogue, and many details of his life are recounted explicitly in his speech. But there are also
more subtle signals. A man who died shot by an arrow will speak of the
words of love as arrows, or bolts, wounding the soul. A man who influen-
tially denounced the flute as an instrument unworthy of a free man's dignity will describe himself as a slave to the enchanting flute-playing of a certain satyr. A man who will deface holy statues compares the soul of Socrates
to a set of god-statues, and speaks of the injustice of rubbing out, or defac-
ing, Socratic virtues. A man who will profane the mysteries puts on trial the
initiate of the mystery-religion of *erōs*. All these connections suggest that
we need to read the work against the background of the already legendary
stories of the life, trying to recover for ourselves the Athenian fascination
with Alcibiades. Only in this way will we grasp the significance of many apparently casual remarks, and, through these, of the whole.

It is commonly charged against Plato that, in the *Symposium*, he ignores the value of the love of one unique whole person for another such

whole person. By treating the person as a seat of valuable properties, and describing love as directed at those repeatable properties, rather than at the whole person, he misses something that is fundamental to our experience of love. Professor Gregory Vlastos, one of the most eloquent expositors of this view, writes:

> We are to love the persons so far, and only insofar, as they are good and beautiful. Now since all too few human beings are masterworks of excellence, and not even the best of those we have the chance to love are wholly free of streaks of the ugly, the mean, the commonplace, the ridiculous, if our love for them is to be only for their virtue and beauty, the individual, in the uniqueness and integrity of his or her individuality, will never be the object of our love. This seems to me the cardinal flaw in Plato's theory. It does not provide for love of whole persons, but only for love of that abstract version of persons which consists of the complex of their best qualities. This is the reason why personal affection ranks so low in Plato's *scala amoris*. . . . The high climactic moment of fulfillment—the peak achievement for which all lesser loves are to be "used as steps"—is the one farthest removed from affection for concrete human beings.[2]

This is all a bit mysterious. We would like to ask just what this uniqueness and individuality come to. Are they merely a subjective impression we have because we have not yet grasped all the properties? Or is uniqueness perhaps the occurrence of certain properties, each itself repeatable, in a hitherto unexemplified combination? Or is it something more elusive and shadowy than this? And yet, despite our questions, we feel that Vlastos must somehow be right. He is certainly pointing to something that we do say and feel about being in love, however unsure we are of what we mean in saying it.

But there is a problem about using this as a criticism of Plato's perceptions. This is that it requires us to treat as Plato's view only the view expressed in the speech of Diotima as repeated by Socrates, and to charge him with being unaware of the rest of what he had written. For following that speech is another speech that claims to tell us the truth—a speech that ends with these words: "One could find many other wonderful things about Socrates to praise. But these same virtues one might attribute to someone else as well. The really wonderful thing about him is that he is not similar to any other man, past or present. . . . This man is so strange—he himself and his speeches too—that you could look and look and find nobody even near him." But that is, more or less, what Vlastos was talking about. If a writer describes a certain theory of love and then follows that description with a counterexample to the theory, a story of intense passion for a unique individual as eloquent as any in literature—a story that says that the theory omits something, is blind to something—then we might want to hesitate before calling the *author* blind. We might want to read the whole of what he has written, and find his meaning emerging from the arrangement of all its parts. I sense that a deep understanding of the *Symposium* will be one that regards it not as a work that ignores the pre-philosophical understanding of *erōs*, but as one that is all about that understanding, and also about why it must be purged and transcended, why Diotima has to come once again to save Athens from a plague. (Perhaps also why she can't save us—or, at any rate, can't save *us*.) In short, a work in which a man who was assassinated by some unknown cohort of the family of Plato gets assassinated by a very well-known cohort of the family of Plato.

We need, then, to be reminded that the *Symposium* is a work about passionate erotic love—a fact that would be hard to infer from most of the criticism written about it. Its only speech that claims to tell "the truth" is the story of a consuming passion, both sexual and intellectual, for a particular individual. There is, indeed, at its heart a speech that challenges or denies these "truths" in the name of the good. But we can hardly hope to understand the motivation for that challenge, or to assess its force, without first understanding Plato's depiction of our actual attachments, and their problems. We have to be willing to explore with this work our own thoughts and feelings about sexual attachment, and to ask whether, having looked at our feelings, we are, like Socrates, ready to be "persuaded" by the revisionary speech of Diotima. That is why we must turn our attention, as Plato's audience would have, to the life and character of Alcibiades.

• • •

II

We can begin with the only one among the original symposiasts who does not praise the speech of Socrates. At the dialogue's end, Socrates attempts to persuade Agathon and Aristophanes that, contrary to popular superstition, one and the same man can be a poet in both the tragic and the comic genres. It is obvious to us that the comic speech of Aristophanes and the tragic (or tragic-comic) speech of Alcibiades contain the most serious objections raised in the *Symposium* against Socrates' program for the ascent of love. These facts suggest that we should study the two speeches together, asking whether they reveal a shared account of the nature of *erōs* and its value, illuminating both one another and the Socratic alternative. Aristophanes never succeeds in telling us his objections to the ascent story, because Alcibiades' entrance disrupts the dialectic. But perhaps it is this entrance, and the ensuing scene, that make known to us the comic poet's most serious reservations.

The comic poet speaks later than originally scheduled. The orderly plan of the symposium is disrupted by a ridiculous bodily contingency: an attack of hiccups. It makes Aristophanes (and us) wonder at the way in which the good order of the body gives way, as though a willing and desiring victim to the most absurd of sub-human noises. Recovered, he offers a story about love that wonders, itself, at the power of the body's contingencies to disrupt and subdue the aspirations of practical reason.

We were once, he tells us, perfect and self-sufficient physical beings. We had the spherical form, "similar in every direction," imagined by early philosophy to be the shape of the god.[3] Now, punished for our overweening attempt to make ourselves rulers of everything, we are creatures cut in half, severed from our other part and made, by a turning of our heads, to look always at the cut, jagged front side of ourselves that reminds us of our lack. And, looking at the contingent loss that cuts us off from the wishes of our imagination — itself still apparently intact — we become preoccupied with the project of returning to the wholeness of our former natures. But to remedy one contingency another piece of luck must happen: we must each find the unique other half from which we were severed. The one hope of "healing" for our human nature is to unite in love with this other oneself, and, indeed, to become fused with that one, insofar as this is possible. *Erōs* is the name of this desire and pursuit of the whole.

The story is comic because, while it is about us and our deepest concerns, it at the same time distances itself from the inner pain of those concerns, asking us to watch ourselves as we watch a species remote from us and our needs. We think, as men, that the human shape is something beautiful; the story gets us to consider that, from the point of view of the whole or the god, the spherical shape may be formally the most beautiful and adequate. A jagged form, equipped with these oddly lumpy and pointy facial features, these ridiculously exposed and dangling genital members, looks like the shape of something that is the object of a joke, or a punishment. From the point of view of desire, the penetration of a penis into some aperture of the loved one's body is an event of excitement and beauty. From the outside it just looks peculiar, or even grotesque; it certainly seems to be without positive aesthetic value. As we hear Aristophanes' distant myth of this passionate groping and grasping, we are invited to think how odd, after all, it is that bodies should have these holes and projections in them, odd that the insertion of a projection into an opening should be thought, by ambitious and intelligent beings, a matter of the deepest concern. How odd that we should have taken as natural and fine this extraordinary fact that our separate bodies actually fit into the insides of other bodies, that bodies are soft and open, not round and shiny-smooth, like stones. (Stone might be the best embodiment of our high ambition.) And, finally, from the inside the disharmony in the nature of these creatures, whose reason still aspires to completeness and control, but whose bodies are so painfully needy, so distracting—from the inside this would feel like torment. From the outside, we cannot help laughing. They want to be gods—and here they are, running around anxiously trying to thrust a piece of themselves inside a hole; or, perhaps more comical still, waiting in the hope that some hole of theirs will have something thrust into it.[4]

And, yet, we are aware that we are those creatures. If the story were told about some completely alien race, in whom we could not see ourselves and our desires, it would be a natural history. If it were told from the inside, it would, as we have said, be tragedy. The comedy comes in the sudden perception of ourselves from another vantage point, the sudden turning round of our heads and eyes to look at human genitals and faces, our unrounded, desiring, and vulnerable parts.

We seem to have in this story much of what Vlastos wanted from an account of love. The objects of these creatures' passions are whole people: not "complexes of desirable qualities," but entire beings, thoroughly embodied, with all their idiosyncrasies, flaws, and even faults. What makes them fall in love is a sudden swelling-up of feelings of kinship and intimacy, the astonishment of finding in a supposed stranger a deep part of your own being. "They are struck in extraordinary fashion by friendly feeling (*philia*) and intimacy and passion (*erōs*), and are hardly willing to be apart from one another even a little time." It is a love that is said to be in and of the soul and body both, and of the soul's longings as expressed in the movements and gestures of the body.

Nor are love objects interchangeable for these people, as seats of abstract goodness or beauty might be. The individual is loved not only as a whole, but also as a unique and irreplaceable whole. For each there is, apparently, exactly one "other half." Although upon the death of the half each will begin a search for a replacement, there is no evidence that this search will bring success. There is nothing like a general description of a suitable or "fitting" lover, satisfiable by a number of candidates, that could serve as a sufficient criterion of suitability. It is mysterious what does make another person the lost half of you, more mysterious still how you come to know that. But there you will find it, both body and soul, not like anyone else in the world. (We can see how close we are to a view of *erōs* frequently expressed in Greek tragedy, if we think of a moment in the *Antigone*. Creon argues for the replaceability of love partners with a crude agricultural metaphor: there are "other furrows" for Haemon's "plow." Ismene answers, "Not another love such as the one that fitted him to her.[5] With their shared emphasis on special *harmonia* [carpenter's fit or musician's harmony], tragedy and Aristophanes seem to capture the uniqueness, as well as the wholeness, that Vlastos found lacking in "Plato" 's view of *erōs*.

But the picture also shows us problems. First of all, Aristophanes' myth vividly dramatizes the sheer contingency of love, and our vulnerability to contingency through love. The very need that gives rise to erotic pursuit is an unnatural, a contingent lack — at least it is seen as such from the point of view of the ambitions of human reason. Here are these ridiculous creatures cut in half, trying to do with these bodies what came easily for them when they had a different bodily nature. The body is a source of limitation and distress: they do not feel at one with it, and they wish they had one of a different sort; or, perhaps, none at all.

Then *erōs*, so necessary to continued life and to "healing" from distress, comes to the cut-up creature by sheer chance, if at all. His or her other half is somewhere, but it is hard to see what reason and planning can do to make that half turn up. The creatures "search" and "come together," but it is plainly not in their power to ensure the happy reunion. It is difficult to accept that something as essential to our good as love is at the same time so much a matter of chance. The creatures would plainly like to believe, with R. B. Brandt, that "If a person is disappointed in love, it is possible to adopt a vigorous plan of action which carries a good chance of acquainting him with someone else he likes at least as well."[6] The comic myth doubts it.

And it is not simply that a particular part of the creatures' good seems to resist control by practical reason. For this component, being absent or unhappily present, causes the creature to lose rational control over all the rest of its life planning. Before the invention of sexual intercourse, the two halves embraced unsatisfied, until both died of hunger and other needs. The possibility of intercourse and orgasm brought both the procreation of children and a temporary respite from physical tension: "Satiety might come to be from intercourse, and they might be assuaged and turn to their work and take thought for the rest of their lives." But this happy possibility indicates to us also that the creature remains always in the grip of these recurring needs, which distract him from his work and the rest of his life, except where satiety provides a small interval of calm.

It emerges, moreover, that the satisfaction achieved in this way is, even as temporary, incomplete. The aim of desire is more intractable. What these lovers really want is not simply the momentary physical pleasure of orgasm, with its ensuing brief respite from bodily tension. Their erotic behavior expresses a deeper need, one that comes from the soul—a need "that the soul cannot describe, but it divines, and obscurely hints at":

> Suppose Hephaistus with his tools were to visit them as they lie together and stand over them and ask: "What is it, mortals, that you hope to gain from one another?" Suppose, too, that when they could not answer he repeated his question in these terms: "Is the object of your desire to be always together as much as possible, and never to be separated from one another day or night? If that is what you want, I am ready to melt and weld you together, so that, instead of two, you shall be one. . . . Would such a fate as this content you, and satisfy your longings?" We know what their answer would be: no one would refuse the offer.

It is a wish for the impossible. However ardently and however often these lovers may enter one another's bodies, they are always going to remain two. No amount of interpenetration will cause even the smallest particle of flesh to fuse with the other flesh. The act of penetration leads inexorably back to separation and inactivity, never to any more lasting or more thoroughgoing union.

But this impossible story of fusing or welding is a simpler miracle than the one that would have to take place if they were really to become one. For these creatures have souls; and their desire for unity is a desire of the soul, a desire of desires, projects, aspirations. (For the lovers' problem to arise they do not, and we do not, need to be dualists. Aristophanes' *psuchē* is probably not an incorporeal substance, but the "inner" elements of a person—desires, beliefs, imaginings—however these are, ultimately, to be analyzed and understood. The operative contrast is the one between the "internal" and the "external." The lovers' problem will arise for anyone who doubts that the external movements, gestures, and speeches of his or her limbs, trunk, face, genitals, always fully and adequately express the person that [s]he feels him or herself to be.)[7] Hephaistus' tools could do nothing to satisfy their desire — unless their souls, in intercourse, had first become thoroughly fused with their own bodies. What would this mean? That each would have to regard his or her bodily movements as fully expressive of and in harmony with the needs and imaginings of the soul or the "insides," so that intercourse was at the same time an interpenetration of imagination with imagination and spirit with spirit. Hephaistus can weld only what is engaged in the bodily act of lovemaking and identifies itself with it. If the mind stands to one side, if it asks, even momentarily, "Is this me?" or, "Is everything that I am in this?" or, "Does that person moving around inside my body really know anything about *me*?", then the welding will be at best a partial welding. There will be a little detached being left on the outside, who resists the craftsman and remains unengulfed, solitary, proud of its secrets. For these creatures, this is almost certain to be the case. Don't they resent the awkwardness of their bodies, those flawed, imperfect surfaces? Don't they pride themselves on the wholeness and beauty of their natures? Then how will they be willing to identify their proud souls with a cut and jagged face, a set of queerly shaped organs? One miracle presupposes a greater miracle: to get to be the whole, you first have to be willing to be the half.

Let us now suppose that, by a miracle, these two fusions have occurred. Each of the lovers makes himself one with his body, and Hephaistus then makes two soul-bodies into one. Locked in each other's arms, penetrating and penetrated, there they lie, for the rest of their lives and on into death, melted into one, immobile. (Let us also suppose that the gap between interpenetration and fusion has really been bridged: they can "die in common"[8] not just in the sense of simultaneity of experience, but in the sense of unity of experience.) Here we meet, unexpectedly, a second comedy. For what they thought they most wanted out of their passionate movement turns out to be a wholeness that would put an end to all movement and all passion. A sphere would not have intercourse with anyone. It would not eat, or doubt, or drink. It would not, as Xenophanes shrewdly observed, even move this way or that, because it would have no reason; it would be complete.[9] *Erōs* is the desire to be a being without any contingent occurrent desires. It is a second-order desire that all desires should be cancelled. This need that makes us pathetically vulnerable to chance is a need whose ideal outcome is the existence of a metal statue, an artifact. It is not accidental that the myth speaks of welding, and uses the tools of the smith instead of the instruments of the doctor. Once we see the self-cancelling character of this *erōs*, we are not at all clear that our first, enthusiastic "yes" to Hephaistus' proposal expressed our deepest wish. But can our deepest wish be to live always in the grip of recurrent needs, and never to reach a stable satisfaction? (As Socrates asks in the *Gorgias*, can we choose the life of leaky jars?[10] We would like to find a way to retain our identity as desiring and moving beings, and yet make ourselves self-sufficient. It takes considerable ingenuity.

This is only a comedy, and only a myth, about distant beings. We are not sure that it is really our story—whether seen one by one, in detail, and from the inside, our loves really look like that. But we are left with questions. We have a sense that there may be some trouble around in the happy land of "uniqueness and integrity," that personal affection may not be in control of the world. We turn now to the speech that attempts to restructure that world, making it safe for practical reason.

III

Socrates never quite says that he is telling us the truth about *erōs*. Nor does he present the account of the ascent of desire in the first person, as a theory of his own, developed through experience and reflection. He introduces it, instead, as an account of whose value he was *persuaded* by a woman, and of whose value he will try, in turn, to persuade others. Diotima's teaching certainly depends in a fundamental way on Socrates' own beliefs and intuitions; like Socrates himself when he examines a pupil, she claims to be showing him what he himself really thinks. But the fact remains that it took an external intervention to convince him that clinging to certain beliefs required abandoning others. Without this, he would presumably have continued living with incompatibles, without seeing how they clash.

Socrates' teacher is a priestess named Diotima. Since she is a fiction, we are moved to ask about her name, and why Plato should have chosen it. The name means "honor the god." Alcibiades had a famous mistress, a courtesan whose name history records as Timandra. This name means "honor the man."[11] Here, then, Socrates, too, takes a mistress: a priestess instead of a courtesan, a woman who prefers the intercourse of the pure mind to the pleasures of the body, who honors divine over merely human things. Diotima's fictional fame and authority derive, Plato tells us, from her benefits to Athens at the time of the great plague, when she succeeded in postponing the catastrophe for ten years. This invention is also significant. Here, says Plato, is a person who is capable of bringing great benefits to the city, even of averting a dangerous illness, if only we will be persuaded to depart, with her as our guide, from our man-centered, man-honoring ways. Plato's picture of the external guide indicates that our salvation may have to come to us from within—i.e., at the cost of abandoning some beliefs and relationships that we, as humans, now cherish. And yet the presentation of Socrates' learning as working through and with his own antecedent beliefs tells us that a need to be so saved is, even now, in us, and will be readily awakened if we can only be brought to a clear vision of our own situation.

The crucial pieces of persuasion work their way unobtrusively into the teaching—both into Diotima's teaching of Socrates and into Socrates' teaching of us. We first discover that we believe (or partly believe) that we love individuals for their repeatable properties by following and being (almost) persuaded by an argument that employs this as a hidden premise. In this argument, whose logical form is unusually perspicuous—it is, for example, one of the easiest in all Plato to formalize, and every step is, usually explicitly, universally quantified—Socrates persuades Agathon that *erōs* is not beautiful. (This argument precedes the explicit introduction of Diotima, but it is clearly the fruit of her teaching, and its premises are further explored in her speech.) At the heart of the argument is a difficulty. We have the following steps:

1. For all y, if y loves, then there is an x such that y loves x.
2. For all y and all x, if y loves x, then y desires x.
3. For all y and all x, if y desires x, then y lacks x.[12]
4. For all y and all x, if y has x, then y does not desire x.[13]
5. For all y and all x, if y has x, y does not love x.
6. For all y and all x: if y loves x, x is beautiful.
7. For all y and all x: if y loves x, y lacks beauty.
8. For all y, if y lacks beauty, y is not beautiful.
9. For all y, if y loves, y is not beautiful.

The trouble comes, for us (though not for Agathon), at step 7. Even if we grant Socrates' controversial claims about the logic of wanting and possessing, even if we grant him, too, that all love objects must be *kalon* (a claim less implausible if we think of the broad moral-aesthetic range of the Greek word), we do not understand how he has reached the conclusions that y lacks beauty. We thought that he was talking about people. We had a situation where some y—let us say Alcibiades—is in love with beautiful Agathon. He wants to possess this beautiful person, and yet he is aware that he does not possess him. If he is lucky enough to be enjoying at present the charms of Agathon, still he cannot count on fully and stably possessing them for the rest of his life. So there is a beautiful person whom he both loves and lacks. This does not, however, show that he himself lacks beauty, even given the earlier premises of the argument. He may be quite beautiful, for all we know. What he lacks is beautiful Agathon. Socrates' conclusion would follow only if we reinterpret step 6—which, in the Greek text, was literally the claim "*erōs* is of the beautiful." From our first interpretation, that the lover's love is for someone (something) that has the property of being beautiful, it follows only that the lover lacks that particular beautiful person (thing). But suppose we now reinterpret step 6 to read:

6 ′. For all y and all x: if y loves x, x is a beauty.

—i.e., an instance of beauty, the beauty *of* some person or thing. From this there follows, at least, the conclusion that there is *an* instance of beauty that the lover does not possess, viz., the instance that he (she) loves. (That this is the correct understanding of the ambiguous sentence is suggested by the ensuing claim that "there cannot be love for the ugly": for, as Vlastos remarks, any whole person has uglinesses and faults. To avoid being directed at ugliness, love must be directed at a property of the person, not the whole. "Love is not for the half of the whole of anything, unless, my friend, that half or whole happens to be good.)

But we are not yet all the way to Plato's conclusion. So far there is some beauty loved by the lover: Alcibiades loves the beauty of Agathon. From this it follows only that Alcibiades lacks *that* beauty—not that he lacks *all* beauty. He might have some other type of beauty. Or he might even have some other token of the same type. The second possibility may not be relevant: it may be part of the psychological claims of the preceding steps that I will not desire something if I have, stably, something that is qualitatively the same, though a countably different instance.[14] But the first seems important: if Alcibiades is *kalon* in physical appearance, can he not still love and lack the beautiful soul of Socrates? What we now see is that Socrates' argument depends on a strong hidden assumption: that all beauty, *qua* beauty, is uniform, the same in kind. All manifestations of the *kalon* must be sufficiently like one another that if you lack one kind it is natural to conclude that you lack them all. The beauty of Alcibiades must be distinct from the beauty of Socrates not qualitatively, but only in terms of contingent spatio-temporal location (and perhaps in *quantity* as well).

And, in fact, this claim about beauty and goodness is explicitly asserted in Diotima's teaching. In her account of the soul's development towards the fullest understanding of the good, the idea of uniformity plays a crucial role. (This section of her speech is introduced as a revelation for the initiate, which will go beyond what Socrates the man could understand on his own. The young lover beginning the ascent—always under the direction of a "correct" guide—will begin by loving a single body, or, more exactly, the beauty of a single body: "Then he must see that the beauty in any one body is closely related to the beauty in another body; and that if he must pursue the beauty of form, it is great mindlessness not to consider the beauty of all bodies to be one and the same."

First, he sees only his loved one's beauty. Then he must notice a close family resemblance between that beauty and others. Then—and this is the crucial step away from the Vlastos view—he *decides* that it is prudent to consider these related beauties to be "one and the same." He then sees that he "must set himself up as the lover of all beautiful bodies, and relax his excessively intense passion for one body, looking down on that and thinking it of small importance." So the crucial step is, oddly, a step of decision, involving considerations of "mindlessness" and good sense. We begin to wonder what sort of need drives this lover. Where, for example, do all these "must" 's come from? Why does he think it foolish not to see things in a way that appears, *prima facie*, to be false to our ordinary intuitions about love? The references to "excessively intense passion" and to a "relaxing" raise the possibility that we are dealing with a strategy adopted for reasons of mental health, because a certain sort of tension has become too risky or difficult to bear. A kind of therapy alters the look of the world, making the related the same, the irreplaceable replaceable. If one "must" (by nature) "pursue the beauty of form," be sexually drawn to bodily beauty, it is most sensible to do it in a way that does not involve this costly tension. And one can do this, if one is determined enough, and has the help of a skillful therapist.

At the next stage, once again, the lover makes a decision to consider something the same and to adjust values accordingly: "He must consider that the beauty in souls is more honorable than that in the body." This judgment must clearly have been preceded, as was the last, by the perception of a relatedness and a prudent decision to treat the related as intimately comparable.[15] And so, in each stage of the ascent, the aspiring lover, aided by his teacher, sees relationships between one beauty and another, acknowledges that these beauties are comparable and intersubstitutable, and emerges with a proportionally diminished, though not fully extinguished, regard for those he formerly prized. The teacher leads him, makes him see, until at last he is able to conceive of the whole of beauty as a vast ocean, whose components are, like droplets, qualitatively indistinguishable:

> And looking towards the great extent of the beautiful, he will no longer, like some servant, loving the beauty of a particular boy or a particular man or of one set of customs, and being the slave of this, remain contemptible and of no account. But turned towards the wide sea of the beautiful and contemplating, he gives birth to many beautiful and grand speeches and reasonings in his abundant love of wisdom.

Education is being turned round, so that you do not see what you used to see.[16] It is also becoming a free man instead of a servant. Diotima connects the love of particulars with tension, excess, and servitude, the love of a uniform "sea" with health, freedom, and creativity. The claim for the change of perception and belief involved in the ascent is not so much that the new ones lead to a *truer* understanding. Questions of truth seem muted; and the gap between "family-related" and "one and the same" suggests that the ascent may be playing fast and loose with the truth as we know it. (Whatever my brother is, he is certainly not "one and the same" with me.) The claim is a claim about health and happiness. It is "great mindlessness" not to embark on the ascent. The person who does so change his world is no longer a no-account slave, and his thoughts bear abundant fruit. At each stage, the teacher convinces the pupil, stuck with his narrow instinctive human perceptions, to be willing to see new unities, to abandon the cherished ideal of irreplaceability in the service of his inner need for health. Socrates is among the convinced; and he is now trying to convince us that our human nature could find no better ally or collaborator than this sort of *erōs*. Once again, we note that what collaborates with my nature would seem not to be a part of my nature. An ally comes from another country to help me win my battles. If the ascent appears remote from human nature, that may be because it is meant that way.

One central feature of the ascent is that the lover escapes, gradually, from his bondage to the contingent. The Aristophanic lover loved in a very chancy way. He or she might never meet the right other in the first place; if she did, the other might not love her, or might die, or leave her. Or she might cease to love; or leave; or retreat; or be tormented by jealousy. Often her passions will distract her from her other plans, and from the good.

Even at the best of times she would be trying to do something both impossible and self-defeating. The philosopher is free of all this. Her contemplative love for all beauty carries no risk of loss, rejection, even frustration. Speeches and thoughts are always in our power, to a degree that emotional and physical intercourse with loved individuals is not. And if one instance of worldly beauty fades away or proves recalcitrant, there remains a boundless sea; we will feel the loss of the droplet almost not at all.

But the final revelation to the initiate lover takes her beyond even this minimal dependence on the world. Like the other advances, this one comes as a new vision. She sees it "all at once," the culmination of all her efforts:

First of all, it is always, and neither comes to be nor passes away, neither grows nor decays; then it is not beautiful in this respect but ugly in this, nor beautiful at one time and not at another, nor beautiful by comparison to this, ugly by comparison to that, nor beautiful here, ugly there, as though it were beautiful for some, and ugly for others. . . . He will see it as being itself by itself with itself, eternal and unitary, and see all the other beautifuls as partaking of it in such a manner that, when the others come to be and are destroyed, it never comes to be any more or less, nor suffers any alteration. . . . This indeed is what it is to approach erotic matters correctly, or to be led to them by another. . . . In this place, my dear Socrates, if anywhere, life is livable for a human being — the place where he contemplates the beautiful itself. If ever you see that, it will not seem to you to be valuable by comparison to gold and clothing and beautiful boys and youths, the sight of whom at present so inflames you that you, and many others, provided that you could see your beloved boys and be continually with them, are prepared to give up eating and drinking, and to spend your whole time contemplating them and being with them. What do we think it would be like . . . if someone should see the beautiful itself — unalloyed, pure, unmixed, not stuffed full of human flesh and colors and lots of other mortal rubbish, but if he could see the divine beautiful itself in its unity? Do you think life would be miserable for a man who looked out there, and contemplated it in an appropriate way and was with it? Or don't you understand that there alone, where he sees the beautiful with that faculty to which it is visible, it will be possible for him to give birth not to simulacra of excellence, since it is no simulacrum he is grasping, but to true excellence, since he is grasping truth? And as he brings forth true excellence and nourishes it, he will become god-loved, and, if ever a human being can, immortal?

So ends Diotima's speech of persuasion. I have quoted it at length not only to indicate the powerfully rhetorical character of her discourse, which moves and persuades us as it does Socrates, but also to show, in it, the signs of deep motivations lying behind the ascent. She speaks, indeed, of truth, and of simulacra. But our thirst for this truth is seen to spring from a practical need, a need for escape from the Aristophanic predicament. The really attractive promise of the ascent, the one she repeatedly stresses, is that, at its end, we will have an object of love and understanding that is perfectly unchanging and always available to be loved and contemplated — a loved one that will to the highest degree satisfy our longing to "be with" the beloved all the time. (*Suneinai* is also the most common word for intercourse.) It will also provide us with a life-activity, an activity expressive of our loving and creative nature, that is itself stable and in our power. The ascent is not "true," if we mean by that that it faithfully articulates our pre-philosophical experience of the world; instead, it teaches us to see the world in a radically different way. And the justification for this remaking is seen to lie in the deep demand of our natures for self-sufficient love. The ascent passage accepts Aristophanes' characterization of the misery and the irrational tumult of personal erotic need, agreeing that it disrupts our rational planning to the point where we would be willing to give up everything else, even health, even life. But that is intolerable. Such a life is not "livable";[17] we must find another way. Instead of flesh and all that mortal rubbish, an immortal object must, and therefore can, be found. Instead of obsessive yearning for a single body and spirit, a blissful contemplative completeness. We are offered no independent reason to think the ascent "true"; its practical truth is that it saves. It is a therapy of vision and intellect that can avert the plague from the persuaded.[18]

As Socrates concludes, we are moved to think back through this story (which, we now recall, is being told to us through Aristodemus, a convert and "lover" of Socrates, as reported by Apollodorus, another formerly wretched person whom philosophy has made happy), and to look at the life and behavior of Socrates as exemplifying the benefits of ascent. It is, first of all, striking that the lives of Socrates and the Socratic narrator appear remarkably orderly and free from distraction. "I used to rush around here and there as things fell out by chance," Apollodorus remembers, at a distance. And his master too seems always remarkably in control of his activities, free from the worldly passions and distractions that trouble most of us. He is reliably virtuous — courageous, just, temperate — all without lapses of weakness or fatigue. And this seems intimately connected with his imperviousness to the distractions of the world. He cares little about clothing, either for beauty or for comfort. We will hear later of his remarkable endurance of cold and bodily hardship. He walks barefoot over the ice, faces the coldest frosts without any coat or hat. This could be interpreted as the behavior of an arrogant man bent on self-display; so, we are told, it was interpreted by the soldiers. But the correct interpretation seems to be that Socrates has so dissociated himself from his body that he genuinely does not feel its pain, or regard its sufferings as things genuinely happening to him. He is famous for drinking without ever getting drunk, and without the hangovers complained of by the others. He does not succumb to the most immediate and intense sexual temptation. He can go sleepless without ever suffering from fatigue. We cannot explain all this by supposing his physiology to be radically different from that of a normal human being. We are invited, instead, to look for the explanation in his psychological distance from the world and from his body as an object in the world. He really seems to think of himself as a being whose mind is distinct from his body, whose personality in no way identifies itself with the body and the body's adventures. Inside the funny, fat, snub-nosed shell, the soul, self-absorbed, pursues its self-sufficient contemplation. We see him, at the beginning of the walk to the party, "turning his attention in some way in upon himself," so that he becomes, at a point, actually forgetful of the world. He falls behind the group; they find him much later, standing in a neighbor's porch, literally deaf to all entreaties. The sounds that enter in at the well-functioning ears never penetrate to the mind. There is a gulf. "Leave him alone," warns Aristodemus. "This is a habit of his. Sometimes he stops and stands wherever he happens to be."

These details have usually been read as intriguing pieces of biography. Perhaps they are. But they are also more than that. They show us what Diotima could only abstractly tell: what a human life starts to look like as one makes the ascent. Socrates is put before us as an example of a man in the process of making himself self-sufficient — put before us, in our still unregenerate state, as a troublesome question mark and a challenge. Is this the life we want for ourselves? Is that the way we want, or need, to see and hear? We are not allowed to have the cozy thought that the ascending man will be just like us, only happier. Socrates is weird. We feel, as we look at him, both awestruck and queasy, timidly homesick for ourselves. We feel that we must look back at what we currently are, our loves and our ways of seeing, and the problems these cause for practical reason. We need to see ourselves more clearly before we can say whether we would like to become this other sort of being, excellent and deaf.

IV

The summit of the ascent, Diotima tells us, is marked by a revelation: "All at once he will see a beauty marvelous in its nature, for the sake of which he had made all his previous efforts." Now, as we begin our reflective descent into ourselves, at this moment when some of the symposiasts are praising Socrates, and Aristophanes is trying to remind us again of his view of our nature, we see another sort of revelation, and another beauty. "And all at once there was a loud knocking at the outer door. It sounded like a drunken party; you could hear the voice of the flute girl. . . . And a minute later they heard the voice of Alcibiades in the courtyard, very drunk and shouting loudly, asking where Agathon was and demanding to be taken to Agathon." The form of the beautiful appeared to the mind's eye alone, looking "not like some face or hands or anything else that partakes in body"; it was "unalloyed, pure, unmixed, not stuffed full of human flesh and colors and lots of other mortal rubbish." Alcibiades the beautiful, the marvelous nature, presents himself to our sensuous imagination, an appearance bursting with color and all the mixed impurity of mortal flesh. We are made to hear his voice, vividly see his movements, even smell the violets that trail through his hair and shade his eyes, their perfume blending with the heavier odors of wine and sweat. The faculty that apprehends the form is preeminently stable, unwavering, and in our power to exercise regardless of the world's happenings. The faculties that see and hear and respond to Alcibiades will be the feelings and sense perceptions of the body, both vulnerable and inconstant. From the rarified contemplative world of the self-sufficient philosopher we are suddenly, with an abrupt jolt, returned to the world we inhabit and invited (by the parallel "all at once") to see this vision, too, as a dawning and a revelation. We are then moved to wonder whether there is a kind of understanding that is itself vulnerable and addressed to vulnerable objects — and, if there is, whether the ascent comprehends it, transcends it, or simply passes it by.

Alcibiades takes up this theme at the very opening of his speech. "You there," says Socrates, "what do you mean to do?" (A question that reverberates ominously for us in view of our greater knowledge of what this man will soon be up to.) "Do you mean to give a mock-praise of me? Or what are you going to do?" The answer is a simple one, though difficult to understand. "I'm going to tell the truth. Do you think you'll allow that?" (Why on earth should anyone, especially a pupil of Socrates, suspect that philosophy might be hostile to the truth?) When, shortly after, he tells us more about his brand of truth-telling, we begin to understand why he is on the defensive. "Gentlemen, I shall undertake to praise Socrates through images. He may think that it is a mock-praise, but the image will be for the sake of the truth, not for ridicule." Asked to speak about Love, Alcibiades has chosen to speak of a particular love; no definitions or explanations of the nature of anything, but just a story of a particular, contingent passion for a particular contingent individual. Asked to make a speech, he gives us the story of his own life: the understanding of *erōs* he has achieved through his own intimate experience. (The concluding words of his speech are the proverbial *pathonta gnōnai*, "understanding through experience" or "suffering.") And, what is more, this story conveys its truths using images or likenesses — a poetic practice much deplored by the Socrates of the *Republic*. (Images lack the power to provide us with true general accounts or explanations of essences.) But his opening remarks indicate that Alcibiades is not simply ignorant of these philosophical objections. He anticipates criticism. He anticipates, in fact, that the philosopher will not *allow* his truths, or not allow their claim to be the truth. And he asserts, in the face of this danger, that, nonetheless, what he will tell will be truth — that the truth can and will be told in just this way, in a story about individuals, and through images.

He seems to be claiming, implicitly, that there are truths about love that can be learned only through the experience of a particular passion of one's own. If one is asked to teach those truths, one's only recourse is to re-create that experience for the hearer: to tell a story, to appeal to his or her imagination and feelings by the use of vivid narrative. Images are invaluable in this attempt to make the audience share the experience, to feel, from the inside, what it is *like* to be that. The comparison of Socrates to the Silenus-statue, for example, takes this man who is not intimately known to the hearer and, by comparing him to something that is a part of everyday experience, makes available to her something of the feeling of what it is like to want and to want to know him. We will examine this and other such cases later on; and we shall also see that Alcibiades, drunk, wound round with ivy, presents himself to our understanding as an image that tells the truth.

We now notice that Alcibiades is offering the material for a defense of the role of literature in moral learning. Certain truths about human experience must be learned by living them in their particularity. Nor can this particularity be grasped solely by thought "itself by itself"; it must be apprehended through the cognitive activity of imagination, emotions, even appetitive feelings. (Wittgenstein said to Rhees that our textbooks of moral philosophy could not teach because they were devoid of examples; they could not touch the imagination. To know what you might say and should choose, you have to put yourself inside a problem and feel it.)[19] But we cannot all live, in our own overt activities, through all that we ought to know in order to live well. Here literature, with its stories and images, enters in as an extension of our experience, encouraging us to develop and understand our cognitive/emotive responses. This exchange of information between texts and life probably works in both directions. From life we learn how to see things in a tragedy or a speech; but from texts we can also attain, in life, to a new correctness of perception.

If this is, indeed, Alcibiades' view, it is not surprising that he is on the defensive in this company. If the symposiasts have anything in common, it is that they seem to believe that *erōs* should be praised in the abstract. Particular stories enter briefly as examples of general principles, but none is described fully or concretely, in a way that would appeal to the sensuous imagination. Aristophanes' myth might be said to teach through an image of human nature; and his poetic gifts are evident in the vividness with which he describes the movements and feelings of the mythic creatures. But the creatures remain anonymous exemplars, and their loved ones, though individuals, are abstractly characterized. We have a hard time seeing ourselves in them, our particular loves in this odd fitting-together. Socrates, meanwhile, has attacked even this limited appeal to lived experience in the name of philosophical wisdom. Nobody loves a half or a whole, unless that half or whole is beautiful and good. Socrates claims to have *epistēmē* of erotic matters; and *epistēmē*, unlike Alcibiades' *pathonta gnōnai*, is deductive, scientific, concerned with universals. (When Aristotle wants to defend the role, in practical wisdom, of a non-deductive intuition of particulars through feeling and experience, he does so by *contrasting* this intuitive grasp with *epistēmē*).[20] The Socratic search for definitions embodying *epistēmē* is, throughout the dialogues, the search for a universal account that covers and explains all the particulars. To answer a Socratic "What is *X*?" question by enumerating particular examples or telling stories is either to misunderstand or to reject his demand. In the early dialogues, examples provide material toward *epistēmē*, material a definition must take into account; they can never on their own embody *epistēmē*. And here in the *Symposium* Socrates' attitude to the particular case seems to be harsher still. Examples are relevant not as complex wholes, but only insofar as they exemplify a property. The correct Socratic lover comes to see each particular only as an instance of something repeatable, one more droplet in the sea. The revelation of the beautiful can count as truth for him only because it is *not* an image and does not present itself through images. Images are contrasted with truth both as objects and as sources of understanding. They block the best kind of seeing. Only with the dulling of the "sight of the body," the senses and the sensuous imagination, does intellect, the "sight of the mind," begin to flourish.

Socratic philosophy, then, cannot allow the truths of Alcibiades to count as truths. It must insist that the non-repeatable aspects of the particular are irrelevant, even a hindrance, to correct seeing. And it is not only the philosophy of Socrates against which Alcibiades must defend his claim to teach. It is any philosophy that demands, for ethics, an abstract simplicity and neatness. Very few philosophers have welcomed stories and images into their art. (One thinks of Aristotle, of Dante, of Nietzsche, of Wittgenstein.)[21] And their openness to literature has been bought, some would say, at the price of giving up philosophy, or of so reducing its high ambition to know the world that it can no longer correctly call itself by that name. At any rate these few, and others similarly interested in looking at their own perceptions, have not produced in the *profession* of philosophy the general spirit of openness and self-questioning that would lead it to listen openly to love stories and the speech of images. Contrasts between the mixed and the pure, between the associative and the analytical, the literary and the philosophical, are as sharply drawn now in many places as they are in this text by Plato—but culpably, because unreflectively, and without Plato's loving recreation of the speech of the other side. Even this mixed piece of writing, which uses the story of Alcibiades as its image, will certainly encounter this. It will be asked by some to prove that it, too, is philosophy, and pure enough to tell the truth.

But to place, in this way, the burden of proof on Alcibiades, to force him to argue with Socrates accepting the Socratic aspiration to systematic *epistēmē*, is itself resolutely not to hear him, not to agree to enter his world. To allow is to enter and to let yourself be entered, to live inside this story and to let it have its way with you, humbly and without decision.

It is, in fact, just a love story. It is, however, not *a* love story, but the story of Socrates, and of the love of Alcibiades for Socrates. Alcibiades, asked to speak about *erōs*, cannot describe the passion or its object in general terms, because his experience of love is an experience that has happened to him this way only once, and in connection with an individual who is seen by him to be like nobody else in the world. The entire speech is an attempt to grasp and communicate that uniqueness, to make credible and imaginable for us an experience and a feeling that is by its nature difficult to describe. He might have begun his answer by enumerating the excellent qualities of this unlikely figure. This would perhaps be all true, but it would not go far towards capturing the particular tone and intensity of the passion; it might even mislead, by implying that another person turning up with these same repeatable properties would make Alcibiades feel the same way. But he doesn't know that. So Alcibiades tells some Socrates stories; he gropes for images and associations to communicate the inside feel of the experience. The speech, disorganized and tumultuous, moves from imaging to describing, response to story, and back again many times over. It is precisely its groping, somewhat chaotic character that makes it so movingly convincing as an account—and an expression—of love.

Two things in the speech, above all, strike us as strange. Using them as clues we may perhaps be able to understand more fully its teaching and its relationship to Socratic teaching. The first is its confusion about sexual roles. Alcibiades begins as the beautiful *erōmenos*, but seems to end as the active *erastēs*, while Socrates, apparently the *erastēs*, becomes the *erōmenos*. The second is Alcibiades' odd habit of incarnation—the way he speaks of his soul, his reason, his feelings and desires, as pieces of flesh that can experience the bites, burns, and tears that are the usual lot of flesh.

The *erōmenos*, in Greek homosexual custom (as interpreted in Sir Kenneth Dover's authoritative study),[22] is a beautiful creature without pressing needs of his own. He is aware of his attractiveness, but self-absorbed in his relationship with those who desire him. He will smile sweetly at the admiring lover; he will show appreciation for the other's friendship, advice, and assistance. He will allow the lover to greet him by touching, affectionately, his genitals and his face, while he looks, himself, demurely at the ground. And, as Dover demonstrates from an exhaustive study of Greek erotic painting, he will even allow the importunate other to satisfy his desires through intercrural intercourse. The boy may hug him at this point, or otherwise positively indicate affection. But two things he will not allow, in the works of art and the literary testimonies that have come down to us. He will not allow any orifice of his body to be penetrated; only hairy satyrs so open themselves. And he will not allow the arousal of his own desire to penetrate the other. In all of surviving Greek art, there are no boys with erections. Dover concludes, with some incredulity, "The penis of the erastes is sometimes erect even before any bodily contact is established, but that of the eromenos remains flaccid even in circumstances to which one would expect the penis of any healthy adolescent to respond willy-nilly."[23] The inner experience of an *erōmenos* would be characterized, we may imagine, by a feeling of proud self-sufficiency. Though the object of importunate solicitation, he is himself not in need of anything beyond himself. He is unwilling to let himself be explored by the other's needy curiosity, and he has, himself, little curiosity about the other. He is something like a god, or the statue of a god.

For Alcibiades, who had spent much of his young life as this sort of closed and self-absorbed being, the experience of love is felt as a sudden openness, and, at the same time, an overwhelming desire to open. The presence of Socrates makes him feel, first of all, a terrifying and painful awareness of being perceived. He wants, with part of himself, to "hold out," to remain an *erōmenos*. His impulse, in service of this end, is to run away, hide, stop up his ears — orifices that can be entered, willy-nilly, by penetrating words. But he senses at the same time that in this being seen and being spoken to, in this Siren music that rushes into his body in this person's presence, is something he deeply needs not to avoid: "There's something I feel with nobody else but Socrates — something you would not have thought was in me — and that is a sense of shame. He is the only person who makes me feel shame. . . . There are times when I'd gladly see him dead. But if that happened, you understand, I'd be worse off than ever." The openness of the lover brings with it so much naked vulnerability to criticism. Alcibiades stands there to be looked at and penetrated, lived in or walked away from. In the closed world of the *erōmenos*, defects and treasures, both, hide comfortably from scrutiny. Being known by the lover can bring the pain of shame, awareness of one's own roughnesses and imperfections. On the other hand this pain, as he dimly sees it, may lead to some kind of growth.

So Alcibiades is thrown into confusion about his role. He knows himself to be, as an object, desirable. "I was amazingly vain about my beauty." He thought of his alliance with Socrates as a decision to grant a favor, while remaining basically unmoved. And yet now he wants, and needs, the penetration and illumination of the other's presence. The sphere has become a thing full of holes.

More confusing still, he feels, at the same time, a deep desire to know Socrates — a desire as conventionally inappropriate as his desire to be

302 known. His speech makes repeated and central use of the image of *opening up* the other: an image which is essentially sexual, and inseparable from his sexual aims and imaginings, but which is also epistemic, intended to convey to us his desire "to hear everything that he knew" and to know everything that he was. Socrates, he tells us, is like one of those toy Sileni made by craftsmen. On the outside they look unremarkable, even funny. But what you are moved to do, what you cannot resist doing once you see the crack running down the middle, is to open them up. (They can be opened up because they have this crack or scar, and are not completely smooth.) Then, on the inside, you see the hidden beauty, the elaborate carving of god-statues. We might imagine the effect to be like that of the amazing mediaeval rosary bead in the Cloisters. On the outside, a decorated sphere, nothing remarkable. Then you pry the two halves apart to reveal "the treasures inside"—a marvelously wrought scene of animals, trees, and men, all carved with the most delicate precision. That something you thought to be a sphere should contain its own world: that is the surprise, and the reason for awe.

Among our first and best-loved toys are things that can be opened to show something on the inside. Even before we can speak, we are trying to open things up. We spend hours sitting on the floor in rapt attention, pulling our spherical balls of wood or plastic apart into their two halves, looking for the hidden ball, or bell, or family. By using such toys as images, Alcibiades reminds us that the urge to open things up, to get at and explore the inside concealed by the outside, is one of our earliest and strongest desires, a desire in which sexual and epistemological need are joined and, apparently, inseparable. We long to probe whatever is secret, to seek out and bring to light what is concealed and obscure; and when we see a crack, that is, to us, a signal that this aim can be fulfilled in the object. Once we notice, in someone to whom we are attracted, this gap or seam, we long to open it up, to make the other's beauty less rounded and more exposed, to walk around inside the world that we imagine to be there for the exploring, coming to know it by means of feelings, emotions, sensations, intellect. Alcibiades sees his sexual aim, the fullest fulfillment of which demands both physical intimacy and philosophical conversation, as a kind of epistemic aim, the aim to achieve a more complete understanding of this particular rich portion of the world.

It is easy enough to see structural parallels between sexual desire and the desire for wisdom. Both are directed towards objects in the world, and aim at somehow grasping or possessing these objects. The fulfilled grasp of the object brings, in both cases, satiety and the temporary cessation of desire: no sphere seduces, "no god does philosophy." Both can be aroused by beauty and goodness, and both seek to understand the nature of that goodness. Both revere the object as a separate, self-complete entity, and yet long, at the same time, to incorporate it. But Alcibiades appears to want to claim something more controversial and anti-Socratic than this parallelism. With his claims that a story tells the truth and that his goal is to open up and to know, he asserts, I believe, that the lover's knowledge of the particular other, gained through an intimacy both bodily and intellectual, is itself a unique and uniquely valuable *kind* of practical understanding, and one that we risk losing if we take the first step up the Socratic ladder.

Socratic knowledge of the good, attained through pure intellect operating apart from the senses, yields universal truths — and, in practical choice, universal rules. If we have apprehended the form, we will be in possession of a general account of beauty, an account that not only holds true of all and only instances of beauty, but also explains why they are correctly called instances of beauty, and grouped together.[24] Such understanding, once attained, would take priority over our vague, mixed impressions of particular beautifuls. It would tell us how to see.

The lover's understanding, attained through the responsive communion of sense, emotion, and intellect (any one of which, once well trained, may perform a cognitive function in exploring and informing us concerning the others) yields particular truths and particular judgments. It insists that those particular intuitive judgments are prior to any universal rules we may be using to guide us. I decide how to respond to my lover not on the basis of definitions or general prescriptions, but on the basis of an intuitive sense of the person and the situation, which, although guided by my general theories, is not subservient to them.[25] This does not mean that my judgments and responses are not rational. Indeed, Alcibiades would claim that a Socratic adherence to rule and refusal to see and feel the particular as such is what is irrational. To have seen that, and how, Socrates is like nobody else, to respond to him as such and to act accordingly, is the deeply rational way to behave towards another individual. The man bound by rules looks, from this viewpoint, like one afraid to see. The Socratic claim to have a general deductive science (*epistēmē*) of the good and of love now begins to appear as weird as Socrates. Perhaps "such cases do not fall under any science or precept, but the agents themselves must consider what suits the occasion, as is also the case in medicine and in navigation. . . . "The universal must come from the particulars; and one of these must have perception, and this is *nous*" (Aristotle, *Nicomachean Ethics*).[26]

It is tempting to try to understand the contrast between these two kinds of knowledge in terms of the contrast between propositional knowledge and knowledge by acquaintance. This would, I believe, be an error. First of all, Socratic knowledge itself is not simply propositional knowledge. Because of Socrates' constant emphasis on the claim that the man with *epistēmē* is the man who is able to give explanations or accounts, the rendering "understanding" is, in general, more appropriate.[27] Second, both kinds of understanding, not just the Socratic kind, are concerned with truths. Alcibiades is claiming not just an ineffable familiarity with Socrates, but the ability to tell the truth about Socrates. He wants to claim that through a lover's intimacy he can produce accounts (stories) that are more deeply and precisely true — that capture more of what is characteristic and practically relevant about Socrates, that explain more about what Socrates does and why — than any account that could be produced by a form-lover who denied himself the cognitive resources of the senses and emotions.

Finally, there is much about the lover's understanding that cannot be captured by either model of knowledge, but can be better conceived as a kind of "knowing how." The lover can be said to understand the beloved when, and only when, (s)he knows how to treat him or her: how to speak, look, and move at various times and in various circumstances; how to give pleasure and how to receive it; how to arouse desire and how to satisfy it; how to deal with the loved one's complex network of intellectual, emotional, and bodily needs. This understanding requires acquaintance, and yields the ability to tell truths; but it does not seem to be reducible to either.

Alcibiades suggests, then, that there is a kind of practical understanding, an understanding of the good and the beautiful, that consists in a keen responsiveness of intellect, imagination, and feeling to the particulars of a situation: an ability to pick out its salient features, combined with a disposition to act appropriately as a result. Of this sort of intuitive practical wisdom the lover's understanding of the particular beloved is a central and particularly deep case — and not only a case among cases, but one whose resulting self-understanding might be fundamental to the flourishing of practical wisdom in other areas of life as well. There is no attempt here to deny that the lover's understanding has many components that are, to a certain degree, independent of the success of his specifically sexual projects. Alcibiades can tell the truth about Socrates' unique strangeness even though his aims were frustrated. And not just any successful lover would have had his intellectual and emotional grasp. But there is no denying, either, that with the failure of sexual intimacy a certain part of practical understanding is lost to Alcibiades. There is a part of Socrates that remains dark and mysterious to him, a depth of intuitive responsiveness to this particular man, an aptness of speech, movement, and gesture, that he can never develop, a kind of "dialectic" that is missing.[28]

It is, then, in his openness to such knowing that Alcibiades stands revealed as no proper *erōmenos*. To receive the other, he must not be self-sufficient, closed against the world, unresponsive to its stimuli. He must put aside the vanity of beauty and become, himself, in his own eyes, an object in the world: in the world of the other's activity, and in the larger world of happenings that affect his dealings with the other. And such an object will know more if it has a crack in it.

This gives us a key to our second puzzle: why Alcibiades should persistently speak of his soul, his inner life, as something of flesh and blood like the visible body. Alcibiades has no particular metaphysical view of the person; he makes it clear that he is uncertain about how to refer to what is "inside" the flesh-and-blood body. What he knows is that this inner part of him is responding like a thing of flesh. He says he feels like a sufferer from snakebite—only he has been "bitten by something more painful and the most painful way one can be bitten: I've been bitten and wounded in the heart or soul, or whatever one should call it, by the philosophical speeches of Socrates." And he tries, without success, to treat Socrates' "whatever" in the same manner, shooting words like lightning bolts in the hope that they will "pierce" him. Whatever is flesh or fleshlike is vulnerable. The mark of body is its ability to be pierced and bitten, to be prey to snakes, lightning flashes, lovers. Alcibiades, without a philosophical view of mind, gives an extraordinary defense of "physicalism" for the souls of lovers:

All and only body is vulnerable to contingent happenings in the world.
I am inwardly bitten, pierced.
Therefore this whatever-you-call-it is bodily (or very like body).

It is an argument that appeals to subjective experience, indeed to subjective suffering, to deny a "Platonic" view of the soul as a thing that is at one and the same time the seat of personality and immortal/invulnerable. The seat of my personality just got bitten by those speeches, so I know it is not *katharon, monoeides, akinēton.* It is obvious that such a line of argument shows us nothing about the souls of philosophers, for whom the Platonic account may, for all Alcibiades knows, be correct.

Both the lover's epistemic aim and his felt vulnerability are captured for us in the central image of Alcibiades' story: the lightning bolt. Images of revelation, appearing, and radiance have been seen before. Alcibiades appears before us "all at once," just as for him Socrates "is accustomed to appear all at once," just when he least thinks he is there, reminding Alcibiades of the inner radiance of his virtues. But now Alcibiades has spoken of the words and gestures of love as things hurled at the other like bolts of lightning. This image knits together, with extraordinary compression, his views about sexual ambition, knowledge, and risk. A lightning bolt strikes all at once, unpredictably, usually allowing no hope of defense or control. It is at one and the same time a brilliance that brings illumination and a force that has the power to wound and to kill. It is, one might say, corporeal light. In the heaven of the philosopher, the Form of the Good, like an intelligible sun, gives intelligibility to the objects of understanding while remaining, itself, unmoving and unchanging.[29] It affects the pure soul only by inspiring it to perform self-sufficient acts of pure reasoning. In the world of Alcibiades, the illumination of the loved one's body and mind strikes like a moving, darting, bodily light, a light that makes its impact by touching as well as by illuminating. It is rather like what happens to the sun in certain later paintings of Turner. No more a pure, remote condition of sight, it becomes a force that does things in the world to objects such as boats, waves, a just man's eyes—all of which are seen, insofar as they are thus illuminated, to be the sorts of things to which happenings can happen. The lover has this light in him to deploy or give, and it is this that he longs to receive, even though it killed Semele. (In the same way one returns again and again to Turner's *Regulus* as though to a temptation, in order to feel the light strike and touch our [Regulus'] eyes. You turn the corner into that room of the Tate, to repeat for yourself the proof that you are not a Platonic soul. That soul is an image too.) If Socrates had carried a shield, its device would have been the sun of the *Republic*, visible image of the intelligible form. Alcibiades, placing on his shield the thunderbolt, marks in his own way the sort of being he claims to be, the sort of understanding he desires.

Our reading has now put us in a position to move from the interpretation of the images *used* by Alcibiades to the interpretation of the image that Alcibiades *is*, as he presents himself before us. He makes his appearance "crowned with a thick crown of ivy and violets," making dress itself an image that tells the truth.[30] The crown of violets is, first of all, a sign of Aphrodite. This hardly surprises us, except for the strange fact (of which we shall speak more later) that this aggressively masculine figure sees himself as a female divinity. It is also, further, a crown worn by the Muses. As he begins his truth-telling through images, Alcibiades, then, presents himself as a poet, and an inspiring god of poets (Plato?). He himself exemplifies the proverbial *pathonta gnōnai*; but, through the intimacy of poetic speeches, it is also possible to learn before you suffer. Philosophy, insofar as it omits this kind of teaching, is incomplete.

But the violet crown stands for something else as well: for the city of Athens herself. In a fragment from Pindar (only one of the poems that use this apparently well-known epithet) she is addressed:

O glistening and violet-crowned and famous in song,
Bulwark of Hellas, glorious Athens,
Fortunate city.

The crown of violets is the delicate, growing sign of the fortunate flourishing of this strange and fragile democracy, now, in the time of Alcibiades, in its greatest danger. By so crowning himself, Alcibiades indicates that his own attentiveness to the particular and the contingent, to persons rather than repeatable properties, intuitions rather than rules, is the fruit of this city's education. This education values the original and the daring, relies on the ability of gifted leaders to "improvise what is required" (Thucydides I. 138), and, instead of commanding humble subservience to law, asks free men to "choose, in their nobility of character " (Thucydides II. 41), a life of virtue and service. Doing away, as it does, with rules, it depends on each man's capacity for practical wisdom and the understanding of the lover. Thucydides' Pericles enjoins the citizens to "look at the city's power day by day and become her lovers." *Erōs*, not law or fear, guides action. But this reliance on *erōs* puts democracy, like Alcibiades, very much at the mercy of fortune, and of the irrational passions.[31] The violet crown is worn by a gifted drunk, who will soon commit imaginative crimes.

The ivy is, of course, the sign of Dionysus, god of wine, god of irrational inspiration. (The ivy is a symbol of the bodily fertility of the inspired lover, who is, and sees himself as, one of the burgeoning and chancy growing things of the natural world, mutable and green.) This god, male in form yet of softly female bearing, exemplifies the sexual contradictions of Alcibiades' aspirations. He embodies, too, another apparent contradiction: he is the patron god of both tragic and comic poetry. This is quite appropriate, since the speech of Alcibiades is both tragic and comic—tragic in its depiction of frustration and its foreshadowing of ruin, comic in the knowing self-humor of the story-teller, who exposes his vanity and illusions with Aristophanic delight. It is already beginning to be evident to us why Socrates should, at the dialogue's end, argue that comedy and tragedy can be the work of a single man. The Aristophanic view of love is of a piece with the vision of Alcibiades in its emphasis on the bodily and contingent nature of human erotic aspiration, the vulnerability of practical wisdom to the world. Now, however, we see a further dimension to the *rapprochement*. Alcibiades is appealing, gripping, and, ultimately, tragic in part *because* he is also the comic poet of his own disaster. If he had told a melodramatic tale of anguish and loss, stripped of the wit, the self-awareness, and the laughter that characterize his actual speech, his story would be less tragic, because we would have less reason to care about him. (A reflection prompted, in part, by the strange experience of Woody Allen's *Interiors*, whose suffering characters, stripped of all laughter, strike us as so self-absorbed and impenetrable that we can hardly think of them as human, much less be moved.) A certain kind of self-critical perception of one's cracks and holes, which issues naturally in comic poetry, is an important part of what we value in Alcibiades and want to salvage in ourselves. So it seems not accidental that Dionysus, god of tragic loss, should stand for both.

There is one more feature of Dionysus to which the ivy crown particularly directs us: he is the god who dies. He undergoes, each year, a ritual death and a rebirth, a cutting back and a resurgence, like the plant, like desire itself. Among the gods he alone is not self-sufficient, he alone can be acted on by the world. And yet, miraculously, he restores himself and burgeons like the ivy. So may, perhaps, the city grow from death. So also, it is hoped, love.

V

All this shows us the case for Alcibiades. But the speech is also, implicitly, Plato's indictment. We have seen him invent a priestess whose job it is to save men from plagues, and we have suggested that personal *erōs* and the lover's knowledge, are this plague. We want now to discover the origins of this condemnation. What makes *erōs* intolerable? What gives rise to this overwhelming need to get above it and away from it?

There are, it must be said, problems for Alcibiades. First there is the problem of what happens to him, and what his curiosity finds. His attempt to penetrate the other encounters an obstacle in the stone of Socratic virtue. It is not without reason that Alcibiades compares Socratic virtues to statues of the gods. For, as we have seen, Socrates, in his ascent towards the form, has become, himself, very like a form—hard, indivisible, unchanging. His virtue, in search of science and of assimilation to the good itself, turns away from the responsive intercourse with particular earthly goods that is Alcibiades' knowledge.

It is not only Socrates' dissociation from his body. It is not only that he sleeps all night with the naked Alcibiades without arousal. There is, along with his remoteness, a deeper impenetrability of spirit. Words launched "like bolts" have no effect. Socrates might conceivably have abstained from intercourse while remaining attentive to the lover in his particularity (like the pairs of lovers in the *Phaedrus*). He might also have had intercourse with Alcibiades while remaining inwardly aloof. There is more than one way to be a statue. But Socrates refuses in every way to be affected. He is stone, and he turns to stone. Alcibiades is to his sight just one more of the beautifuls, a piece of the form, a pure thing like a jewel.

So the first problem for Alcibiades is that his own great openness is denied. He is a victim of *hubris* pierced, mocked, dishonored.[32] This is, of course, just a story, and the story of a unique problem. There are not many stones like Socrates. But there are, on the other hand, many varieties of stone. If there is, by luck, responsiveness on both sides now, still there may be change, estrangement bringing painful loss of knowledge. As even Diotima concedes, before proposing the method of ascent that will try to remedy the problem, souls, with their thoughts, feelings, and desires, are no more stable than bodies. "Our understandings come into being and pass away, and we are never the same even in our understandings, but every single understanding suffers this." Even if there is rare stability in understanding and response, there will surely still be death to put knowledge to sleep. They never really do die "in common," either.

So happenings plague the lover; and we might begin to wonder how contingent these happenings are. But let us suppose, for a moment, that Alcibiades is deeply involved in a mutually passionate love, in which both parties are lovers, each trying to explore the world that the openness of the other makes available. We want to know whether Diotima has reason to see personal *eros* as, in its nature, a plague, or whether her criticisms work only against the unhappy cases, and speak only to those of us who either fear or are enmeshed in such experiences. Let us, then, imagine Alcibiades happy in love. Is he, then, in love, truly happy or good? The dialogue makes us wonder. No present fortune is guarantee of its own stability. Therefore, as the dialogue indicates, fears, jealousies, and the threat of loss may be an intimate part of even the best experiences of loving. The playfully threatening banter between Socrates and Alcibiades, the mock violence that points to the real violence to come, the drunken lack of control, are not necessarily to be read against the background of their estrangement. In the best of times such dangerous emotions could be summoned by the fear of the other's separateness. There is a strong possibility that Alcibiades *wants* Socrates to be a statue—a thing that can be held, carried, or, when necessary, smashed. There is a strong possibility that this sort of intense being-in-love cannot tolerate, and wishes to kill, autonomous movement. The sentimentalized lover of Greek erotic painting greets the boy by affectionately touching him on face and genitals, indicating in this tender gesture respect and awe for his whole person.[33] The gesture of Alcibiades—the violent smashing of holy faces and genitals—may be, the dialogue suggests, a truer expression of unregenerate *erōs*.

There is also the equally troublesome possibility that it is precisely the stoniness of the other that attracts. The remote, round, brilliant thing, gleaming like a form, undivided, lures with the promise of secret richness. It's nothing to open something that has a crack. But the perfect thing—if you could ever open that up, then you would be blessed and of unlimited power. Alcibiades loves the stone beauty that he finds: only that temperance is worthy of him, because only that beautifully eludes him. So, perhaps, practical reason, reaching for power, dooms itself, repeatedly. When the light of Socrates "appears all at once" for Alcibiades, it is the sort of light that, radiantly poured round the aspiring body, may seal or freeze it in, like a coat of ice. That is its beauty.

All this leads us to ask most seriously whether personal *erōs* can have, after all, any place in a life that is to be shaped and ruled by practical reason. We tried to think of a life in which *erōs* would play its part along with other component goods—intellectual, political, social. But the nature of personal erotic passion may be such as to be always unstable, always threatening, when given a part, to overwhelm the whole. Aristophanes said that the erotic needs of his mythical creatures made them indifferent to eating, drinking, and "all other pursuits." We see Alcibiades' jealous and exclusive passions making him indifferent to truth and goodness. Practical reason shapes a world of value, and prides itself both on the worth of its world and on its efficiency in making it actual. But to make yourself a lover is to accept the reality and the power of another world. Here is this other reasoning being outside me, itself a maker of a world. My love for this being is a desire to explore and be explored by that other as other; it essentially involves (although it also struggles against) respect for the autonomy of the other's reason. But this respect presupposes the acknowledgment that I am not the whole world. I make myself cracked, put myself into the power and under the judging, defining eye of the other outside me. (At the same time I entrust myself also to equally uncontrollable forces within me.) To feel so great a commitment to and power from what is external to your practical reason can feel like slavery, or madness. Alcibiades compares himself to someone who is gripped by something and out of his senses. His soul is in a turmoil. He is angry at himself for his slavish condition. "I had no resource," he concludes, "and I went around in slavery to this man, such slavery as has never been before." The past is still actual. To be a slave is to be without autonomy, unable to live by the plans of your own reason, perhaps unable even to form a plan. It is no wonder that, as we look on the man who will live, to the end, a disorderly, buffeted life, inconstant and wasteful of his excellent nature, we are tempted to say, with Socrates: "I shudder at his madness and his passion for love."

We now begin to understand Plato's strategy in constructing this dramatic confrontation. Through Aristophanes, he raises certain doubts in our mind concerning the erotic projects to which we are most attached. And yet the speech of Aristophanes still praises *erōs* as most necessary, and necessary for the success of practical reason itself. He then shows us, through Socrates and Diotima, how, despite our needy and mortal natures, we can transcend the merely personal in *erōs* and ascend, through desire itself, to the good. But we are not yet persuaded that we can accept this vision of self-sufficiency and this model of practical understanding, since, with Vlastos, we feel that they omit something. What they omit is now movingly displayed to us in the person and the story of Alcibiades, which is also our story. We realize, through him, the deep importance unique passion has for us; we see its irreplaceable contribution to understanding. But the story brings a further problem: it shows us clearly that we cannot simply add the love of Alcibiades to the ascent of Diotima; indeed, that we cannot have this love and the kind of stable practical rationality, the orderly and respectful goodness, that she revealed to us. Socrates was serious when he spoke of two mutually exclusive varieties of vision.

And now, all at once, *exaiphnēs*, there dawns on us the full light of Plato's design, his comic tragedy of choice and practical wisdom. We see two kinds of value, two kinds of knowledge; and we see that we must choose. One sort of understanding blocks out the other. The pure light of the eternal form eclipses, or is eclipsed by, the flickering lightning of the opened and penetrating body. You think, says Plato, that you can have this love and goodness too, this knowledge of and by flesh and good-knowledge too. (Gregory Vlastos thinks that we can love particular individuals with the intensity of Alcibiades and still be rational men and philosophers.) Well, says Plato, you can't, and he can't. You have to blind yourself to something, give up some beauty. "The sight of reason begins to see clearly when the sight of the eyes begins to grow dim"—whether from age or because you are learning to be good. You cannot have all value, all knowledge.

But what, then, becomes of us, the audience, when we are confronted with the illumination of this true tragedy, and forced to see everything? We are, Alcibiades tells us, the jury. And we are also the accused. As we watch the trial of Socrates for the contemptuous overweening of reason, which is at the same time the trial of Alcibiades for the contemptuous overweening of the body, we see what neither of them can fully see — the overweening of both. And we see that it is ours, part of the way we must go if we are to follow either one or the other. But so much light can turn to stone. You have to refuse to see something, apparently, if you are going to act. I can choose to follow Socrates, ascending to the vision of the beautiful. But I cannot take the first step on that ladder as long as I *see* Alcibiades. I can follow Socrates only if, like Socrates, I am *persuaded* of the truth of Diotima's account; and Alcibiades robs me of this conviction. He makes me feel that in embarking on the ascent I am sacrificing a beauty; so I can no longer view the ascent as embracing the whole of beauty. The minute I think "sacrifice" and "denial," the ascent is no longer what it seemed, nor am I, in it, self-sufficient. I can, on the other hand, follow Alcibiades, making my soul a body. I can live in *erōs*, devoted to its violence and its sudden light. But once I have listened to Diotima, I see the loss of light that this course, too, entails—the loss of rational planning, the loss, we might say, of the chance to make a world. And then, if I am a rational being, with a rational being's deep need for order and for understanding, I feel that I *must* be false to *erōs*, for the world's sake.[34]

The *Symposium* now seems to us a cruel and terrifying book. It starkly confronts us with a choice, and at the same time it makes us see so clearly that we cannot choose anything. We see now that philosophy is not fully human; but we are terrified of our humanity and what it leads to. It is *our* tragedy: it floods us with light and takes away action. As Socrates and Alcibiades compete for our souls, we become, like their object Agathon, beings without character, without choice. Agathon could stand their blandishments, because he had no soul to begin with. We did have souls, and we feel they are being turned to statues.

So they go their ways—Socrates, sleepless, to the city for an ordinary day of dialectic, Alcibiades to disorder and to violence. The riot of the body conceals the soul of Alcibiades from our sight. He becomes from now on an anonymous member of the band of drunken revellers; we do not even know when he departs. The ambitions of the soul conceal the body of Socrates from his awareness. Just as drink did not make him drunk, cold did not make him freeze, and the naked body of Alcibiades did not make him erect, so now sleeplessness does not make him stop philosophizing. He goes about his business with all the equanimity of a rational stone. Meanwhile, the comic and tragic poets sleep together, tucked in by the cool hand of philosophy. *Those* two—philosophy and literature—cannot live together or know each other's truths, that's for sure. Not unless literature gives up its attachment to the contingent and the vulnerable, and makes itself an instrument of Diotima's persuasion. But that would be to leave its own truths behind.

Between one telling of the story and another, or perhaps during the second telling itself—and, for us (in us?) during the time we take to read and experience this work—Alcibiades has died. With him dies a hope that *erōs* and philosophy could live together in the city and so save it from disaster. This was, perhaps, Apollodorus' hope, his companion's hope. It was also ours, for ourselves, for our city. Plutarch tells us that the night before his death Alcibiades dreamed that he was dressed in women's clothes. A courtesan was holding his head and painting his face with makeup. In the soul of this proudly aggressive man, it is a dream that expresses the wish for passivity, the wish to lose the need for practical reason, to become a being who could live entirely in the flux of *erōs* and so avoid tragedy. But at the same time it is a wish to be no longer an erotic being; for what does not reach out to order the world does not love, and the self-sufficiency of the passive object is as unerotic as the self-sufficiency of the god. It is, we might say, a wish not to live in the world. After the arrow had killed him, the courtesan Timandra, "Honor-the-Man," wrapped his bitten body and his soul of flesh in her own clothes and buried him sumptuously in the earth.

314   When Alcibiades finished speaking, they burst out laughing at the frankness of his speech, because it looked as though he was still in love with Socrates. He stood there, perhaps, with ivy in his hair, crowned with violets.

Notes

[1] These stories, though probably not all true, are representative of the popular legends about Alcibiades that form the background for the dialogue. All sources are in general agreement about his character and the main facts of his life. From Thucydides come the account of his career, the spectacle-giving, the military and political abilities, as well as the Olympia story and the remarks about love of country. From Plutarch's *Life* come the stories about the flute, the resident alien, and the dog.

[2] G. Vlastos, "The Individual as Object of Love in Plato's Dialogues," in *Platonic Studies* (Princeton: Princeton University Press, 1973), pp. 1–34. T. Irwin's *Plato's Moral Theory* (Oxford: Clarendon Press, 1977) criticizes some aspects of Vlastos's interpretation, but seems to agree with him in this criticism of Plato. One recent interpreter who gives due weight to Alcibiades' speech and its criticisms of Socrates is M. Gagarin, "Socrates and Alcibiades," *Phoenix* 31 (1977): 22–37.

[3] Xenophanes (frags. B 23–26) imagines a god "not similar in shape to mortal men." Aristotle frequently cites the spherical as the most perfect shape and the shape most suited for the divine. Also relevant here are the arguments of the *Philebus* 51b–c against the forms of representational art.

[4] Contrast Milton's extraordinary account of the sexual life of angels, who "obstacle find none/of membrane, joint, or limb" (*Paradise Lost* VIII, 620ff.). (I am indebted to John Hollander for bringing this passage to my attention.)

[5] Sophocles *Antigone* 568–70.

[6] R. B. Brandt, "The Morality and Rationality of Suicide," in J. Rachels, ed. *Moral Problems* (New York: Harper and Row, 1975), pp. 363–87.

[7] Even at 207e, the contrast between *psuche* and *soma* is not the contrast between the material and the immaterial—or at least not as this contrast is usually drawn by Plato in other middle-period dialogues. *Psuche* includes habits, character, opinions, appetites, pleasures, pains, fears, understandings.

[8] For the sexual association of "die" and related words in Greek, see, for example, Heraclitus, frags. 15, 77, 117, perhaps 85, and the elaborately metaphorical ending of Aristophanes' *Acharnians*.

[9] Xenophanes B 25, cf. *Republic* 382d–e.

[10] *Gorgias* 492d ff. To Socrates' claim that the happy life is a self-sufficient life without recurrent needs, Callicles responds, "In that case, stones and corpses would be supremely happy" (492e).

[11] It is barely possible that Timandra was invented by Plutarch (who knew the *Symposium*) to correspond to Diotima, rather than the other way round. Although we cannot entirely rule this out, what we can say is that in this case Plato's invented name will still be meaningful, though in a more abstract way; and Plutarch will have shown himself to be an extraordinarily sharp interpreter.

[12] There is an extra step here, in which they agree that the implication holds necessarily.

[13] *Endees estin*, "lacks," "is in need of," is, throughout, used interchangeably with *ouch*

echei, "does not have." I omit here the interesting digression in which Socrates concedes that an agent may desire something that (s)he does now have, but argues that what (s)he really desires in such cases is something (s)he does not now have, viz. the continued future possession of the object.

[14]It is not at all clear what Plato would say about the well-known Aristotelian problem of the individuation of items in non-substance categories.

[15]There is some language that suggests qualitative distinctions: "more honorable" at 210b7, perhaps "gold for bronze" at 219a1. But most of the language is quantitative, as, indeed, the view seems to require: "considering it small" (210b6, 210c5), "the vast amount (*to polu*) of beauty" (210d1), "the vast sea of beauty" (d4). At 218e, Socrates ascribes to Alcibiades the desire "to make an exchange of beauty for beauty," and, since Socrates' beauty is "entirely surpassing" (e3), accuses Alcibiades of *pleonexia*, "greed," "desire to have *more*."

[16]*Republic* 521c ff.

[17]*Biotos* means "livable," "worth the living." It is most often found negated, frequently in connection with the willing acceptance of death, or even suicide. Joyce's translation, "and if, my dear Socrates, man's life is ever worth the living," is correct. W. Hamilton's "the region where a man's life should be spent" is deficient; it misses the force and the nature of the argument.

[18]Irwin and J. Moravcsik ("Reason and *Eros* in the Ascent Passage of the *Symposium*," in J. Anton and G. Kustas, eds., *Essays in Ancient Greek Philosophy* [Albany: State University of New York Press, 1972], pp. 285–302) also stress the role of need and dissatisfaction in moving the agent from one level to another. Neither discusses the precise nature of the propelling practical needs or points out the enabling role of questionable judgments of qualitative similarity. But Moravcsik's very interesting discussion of the role of aspiration and discontent in the ascent seems in no way incompatible with my observations (as the author now assures me). Another valuable discussion, focussing on the nature of erotic creativity in the ascent, is L. A. Kosman, "Platonic Love," in W. H. Werkmeister, ed., *Facets of Plato's Philosophy* (Assen: Van Gorcum, 1976), pp. 53–69.

[19]This is a reference to the conversation on ethics between Wittgenstein and Rhees that is reported by Rhees in "Wittgenstein's Lecture on Ethics," *Philosophical Review* 74 (1965): 3–21. It is discussed further in another part of the longer manuscript from which this paper is taken.

[20]*EN* 1142a23 ff.

[21]This is not, of course, meant to imply that all write, themselves, poetically; why Aristotle, holding the views he holds, writes as he does is a deep question for any interpreter of his view of philosophy.

[22]K. J. Dover, *Greek Homosexuality* (Cambridge: Harvard University Press, 1978), esp. II.C.5. This courageous and masterful piece of scholarship by one of our most distinguished living classicists supercedes all previous attempts to interpret these phenomena. (See also the review by Bernard Knox, *New York Review of Books* 25 [1979]: 5–8.)

[23]Ibid., p. 96.

[24]Cf. *Euthyphro* 11a–b.

[25]For some interesting remarks about "lover's knowledge" and its relationship to the analytical, see Lionel Trilling, "The Princess Casamassima," in *The Liberal Imagination* (New York: Scribners, 1950), pp. 86 ff.

[26]See my "Practical Syllogisms and Practical Science," in *Aristotle's De Motu Animalium*

(Princeton: Princeton University Press, 1978), Essay 4, and D. Wiggins, "Deliberation and Practical Reason," *Proc. Arist. Soc.* 76 (1975-76): 29-51.

[27]This is the theme of several recent pieces on both Plato and Aristotle: especially J. Moravcsik, "Understanding and Knowledge in Plato's Dialogues," *Neue Hefte für Philosophie* (1978), and M. F. Burnyeat, "Aristotle on Understanding Knowledge," Symposium Aristotelicum 1978, proceedings forthcoming.

[28]For uses of *dialegesthai* of sexual relations, see references in J. J. Henderson, *The Maculate Muse* (New Haven: Yale University Press, 1975), p. 155.

[29]*Republic* VI-VII, 504a ff.

[30]See the illuminating discussion of related questions in Anne Hollander, *Seeing Through Clothes* (New York: Viking, 1978). Alcibiades later removes the garlands that were attached to the wreath and puts them on the heads of Agathon and Socrates. But the Greek text indicates that the garlands were a separate item (cf. 212e2), and it appears that the violet/ivy wreath is worn throughout his speech. On this point Joyce's translation is correct, Hamilton's misleading.

[31]See A. Lowell Edmunds, *Chance and Intelligence in Thucydides* (Cambridge: Harvard University Press, 1975).

[32]*Hubris*, ironically, is also a legal and popular term for sexual assault: see *LSJ* s.v., Henderson, p. 154, and Gagarin, "Socrates and Alcibiades."

[33]See the discussion and illustrations in Dover, pp. 94-95, and plates. This "most characteristic configuration of homosexual courtship" (Dover, p. 94) was previously described in Sir John Beazley's important article, "Some Attic Vases in the Cyprus Museum," *Proceedings of the British Academy* 33 (1947): 195-244.

[34]Compare Shakespeare, *Othello* IV, iii. This entire discussion should be compared with the reading of Othello in Stanley Cavell's *The Claim of Reason* (New York: Oxford University Press, 1979), and "Epistemology and Tragedy: A Reading of *Othello*," *Daedalus* 108 (1979): 27-43.

Jerome Neu
Plato's Homoerotic Symposium

Jerome Neu is professor of philosophy at the University of California, Santa Cruz, the author of Emotion, Thought and Therapy, *and editor of* The Cambridge Companion to Freud.

Plato's *Symposium*, the greatest book ever written about the nature of love, centers on homoerotic desire. Does that make a difference? What it says is certainly shaped by the assumptions of the society in which it was written and by the interests of the man who wrote it. Not only are the exemplars of love discussed most often homosexual, they are also exemplars of a very special socially sanctioned form of pederasty, characteristic of Plato's time and class. Does that affect what can be learned from it by individuals in other times and other societies, with other assumptions, customs, and interests?

Homoerotic Love — Pausanias

Several of the speakers at this feast of speeches in praise of love make explicitly clear that, in their view, the ideal love relationship is between a male and another male. Some of them suggest that the reason for this is to be found in the social benefits of the practice. Thus Phaedrus argues that an army of lovers would be undefeatable, since a lover would be ashamed to show lack of courage before his beloved (178D–179D). That this should be regarded as important in a world of many divided city-states in frequent armed conflict with each other is hardly surprising. And if in modern wars soldiers are supposed to be inspired by concern for loved ones back home, surely there is something to be said for the power of concern for loved comrades by one's side. But this is no less an argument in favor of women in the military (and a liberal attitude toward "fraternization" in the ranks) than in favor of particular gender alignments in love relations. Other speakers point to social advantages beyond the narrowly military. Aristophanes maintains that youths who pursue other males "are the best of boys and lads, because they are the most manly," citing in proof that "these are the only kind of boys who grow up to be politicians" engaged in public life

318 (191E-192A). But the endorsement here may be ironic, and more important, the benefits to public life might be equally achievable by other practices, given a different social context. Plato himself (through Socrates/Diotima) speaks of the beauty of a beloved boy as the catalyst for the creation of wisdom and virtue, poetry and laws (208E-209E, 211B). But if, as Plato insists, there is a single Form of Beauty instantiated in all beautiful things (however otherwise diverse), the gender of the bearer of inspirational beauty should be irrelevant to its power. (Thomas Mann's Aschenbach has his Tadzio, Dante has his Beatrice.) In our time, Freud too has suggested that homosexual erotic energy might contribute to socially spirited and productive activity; though unlike the Greeks, Freud seems usually to think it is the sublimated forms of that energy that are most effective.[1] Plato's own view of sexual sublimation is complex and will need closer scrutiny.

Pausanias gives a fuller picture of the ideal love relationship in classical Athens. It is unsublimated, but it is crucially asymmetrical. Although the lovers are of the same gender, they are of different ages. The ideal love relationship is between an older man and an adolescent youth (described as "beardless" by Phaedrus [180A] and as "showing the first traces of a beard" by Pausanias [181D]). The needs that are fulfilled by the relationship are also thought to be different. While the youth (the beloved, *eromenos*) offers his beauty and sensual satisfaction, the older man (the lover, *erastes*) is supposed to provide moral instruction, spiritual and intellectual guidance. The relationship is importantly educational.

Pausanias spells out the assumptions of the Athens of his time in connection with a contrast he draws between two types of love, Heavenly and Common. The lower form of love is aimed purely at physical pleasure and may be directed at very young boys or even women. (Women are generally denigrated throughout the theoretical discussions of the *Symposium*, though a few—such as Alcestis and Diotima—are accorded respectful treatment.[2]) Because Common love is inspired by physical attractions, which inevitably fade, it is unreliable and of short duration. Heavenly love differs in aim, object, and duration. Although it may include physical intimacy (the lover desires "favors"), it centrally aims at spiritual communion and the development of the beloved. Its objects are older youths of high spirit and high intelligence, and the love is stable and of lasting duration. Indeed, the key test for differentiating Heavenly from Common love involves time and the overcoming of obstacles, provided through a whole etiquette of courtship and interaction. The youth is expected to be at first coy and to avoid giving in too soon or for base motives (as would be suspected were he to give in to a rich or famous person who could not offer a suitable mentor relationship in pursuit of virtue and excellence). The ideal structure involves a bargain, but (on Pausanias' account) a long-term and high-minded one. Some of Pausanias' statements may be self-serving; he is, as Aristophanes indicates (193C, cf. *Protagoras* 315D-E), the long-term lover of Agathon, the honored tragic poet and host of the feast. Diotima's later praise of pederasty ("loving boys correctly," 211B), however, must be regarded as disinterested.

The sexual asymmetry in the relationship deserves a note of emphasis. In Pausanias' picture the youth is not supposed to be particularly physically attracted to the older man, and in any case sexual gratification is not his aim. Aristophanes, by contrast, seems to allow that the youth may enjoy the physical aspects of the relationship ("While they are boys . . . they love men and enjoy lying with men and being embraced by men" [191E]). The conventional attitude was that the youth was expected not to enjoy the physical intimacy as such, indeed the range of physical interaction (at least in conventional depictions, as on vases) was rather limited. The assuming of what to the ancient Greeks as to many modern "macho" cultures would appear a passive and so womanly sexual role was problematic and was supposed to be a passing phase (the youth eventually becoming *erastes* to another youth and husband to a wife) — the gratifications involved were supposed to be nonsexual. A strong statement of the view is attributed to Socrates in Xenophon's *Symposium* (8.21): "The boy does not share in the man's pleasure in intercourse, as a woman does; cold sober, he looks upon the other drunk with sexual desire."[3] Of course depictions of cultural expectations should not be mistaken for accounts of actual practice and experience.

In a remarkable passage, in the course of praising the Athenian arrangements, Pausanias directly links sexual repression with political repression. The idea is now a familiar one, from the work of Marcuse and many others, but Plato's Pausanias is the first (so far as I am aware) to make the link. He explains that:

the Persian empire is absolute; that is why it condemns love as well as philosophy and sport. It is no good for rulers if the people they rule cherish ambitions for themselves, or form strong bonds of friendship with one another. That these are precisely the effects of philosophy, sport, and especially of Love is a lesson the tyrants of Athens learned directly from their own experience: didn't their reign come to a dismal end because of the bonds uniting Harmodius and Aristogiton in love and affection?

So you can see that plain condemnation of Love reveals lust for power in the rulers and cowardice in the ruled. (182B–182D, trans. Nehamas & Woodruff)

Matching Halves — Aristophanes

At the start of his *Three Essays on the Theory of Sexuality,* the greatest book ever written about the nature of sex, Freud speaks of "the poetic fable which tells how the original human beings were cut up into two halves — man and woman — and how these are always striving to unite again in love." If this refers to Aristophanes' speech in the *Symposium,*[4] Freud's account is seriously misleading. After specifying the two halves as "man and woman," Freud goes on to say, "It comes as a great surprise therefore to learn that there are men whose sexual object is a man and not a woman, and women whose sexual object is a woman and not a man." But, of course, this is no surprise on Aristophanes' theory. His story of the division of the original human beings into two halves and their subsequent quest to reunite in love, allows for all three alternatives. Aristophanes starts with *three* original sexes: double-male, double-female, and "androgynous." Thus the myth offers an explanation (the *same* explanation) of homosexuality and lesbianism as well as heterosexuality.

The Greeks in general tended to think of sexuality as involving a single desire aimed at the beautiful, whether the beauty is embodied in a male or female, and they thought of attraction to a person of the same or the opposite sex as equally natural.[5] This accords with Freud's own preferred view:

Psycho-analysis considers that a choice of an object independently of its sex — freedom to range equally over male and female objects — as it is found in childhood, in primitive states of society and early periods of history, is the original basis from which, as a result of restriction in one direction or the other, both the normal and the inverted types develop. Thus from the point of view of psycho-analysis the exclusive sexual interest felt by men for women is also a problem that needs elucidating and is not a self-evident fact based upon an attraction that is ultimately of a chemical nature.[6]

For psychoanalysis, as for Aristophanes in the *Symposium,* heterosexuality and homosexuality are equally in need of explanation, and the same type of explanation is offered for both. No special explanatory factors or pathology is involved in either object choice.

Aristophanes' myth shares another important feature with Freud's views: for both, love involves "a need to restore an earlier state of things."[7] So far as later objects are imperfect substitutes for the original object (one's "matching half" [191D]), one's striving for wholeness may have to remain incomplete and restless.[8]

The obsessiveness of love may have an even deeper source. Although Aristophanes' picture of the restoration of oneness, a blissful merging, as the aim of love resonates through later literature and meshes with much individual experience, a close reading of Aristophanes' myth makes it questionable whether lovers, even on his account, ultimately aim at oneness alone. Anne Carson suggests that "Aristophanes' judgment ("no lover could want anything else") is belied by the anthropology of his own myth. Was it the case that the round beings of his fantasy remained perfectly content rolling about the world in prelapsarian oneness? No. They got big ideas and started rolling toward Olympus to make an attempt on the gods (190b-c). They began reaching for something else. So much for oneness."[9]

Incompleteness (and also triangles) may form an inevitable aspect of the bittersweetness of eros. Restless striving may be part of its nature. When Plato moves us from Aristophanes' myth to Diotima's transcendental erotics, it becomes explicitly clear that the aim of erotic desire is not the *possession* of the beautiful, but "reproduction and birth in beauty" (206E). (The aim never was simple intercourse, even on Aristophanes' account: "No one would think it is the intimacy of sex—that mere sex is the reason each lover takes so great and deep a joy in being with the other" [192C-D].) Beauty is the object (both on the conventional Greek and the etherealized Platonic accounts), but creativity is the aim of love. Desire is endless, not only because its object (as in Aristophanes' myth) is a forever lost and unrecoverable earlier state, not only because its object (as in Socrates-Diotima's vision) is a transcendental Form, but because what is wanted is creativity inspired by beauty, an activity (not passive ownership).[10]

The aestheticizing of the object of sexual desire may seem puzzling. But it was not for the Greeks in general, who assumed the beautiful is desirable, not for Plato in particular, who enshrined the Form of Beauty as the ultimate object of desire. Yet so far as "the beautiful" picks out an objective type (especially a visual type), it is not clear that desire in fact always aims at beauty as its object. (Socrates himself was notably ugly; only a shift in gaze from the outer to the inner man enabled Alcibiades to see him as

"beautiful" [215B, 217A].) The objects of desire (in particular sexual desire) are subject to all sorts of psychological conditions, "beauty" being only
one possibility. It might be a particular scar or a turn of speech that appeals, despite a person's ugliness. Of course if one defines beauty in terms of
desirability to the individual, it will follow that whatever one desires, one
will believe to be beautiful. (Cf. Sappho.) Freud suggests such a subjectiviz-
ing standard when he writes: "There is to my mind no doubt that the concept of 'beautiful' has its roots in sexual excitation and that its original
meaning was 'sexually stimulating.'"[11] This is a familiar philosophical
move in relation to "good" (defining goodness in terms of desirability). But
Plato's Form of Beauty is not subjective; his metaphysics insists on objective
standards. So understood, desire need not always in fact aim at beauty.
Moreover, there are subjective notions of beauty which do not tie beauty directly to desire. Thus desire need not always aim at beauty—whether one
takes beauty itself as subjective or objective. Nonetheless, the special place
Plato gives to Beauty (and Goodness) in his account of love may help us
better understand the place of idealization in our experience of love.

Longer Is Better, Forever Is Best—
Socrates and Diotima

Diotima's vision of "rising stairs," which take the lover on an ascent from
particular beautiful bodies, to beautiful souls, activities and laws, and ultimately to knowledge and the very Form of Beauty (210A–211C), contains
both unexamined bias and fruitful insight. The progressive abstraction in
the objects of love, which may have connections with the special educational functions of homosexual love in Plato's time, moves the lover away
from that passionate attachment to a particular person that is perhaps
most characteristic of modern views of erotic love. The loss in such detachment is very real (and we will come back to it in relation to Alcibiades). On
the other hand, the move toward an ideal object as one ascends Diotima's
ladder may reveal some of the importance of the idealization of the object
perhaps most characteristic of modern views of romantic love (discussed,
for example, by Stendhal in terms of "crystallization"). An ideal abstract
object and idealization of a particular object are not the same, but metaphysics and romantic fantasy may here share a common aspiration.

The aim of love according to Plato is creativity, the achievement of immortality through "reproduction and birth in beauty." Given the homoerotic context, it is perhaps not surprising that the principle of procreation
is male (though it is presented in the female voice of Diotima, as reported

by Socrates): It is the men who are "pregnant," both in body and in soul, and spiritual and intellectual children are to be preferred to the fleshly variety (208E–209E). The beauty of the beloved is the catalyst for the creativity. There is in Plato's account, in addition to a bias for the male, a bias for the abstract and for the eternal. Creativity might in the ordinary Greek practice be expressed through the education and cultivation of the beloved, and this may involve overvaluation, an idealization of the object of love. Plato makes no direct mention of such overvaluation in the *Symposium* (romantic idealization of a particular individual would seem shortsighted delusion in the face of the Forms), but he recognizes it quite clearly in the *Phaedrus* as involving a projection of desired characteristics (252D–253C).[12] Diotima insists that love depends on the ideal, and Alcibiades idealizes Socrates (although it is a question whether rightly or as a delusion).

Idealization of the object of love is later crucial to the nature of love according to Stendhal, Proust, Freud, and countless others. Freud suggests that such overvaluation of the beloved is the result of transferred narcissism,[13] and the importance Plato attaches to an egoistic desire for immortality (even in the case of Alcestis' sacrifice of her life — apparently — for her husband's sake [208C–E]) accords with such a source (though Plato would deny that the "idealization" involved when the Forms, rather than particular individuals, are the objects of love constitutes *over*valuation). If the source seems low, the aspiration remains high. Idealization points to a value beyond the immediate object. Plato makes an important contribution in distinguishing the two. The problem emerges when one considers whether the value of the manifest image of the transcendent is itself enhanced or diminished in virtue of its intermediary role. In the *Symposium*, the message is that those who see aright will recognize that the immediate object of love really stands in for or represents an ultimate value. The unfortunate implication is that once this is understood, the particular individual can drop out of the picture. Thus, Socrates rejects Aristophanes' notion that we love the missing part of ourselves in the other, and insists that we love only the good in the object (205E). The particular beautiful object is used to move to the vision of the Form, which in itself is not visible to the senses, having neither face nor hands nor "anything else that belongs to the body" (211A). On this account, what gets left out is love of the individual as a whole (with and even despite his faults), love of the individual as (perishably) embodied, and love for the sake of the beloved (as opposed to for the good of the lover).[14]

The Platonic ascent sublimates particular attachments in favor of what results in a kind of social creativity (yielding poetry and laws), but it is motivated in his account by an egoistic desire for immortality. In this we see his bias for the eternal.

That more stable, long-lasting relationships are better is an assumption built into Pausanias' test for Heavenly love. Surely if longer is better, forever is best. But people change and ultimately perish. The highest objects of love for Plato are unperishing. Individuals aim at immortality for themselves, and in their objects seek the immortal. People inevitably drop out of the picture altogether. Even when it has a place—at the bottom of Diotima's ladder—love of particular people is aimed only at the good in them, and loving them is only a way to the Forms. Plato (and hordes since) makes a profound assumption that in love, and in everything else, the everlasting is better, the unchanging is better. Is it? Plato speaks of the absolute Form of Beauty as "not polluted by human flesh or colors or any other great nonsense of mortality" (211E). But is an artificial rose that lasts indefinitely "better" than a living rose, with its ephemeral, passing beauty? And, in case one thinks an artificial rose is a thing different in kind from a rose, would a rose that lasted forever, that never wilted or withered, inevitably be better? Is it unthinkable that part of the beauty and appeal of a rose lies precisely in its natural cycle from bud to bloom through death? Would the shape of a human life necessarily be more satisfying if it had no end?[15] Ideas of immortality and the desire for a reliable (ultimately unchanging) object seem tied to narcissistic desires for self-sufficiency which may be incompatible with love as a relationship. The aspirations in Plato's vision, like Spinoza's "intellectual love of God," may lead to a life in which individual relationships and individual persons as objects of love drop out. The philosopher contemplating the Forms is a model of self-sufficiency, like "Socrates, who was impervious to drink, to cold, to the naked body of Alcibiades."[16]

Why Say No to Alcibiades?

When Alcibiades joins the company, we learn from him that years before, Socrates had rejected his advances. At the time, Alcibiades had been commonly viewed as the most promising, beautiful, and desirable youth in Athens, and Socrates (as presented in Plato's portrait) was the wisest and the best man. So the relation, if consummated, would have exemplified what Pausanias had described as the ideal: a relation for mutual benefit between an older man and a younger boy, the man enjoying the youth's sensual beauty and the youth receiving valuable instruction. What is unusual in Alcibiades' story in terms of Athenian ideals is the reversal of conventional courtship roles, with the younger man pursuing the older. But surely this was not enough to make Socrates turn away, especially since it is clear that Alcibiades was as desirable to him as to everyone else.[17] Why then did Socrates' view of love require him to reject Alcibiades?

When Socrates rejects Alcibiades, he speaks contemptuously (ironically?) of being asked to give "gold in exchange for bronze" (219A). But is Socrates in fact being offered an unfair bargain? Granting the evaluation of his and Alcibiades' assets in terms of gold and bronze, what would Socrates be giving up? For unlike gold, which once given is gone, wisdom can be given to another and yet retained, that is, shared without loss or sacrifice. (If Socrates' point is that he lacks the wisdom Alcibiades means to be bargaining for, that in itself is no reason not to indulge in sexual relations — so long as fraud and deceit are avoided.) Perhaps the problem is not supposed to be the unfairness (what Socrates would have to give up), but the insufficiency of the inducement. On Diotima's account, the enlightened lover would have no desire for what Alcibiades was offering. That is, on one reading, once one has achieved later and higher stages on the ascending ladder of love, one would have abandoned the earlier and lower ("When he grasps this, he must become a lover of all beautiful bodies, and he must think that this wild gaping after just one body is a small thing and despise it" [210B]).

But why should that be so? Why should there not be room for both interests, even if one is thought of as higher and the other as lower (because of a bias for the eternal)? Aristotle, and many others before and since, have insisted that human beings are of mixed nature. Although partaking in the nature of both gods and animals, we are not simply either. We may achieve insight into the eternal Forms, but we are also embodied creatures with mortal needs. No one can live a life devoted exclusively to doing mathematics or contemplating the Forms — even if such moments constitute the high point of particular days. Even Socrates himself, with his great powers of concentration and in his extreme self-composure, is better considered not as a person beyond temptation, but as a person of extraordinary temperance and self-control and of extraordinary calm and contentment within his self-control.[18]

Perhaps Socrates means to be teaching Alcibiades a lesson. What then is it? Alcibiades' own desires seem already to fit the hierarchy in Diotima's ladder. Alcibiades' feelings for the outwardly unattractive Socrates reveal that he has already moved beyond the first step, love of mere bodily beauty.

In approaching Socrates he says: "Nothing is more important to me than becoming the best man I can be, and no one can help me more than you to reach that aim" (218D). He comes seeking intellectual instruction, improvement of his soul (not gross physical pleasure) from Socrates. He is clearly not acting out of simple lust or for the sake of money or some other low aim.[19] So when Socrates denies himself sensual pleasure, he is *not* showing Alcibiades that he should seek higher things than sensual pleasure. Alcibiades already knows that and in offering himself to Socrates is trying to further the pursuit of those very higher things at which Diotima and Socrates would have him aim. As noted, Alcibiades' design also seems to fit Pausanias' ideal (in which a youth exchanges beauty and sensuousness for a mature man's wisdom and instruction). Perhaps then the ideal described by Pausanias was not in fact pervasive in the Athens of his time (despite much corroborating evidence),[20] or even if it was, perhaps Socrates wished to reject that ideal: either regarding it as incompatible with the contemplation of higher things or simply regarding it as unseemly for a dignified older man to be in hot pursuit of pretty boys, however much he might enjoy the distraction from his more demanding intellectual pursuits.

There is in fact a speech to that effect in the *Phaedrus*, where Plato has Socrates criticize "May-December" romances in terms of divergent interests, compulsive behavior, and "unseasonable fulsome compliments" (*Phaedrus* 240C–E, trans. Hackforth; cf. Xenophon *Memorabilia* i 2.29f). But that speech is later repudiated, at least in part, in favor of the divine madness of love. Still, despite the approval of passionate attachment in Socrates' more considered speech (his speech of recantation), there abides an antipathy to physical gratification of love—and it should be noted that it extends to intercourse of any kind, whether homosexual (*Phaedrus* 256A–B) or heterosexual (*Phaedrus* 250E).[21] That repugnance, quite apart from issues of age difference, may account for Socrates' rejection of Alcibiades' embraces as he sleeps through the night beside him.

If Socrates meant to be giving Alcibiades a lesson in abstinence, then Diotima's ideal differs from Pausanias' in more than just its vision of the Form. Pausanias would allow the beloved to grant "favors" and perform "any service for a lover who can make him wise and virtuous" (184D). The question becomes why Diotima's ideal calls for abstinence, either through the despising and abandoning of earlier objects or, more peculiarly, through precise sexual limitations. The abstinence (as spelled out most clearly in the *Phaedrus*) is required only beyond a certain point, marked by intercourse.[22] Why?

To start on the path to contemplation of true Beauty, there must be self-denial and self-control, and specifically there must be physical abstinence. Socrates' dissociation from his own body as he ascends the ladder is evidenced in many of his distinctive characteristics, from imperviousness to alcohol and cold to imperviousness (beyond a certain point) to the charms of Alcibiades. But Socrates did not feel obliged to abstain from alcohol. Why should sexual relations seem more threatening? Perhaps because he was more susceptible to their appeal. Certainly sexual arousal had greater power to disturb his equanimity (see *Charmides* 155C–E). Still, more may be at stake than Socrates' (or any would-be philosopher's) self-sufficient impregnability and imperturbability. Plato, at various points in his development, subscribes to beliefs that might make him (and Socrates in his account) shy away from intercourse with a beloved. In the *Phaedrus*, despite initial lust for "a monstrous and forbidden act," the lover exercises restraint because of "modesty" and "awe and reverence" for the Form of Beauty reflected in the beloved (254A–B) and ultimately because of "reverence and awe" for the beloved himself (254E). Later, despite mutuality of desire, caresses stop short of intercourse because of "reverence and heedfulness" and the desire for "self-mastery and inward peace" (256A–B). Yet it is difficult to see how this is based on anything other than the sort of suspicion of the body and antipathy to intercourse that pervade Plato's works (as well as, of course, later Christianity).[23]

The specific problem of intercourse for Plato (recall that passionate physical interaction, up to but not including intercourse, is permitted in the *Phaedrus*), may be based on the specially intense pleasure of orgasm. Regarding the soul as the prisoner of the body, and believing that intense pleasure nails the soul to the body, making it impossible to detach and free oneself and distorting one's sense of reality (*Phaedo* 82D–83D), Plato understandably has a metaphysical horror of such experience.[24] But it is a false metaphysics that seeks to separate the mind from the body, and it is a false respect that seeks to separate out disembodied virtues of the beloved. In addition, in the *Laws* and elsewhere, Plato explicitly regards homosexual intercourse (though not homosexual desire in general) as "unnatural" (cf. *Phaedrus* 250E, *Republic* 403B–C, *Laws* 636, 836B–841E). That view is of course, where intelligible, untenable: animals do engage in such intercourse; and, whatever is true of other animals, one must remember that humans and their diverse desires are also part of the natural order.[25]

Whatever Plato may have believed, false respect and false natural lines (and behind them, the need for control and the need to avoid passivity) cannot be taken by us as proper grounds for guiding behavior. If physical limits placed on passionate attachment are not to be based on false beliefs or on a simple and unjustified rejection of sexuality in general, other matters must come into consideration. In addition to issues of the "exploitation" of youth (after Freud it is not possible to deny the presence of sexual desires in even the very young, but neither is it possible to assume they take the same form as adult sexual desires),[26] there may be implicit in Plato's views a doctrine of sublimation, in which energy with a certain object and aim gets deliberately turned to higher objects and aims, strengthening the passionate pursuit of knowledge and virtue (cf. *Republic* 485D). This sexual energizing of the quest for the transcendental ideal would in some ways anticipate the explicit doctrine of sublimation in Freud, which goes beyond Plato's both in scope (Freud adds the complications of infantile pregenital sexuality; Plato restricts only certain consummating activities of adult sexuality and not the correlative desires or homosexual activity in general) and in operation (Freud introduces unconscious mechanisms; Plato is concerned with self-conscious self-control).[27]

It might be suggested that Socrates also objected to the double standard built into the Athenian ideal of his time. Pausanias' model includes a double standard, which, while focused on age rather than gender, is not wholly unlike the more familiar Victorian variety. Older men are encouraged to pursue younger boys, but the boys are encouraged to play hard to get. This is, according to Pausanias, to test the seriousness of the man's intentions; but it may also reflect a natural variation, in a society where women were segregated, of the same conventions that governed a later society where women were allowed more freedom of movement.[28] Finally, it may reflect in the conventional terms of the time the seductiveness of unattainability, the essential tension of erotic desire that connects attractiveness with lack and obstacle.[29] Whatever the significance of the double standard ("we do everything we can to make it as easy as possible for lovers to press their suits and as difficult as possible for young men to comply" [184A]), if Socrates did object to it there is no evidence that he did in the *Symposium*. Alcibiades in fact switches traditional roles in relation to Socrates ("as if I were his lover and he my young prey" [217C]), and there is nothing in the *Symposium* to suggest that Socrates (or Diotima in her quoted speech) rejects the hierarchy of age and status, not to speak of the sexual asymmetry, between lovers generally accepted in Greek society.[30]

Plato's emphasis on creativity rather than on possessiveness in love, the sublimation of physical desire, and the move to an ideal object are all truly distinctive, but they do not come tied to any notion of equality or reciprocity in love. Indeed, not only is the model of love in the *Symposium* generally between unequals, but as one ascends Diotima's ladder other people drop out as the object of love, their place taken by the Forms — and Forms *cannot* reciprocate love. The question then becomes whether one can make the ascent alone, without the company of (human) lovers (whether equal or unequal). Socrates himself has a guide or teacher, namely Diotima, on the way to the highest vision of love; and a beautiful inspiration seems important at least in the earliest stages (according to the account in the *Symposium*) and perhaps throughout the quest (according to the account in the *Phaedrus*). The question nonetheless remains whether one can make sense of an erotic love in which ultimately the lover does not himself desire to be loved.

We have noted that one cannot explain Socrates' rejection of Alcibiades by a lack of homosexual desire in general or an attraction to Alcibiades in particular. And Socrates' view of love, like the conventional one of his time, included neither horror at homosexuality nor modern notions of equality between lovers. By the time Plato wrote the *Symposium*, however, he and his audience would have been aware that Alcibiades had come to a bad end (he was murdered in 404 B.C., after betraying Athens and contributing to its defeat in the Peloponnesian War; the likely composition date for the *Symposium* is between 385/4 and 379/8 B.C.).[31] If we suppose Socrates at the time of the attempted seduction had a premonition of Alcibiades' bad end, he would have been rejecting Alcibiades for his (later) bad character. Although this might accord with the notion of loving only the good in the beloved (which Socrates insists on in opposition to Aristophanes' notion of love of one's other half), he makes no mention of it. Moreover, it does not accord with love of whole persons (with or despite their faults). Not that all faults must be accepted, but if people are all mixed in character, the result for Socrates would be that individuals (even with minor flaws) disappear as objects of love (for moral as well as metaphysical reasons).

Some in Athens doubtless blamed Socrates for the corruption of Alcibiades and other of his followers (cf. the *Apology*), and some might read the *Symposium* as a response to the charge, showing preexisting flaws in the pupil who preferred political glory to philosophical pursuits — but then it could also be read as revealing Socrates' failure as a teacher. For he failed to give Alcibiades whatever was needed to change him (whether or not he should be blamed for his "corruption"); unlike his teacher Diotima, it could be said he frustrated his students with his insistent disavowal of knowledge. And the failure here may be thought of as a failure of love.[32]

Conclusion

Does the fact that Plato's *Symposium* focuses on homosexual love affect what it has to teach us about erotic desire? The perhaps obvious answer is: in some ways yes, in some ways no. The advantages of homosexual relations as perceived by Plato's symposiasts, like the perceived disadvantages of homosexual relations in some modern societies, are largely social artifacts, the variable and changeable effects of local customs and attitudes. Attraction to members of one's own or of the opposite sex is, as Aristophanes' myth suggests and as Freud's theory confirms, explainable in terms of a single underlying set of factors; neither preference is to be regarded as more natural than the other. And as the classical Greek practices reveal, neither preference need be exclusive or fixed for life. Plato's preference emerges in Diotima's image of male pregnancy. The gender of the immediate object of love certainly affects the possibilities of procreation, and dubious presumptions about the superiority of the male and the spiritual as opposed to the female and the bodily come into play, but the distinguishing of an ultimate object beyond the immediate one as well as the nature of that ultimate object and of the aims of erotic desire (whether or not one accepts Plato's particular account) remain unaffected. Plato's emphasis on creativity in love may indeed have been influenced by the educational functions of the homoerotic practices of his time. Even the refusal of the sort of physical consummation that Pausanias' ideal would have allowed may be seen as aimed at strengthening the passionate pursuit of knowledge and virtue, thus according with the educational aims while revising the practices.

But the case for (what through modern eyes must be seen as) intentional sublimation rests neither on Plato's personal preferences nor the customs of his time. The Forms as the ultimate objects of love and the restrictions on sexual activity are based on Plato's metaphysics, a metaphysics that makes the Forms the supreme reality and that sees the human body as an ephemeral prison for the soul. Plato's call for sublimation can be no more persuasive than that metaphysics. Nonetheless, Plato's expansion of the scope of eros (205A–D), like Freud's later expansion of the scope of sexuality, offers explanatory insight. Plato's metaphysical flight up Diotima's rising stairs takes us away from the conventional objects of love (of our own and also, it should be emphasized, his own time), but takes us closer to understanding both the obsessiveness (due to the unobtainability of the ultimate object and aim) and the overvaluation (due to the ultimate value represented by the immediate object) characteristic of erotic love. And other insights, such as those concerning the role of creativity as opposed to possessiveness in love and the one voiced by Pausanias concerning the relations of sexuality and politics, are independent of social convention and individual preference; indeed, they help us understand such conventions and preferences.[33]

Notes

[1]For example: "After the stage of heterosexual object-choice has been reached, the homosexual tendencies are not, as might be supposed, done away with or brought to a stop; they are merely deflected from their sexual aim and applied to fresh uses. They now combine with portions of the ego-instincts and, as 'attached' components, help to constitute the social instincts, thus contributing an erotic factor to friendship and comradeship, to *esprit de corps* and to the love of mankind in general. How large a contribution is in fact derived from erotic sources (with the sexual aim inhibited) could scarcely be guessed from the normal social relations of mankind. But it is not irrelevant to note that it is precisely manifest homosexuals, and among them again precisely those that set themselves against an indulgence in sensual acts, who are distinguished by taking a particularly active share in the general interests of humanity— interests which have themselves sprung from a sublimation of erotic instincts." (Sigmund Freud, *Psycho-Analytic Notes on an Autobiographical Account of a Case of Paranoia* [1912], *Standard Edition*, XII, p. 61.)

While the usual connection that Freud makes is between social feeling and sublimated homosexuality (rather than active homosexuality), he frequently points out the great social contributions of homosexuals in history, sometimes even tying the contributions to the sexual orientation itself, deriving social energies from homosexual inclinations, e.g.: "It is well known that a good number of homosexuals are characterized by a special development of their social instinctual impulses and by their devotion to the interests of the community. . . . the fact that homosexual object-choice not infrequently proceeds from an early overcoming of rivalry with men cannot be without a bearing on the connection between homosexuality and social feeling." (Sigmund Freud, "Some Neurotic Mechanisms in Jealousy, Paranoia and Homosexuality" [1922], *Standard Edition* XVIII, p. 232.)

[2]This goes with the importance attached to military prowess, the segregation of women of citizen families (women available outside of marriage were not likely to be "respectable"), attitudes toward sexual passivity, and other assumptions of the time. Plato's own rather mixed attitude toward women, expressed in *The Republic* and other works, is convincingly sorted out by Gregory Vlastos, "Was Plato a Feminist?" *Times Literary Supplement* (March 17-23, 1989), pp. 276 and 288-289. On Diotima's presence (and absence) in the *Symposium*, see David M. Halperin, "Why is Diotima a Woman?" in his *One Hundred Years of Homosexuality and Other Essays on Greek Love* (London: Routledge, 1989).

[3]Quoted by K. J. Dover in his authoritative work, *Greek Homosexuality* (London: Duckworth, 1978), p. 52 (cf. p. 76). Dover notes the dominance of intercrural frottage, as opposed to other physical interactions, and the absence of erections in the *eromenoi* ("even in circumstances to which one would expect the penis of any healthy adolescent to respond willy-nilly")

in depictions on vases (pp. 91-109). See also Michel Foucault, *The Use of Pleasure* (volume 2 of *The History of Sexuality*) (New York: Vintage Books, 1986), pp. 215-25; and Halperin, "Diotima," section 6. And despite the comment of the character Aristophanes in the *Symposium* (191E), in actual Aristophanic comedies to assume a passive role in homosexual activity was to become the butt of jokes.

[4]The normally highly reliable editors of the *The Standard Edition of the Complete Psychological Works of Sigmund Freud* claim in a footnote to the passage that it does ([1905], VII, p. 136); but one should note that there is an Indian version of the myth that may conform better to Freud's account, and Freud explicitly refers to it later in *Beyond the Pleasure Principle* ([1920], XVIII, pp. 57-58).

[5]Dover, *Greek Homosexuality*, pp. 65-66; Foucault, *Use of Pleasure*, pp. 187-92. For a reading of the evidence that points to greater conflict in attitudes, see David Cohen, "Law, Society and Homosexuality in Classical Athens," *Past and Present*, no. 117 (Nov. 1987): 3-21.

[6]Sigmund Freud, *Three Essays on the Theory of Sexuality* (1905), *Standard Edition* VII, pp. 145-46n.

[7]Freud, *Beyond the Pleasure Principle* (1920), p. 57. Freud makes this statement in the context of his later theorizing about the repetition compulsion and the death instinct, but the notion of a return to an earlier state is present even in the *Three Essays* (1905), where Freud writes "The finding of an object is in fact a refinding of it" (p. 222). As Dover notes, in Aristophanes' myth, "as commonly in the folktale genre, the time-scale is ignored and the distinction between species and individual is blurred." (Dover, *Greek Homosexuality*, p. 62; cf. idem, "Aristophanes' Speech in Plato's *Symposium*," *Journal of Hellenic Studies*, 86 [1966]: 41-50, esp. 44.)

[8]Cf. Sigmund Freud, "On the Universal Tendency to Debasement in the Sphere of Love" (1912), *Standard Edition* XI, pp. 188-89.

[9]Anne Carson, *Eros the Bittersweet* (Princeton, N.J.: Princeton University Press, 1986), p. 68.

[10]On the complications in Plato's understanding of erotic object and aim, and especially on the contrast of physical appetite and value-laden desire, see David M. Halperin, "Platonic *Erōs* and What Men Call Love," *Ancient Philosophy* 5 (1985): 161-204.

[11]Freud, *Three Essays*, p. 156, n.2 (cf. p. 209). For Sappho's view, see C. M. Bowra, *Greek Lyric Poetry from Aleman to Simonides*, 2d. rev. ed. (Oxford University Press, 1961), p. 180.

[12]"So each selects a fair one for his love after his disposition, and even as if the beloved himself were a god he fashions for himself as it were an image, and adorns it to be the object of his veneration and worship. . . . But all this, mark you, they attribute to the beloved, and the draughts which they draw from Zeus they pour out, like Bacchants, into the soul of the beloved, thus creating in him the closest possible likeness to the god they worship" (*Phaedrus*, 252D and 253A, trans. Hackforth). While in this passage the lover may not risk mistaking the boy for the Form, he does seem (contra Gregory Vlastos, "The Individual as an Object of Love in Plato," *Platonic Studies* [Princeton, N.J.: Princeton University Press, 1973], p. 30, n. 88) to idealize the boy by attributing to him virtues he does not have. (Cf. A. W. Price, *Love and Friendship in Plato and Aristotle* [Oxford: Oxford University Press, 1989], pp. 215-22.)

[13]Sigmund Freud, "On Narcissism: An Introduction" (1914), *Standard Edition* XIV, pp. 88ff.; *Group Psychology and the Analysis of the Ego* (1921), *Standard Edition* XVIII, pp. 112-114. In addition to their relation to one's ego or ego ideal, both transcendental objects

and idealized individuals may owe some of their overvaluation to their relation to those earlier objects of which they are a "refinding."

Narcissism is also at the center of Freud's later theorizing about the mechanism of sublimation, in which the ego "begins by changing sexual object-libido into narcissistic libido and then, perhaps, goes on to give it another aim" (*The Ego and the Id* [1923], *Standard Edition* XIX, pp. 30, 44–47).

[14]See Vlastos, "The Individual as an Object of Love in Plato," pp. 3–42.

[15]If finite life is meaningless or absurd, might not unending life be infinitely meaningless or infinitely absurd? (See Thomas Nagel, "The Absurd," *Mortal Questions* [Cambridge: University Press, 1979].) And it has been argued that eternal life, far from being desirable, would inevitably be boring. (See Bernard Williams, "The Makropulos Case: Reflections on the Tedium of Immortality," *Problems of the Self* [Cambridge: University Press, 1973].)

Freud, here as elsewhere, offers valuable insight. Writing in the midst of World War I, he argued against the "view that the transience of what is beautiful involves any loss in its worth. On the contrary, an increase! Transience value is scarcity value in time. . . . The beauty of the human form and face vanish forever in the course of our own lives, but their evanescence only lends them a fresh charm. A flower that blossoms only for a single night does not seem to us on that account less lovely" ("On Transience" [1916 (1915)], *Standard Edition* XIV, pp. 305–6). Similarly, certain ancient authors argued that it was precisely the fleetingness of the bloom of youth that was part of its appeal, making desire directed at youthful beauty (particularly that of boys) more poignant and more intense (see Achilles Tatius, 2.33–38; cf. Foucault, *Use of Pleasure*, pp. 199–201).

[16]Martha Nussbaum, " 'This Story Isn't True': Madness, Reason and Recantation in the *Phaedrus*," ch. 7 in her *Fragility of Goodness* (Cambridge: Cambridge University Press, 1986), p. 203. See also "The Speech of Alcibiades: A Reading of the *Symposium*," ch. 6 in the same volume, pp. 183–84, 199.

[17]Diotima describes his interest, at the time of their meeting, in "beautiful boys and youths — who, if you see them now, strike you out of your senses, and make you, you and many others, eager to be with the boys you love and look at them forever, if there were any way to do that, forgetting food and drink, everything but looking at them and being with them" (211D). And Alcibiades, at the *Symposium* itself, describes Socrates as "crazy about beautiful boys; he constantly follows them around in a perpetual daze" (216D), adding, in the course of their playful rivalry over Agathon, "when Socrates is around, nobody else can even get close to a good-looking man" (223A). The passages throughout Plato's writings describing Socrates' interest in beautiful youths are plentiful (e.g., *Charmides* 155C–E, *Meno* 76C), and in particular he is described at the start of the *Protagoras* as coming "from pursuit of the captivating Alcibiades" (309A, trans. Guthrie); he describes himself in the *Gorgias* as "erastes of Alcibiades and of philosophy" (481D, trans. Dover, p. 156).

[18]See Gregory Vlastos, "Socratic Irony," *Classical Quarterly*, 37 (1987); 79–96, esp. 90–92.

[19]Martha Nussbaum reads Alcibiades' speech as "a story of complex passion, both sexual and intellectual, for a particular individual" ("The Speech of Alcibiades," p. 167). Less plausibly, she also presents it as an alternative ideal offered by Plato.

[20]See Dover, "Eros and Nomos," *Bulletin of the Institute of Classical Studies* 11 (1964): 31–42.

[21]There is some controversy about *Phaedrus* 250E. Vlastos argues that the passage, in context, should be read as critical only of homosexual intercourse (*Platonic Studies*, p. 25,

n.76). Dover and most other commentators do not accept that limited reading (*Greek Homosexuality*, p. 163, n.15). Whatever the import of the particular passage, strictures against the body and restrictions on intercourse (though most often put in eugenic terms) pervade Plato's writings.

²²On "Sex in Platonic Love," see Vlastos, *Platonic Studies*, pp. 38–42, where he expands on the view that "Plato discovers a new form of pederastic love, fully sensual in its resonance, but denying itself consummation, transmuting physical excitement into imaginative and intellectual energy" (pp. 22–23).

²³See, e.g., *Phaedo* 64D–67B and passages cited in text. On Christianity, see Peter Brown, *The Body and Society: Men, Women and Sexual Renunciation in Early Christianity* (New York: Columbia University Press, 1988).

²⁴See Vlastos, "Socratic Irony," p. 91.

²⁵See John Boswell, *Christianity, Social Tolerance, and Homosexuality* (Chicago: University of Chicago Press, 1980); R. H. Denniston, "Ambisexuality in Animals," in J. Marmor, ed., *Homosexual Behavior* (New York: Basic Books, 1980), pp. 25–40; Dover, *Greek Homosexuality*, pp. 167–70; A. W. Price, *Love and Friendship*, pp. 229–35; Michael Slote, "Inapplicable Concepts," *Philosophical Studies*, 28 (1975): 265–71; John J. Winkler, "Unnatural Acts," *The Constraints of Desire: The Anthropology of Sex and Gender in Ancient Greece* (New York: Routledge, 1990).

²⁶Concern about exploitation emerges in *Charmides* 155D–E and *Phaedrus* 238E–241D (in Socrates' later repudiated speech) and can be seen in Pausanias' discussion of Common love (the superior lover, by contrast, is said not to "aim to deceive [the young man] — to take advantage of him while he is still young and inexperienced and then, after exposing him to ridicule, to move quickly on to someone else" [181D]) and the protections against it ("fathers hire attendants for their sons as soon as they're old enough to be attractive . . ." [183C]). It is most explicit in Xenophon's portrayal of Socrates (*Memorabilia* 2.6, *Symposium* 8). And one should remember the special stigma that attached in ancient Greece to sexual passivity ("It is not only by assimilating himself to a woman in the sexual act that the submissive male rejects his role as a male citizen, but also by deliberately choosing to be the victim of what would be, if the victim were unwilling, hubris" [Dover, *Greek Homosexuality*, pp. 103–4]). See Vlastos, "Socratic Irony," pp. 95–96.

²⁷J. M. E. Moravcsik denies the link between Plato's theory of eros and Freud's theory of sublimation ("Reason and Eros in the 'Ascent'-Passage of the *Symposium*," in J. P. Anton and G. L. Kustas, eds., *Essays in Ancient Greek Philosophy* (Albany: State University of New York Press, 1971), pp. 285–302, p. 291). But that offers no account for the call for abstinence from sexual intercourse illustrated in the relation of Alcibiades and Socrates in the *Symposium* and made explicit in the doctrine of love of the *Phaedrus*. Neither "unnaturalness" nor "sublimation" is mentioned in the *Symposium*, but both doctrines may be in play. E. R. Dodds, among others, does see the link between Platonic eros and Freudian libido and sublimation, and interestingly remarks that Plato never "fully integrated this line of thought with the rest of his philosophy; had he done so, the notion of the intellect as a self-sufficient entity independent of the body might have been imperilled, and Plato was not going to risk that" (*The Greeks and the Irrational* [Berkeley: University of California Press, 1951], pp. 218–19). Valuable discussion of the paradoxes and problems of sublimation can be found in Norman O. Brown, *Life Against Death* (Middletown, Conn.: Wesleyan University Press, 1959), Part Four.

²⁸See Dover, *Greek Homosexuality*, pp. 81–91.

[29]Carson, *Eros the Bittersweet*, pp. 23–25. "This erotic code is a social expression of the division within a lover's heart. Double standards of behavior reflect double or contradictory pressures within erotic emotion itself" (p. 24). "Such societal and aesthetic sanction given at once to lover's pursuit and beloved's flight has its image on Greek vases as a moment of impasse in the ritual of courtship, its conceptual ground in the traditionally bittersweet character of desire" (p. 25).

[30]David Halperin ("Diotima," Section 6, and "Plato and Erotic Reciprocity," *Classical Antiquity*, 5 (1986): 60–80; cf. Foucault, *Use of Pleasure*, pp. 229–46) claims to discern in Plato a move from hierarchy to reciprocity in eros, but the evidence is rather thin. There is none in the *Symposium* (unless one assumes Aristophanes' speech represents Plato's preferred view), and the import of the passage from the *Phaedrus* (255C–E) that Halperin emphasizes may be stretched. As Dover puts it, the conventional view allows that when the erastes succeeds in his aim, "there is indeed love on both sides, but eros on one side only"(*Greek Homosexuality*, p. 53). The responsiveness of the eromenos is specifically not erotic; it is based on "affection, gratitude and admiration" (Dover, ed., *Plato: Symposium* [Cambridge: Cambridge University Press, 1980], p. 4). Even in the *Phaedrus* passage, which may go beyond the views of its time by allowing for mutuality of desire, if eros is returned, it is an eros that has been desexualized, dissociated from the sexual activity (and passivity) of intercourse. And there is no notion at all in Plato of equality between lovers of the sort Aristotle (writing later) thinks necessary between persons capable of true friendship.

Plato's point about the lovers in *Phaedrus* 255C–E may be that in loving each other, they love the same thing. On one reading, this same thing is the eromenos (his counter-eros is of himself reflected in the lover: "his lover is as it were a mirror in which he beholds himself"). On another, it is the Form, that is the ultimate object participated in or represented by the immediate object ("the stream of beauty turns back and re-enters the eyes of the fair beloved"). On no reading do the two become one (as in Aristophanes' account), nor does the eromenos see and so love his lover as instantiating the Form (in which case there *would* be reciprocity, each loving in the same way). In none of this, of course, is there a critique of double standards in courtship.

[31]K. J. Dover, "The Date of Plato's *Symposium*," *Phronesis*, 10 (1965), 2–20.

[32]See Gregory Vlastos, "The Paradox of Socrates" (1958), in *The Philosophy of Socrates*, ed. idem. (Notre Dame, Ind.: University of Notre Dame Press, 1980), pp. 16–17; Michael Gagarin, "Socrates' *Hybris* and Alcibiades' Failure," *Phoenix*, 31 (1977); 22–37; and Nussbaum, "The Speech of Alcibiades."

[33]I wish to thank Norman O. Brown, David Halperin, Gregory Vlastos, and Carter Wilson for helpful critical discussion.

Louis Mackey

Eros into Logos: The Rhetoric of Courtly Love

Louis Mackey is professor of philosophy at the University of Texas at Austin. He is the author of Kierkegaard: A Kind of Poet, Points of View: Readings of Kierkegaard, *and articles on topics in medieval philosophy and literary theory.*

> Meum pectus sauciat
> puellarum decor,
> et quas tactu nequeo,
> saltem corde mechor.
> (The girls are so pretty it hurts. But even though I can't touch them, at
> least I can commit adultery in my heart.)
>   — *The Confession of Golias*

The Middle Ages were much preoccupied with eros. Championing the ascendancy of spirit over flesh, the church found it necessary to restrain or channel the power of sex in various ways. Contained within the bonds of matrimony, sexuality was a useful instrument of social production (offspring) and social control (taming unruly passions, assuring the orderly transfer of property through patrilineal inheritance, and so on). In celibate religious communities, sublimated (sublimed) erotic desire could be indulged as a symbol of the love of Christ the heavenly bridegroom for his spiritual bride: the church or the holy soul. In secular literature like the Carmina Burana, unlicensed by the church but composed for the most part by clerics, love was celebrated as the source of an illicit but ecstatic delight, the transience and irregularity of which compounded sexual pleasure with the poignancy of mortality and the fear of retribution. Though it could not authorize the expression, carnal or verbal, of free sexuality, neither did the church regard it as a serious threat to its own moral theology: sinners could be expected to sin.

The configuration of attitude, ideals, and beliefs that has come to be known as courtly love was another matter. Theologians decried it, and preachers inveighed against it. Openly defiant of the church's teaching (the courtly relationship is normatively adulterous), with its own ideology and its own cult (the rules of love and the courts of love), *fin' amors* was perceived as a rival religion. Normally expressed in song—the lyrics of the troubadours, the trouveres, and their counterparts in Italy and Germany—courtly love has its theorists, of whom the prince is Andreas Capellanus. My intention in this essay is to examine the theory and practice of courtly love as propounded in his treatise, to expose its motives and effects, and to explicate its relationship to medieval Christianity.

Andreas Capellanus was a cleric. His name, plus his association with the court of Champagne, suggests that he was a chaplain in service to the Countess Marie, who governed as regent after the death of her husband and during the minority of their sons. He describes himself as "chaplain of the royal court." The claim cannot be verified. But in view of the fact that King Philip Augustus was half-brother to Marie and the Queen Mother sister to Marie's husband Henry, relations between Paris and Troyes were very close and Andreas may be telling the truth.[1]

Andreas's text—*De amore* or sometimes *De arte honeste amandi* (c. 1185)—is written in the form of a letter to a (real or fictional) friend named Walter (Gualterius). Its avowed purpose is to advise Walter on how to conduct a love affair: how to get love, how to keep it, and (if need be) how to get out of a relationship unscathed. Recently smitten by love, Walter does not know how to manage his passion and has asked Andreas for counsel. Andreas therefore offers him the wisdom gleaned from his own wide and varied experience. He is moved to do this by affection for his young friend, though he also admonishes him (in the Preface to his treatise) that it is neither fitting nor expedient to offer oneself to the service of love:

> For I know, having learned from experience, that it does not do the man who owes obedience to Venus's service any good to give careful thought to anything except how he may always be doing something that will entangle him more firmly in his chains; he thinks he has nothing good except what may wholly please his love. Therefore, although it does not seem expedient to devote oneself to things of this kind or fitting for any prudent man to engage in this kind of hunting, nevertheless, because of the affection I have for you, I can by no means refuse your request; because I know clearer than day that after you have learned the art of love your progress in it will be more cautious, in so far as I can I shall comply with your desire.(27)

It is impossible not to detect a note of irony in these words. "Entangle him more firmly in his chains": Is love a kind of self-incurred bondage? And that last clause. Does it mean that Walter will be more adept in love once he has learned the art of it? Or is Andreas saying: The more you know about the trials of love, the less disposed you will be to rush precipitously into the lists? If Andreas is ironical here, what is the force of his irony? Does he seriously intend to introduce Walter to the mystery of love only in order to warn him against it? Book III (The Rejection of Love) suggests as much. But the brief diatribe against the *evils* of love (read: against women) in Book III is not obviously consistent with—nor an adequate antidote to— the expansive and enthusiastic exposition of the *art* of love in Books I and II. There is a problem about the integrity of this work. Of which more later.

At the outset of Book I Andreas defines love as "a certain inborn suffering derived from the sight of and excessive meditation upon the beauty of the opposite sex" (28). Every element in this definition calls for comment. First, love is suffering. Specifically fear: fear that one will not attain one's object or that, having attained it, one will lose it (28–29). It is clear from his language that what Andreas calls love is what St. Augustine calls lust. Andreas would have been aware that Augustine had defined lust (*libido* or *cupiditas*) as the love of those things (e.g., a mistress) that one can lose against his will and had opposed it to the love of God, of whose favor one cannot be unwillingly deprived.[2] Andreas knows what he is talking about: not the ordinate love of God to which Christians are enjoined and by which they are beatified, but the inordinate love of created things from which they are urgently dissuaded and in which they experience nothing but misery and frustration.

Second, love is innate. Just as the cause of sin is not created things but the soul's immoderate devotion to them, so erotic passion is aroused not by its occasion (the sight of a beautiful example of the opposite sex) but by the mind's "excessive meditation" upon what it sees. The real object of sexual desire is not woman but the representation of woman. As opposed to *caritas*, which is a selfless love of the other, whether God or neighbor, sexual love (*amor*) is always self-love—a fascination with one's own imaginings. And so (perhaps) it ruptures two commandments at once. Flouting the sixth, it also undermines the first by idolizing the self and its desires.

Wherefore (third) Andreas proceeds to explain the growth of love in terms of the common medieval notion of the three stages in the genesis of sin: suggestion, delight, and consent. Suggestion: upon sighting a comely woman the lover-to-be immediately begins to "lust after her in his heart." Delight: the more he thinks about her ("fuller meditation") the more his passion is inflamed, until he comes at last to a "complete meditation": he contemplates her form, imagines all her bodily parts and their functions, and desires to put each of her members to "the fullest use." Consent: having thus incited himself to lust, the lover "proceeds at once to action," and begins to plan the strategies by which he may possess the object of his desire (29).

Since the genesis of love is structurally identical with the genesis of sin, you prevent love the same way you prevent sin: by avoiding the occasions of it. If the occasion nevertheless presents itself, you do not follow through. So Andreas, at the other end of his argument, advises:

> Never let your thoughts . . . lead you to the delight of the flesh, and always take care wholly to avoid places, times, and persons which may excite your passions or give occasion for lust. If a convenient place and some unexpected happening urge you on to the work of the flesh by putting the thought of some woman into your head, be careful to restrain your passion like a man and to get away from the tempting place. Even if carnal incitements have commenced to vex you, take care that they do not lead you to action, or that the combination of circumstances does not cause you to sin. (197)

Walter's objective — to be succesful in love — is imprudent. Christ admonished his auditors to stop short of the first promptings of eros, for even to lust after a woman in one's heart is already adultery.[3] But Andreas's description of the progress of carnal love is medieval commonplace. He is not recommending that one become embroiled in love affairs. Teaching what experience has taught him, he is telling Walter, who is already past the stage of suggestion and has presumably achieved a "complete meditation," how to handle his passion and — eventually — get rid of it. Or so at least he would have us believe.

Everything Andreas says by way of characterizing love is consistent with Augustine's description of lust. "Love is always either increasing or decreasing": Erotic love is inherently mutable and unstable, as opposed to the love of God, eternal and unchanging. Love is a kind of bondage,[4] as opposed to the liberating service of God (31). Love may be ennobling, but it is unreliable and seldom fair, as opposed to the love of God, which is always uplifting, always constant, and always just (31–32). There are people who are unfit for love—the very young, the very old, the blind, the overly passionate—but no one is excluded from the love of God (32–33).

Most perfectly Augustinian, though less obviously so, is Andreas's account of the means by which love may be acquired. Throughout the *Confessions* Augustine calls attention to the intimate connection between language and character. The deceitful language of the serpent precipitates the fall, and the language spoken by men ever after perpetuates its effects. The rhetoric that Augustine learned in school and later, as *vendor verborum*, retailed to his students is only the most corrupt (because most effective) form of a language corrupted from the beginning. After his conversion Augustine endeavored to free language from slavery to selfish desire (rhetoric) and return it to the service of God (prayer). The rightful use of words is to commemorate that Word by which the world was created and by which, incarnate, it was redeemed. But as long as human history is the history of sin, human language will continue to be the instrument of lust. It is this capacity of language to further the cause of eros that Andreas advises the lover to exploit.

There are, he tells us, five ways generally recognized by which the lover may get what he wants: "a beautiful figure, excellence of character, extreme readiness of speech, great wealth, and the readiness with which one grants that which is sought" (33). The last two he rejects as unworthy to appear in the courts of love. Of the remaining three he ranks character first. Beauty elicits an easy and incautious love at best; at worst it is nothing but cosmetic fakery, and in any case it is evanescent. "Character alone . . . is worthy of the crown of love" (35). However, Andreas adds, "fluency of speech . . . creates a presumption in favor of the excellent character of the speaker" (35). Only a lover of good character deserves to be requited, but facility in speech is the principle datum from which, rightly or wrongly, character is inferred. Andreas will not go so far as to say that character *is* rhetoric, but rhetoric produces the effects of character—its appearances—and in an erotic relationship it is appearances that count. For this reason Andreas devotes most of his treatise to the art of amatory discourse. Inverting and perverting Augustine's program for the redemption of rhetoric, exploiting rather than converting the language of sin, Andreas simultaneously declares his own commitment to the terms and parameters of the Augustinian tradition.

More than half of Andreas's text—106 out of 186 pages in the English translation—consists of exemplary dialogues of seduction and, embedded in them, numerous stories of fabulous loves and lovers. There are no explicit descriptions of sexual encounters of the sort one gets in contemporary fiction. Nor does Andreas's work, like a modern sex manual, enumerate and illustrate the techniques of intercourse. That is not his concern. What he does provide are two lists of the "rules" of love (81-82, 184-86), a long chivalric narrative recounting the discovery of these rules (177-86), and records of judgments handed down in the courts of love by Countess Marie, Queen Eleanor, and other authoritative judges. In short: language and lots of it. Not the language of pornography or the language of sexual technology, but the language of seduction and erotic adventure. The medium has become the message. The reality of sex is sublated and sublimated in the discourse of love. Eros is subsumed without remainder into logos.

According to Kenneth Burke, the paradigmatic rhetorical performance—the quintessence of persuasion—is the act of courtship: seduction lifted from the carnal to the verbal level, and perhaps consummated there. Courtship is the "spiritualization" of seduction, the spirituality of which is the spirituality of its linguistic medium.[5] So in Andreas's text love is spiritualized—made "courtly" or *honestus*—by its translation into language. Courtly love becomes thereby the inverse (and no doubt perverse) counterpart of the heavenly love imagined in monastic commentaries on *The Song of Songs*. Each is a purified eros directed at an ideal object, in the one case God and in the other a lady who, in her unapproachable remoteness, is the intentional (albeit not the actual) equivalent of God. Both the love of God and the love of woman are *meant* to produce a certain perfection of character in the lover: single-minded chaste devotion to the beloved. Both *result in* the elaboration of a distinctive rhetoric. In both its courtly and its monastic transformations, love is a matter of character and character in turn is a matter of language.

Courtly love expresses itself in a series of formal postures and a system of linguistic conventions. That is why Andreas advises Walter: Do not try to court peasant women. His brief remarks on this head (149-50) are motivated by aristocratic disdain and a regard for feudal order: If (*contra naturam*) farmers cultivate the art of love rather than the art of agriculture, the upper classes will get nothing to eat. Along with these economic proprieties, there is the fact, decisive for the theorist of courtly love, that a peasant woman *cannot* be courted. Crude and illiterate, she is incapable of responding to the finer solicitations of language and—if one is so incautious as to desire her—may simply be taken by force.

An even closer association of economic and rhetorical motives is evident in Andreas's attitude toward commerce with prostitutes and other women who give their "solaces" in return for money (144–48, 150). His abhorrence of such relationships is unqualified: "This most precious gift of love cannot be paid for at any set price or be cheapened by a matter of money. . . . The love which seeks for rewards should not be called love by anybody, but rather shameful harlotry and greedy wantonness" (144, 145). Andreas's contempt for the oldest profession symptomizes the incommensurability of the feudal ideal, formally committed to chivalric relations between the sexes, and the capitalist economy of the future, in which the prostitute's medium of exchange, money, will replace language as the universal means of communication and the sole spiritual bond among men. Even within the feudal economy, marital contracts are based on considerations of property rather than personality, so that, although a man should not court a woman he would be ashamed to marry (81, 185), courtly relations are normally extramarital (187–88) and the courtly lover careless of his property (191).

Spiritualized by its transformation into logos, eros becomes (1) an exchange of set speeches from a repertory of prescribed dialogues between lover and beloved, aimed at eventual consummation; (2) a code of rules to be followed and a set of poses to be assumed by lady and leman on the way to sexual congress; (3) stories of noble loves and lovers, *exempla* of successful seduction; and (4) judgments rendered in the courts of love, legitimizing honorable conjunctions. In short: an art—or artificiality—of speech and gesture all directed—presumably—toward the single end of carnal union.

Presumably. For the union in question, though carnally imagined, is not copulation in general or without qualification. Intercourse between husband and wife is excluded (106–7, 156, 171, 175), as is intercourse between peasants, intercourse between peasants and nobles, and intercourse with prostitutes or other venal women. The *immediacy* of sexual union is not what matters. What matters is *context*: an artfully contrived setting for erotic adventure and the artful arrival at sexual fulfillment. An overabundance of lust is incompatible with courtly love (33). Orgasm is better if postponed as long as possible, infrequently enjoyed, and difficult to procure. It is only fully satisfying if accomplished by artistic means and relished for its aesthetic value.

Indeed, it need not occur at all. Andreas distinguishes what he calls "pure" love from an inferior form called "mixed" love (122, 164). Mixed love goes all the way. Pure love appears to be something like heavy petting that permits the nude embrace but stops short of copulation. Copulation adulterates love because it terminates the dialogue of seduction. Orgasm is notoriously wordless. Accompanied by nothing more articulate than moans and groans and cries of ecstasy, it blocks the flow of language and curtails the (otherwise endless) opportunities for rhetoric. But the show must go on. Therefore, in Andreas's text, copulation is not even named but only suggested by a glossary of euphemistic designators: the work of Venus, sweet solaces, the regular solaces, the final solace, the ultimate solace, the yielding of the whole person, and so on. In its courtly transfiguration, sexual intercourse becomes a purely rhetorical exchange and orgasm ideally a rhetorical climax. Courtly lovers don't mate, they flirt. And instead of coming, they go on and on and on. . . .[6]

Under the sign of paradox, the rhetoric of courtly love threatens to deconstruct itself. Ostensibly a mode of discourse and a style of comportment aimed at gratifying desire, it is nevertheless so designed that it postpones gratification indefinitely and distances the immediacy which is its (ostensible) consummation. Without sexual desire, courtly love could not exist. But it cannot tolerate the satisfaction of the desire that sponsors it. Intercourse itself, if it does occur, is not enjoyed immediately[7] — for that purpose the occasional peasant girl would no doubt be better — but savored as the finishing touch on a successful work of art.

The linguistic technique which intends to overcome difference and effect unity institutionalizes difference and interdicts unity. Such is the paradox of courtly rhetoric. The union of lover and beloved, which is the purpose of courtship, is indefinitely deferred by the transformation of eros into logos. The union of flesh and spirit that would render love "courtly"—make sexual intercourse honorable — is achieved only at the level of spirit (language) and thereby distanced from the immediacy of the flesh and its desires. The rhetoric of courtly love is a rhetoric of *différance*: the transcendence of carnal reality necessitated by the requirements of courtliness iterates the difference (of lover and beloved, flesh and spirit) it is meant to repair and defers the consummation it is meant to facilitate. Courtly love is a failed incarnation — a disincarnation — in which the flesh becomes word, and for that reason, among others, the antithesis of the Love which prompted the Word to become flesh.

The topos of the celestial bridegroom and the divine nuptials (a commonplace of monastic spirituality) with which Andreas ends his work (211–12) is simply the ultimate act of transcendence: the projection of erotic fulfillment from the courts of love into the court of the heavenly King. It is also the ultimate *différance*, as heaven is infinitely remote from earth in

space and time alike. But—and this is typical of the rhetoric of religion—
the language and the imagery imply that in the heavenly union of Christ
and the soul, the immediacy forfeit in this world is recovered in the next.
The joys of mystical marriage are at once the purest and most fulfilling. In
the bridal chambers of Zion, the perfection of *fin' amors* and the gratification of desire coincide in a single everlasting and wholly spiritual orgasm.
But there is a price. Just as the elevation of love to the level of *courtoisie* demands the suppression of gross carnality, so admission to the heavenly nuptials demands the renunciation of courtly love. Therefore, Andreas, having
spent 160 pages explaining love—what it is, how to get it, how to keep it—
adds 26 pages counseling "The Rejection of Love."

At the outset of Book III Andreas tells Walter: you now "lack nothing
in the art of love, since in this little book we gave you the theory of the subject, fully and completely" (187). Whereupon he adds:

> We did not do this because we consider it advisable for you or any other
> man to fall in love, but for fear lest you might think us stupid; we be-
> lieve, though, that any man who devotes his efforts to love loses all his
> usefulness. Read this little book, then, not as one seeking to take up the
> life of a lover, but that, invigorated by the theory and trained to excite
> the minds of women to love, you may, by refraining from so doing, win
> an eternal recompense and thereby deserve a greater reward from God.
> For God is more pleased with a man who is able to sin and does not,
> than with a man who has no opportunity to sin. (187)

The Scriptures admonish us again and again: Be not hearers of the
word only but doers as well, for it is not understanding that pleases God but
obedience. Many a medieval text repeats this admonition, urging its readers to move through contemplation to action. Andreas's skewed relationship to his own tradition requires him to turn this familiar trope against itself. Echoing and clarifying the language of his Preface ("after you have
learned the art of love your progress in it will be more cautious"), he makes
his meaning plain: You are to become expert in the art of love in order *not*
to practice it. By refusing to do what you have been trained to do ("excite
the minds of women to love"), you will gain an eternal reward. For God is
better pleased with a man who can sin and won't than He is with a man
who just can't.

But the clarification only intensifies the irony of Andreas's text and ag-
gravates the problem of its integrity. Granted that incapacity (impotence?)

is no virtue. Does he really mean that one should learn to sin in order not to, so that, not doing the evil one might, one acquires greater merit thereby? How does this—cultivating the art of love—differ from that "fuller meditation" which, in the genesis of sin, leads from suggestion to consent? Wouldn't it be better, as Andreas advises a few pages on, simply to avoid the occasions of evil in the first place? "For lust is the sort of thing that overcomes us if we follow it, but is driven away if we flee from it" (197-98). Book III appears to stand in irreconcilable contradiction with the main body of the text.

One may of course suppose that Andreas, as a cleric, was just protecting himself—summarily recanting what he had taught in order to maintain the appearance of regularity. Assumptions of this sort come easily to the modern mind, but they may be too easy. Accusing the author of bad faith, they do nothing to integrate his work. In any event, it seems evident that Andreas's superiors, if they worried about such things, would not have been deceived by so obviously cynical a gesture. Therefore, another solution recommends itself: In his terminal revocation Andreas may, in all sincerity, be confronting the courtly *ideal* of love with the brutal *actuality* of sex. The courtly ideal is a vision of eros conceived and consummated in logos: a rhetoric of romance. The actuality would be the church's normative view of sexual relations, opposing to the romantic glorification of a woman a misogynist conception of her historical reality. For while it had to condone marriage as a sacrament instituted by God and confirmed by Christ, the medieval church could not forget that women, ever since Eve, had tried to distract men from their divinely ordained destiny, displacing and replacing God as the supreme object of their desire and the only source of true happiness.

This reading of the text is recommended by the fact that the bulk of Andreas's third book is occupied with denigrating woman and itemizing the miseries entailed by sexual infatuation. Andreas has a whole arsenal of reasons for abstaining from the love of woman. (1) As Holy Scripture tells us, the "foul and shameful acts of Venus" (188) are hateful to God. (2) The love of woman causes men to neglect their duty to their neighbors. These two arguments, taken together, should be sufficient. By yielding to sexual temptation we violate the two great commandments: "Thou shalt love the Lord thy God . . . and thy neighbor as thyself."[8] But Andreas has just begun. (3) Sexual attachments ruin masculine friendships. Andreas was neither the first nor the last to complain that the love of woman ruptures male bonding. (4) Love defiles body and soul alike. (5) The lover is enslaved to fear and jealousy: The suffering which defines love (28) is also one of its chief faults. Naturally enough: Having described love in the terms used by Augustine to characterize lust, Andreas, in order to disparage love, has only to reaffirm his solidarity with the tradition from which, even in subverting it, he has never really departed. (6) The lover is impoverished by the service of his lady, and by his poverty he is (like the addict) impelled to crime in order to maintain his habit. (7) The lover suffers constant torments, both temporal and spiritual. (8) Love (= lust) is universally acknowledged to be a vice, opposed to the corresponding virtues of temperance and chastity. (9) Love incites its devotees to every kind of crime. (10) Much evil but no good comes from love. (11) Love deprives men of worldly honor and heavenly reward.

At this point Andreas breaks off enumerating arguments (already redundant) and embarks on an extended and impassioned exhortation to chastity. But eventually he resumes his bill of particulars. (12) The act of love (where have we heard this before?) weakens the body. (13) Love robs a man of his wisdom. Andreas is thinking of David and Solomon, both deranged by lust. Had he also heard of Abelard, whose dalliance with Heloise caused him to neglect his studies? (14) Not quite finally, Andreas argues that women are incapable of true love by reason of their many faults. To be precise: Every woman is avaricious (she's after your property), envious, slanderous, greedy, gluttonous (there's nothing she won't do for a free meal), inconstant (*la donna è mobile*), deceitful, disobedient to God and her husband, arrogant, vainglorious, mendacious, bibulous, loud-mouthed, incapable of keeping a secret (telephone, telegraph, tell a woman), wanton, faithless, and—like the Greeks, who built a shrine to the god they might have overlooked—Andreas adds: prone to every sort of evil. From which (surely exhaustive) catalogue of vices it follows that no woman is capable of a pure and sincere love. To which, as if more were necessary, Andreas subjoins (15): love itself is unjust and will not constantly reward even the most consistent lover with the satisfactions he seeks. Clearly, he says, these are "conclusive reasons why a man is bound to avoid [love] with all his might and to trample under foot all its rules" (210).

Clearly. Yet these considerations, while they do epitomize the received opinion of sex and woman in the Middle Ages, only exacerbate the contradiction in Andreas's text between its apparent recommendation of love and its terminal renunciation. They represent but do not reconcile the conflict between the courtly ideal and the Christian norm. However, it must be remembered, first, that the monstrous female of Book III is just as much a rhetorical ideal as the romanticized lady of Books I and II. The woman maligned in Book III is a masterpiece of wickedness and a virtuoso in "every sort of evil" (208). She is, as Andreas more than once reminds us, a perfect Eve (203, 205): the object of a love that will finally betray our trust and disappoint our expectations. Her counterpart in Books I and II is likewise a rhetorical entity: the incarnation of a remote perfection with whom the lover seeks to be united and from whom he is repelled in the seeking. An inverse image of the Blessed Virgin, who for Christians is the historically actual paradigm of womanhood, she is at once the joy of every man's desiring and the *ewige Weibliche* who is never possessed. Supremely alluring and cruelly aloof, the beloved lady of the troubadours welcomes all her courtiers and remains disdainfully indifferent to their entreaties.

The contradiction *between* the repulsive woman of Book III and the enticing woman of Books I and II iterates the contradiction *within* the woman of Books I and II. The antagonism of the (theologically) real and the (courtly) ideal repeats and potentiates the tension already present in the ideal. And both — both women and both contradictions — are projections of the contrary vectors in the rhetoric of courtly love, a rhetoric designed to prevent the attainment of the end it seeks. The two faces of woman are just the two poles of a rhetoric which at once attracts and repels, and the two women (of Books I and II and of Book III) are contradictorily coherent with each other and with an ambivalent language which simultaneously proposes unity and perpetuates difference.

From this point of view it is not difficult to understand why courtly love was both so attractive and so threatening to the medieval mind.[9] Courtly love and Christianity were rival religions because they were rival rhetorics. For the Christian religion, though it offers itself as revealed truth commanding men's allegiance, is never more than a representation of revealed truth. Holy Scripture, accepted by believers as the one true story of the world, inspired by the Holy Spirit, is nevertheless the work of human authors, composed in the language of fallen man. Sacred history is not literally recounted but figuratively represented, wrapped in an artful *integumentum* that exploits all the tropes of rhetoric from allegory to zeugma. Only in this way can human beings receive it. Likewise Christian doctrine is not simply the truth about God and the economy of redemption, but a figuration of that truth mediated by the forms of human thought and by human modes of expression.

Christianity itself is a rhetoric of salvation, its figurative character necessitated by fallen man's alienation from the unmediated vision of God. For the faithful it is the rhetoric of truth, over against which the rhetoric of courtly love could only be perceived as the rhetoric of deviance and error. From a Christian point of view the lady imagined in the literature of courtly love would have to be either the apotheosis of Eve or a degradation of the Blessed Virgin — and unacceptable under either description. But the relation between Eve, the executrix of damnation, and Mary, the mediatrix of salvation, is just as ambiguous as the relation between the courtly lady of Books I and II and the vile creature anathematized in Book III. Though opposed as figures of sin and grace respectively, they are both women. And as it was woman's disobedience that succumbed to the blandishments of the serpent, so it was the seed of woman's obedience who trampled the serpent under his feet. The Blessed Virgin, who is the opposite of Eve, is also the redemption of Eve, just as Christ is Adam's antitype and his redeemer. And from a historical point of view the crime of Eve (the original sin) is always already past just as the achievement of Mary (the final restoration of human nature) is never yet present. Christianity, like courtly love, is not only a rhetoric, but a rhetoric of *différance*. Presupposing difference (the alienation of sin), it promises union (atonement), but in fact — until the end of history — reiterates difference and postpones reconciliation. The bitterness of the rivalry between courtly love and Christianity is a function of their complicity — both are rhetorics of reunion — and their complicity is the effect of their common duplicity — both are rhetorics of difference and deferment.

Though it has non-Christian (e.g., Islamic) antecedents, the ideology of courtly love as expounded by Andreas Capellanus is obviously parasitic on the Christianity with which it competes. Not only are its values defined by Christianity — courtly *amor* is the negative image of Christian *caritas*, Andreas's "love" is Augustine's "lust," and the courtly lady a blasphemous conjunction of the mother of men and the Mother of God — but also its ultimate goal is reunion with the Christian ideal of which it is the travesty and to which it pays tribute thereby. This duplicity is, *faute de mieux*, the source of whatever integrity may be found in Andreas's text.

At the end of Book III Andreas himself admits there is a problem and offers a solution. "This doctrine of ours," he tells Walter, "will . . . seem to present two different points of view" (210–11). In the first part of this work, he says, "we tried to assent to your simple and youthful request" (211) by explaining the art of love in detail and in order.

If you wish to practice the system, you will obtain, as a careful reading of this little book will show you, all the delights of the flesh in fullest measure; but the grace of God, the companionship of the good, and the friendship of praiseworthy men you will with good reason be deprived of, and you will do great harm to your good name, and it will be difficult for you to obtain the honors of this world. (211)

But in the latter part of the work,

we were more concerned with what might be useful to you, and of our own accord we added something about the rejection of love, although you had no reason to ask for it, and we treated the matter fully; perhaps we can do you good against your will. (211)

Books I and II are really to be ascribed to Walter, in response to whose simple and youthful (albeit misguided) entreaties they were written, that Andreas might prove his diligence and his friendship. Only Book III is Andreas's own work, added not to please his friend by providing him the illusory good he craves but (in the spirit of true friendship) to help him (albeit against his will) obtain the good that satisfies eternally. But it's all one. If Walter practices the art of love, he will enjoy the pleasures of the flesh "in fullest measure" but forfeit all spiritual and temporal well-being. If he abstains from it, he will merit worldly success and earn the favor of the heavenly King. Whatever his choice, he will learn what he needs to know. Enrolled in the service of love, he will learn from bitter experience that he has made a mistake. Adopting the counsel of Book III, he will learn, honorably and without pain, the evils of carnal love. Consistent in spite of appearances to the contrary, the *De amore* offers Walter two ways to learn one and the same lesson: renounce the love of woman and cultivate the love of God.

If he is wise, therefore, Walter will ignore the solicitations of Venus and obey the commandments of God. By so doing he will keep himself (wise virgin) in readiness for the advent of the heavenly bridegroom, a worthy candidate for the joys of celestial marriage.

Therefore, Walter, accept this health-giving teaching we offer you, and pass by all the vanities of the world, so that when the Bridegroom cometh to celebrate the greater nuptials, and the cry ariseth in the night, you may be prepared to go forth to meet Him with your lamps filled and to go in with Him to the divine marriage, and you will have no need to seek out in haste what you need for your lamps, and find it too late, and come to the home of the Bridegroom after the door is shut, and hear His venerable voice.

Be mindful, therefore, Walter, to have your lamps always supplied, that is, have the supplies of charity and good works. Be mindful ever to watch, lest the unexpected coming of the Bridegroom find you asleep in sins. Avoid then, Walter, practicing the mandates of love, and labor in constant watchfulness so that when the Bridegroom cometh He may find you wakeful; do not let worldly delight make you lie down in your sins, trusting to the youth of your body and confident that the Bridegroom will be late, since, as He tells us Himself, we know neither the day nor the hour. (211–212)

As love becomes rhetoric in Books I and II, so the rejection of love is an exercise in the rhetoric of renunciation and postponement: Give up pleasure in favor of virtue (here and now), so that you may (there and then) enjoy both in fullest measure. The problem of the unity of this text is a problem in rhetoric: how to align the rhetoric of "what you want" with the rhetoric of "what is good for you." Andreas's solution—and here the language of courtly love rejoins the language of monastic spirituality—is to invoke the rhetoric of transcendence and merger (deferment): *In heaven* what you want and what's good for you will be the same, and the rhetoric of victimage (difference): *Until then* curb your desires and seek the good.[10] When your Lover comes, you will have it all. The cravings of the flesh and the needs of the spirit are proleptically reconciled, by the rhetoric of religion, in the world (ever yet) to come. There the fulfillment of the divine mandates will be the satisfaction of desire. But in this life we are caught in the dialectical standoff of the rhetoric of desire and the rhetoric of virtue. And this dialectic—projected as contradictory perspectives on the nature of woman but rooted in the differential logic of the rhetorical project itself—is the only integrity Andreas's text can hope to achieve. "A scar is what happens when the word is made flesh."[11] And when eros is taken into logos, the wound of renunciation is not healed save in expectation.

Notes

[1]For a full discussion of Andreas and his work in their historical setting, see the editor's Introduction to John Jay Parry, trans., *The Art of Courtly Love* (New York: W. W. Norton, 1969). Parenthetical page references in my text are to this edition, which reprints the first edition, by Columbia University Press (1941), in its Records of Civilization series.

[2]Cf. St. Augustine, *De Libero Arbitrio Voluntatis*, 1. 4. 31.

[3]Matthew 5: 27–28.

[4]Andreas, following Isidore of Seville (*Etymologies*, 10. 1. 5), derives *amor* (love) from *(h)amus* (hook). This may be the origin of the "tender trap."

⁵Cf. Kenneth Burke, *A Rhetoric of Motives* (Berkeley and Los Angeles: University of California Press, 1969), pp. 174-80, 208-12.

⁶As Kenneth Burke might say, they are dancing an attitude. The lovers execute a *pas de deux* in the larger ballet of courtly demeanor: a performance compounded of stylized poses, prescribed ripostes, rhetorical thrust and parry, and so on—all carried out in obedience to purely formal demands and in the service of purely formal ends.

⁷Is it ever? Desire is always the reflection of desire and its object the representation of its object. In any case, it is tautologous but tragic that no desire survives its own gratification. Eros that is not subsumed into logos is consumed by thanatos.

⁸Matthew 22: 37-39, Mark 12: 30-31, Luke 10: 27.

⁹And for that matter to some modern minds. The extreme case is D. W. Robertson, Jr., who denies the existence of a courtly love tradition. See his *Preface to Chaucer* (Princeton: Princeton University Press, 1962), Part V; and his *Essays in Medieval Culture* (Princeton: Princeton University Press, 1980), esp. pp. 151—65, 202—6, and 257—72. Others, like C. S. Lewis in *The Allegory of Love* (New York: Oxford University Press, 1936), esp. pp. 1-43, simply acknowledge the conflict between Christianity and courtly love and declare it irreconcilable.

¹⁰Cf. Kenneth Burke, *A Grammar of Motives* (Berkeley and Los Angeles: University of California Press, 1969), pp. 402—43.

¹¹Leonard Cohen, *The Favorite Game* (New York: Avon Books, 1965), p. 9.

Amelie Rorty

Spinoza on the Pathos of Idolatrous Love
and the Hilarity of True Love

Amelie Rorty is Matina Horner Visiting Professor of philosophy at Rad-
cliffe College and professor of philosophy at Mt. Holyoke College. She is
the author of Mind in Action *(1988) and coeditor of* Identity, Character,
and Morality *(1990)*.

In memory of Laszlo Versenyi
Hungary, 1929–Williamstown, Mass., 1988

> ["In reflecting on love], I was led far beyond my individual life and
> time, to the point where . . . [I] became no more than an accidental fo-
> cal point of something much larger; a mere vantage point for seeing
> and ranging over a landscape that has no clear boundaries."
>   Laszlo Versenyi, *Going Home*

Differ as we do about its nature, its causes and effects, its
proper objects, we all agree that love is—or can be—the beginning of wisdom. But wisdom about what? Spinoza wrote not only truthfully but wisely
about love, about its travails and dangers, about its connection to knowledge and power, about individuality and the disappearance of the self. To
understand what is vital and what is mortifying about the passions, to trace
the movement from the bondage of passivity to the freedom of activity, we
could do no better than follow his investigations. In the nature of the case,
each of us necessarily understands him—as we do all else—from the parti-
ality of our own perspectives. We shall follow Ariadne's thread, into the
heart of the labyrinth, first speaking with the vulgar, telling fragmentary
tales about appearances. Then we must follow the thread out again, thinking with the learned, gaining scientific understanding of what we really
are; and finally we must put these two—vulgar appearance and scientific
explanation—together to tell the real story, the story of reality.

Speaking with the Vulgar about Appearances:
Fragmentary Images of Passivity, Idolatry, Partiality

Spinoza is, first and last, a particularist: The world is composed wholly and entirely of particular individuals, so interrelated that they form a complex individual, a unified system. To understand the pathos of love, we must therefore begin with a particular story; it will, of course, be merely a fragmentary image, only partially true, because it is, perforce, only part of the story. Nevertheless, following it where it must go will bring us to an increasingly adequate understanding of love, of the characters in our story, and of ourselves, as we love.

Ariadne loves Echo, loves him, as she thinks, for the subtlety of his interpretation of Spinoza, for his wry speech, the precision and delicacy of his courtesy, his way of looking at her with those eyes of his, and perhaps most important of all, as is the way of these things, for she knows not what.

As Spinoza would see it, Ariadne's love is an elation—a sense of well-being—that she thinks Echo brings her. She feels herself more fully herself, freer to write clearly and fluently, to move gracefully because of him. ("Love is elation accompanied by the idea of an external cause" [III. app. D. 6].)[1] But if she thought that her University or a particular landscape were the causes of her elation—her exhilarated enhancement—she would love her University or that landscape. Although each love—indeed each moment of love—is unique, there are as many types of love as there are types of individuals. ("There are as many kinds of . . . love . . . as there are kinds of objects by which we are affected. Any affect of one individual differs from that of another in the extent that the essence of one individual differs from the essence of the other" [III. 56–57].) The elation of love is the ideational or psychological expression of a change in Ariadne's bodily thriving. Indeed every "affect is a modification of the body by which the body's power is increased or diminished, assisted or checked, together with the ideas of these modifications. If we are the adequate cause of an affect, then the affect is active; if we are not, it is passive" (III. D. 3). So in truth, Ariadne's love is her body's elation, psychologically expressed. To the extent that she thinks of this elation as externally caused, her affect is passive; to the extent that she thinks of it as a function of her own nature, her love is active.

Spinoza's *affectus*—usually translated as "affect" or "emotion"—is obviously a much broader and more encompassing notion than the contemporary class of *emotions* that is commonly contrasted to *beliefs* and *desires*. Affects include desires, wishes, a sense of health or debility: They are ideational indicants of bodily thriving or declining. A condition is passive when its cause is (regarded as) external, active when internal, to the body. So, for instance, a healing process which is a function of the body's own "internal" defensive immune system is a modification of the body, registered in the mind as an active affect; a healing process "externally" produced by medication is a modification of the body, registered in the mind as a passive affect.

So far, so good: Love is a particular sense of health, with a diagnosis of its cause. But troubles soon begin. Elation is an active contrast to a previous state; it must, in its very nature, escalate. ("Elation is . . . a passage or transition from a state of less to a state of greater perfection or vitality" [III. app. D. 2].) Ariadne will try to secure Echo for herself in whatever ways she can, acting to preserve her elation and to oppose or to destroy whatever might bring dejection. ("We endeavour to bring about whatever we imagine to be conducive to elation; [and] endeavor to remove or destroy whatever we imagine to be opposed to it and conducive to dejection" [III. 26–28].) One of the ways Ariadne will attempt to secure him is to think of him a lot. When Echo is not actually around discussing Spinoza with her, she will have fantasies of their increasing intimacy, an intimacy that would still further enhance and elate her. But she will—she must—go further than fantasy: She will attempt to control Echo so that those aspects of his character that enhance her are strengthened, those that debilitate her are weakened. There is nothing special about love in this; all psychological conditions are active, relational, and dynamic. Thoughts and passions alike are individuated in a field of forces. Each individual is so constituted as to attempt to perpetuate and enhance his nature, in relation to other individuals. ("Everything . . . endeavors to persist in its own being. . . . The mind endeavors as far as it can to think of those things that increase or assist the body's power of activity" [III. 6–9, 12].) Indeed, the details of all an individual's activities in self-preservation, taken together, constitute its *conatus*, its essential nature. A person's thoughts and passions are the traces—the expressions and reflections—of all this activity.

Of course the satisfaction of Ariadne's desires will depend on her psychological canniness, on how well she understands Echo and herself. If Echo does not reciprocate her affections—if that way of looking at her turns out to be nearsightedness, if the intricacies of his interpretations are merely constructed to impress Ariadne in her persona as department head — her love will be short-lived, likely to be replaced by hatred for someone who has diminished her sense of herself. But would Spinoza expect their apparent happiness to continue if Echo returns her affections? The natural story of the best of such love relatively quickly leads to ambivalence, confusion, unhappiness. ("Emotional distress and unhappiness have their origin especially in excessive love towards anything subject to considerable instability, a thing which we can never completely possess. For nobody is disturbed or anxious about any thing unless he loves it, nor do wrongs, suspicions, enmities, etc. arise except from love towards things which nobody can truly possess" [V. 20. S].) Ariadne and Echo are complex people, with complex relations to others. She has her work, he has his; she has one set of friends, he has another. Their relations to one another are necessarily affected by the constant and subtle changes in their interactions with the rest of the world. If their friends and acquaintances endorse their mutual esteem, their love will, for a time, be reinforced. But if their common acquaintances do not respect Echo, Ariadne's love will be weakened. If, on the other hand, he is commonly thought to be too good for her, she will begin to fear — and to perceive — a change in his attentions. When his affection fluctuates, her sense of assurance falters, her grace and style crack. She will sense herself diminished and her estrangement will begin.

In loving Echo, Ariadne comes to redefine her relations to the rest of the world: Her interactions with others will be mediated, skewed by how she imagines they affect Echo and above all by how they affect Echo's relation to her. She will love what she believes enhances his love for her, hate what endangers it, become jealous of what draws his attentions away from her, envy those whom Echo envies. It is this feature of love — that it generates tangential, perspectivally fragmented relations to the world — that makes it especially blinding. The bondage of Ariadne's passive love ramifies beyond her perspectivally distorted perceptions of the complexities of Echo's qualities to similar distortions about the complex qualities of all that interacts with Echo.

For their happiness to continue, their constant changes must remain in harmony. Each must exactly register and adapt to the constant transformations in the other, and those transformations must remain mutually enhancing. Ariadne's growing reputation must somehow stand in continuous harmony with the changes that affect Echo, the reviews of his commentary on Spinoza, the adoration of his women students. As we fill in the familiar details of such stories, it becomes harder and harder to imagine the two continuing to enhance one another. How do they perceive one another's attentions to the rest of the world? Every unshared moment of delight becomes the occasion for fear, envy, and jealousy. Every shared moment introduces a subtle struggle for power. But even if all goes well—and of course if it does, we have moved from a familiar story to a fairy story—things are at best precarious. Every moment of love occurs within a larger context. But since affects that are accidentally associated remain associated, the elation of love readily becomes linked with a sense of debility. ("Anything can accidentally be the cause of elation, dejection or desire" [III. 15]. "If the mind has once been affected by two passions at the same time, when it is later affected by one it will also be affected by the other" [III. 14].) For instance, if Ariadne tended Echo during an illness, comforted him during some disappointment, or protected him from his crippling sense of insecurity, his affection will remind him of debilities that he naturally prefers to forget. It gets harder and harder to prevent elation from sliding to ambivalence, and ambivalence from sliding to the disintegration that is associated with erratic and vacillating impulsive movements. Any love that focuses on a particular individual is idolatrous; and because idolatrous love is fetishistic and partial, it inevitably brings ambivalence and frustration.

Ariadne's natural vitality will combat disintegration; she straightway moves to preserve herself, to overcome pathology in whatever way she can. Of course she has ways to combat debility; indeed she'd have disintegrated long ago if she'd not been naturally constructed and organized in such a way as to overcome debility, to preserve her integrity. Ariadne could not be cured of envy, jealousy, fear, just by trying to stop loving Echo. After all, every chance joy and enhancement brings love with it. She must in some way go to the root of the matter of her dreadful and tiresome tendency to fall in love, always and invariably, time and again, to fall in love. Nor—however tempting that might seem—will it help her to attempt to transform her love to contempt, disdain, hate. As love is a sense of enhancement, of elation, hate is a sense of dejection, accompanied by an idea of its cause (III. app. D. 7). But no one can be enhanced by an affect that is itself an expression of a variety of diminution.

Ariadne can only redirect her passive love through a more powerful emotion. ("An affect or emotion cannot be checked or destroyed except by a contrary emotion which is stronger than the emotion to be checked" [IV. 7].) It will not help Ariadne to love a more powerful person, (say) Abraham, or to acquire a more dominating passion, for (say) fame, or a passion for a more stable object, (say) Sung vases. All idolatry—any focus on a single object—brings the miseries of pathology in its wake. Love is love, with the same structure and the same consequences, even if each moment of elation is uniquely determined by the details of that moment. If she is astute, Ariadne will know that she cannot avoid the disintegration of one pathological love by finding another.

Thinking with the Learned about the Structure of Appearances: From the Bondage of Passivity to the Freedom of Activity

Let us suppose that Ariadne is psychologically canny, that she has considerable natural endowments—some of them constitutional, some acquired by the fortune of her upbringing. Central among them is a certain capacity for and energy toward clarity in reflection. She knows that idolatrous love, focused on a particular individual, necessarily involves misperception. Not that Echo wasn't what he seemed: He did have a wry turn of mind; he did have a sound understanding of Spinoza. But in fact the elation he first brought her was not just a function of *his* character: it was, rather, the expression of the fit between his traits *and* hers. Had she been the star of a hardrock music group, she'd not have been charmed by Echo's charms. Since she is canny—and this is just what it means to be canny, neither more nor less—she has a hunger for further explanations, an active passion for understanding. In fact her hunger for further explanation is another way of expressing her activity in integration, her moving from the debilities of love and its consequences. That hunger, her reflections, her drive to integrity are all different ways of describing the same thing: the active energies exercised in preserving and enhancing her existence.

Explanation-hungry as she is, Ariadne has also come to realize a number of things about herself and Echo: that she and Echo—and anyone or anything else she might love—are complex, constantly changing, compounded entities. Every aspect of their individuality is affected by their interactions with other equally historically conditioned, dynamic individuals. The details of all these interactions are themselves expressions and reflections of the details of their past history, the active traces, as it were, of many different layers of previous interactions, stretching far beyond their individual lives. Echo's interest in Spinoza expresses his grandmother's attitudes toward the world; his eyes and the look of his eyes reflect his biological inheritance. Ariadne's own penchant for fellows with a wry turn of mind derives from some of her childhood attachments, and the timbre of her voice reflects not only her constitution but also her family's passion for folksongs.

Gradually, Ariadne comes to see herself and Echo in a different light. In fact, she begins to suspect—though she has as yet no way of making this suspicion anything but a vague hunch—that she and Echo just *are* the active traces of all that has happened to them, stretching far backward before their births, and far outward to distant interactive individuals. She gives up her idolatrous modes of thinking about Echo and herself as "closed and bounded entities" and instead comes to think of all individuals as complex, dynamic compounds, individuated by their history and their interactions. By changing her thoughts in this way, Ariadne's image-ideas have become reflective ideas, ideas which, besides including their direct objects, also include reflections on the relations between the idea of their direct objects and other ideas. So in thinking of Echo, Ariadne now thinks of the interrelations between her ideas of Echo and her ideas of her brother, his grandparents, folksongs of a certain era; in thinking of herself, she now thinks of her ideas of Echo, of her grandmother, and so on.

All of these reflections give her some relief from ambivalence and its inevitably erratic behavior. Because she has traced the disparate sources of the various strands that have formed Echo, she has dispersed the intensity of her attachment. Since she now sees Echo as a mediating transmitter rather than as a Substance, her idea of the causes of her elation has correspondingly changed. The train of associated passions—fear, envy, jealousy—is deflected by this change. Her greater understanding gives her an increased sense of her own powers; and her new sense of power gives her a new source for elation. She has, for one thing, turned inadequate ideas—images—into increasingly adequate ideas. In following her own nature, in affirming the truth about its history and constitution, she has become active rather than passive. She is, in fact, active in exactly the degree to which her ideas are adequate rather than inadequate. Instead of imagining herself to be the recipient of the benefits of Echo's charms, she actively identifies herself with the system of interactive causes that have determined her. In so affirming her identity, she recognizes that what she had thought of as a passive passion, a modification produced by an external cause, actually in part also proceeds from her own nature. ("Insofar as the mind has adequate ideas, it is necessarily active; insofar as it has inadequate ideas, it is necessarily passive" [III. 1]. "We are active when something takes place in us or externally to us of which we are the adequate cause, that is, when it follows from our nature. . . . We are passive when something takes place in us, of which we are only the partial cause" [III. D. 2]. "The more active a thing is, the more perfect it is" [V. 40].)

It now seems as if Ariadne's original passive elation—her love of Echo—is as nothing in comparison to the active elation she has in discovering the real nature of individuals, in understanding how she and Echo came to interact as they did. ("The greater the number of causes that simultaneously concur in arousing an emotion, the greater the emotion" [V. 8].) There is no better cure for idolatry than the analysis of its causes and objects, no better cure for the fetishism of idolatry than its dispersed and ramified redistribution. But the movement that locates the particular in its place in a pattern loses neither the particularity nor love: It transforms inadequacy into adequacy, passivity into activity.

We've talked as if Ariadne's discoveries and reflections are things *she* did in attempting to persevere, to integrate herself. In a way that is right; Ariadne's nature just is of this kind: She is psychologically canny and historically reflective. Her researches, inquiries, and reflections are, however, just as much an expression of—a determination of—her constitution and her history as are the timbre of her voice and her taste for wry minds. Her insight has—and does not have—a special status. In one sense, she neither generates nor controls it; for it, too, follows from the interactive nexus of individuals. Even her insight is nothing more (or less) than the complex and dynamic active traces of her genetic constitution and personal history. Still, if she is so fortunate as to be an active inquirer, her insight is more expressive of her nature than is the timbre of her voice or her taste for wry minds. The centrality of insight is not (alas) assured because insight lasts longer than the timbre of a voice. Treated as facts, both are timeless and unchangeable; treated as properties, both are contingent, susceptible to disease and debility. Insight does not cure or prevent senility; nor does it empower an individual mind by elevating it to transcendent objects. It is nothing more (or less) than the detailed activity of integrating ideas. It consists of painstakingly putting two and two together, and then tracing the functions of four in the system of natural numbers. There is nothing more mystical to it than that: The power of a mind is expressed in its comprehensive activity in integration.

In pursuing her liberation from the pathology of love, Ariadne is not a *homuncula* somewhere at the center of her essence, willing herself to be whole and intact, directing the strategies designed to free her from the disintegrative suffering of love. Ariadne knows better; she knows that she does not will the direction of energy. Just as Echo is not the onelie begetter of her elation, so too she is not the only begetter of her liberation. All these active reflections are just the fortune of her history and interactions, working in and through her. Even her realization that she necessarily is (no more and no less) than the totality of the accidents of her history and her interactions is the fortune of her history and interactions. If she has the good fortune to identify herself *with* and *as* all those dynamic interactions which have made her who she is, she will no longer think of herself as having been formed *by* them, as if she could mysteriously have been the same essential core, with a different history. Her characteristics will follow from her nature because they *are* her nature. This reflection is not a further thought; it is just the self-conscious realization of the connected significance of all the thoughts that she is.

Ariadne's conception of herself—her idea of her mind as a structure of ideas—is exactly coordinate with her conception of the boundaries that distinguish her essence from those of other individuals. It therefore exactly defines the scope of her passive affects, those she imagines to be externally caused, in contrast to her active affects, those that she thinks of as following from her nature. A person's passions are functions of her conceptions of her essential nature. It is ambiguous and misleading to say that a person bent on liberation from the pathology of passion must transform and enlarge her conception of her individuality. It suggests that there are two distinct lines of thought, one's conception of oneself on the one hand, and the range of one's affects on the other. But these are different ways of describing the same thing. To have a clearer conception of oneself just *is* to have turned and to be turning passive into active affective states, seeing them as parts of one's nature rather than as invasions. To recommend a better conception of oneself misleadingly suggests that there is a core person deciding to correct her self-image. But these processes of correction are just the various strands in the person's complex nature, expressing themselves in the many ways a complex *conatus* acts to persist in its own nature.

As we have told it so far, the story of Ariadne's increased awareness of the complex dynamic relations between herself and Echo is, in every sense of the word, a vulgar story. But in her larger understanding, Ariadne sees that there is a tale of necessity within every vulgar story. The vulgar story of love—with its trials and tribulations—is told in a very confused and as we might say, provisional language, within the realm of *imaginatio*. It is partial, fragmentary. Even Ariadne's increased self-awareness is, as the story first unfolds, a case of narrative discovery, tracing more and more of the vast expanding network of the historical and relational details that determine Echo and herself. The language of psychological canniness, even that of historical astuteness is still quite inadequate to express the deeper structures of these appearances. If Ariadne follows Spinoza's therapeutic recommendations in liberating herself from passive love, she detaches her love from her confused imagistic thought of Echo, and concentrates instead on understanding how her emotions formed an interdependent pattern. First she might think of family histories and family resemblances; then she begins to form rough generalizations about academics and men, about the relation between love and dependence, weakness and fear, envy and jealousy. ("The power of the mind over the emotions consists in . . . detaching the affect from the thought of their external cause, which we imagine confusedly; and in . . . knowing the . . . order and connection among the affects" V. 20. S.) Actively engaging in this sort of sociopsychological investigation helps Ariadne become less prey to the demons of associated passive affects. She becomes actively thoughtful. Although such rough generalizations are, to be sure, genuinely central to understanding Ariadne's condition, we — and if she is fortunate, she — can get further.

Ariadne's active elation in the power of her psychological and historical understanding can be still further enhanced by her understanding of biology and eventually of mathematical physics. Before we have a full understanding of Ariadne's love, and before we return the particularity of Ariadne's love to her, we must stop speaking with vulgar and leave appearances and the language of appearances behind. In truth, Ariadne and Echo are human bodies, organisms delicately and dynamically structured in such a way as to conserve and preserve their continuing complex activities in their interactions with other bodies surrounding them. Organic processes are themselves expressions of the activities of basic entities, the simple particulars (*corpora simplicissima*) of which the world is composed, no more, no less. The organization and activity of human bodies — the interactions between Ariadne, Echo, and other bodies — are functions of the dynamic interactions among the *corpora simplicissima* that compose them (II. 13).

In truth, then, Ariadne and Echo (it is now more appropriate to ignore their individual histories and to call them *A* and *E*) are compound bodies whose properties are functions of the character of extension. Their individual minds — that is, their ideas of themselves and of one another — are ideas of the ideas of their bodies. More fully and adequately understood, the order of Ariadne's ideas — the rationale of her thoughts and affects — is the same as the order of the properties of bodies. ("The order and connection of ideas is the same as the order and connection of things. . . . The . . . human mind is basically nothing else but the idea of an individual actually existing thing. . . . The object of the idea constituting the human mind is the body, a definite mode of extension, and nothing else. . . . The idea which constitutes . . . the human mind is nothing simple, but composed of very many ideas" [II. 7, 11–13, 15].) What *A* knows of herself—in contrast to what she may imagine—is a set of ideas of the condition of a compound body (vulgarly called *hers*) which is itself a reflection of the interaction between her compound body and other sections of extension, including that compound vulgarly called Echo. What she knows of the world, she knows only through her body; her ideas are just the intellectual articulations of bodily states. Yet Spinoza's psychophysicalism is not reductive, but correlative. Relations among ideas are the articulations of the relations among parts of extension; and the relational properties of extension are the expressions—the spatial projections—of the relational structures of ideas. The properties of extension can only be characterised, can only be expressed as relations among ideas; but the relations among ideas are just the expressions of the dynamic properties of extension, nothing more and nothing less. Spinoza's insistence on the relational and dynamic character of both thought and extension preserves him from sliding into a reductivist position, either on the side of materialism or on that of idealism.

For all its graces, *A*'s mind is nothing special. All her ideas—including her love and other affects or emotions—are articulations, expressions of the activities of her body. But that body—that relatively self-preserving organism—is, like every other extended individual, an active nexus of *corpora simplicissima* interrelated, concatenated in such a way that they preserve a particular ratio of motion and rest. Some of the central properties of *A*'s body are properties which she has in common with all other bodies: They are properties that are as attributable to any part of her as they are to the whole of her, attributable to any part of extension as they are to the whole of extension (II. 37). Now since the order of extension is necessarily expressed in ideas, *A*'s mind necessarily has (is in part composed of) self-evident ideas of these common properties of extension. Her body is composed of these properties; and her ideas are ideas of the properties of her body. Since such common ideas are not fragmentary or perspectival, not qualified by their dependence on other ideas—since they are ideas of the properties of *every* body—they are adequate, necessarily and self-evidently true (II. 38–40). Like every idea, common ideas are relational, determined by their interconnection in the system of ideas. But since common ideas are universally instantiated, the ideas which determine them are identical to them. The grounds or conditions for common ideas are therefore represented within them; and since they are the bearers of their own determination, they are self-evident. Since A's power and activity is a function of the adequacy of her ideas, her power—her elation—is increased by her knowledge of the unqualifiedly necessary properties of bodies.

Every individual mind has (is partially composed of) a set of adequate ideas of extension, the common notions that express "her" body, as they do every body. To the extent that she focuses on these adequate ideas, A has a more adequate understanding of her relation to E than she has from her psychological and historical understanding, which at best forms a contingent narrative, a set of generalizations from likely stories. The common notions of mathematical physics take A beyond psychological and historical insight to *ratio*, to a necessary and deductive scientific demonstrative science of extension. All that was particular—that is, all that was merely conditional and perspectival—about Echo and herself, and all the sound but incomplete generalizations of folk psychology and history can now be supplemented by a rigorously deductive science. A now has a much more powerful idea of her own mind, because she now has placed her idea of her mind in a system of interrelated ideas: She knows *what it is to be a mind*. In focusing on these adequate ideas, in bringing them to light, she has in a sense enlarged her mind; she not only has a clear idea of how things are, but also why they are like that. She now has two quite different types of explanations of the phenomena. The first was afforded by the reflections that moved her from confused images to psychological and historical generalizations. The second is afforded by the rationally demonstrative science of extension.

In a sense A is no longer merely the passive person she was. As a mind which has realized her adequate ideas of itself, she affirms what necessarily follows from her nature. As a psychological historian, she affirmed herself as the active traces of all that made her what she is: acknowledging herself as identical with what—the world being what it is—she was caused to become. But as a mathematical physicist, A is the active expression of principles much more powerful than the relatively finite temporal incidents in the life of Ariadne and Echo, even as they might be extended to their ancestors and their communities. Her idea of herself—which was in any case nothing more than the idea of the nexus of her ideas of her body (II. 15)—now includes an idea of herself as a systematically organized set of adequate ideas. Her idea of her mind is still exactly correlated with her idea of its "boundaries." Insofar as she is a mind composed of adequate ideas of the properties common to every part of extension, she does not conceive of anything falling outside her boundaries, her nature. Although all properties — including those that are universally instantiated — are relational, the interdependence of common properties does not make them conditional; they interact with properties that are exactly identical to them. It is for this reason that, despite their place in the nexus of ideas, adequate ideas can be self-evident. They are conditional on something identical with them.

A is active to the extent — but only to the extent — that she identifies herself as a mind composed of adequate ideas. What a powerful and integrated system of adequate ideas (and their logical consequences) she now is! The crude psychological egoism with which Ariadne began — the egoism sketched in the first, preliminary accounts of *conatus* — is by now strikingly modified, reinterpreted. The power of Ariadne's *conatus* is expressed in its actively expanding its original, narrow, and necessarily defensive conception of its boundaries. The more narrowly defined is an individual's conception of her boundaries, the more readily is she overcome by the vast number of external forces. But the more broadly she identifies herself with other free rational minds, the more actively powerful she becomes: Her nature is not then bounded by, but agrees with others (IV. 35–37). "It is of first importance to [men] to establish close relationships [with other rational men] and to bind themselves together . . . unite[d] in one body . . . to act in such a way as to strengthen friendship" (IV. app. 12).

Compared to the exhilaration of *this* rationally extended sense of her activity and action, the elation of Ariadne's original relation to Echo — even as it became extended to her activities as an inquirer into the constitution and history — was really child's play. What elation can Echo bring to *A*, who identifies herself with other free, rational citizens who recognize universal and timeless truths about the basic structure of Nature? After all, modestly speaking, without any trace of megalomania, she now sees that as part of an aspect of God, she cannot be enhanced or diminished by the flotsam and jetsam of *la vie quotidienne*.

We have skipped and condensed quite a bit, but in any case, we are far from through. First of all there is the extremely difficult question of just how *A* came to realize her adequate ideas, how she came to have a more adequate idea of herself as a mind composed of both adequate ideas and a history of confused ideas. After all, what is self-evident — even what is demonstrated as self-evident — is not always obvious. Even if *A* timelessly was the person she — as we confusedly say — came to be, how did the timeless story come to be just what it always was, a timeless story that seems to have *befores* and *afters* and *becauses?* Even if Ariadne's intellectual biography provides a psychohistorical answer to that question, can there be a properly scientific answer to it? It is all very well to say that *A*'s complex condition can be explained backward historically, and outward by a nexus of interactive causes. Can it also be generated downward from adequate ideas of common properties? Having fully adequate ideas, can *A* demonstrate the particular set of events that caused and constituted her loving Echo? Can she have adequate ideas about such contingent, conditional matters, rather than relatively vague generalizations about the nature of love in this or that historical era? Evidently not, for it is impossible to deduce particular temporal events from ideas that are by definition common to absolutely every event. But doesn't this mean that the promise of explanation—and therefore the promise of freedom—was false, a misleading confused promise? To answer these rhetorical questions, we must move from *ratio* to *scientia intuitiva*, the highest level of knowledge that grasps the interconnections of individual essences within one unified system.

Having It All: Back to Love
with Vulgarity and Learning

What happened to the confusions of the imagination, perceptions, rough generalizations, passive affects? Have they utterly disappeared? How do we preserve the particularity of appearances with which we began? What happened to individual essences and the essence of individuality? If confused ideas of the boundaries among individuals are necessary, isn't there a sense in which a timeless understanding of the order of things—of the whole of reality—must include a timeless understanding of these partial and confused appearances? And what happened to love, to the promised *hilaritas* of true love?

Ariadne has not, thank god, been intransformed into a pure abstract mind, a divine geometer, not Spinoza's Ariadne, at any rate. She is, was, and will be the *particular* very finite collection of ideas reflecting a particular body. All *A*'s mathematical knowledge of the *corpora simplicissima* is knowledge of the properties that are *common* to all bodies. Those properties—and the ideas of those properties—are still particular. What distinguishes them from other particular ideas is simply their universality and their self-evident necessity. So in having adequate ideas, in becoming actively affected, *A* is still Ariadne, and she still loves. For that matter she still loves Echo; but her active love is a far, far better love than she has ever loved before. It is, of course, not better in being purer or more self-sacrificing; nor scandalously, is it more perfect. Indeed on the contrary, far from being purer, it is more comprehensive in every sense of that term. Not only does she love Echo, but she loves Echo-as-a-particular-expression-of-the-vast-network-of-individuals that have affected him; through him, she loves all that has made him. Far from being self-sacrificing, her active love of Echo—now more truly, adequately understood by her—is self-expressing. In loving him, she loves herself. Nor is her truthful love more perfect, because *the idea of perfection is an inadequate idea*, formed from a fragmented, particular perspective.

It is time to unwrap Spinoza's irony. Ariadne's liberation has been described as a movement to greater perfection. That's vulgar talk. (In truth "Men are accustomed to call natural things perfect or imperfect more from prejudice than from true knowledge of those things. . . . Nature does nothing on account of an end. . . . Perfection and imperfection are only modes of thinking, that is, notions we are accustomed to feign when we compare individuals of the same species to one another. . . . Insofar as we attribute something to them that involves negation, —like a limit, and end or lack of power—, we call them imperfect, because they do not affect our mind as much as those we call perfect, not because something is lacking in them which is theirs" [IV. Preface]. "Nothing happens in nature which can be attributed to a defect in it" [III. Preface].) The idea of perfection is a mote in the eye of the perceiver, an idea which—like all other ideas—is a reflection of the order of things. But it is a confused and partial idea. In truth, since each thing is what it must be, nothing is, in and of itself, either less or more than it is or can be. Seen in this way, Ariadne's pathological love, necessitated as it was by the order of things, could not have been a *defect* in her.

All along Ariadne is, even with her transformation into a psychohistorian and mathematical physicist, a particular interactive finite body, a particular finite system of ideas. Now we saw that rational demonstration—the system that expresses the relations among adequate ideas—is not hospitable to such variables as *Ariadne*, let alone *Ariadne's love of Echo at a particular time*. How can the *corpora simplicissima* that compose *A* and *E* rub together to produce the explosion of a particular love? Increasing the number of *corpora* to form compounds does not increase their explanatory power, nor does increasing the complexity of the relations between their respective ratios of motion and rest. There can be no mathematical demonstration that concludes with Ariadne's love for Echo. Yet she did passively love Echo, and that passive love was interactively necessitated. ("Inadequate and confused ideas follow by the same necessity as adequate or clear ideas" [II. 36].) Although *A*'s rational knowledge as a mathematician gives her necessary knowledge of what she has in common with all other bodies, it cannot, in the nature of the case, provide a demonstration of the necessity of her confused, inadequate, partial, perspectival ideas. ("Whatever ideas follow in the mind from adequate ideas are also adequate" [II. 40].) It should not be surprising that we cannot derive the dynamic, relational, historical particular from what is timeless, necessary, and invariant.

Fortunately there is, besides psychohistorical knowledge and mathematical physics, yet another knowledge—*scientia intuitiva*—which combines the other two in a single active act of understanding. *Scientia intuitiva* involves apprehending the vast system, the network of particular individuals (including of course all the properties they have in common) as a unified individual. Since there is no such thing as abstract Being as such, *scientia intuitiva* is not mystical insight into the abstract nature of Being. On the contrary, this insight preserves all particularity: Reflective ideas— ideas of ideas—retain their particularity when they are systematically interconnected to form the increasingly more encompassing particular that is *A*'s individual mind. (As, for instance, the *corpora simplicissima* of which *A*'s body is composed retain their particularity even though they are organized to form another individual, Ariadne's body.) *A* cannot have an adequate idea of Echo, treated merely as a finite mode, an isolated fragment of the world; but since she can have increasingly adequate ideas of him as part of the system of ideas, and since she can treat the system of her ideas as a particular, she can have *scientia intuitiva* of the unified system of which Echo is a fragment. (Compare: While there is no *ratio* [scientific knowledge] of a particular corpuscle of hemoglobin, taken in isolation as a fragment of extension, there is scientific knowledge of hemoglobin, treated as a functional part of organic systems. Going beyond the *ratio* of discursive biochemistry, *scientia intuitiva* fuses all that is discretely encompassed by *ratio*, recognizing that it forms a unity, a particular individual.)

How does intuitive insight—psychohistorical knowledge and demonstrative rationality all wrapped into a bundle and seen as a unified, self-sustaining, self-evident whole—free us? It is, as are all ideational states, the expression of a bodily condition, one in which the body is, as it were, enlarged because "the individual body" is no longer artificially separated as a bounded, separate entity. Nevertheless, each condition of any "particular part" of extension necessarily has the properties it has, by virtue of its interconnections with all other parts. So the sense of boundary—Ariadne's experiencing herself as a bounded particular individual—is *itself* the necessary outcome, the expression of all that exists, no more and no less. Ariadne's passivity and defensiveness are, despite their being confused and conditional ideas, necessary (II. 36). When she realizes this, she actively rather than passively preserves all the details of her individuation because she recognizes that those details, too, follow from her nature (V. 27). Ariadne actively expresses rather than passively suffers whatever follows from the necessities of her nature; so Ariadne does not *suffer* the pathology of love, the Goyaesque furies of any passive passion. Does that mean that she will not suffer ambivalence, envy, fear, despair? Well, yes, she will not passively suffer the Goyaesque furies; but, depending on her circumstances and condition, she may nevertheless enact some of them.

Like all Stoics, including Freud, Spinoza speaks with forked tongue about whether those who have reached the most active and comprehensive knowledge have no passive love, ambivalence, and the rest of the furies. On the one hand, those passions are, even in their experienced passivity, *necessary* natural events. On the other hand, "The truth shall make you free" is absolutely true; and there is, in principle, absolutely no barrier between any individual and truth. Affects that follow from adequate ideas are not passive, and at least some affects only follow from inadequate ideas. An individual is free and active just to that degree that she has adequate ideas. ("If we remove an agitation of the mind, or emotion, from the thought of its external cause and join it to other thoughts, then . . . the vacillations that arise from these affects will be destroyed. . . . There is no affection of the body of which we cannot form a clear and distinct conception" [V. 2, 4].) Can Ariadne turn all her inadequate ideas into fully adequate ideas? It seems not; but if she is fortunate, she can make them more adequate, and if she is even more fortunate, she can focus primarily on her adequate ideas. ("[If *scientia intuitiva*] does not absolutely remove passive affects, it at least brings it about that they constitute the smallest part of the mind" [V. 20. S].)

But we have in a way been dodging the real question. Does knowledge always liberate us from suffering? What are we to make of all our wise friends whose love is passive and who suffer in loving? Here Spinoza reveals his Socratic face: Not all those who mouth knowledge genuinely have it. In the first place, *being able to discourse fluently* isn't necessarily *knowing*. Only knowledge that pervades a person's psychology and that expresses an appropriate bodily state counts as real knowledge. Knowledge is not an attitude toward propositional content: To know p is to engage in a vast number of activities of integrating *p* within a system of ideas, beliefs, desires. Unless an intellectual attitude really transforms the way a person thinks and acts, it does not qualify as knowledge. (Compare: Knowing a mathematical technique is not merely a matter of being able to state and defend it clearly. To qualify as knowing a technique, one must actually use it in constructions and proofs.)

In the second place, not everyone who wishes to know, not everyone who dreams of *scientia intuitiva* is in a position—a constitutional, and psychohistorical position—to have it. Whether or not a particular bit of understanding succeeds in being knowledge at any given time is—like everything else—a function of person, time, and circumstance. It is not only our own activity, but our activity in dynamic relation to what surrounds us that determines our condition. ("The force and growth of any passion, . . . are not defined by the power by which we strive to persevere in existing, but by the power of an external cause compared with our own" [IV. 5]. "It is necessary to come to know both our nature's power and its lack of power to determine what reason can do—and what it cannot do—in moderating the affects" (IV. 17. Scholium].) In any case, even our wisest friends are finite individual minds, composed of a mixture of adequate and inadequate ideas. ("The human mind does not involve an adequate knowledge of the component parts of the body . . . [or] of an external body" [II. 24-31]. "Desire which arises from knowledge of good and evil insofar as it concerns future . . . or contingent things . . . can be easily restrained by desires for things which are present" [IV. 16-17].) Starkly, not even *A*—that superb mathematical physicist—is, at any and every moment of her life, focused only on her adequate ideas, let alone engaged in *scientia intuitiva*. Although compared individually adequate ideas and active passions are much more powerful than inadequate ideas and their corresponding passive passions, a large number of inadequate ideas and passive passions can deflect the directions of active desires.

In the third place, we should not confuse suffering with *suffering*. When Spinoza contrasts activity with passivity, freedom with bondage, he does not identify—though he does associate—passivity and bondage with *pain*. To begin with, many passive affects are delightful. And by Spinoza's lights, however uncomfortable they may be, healthy growing pains are not *sufferings*, unless an adolescent thinks of his body as an external cause of his condition. Similarly, the hardships of difficult thought are not sufferings, unless a scholar thinks of himself as invaded or obsessed by them.

But what, you may ask, is the point of being free? Why isn't mucking along in trouble and travail, in ambivalence and uncertainty, in the pathology of idolatry, fragmentation, and fetishism good enough? Since that is what the particularity of life is, and since there is nothing but particularity, why want more? Maybe life is not directed to the hilarity of integration, but just to living. In a way Spinoza agrees. It is not a question of striving for a better, nobler form of life. We each live according to the life force within us. Those whose constitution and circumstances make them relatively vulnerable to forces they experience as external to them will indeed suffer love and hate. Others are, by the fortune of their situation, capable of what liberation their circumstances allow. In any case, both those who are relatively passively weak and those who are relatively actively strong alike attempt to live as fully as they can. There is no teleology in the matter, no salvation, and in a way, no liberation. We are what we are no matter what. We are the extent and manner of our striving toward harmonic integration.

Still, be that as it must be, Spinoza thinks that liberated love is superior to bonded love: Wise lovers are not only more joyous, but more effective and beneficent than unenlightened lovers. How do the wise act on behalf of those they love? To be sure, they desire to unite with what they love. But that is, according to Spinoza, a consequence rather than the essential definition of love (III. app. D. 6, Explication). In any case that desire does not define any particular action; it might, for instance, generate civic as well as sexual unity and harmony. Ariadne's desire to unify herself with Echo is a desire to conjoin her own welfare with his to form a single well-structured whole (IV. 35–37, 62–66). But passive love generates a desire to control, rather than to act on behalf of a common good. Promoting the real—rather than the partial and imagined—welfare of an extended self properly arises from a rational recognition of interdependence (IV. 73). Since passive love is ambivalent, mingled with hate and envy, disdain, and fear, the behavior that expresses it will be erratic, each moment undermining the next. Well-formed action arises only from well-formed attitudes, from adequate ideas.

And the hilarity, the promised hilarity of true love? True love is the elation that comes of true knowledge, an intuitive grasp of the world, seen as a whole, immanent within one's ideas. Because such love is the expression of an individual's most vital activity, it carries the greatest possible self-realization. But an elation that affects the individual as a whole *is* hilarity (III. 11. Scholium). Like true knowledge, hilarity can never be excessive; when it is seen as actively following from an individual's own nature, it can never bring bondage in its wake (IV. 42).[2]

Notes

[1] I have used two translations, turning sometimes to E. M. Curley, *The Collected Works of Spinoza* (Princeton, N.J.: Princeton University Press, 1985) and sometimes to Samuel Shirley, *The Ethics*, ed. Seymore Feldman (Indianapolis: Hackett, 1982). But I have also substituted some translations of my own. Rather than following Shirley's *pleasure* or Curley's *joy*, I render *laetitia* as *elation* because I believe that it better captures Spinoza's view that love, like other affects, is an expression of a *change*, an increase, in the body's powers or vitality. Spinoza distinguishes two varieties of *laetitia*: *titillatio* and *hilaritas*. Titillation involves an increase of activity or power in one part of the body more than in another (the early stages of sexual excitation, for example); *hilaritas* marks an increase in vitality that affects all parts of the body equally (radiant health, for example). The corresponding distinctions for varieties of *tristitia*, which I translate as *dejection* (rendered by Shirley as *pain* and by Curley as *sadness*), are *dolor* (pain), a change which affects one part of the body more than another (a wound, for example), and *melancholia*, a change which affects all parts equally (anemia, for example). Spinoza undertakes to show that all affects arise from the three basic affects of elation, dejection, and desire (III. 11. S).

[2] I am grateful to Alan Hart for detailed, incisive comments, to Tom Cook and Genevieve Lloyd for many illuminating conversations. This paper was prepared for a conference on "Theoretical Perspectives on Love and Friendship" at the National Center for the Humanities. I enjoyed and benefited from Tom Hill's acute and searching discussions. Annette Baier helpfully suggested some issues that needed elaboration: Spinoza's avoidance of both reductive materialism and reductive idealism, and the problem of how the adequate ideas of common notions can be both relational and self-evident. Martha Nussbaum pressed me to give an account of the directions — and the limits — of what she sees as Spinoza's psychological egoism.

Elizabeth Rapaport
On the Future of Love: Rousseau and the Radical Feminists

Elizabeth Rapaport teaches law and public policy at Duke University.

1. Introduction

Love can make people happy or miserable. It can be mutual or one-sided. It can be asymmetrical, two people loving each other in the same way, or asymmetrical. Love can express itself in the sharing and fusing of lives or in pathological dependence one upon another. Radical feminists tend to portray love as we know it as a one-sided pathological dependency of women on men. Can there be, could there be, mutual, symmetrical, nonpathological love between men and women?

Feminism, even a moderate feminism, is a doctrine with very radical implications. It is all the more surprising that radical feminist ideas have gained very large numbers of more and less unreserved adherents. It seems that virtually everyone now understands and agrees with the feminist slogan that "The personal is political." Nowhere is the political more personal than in sexual love between men and women. I have been surprised to find therefore that radical feminists tend to have temperate, even conservative views, on the possibility of love between men and women. Radical feminists for the most part present variants of a common analysis and critique of love. The analysis supports the conclusion that love between men and women is extremely difficult if not impossible in the present. But it also supports the conclusion that in a future in which women's liberations has been effected through radical economic and social reorganization, especially of our sexual, familial and childrearing institutions, love between men and women will be possible. Not only will it be possible but it will be one of the principal, if not *the* principal supports and expressions of human happiness. It is striking that while feminists stigmatize love as we know it as a central cultural mechanism through which women's oppression operates and by which it is mystified and legitimated, love retains in the society of the future that same place at the pinnacle of valuable human experience that our culture ascribes to it.

The analysis of love as we now know it, which I'm calling the radical feminist analysis, pictures love as a destructive dependency relationship. Or rather women's love is pictured as a destructive dependency upon men; men are pictured as neither harmed by nor dependent upon the women they love, if they love at all. Love is not seen as a structurally symmetrical relationship in which men and women love each other in the same way and have a similar or identical experience of love. Why don't radical feminists make their quietus with love present and future? There seem to be features of the experience of love which would incite a flat denial that love could lead to anything but heartbreak or suffocation.

My aim in writing this paper is to vindicate radical feminist optimism about the future of love. I want to compare three theories: that of Rousseau with that of two radical feminist writers, Ti-Grace Atkinson and Shulamith Firestone. Atkinson presents a rare truly denunciatory radical feminist rejection of love now and forever. Firestone is perhaps the most influential contemporary American radical feminist to have written on love. Her views are representative of that combination of optimism for the future and condemnation of the present possibility of love which I attributed to most radical feminists above.

Rousseau, that arch-wallower in sentimentality, author of two best-selling blockbuster love stories, *La Nouvelle Héloïse* and *Emile*, in which the love of Emile and Sophie is chronicled, had despite these credentials a theory of love which vividly elaborates the negative features of love. He depicts love as an inherently pathetic or perhaps tragic loss of personality and destructive dependency relationship for both men and women. Yet love has for him precisely that feature of mutuality, of symmetry of quality or character for men and women the lack of which the radical feminists claim is a chief flaw of love as we know it. Mutuality is apparently not enough for the rehabilitation of love, unless landing men and women in the same soup is sufficient for its reclamation.

2. Atkinson on Love

It is not easy to imagine a more extreme view of sexual love than Atkinson's.[1] Yet she argues from some premises which are the common ground of radical feminists. Allow me to present a reconstruction of her argument in schematic form:

(1) There is no basis in essential or essentially different biological or psychological traits for the differences in social role and personality be-

374 tween men and women save one: women can bear children and men cannot. Otherwise, male and female roles and traits are cultural, not natural.

(2) Culturally acquired sexual roles and traits have a political origin. Very early in human history "men" took advantage of the one biologically different aspect of "women," childbearing, and the relative weakness and vulnerability that pregnancy entails to impose a differentiation of social function on "women." "Women" were forced to accept confinement and social definition in the ramified role of reproducing the species—childbearing, child-tending and familial service. This political imposition created men and women.

(3) Since male and female roles and traits are wholly the product of political oppression they can and should be eliminated in favor of a sexually undifferentiated human personality, culture and social system. "Men" and "women" must be destroyed.

(4) The politics and culture of sexual oppression is made possible by the sexual reproduction of the human species. A necessary step in extricating men and women from their present conditions of oppressor and oppressed is to eliminate sexual reproduction in favor of extra-uterine conception and incubation, now technically feasible. Sexual intercourse is not a human need but a social institution. Allegedly natural or biological sexual drives or needs would disappear with the elimination of their reproductive and political functions. "Sexual 'drives' and 'needs' would disappear with their functions."[2]

(5) Sexual love is wholly and inextricably bound up with the pathological deformations of human personality and its potentialities for realization associated with the humanly deplorable conditions of being a man or a woman. When sex goes, sexuality and sexual love go with it, and good riddance.

Atkinson says of sexual love, which for her has no human future:

The most common female escape (from their imprisonment in the female role and the denial of their humanity) is the psychopathological condition of love. It is a euphoric state of fantasy in which the victim transforms her oppressor into her redeemer: she turns her natural hostility towards the aggressor against the remnants of herself—her Consciousness—and sees her counterpart in contrast to herself as all powerful (as he is by now at her expense). The combination of his power, her self-hatred, and the hope for a life that is self-justifying—the

goal of all living creatures — results in a yearning for her stolen life — her   *375*
Self — that is the delusion and poignancy of love. "Love" is the natural
response of the victim to the rapist.[3]

What gives Atkinson's argument an air of the incredible is her attack on
sexual intercourse itself.[4] She speculates that in a human future there may
be some human value in "cooperative sensual experience" whose function
and value would be a social and public expression of approval of the sensu-
ally gratified subject. She says that "the outside participant expresses by its
presence an identification with the recipient's feelings for itself. This could
serve as a reinforcement to the ego and to a generalization from the attitude of the agent towards the recipient to the attitude of the public as a
whole toward the recipient."[5] Note that she is speculating not about the
sexual future but the sensual future and that the kind of experience she envisions is not reciprocal but the gratification of one subject by another who
represents the social community. Although Atkinson does not banish sensuality, this cannot be construed as a rehabilitation of love.

(1)-(3) are common ground for many feminists. Atkinson's uniqueness
is her insistence that all aspects of sexuality including sexual intercourse itself are humanly eliminable, destructive cultural constructs. The question
arises, why do not all feminists who share the view that maleness and femaleness are oppressive social constructs share the view that with the elimination of these constructs must come the elimination of if not human sexual contact then at least sexual intercourse between "men" and "women"?
Can sexuality and sexual love be separated from "maleness" and "femaleness" as they have been socially constructed?

Atkinson's remarks about "cooperative sensual experiences" suggest the
following theory about that complex emotional and sexual relationship we
call romantic or sexual love. Sexual love is a destructive dependency relationship. It is incompatible with human autonomy, with the recognition by
the self and others of the independent worth of the individual for that human individual to be dependent upon any other particular individual or
individuals for the fulfillment of its needs or the affirmation or conferral of
its value. A human individual may need, however, or be enhanced in its
sense of worth by, the generalized social recognition of its worth and the legitimacy of its needs. Therefore in an androgynous human future it would
be wrong to expect what would formerly have been identified as "men" and
"women" to want or have experiences of sexual love for people of the same
or the opposite "sex." There is something wrong with love in addition to

sexual oppression. It is a dependency relation which robs the lover of its autonomy, something that will be no more desirable when we are freed from the pathology of sexuality than it is now. Fortunately we will have no inclination for love once freed of the political and cultural compulsion to act out the roles of male and female, oppressor and oppressed.

This seems to me to be a not implausible theory for anyone who holds that love is a destructive dependency relationship and that "men" and "women" should be superceded. It certainly does induce shudders in anticipation of a world even more bereft of intimate contact than the isolation we presently endure and before which the contemporary spirit already quails.

I now want to turn to the kind of view of love which has more preponderant radical feminine support. We will see that it is Firestone's willingness to see dependency relationships rehabilitated that permits her to be both a good feminist and a partisan of a future for love.

3. Firestone on Love

I said in my introduction that for the radical feminist love is now impossible, but will be possible in a liberated human future. This is not quite accurate. The radical feminist thesis is that love as we now know it is a culturally pathological dependency relationship but that love can be a healthy and enriching dependency relation in the revolutionary future. The distinction is really between healthy and destructive love, not between love and no love. In the section on Rousseau below, we shall see a challenge to the claim that dependency relationships can be rehabilitated. Rousseau, like Atkinson, holds that all dependency relationships are destructive. Let us examine both the bad love of the present and the good love of the future as portrayed by Firestone.[6] I will begin by setting forth what I take to be Firestone's requirements for healthy love and then show why and how she thinks love as we know it differs from healthy love.

Mutuality

"Love between two equals would be an enrichment. . . ."[7] The love relationship must be symmetrical in that both man and woman love each other in a similar or identical fashion. But another sort of mutuality is required if this is to be possible. Both man and woman must be and recognize themselves and each other as free-standing independent beings possessing equal and unqualified human worth as persons. Love has a precondition of self-

respect and respect for the beloved's status as a free and equal human being.

Vulnerability, Openness, Interdependency

"Love is being psychically wide-open to another. It is a situation of total
emotional vulnerability."[8] An individual cannot be open, not to say wide-
open, to another unless he or she respects himself. To be vulnerable is to
recognize our need and desire for the other person. It is also caring for or
prizing the other as much as ourselves because of his or her unique value
for ourself. Love is thus both selfish and unselfish,[9] a feature of love
founded in the recognition of our vulnerability. In healthy love dependency
is not merely tolerable. It is essential.

Idealization

"The beauty/character of the beloved, perhaps hidden to others under layers of defenses is revealed."[10] Firestone emphasizes that the vulnerability of
love makes it possible for lovers to reveal the best of themselves to each
other, permitting an idealization more in the sense of a prizing of what is
really there for each other rather than an over-estimation of the qualities of
the beloved. Others have noticed another possible aspect of a not unrealistic or falsifying idealization of the beloved. Love may provide an opportunity for the recognition by the self of qualities he or she did not know he or
she possessed before the lover discovered them and revealed them. Love
may also occasion the growth and positive development of personality.[11]

The Fusion of Egos, the Exchange of Selves

Love between two equals would be an enrichment, each enlarging himself through the other: instead of being one, locked in the cell of himself
with only his own experience and view, he could participate in the existence of another — an extra window on the world. This accounts for the
bliss that successful lovers experience: Lovers are temporarily freed
from the burden of isolation that every individual bears.[12]

Firestone argues that love as we know it does not satisfy any of these conditions. She claims that women love pathologically and men don't love at all.
Firestone is in essential agreement with points (1)-(3) set forth in my reconstruction of Atkinson's argument above. We may therefore take (1)-(3) as
the first installment of Firestone's analysis of love as we know it. The remaining crucial stages of the argument which provides the context for Firestone's critique of love are these:

(4') The political origins of the oppression of women by men have long been forgotten by both sexes. It is generally believed that the politically conditioned sexually differentiated social roles and statuses of men and women are essential or natural features of the two sexes. This is expressed as the ideology of male supremacy. Men are seen as powerful, active, self-sufficient and fully human; women as weak, passive, and dependent — support players in the essentially male human drama. Male nature is human nature, female nature is to be helpmeet of man.

(5') The ideology of male supremacy corresponds to the real economic, social and political condition of men and women in the present and through most of human history. Women *are* dependent on men. For the most part whatever women may achieve socially and economically in the real world of oppression in which we live is through their acceptance by and associations with men.

(6) Many of the changes introduced by modern industrial society have tended to undermine the power of men over women as well as the ideology of male supremacy — e.g., birth control technology, the possibility and the desirability of women having fewer children, women entering the paid labor force in massive numbers. "Romanticism develops in proportion to the liberation of women from their biology."[13] The love of women for men has the function of mystifying and reinforcing patriarchal hegemony. The function of romantic love is therefore the reinforcement of an otherwise weakened male hegemony.

(7) In the modern industrial world it is possible for women, by acting in concert politically and to a much lesser extent through individual action, to establish lives for themselves as independent, active social and economic beings. Love induces them to try to live for and through men instead. Love robs them of the will, strength and insight into political realities and human possibilities necessary to attempt to overthrow male hegemony.

Firestone argues that under such conditions the love of woman for man can only be pathological and that men cannot love women at all. The mutual self-respect which is necessary for healthy love is impossible where neither men nor women regard women as genuine and autonomous persons. They cannot, therefore, be mutually wide open to each other. Men do not see a person worthy of the effort. Women's self-contempt precludes seeing themselves as having any personal substance and worth to reveal. They hope to gain substance and worth through the love of men.

Firestone claims that it is not generally the case that women idealize the men they love, although men tend to idealize the women they fall in love with. ("Falling in love" is very different from "loving" for Firestone, as I shall momentarily explain.) "Idealization occurs much less frequently on the part of women. . . . A man must idealize one woman over the rest in order to justify his descent to a lower caste. Women have no such reason to idealize. . . ."[14] They regard themselves as defective and men as full human beings. All men are in a sense idealized in female eyes. They all possess the value of being self-sufficient, authentic, human subjects which women concur in believing is not true of themselves. However, it is not true that any woman can love any man. Social and economic status make some men more lovable than others.

Men, Firestone claims, don't love, they fall in love. They see special virtues in one woman, which she for her part knows are not there and so lives in terror of his disillusionment, which comes often enough. Firestone accepts the Freudian thesis that men at least are seeking an ego-ideal and substitute for the forbidden mother in the women they fall in love with. Freud himself seems to support Firestone. He holds that the satisfaction of love's desire lessens or leads to the cessation of love. Firestone and Freud find men fickle and prone to disillusionment. Firestone claims men fall in love rather than love both because they undervalue all women and unrealistically idealize the woman they fall in love with. Both prevent the intimate and open interaction with women that love requires. Women on their side prevent real contact by desperately trying to shore up men's illusions about them in order to hold their love.

Firestone has another reason for claiming men do not love and why when they fall in love they are wont to fall out of love soon after: Men fear dependency. Their model for vulnerability is not the openness of genuine love but the dependency-love of women as they know them. They associate dependency with weakness and insufficiency. They have good cause to fear the love women offer them as well. Women are after all seeking to devour men's independent substance. Without openness or respect on either side there can of course be no fusion of egos. In no way is love as we know it the genuine article.

I find Firestone's stigmatization of love as we know it as serving the function of legitimating and reinforcing male hegemony convincing. I also believe that there is much to be said for her distinctions between destructive and healthy love. Her account does not however deal adequately with the social psychological issue of the possibility of non-destructive dependency relationships. Rousseau's account of destructive love locates the pa-

380   thology of love precisely in the destructive character of all dependency relationships. It is a critique of this sort of psychology which partisans of love's
future must provide. Rousseau's account of destructive love also supplies a
needed corrective to the radical feminist claim that men do not love. The
pathology of destructive love engulfs both men and women.

Rousseau on Love

Rousseau's theory of love might be captured by the traditional adage of
husbands, "I can't live with her and I can't live without her," were the adage not so wry. The climate of love for Rousseau is bathed in intense feeling. Sexual love is portrayed by Rousseau as mutually destructive to men
and women. Sexual love is at the center of Rousseau's account of social relations. It is the first other-regarding emotion that the developing human
individual experiences and the paradigm of social relations with others.
Sexual love is an inescapable human need. But the pursuit of love inevitably leads to frustration and unhappiness. The way we love inevitably de-
feats the ends of love. Defeat in love engulfs our whole personality. It destroys not only love but the lovers as well. For Rousseau man's love is like his
sociality. Man is naturally social. But social living, the condition of human
development and self-realization, is the irredeemable cause of human misery. To be happy we must be self-sufficient. But because we are human we
need others. We are therefore happy neither in isolation nor in company.

   Love, according to Rousseau's psychology, is a natural but not an original human need or desire. The distinction between original and non-
original elements in the human constitution is crucial in Rousseau's psychology. For Rousseau ontogeny recapitulates phylogeny. The nature of the
human species and the human individual can only be understood in terms
of their identical developmental courses. Savage man is not natural man
but natural man at the beginning stages of human development. He has
the potential to develop intellectual and moral capacities which will carry
the human race from the savage to the civilized state. The development of
these capacities is necessary for the full realization of human possibilities.
Savage man is an isolate, a self-sufficient creature, with minimal, peaceful
and uneventful interactions with others of his kind. He develops the characteristic and essential human capacities of reason and conscience as his
world becomes social. As human life becomes social, he comes to need and
depend upon others. He gains his humanity but loses his self-sufficiency.
The quality of his life depends on the quality of his society. The human
personality requires social living for its development. Its contours and con-

tents vary with different sorts of society, some of which suit the inborn features of human personality very much more comfortably than others. A bad fit produces much avoidable misery. But societies cannot be torn off and replaced like ill-fitting suits of clothes. Tragically the best fit is not nearly good enough to prevent human misery. Why this is so can be seen by tracing out the parallel ontogenetic developmental course.[15]

The human child like the human savage is an essentially asocial creature. Rousseau sees the human adult as ruled and motivated by two "sentiments" which organize and color his affective structure, *amour de soi*— rendered in English as "self-preservation," "self-love" or "proper self-love"—and *amour propre*, rendered in English as "pride," "selfishness" or "egotism." *Amour propre* is not yet an active principle in the infant and child. He is wholly a creature of self-love. *Amour de soi*, in savage and child, Rousseau regards as a benign principle. *Amour propre* is regarded as a pernicious principle that always leads to personal unhappiness and interpersonal conflict. The whole strategy of childhood education that Rousseau sets out in his *Emile* revolves around allowing the child to develop the powers to satisfy the desires of self-love in such fashion as to be as far as possible autonomous and self-sufficient. Both the powers and desires are naturally given and naturally develop commensurately so that the powers are adequate for the satisfaction of desire. Of course the child will need adult help and guidance. But adult help and guidance should be aimed at increasing his autonomy as well as perhaps the illusion of a greater autonomy than he really has. "True happiness consists in decreasing the distance between our desires and our powers, in establishing a perfect equilibrium between power and will."[16] Happiness will therefore be possible for the well-educated child as it never will be for the man in any possible human society.

If the child is made to feel dependent on the will of others, whether they are generous with him, over-generous, or whether they deny him, he will develop hostile feelings towards those around him. Worse, his personality structure will be adversely affected. He will be by turns servile and domineering in his attempts to gain his will through those on whom he is forced to depend. Rousseau's doctrine is that both tyranny and servility stem from impotence and breed hatred for those with the power to satisfy and withhold satisfaction of our desires. Tyrannical or servile, the frustrated child is equally miserable.[17]

Amour propre, sexual desire and the capacity for sexual love, all develop at the same time, at puberty, and bring in their train the develop-

382 ment of genuinely other-regarding emotions and social interactions which go beyond an awareness of others as simply helps or obstacles to the child's own ends.

> As soon as man needs a companion he is no longer an isolated creature, his heart is no longer alone. All his relations with his species, all the affections of his heart, came into being along with this. His first passion soon arouses the rest.[18]

Sexual love is a natural but not an original desire. The sexual desire is original but can be satisfied indifferently by any one of the opposite sex. Savages meet and couple in passing. They form no sexual relationships which endure beyond the desires of the moment. Sexual love involves choice of a lover. This choice involves comparison and preference. These preferences require standards of beauty and virtue. These standards of beauty and virtue are products of social living and culture.

> All women would be alike to a man who had no idea of virtue and beauty, and the first comer would always be the most charming. Love does not spring from Nature, far from it; it is the curb and law of her desires; it is love that makes one sex indifferent to the other, the loved one alone excepted.[19]

But the lover desires to be loved in turn. And here is where *amour propre* enters, like the snake into the Garden of Eden.

> We wish to inspire the preference we feel; love must be mutual. To be loved we must be worthy of love; to be preferred we must be more worthy than the rest, at least in the eyes of our beloved. Hence we begin to look around among our fellows; we begin to compare ourselves with them, there is emulation, rivalry and jealousy.[20]

The lover wants his love to be reciprocated. She must see him as preeminent in virtue and beauty, if he is to succeed. This necessarily activates the human capacity for *amour propre*, for jealousy, rivalry and the desire to gain an invidious esteem. He must strive to be or at least appear to be in her eyes the preeminent possesser of the qualities she prizes most. His child's autonomy, were he lucky enough to have achieved it, falls away. It is perilous to human autonomy to need another. But love, were it possible, would more than fully compensate. The lover loses his autonomy in a deeper sense. He must give up a life guided by *amour de soi*, by the pursuit of the natural desires that his heart has and which would realize the potentialities of his personality, and assume the straightjacket of being or appearing to be the man of her heart's desire. So it is with love and so it is in all other human relations in which the affections and esteem of others are courted. They necessarily make rivals of men, force us to give up independent standards of self-esteem for socially imposed standards of our worth. We lose touch with our natural feelings, forfeit the chance for self-actualization. We lose ourselves and present a false self in the lists of social competition. While it does not prevent feelings of affection or continual growth of sympathy for others, it does neutralize or prevent affection and concern for others whenever one's own desire for the affection and esteem of others is active. *Amour propre* haunts and destroys all our attempts to reach out and make genuine contact with others.

With these psychological doctrines as necessary background, let us look at Rousseau's theory of love, at what a benign and happy love would be like and of what love must become in the irremediable circumstances of human social living.

Natural Attraction, the Fusion of Egos

Rousseau emphasizes the affective aspects of love. The goal of love is the fusion of two personalities. For this union to occur there must first be an initial attraction founded in like sensibility. This initial recognition of one's male or female counterpart provides the sentimental basis and the pull which draws us into union. Julie writes to her lover, Saint-Preux,

> Our souls touch, so to speak at all points, and we feel an entire coherence . . . hence forward we shall have only mutual pleasures and pains; and like those magnets of which you were telling me that have, it is said, the same movements at different places, we shall have the same sensations though we were at the two poles of the earth.[21]

Dependency

Love begins with the recognition of a need for another, with the discovery of the radical insufficiency of the self and one's own powers for self-realization. The lover recognizes and feels his lack of or loss of autonomy. Saint-Preux writes to Julie, "I am no longer master of myself, I confess, my estranged soul is wholly absorbed in yours."[22]

Mutuality

Love would be mutual. Saint-Preux wants to possess as well as be possessed by Julie. If love is to be returned both man and woman must regard each other as worthy of love. Rousseau is certainly a male supremacist. He holds male and female natures are essentially different. Woman was made for man. The essence of womanhood was to serve, to please and to nurture man. Yet men value and respect the complementary and alien submissive virtues of women despite the defectiveness of female nature when judged by the standard of male nature. All the intellectual and moral inequalities of the sexes are neutralized by the mutual recognition of the need for love. Men do not respect women as full persons in the male sense. But they respect the terrible power women have to give or withhold the love they need. Men and women are equal in love. They are equally vulnerable and equally powerful.

Idealization

Love begins with the attraction and recognition of a like sensibility which seems to hold out the possibility of fusion of personalities. But love also requires that we see in the other and continue to see features of personality radically different from our own. The lover must find the perfections of the other and alien sex in the beloved, the perfections he or she necessarily lacks. Since love involves choice and standards of compassion between members of a sex, love's choice is for the man or woman pre-eminent of their sex. The standard of perfection will be a mixture of the personal and the public. It will be public insofar as canons of male and female beauty and virtue are cultural norms. It will be personal insofar as it involves placing a high value on the possession of certain qualities which may be found in either sex and which the lover finds in both himself and the beloved. These make possible the natural affinity of particular men and women for each other.

Exclusivity

If one man or woman is found perfect and finding perfection is a requirement for loving, there must be exclusive, complete fusion with and absorption in another. A multiplicity of love relations is precluded.

Rousseau holds that the achievement of love is illusional or delusional. To see why we must look at one more feature of love.

The Logic of Dependence

The lover is dependent, entirely, terribly dependent on his beloved for something he needs, the reciprocity of his love. Therefore loving falls under the domain of *amour propre*, not *amour de soi*. The lover cannot achieve love's desire, reciprocity, by the exercise of his own powers. He will only be loved if she finds him pre-eminent. He must present himself in the guise in which she would see her beloved. This leads to a false presentation of the self and the chronic fear of exposure and loss of love. Along the way the lover loses himself and necessarily the opportunity to gain love for this lost self.

But what of the fortunate possibility that a pair of lovers actually possess the very virtues that they seek and find in each other? Might not fortunate couples each rich in personal merit not escape the predicament of self-falsification and self-loss in love? The answer, I think, must be no. Love operates in the domain of *amour-propre*, not *amour de soi*. The reciprocity of need and dependence cannot prevent the disastrous working out of the effects of dependence in the human personality. To be happy we must be autonomous. But we are not autonomous in love. Therefore we cannot be happy in love. Love operates in the domain of *amour-propre*. Human beings can only act in a fashion not self- and mutually destructive when they are motivated by desires whose satisfaction is within their own powers. If we need another, the terrible possibility remains that their gratification of our need will be withdrawn. Even if love has been met with complete responsiveness, there is the future to dread. It is not within our power to secure the future love of our beloved against surfeit, disillusionment, or a rival found more worthy. Therefore, the lover is in a position of weakness, of impotence. Impotence forces him to employ tyrannical or servile means in futile attempts to secure what cannot be secured. The lover becomes a tyrant or a slave because of his impotence. In so doing he must both become and reveal a personality lacking in the perfections the lover sought and that he or she had found. In his weakness he confirms or creates the very doubts about his worthiness he feared his beloved was entertaining. Even if the doubts and fears that consume lovers and the jealous and craven responses they make do not result in the withdrawal of love, these feelings themselves, together with the sense of impotence they spring from, make the lover miserable. Such is certainly the case with Saint-Preux, who is given to depressive fits of jealous rage against his friend and protector, Lord Edward. Love is an illusion or a delusion. Or if you prefer, love is a genuine enough human experience, but a miserable one. Lovers may possess each other and consume each other, but they lose themselves.

I believe that Rousseau's two great fictional accounts of love, the story of Emile and Sophie and of Saint-Preux and Julie, support my interpretation of Rousseau's theory of love if properly read. Despite the undeniable aspects of the sentimental celebration of romantic love characteristic of these works and which largely account for their tremendous popular success, love is portrayed as a tragic disappointment in both. Rousseau had what has been called a bourgeois conception of love.[23] The ideal is married love. In one of his two great love stories the hero marries the girl and loses her. In the other he simply loses her. Both losses propel the male lovers, whose side of the story Rousseau identifies with and treats more fully, into massive depressions and sends them off on years-long travels to try to forget and heal their wounds. Both Emile and Saint-Preux are depicted as men of unusual pasts and merits. Emile is unusual in that he has been carefully educated for the attainment of happiness and virtue despite, and in the midst of, what Rousseau regarded as a deplorable social environment. Saint-Preux is portrayed as a man of unusual talents and qualities. Both, as a result of loving, succeed in doing nothing of any note in the world, more significant in Saint-Preux's case, and feeling nothing but intense misery, more significant in Emile's case.

Julie writes to her lover Saint-Preux:

> Love is accompanied by a continual uneasiness over jealousy or privation, little suited to marriage, which is a state of enjoyment and peace. People do not marry in order to think exclusively of each other, but in order to fulfill the duties of civil society jointly, to govern the house prudently, to rear their children well. Lovers never see anyone but themselves, they incessantly attend only to themselves, and the only thing they are able to do is love each other.[24]

Despite his bourgeois ideal of love, it seems to be Rousseau's opinion that even the slight requirements for the fulfillment of women's social role are incompatible with love, while potentially great and virtuous men have their capacity to act in the world as well as their happiness destroyed by love. In the little read and as far as I know untranslated sequel to *Emile*, *Emile et Sophie*, the tragic dissolution of Emile's marriage is portrayed. Emile's marriage falters because that paragon of virtue is distracted by Parisian pleasures and neglects his wife. It seems that when a social evil is not introduced as an obstacle to love's desire (Saint-Preux's low birth prevents his marriage to Julie), and even when the best of men and women have the best of chances for success love fails. His desire realized, Emile loses interest in his wife until her unfaithfulness revives the fires and torments of love.

5. The Future of Love:
Sexual Love and Social Psychology

I have been writing about love as if there were one kind of experience of love that was uniform for all people or among all people of the same sex. This is almost certainly not the case. No doubt there are very different sorts of sexual love. But the theories I have been considering focus on certain core features of sexual love that reflect either psychological invariance or the differential impact on men and women of social conditions and cultural norms. These features permit considerable latitude for talking about the experience of men and women in love in a univocal way without inadmissible abstraction or distortion.

There is something to be learned from both Firestone's and Rousseau's accounts of love. We can make at least a beginning to identifying the causes of the pathologies that disfigure sexual love and point the way to its rehabilitation. Radical feminism need not lead to the excesses of Atkinson or to the denial that men as well as women are the victims of love as we now know it.

It seems to me that Firestone's account of the pathology of women's love is essentially accurate. Without self-respect and the respect of men grounded in the social and economic equality of the sexes, men and women cannot meet on the terrain of mutual openness and appreciation which love requires. Although Firestone claims that men can't love, her account of man's sexual and romantic encounters with women and Rousseau's are in fact much closer than this startling claim would seem to suggest. Firestone traces male inability to love to the fear of dependency. Rather than inability to love, we should follow Rousseau in identifying the distinctive pathology of male love as precisely that fear of dependency which he claims is the explanation for the dysfunctional character of love for *both* men and women. We should retain however a Firestonean perspective on the distinctiveness of male and female experience of love and their roots in the social inequality of the sexes.

If love is to be rehabilitated, something must be very wrong with the Rousseauvian thesis that dependency relationships are always self- and mutually destructive. Something *is* very wrong with this thesis. The radical feminist Thesis I, which explains the pathology of love as we know it as the product of sexual inequality must be supplemented by an elaboration and substantiation of Thesis II. Dependency relations need not be destructive if our social psychological natures and the social conditions which they reflect are transformed.

There is a paradox at the heart of Rousseau's account of social relations. To be humanly happy we need others. But if we need others we are lost. Rousseau wanted to repudiate the kind of psychological egoism which regarded human beings as wholly selfish and as having purely instrumental interactions with each other, interactions whose goal was the satisfaction of the self, a self which was only in peripheral ways effected by or a product of its society and culture. But he was too deeply mired in individualism to make more than a very partial break with its social and psychological theory. He was able to project the essential effects of social living on the individual's personality structure only as threats to the integrity and happiness of the self. The result is a theory which posits the insufficiency of the human individual to achieve his or her self-realization in society. But what is really wanted is a theoretical critique of the insufficiency of individualism. This is a very large and a very difficult theoretical task which it goes without saying I cannot undertake here. But a few remarks will show the relevance of this critical task to the rehabilitation of love.

If autonomy from the need for others is posited as a necessary condition for human happiness, all dependency relations are necessarily pernicious. Add that they are unavoidable and you have the plight of Rousseauvian love. But suppose that the just fear of dependency of men on women and women on men that now obtains is the product of dysfunctional economic and social relations not just between the sexes but throughout social life, not the product of some deficiency in human nature. Suppose that the fear of dependency is a variable feature of human personality attributable to social conditions which drive them into invidious competition for the social status and esteem which could be accorded everyone in a society where cooperative institutions supported fruitful and healthy interdependency. Suppose that the thesis is false, that love, respect, and esteem are only given to him who is so pre-eminent in the eyes of others as to scarcely seem to require the further perfection of being loved by others. Suppose we could grant our love on some basis other than the supposed absolute pre-eminence of the beloved. Under conditions in which lovers did not seek pre-eminence according to social norms of attainment in those whom they loved, dependency would not have the terrible aspect of courting almost certain exposure and failure. Love's eye could still seek and find the special qualities that lead to preferment, draw affection and nourish the growth of personality in lovers. Human differences and variety in sensibility and qualities would still guide and motivate love-choices. Such encounters would still be fraught with the perils of rejection and failure but not hopelessly and inevitably so. What I am proposing is a socialist theory of social psychology, of which we have now only the barest sketch. Love may be rehabilitated if the just fear of dependency relations we learn from love as we know it turns out to be grounded not in fear of ourselves but the pathological distortions of human personality produced by an unjust, destructive and successfully alterable social order.

Radical feminists have forced an admission on the part of many socialists that traditional socialist programs are insufficient for achieving women's liberation. The insufficiency of a feminist program alone to give love a future shows that this most personal of political problems requires more than sexual equality for its solution.

Notes

My thanks to Joseph Agassi and Alice Jacobs for discussions we had about love; and to editors Carol Gould and Marx Wartofsky.

[1]Ti Grace Atkinson, "Radical Feminism" and "The Institution of Sexual Intercourse," both in *Notes From the Second Year: Women's Liberation* (Boston: 1969).

[2]Atkinson, "The Institution of Sexual Intercourse," p. 45.

[3]Atkinson, "Radical Feminism," pp. 36–37.

[4]Atkinson's attack on sexual intercourse is part of her contribution to the debate about Female sexuality and in particular, the vaginal orgasm. She writes, "The theory of vaginal orgasm was created quite recently to shore up that part of the foundation of a social institution that was being threatened by the increasing demand by women for freedom for women. The political institution I am referring to is the institution of sexual intercourse. The purpose, i.e., the social function, of the institution is to maintain the human species." (Ibid., p. 42.)

[5]Atkinson, "The Institution of Sexual Intercourse," p. 47.

[6]Cf. *The Dialectic of Sex* (New York: Bantam Books, 1970), especially Chapters 5 and 6, "Love" and "The Culture of Romance."

[7]Ibid., p. 128.

[8]Ibid., p. 128.

[9]Cf. J. O. Wisdom, on the paradoxically selfish and unselfish quality of love, "Freud and Melanie Klein: Psychology, Ontology and Weltanschauung," in *Psychoanalysis and Philosophy*, ed. C. Hanley and M. Lazerowitz (New York: 1970), pp. 349–54.

[10]Firestone, p. 132.

[11]Cf. Wisdom, p. 383. See also Simone de Beauvoir, *The Second Sex* (New York, Bantam Books, 1953).

[12]Ibid., p. 128.

[13]Ibid., p. 146.

[14]Ibid., p. 131.

[15]Cf. Rousseau's *A Discourse on the Origin of Inequality*, for his phylogenetic account.

[16]*Emile*, Everyman Library, p. 44.

[17]Cf. *Emile*, Part II.

[18]Ibid., p. 175.

[19]Ibid.

[20]Ibid., p. 176.

[21]*La Nouvelle Héloïse* (University Park: Pennsylvania State University Press, 1968), p. 47.

[22]Ibid., p. 83.

[23]Denis de Rougemont, *Love in the Western World* (New York: Pantheon, 1956).

[24]*La Nouvelle Héloïse*, p. 261–262.

Kathryn Pauly Morgan
Romantic Love, Altruism, and Self-Respect:
An Analysis of Beauvoir

Kathryn Pauly Morgan is associate professor of philosophy and women's studies at the University of Toronto.

In her analysis of "The Woman in Love" in *The Second Sex*, Beauvoir quotes three men:[1] Balzac says,

> Among the first-rate, man's life is fame, woman's life is love. Woman is man's equal only when she makes her life a perpetual offering, as that of man is perpetual action. (SS, 742)

Byron claims,

> Man's love is of man's life a thing apart;
> 'Tis woman's whole existence. (SS, 712)

And Nietzsche writes in *The Gay Science*,

> The single word love in fact signifies two different things for man and woman. What woman understands by love is clear enough: it is not only devotion, it is a total gift of body and soul, without reservation, without regard for anything whatever. . . . As for man, . . . he is . . . far from postulating the same sentiment for himself as for woman; if there should be men who also felt that desire for complete abandonment, upon my word, they would not be men.

In contrast, Beauvoir's own view is that the womanly *vocation* of loving involves massive self-deception which can lead to personal annihilation for the woman involved.

In the first part of this discussion I examine central philosophical assumptions which frame her analysis of the intersubjective dynamic of romantic love. This dynamic generates four double-bind paradoxes, leading ultimately to servility in the woman who loves. In the second part I ask whether it is wrong for a woman to aspire to and/or choose this form of servitude. I distinguish two kinds of considerations: (1) those having to do with the intrinsic moral nature of the commitment or decision, and (2) those based on harm.

Part I: Philosophical and Empirical Assumptions

Beauvoir explores the conceptual assumptions in the writings of the authors cited earlier. Such thinkers hold that, for men, love must be seen merely as a diversion, as a phenomenon to be experienced only on the periphery of a real man's life, because it is a dangerously privatizing emotion. At no time must love be seen as definitional of his identity and his worth, which must be focused on action and recognition in some public realm. Not so for women. Beauvoir argues that from a woman's point of view loving can be a woman's central *vocation*, that loving a superior being can be what confirms a woman in her *womanliness* (as contrasted with her biological *femaleness* which is confirmed through maternity and lactation),[2] and that loving generates unconditional *person-specific altruism* as a life-governing moral principle. For women, romantic love can forge a crucial link between altruism, self-respect, and womanliness. In *The Second Sex*, Beauvoir works with three important dualisms in addition to the central dualism of Self and Other. Each of these dualisms permanently assigns women to the category of a secondary "Other," in contrast to genuine "selves" who are the locus of authentic self-originating activity.

Dualism 1: Life versus Spirit

The first dualism involves a distinction between a life oriented toward Life and a life of the Spirit.[3] For an individual committed to life and life processes, life-giving and life-sustaining are the dominant values. Activities such as giving birth, nursing a child, and preparing food are paradigmatic life-oriented activities. Central to the focus on life is a commitment to the domain of the temporal and the ephemeral, involving processes largely out of one's control, requiring waiting and passivity. A life oriented toward Life is essentially a life lived in common with other animals because its ultimate goal is simply the *replication* of life. It is not a genuinely creative, properly *human* life.[4]

By contrast, the life of Spirit rises above the biological level. The individual oriented toward the Spirit would be interested in creative adventure, in experimentation, perhaps even to the point of risking life. We can identify a life committed to Spirit, Beauvoir suggests, by noting the primacy placed on inventions, technology, symbols, and idealized values, i.e., entities whose permanence often outlasts and transcends the perishable domain of biological life, whether it be that of the individual or the species.[5] This commitment is manifest in situations in which an individual is willing to risk biological life for a higher value such as the Nation or Peace or the Public Good or Justice. One of Beauvoir's primary projects in *The Second Sex* is to argue that women are entitled to full legitimate access to the life of the Spirit. As she says, "It is regardless of sex that the existent seeks self-justification through transcendence—the very submission of women is proof of that statement. What they demand today is to be recognized as existents by the same right as men and not to subordinate existence to life, the human being to its animality" (SS, 73).[6]

Dualism 2: Immanence versus Transcendence
This distinction emphasizes the underlying psychological structures of consciousness, their metaphysical correlates, and the accompanying existential emotions. The sphere of immanence involves lived repetition.[7] According to Beauvoir, the physically confined and repetitious life of many women is simply the material replica of their psychological confinement, in which one thinks within predetermined limits, within already established conditions and conventions, submitting to identity-determining roles which are perceived as necessary and given. It is a life without adventure, without risk. Metaphysically speaking, it means living a life immersed and trapped within the domain of the *given*—the present and the immediate—which is then equated with all that is real. Thus carried to its ultimate limit, it approximates the predictable life of the nonhuman object. For Beauvoir, a life of immanence is a life of human stagnation and living death, though tempting because of its very predictability and security.

A life directed towards transcendence, by contrast, is a life open to the future, a life self-originated rather than based on a preexisting identity. Transcendent subjects invent, act, make choices. They view the future as something indeterminate to shape and bring into existence rather than as a fate to which one can only submit. They think of themselves as self-determining, as having the power to create. Metaphysically speaking, the transcendent subject is oriented towards the domain of the *possible*. Concomitant with this experience of the self, however, is a pervasive feeling of dread at the resulting responsibility for one's life and identity. Again it is clear that for Beauvoir only the life of transcendence is worthy of human respect.[8] She also notes that one or another form of a life of immanence is built into virtually all the acceptable roles open to women.

Dualism 3: Life Situations of Women and Men

As Beauvoir studies the life-determining situations and roles of adolescent girls, married women, mothers, and aging widows, she argues that women's acceptable roles constantly direct a woman's consciousness to concerns which are concrete, immediate, and particular, and hence, to lives of immanence. Beauvoir both devalues and mourns such lives.[9] Further, she claims that the actual life situations of women define the heterosexually desirable feminine woman in terms of dependency, vulnerability, and submissiveness, whose moral sensibility is one of self-sacrifice. Insofar as a life of autonomy or self-determination calls for independence, strength, a sense of personal integrity, and a deep commitment to development of self, the notion of an autonomous desirable *feminine* woman is a living impossibility. On the contrary, the social situations of men characteristically require a "masculine" boy or man to strive to be independent, achievement-oriented, courageous, assertive, and decisive; to have a sense of adventure and risk-taking; and to be rational.[10] As Beauvoir says,

> The advantage man enjoys, which makes itself felt from his childhood, is that his vocation as a human being in no way runs counter to his destiny as a male. Through the identification of phallus and transcendence, it turns out that his social and spiritual successes endow him with a virile prestige. He is not divided. Whereas it is required of woman that in order to realize her femininity she must make herself object and prey, which is to say that she must renounce her claims as sovereign subject. It is this conflict that especially marks the situation of the emancipated woman. She refuses to confine herself to her role as female, because she will not accept mutilation; but it would also be a mutilation to repudiate her sex. (SS, 758)

Three Contributing Factors

Within this general dualistic framework, Beauvoir argues that three further factors often combine to generate in women desire for romantic love: (1) the general human desire to avoid a life of responsible self-determination (the phenomenon of bad faith or *mauvaise foi*), (2) the specific social and economic circumstances of many women, and (3) a romantic ideology which is carefully inculcated in girls and women from an early age.

(1) Bad Faith: The first factor contributing to women desiring romantic love is what Beauvoir and other existentialist thinkers see as a primary, universal, defining form of motivation in human subjects, *viz.*, the desire for inauthenticity, objectification, or bad faith (*mauvaise foi*). Basically, this notion refers to the desire of any conscious subject to flee from a life of self-determination in which we continually strive to surpass our given self. Glimpsing the uncertainty and concomitant dread which characterize this work of self-determination, we sink softly and securely into some self-deceptive form of objecthood.

There are at least four ways in which a woman can be tempted into bad faith. Unfortunately these ways are not mutually exclusive.[11] The *first form* involves regarding the received values which permeate and regulate one's life as absolute and necessary instead of open to revision and change. For example, a woman might think, "As a woman, I *must* be nurturant, compassionate, self-sacrificing. I have no choice." A *second form* of bad faith consists in completely identifying with a role or set of roles and, again, pretending that that role is *normatively* binding. For example, the woman who says that "As a good Christian mother, I must do X, feel Y . . ." or that "As the wife of Professor X, I must always say . . ." or thinks "As a feminist, I must feel . . ." would be practicing self-deception. A *third form* of bad faith involves *subordinating oneself to the status of instrument or object*. The *fourth form* of bad faith which particularly tempts women is that of *becoming an identity parasite*. This fourth form, Beauvoir argues, must be invoked in order to explain the desire that some women have for a great romantic love either with a human being or, through mysticism, with a divine being. It is this fourth form that particularly interests Beauvoir in her discussion of the woman in love.[12]

(2) General Social and Economic Circumstances of Women: In explaining the appeal of romantic love to women, it is important to note general oppressive features of women's lives which lead women in many cultures to see romantic love as one form of salvation. At least three such circumstances need to be mentioned. First, women are often relegated to the essentially repetitive low status tasks of domestic labor. Secondly, women are devalued because of their primary definition in terms of their family in an ideological context which views the family as natural, precultural, and private and sees women affiliated with children as similarly emotional and irrational. Thirdly, young girls are taught that their lives as women are,

properly, lives destined to be lived for others. A girl's social position and her economic security are essentially bound up with the social and economic position of her father, husband, or other significant male kinship figure. Her own situation, as an individual woman, is usually one of minimal public power. In this context, falling in love and being loved by a superior being come to be seen as a desirable and liberating way of acquiring identity and access to power.

(3) Beliefs Which Are Central to a Romantic Ideology: "It is agonizing for a woman to assume responsibility for her life. It is man's good fortune to be obliged to take the most arduous roads, but the surest; it is woman's misfortune to be surrounded by almost irresistible temptations; everything incites her to follow the easy slopes; instead of being invited to fight her own way up, she is told that she has only to let herself slide and she will attain paradises of enchantment" (SS, 715). According to Beauvoir, girls and women, particularly in Western cultures, are bombarded with a complex belief set which one can refer to as the Romantic Ideology. As mentioned earlier, three beliefs are central to a patriarchal conception and dynamic of romantic love. These are (1) the belief that loving is a woman's central vocation; (2) the belief that loving is what confirms a woman in her womanliness; and (3) the belief that the proper moral principle in this situation is unconditional person-specific altruism. In order to explain why a woman comes to accept and deeply internalize these beliefs, Beauvoir argues that two additional convictions are necessary. First, it is necessary to convince the young girl that because she is a female throughout her life she will be seen as less important and less valuable than a male, and to assure her that this situation is normal. *This is the crucial assumption of male supremacy.*

Second, it is crucial that she come to experience herself as essentially incomplete as a single woman who lacks affiliation with a male. Her life is passing in a state of suspension because the locus of her identity has not yet appeared or, perhaps, never will. Encouraged by the popular and religious mythologies of the culture, she dreams of being found by the appropriate Prince Charming (Charles?) who will confer a sense of achieved and privileged heterosexual identity upon her along with, in many cases, social and economic status.[13] *This is the crucial heterosexist assumption of asymmetric complementarity.*

Beauvoir argues that if these beliefs are internalized it is easy to understand what motivates a woman to want to love. *First, a woman wants to fall in love to find out who she is.* Women are taught that until they fall in love with a superior being who has already formed an identity of his own, they do not have an identity. A woman's *second* important motive is that in the process of loving and acquiring her identity, *a woman's past and present become meaningful* in relation to the loved one. What had been indeterminate now has significance. Think, for example, of the positive value assigned to Lady Diana Spenser's virginity prior to her marriage to Prince Charles. As a biological state of the organism, one might regard virginity as a value-neutral property. In the eye of the royal lover, it obviously became of prime importance. The *third* important motive for the woman to love is that it provides for the possibility of *legitimizing and integrating her sexuality with her sense of her own identity.* Beauvoir points out that in a situation devoid of affection and commitment, many women who are taught to regard their own erotic responses as forms of animallike debasement feel used by men as sexual instruments. Sexual fervor in the context of love legitimizes a woman's erotic passion; sexual pleasure can be experienced in a genuinely human way. Her *fourth* important motive is *to acquire a locus of values.* Ideally, the woman in love looks to her lover to be her *world.* The extent to which this can take place is limitless. As Beauvoir describes it,

> the measure of values, the truth of the world, are in his consciousness; hence it is not enough to serve him. The woman in love tries to see with his eyes; she reads the books he reads, prefers the pictures and the music he prefers; she is interested only in the landscapes she sees with him, in the ideas that come from him; she adopts his friendships, his enmities, his opinions; when she questions herself, it is his reply she tries to hear. . . . Her idea of location in space, even, is upset: the centre of the world is no longer the place where she is, but that occupied by her lover; all roads lead to his home and from it. (SS 724)

In sum, for the woman in love, her lover becomes the person who is the source of identity, meaning, and significance in her world, the person who legitimizes her erotic nature, who functions as the limits of her world, the infallible judge of her life, and the locus of her own freedom.[14]

Beauvoir argues that what is particularly treacherous about this whole situation is that inauthenticity and self-deception are being directly camouflaged in the powerful guise of "freedom," fulfillment, and self-realization. The woman in love desires and seeks love as a form of liberation, as one of the few genuinely creative acts open to her, as the closest, gender-appropriate way of approximating the Life of the Spirit to which she, as a naturally inferior human subject, can aspire. Rather than being identified

398 as a form of temptation, the ideal of the woman in love is advanced not only as an ideal worthy of any woman, but as the highest form of existential aspiration open to her. This is why Beauvoir's critique is so ruthless. She is committed to exposing romantic love as an existential fraud. Whereas the woman in love sees in her love a form of transcendence, a form of genuine liberation, Beauvoir sees it as an inevitable downward spiral into abject servility incompatible with any surviving remnant of self-respect.

The Phenomenology of Romantic Love:
Problems and Paradoxes
Phase One: Identification

Beauvoir distinguishes various phases or moments which generate devastating paradoxes. She holds that the deepest, most important motives which lead a woman to seek out a great love are the acquiring of identity, value, erotic integration, and meaning. In her love for a superior being who instantiates all that is desired by way of freedom, the woman in love sees *herself* as creative, as transcending her initial situation of immanence and feminine powerlessness. Moreover, in glorying in her love and serving this superior person, she glories in her essential womanliness. This is the initial experienced state of loving as a vocation.

The woman in love abandons herself, in a blaze of unconditional altruistic splendor, to loving immersion in and submissive identification with the loved one, so that her transcendence is achieved through participation in his. Through this process, however, the woman in love succeeds only in becoming a metaphysical *dependent*: for genuine transcendence requires *action*, a sense of authority, and independence. As the woman in love identifies more and more passively with the agency of her lover—which is how she *defines* "falling in love"—she loses and destroys the very possibility of ever having her own identity. This is, then, the first paradox: that in seeking transcendence, the woman in love chooses precisely those means which annihilate the possibility of her transcendence (SS, 722).

Phase Two: Inversion

Beauvoir believes that every human subject desires to experience self-determination. Although the woman in love initially celebrates her vulnerability and dependency as proof of the intensity of her love, she gradually comes to perceive her need for some power and control in the relationship. This desire becomes more urgent as the woman in love comes to see the fragility of her situation. Having given all, she is in a position to lose all should her lover abandon her. In response to a resurgence of her desire for genuine transcendence, the woman in love strives to invert the power situation through her sacrifice.[15] She conveys to her lover the magnificence of the gift of her love, the totality of the gift of herself, and the absoluteness of her devotion. Ever more sensitively, more completely, the clever woman in love strives to become indispensable to her lover, sometimes even cultivating wants in him that only she can satisfy.[16] Should the lover feel uneasy about this situation, he has little recourse. It is virtually impossible for him to resist without appearing brutishly ungrateful. Nevertheless, a mortal struggle is taking place here: ". . . the woman requires him to accept gratefully the burdens with which she crushes him" (SS 729).

But the woman in love cannot logically emerge victorious in this struggle. This is the *second paradox*: If she *succeeds* in gaining control at this stage of the relationship, if she takes camouflaged possession of her lover, then he ceases to be a *worthy* object of her love. She has destroyed that transcendence which attracted her to him in the first place. She is lost. She is degraded and unhappy. She knows that a truly transcendent free subject could not be so controlled. If she succeeds, she demonstrates her own poor judgment in her choice of a mediocre lover, the relationship is shattered, and her sacrifice is exposed as worthless. If, on the other hand, the woman in love *fails*, if her lover remains free of the tyranny of her devotion, the woman in love faces her own powerlessness, her failure as a free subject. Thus, she is unhappy with this second alternative as well. In short, either way she loses. According to Beauvoir, the woman in love is subject to two powerful temptations at this stage.

Temptation 1: Lying. Acknowledging her own vulnerability, the woman in love tells herself that their love is a genuinely reciprocated relationship of mutuality, that her lover is just as dependent on her as she is on him. But the relief and satisfaction provided by this state of deception is short-lived. It cannot be sustained without generating a *third paradox* similar to the second. It is this: What attracted the woman in love to her lover initially was his sense of *separate and complete* identity, his sense of superiority and independence which had been achieved quite apart from her. Demonstrating a relation of mutual interdependence destroys precisely those features of the lover which she believes make him worthy of her love. If, on the other hand, what she is telling herself is the truth, namely, that her lover *is* dependent upon her, that her existence and identity are just as central to his sense of himself as his are to hers, then the lover has lost the strength, the sense of independence, of the transcendent subject. He is no longer free. He has become a fallen idol no longer worthy of her love.

Temptation 2: Jealous Manipulation. Beauvoir argues that the experience and significance of jealousy are metaphysically different for the woman in love than for her lover.[17] The lover's identity and sense of self-worth are presumed to be formed prior to entering into this relationship. Thus, the loss of his loved woman, at best, might be akin to the loss of an ego-incorporated servant, mirror, or highly-treasured possession. If all three are involved, we would have some explanation for the consuming violence of jealous male behavior without postulating the separate subjectivity of the woman concerned, especially when the outcome of such behavior is the annihilation of that woman's subjectivity. Thus while the jealous lover may be moved to rage or violence, the definition of romantic love necessarily prevents his loss from being of any greater *intersubjective* significance for him. (Think of his behavior when his prized car or stereo equipment is threatened or damaged.) Should the loss prove more profound, this would testify to his lack of transcendent completeness and would be evidence of his existential inferiority. Such a lover would not be worth feeling jealous over. The woman in love, on the other hand, ". . . loving her man in his alterity and in his transcendence, feels in danger at every moment. There is no great distance between the treason of absence and infidelity. . . . Her entire destiny is involved in each glance her lover casts at another woman, since she has identified her whole being with him. . . . She has received all from love, she can lose all in losing it" (SS, 736).

Because she has, literally, come into existence through this relationship, if she loses it, she loses all that she is: her sense of identity, her sense of herself as a person of value, her social world, and often her sense of economic security. Because of the nature of her experience of jealous terror and her fear of its consequences, the woman in love is tempted to engage in one of two manipulative tactics. She might try returning to the attempts to control characteristic of the inversion stage of the relationship, this time in more hyperbolic form using more gentleness, more devotion, more smiles, more mystery. "Even a proud woman is forced to make herself gentle and passive; maneuvering, discretion, trickery, smiles, charm, docility, are her best weapons. . . . Party clothes, weapons of war!" (SS, 738) This tactic is likely to fail. This time, the very servility embodied in the tactic itself will undermine her efforts. For, as Beauvoir notes, "giving herself blindly, the woman has lost that dimension of freedom which at first made her fascinating.

The lover seeks his reflection in her; but if he begins to find it altogether too faithful, he gets bored" (SS, 738).

A slightly more subtle maneuver is for her to feign a lack of interest in the lover in order to conjure up a tantalizing dimension of freedom. Often she will simultaneously engage in flirtation and seduction with others in hopes of rekindling his interest. But this situation leads to the *fourth paradox*: If either of these manipulative strategies succeeds and the lover fails to see through them, she cannot help but see how gullible and lacking in perception he is, and hence he is exposed as a pseudotranscendent fraud. If, on the other hand, her maneuvers fail and the perceptiveness of the lover is thereby revealed, so too are her manipulations seen for what they are, games played by an abject and fearful dependent.

In sum, though praised and celebrated for her love, the woman in love often becomes in reality pitiful, insecure, dependent, and powerless through her loving. Her own life tends toward one of servility, increasingly devoid of even the conditions of the possibility of self-respect. As Beauvoir puts it, "It is, again, one of the loving woman's misfortunes to find that her very love disfigures her, destroys her; she is nothing more than this slave, this servant, this too ready mirror, this too faithful echo. . . . Her salvation depends on this despotic free being that has made her and can instantly destroy her. . . . Love is a supreme effort to survive by accepting the dependence to which she is condemned; but even with consent a life of dependency can be lived only in fear and servility" (SS 738, 742). Beauvoir believes that if a woman genuinely chooses romantic love, she chooses a clear moral evil. If it is not a choice but is experienced as a personal, social, or economic "necessity" resulting from oppressive social and economic circumstances and the internalization of a mythology of romantic love, it is still a destructive form of self-delusion. In either case, it is morally wrong.

The question then arises: What of those individuals who do not operate within an existentialist conceptual and moral universe of discourse? How would they answer the central moral question: Is it morally wrong to aspire to and choose a life commitment to romantic love? They might maintain that a life of romantic love is either morally neutral or, like Balzac, claim that it is the unique source of woman's genuine equality with man. I now turn to a further exploration of the morality of romantic love as defined in this paper.

Part II: Assessment by a Moral Eclectic

At the first stage of the assessment it is important to determine whether or not the choice is really a choice, and whether the necessary preconditions of genuine choice have been satisfied: knowledge, freedom from coercion, and access to other real alternatives.

Turning first to the question of coercion, one can distinguish at least two types. One is the knife-at-your-throat, razor-at-your-nipple variety of overt physical coercion. Usually this form of coercion is not at work in romantic love. Two other forms need to be considered: covert deliberate coercion and unintentional institutional coercion.[18] Both can take subtle and insidious forms. Human beings grow up and are socialized in a culture which indoctrinates them into a complex set of beliefs about what their essential nature is, what their corresponding permitted and proper roles will be, and how access to economic and social privileges can be gained. Described in a formal way, this process appears (relatively) morally neutral. Consider, however, someone being socialized in a culture in which white supremacy is generally accepted as an "empirical truth." When faced with a significant choice, persons of color who believe in white supremacy may believe that it is "fitting and right" to choose an inferior self-effacing position on the grounds that this is commensurate with their abilities. To do otherwise would be a display of deplorable and punishable social and moral arrogance. Deference and institutionalized inferiority are seen as the appropriate postures for them to assume.[19] In this situation, the individual's self-image has been shaped in powerful ways.[20] Even if we omit the negative social consequences of choosing otherwise, I think it is fair to say that although a particular choice is alleged to be "open," persons of color who have been indoctrinated into a belief in white supremacy would experience strong internal psychological pressure in the direction of an inferior alternative.

Not all female babies are given complete sets of Harlequin Romances at birth. Nevertheless, women in many cultures are socialized, profoundly and sometimes violently, into heterosexist ideologies of male supremacy. In some cultures and in some historical periods, this ideology is supported by the more specific patriarchal ideology of romantic love. Again, central to this romantic ideology is the axiom of male supremacy and essential female inferiority.[21] Raised in a male supremacist society, a woman comes to have an image of herself as inferior. This internalized perception is lived out in the selection of inferior roles and alternatives.[22] Such "choices" then reinforce the perception of women as inferior and provide material support to existing male supremacist practices. In such circumstances a woman's "choice" of romantic love, defined as including affiliation with a superior male, is not a genuinely free choice.

Similarly, a strong case can be made that in many cultures women do not have genuinely human alternatives from which to choose. Any culture which *defines* women totally in terms of reproductive and domestic roles and analogous service roles in the domain of paid labor cannot be said to offer women a full range of alternatives.[23] If romantic love is in fact a necessary catalyst in leading a woman into her life as a domestic reproducer and that is the only legitimate life held open to her, then the choice of romantic love is, again, not a genuine choice. Finally, it is clear that where knowledge of the consequences is lacking, a person cannot be said to have made an informed free choice. In many cultures, the alleged glories of romantic love are sung, celebrated, and eulogized. The actual consequences often remain camouflaged.[24] A woman who has accepted the illusory message of romantic love as literal truth cannot be said to be informed about the situation. Again, her choice is not a free one.

Suppose, however, that we consider the morally difficult case. Let us assume a woman whose choice has not been coerced, either overtly or covertly, who has other significant alternatives in her life, and who has knowledge of the consequences of her choice. She has read and understood *The Second Sex*; she has even read this paper. She has seen numerous friends disappear into the quagmires of romantic servility and she does not regard herself as, in some way, idiosyncratically exempt from the servile consequences. *Is it immoral for her to choose a life of romantic love if HE (or SHE) comes along?* I believe it is immoral for two very different sorts of reasons: first, because the choice of romantic love is ultimately the choice of an intrinsic though often camouflaged evil; and, second, because the life of romantic love leads to significant harm.

Claim 1: Romantic love is intrinsically evil. This type of objection can be found in the writings of a variety of moral theorists. For example, in *On Liberty* John Stuart Mill argues that one cannot, with moral approbation, knowingly enter into a relationship or situation which will terminate the very possibility of moral choice.[25] That is, voluntary servitude is always immoral. This moral evaluation is based on a view of human nature (not entirely dissimilar to that of Beauvoir) in which the making of moral choices is central to any life properly regarded as a human life, so that it is immoral for any human beings to use their human capacity for choice in such a way as to annihilate that capacity for choice. This moral voluntarism prohibits choosing a life of committed inevitable servility whether it is in the form of romantic self-abasing attachment or in some other form of servitude such as economic slavery *when one has other real options which might preserve and even enhance one's capacity and range of choice.*[26] From this perspective, then, the choice of romantic love as a life-determining form of voluntary servitude must be regarded as an intrinsically immoral choice.

Claim 2: Romantic love leads to harmful consequences. We can distinguish at least four possible categories of harm: (1) harm to the woman who loves, (2) harm to the lover, (3) harm to the quality of the relationship, and (4) harm to the social community ("the greatest number").

(1) *Romantic love harms the woman who loves.* As noted in Part I, when the woman in love begins to fear the loss of her lover, she often uses the only form of power usually available to her: manipulative power. This can be roughly characterized as power the successful exercise of which depends essentially on its remaining unperceived. The effect of the exercise of covert power on the manipulator is a complicated issue.[27] But in this context the crucial point is that anyone who uses manipulative power in a situation in which no other forms are available to them (because they are not of the "right" gender or the "right" race) will be crippled and mutilated through the very use of that power. The manipulating woman must simulate a posture of weakness and vulnerability. This has the harmful consequence that even though the particular manipulative tactic may work, the woman herself can only continue to be falsely perceived as weak and powerless and, hence, open to exploitation. Often the woman internalizes this perception of herself (this may be precisely why she turns to manipulation in the first place) and comes to see herself as genuinely weak. Furthermore, because she will be seen as a *typically* "weak woman," a normal member of "the weaker sex," the property of being naturally weak will continue to be ascribed to other women as well. Moreover, the use of manipulative power is seldom cumulative. Because the manipulative woman is not usually perceived as powerful by those whom she manipulates, she is not accorded the minimal amount of respect directed toward individuals who use power in publicly acknowledged ways. (Needless to say, the person manipulated, in this case the lover, is also harmed by this use of power. By being deceived, the person's capacity for self-determination is being undermined.)

(2) *Romantic love is harmful to the lover.*[28] As seen in Part I, the ideology of romantic love calls for the lover to be an incarnation of an ideal transcendent hero. Romantic love requires that the appropriate loved person be a *world-constituting, meaning-conferring* subject. This cannot help but be a deeply falsifying picture of the lover. Even when the social accept-

ability of the demands of masculinity supports the development of such characteristics in males, it is difficult to imagine any human beings able to satisfy, unwaveringly, the demands made of them by a woman in love. In short, no one can *be* the transcendent existentialist hero that the woman in love requires to justify her passion and her commitment. This is the first sort of harm that is done to the lover: impossible and falsifying demands are placed upon that person.

Moreover, the lover is invited to participate in a situation of double metaphysical duplicity. If the lover is male, he is encouraged, often both by the culture and by the woman who loves him, to believe that he really *is* the "Hero," this superior being. Forbidden any weakness, he himself may well forget that he too, like any other subject, is vulnerable, fragile, and subject to anguish. Thus not only is he being forced into a mold by his lover (and his culture) as a foil for her weakness; he is praised for accepting this falsifying perception of himself. Although some beneficial consequences might result (for example, he might be likely to act more courageously or more steadfastly than if he did not have this view of himself), this situation is harmful because it makes genuine self-knowledge impossible.

In addition, it is a perception which encourages and legitimizes exploitative arrogance in the name of "normal" love. Romantic ideology instructs a male, as the potential legitimate recipient of this love, to regard his arrogance as the normal behavior of a superior individual. In a situation like this, the avoidance of arrogant exploitation is almost impossible.[29] Thus, romantic love requires a falsification of the lover which is harmful because it prevents genuine self-knowledge and leads to the further harm of camouflaging the vice of arrogance as an indelible mark of superior virtue. Arrogance, though less oppressive than servility, can be just as morally corrupting.

(3) *Romantic love harms and can destroy any relationship of love.* I now argue that the *relationship* of love itself suffers accordingly with yet more resultant harm to the participants. One way in which the quality of the relationship might be harmed occurs when the woman in love attempts to carry out her inversion of the original power relationship by preserving or even cultivating emotional primitiveness in her lover. This is designed to establish the woman's indispensability as a kind of empathic companion and expert in the life of the emotions, an expertise often conveniently already assigned to her in many Western capitalist societies.[30] Blum et al. (1976) discuss the harmful effects this process can have for wife and husband. This dynamic can occur in a relationship of romantic love as well.

Although the woman in love may be successful in cultivating such emotional dependency, in so doing, she harms the quality of the relationship because such an asymmetrical relationship is bound to remain emotionally primitive while potential for emotional growth and intimacy is stunted and thwarted for both participants. I see this as a clear case of harm.[31]

More generally the relationship of romantic love is claimed not only to *be* a love relationship but, for a woman, her most significant and fulfilling adult relationship.[32] I would hold that, at the minimum, any genuine love relationship should provide support and caring in an atmosphere of mutual trust and communication. The lovers should strive to be present to the other in a forthright way so that the relationship can be based on shared and mutual knowledge—albeit partial and open to change. In romantic love lovers are incapable of satisfying these minimum conditions for genuine love. So the relationship of love suffers. Instead of knowledge, we find double illusions necessary to sustain the dynamic of romantic love. Instead of trust, we find, at best, an intermingling of dependency, fear, and manipulation on the part of the woman in love, and a prohibition of genuine intimacy and sharing by the lover. Instead of mutual support, we find a situation of double-victimization involving the woman whose total dependency is encouraged and in the lover whose solitary self-sufficiency is required as the *raison d'être* of the relationship.

(4) *Romantic love produces social harm.* I assume that interpersonal alienation is bad, and that any process that produces alienation on a large scale by creating an atmosphere of fear and hostility should be avoided if possible. More specifically, where participation in a particular dynamic diminishes the potential for caring and trust among human beings and intensifies loneliness and dependency, I would argue that this dynamic is harmful. I would, like Beauvoir, argue that the love provides an illustration of such a dynamic. As mentioned in the discussion of jealousy, the woman in love is likely to fear abandonment. Her situation is, psychologically, a life and death situation for her. Thus, at the very least, prudence would seem to require that she monitor her environment for potential threats. Given both identity and a feeling of worth through her love, the woman in love exists in a state of metaphysical dependency upon her lover. Should he leave her for another, in an important sense she, *qua* individually defined consciousness, perishes. For the most part, women form the threatening social group.

In this context, it is important that the heterosexual woman in love be able to assess other women in *male-identified* terms using those categories which she knows attract her male lover (which might be quite distinct from those categories she herself employs when she finds another woman attractive and valuable.)[33] In this evaluation process, it is crucial that the woman in love be able to see other women *through* her lover's eyes. Two categories of women emerge: women who are assessed as (potential, illusory, or real) threats and women who appear to be "safe." The woman in love knows that this latter judgment is never infallible. There is always the lurking suspicion that even "safe" women are capable of being metamorphosed by the "right" lover into potential threats. Thus, in principle, no woman is completely safe for the woman in love.

This leads to at least two harmful consequences. First, the woman in love employs—and must employ—standards of assessment derived from male criteria of attractiveness and desirability (and is herself continually being evaluated by these criteria by *other* women in love). In the best of all possible worlds, male-derived criteria of assessment can lead only to a partial perception of any individual woman. What is more likely is that in a male supremacist culture these criteria of evaluation are seen, both by the woman in love and the culture at large, as the *only* standards of evaluation worth employing. Thus the use of these standards not only distorts but simultaneously devalues women on a large scale, thereby reinforcing male supremacist attitudes and practices. Secondly, since the woman in love carries out this process of monitoring in the name of assessing threats, any positive assessment of another woman by her is bound to generate feelings of suspicion, fear, and hostility—feelings which make it impossible to form significant relationships of support and affection with any of these women. Since in Western popular culture and in many others romantic love is encouraged on a large social scale, the resulting social alienation and hostility between women is potentially massive. The political implications of this situation for women are not incidental.[34] Romantic love should be avoided because of its profoundly harmful effects to the social community at large. I conclude, then, that the choice of patriarchal romantic love can be seen as morally bad in a variety of moral frameworks: existential, deontological, and consequentialist.

Is There Hope?

But is the reader convinced? Indeed, is the author convinced by her own arguments? Is it possible to be an optimist, yet avoid the epithet "Romance Junkie"? Unlike Sartre, Beauvoir clearly holds out the possibility of stable authentic love, a love which respects, as she puts it, "the strange ambiguity of existence made body," an ambiguity which is lived in a variety of fashions. For Beauvoir, what this requires is that both should "assume the ambiguity with a clear-sighted modesty, correlative of an authentic pride" in which each would be seen as an equal in their erotic drama.

While it is difficult to disagree with Beauvoir's brief but hopeful description, I can't help but feel that it is somewhat on the anemic side; that it is praiseworthy but devoid of the scarlet smoldering, the fiery icicles, and the wrenching tenderness that any romantic love must have to be worthy of the name (or the price). For further illumination, perhaps we should turn once more to a more contemporary philosophical analysis. Consider, for example, the words of Newton-Smith:

> An idea of these concepts can be gained by sketching a sequence of relations, the members of which we take as relevant in deciding whether or not some given relationship between persons A and B is one of love. . . . The sequence would include at least the following:
> (1) A knows B (or at least knows something of B)
> (2) A cares (is concerned about) B
> A likes B
> (3) A respects B
> A is attracted to B
> A feels affection for B
> (4) A is committed to B
> A wishes to see B's welfare promoted.[35]

Does this brittle, arid prose really lead to greater understanding? While I do not want to insult my fellow philosophers, perhaps it is best simply to admit that, *qua* philosophers, we are ill-suited to capture the magic, the passion, and the particularity of romantic love. This paper began with poetry. Perhaps it is best to end with poetry, to turn to a wise woman who has written about love in a way that speaks, that crackles, that sings and resonates with her lived experience.

> Love dwells in the major caves of the psyche
> chewing on the long bones of the limbs of courage.[36]

Why should that be? What does love demand, what does it require?

> Trying to enter each other,
> trying to interpenetrate and let go.

Trying not to lie down in the same old rutted bed
part rack, part cocoon.

We are equal only if you open too on your heavy hinges
and let your love come freely, freely, where it will never be safe,
where you can never possess.[37]

But not all is so serious. In a whimsical poem entitled "A private bestiary," Piercy writes,

I want us to be dolphins
together whose whole envelope
of skin sensitive as nipples
crinkles in joy, who roll over
and over borne up in the cradle
of water, sensuous, grinning at play. . . .
lion meets lion while lamb greets lamb.[38]

But, you ask, can it last? Should it last? For at least one woman, the answer is "Yes":

For three years we have loved, now well,
now badly, now a love of honey and fire,
now of bone and rust, now of pick handles
entwined with red roses. I hold my breath
. . . eager now
as the first night, the first month
the first summer and fall and winter.[39]

Courage, equality in vulnerability and trust, freedom, joy, desire, pleasure, play, breathlessness, strength, growth—love formed out of honey and fire, bone and rust. That sounds more like it. Philosophers have always been satisfied that universal claims can be seriously called into question by a convincing, living, breathing counterexample. Marge Piercy is one such welcome counterexample.

Notes

[1]All references to Simone de Beauvoir in this paper are to *The Second Sex*, trans. and ed. H. M. Parshley (New York: Random House, 1952), and will be abbreviated as SS.

[2]For the remainder of this paper I will be using the term "man" in place of "superior being" because Beauvoir assumes (uncritically) a heterosexist model throughout. Insofar as the

socialization of males is directed toward producing a sense of superiority and male supremacy as an ideal end state, an "appropriately" socialized male will be more likely to be perceived as the "proper" recipient of love. However, I do not believe that Beauvoir's analysis applies solely to heterosexual situations. What is necessary to generate the dynamic under discussion is the presence of someone (more likely a woman) who has internalized these three central assumptions of romantic ideology. That this same dynamic can be generated between two women is clear from Kate Millett's account in *Sita* (New York: Farrar, Straus and Giroux, 1977). Whether it is likely to be generated between two men, neither of whom has been socialized into this set of beliefs, is an open question at this point, although recent discussion in *The Body Politic* suggests that it occurs in the gay community as well.

[3]See the chapter "The Nomads," SS, pp. 69–73, for a fuller discussion of this distinction.

[4]For a sustained and convincing analysis of birthing as a properly human activity, equivalent in importance to the existential emphasis on death, see Virginia Held, "Birth and Death," *Ethics* 99 (1989): 362–88. Beauvoir would likely see the intense technologizing of human reproduction as shifting it into the domain of the life of the Spirit. Cf. Sherry Ortner, "Is Woman to Man as Nature Is to Culture?" in *Women, Culture, and Society*, ed. Michelle Zimbalist and Louise Lamphere (Stanford, Calif.: Stanford University Press, 1974), pp. 265–80, for a discussion of the theme of the partial identification of women with Nature, accepting Beauvoir's devaluation of the natural domain. It should be noted that there are at least two critical ways of dealing with the claim that women are closer to Nature and therefore inferior. One way is to argue against the primary association of women and Nature; the second is to challenge the consequent assessment of inferiority alleged to follow from this association. Susan Griffin adopts this second tactic in *Woman and Nature, the Roaring Inside Her* (New York: Harper and Row, 1978).

[5]In the Chapter on "Situation and Character," Beauvoir expands this distinction into a full theory of human consciousness in which characteristic feminine and masculine sensibilities are sharply differentiated along cognitive, emotional, physical, moral, political, and metaphysical lines.

[6]To many contemporary feminist thinkers, much of Beauvoir's discussion of this dualism with its Platonic commitment to the noncorporeal appears to be not only somatophobic but misogynistic. See, for example, Mary Lowenthal Festiner's discussion in "Seeing *The Second Sex* through the Second Wave," *Feminist Studies*, vol. 6, no. 2 (Summer 1980), pp. 247–76. I concur with this assessment.

[7]An example which Beauvoir examines at length is the situation of a housewife in industrialized societies whose labor is entirely of a domestic sort. She is involved in noncumulative cyclical processes of cleaning and cooking, cleaning and cooking with no obvious product of any sort to show for this labor. Clearly Beauvoir's account needs revision in the light of Marxist and socialist feminist reevaluations of reproductive domestic labor.

[8]"Every subject plays his part as such specifically through exploits or projects that serve as a mode of transcendence; he achieves liberty only through a continual reaching out toward other liberties. . . . Every time transcendence falls back into immanence, stagnation, there is a degradation of existence into the '*en soi*'—the brutish life of subjection to given conditions—and of liberty into constraint and contingence. This downfall represents a moral fault if the subject consents to it; if it is inflicted upon him, it spells frustration and oppression. In both cases, it is an absolute evil" (SS, xxxiii).

[9]Note that one can accept Beauvoir's descriptive analysis of women's situations and roles

without accepting her value judgments. Such an approach has been attempted recently, with admirable success, in Sara Ruddick's "Maternal Thinking," *Feminist Studies*, vol. 6, no. 2 (Summer 1980), pp. 342–67, and *Maternal Thinking: Toward a Politics of Peace* (Boston: Beacon Press, 1989). For a subtle philosophical collection of papers on this topic, see Joyce Trebilcot, ed., *Mothering: Essays in Feminist Theory* (Totowa, N.J.: Rowman and Allanheld, 1983).

[10]This is not to say that the actual lives of all men are those of authentic human subjects — Beauvoir herself cites the example of the *petit bourgeois* white-collar male worker as exemplifying some of the worst aspects of a life of immanence. Rather, it is a claim that it is only within the *kind* of situations which, until now, have been available only to (white) men that any form of a life of transcendence is possible. Whether this caveat ultimately saves Beauvoir from the charge of male identification is unclear.

[11]This notion of bad faith has recently been lifted out of its existentialist theoretical framework and is marketed in Collette Dowling's best seller, *The Cinderella Complex, Women's Hidden Fear of Independence* (New York: Simon and Schuster, 1981).

[12]In general, I believe it is fair to say that the second half of *The Second Sex* consists of an extended analysis of the ways in which the various roles ascribed to women, as lived by "normal women," generate situations of bad faith, lives which are less than fully human. Beauvoir is convinced that the "normal," "good" woman, as defined in patriarchal cultures, must live in bad faith and cannot be fully human. Her analysis of the woman in love is simply one form of a much larger sustained feminist project. The careful reader of Beauvoir must be ever on guard against uncritically adopting a Victimization Model of women's history and social situation. As Marilyn Frye points out, "one can conjure the appearance of the female as parasite only if one takes a very narrow view of human living — historically parochial, narrow with respect to class and race, and limited in conception of what are the necessary goods. One can and should distinguish between a partial and contingent material dependence created by a certain sort of money economy and class structure, and the nearly ubiquitous spiritual, emotional, and material dependence of males on females. . . . Females provide and generally have provided for males the energy and spirit for living; the males are nurtured by the females. And this the males apparently cannot do for themselves, even partially" ("On Separatism and Power," *The Politics of Reality: Essays in Feminist Theory* [Trumansburg, N.Y.: The Crossing Press, 1983] p. 99; essay first published in *Sinister Wisdom* 6 [Summer 1978]).

[13]This view of the formation of female identity has been labeled "normal" by the influential psychologist Erik Erikson. Erikson claims that women cannot resolve their primary identity crisis until their primary relationship with a man has been determined. Who she is and what her life will be await the formation of this primary relationship. This entails that women who remain single never really form an identity (which, unfortunately, still appears to be true in many cultures which deny an identity to married women). See Erikson, "Identity and the Life-Cycle," *Psychological Issues* 1 (1959). The danger in advocating such a theory as normative is that girls and women who strive to acquire an identity of their own apart from a male are labeled "abnormal" and "masculine" and subjected to various forms of clinical and social disapprobation.

[14]Although Beauvoir's descriptions here might seem to be hyperbolic, something like her theory is needed to account for the profound loss of identity experienced by women who are suddenly abandoned or widowed, a loss which does not always diminish with time. Translated

into a social custom, the suttee as it is practiced and understood in India illustrates the total identification expected of a wife with her husband.

[15]In this and other sections of *The Second Sex*, Beauvoir's debt to Hegel's analysis of the master-slave dialectic in *The Phenomenology of Spirit* is clear.

[16]The devastating moral consequences of this process have been explored in a perceptive article by Larry Blum et al., "Altruism and Women's Oppression," in *Women and Philosophy*, ed. Carol Gould and Marx Wartofsky (New York: G. P. Putnam's Sons, 1976), pp. 222–47.

[17]For interesting alternative accounts of jealousy see R. B. de Sousa, *The Rationality of Emotions* (Cambridge, Mass.: MIT Press, 1981); and Jerome Neu, "Jealous Thoughts," in *Explaining Emotions*, ed. A. O. Rorty (Berkeley: University of California Press, 1980), pp. 425–64. It should be noted that alternative readings of this situation are possible. Frye ("On Separatism," p. 99), for example, claims that the panic, rage, and hysteria that men display is evidence of the man's parasitism on the woman and indicates his response to the thought of being abandoned by women.

[18]For an analysis of this coercion see Richard Wasserstrom, "Racism, Sexism, and Preferential Treatment: An Approach to the Topics," *U.C.L.A. Law Review* (Feb. 1977), pp. 581–615.

[19]Thomas E. Hill suggested an analogous example. See his exceedingly generative article, "Servility and Self-Respect," *Monist*, vol. 57, no. 1 (Jan. 1973), pp. 87–104.

[20]Sandra and Daryl Bem make this point in their discussion of the socialization of American women ("Training a Woman to Know Her Place: The Power of a Nonconscious Ideology," in *Roles Women Play: Readings Toward Women's Liberation*, ed. Michele Garskof [Belmont, Calif.: Wadsworth Publishing Co., 1971], pp. 84–96). In their discussion of the claim that American women are perfectly free to choose among a variety of roles, they say that "this argument conveniently overlooks the fact that the society which has spent twenty years carefully marking the woman's ballot for her has nothing to lose in that twenty-first year by pretending to let her cast it for the alternative of her choice. Society has controlled not her alternatives, but her motivation to choose any but one of those alternatives. The so-called freedom to choose is illusory . . ." (pp. 88–89). See also Sandra Bartky, "On Psychological Oppression," in *Philosophy and Women*, ed. Sharon Bishop and Marjorie Weinzweig (Belmont, Calif.: Wadsworth Publishing Co., 1979), pp. 33–41.

[21]This consideration leads me to distinguish morally and politically between heterosexual romantic love and lesbian romantic love. Although lesbian romantic love may involve some of the same emotional and moral pitfalls from the point of view of Beauvoir's analysis, the situation of a woman committed profoundly and completely to another woman challenges at its very core the premise of male supremacy.

[22]Think of the documented tendency of women in sexist capitalist societies to name lower starting salaries for themselves than their male counterparts as a result of an internal devaluation of themselves as workers.

[23]For an extended analysis of the ways in which coercive pronatalist ideology operates, see Martha E. Gimenez, "Feminism, Pronatalism, and Motherhood," in Trebilcot, ed., *Mothering*; and Margaret Simons, "Motherhood, Feminism and Identity," in *Women's Studies International Forum, Hypatia* 7 (Special Issue, 1984): pp. 349–60.

[24]An analogous point can be made concerning the anomaly of participating in a marriage contract which neither of the participants sees. For an interesting discussion of this issue, see Sara Ann Ketchum, "Liberalism and Marriage Law," in *Feminism and Philosophy*, ed. Mary

Vetterling Braggin, Frederick Elliston, and Jane English (Totowa, N.J.: Littlefield, Adams, 1977), pp. 264-76.

[25]See Chapter 5 of Mill's *On Liberty*, ed. Elizabeth Rapaport (Indianapolis: Hackett Publishing Co., 1978), pp. 99-101, for his discussion of this issue. It is interesting to note that Mill objects less to actual suicide than to lives of voluntary servitude.

[26]This is a crucial assumption. The actual life situation of any particular woman must be carefully looked at to determine whether real alternatives exist before one passes moral judgment. For many women, this condition may not be met although, to be sure, girls and women in many cultures enter into—or are entered into—marriages devoid of romantic love and completely circumscribed by domestic toil. Whether this latter situation is a more or less desirable form of servitude than advanced romantic love is an open question. My present feeling is that in relationships devoid of romantic love at least a woman stands a chance of having her identity left more intact. The extent to which her situation is one of social and economic oppression coupled with domestic violence will be determining factors here.

[27]See my "Morality of Manipulative Power" (forthcoming).

[28]I am speaking here specifically of a male lover because it is not entirely clear to me that the same harm is done to a lover who is a woman.

[29]An analogous argument is made by R. M. Hare regarding the moral well-being of slave owners in "What Is Wrong with Slavery," *Philosophy and Public Affairs*, vol. 8, no. 2 (1979), pp. 103-17.

[30]See Eli Zaretsky, *Capitalism, the Family, and Personal Life* (New York: Harper & Row, 1976), for a general discussion of the rise of this perception of women as emotional experts.

[31]Similarly, if the woman in love is led to overlook real difficulties in the relationship or to excuse them because sustaining that relationship is the most important part of her life, then she is undercutting the potential for change and growth in the relationship. A similar point is made by Blum et al., "Altruism." I see this as a major temptation for women who are uncritically socialized into an "ethics of care." For the original articulation of this term, see Carol Gilligan, *In a Different Voice: Psychological Theory and Women's Development* (Cambridge, Mass.: Harvard University Press, 1982); and Nel Noddings, *Caring: A Feminist Approach to Ethics and Moral Education* (Berkeley: University of Calif. Press, 1984). For recent critiques of this ethical model, see Morgan, "Women and Moral Madness," in *Feminist Perspectives: Philosophical Essays in Methods and Morals*, ed. Lorraine Code, Sheila Mullett, Christine Overall (Toronto: University of Toronto Press, 1987), and "Strangers in a Strange Land: Feminists Visit Relativists," in *Moral Relativism* (tentative title), ed. C. Stewart (Toronto: Agathon Press, 1990); Barbara Houston, "Gilligan and the Politics of a Distinctive Women's Morality," in Code et al., and "Rescuing Womanly Virtues: Some Dangers of Moral Reclamation," in *Science, Morality, and Feminist Theory: Special Issue, Canadian Journal of Philosophy*, ed. Marsha Hanen and Kai Nielsen (1987); Marilyn Friedman, "Care and Context in Moral Reasoning," in *Women and Moral Theory*, ed. Eva Feder Kittay and Diana Meyers (Totowa, N.J.: Rowman and Littlefield, 1987), pp. 190-204, and "Beyond Caring," in Hanen and Nielsen, eds., *Science*, pp. 87-110, as well as other discussions in Kittay and Meyers.

[32]This is to be distinguished from a possible relationship she might have with a child which many (of the same) theorists argue is—or ought to be—a woman's most fulfilling relationship per se.

[33]Here again important gender differences might be drawn between heterosexual and lesbian romantic relationships. In a lesbian relationship, although the potential for abandon-

ment may be present, the woman in love does not need to use male generated criteria of assessment in calculating her risks. This removes at least one layer of alienation from the situation.

[34]Now it may be that the prevention of significant forms of political and social bonding among women is precisely one of the main consequences desired in a patriarchal situation. It is important to test the hypothesis that a stress on the importance of heterosexual romantic love is inversely correlated with high social expectations and approval of friendships between women. For work already done in this area, see, for example, Lillian Faderman, *Surpassing the Love of Men: Romantic Friendship and Love between Women from the Renaissance to the Present* (New York: William Morrow and Co., Inc., 1981); Adrienne Rich, "Compulsory Heterosexuality and Lesbian Existence," *Signs: Journal of Women in Culture and Society*, vol. 5, no. 4 (1980), pp. 631–60; and Carroll Smith-Rosenberg, "The Female World of Love and Ritual: Relations between Women in Nineteenth-Century America," *Signs*, vol. 1, no. 1 (1976), pp. 1–29.

[35]W. Newton-Smith, "A Conceptual Investigation of Love," in *Philosophy and Personal Relations*, ed. Alan Montefiore (London: Routledge and Kegan Paul, 1974), pp. 119–590.

[36]Marge Piercy, "The back pockets of love," in *Stone, Paper, Knife* (New York: Alfred A. Knopf, 1983).

[37]Piercy, "Doing It Differently," in *To Be of Use* (New York: Doubleday, 1974).

[38]Piercy, *Stone, Paper, Knife*, pp. 114–15.

[39]Piercy, "The name I call you," in ibid., p. 97.

iv

Robert Nozick

Love's Bond

Robert Nozick is Arthur Kingsley Porter Professor of Philosophy at Harvard University and the author, most recently, of Philosophical Explanations *and* The Examined Life.

The general phenomenon of love encompasses romantic love, the love of a parent for a child, love of one's country, and more. What is common to all love is this: Your own well-being is tied up with that of someone (or something) you love. When a bad thing happens to a friend, it happens to her and you feel sad for her; when something good happens, you feel happy for her. When something bad happens to one you love, though, something bad also happens *to you*. (It need not be exactly the same bad thing. And I do not mean that one cannot also love a friend.) If a loved one is hurt or disgraced, you are hurt; if something wonderful happens to her, you feel better off. Not every gratification of a loved one's preference will make you feel better off, though; her well-being, not merely a preference of hers, has to be at stake. (Her well-being as who perceives it, she or you?) When love is not present, changes in other people's well-being do not, in general, change your own. You will be moved when others suffer in a famine and will contribute to help; you may be haunted by their plight, but you need not feel you yourself are worse off.

This extension of your own well-being (or ill-being) is what marks all the different kinds of love: the love of children, the love of parents, the love of one's people, of one's country. Love is not necessarily a matter of caring equally or more about someone else than about yourself. These loves are large, but love in some amount is present when your well-being is affected to whatever extent (but in the same direction) by another's. As the other fares, so (to some extent) do you. The people you love are included inside your boundaries, their well-being is your own.[1]

Being "in love," infatuation, is an intense state that displays familiar features: almost always thinking of the person; wanting constantly to touch and to be together; excitement in the other's presence; losing sleep; expressing one's feelings through poetry, gifts, or still other ways to delight the beloved; gazing deeply into each other's eyes; candlelit dinners; feeling that short separations are long; smiling foolishly when remembering actions and remarks of the other; feeling that the other's minor foibles are delightful; experiencing joy at having found the other and at being found by the other; and (as Tolstoy depicts Levin in *Anna Karenina* as he learns Kitty loves him) finding *everyone* charming and nice, and thinking they all must sense one's happiness. Other concerns and responsibilities become minor background details in the story of the romance, which becomes the predominant foreground event of life. (When major public responsibilities such as commanding Rome's armies or being king of England are put aside, the tales engross.) The vividness of the relationship can carry artistic or myth is proportions — lying together like figures in a painting, jointly living a new tale from Ovid. Familiar, too, is what happens when the love is not equally reciprocated: melancholy, obsessive rumination on what went wrong, fantasies about its being set right, lingering in places to catch a glimpse of the person, making telephone calls to hear the other's voice, finding that all other activities seem flat, occasionally having suicidal thoughts.

However and whenever infatuation begins, if given the opportunity it transforms itself into continuing romantic love or else it disappears. With this continuing romantic love, it feels to the two people that they have united to form and constitute a new entity in the world, what might be called a *we*.[2] You can be in romantic love with someone, however, without actually forming a *we* with her or him — that other person might not be in love with you. Love, romantic love, is *wanting* to form a *we* with that particular person, feeling, or perhaps wanting, that particular person to be the right one for you to form a *we* with, and also wanting the other to feel the same way about you. (It would be kinder if the realization that the other person is not the right one with whom to form a *we* always and immediately terminated the desire to form it.) The desire to form a *we* with that other person is not simply something that goes along with romantic love, something that contingently happens when love does. That desire is intrinsic to the nature of love, I think; it is an important part of what love intends.

In a *we*, the two people are not bound physically like Siamese twins; they can be in distant places, feel differently about things, carry on different occupations. In what sense, then, do these people together constitute a new entity, a *we*? That new entity is created by a new web of relationships between them which makes them no longer so separate. Let me describe some features of this web; I will begin with two that have a somewhat cold and political-science sound.

First, the defining feature we mentioned which applies to love in general: Your own well-being is tied up with that of someone you love romantically. Love, then, among other things, can place you at risk. Bad things that happen to your loved one happen to you. But so too do good things; moreover, someone who loves you helps you with care and comfort to meet vicissitudes — not out of selfishness although her doing so does, in part, help maintain her own well-being too. Thus, love places a floor under your well-being; it provides insurance in the face of fate's blows. (Would economists explain some features of selecting a mate as the rational pooling of risks?)

People who form a *we* pool not only their well-being but also their autonomy. They limit or curtail their own decision-making power and rights; some decisions can no longer be made alone. Which decisions these are will be parceled differently by different couples: where to live, how to live, who friends are and how to see them, whether to have children and how many, where to travel, whether to go to the movies that night and what to see. Each transfers some previous rights to make certain decisions unilaterally into a joint pool; somehow, decisions will be made together about how to be together. If your well-being so closely affects and is affected by another's, it is not surprising that decisions that importantly affect well-being, even in the first instance primarily your own, will no longer be made alone.[3]

The term *couple* used in reference to people who have formed a *we* is not accidental. The two people also view themselves as a new and continuing unit, and they present that face to the world. They want to be perceived publicly as a couple, to express and assert their identity as a couple in public. Hence those homosexual couples unable to do this face a serious impediment.

To be part of a *we* involves having a new identity, an additional one. This does *not* mean that you no longer have any individual identity or that your sole identity is as part of the *we*. However, the individual identity you did have will become altered. To have this new identity is to enter a certain psychological stance; and each party in the *we* has this stance toward the other. Each becomes psychologically part of the other's identity. How can we say more exactly what this means? To say that something is part of your identity when, if that thing changes or is lost, you feel like a different person, seems only to reintroduce the very notion of identity that needs to be explained. Here is something more helpful: To love someone might be, in part, to devote alertness to their well-being and to your connection with them. (More generally, shall we say that something is part of your identity when you continually make it one of your few areas of special alertness?) There are empirical tests of alertness in the case of your own separate identity—for example, how you hear your name mentioned through the noise of a conversation you were not consciously attending to; how a word that resembles your name "jumps out" from the page. We might find similar tests to check for that alertness involved in loving someone. For example, a person in a *we* often is considerably more worried about the dangers of traveling—air crashes or whatever—when the other is traveling alone than when both travel together or when he himself or she herself is traveling alone; it seems plausible that a person in a *we* is alert, in general, to dangers to the other that would necessitate having to go back to a single individual identity, while these are made especially salient by a significant physical separation. Other criteria for the formation of a joint identity also might be suggested, such as a certain kind of division of labor. A person in a *we* might find himself coming across something interesting to read yet leaving it for the other person, not because he himself would not be interested in it but because the other would be more interested, and one of them reading it is sufficient for it to be registered by the wider identity now shared, the *we*. If the couple breaks up, they then might notice themselves reading all those things directly; the other person no longer can do it *for them*. (The list of criteria for the *we* might continue on to include something we discuss later, not seeking to "trade up" to another partner.) Sometimes the existence of the *we* can be very palpable. Just as a reflective person can walk along the street in friendly internal dialogue with himself, keeping himself company, so can one be with a loved person who is not physically present, thinking what she would say, conversing with her, noticing things as she would, for her, because she is not there to notice, saying things to others that she would say, in her tone of voice, carrying the full *we* along.

If we picture the individual self as a closed figure whose boundaries are continuous and solid, dividing what is inside from what is outside, then we might diagram the *we* as two figures with the boundary line between them erased where they come together. (Is that the traditional heart shape?) The unitive aspects of sexual experience, two persons flowing together and intensely merging, mirror and aid the formation of the *we*. Meaningful work, creative activity, and development can change the shape of the self. Intimate bonds change the boundaries of the self and alter its *topology*—romantic love in one way and friendship (as we shall see) in another.

The individual self can be related to the *we* it identifies with in two different ways. It can see the *we* as a very important *aspect* of itself, or it can see itself as part of the *we*, as contained within it. It may be that men more often take the former view, women the latter. Although both see the *we* as extremely important for the self, most men might draw the circle of themselves containing the circle of the *we* as an aspect *within* it, while most women might draw the circle of themselves within the circle of the *we*. In either case, the *we* need not consume an individual self or leave it without any autonomy.

Each person in a romantic *we* wants to possess the other completely; yet each also needs the other to be an independent and nonsubservient person. Only someone who continues to possess a nonsubservient autonomy can be an apt partner in a joint identity that enlarges and enhances your individual one. And, of course, the other's well-being—something you care about—requires that nonsubservient autonomy too. Yet at the same time there is the desire to possess the other *completely*. This does not have to stem from a desire to dominate the other person, I think. What you need and want is to possess the other as completely as you do your own identity. This is an expression of the fact that you *are* forming a new joint identity with him or her. Or, perhaps, this desire just *is* the desire to form an identity with the other. Unlike Hegel's description of the unstable dialectic between the master and the slave, though, in a romantic *we* the autonomy of the other and complete possession too are reconciled in the formation of a joint and wondrous enlarged identity for both.

The heart of the love relationship is how the lovers view it from the inside, how they feel about their partner and about themselves within it, and the particular ways in which they are good *to* each other. Each person in love delights in the other, and also in giving delight; this often expresses itself in being playful together. In receiving adult love, we are held worthy of being the primary object of the most intense love, something we were not given in the childhood oedipal triangle.[4] Seeing the other happy with us and made happy through our love, we become happier with ourselves.

To be englowed by someone's love, it must be we ourselves who are loved, not a whitewashed version of ourselves, not just a portion. In the complete intimacy of love, a partner knows us as we are, fully. It is no reassurance to be loved by someone ignorant of those traits and features we feel might make us unlovable. Sometimes these are character traits or areas of incompetence, clumsiness, or ignorance; sometimes these are personal bodily features. Complex are the ways parents make children uncomfortable about sites of pleasure or elimination, and these feelings can be soothed or transformed in the closest attentive and loving sexual intimacy. In the full intimacy of love, the full person is known and cleansed and accepted. And healed.

To be made happy with yourself by being loved, it must be you who is loved, not some feature such as your money. People want, as they say, to be loved "for themselves." You are loved for something else when what you are loved for is a peripheral part of your own self-image or identity. However, someone for whom money, or the ability to make it, was central to his identity, or for whom good looks or great kindness or intelligence was, might not be averse to love's being prompted by these characteristics. You can fall in love with someone because of certain characteristics and you can continue to delight in these; but eventually you must love the person himself, and not *for* the characteristics, not, at any rate, for any delimited list of them. But what does this mean, exactly?

We love the person when being together with that person is a salient part of our identity as we think of it: "being with Eve," "being with Adam," rather than "being with someone who is (or has) such-and-such. . . ." How does this come about? Characteristics must have played some important role, for otherwise why was not a different person loved just as well? Yet if we continue to be loved "for" the characteristics, then the love seems conditional, something that might change or disappear if the characteristics do. Perhaps we should think of love as like imprinting in ducks, where a duckling will attach itself to the first sizable moving object it sees in a certain time period and follow that as its mother. With people, perhaps characteristics set off the imprint of love, but then the person is loved in a way that is no longer based upon retaining those characteristics. This will be helped if the love is based at first upon a wide range of characteristics; it begins as conditional, contingent upon the loved person's having these desirable characteristics, yet given their range and tenacity, it is not insecure.

However, love between people, unlike imprinting with ducks, is not unalterable. Though no longer dependent upon the particular characteristics that set it off, it *can* be overcome over time by new and sufficiently negative other characteristics. Or perhaps by a new imprinting onto another person. Yet this alteration will not be sought by someone within a *we*. If someone were loved "for" certain desirable or valuable characteristics, on the other hand, then if someone else came along who had those characteristics to a greater extent, or other even more valuable characteristics, it seems you should love this new person more. And in that case, why merely wait for a "better" person to turn up; why not actively seek to "trade up" to someone with a "higher score" along valuable dimensions? (Plato's theory is especially vulnerable to these questions, for there it is the Form of Beauty that is the ultimate and appropriate object of love; any particular person serves merely as a bearer of characteristics that awaken in the lover a love of the Form, and hence any such person should be replaceable by a better awakener.)

A readiness to trade up, looking for someone with "better" characteristics, does not fit with an attitude of love. An illuminating view should explain why not, yet why, nevertheless, the attitude of love is not irrational. One possible and boring explanation is economic in form. Once you have come to know a person well, it would take a large investment of time and energy to reach the comparable point with another person, so there is a barrier to switching. (But couldn't the other person promise a greater return, even taking into account the new costs of investment?) There is uncertainty about a new person; only after long time and experience together, through arguments and crises, can one come to know a person's trustworthiness, reliability, resiliency, and compassion in hardships. Investigating another candidate for coupledom, even an apparently promising one, is likely eventually to reach a negative conclusion and it probably will necessitate curtailing or ending one's current coupled state. So it is unwise to seek to trade up from a reasonably satisfactory situation; the energy you'd expend in search might better be invested in improving your current *we*.

These counsels of economic prudence are not silly—far from it—but they are external. According to them, nothing about the nature of love itself focuses upon the particular individual loved or involves an unwillingness to substitute another; rather, the likelihood of losses from the substitution is what militates against it. We can see why, if the economic analysis were so, we would welcome someone's directing an attitude of love toward us that includes commitment to a particular person, and we can see why we might have to trade the offering or semblance of such an attitude in order to receive it. But why would we want actually to give such a commitment to a particular person, shunning all other partners? What special value is reached through such a love relationship committed to particularism but in no other way? To add that we care about our partners and so do not want to cause them hurt by replacing them is true, yet does not answer the question fully.

Economic analysis might even provide somewhat more understanding. Repeated trading with a fixed partner with special resources might make it

rational to develop in yourself specialized assets for trading with that partner (and similarly on the partner's part toward you); and this specialization
gives some assurance that you will continue to trade *with that party* (since
the invested resources could be worth much less in exchanges with any
third party). Moreover, to shape yourself and specialize so as to better fit
and trade with that partner, and therefore to do so less well with others, you
will want some commitment and guarantee that the party will continue to
trade with you, a guarantee that goes beyond the party's own specialization
to fit you. Under some conditions it will be economically advantageous for
two such trading firms to combine into *one* firm, with all allocations now
becoming internal. Here at last we come to something like the notion of a
joint identity.

The intention in love is to form a *we* and to identify with it as an extended self, to identify one's fortunes in large part with its fortunes. A willingness to trade up, to destroy the very *we* you largely identify with, would
then be a willingness to destroy your self in the form of your own extended
self. One could not, therefore, intend to sink into another *we* unless one
had ceased to identify with a current one—unless, that is, one had already
ceased to love. Even in that case, the intention to form the new *we* would be
an intention to *then* no longer be open to trading up. It is intrinsic to the
notion of love, and to the *we* formed by it, that there is not that willingness
to trade up. One is no more willing to find another partner, even one with a
"higher score," than to destroy the personal self one identifies with in order
to allow another, possibly better, but discontinuous self to replace it. (This
is not to say one is unwilling to improve or transform oneself.) Perhaps here
lies one function of infatuation, to pave and smooth the way to uniting in a
we; it provides enthusiasm to take on over the hurdles of concern for one's
own autonomy, and it provides an initiation into *we*-thinking too, by constantly occupying the mind with thoughts of the other and of the two of you
together. A more cynical view than mine might see infatuation as the temporary glue that manages to hold people together until they are stuck.

Part of the process by which people soften their boundaries and move
into a *we* involves repeated expression of the desire to do so, repeatedly telling each other that they love each other. Their statement often will be tentative, subject to withdrawal if the other does not respond with similar
avowals. Holding hands, they walk into the water together, step by step.
Their caution may become as great as when two suspicious groups or
nations—Israel and the Palestinians might be an example—need to recognize the legitimacy of one another. Neither wants to recognize if the other

does not, and it also will not suffice for each to announce that it will recognize if the other one does also. For each then will have announced a conditional recognition, contingent upon the other's unconditional recognition. Since neither one has offered this last, they haven't yet gotten started. Neither will it help if each says it will recognize conditional upon the other's conditional recognition: "I'll recognize you if you'll recognize me if I'll recognize you." For here each has given the other a three-part conditional announcement, one which is contingent upon, and goes into operation only when there exists, a two-part conditional announcement from the other party; so neither one has given the other exactly what will trigger that other's recognition, namely a two-part announcement. So long as they both symmetrically announce conditionals of the same length and complexity, they will not be able to get started. Some asymmetry is needed, then, but it need not be that either one begins by offering unconditional recognition. It would be enough for the first to offer the three-part recognition (which is contingent upon the other's simple two-part conditional recognition), and for the second to offer the two-part conditional recognition. The latter triggers the first to recognize outright and this, in turn, triggers the second to do the same. Between lovers, it never becomes this complicated explicitly. Neither makes the nested announcement "I will love you if you will love me if I will love you," and if either one did, this would not (to put it mildly) facilitate the formation of a *we*. Yet the frequency of their saying to each other, "I love you," and their attention to the other's response, may indicate a nesting that is implicit and very deep, as deep as the repeated triggering necessary to overcome caution and produce the actual and unconditional formation of the *we*.

Even after the *we* is formed, its motion is Aristotelian rather than Newtonian, maintained by frequent impetus. The avowals of love may not stop, and neither may romantic gestures, those especially apt actions, breaking the customary frame, that express and symbolize one's attachment to the *we* or, occurring earlier, the desire to form it.

Granting that a willingness to trade up is incompatible with love and with the formation of a *we* with a particular person, the question becomes one of whether it is rational to love in that particular way. There is the alternative of serious and significant personal ties without a joint identity, after all — friendships and sexual relationships, for instance. An answer could be given by the long and obvious list of the things and actions and emotions especially made possible and facilitated by the *we*. It is not unreasonable to want these, hence not irrational to enter into a *we* including forgoing the option of trading up. Yet it distorts romantic love to view it through the lens of the egoistic question "What's in it for me?" What we want when we are in love is to be with that person. What we want is to be with her or him — not *to be someone who is with her or him*. When we are with the other person, to be sure, we are someone who is with that person, but the object of our desire is not being that kind of someone. We want to make the other person happy, and also, but less so, to be the kind of person who makes her or him happy. It is a question of the emphasis, of how we describe what we want and seek — to use the philosophers' language, a question of the intentional object of our desire.

The way the egoistic question distorts romantic love is by switching the focus of attention from the relation between the lovers to the way each lover in the relation is. I do not mean that the way they are then is unimportant; how good reciprocated romantic love is for us is part of the reason why we desire and value it. But the central fact about love is the relation between the lovers. The central concern of lovers, as lovers, what they dwell upon and nurture, is the other person, and the relation between the two of them, not their own state. Of course, we cannot completely abstract a relation from whatever stands in it. (Contemporary extensional logic treats a relation simply as a set of the ordered pairs of things that — as we would say — stand in the relation.) And in fact, the particularity of a romantic relation does arise from the character of the lovers and then enhances that. Yet what is most salient to each is the other person and what holds between the two of them, not themselves as an endpoint of the relation. There is a difference between wanting to hug someone and using them as an opportunity for yourself to become a hugger.

The desire to have love in one's life, to be part of a *we* someday, is not the same as loving a particular person, wanting to form a *we* with that person in particular. In the choice of a particular partner, reasons can play a significant role, I think. Yet in addition to the merits of the other person and her or his qualities, there also is the question of whether the thought of forming a *we* with that person brings excitement and delight. Does that identity seem a wonderful one for you to have? Will it be *fun*? Here the answer is as complicated and mysterious as your relation to your own separate identity. Neither case is completely governed by reasons, but still we might hope that our choices do meet what reasoned standards there are. (The desire to continue to feel that the other is the right partner in your *we* also helps one surmount the inevitable moments in life together when that feeling itself becomes bruised.) The feeling that there is just "one right person"

in the world for you, implausible beforehand—what lucky accident made
that one unique person inhabit your century?—becomes true after the *we* is
formed. Now your identity is wrapped up in that particular *we* with that
particular person, so for the particular *you* you now are, there *is* just one
other person who is right.

In the view of a person who loves someone romantically, there couldn't
be anyone else who was better as a partner. He might think that person he
is in love with could be better somehow—stop leaving toothpaste in the sink
or whatever—but any description he could offer of a better mate would be
a description of his mate changed, not one of somebody *else*. No one else
would do, no matter what her qualities. Perhaps this is due to the particularity of the qualities you come to love, not just a sense of humor but that
particular one, not just some way of looking mock-stern but that one. Plato
got the matter reversed, then; as love grows you love not general aspects or
traits but more and more particular ones, not intelligence in general but
that particular mind, not kindness in general but those particular ways of
being kind. In trying to imagine a "better" mate, a person in romantic love
will require her or him to have a very particular constellation of very particular traits and—leaving aside various "science fiction" possibilities—no
other person *could* have precisely those traits; therefore, any imagined person will be the same mate (perhaps) somewhat changed, not somebody
else. (If that same mate actually alters, though, the romantic partner may
well come to love and require that new constellation of particulars.) Hence,
a person in romantic love *could not* seek to "trade up"—he would have to
seek out the very same person. A person not in love might seek someone
with certain traits, yet after finding someone, even (remarkably) a person
who has the traits sought, if he loves that person she will show those traits in
a particularity he did not initially seek but now has come to love—her particular versions of these traits. Since a romantic mate eventually comes to
be loved, not for any general dimensions or "score" on such dimensions—
that, if anything, gets taken for granted—but for his or her own particular
and nonduplicable way of embodying such general traits, a person in love
could not make any coherent sense of his "trading up" to *another*.

This does not yet show that a person could not have many such different focused desires, just as she might desire to read this particular book and
also that one. I believe that the romantic desire is to form a *we* with that
particular person *and* with no other. In the strong sense of the notion of
identity involved here, one can no more be part of many *wes* which constitute one's identity than one can simultaneously have many individual iden-

428   tities. (What persons with multiple personality have is not many identities but not quite one.) In a *we*, the people *share* an identity and do not simply each have identities that are enlarged. The desire to share not only our life but our very identity with another marks our fullest openness. What more central and intimate thing could we share?

The desire to form a *we* with that person and no other includes a desire for that person to form one with you yourself and with no other; and so after sexual desire links with romantic love as a vehicle for its expression, and itself becomes more intense thereby, the mutual desire for sexual monogamy becomes almost inevitable, to mark the intimacy and uniqueness of forming an identity with that one particular person by directing what is the most intense physical intimacy toward her or him alone.

It is instructive here to consider friendship, which too alters and recontours an individual's boundaries, providing a distinct shape and character to the self. The salient feature of friendship is *sharing*. In sharing things— food, happy occasions, football games, a concern with problems, events to celebrate—friends especially want these to be had together; while it might constitute something good when each person has the thing separately, friends want that it be had or done by both (or all) of them *together*. To be sure, a good thing does get magnified for you when it is shared with others, and some things can be more fun when done together—indeed, fun, in part, is just the sharing and taking of delight in something together. Yet in friendship the sharing is not desired simply to enlarge our individual benefits.

The self, we shall see later, can be construed as an appropriative mechanism, one that moves from reflexive awareness of things to *sole* possession of them. The boundaries between selves get constituted by the specialness of this relation of possession and ownership—in the case of psychological items, this generates the philosophical "problem of other minds." Things shared with friends, however, do not stand in a unique and special relationship to any one self as its sole possession; we join with friends in having them and, to that extent at least, our selves and theirs overlap or the boundaries between them are less sharp. The very same things— experiences, activities, conversations, problems, objects of focus or of amusement—are part of us both. We each then are related closely to many things that another person also has an equally close relationship to. We therefore are not separate selves—not so separate anyway. (Should we diagram friendship as two circles that overlap?)

A friendship does not exist *solely* for further purposes, whether a political movement's larger goals, an occupational endeavor, or simply the participant's separate and individual benefits. Of course, there can be many further benefits that flow within friendship and from it, benefits so familiar as not to need listing. Aristotle held one of these to be most central; a friend, he said, is a "second self" who is a means to your own self-awareness. (In his listing of the virtuous characteristics one should seek in a friend, Aristotle takes your parents' view of who your friends should be.) Nevertheless, a relationship is a friendship to the extent that it shares activities for no further purpose than the sharing of them.

People seek to engage in sharing beyond the domain of personal friendship also. One important reason we read newspapers, I think, is not the importance or intrinsic interest of the news; we rarely take action whose direction depends upon what we read there, and if somehow we were shipwrecked for ten years on an isolated island, when we returned we would want a summary of what had happened meanwhile, but we certainly would not choose to peruse the back newspapers of the previous ten years. Rather, we read newspapers because we want to *share* information with our fellows, we want to have a range of information in common with them, a common stock of mental contents. We already share with them a geography and a language, and also a common fate in the face of large-scale events. That we also desire to share the daily flow of information shows how very intense our desire to share is.

Nonromantic friends do not, in general, share an *identity*. In part, this may be because of the crisscrossing web of friendships. The friend of your friend may be your acquaintance, but he or she is not necessarily someone you are close to or would meet with separately. As in the case of multiple bilateral defense treaties among nations, conflicts of action and attachment can occur that make it difficult to delineate any larger entity to which one safely can cede powers and make the bearer of a larger identity. Such considerations also help explain why it is not feasible for a person simultaneously to be part of multiple romantic couples (or of a trio), even were the person to desire this. Friends want to share the things they do *as* a sharing, and they think, correctly, that friendship is valuable partly *because* of its sharing—perhaps specially valuable because, unlike the case of romantic love, this valued sharing occurs *without* any sharing of identity.

We might pause over one mode of sharing that, while it is not done primarily for its own sake, produces a significant sense of solidarity. That is participating with others in joint action directed toward an external goal—perhaps a political cause or reform movement or occupational project or team sport or artistic performance or scientific endeavor—where the participants feel the pleasures of joint and purposeful participation in something really worthwhile. Perhaps there is a special need for this among young adults as they leave the family, and that in part constitutes youth's "idealism." Linked with others toward a larger joint purpose, *joined* with them at the same node of an effectual casual chain, one's life is no longer simply private. In such a way citizens might think of themselves as creating together, and sharing, a memorable civilization.

We can prize romantic love and the formation of a *we*, without denying that there may be extended times, years even, when an adult might best develop alone. It is not plausible, either, to think that every single individual, at some or another time in his life, would be most enhanced as part of a romantically loving *we*—that Buddha, Socrates, Jesus, Beethoven, or Gandhi would have been. This may be, in part, because the energy necessary to sustain and deepen a *we* would have been removed from (thereby lessening) these individuals' activities. But there is more to say. The particular vivid way these individuals defined themselves would not fit easily within a romantic *we*; their special lives would have had to be very different. Of course, a *we* often falls short of its best, so a prudent person might seek (or settle for) other modes of personal relationship and connection. Yet these extraordinary figures remind us that even at its best a *we* constitutes a particular formation of identity that involves forgoing some extraordinary possibilities. (Or is it just that these figures needed equally extraordinary mates?)

Just as the identity of the self continues over an extended period of time, so too is there the desire for the *we* to continue; part of identifying fully with the *we* is intending that it continue. Marriage marks a full identification with that *we*. With this, the *we* enters a new stage, building a sturdier structure, knitting itself together more fully. Being a couple is taken as given though not for granted. No longer focusing upon whether they *do* constitute an enduring *we*, the partners now are free confidently to build together a life with its own focus and directions. The *we* lives their life together. As egg and sperm come together, two biographies have become one. The couple's first child is their union—their earlier history was prenatal.

A *we* is not a new physical entity in the world, whether or not it is a new ontological one. However, it may want to give its web of love relationships a physical incarnation. That is one thing a home is about—an environment that reflects and symbolizes how the couple feel (and what they do) together, the spirit in which they are together; this also, of course, makes it a happy place for them to be. In a different way, and to a much greater extent, children can constitute a physical realization of the parents' love, an incarnation in the world of the valuable extended self the two of them have created. And children might be loved and delighted in, in part as this physical representation of the love between the parents. However, of course and obviously, the children are not merely an adjunct to the parents' love, as either a representation of it or a means of heightening it; they primarily are people to be cared for, delighted in, and loved for themselves.

Intimate bonds change the contours and boundaries of the self, altering its topology: in love, as we have seen, in the sharings of friendship, in the intimacy of sexuality. Alterations in the individual self's boundaries and contours also are a goal of religious quest: expanding the self to include all of being (Indian Vedanta), eliminating the self (Buddhism), or merging with the divine. There also are modes of general love for all of humanity, often religiously enjoined—recall how Dostoyevsky depicts Father Zossima in *The Brothers Karamazov*—that greatly alter the character and contours of the self, now no longer so appropriately referred to as "individual."

It may not be an accident that people rarely do simultaneously combine building a romantic *we* with a spiritual quest. It seems impossible to proceed full strength with more than one major alteration in the self's topology at a time. Nevertheless, it may well be important at times to be engaged in *some* or another mode of change in the boundaries and topology of the self, different ones at different times. Any such change need not be judged solely by how it substantively feeds back into the individual self, though. The new entity that is created or contoured, with its own boundaries and topology, has its own evaluations to make. An individual self justifiably might be proud to be supple enough to enter into these changes and exfoliate them, yet its perspective before the changes does not provide the only relevant standard. It *is* in the interests of an individual sperm or egg cell to unite to form a new organism, yet we do not continue to judge the new life by that gamete's particular interests. In love's bond, we metamorphose.

Notes

[1] A somewhat sharper criterion can be formulated of when another's well-being is *directly* part of your own. This occurs when (1) you say and believe your well-being is affected by significant changes in hers; (2) your well-being is affected in the same *direction* as hers, an improvement in her well-being producing an improvement in your own, a decrease, a decrease; (3) you not only judge yourself worse off, but feel some emotion appropriate to that state; (4)

you are affected by the change in *her* well-being directly, merely through knowing about it, and not because it symbolically represents to you something else about yourself, a childhood situation or whatever; (5) (and this condition is especially diagnostic) your *mood* changes: you now have different occurrent feelings and changed dispositions to have particular other emotions; and (6) this change in mood is somewhat enduring. Moreover, (7) you have this general tendency or disposition toward a person or object, to be thus affected; you *tend* to be thus affected by changes in that person's well-being.

²For a discussion of love as the formation of a *we*, see Robert Solomon, *Love* (Garden City, N.Y.: Anchor Books, 1981).

³This curtailment of unilateral decision-making rights extends even to a decision to end the romantic love relationship. This decision, if any, you would think you could make by yourself. And so you can, but only in certain ways at a certain pace. Another kind of relation might be ended because you feel like it or because you find it no longer satisfactory, but in a love relationship the other party "has a vote." This does not mean a permanent veto; but the other party has a right to have his or her say, to try to repair, to be convinced. After some time, to be sure, one party may insist on ending the relationship even without the other's consent, but what they each have forgone, in love, is the right to act unilaterally and swiftly.

⁴Another Greek tale, that of Telemachus at home with Penelope while Odysseus wanders, provides a different picture of the family triangle's character. A father is a needed protector, not just someone to compete with for the mother's love. If the mother is as attractive as the child thinks, in the absence of the father other suitors will present themselves before her. And unlike the father, who will not kill the competitive child or maim him (despite what the psychoanalytic literature depicts as the child's anxieties), these suitors *are* his enemies. Telemachus *needs* his father—to maintain the *safe* triangle—and so he sets out to find him.

Annette Baier

Unsafe Loves

Annette Baier is professor of philosophy at the University of Pittsburgh and the author of Postures of the Mind: Essays on Mind and Morals *(1985) and* A Progress of Sentiments *(1988).*

> Destroy love and friendship; what remains in the world worth accepting?
> *David Hume*[1]

What is it to love another person, and is it ever a good idea? The ones who have told us most or most insightful things about love are poets and novelists. Philosophers, although they are supposed to be lovers of a sort, tend to be all thumbs when it comes to handling love. But since I am only a philosopher I will look at some of their attempts. According to a recent book-length philosophical analysis of love, "what makes love unusual among the emotions is the human inability to do without it."[2] If this is right, then let us hope that love can be a good thing for us, otherwise it will have to count as an unfortunate addiction, something we cannot do without but that does not bring us anything positively good, either, and that may bring us much sorrow. Robert Brown, the philosopher I quoted, thinks it does usually bring "an immense amount of satisfaction" and yet "often produces as much pain as pleasure. For love is always subject to frustration and rejection, and commonly bound together with such dangerous emotions as jealousy, hate, fear."[3] We could in a sense "do without" those emotions—that is, we might prefer to be without them, but we would not, Brown believes, choose to be without the love that commonly brings them. Nor is it only emotions dangerous to our fellows, the aggression-feeding emotions of jealousy, hate, and fear of rivals that love commonly brings with it. There are also those more "dangerous" to the lover than to others, paralyzing grief or reckless despair at the loss or death of loved ones, retreat into a sort of psychic hibernation when cut off from "news" of them, crippling anxiety when they are in danger, helpless anguish when they are in pain, crushing guilt when one has harmed them, deadly shame when one fails them. All of these "dangers" to the lover must be weighed against that immense satisfaction love can bring. And then there are the dangers to the ones who are loved—the danger of overprotection, of suffocation, of loss of independence, toughness and self-reliance. When love is reciprocal each faces the dangers of lovers combined with those of beloveds. As we catalog the risks of loving, we may begin to sympathize with the conclusion of Jerome Shaffer, who in an article "assessing" the role of emotions in our lives comes down against the lot of them, and in particular against love: "The world might have become a better place when Scrooge found love, but perhaps not in the case of Anna Karenina, and probably not in the case of King Kong. Love like other emotions has no general claim to value or importance in our lives."[4]

Nor is Shaffer alone among what we might call the philosophical "mis-amorists," the distrusters of the claims of love. Kant too more or less advises us to keep ourselves to ourselves, *not* to link our fate unnecessarily closely with that of other persons, to remain detached—respecting others, but not getting too mixed up in their lives. Kant does recognize a moral duty of philanthropy, love of our fellows, yet he construes this not as involving feeling or emotion, but solely as goodwill, benevolence, willingness to do things for others, to draw close enough to them to help them. Kant says that in the moral world there is an analogy to the attraction and repulsion that operate in the physical world. "The principle of *mutual love* admonishes men constantly to *come nearer* to one another; that of the respect which they owe each other, to keep themselves at a *distance* from one another."[5] Although he finds room for a duty of love as well as a duty of respect, a duty to draw close and a duty to keep one's distance, his way of harmonizing them is to weaken the "law of love" into a duty to help one's neighbor, with the understanding that one's neighbor does *not* want to be any closer to one—one helps him best by helping him keep his self-respect, keep his sense that he merits respect, is a person one would hesitate to come too close to. So, says Kant, if we express our philanthropy by being generous to a poorer person, "it is our duty to behave as if our help is either what is merely due him, or but a slight service of love, and so to spare him humiliation and maintain his self respect."[6] This recognizes another danger in love, or rather in being loved—the danger of humiliation, of being seen to need the services of others. Beware lovers bearing gifts—they may be gifts of what you need!

Kant finds another danger closely associated with humiliation lurking in the vicinity of love, especially of emotional and felt love—the danger of self-exposure and vulnerability to harm from others. He speaks in his *Lectures on Ethics* of friendship as "a man's refuge in this world from his distrust of his fellows,"[7] and advocates caution in taking such refuge. "We must so conduct ourselves towards a friend that there is no harm done if he should turn into an enemy."[8] Kant grants that "we all have a strong impulse to disclose ourselves, and enter wholly into fellowship; and such self-revelation is further a human necessity for the correction of our judgments. To have a friend whom we know to be frank and loving, neither false nor spiteful, is to have one who will help us to correct our judgment when it is mistaken. This is the whole end of man, through which he can enjoy his existence. But even between the closest and most intimate of friends there are still things that call for reserve."[9] Reserve is called for, Kant says, as much for the other's sake as for one's own since "we have certain natural frailties which ought to be concealed for the sake of decency, lest humanity be outraged. Even to our best friend we must not reveal ourselves in our natural state as we know it ourselves. To do so would be loathsome."[10]

A great danger in loving friendship, as Kant describes it, is that it will tempt the friends into too great a candor, a candor that is both inconsiderate and imprudent. Polite and prudent reserve, carefully measured "disclosure," is what Kant recommends even toward one's best friends, those toward whom one is frankest and most loving. Kant says that true friendship is merely an Ideal, or an Idea, in Plato's sense. At least twice he quotes the ancient Greek adage, "My dear friends, there are no friends" (once attributing it to Socrates, once to Aristotle). In the real world there are false friends and lovers and ex-friends and lovers, ones who either from carelessness or from spite reveal to others what was disclosed to them alone, whose love is likely to turn to loathing if the once-loved person fails to keep defects secret or at least out of view. In the real world hot-headed intimates turn confidences into weapons; an intimate can "be capable of sending us to the gallows in a moment of passion, while imploring our pardon as soon as he cools down." Kant clearly thinks that the duty of respect, of keeping due distance, trumps the ideal of loving fellowship. "The whole end of man" is correct judgment, not fellowship. Fellowship is merely a means to this end, and a risky one.

Kant's ambivalence about love—his simultaneous acceptance of a "true" and "very necessary" idea of mutual love and friendship and his "misamorism" as far as human love goes, his warnings to us not to expect to find any examples of real love in our experience—is the culmination of a long philosophical tradition, which we could call the theological tradition.

In Plato, in St. Augustine, in Descartes, we get a similar sort of combination of a very strong definition of what the real thing would be, and a claim that no love between human persons will satisfy this definition. All human loves are doomed to failure. At their worst, they degenerate into mutual loathing, betrayal, and enmity; at their best, they are interrupted by death and end in separation and bereavement. The moral, for these "theological" pessimists about human love, is not the very drastic moral that Shaffer draws—that we should try to discover and then to take a medicine that would make us "love-proof"—but rather that we should restrict our love for the "right" object of love, namely God. Love of God will be a sort of live vaccine that will block any riskier loving. We are to find a person who because omnipresent cannot "forsake" us, who because already all-knowing cannot be surprised or shocked at what we reveal of ourselves, who because all powerful has us already in His power, whether or not we give love, so that in loving Him we renounce no independence that we ever had or could have.

Not every variant of this theological tradition, that advises us that love of God is the best love for us, says that it will be in any way a reciprocated love. Even the orthodox Christian version of the tradition, which does say that human love of God is to be a response to God's love for man, cannot say that there is much in common between the way we love God and the way God loves us. For our love is love by the ignorant of a fully knowledgeable one, love by the powerless of an all-powerful one. It would be impossible for us even to try to love God in the way God is claimed to love us— powerfully, knowledgeably, generously; the highest being condescending to love lesser beings. If we were to try to imitate that sort of love it would have to be by ourselves loving less powerful and less knowledgeable beings—our infant children, or our domestic pets. So if we are to try to imitate divine love for us, to let it serve as an ideal or example for us, we will *have* to love someone besides God; we will have to find some even more vulnerable being to love. There is some tension in the Christian story about the sort of reciprocity love at its best involves and about the relation between human love for God and our love for other mortals. If God's love is the best love, *which* of God's loves is the best—that of the Father for other Persons of the Godhead, or that of God for human souls? Which, if any, should we try to imitate?

Tensions in theology are, if Feuerbach and Freud are right, reflections of tensions in our understanding of our own human situation. Love of an all-powerful God may be seen as a displaced version of love of a more powerful human father. Uncertainties about reciprocity, about whether it is appropriate to expect return divine love, and if it is, if that return love should serve as a model for one's own love, will reflect uncertainties about the human father-child relation. Retreat to love of God after disillusion with human adult loves may be a sort of nostalgia for some recalled or fantasized infant security in the strong arms of a loving parent. Thus we can learn something about our own ambivalent attitudes to love by looking at the tensions in the theological tradition, even if we want eventually to demystify it, to bring it back to earth.

Descartes, who can be said to be a heretical adherent of this tradition, gave us a pretty full account of our passion-repertoire and gave love pride of place in his account. He describes it as an emotion that impels us to "join ourselves willingly" to the loved thing or person, and he adds a gloss on this willingness: "I mean the assent by which we consider ourselves henceforth as joined with what we love in such a manner that we take ourselves to be only one part, and the thing loved to be the other."[11] He later adds that in many sorts of love, such as parental love and deep devotion to a nobler person, the lover may take himself to be not the *better* part of the imagined whole, so as not to be afraid of sacrificing himself to save the loved one, even giving his life. But many male lovers take themselves to be the better parts of the unions they make with women and can be ambivalent about any such union, any treating of oneself as mere "part."

Descartes gives an example of such a love when he portrays for us a grief-stricken husband mourning his dead wife, a husband who while he weeps with sincere distress, also experiences "at the same time a secret joy in his innermost soul," and "would be sorry to see her brought to life again."[12] Descartes seems to be ambivalent about love, or at any rate about love of fellow human persons. He defines it in strong and apparently approving tones ("Love can never be too great," he says), but he also seems to endorse a cautious avoidance of it and shows sympathy with the person who rejoices at escape, at regaining his freedom, after experience of the sort of willing union that at least marriage involves. This is not surprising after his sardonic account of adult heterosexual attraction, whose willing endorsement counts as heterosexual love: "Nature . . . brings it about that at a certain age and time we regard ourselves as deficient—as forming only one half of a whole, whose other half must be a person of the other sex. . . . Nature represents, in a confused manner, the acquisition of this other half as the greatest of all goods imaginable."[13]

Descartes says almost nothing about reciprocity in love. He mentions

438   return love only in passing, and Spinoza, who had read him carefully, spells out explicitly what Descartes had implied both by what he said and by what he did not say: that the one who loves the best object of love, namely God, cannot hope for return love, but at best for modest participation in divine self-love. Love of God, on this account, is ultimately a form of prudent withdrawal from human loves, especially sexual ones. Even if it does not lengthen our earthly life, it is at least safe from any nasty surprises of the sort we sometimes get from human loved ones, when their response, even their return love, takes forms that upset, distress, or harm us.

I have labeled Kant's, Descartes's, and Spinoza's accounts of love "theological" and called them "misamorists" as far as love between human beings goes. The common feature is a strong sense that human persons are unlovable. We can love, but only our betters, and our fellow persons are rarely much better. So Kant can suppose that respect depends upon averting one's gaze from the possibly "loathsome" full actuality of the respected person. Friendship and love between human persons is dangerous because it risks mutual knowledge. Descartes, although he does not, like Kant, give such free rein to expressions of disgust for normal human persons, does not encourage us, even when lovers, to expect to be loved. Presented in this (admittedly unsympathetic) way, this sounds pretty sick stuff. What features of the human situation might explain this peculiar theological ideal of love of a superior who must not be expected to love back and this conviction that we are too defect-filled and inferior to be loved once fully known? Were these great philosophers of our tradition the victims of early childhood traumas of parental rejection, of exposure to scorn and contempt? Did they never experience the great satisfactions of reciprocated love between parent and child, or between human lovers? What soured them? Human persons are of course faulty, but roughly equally faulty, so they need not scorn or be disgusted by each other once they know each other. Nor do we have to be perpetually intent on mutual fault finding and shaming—there can be time also for some mutual admiration and some mutual teasing. I am not going to try to diagnose the causes of the misamorism of these philosophers, tempting though it is to speculate, on the basis of what information we have (Descartes's mother's death in his early infancy and his daughter's early death, Spinoza's rejection by his own community, Kant's puritan upbringing). Rather I am going to turn to some less theological thinkers, ones who do not conceive of us primarily as souls in relation to other sinful souls or to a sovereign God, but rather as intelligent mammals, at birth literally "attached" to a mother, who then may feed us at her breast. I turn from the *supernatural* theological philosophers of love to the naturalist philosophers of love, those who take umbilical cords, navels, and other basic anatomical reminders of our mammalian condition more seriously than they take our immortal and sinful souls.[14]

David Hume stands out as a philosopher who gives a purely naturalist account of human love. In his *Treatise of Human Nature* he devotes Part 2 of Book Two (about 70 pages, almost as much space as he gives to causation) to analyzing its forms (and those of hate). What is striking in his account, if we compare it with that of Descartes and Kant, is that he takes the forms of human love to be variants on what he calls "love in animals." (Earlier he had related our reason to "reason in animals," our pride to "pride in animals.") Our biological nature, as well as our social organization, sets the stage for our loving. Hume devotes a section to *Love of relations*. He calls "the tie of blood . . . the strongest tie the mind is capable of," and he associates our understanding of all "relations," in however abstract a sense, with this one "relation of a different kind," the blood tie. He makes some interesting remarks about a child's love for his mother, his limited toleration of brothers and sisters sharing that love, his intolerance of stepfathers, calling these "pretty curious phenomena." He gives a glowing description of the sort of intimacy loving friends, loving relatives, loving parent and child, may have, and of our need for such intimacy. In the company of a loved and trusted intimate, he says, the mind "awakes as from a dream: the blood flows with a new tide: the heart is elevated: and the whole man acquires a vigor which he cannot command in his solitary and calm moments."[15] We rejoice, he says, in the presence of a "Being like ourselves, who communicates to us all the actions of his mind; makes us privy to his inmost sentiments and affections, and lets us see, in the very instant of their production, all the emotions which are caused by any object."[16] Kant might well have been lecturing the ghost of Hume in his warnings about the danger of unguarded intimacy and the likely fate of such unashamed and trusting fools as Hume describes. Hume seems unworried that these candid intimates may find what is revealed "loathsome." Where Kant issues the rule "Don't treat your friends in ways you will regret if and when they cease to be your friends," Hume in fact gives the reverse rule: "Don't treat strangers in ways you will regret should they become your friends."[17] Hume's account of love, and his apparent recommendation of its delights, must seem *reckless* to the Kantian. Risks of betrayal, of looking silly or even loathsome, of getting caught up in others' troubles, of being attacked while your guard is down are not mentioned at all by Hume. For him these risks of love seem to be outweighed by the evil of solitude. He echoes what Seneca and Boethius said, "A perfect solitude is, perhaps, the greatest punishment we can suffer. Every pleasure languishes when enjoy'd apart from company."[18] Is it that Hume does not see the dangers that Kant finds in human loves, or is it that he accepts those risks as a fair price to pay for waking from the bad dream of solitude? "Let all the powers and elements conspire to serve one man . . . the sun rise and set at his command. . . . He will still be miserable till you give him one person at least with whom he may share his happiness and whose esteem and friendship he may enjoy."[19]

Hume seems not to share Kant's worries that close friendship, with the mutual candor that it encourages, will destroy mutual esteem. "Love," in Hume's wide sense, has esteem as one of its forms. To love someone, by Hume's definition, is simply to find something attractive or "fine" in that person. He distinguishes different sorts of love both by the *sort* of fine thing found (power, beauty, wit, good nature) and by the perceived social or biological relationship of the lover to the one in whom he finds "fine" qualities. So we "respect" those we consider our superiors but feel other sorts of love for equals, or for "weaker" ones. Parental love is for those who depend upon us in ways we do not depend on them. Hume thinks adults *do* depend on their children, and on other relatives, in many other ways. Children can be "subjects" of their parents' pride and can sustain their parents' pride, whatever it is taken in, by their sympathy and love. Hume thinks that a person's family's opinion of her matters to her in a special way. "We are most uneasy under the contempt of persons who are both related to us by blood and contiguous in place."[20] He tries to give us an account of love that fits in with his account of proper pride. One of the benefits of mutual love is the mutual sustaining of proper pride.

Hume's account of sexual love is pretty straightforward and brings into prominence a basic biological fact about it that links with his earlier discussion of "the tie of blood." Parental love is the first of love's variants that he discusses, and he ends with "the amorous passion or love betwixt the sexes." What he takes to be distinctive in this form of love, a form which deserves our attention in part "on account of its force and violence," is that it combines three passions—general good will arising out of esteem for "the merit or wit" of the loved person, admiration for the loved one's beauty, and what he calls "the appetite for generation," "the bodily appetite," or lust. Whether or not there is a felt desire for "generation" as such, the satisfaction of this appetite is, at least in the forms of the amorous passion tolerated in Hume's culture,[21] likely to have that result.

Hume, the biologically realistic philosopher of love, puts "generation" pretty squarely in the center of his account of human love (and of his account of marriage as an institution).[22] This love is not merely, as for Descartes, a matter of a willing uniting with one other person to form "a whole," it is also a matter of willingness to jointly generate a third person, as children's love of parents is a response to those who generated them, to parents and progenitors. There is no "one whole"; there are ongoing families and successive generations. Hume does not of course *restrict* love to love between those linked or about to be linked by some "generative" tie (any more than he restricts lust to procreative intent), but he is very clear that, to understand love, we must understand our "blood ties," and the mammalian nature of our "descent" and our genealogy. He discusses the way we like to trace descent and boast of the antiquity of our family; he wonders why we care whether we descend from notable ancestors through the maternal or the paternal line and why we take our father's, not our mother's, family name.[23] One might almost say that Hume is *obsessed*, in his account of love, with the circumstances of human generation. But that comes as a relief after the careful avoidance of or disdain for such "unspiritual" matters that we get in Descartes and in Kant.

Darwin read Hume and quotes him with approval, and Darwin's disciple T. H. Huxley wrote a book about Hume's *Treatise*, with particular praise of its naturalism and particular emphasis on the short chapters on reason, pride, and love in animals. Darwin discusses human love not just in the *Descent of Man* but also in *The Expressions of Emotion in Man and Animals*. Naturally his main focus is on the sexual love that is "generative," and on parent-child love, particularly mother-child love, and its expression. Although he does not find love to have the typical "face" that anger, fear, and disgust have, he does suppose that it shows in the eyes and in the voice, and he suggests that the power of music to rouse emotions may lie in its power to dimly evoke memories in us, race memories of mating cries as well as individual memories of the intonations of soothing motherly voices. Darwin postulated, indeed, that before we were a talking species we were a singing species. Our first songs were without words; later came songs with words, and lastly, intoned sentences. Our first songs would be love songs, but there would also be marching-off-to-the-hunt rhythmic songs, rousing battle hymns, and so on, which exploited the innately expressive power of tone of voice and of repetition of calls. Here Darwin could have called on Descartes for support, for Descartes had both explored the inner and outer bodily effects of love and other emotions (love "speeds the digestion" and produces a warm, steady heat in the chest) and had noted how music stirs emotions and how, for this purpose, the human voice is the best musical instrument.

What Darwin says about mother-child love echoes Hume's discussion of it. It is not so much that there is a special face or posture which is the face of mother love, nor even one voice the voice of mother love. It is rather that there is immediate responsiveness to the *range* of faces and voices that the child displays. Love makes us more *aware* of the emotions of the loved one than we would otherwise be and makes us quicker to make helpful responses. So the face of mother love will be a mobile face—anxiety, relief, pride, contentment will show there, coordinately with the expressed emotions of the child. Similarly, the child will follow the mother's face and voice—love is as much this sort of coordination of emotions between lovers, as itself a special emotion. Hobbes, Descartes, Hume, Darwin, and many others included love on their lists of human emotions, but, like a mood, it seems as much an activator of other emotions and of response to the other's emotion, as itself an emotion. Hume treated sympathy not as a special emotion but as a disposition or "principle" that communicates emotions from person to person—that "spreads" our distress or our joy to sympathetic companions. Love may be as much like sympathy as it is like the emotions that sympathy can spread. It is a *coordination* or mutual involvement of two (or more) persons' emotions, and it is more than sympathy, more than just the duplication of the emotion of each in a sympathetic echo in the other.

A sympathetic person tends to share the sorrows and joys of all her fellows, as far as she is in a position to recognize them. Sympathy increases joys and sorrows in much the same proportion. Only the person whose own personal ratio of joy over sorrow is exceptionally high or who is surrounded only by those whose misery is exceptionally great will "lose" anything by being a sympathetic person, one whose psyche reverberates, in Hume's phrase, to others' fates. A sympathetic person may in an age of mass communication come to bear the world's sorrows on her shoulders, but also share the world's rejoicings (except that they are less fully reported—weep and the TV world weeps with you, laugh and you laugh alone). One's life will be enriched by a capacity for sympathy, and the more enriched the wider the scope of one's sympathy, but the overall balance of joy and sorrow one experiences need not be affected by how prone one is to sympathize in Hume's sense, that is to empathize, with others. Love is different. It *will* make a difference to the balance, and it is risky and "unsafe" precisely because one does not know, cannot know, just how one's life will be affected by the strong sort of involvement in the life of another that it brings. It is "for better, for worse." It is not just that one takes on an extra set of joys and sorrows to one's own—one does that if one has sympathy for a person over a period of time whether or not one loves her. When one loves, one's occasions for joy, sorrow, and other emotions will become "geared" in a more complex way than just sympathy to those of the loved person, and this may indeed affect the balance of joy over sorrow in one's life. The loved person's indifference will hurt, her boredom will disappoint, her premature withdrawal will grieve one. Her enthusiasms also may shock and disturb one, the intensity of her embrace may maim one, the diseases she carries may kill one, and one may know that they are killing one.

Even in the womb the child may be affected not just by the mother's physical state but by her changing emotional states. The child may then show a certain kind of psychophysical "sympathy" to the mother's state of mind. Its states may correlate with her states, but not in the complex coordinated way they will correlate when, say, the mother and child *play* together when the child is about one year old. The response then is not just sympathetic sharing of expressed emotions, it is also appropriate *follow-up* responses to what one knows by sympathy that the other is feeling—mischievous delight at the other's temporary bafflement, a frisson of fear at their feigned aggression, glory in the other's surrender. There will be a heightened ability to anticipate the next emotional move of the other, to watch for it and to be ready for it.

The coordination of emotions between intimates, in fun and in more serious contexts of repentance and forgiveness, is a much more complex matter than just a duplication of the expressed emotion of one in a sympathetic echo-emotion of the other—and indeed it may not even require sympathy on both parts. Some sort of knowing how the other feels that stops short of sympathetic fellow-feeling may be all that is needed for these mutually responsive feelings—just as when the cello replies to the violin in a duo it need not first re-sound the violin's notes. When lovers forgive one another (or one the other) there need not first be felt sympathy with the other's repentance, simply familiarity with that feeling and recognition that this was an occasion for the other to feel it. When lovers laugh at each other's familiar endearing weaknesses—and lovers do laugh at the sorts of weakness that it would be offensive to draw attention to in a stranger—they need not each laugh at *hirself*.[24] Each laughs at the other, but neither need laugh *with* the other, finding lovably ridiculous what the other so finds.

Otherwise love would entail self-love and "self so self-loving were iniquity."[25] We do not invite others to empathize or sympathize with our loving of our beloved,[26] and we do not expect it of the beloved either. "Love me, love my dog," "Love me, try to love my other loved ones," maybe. But not, or only for metaphysical poets, "Love me, love all my loved ones, and so love yourself." As Hume put it, "when we talk of self-love tis not in any proper sense, nor has the sensation it produces anything in common with that tender emotion which is excited by a friend or mistress."[27] Hume may be optimistically ignoring narcissists who do feel tenderly about themselves, but surely he is right that love proper is for another, and what we hope for is that the other *reciprocates*, rather than sympathizes with, our love. So we can find tender amusement in our loved ones' harmless faults without wanting them to be tenderly amused at themselves. Lovers clown for each other or are willing to be cast as clowns, but clowns are not expected to be amused at their own antics. The capacity to laugh at oneself which we welcome in each other is not exactly a capacity to find oneself an amusing spectacle. As it is bad form to laugh at one's own jokes, so it is at least dubious form, incurring risk of a charge of narcissism, to laugh with real amusement at oneself, even on those occasions when one welcomes a lover's amusement. If one laughs with one's lover at oneself and one's defects, it should be untenderly, "against that time, if ever that time come, when I shall see thee frown on my defects."[28] To love is to give another the permission to laugh at one, hopefully tenderly, when no one else, not even oneself, has quite that same permission. One of the risks of love, as Kant rightly saw, was that the permitted laughter may lose its tenderness, may take on more of the tough, unamused, almost sardonic character it is supposed to have when we are sometimes urged by character-improvers to see how ridiculously we are acting and reacting, to do a bit of unfriendly jeering at ourselves. Love complicates the occasions for laughter as greatly as it complicates the occasions for anger, for curiosity, for disappointment, for shame at failure, for sorrow. It adds to the varieties of all of these and so to the degree of delicacy needed for showing the right variety on the right occasion.

Love is not just an emotion people feel toward other people, but also a complex tying together of the emotions that two or a few more people have; it is a special form of emotional interdependence.[29] That love involves some sort of tie, relationship, attachment is a commonplace. Both the theological and the biological accounts relate love the felt emotion to some sort of more-than-emotional tie between persons. For the Christian tradition it is the creator-creature tie which *grounds* love of God, which is a feeling endorsing that ontological attachment. For Descartes, felt love is a will to be or remain attached in a strong, ontological way with a more perfect being. For Hume, Darwin, and after them Freud, one form of felt love, the fundamental form, is grounded in the human child's past, literally physical, tie to a maternal parent, and hers to the child; and other forms of felt love create an actual dependency, at least of emotions and occasions for emotions, which goes beyond any that is "willed" by the lover. The fact of the attachment grounds the feeling of attachment and may exceed the desire for attachment. Love the emotion is not the wish for a relationship, it is the acknowledgment and endorsement of one. Love the tie is not produced by our feelings of love, it is what is endorsed and sustained by them. We may have no say in the coming into existence of the tie — children do not choose their mother, nor she them. Adolescent and adult love is something we are said to "fall" into (and out of), something that happens to us. There may always be some choice about sustaining it, but not always about initiating it. As Richard Wollheim says, we choose our friends, make friendships, but "love is a response to a felt relation,"[30] and one we may have had no say at all about initiating.

It may be objected that this may make sense for mother-infant love, but less good sense for mature sexual love. Surely we *do* initiate sexual relationships (these days it had better be the woman who does the proposing, the man the accepting or refusing). Yes, but as Hume pointed out, sexual desire, or "the appetite for generation" is only *one* component of "the amorous passion." The "felt relation" to which sexual love is a response is not just the temporary and voluntarily entered into "relation" of sexual intercourse. A one-night stand is not the sort of relation whose acknowledgment and endorsement would count as love, otherwise gigolos and other prostitutes would count as lovers. The "relationship" that, when felt and positively responded to, is sexual love is a mutual involvement that is physical, emotional, cognitive, and conative — it is mutual dependency in pleasures, in hopes, in griefs, in intentions for the future. This is not to say that it must be for a very long future — there are "brief loves" that are from the start known to the lovers as likely to be brief. But they are not mere agreements for mutual erotic services for a limited time. (Kant notoriously took marriage to involve such a mutual agreement, for life.) Where people do "use each other" for erotic pleasure, without any other mutual dependency, there all the current advice about "safe sex" will be appropriate, especially as these pleasure-seekers will often welcome the contraceptive "protection" these health protecting measures will also bring. But will *lovers* want safe sex? Their unsafe sex may be a fitting expression of their in any case unsafe love. Risking their own health is something lovers have always done. Think of all the women who died in childbirth, and who in loving knew quite well the chances that they would so die. Think of the venereal and other diseases that spouses got from one another and passed on to their children. Our loved ones inherit from us, and sometimes inherit our diseases. Of course a lover will, if she lovingly can, avoid "communicating" any disease to her loved one and to her child, but if it takes withdrawal from the love relation to do that, then she will not have opted for "safe loving," however "safe" her sexual and other practices.

It is not very "safe" to love another. If safety is what one values most, the womb or the grave are the best places for one, and, between them, one will want the best approximations one can get to these places where one is sheltered from or beyond hurt. One will opt for places where one cannot respond emotionally to the emotions and other states of mind of others, cannot be pleased by their pleasure, disappointed at their lack of pleasure, hurt by their indifference, angry at their failure to be angered by insults, saddened by their choice to withdraw rather than forgivably harm, and so on. There is no safe love.

Should we therefore avoid love? We should of course do what we can to "protect third parties," and in love there are always third parties, future lovers, children who may be born to one of the lovers, their lovers, and their children. Love tends to be generative and cannot be confined to romantic Romeo and Juliet couplings. The mutual love of couples like Romeo and Juliet is not secure from the generations before them, nor are later generations secure from their love. So of course some sort of "third (or fourth or fifth) party insurance" is incumbent on lovers, and they will want health for the children of their love, but neither venereal nor any other kind of safety is something they can promise each other, their future children, nor other persons affected or infected by their love. If all the world (except misamorist philosophers) is to keep loving lovers, it will have to come to accept risk, too, and to be willing to share the risk, and to help care for the victims of the worst risks.

Only in the theological tradition has love ever been thought of as life-prolonging for the human lover, as a measure against mortality. On a biological view, mortality and natality go together, setting the framework for human love. Human love sometimes generates new lives and has generated some great sonnets. It typically tries to sustain the flourishing life of loved ones, and it makes memorials for dead loved ones, but it does not aim to lengthen the lover's life. Risk of earlier death because of their love is a risk lovers always had to be willing to run and still must (just as seafarers risk shipwreck, promiscuous seekers of sexual pleasure risk venereal diseases, city dwellers risk air pollution, and citizens risk being involved in their nations' wars). Women were once taught to accept the risk of dying in childbed as a risk that went with their honorable station as loving wives, as prostitutes and their customers accepted the risk of an early death from venereal disease contracted from their less honorable (and contractual) activities, and as all able-bodied men were taught to accept the risk of dying on the battlefield as an occupational risk that went with their honorable station as protective males. There were always of course also some civilian deaths in wars, some virtuous wives whose marriage settlement from their husbands included venereal disease, and many children who were bequeathed their parents' diseases. (No men died in childbirth.) Now the risks are less concentrated on special groups. Death in childbed is not so frequent, and the other threats are fairly widely spread. We all, not just male militants, now have to accept the risk of dying in the quarrels our motherlands and fatherlands get into. The main health risk in loving lies now not in childbed but in other painful beds that may come after the love bed. This risk is not so high for "true lovers" as for mere promiscuous pleasure seekers, but it is not negligible. Love is now as risky to the health for all of us as it has always been for women. Now all is fairly fair in love and war, no more special exemptions.

Most of us believe we should do what we can to reduce the chances of war, especially as we have little reason to hope to be able to confine the risks of unprevented war to a limited population of professional militants. Should we do what we can to reduce the chances of love, given that its risks are also hard to confine? We surely should do what we can to reduce those health risks, but to try to confine them by attempted quarantine would be to restrict love, to outlaw some loving relationships, as some feminists want to morally outlaw love of men, the ones whose forefathers so long oppressed women, infected women, exploited women, and wore them out bearing children to carry on their father's name. Such responses to the risks of love amount to a retreat from generative love, a retreat which, carried to its extreme, would be an attempt to be a monad, to withdraw into safe solitude, into solitary vice. We need not fear nor expect many to respond this way— as Brown says, love is something some form of which we cannot do without. And as Wollheim says, love is a response to a felt relationship between oneself and another or others, a relationship we find there to be responded to.

Both the relations of interdependency and our responses to them, when we will their continuation, are fraught with risks — risks of mutual maiming, of loss and heartbreak, of domination, of betrayal, of boredom, of strange fashions of forsaking, of special forms of disease, and of disgrace. But they are also big with the promise of strengths united,[31] of new enthusiasms, special joys, of easy ungloved intimacy, of generous givings and forgivings, of surprising forms of grace. And as in justice, so in love, it may be impossible to separate the good from the ill.[32]

I said at the start that philosophers have a bad track record when they talk about love, and my own discourse has degenerated into a sermon. My sermon secularized and naturalized a very old story. My endorsement of the "biological" approach of Hume, Darwin, and some Freudians seems to bring me to a perhaps surprising agreement with the natural law tradition that they had little time for, agreement in putting generative love, and love of progenitors and of progeny, at the center of the cluster of kinds of love. It makes a pretty big difference, however, when we drop not just the theology but the patriarchal bias of that version of love. Just how much of a difference this will make we are still finding out. Experiments in loving, in love without domination, are a feature of our time. They may succeed not just in eliminating the special sort of domination that contaminated love in its patriarchal and phallocentric versions but in reducing the danger of any sort of domination in love. But even without domination there will still be some power play, for that seems to be essential to the play we all enjoy. Sometimes the play will turn vicious, sometimes the love will go sour. Those are risks we lovers run. Even if some loves are unlucky loves, some loves false loves, still,

> The water is wide, I cannot get o'er,
> And neither have I wings to fly;
> Give me a boat that will carry two;
> And both will row, my love and I.[33]

Notes

[1]Hume, "Of Polygamy and Divorces," in *Essays Moral Political and Literary*, ed. Eugene F. Miller (Indianapolis: Liberty Classics, 1985, p. 185.

[2]Robert Brown, *Analyzing Love* (Cambridge and New York: Cambridge University Press, 1987), p. 126.

[3]Ibid.

[4]Jerome Shaffer, "An Assessment of Emotion," *American Philosophical Quarterly*, vol. 20, no. 2 (April 1983), p. 171.

[5]Immanuel Kant, *Metaphysics of Morals* (Indianapolis: Bobbs Merrill Co., 1964), Part 2, sec. 24.

[6]Ibid., sec. 23.

[7]Kant, *Lectures on Ethics*, trans. L. Infield (New York: Harper & Row, 1963), p. 207.

[8]Ibid., p. 208.

[9]Ibid., p. 206.

[10]Ibid.

[11]René Descartes, *Passions of the Soul*, trans. J. Cottingham, R. Stoothoff, and D. Murdoch (Cambridge and New York: Cambridge University Press, 1988), arts. 79 and 80.

[12]Ibid., art. 147.

[13]Ibid., 3, art. 90.

[14]I am drawing a sharp contrast between theological and naturalistic views, but they can be combined in one philosopher. St. Augustine is a good case of a thinker who takes our natural condition seriously enough, but goes on to superimpose a supernatural framework on it, in a platonistic way working up from childhood experience of love between mother and child, through love of comrades, experience of sexual love, and what he in the *Confessions* calls "the madness of raging lust," to transcend all these in eventual love of God.

[15]David Hume, *A Treatise of Human Nature*, ed. L. A. Selby-Bigge and P. H. Nidditch (Oxford: Clarendon Press, 1978), p. 353.

[16]Ibid.

[17]See Ibid., p. 581. "A man that lies at a distance from us may in a little time become a familiar acquaintance."

[18]Ibid., p. 363.

[19]Ibid.

[20]Ibid., p. 322.

[21]In "A Dialogue," (Hume, *Enquiries*, ed. L. A. Selby-Bigge and P. H. Nidditch [Oxford: Clarendon Press, 1975]), Hume discusses homosexual love as Plato knew it and treats it much more sympathetically than he elsewhere (for example in "Of Polygamy and Divorces") treats some forms of heterosexual love, such as that of a sultan for his harem.

[22]See Hume, *Treatise*, "Of Chastity and Modesty" and "Of Polygamy and Divorces."

[23]Ibid., pp. 308-9.

[24]Hirself = her or him self.

[25]William Shakespeare, *Shakespeare's Sonnets*, Sonnet 62 (New Haven, Conn.: Yale University Press, 1977).

[26]I discuss this feature of love in "What Emotions are About," *Philosophical Perspectives 4: Action Theory and Philosophy of Mind*, ed. James E. Tomberlin (Atascadero, Calif.: Ridgeview Publishing Co., 1990).

[27]Hume, *Treatise*, p. 327.

[28]Shakespeare, Sonnet 49.

[29]A similar view is taken also by Robert C. Roberts, in an article which came to my attention after I had written this paper. He writes "the responses characteristic of such attachment are too various and conflicting for it to be an emotion. They can be joy when the beloved is flourishing, indignation when she is insulted, gratitude when she is benefited, fear when she is threatened, hope when her prospects are good, grief when she dies and much more. Love in this sense is not an emotion but a disposition to a range of emotions" ["What an Emotion Is: A Sketch," *Philosophical Review* (April 1988), p. 203].

[30]Richard Wollheim, *The Thread of Life* (Cambridge, Mass.: Harvard University Press, 1984), p. 279; see also p. 212.

[31]Thomas Hobbes, *Leviathan* (New York: Everyman's Library, 1973), Chap. 10. "To have friends is power, for they are strengths united."

[32]Hume, *Treatise*, p. 497.

[33]This is a revised version of a talk given at a conference on "Love" organized by John O'Connor, held at William Paterson College in February 1988. I have been helped by the discussion on that occasion, by perceptive criticisms by Lynne Tirrell, and by editorial suggestions from Robert Solomon and Kathleen Higgins. Would that they, or some other transforming agency, could have effected a magic replacement of my preachy prose by a pointed short story, a well-turned sonnet, or a simple telling lyric, like this Elizabethan song whose first verse I have borrowed.

William Gass

Throw the Emptiness out of Your Arms: Rilke's
Doctrine of Nonpossessive Love

William Gass is David May Distinguished Professor in the Humanities and director of the International Writers Center at Washington University in Saint Louis. His most recent book of essays, Habitations of the Word, *won the National Book Critics Circle Award.*

For a wide range of reasons, writing about love is a risky undertaking. It can't help but be revelatory. The point at which you begin, the assumptions you make, the elements you omit or ignore, emphasize or distort, the sorts of expository steps you take, the conclusions you draw: each choice will add a line to your portrait, as will the lyricism you display, your cynicism, scorn, or derision, whether you approach your subject as a psychologist, philosopher, or poet, and whether you adopt a scholar's scrupulosity, a theorist's elevation, the artist's ardency, or a politician's pose.

It is a word, furthermore, which the hypocrisies of society have corrupted. It has been suspiciously in the service of too many masters, the whole time wearing a most welcoming face, while want, desire, lust, need, pleasure even, reassurance, respect, admiration, friendship—as problematic as each is—concern, devotion, sacrifice, fidelity, passion, jealousy, and other states of character and feeling rise and fall in interest or estimation because everyone wants to hire love—of mother, country, God—to front for them, to do their business and support their cause.

One would suppose that love's opposite number would be hate, but this is rarely the case, although to love your country, at the very least, means to mistrust every other nation. More often death has the other star part, or sometimes loss does, or ennui.

Our language suggests that love is a wholly engrossing condition and can be expected to call upon the full range of our faculties, to demand our deepest and most continuous attention. Love absorbs the way the best paper towels are said to absorb. Love obsesses as if brought on by a whiff of se-

The translations of Rilke are by the author.

ductive perfume. It cancels comradeship, replaces respect, absolves duty, supercedes every other inclination. The poet says that love feeds on itself like a fire, and must be fed its own flames, as if Prometheus were to dine on his own entrails instead of being pecked by the beaks of those vulturous birds. Is love then a punishment for the theft of a heart? Well, perhaps. It's also been argued that love's true opposite is justice.

Is there another state of soul that accepts the same class of modifiers, that demands a similar set of objects, that surrounds itself with prepositions of the same kind? Grammatically, being in love seems like being in pain. One is simply found there or thrown there like a cat in heat or a criminal in prison. But love's resemblance to pain is not perfect: I cannot have a love in my foot or a great pain for Jan Sibelius. Want and need might run on parallel syntactical tracks, but only for a time, because, although we fall in love as though it were an opening in the earth, and out of love as though it were a tree, want and need are simply too low down to fall from and too instinctive to fade. Sometimes it is sudden as a slap . . . the onset of love; sometimes we Alice into it, and fall through long parts of life as through a dream.

I can be peeved by you, and I can peeve you too, but I cannot be in peeve, only in a pet, in a state, in a snit, in a stew. I can find myself full of hate or I can run out of love as though both were a fuel; however, I can't make hate the way I make time, or make do, or make haste, or make love, as if hate or love were a hat. To make love is to "have" sex the way one might have a second helping of potatoes, but hate has no program to be fulfilled; there are no guidelines, no handbooks, for hate. And if sex didn't hide inside of love like a weevil in a biscuit, love and hate would be one of grammar's twins. However, hate is not a thing, like tracks, that can be made by putting a foot down. Hate has no space. Hate appears and disappears in us like a fever, whereas love is like a trap waiting to be sprung. Almost like a season, it has its time; almost like a climate, it has its place.

What more can usage tell us? That cupid has his bow, but only anger can be aimed. That "lovely" has no more to do with "love" than "like" with "likely." It's true that "like" is a love-like word, yet I can like Mike and still not do anything for the like of Mike. Certainly, joy is not its linguistic image, because joy is verbally passive; it's not jealousy, which is never a verb; it's not glee, which is never a noun; it's not envy, which can't be sent through the mail like a letter-bomb.

Some people claim that love resembles death because both involve the loss of self (our small deaths are the culminations of sex the way our one large and lasting death is the completion of life), whereas others will argue that our love of our neighbor is adulterous self-love in disguise and that the beloved is merely a mirror. Love is a form of flattery, of systematic overestimation. It is a power play, a ploy in the game of seduction. It is the parent we thought we wanted. Were we a grapefruit, it would be our other half. It is simply a hormonal imbalance and something we suffer at sixteen like acne, angst, and insecurity. It is the mutual adjustment of people to one another for their joint comfort. It is the highest condition of the soul. It is the desire to turn the other cheek as if spanking were a pleasure. It is a jangle of the genitals like a jingle of keys. It is one thing for women — tender and prolonged — another for men — brutal and brief. It is sacrificial and a state of devotion. It is a humiliating illness. It is union; it is takeover; it is buyout. Above all, it is big business. The commercialization of love has become so complete, it is now a word embarrassing to speak. Among teenagers, the term is reserved exclusively for french fries and phonograph records. It is uncool as can be.

Love wears out like a suit of clothes. Love comes and goes like the clouds. Love is the lie of the lover and the belief of the beloved. "To love" and "to believe" have the same etymological companions: "leman," or dear one, of course, and "lief" as in "leave" or permission to be absent.

Despite such roots, love is supposed to be a long-term proposition like loyalty, obedience, and trust, and therefore unlike lust, which is expected to be as brief as the flare of a match, and to be indelicate if prolonged beyond that. In addition, love is initially reserved for elevated objects: husbands, nations, gods, ideals; so that one's love of the Buick car is a case of commercial hyperbole; so that, of boating or broccoli, one is properly only fond; but, if the objects of love begin by being high and mighty — put on a pedestal like a poop spot for pigeons — they are not necessarily perfect, nor is their position permanent, because they will descend from their eminence in time; they will decline — indeed, they are this moment being seen through; they have, in fact, sagged like a slowing line of fast talk. To repeat an old saw: Familiarity seeds every intimacy with contempt. So the romantic realms of love grow unworthy like gardens overwhelmed with weeds. What then, about the so-called objects of love, is honestly lovable? Among husbands, is it their bankrolls? Concerning boyfriends, is it their biceps, or the rumbleseats of their runabouts? And the pubic patch of the girl next door, is it not the real source of one's youthful wonder and despair?

I know of no more frequently cited word in *The Oxford Dictionary of Quotations* than "love," and the situation with *Bartlett's* is the same. Shouldn't this support the suspicion, along with rump-shaped hearts on bumper stickers, *billets-doux* and lying valentines, billboards, broadcasts, and inflammatory photos, that in our language there may be no more bankrupt a word? Still, these days, bankruptcy does not prevent one from continuing to do a very profitable business.

The poet Rainer Maria Rilke grew up surrounded by many examples of the fraudulent usage we are now accustomed to. Just because we're born, and even at the moment of our initial outcry, we are beloved: by God as a fresh soul to be saved; by the Nation as another mother or a future man-at-arms; by the Economy as an eventual customer; by each parent because they admire the miracle of their loins and because to do otherwise than love their child is unnatural; but also because a son will attest to his father's virility; he will carry on the family name and follow in his father's footsteps; because daughter will doubtless be beautiful, marry money, and care for papa in his gouty age, mama in her weeds; thus, in this way, the circle of beloving will widen to include every local aunt and uncle, grandthis and grandthat, peekaboo and kissing cousins, family chums and other seducers; since clearly the family comes first—it is the human nest—and whatever enlarges the family enlarges life, increases its clannish power, multiplies the number of hands for profitable labor.

What a fortunate child—to be bound by so many lines of love! lifted up by so many helping hands!

Rilke's parents had lost a daughter the year before they begot Renée, hoping for another daughter to replace her, and, until he was ready to enter school, his mother got him up girlishly, combed his curls, encouraged him to call his good self Sophie, and handled him like a china doll, cooing and cuddling his shiny porcelainities until such time as he was abruptly put away in a drawer. Later, with a recognition that resembled Gertrude Stein's, Rilke realized that someone else had had to die in order to provide him with a place in life.

His mother had aspired, when she married, to something grander than she got, though she poured cheap wine in better bottles and in other ways tried to keep up appearances. During his first year, Rilke's nurses came and went like hours of the day. His time as a toy continued. Affection, lit like a lamp, would be blown out by any sudden whim. As his parents drew away from one another like the trains his father oversaw, Rilke was more and more frequently farmed out by his mother, for whom a small boy was a social drag, to this or that carrier of concern. The child began to believe that love, like money, time, and food, was in limited supply and that what went into one life could not go into another.

My mother spread her presents at the feet
of those poor saints hewn of heart wood.
Mute, unmoving, and amazed, they stood
behind the pews, so straight and complete.

They neglected to thank her, too,
for her fervently offered gift.
The little dark her candles lift
was all of her faith they knew.

Still my mother gave, in a paper roll,
these flowers with their fragile blooms,
which she took from a bowl in our modest rooms,
in the sight and longing of my soul.

His mother's religiosity was always on simmer, if not on boil, but its turbulence took place, Rilke increasingly felt, in a shallow pot. "I am horrified," he wrote Lou Salomé, "by her scatter-brained piety, by her pigheaded faith, by all those twisted and disfiguring things to which she has fastened herself, she who is as empty as a dress, ghostlike and terrible. And that I'm her child, that I came into the world through a scarcely perceptible hole in the paper of this faded wall. . . ."

This is love, we are told: Here are mother and father being nice to one another, exchanging gifts, loving their furniture, their cat, their child; here is a faintly smiling madonna, and there a stern saint, and now a priest, and then a nurse, a friend, a dog whose tail wags; but on top of what we are told, like a cold hand, soon lies what we see and feel and finally know: the mother who picks us up and puts us down like a hand of cards; the joyful union that parts, perhaps like wet paper, without a sound, in front of our fearful eyes; the cat who sings its sex in the night and runs away; those saints who swallow only candlesmoke and say nothing; the dog whose devotions knock us down; or the priest, with a forced warmth heating his polished face, who twists the arm of an unruly acolyte because the boy doesn't dare yelp during the service; the nurse who says "good night, sleep tight" over the closing latches of her traveling bags; and finally those friends . . . those friends who skip scornfully away to play with children who have called us dreadful names: which layer is the layer of love? Is it only made of words — that kiss called "lip service," that caress called "shake hands," that welcome that feels like "good-by"?

During childhood, contradiction paves every avenue of feeling, and we grow up in bewilderment like a bird in a ballroom, with all that space and none meant for flying, a wide, shining floor and nowhere to light. So out of the lies and confusions of every day the child constructs a way to cope, part of which will comprise a general manner of being in, and making, love. So from the contrast between the official language of love and the unofficial facts of life is born a dream of what this pain, this passion, this obsession, this belief, this relation, ought to be. Yes, love is some sort of ideal relation, but does it have a price and a payoff like that of husband and wife; ought it to resemble that of the master and the slave; is it the connection of con to conned, of the fanatic to his faith?

Rilke eventually learned what he thought it was, because, when he sought a mother in his mistress instead of a mistress, leaning, as one into the wind, on Lou Salomé's spirit, she finally sent him off into the world again—out of her schoolroom, bed, and maternal hug—she did so, she said, because of his increasing dependency, because of her need for freedom to develop, because of a similar hope on her part for himself and his art; and, although he did not realize it all at once, he would come to understand how we constantly endeavor to match the ideology of love we've learned with the reality of its practice; to harmonize our own mutilated methods with those we've dreamed. We seek to reconstitute an improved past in the present. Not only do we search for surrogate parents—parents who would neither intimidate nor disappoint—but we attempt to create an environment in which our reenactments will correct every error and put the world right. We regress to rework and repair, because, inside of each of us, for a long time, lives an ear which still trusts what it heard, and an eye which still wishes to see such things as have been said to be. Yet day by day that child disappears until we enter the end without our heartfelt and hoped for beginnings; not because we've grown out of our need for teddy bears, but because our spirit no longer has the strength for that kind of complete and innocent embrace.

Our enterprises meet defeat again and again. In order to repair the past we must recreate the essential conditions of its breakdown. Then the same face appears, saying the same cruel words, doing the same disenchanting things, and we helplessly repeat our response—Freud says compulsively—and in that way enrich another bad habit at the expense of our happiness.

Rilke sought solace in an art colony called Worpswede, which was located in the bog country not far from Bremen—a spare, flat land valued for its isolation and its light. There he met his future wife as well as the painter, Paula Becker, whom he fancied first. The rapidity with which these relations were secured can be accounted for, in part, by the cruise ship atmosphere such colonies often have, but mainly because Rilke simply threw himself in the air and cried "Catch!"

Carla Westhoff caught him; a cottage caught him; domesticity seemed to swaddle him and protect him with its warmth. Love is always dreamed before it is performed, and Rilke imagined himself in soft lamplight standing before his stove preparing a simple supper for his beloved—perhaps a vegetable, he writes her, perhaps a bit of porridge. He envisions a dish of honey gleaming on the table, butter pale as ivory, a long, narrow platter of Westphalian ham "larded with strips of white fat like an evening sky banded by clouds," and wheat-colored tea in glasses, too, all standing on a Russian cloth. Huge lemons, reddish tangerines, silver saucers are invited, and then long-stemmed roses, of course, to complete this picture of quiet, unanxious sensuality. We need not describe the layer of boring chores, the clutter of mismated china, sticky pots, and soiled silver, annoying habits and nervous tics, which will cloud the rich cloth when reality arrives; and the bellowing of the baby, her repeated poops, the sighs of reproach, the pure passages of self-pity which will violin from one small room to another before disappearing out the door—a poor smell seeking to improve itself by flight.

He possesses his wife. Her friends observe it: how he has enthralled her. Whereas she first encompasses and then possesses the child. On the other hand, when the couple appears in public, the large and robust Clara seems to have her little Rilke beneath her arm (a few wrote) like a pet pooch. Routines take over. How in the world can three live as one? In the same pout spot, the boudoir, in the same pantry? Clara concentrates on Rilke, and it compacts him. He feels himself growing hard, rindlike, remorseless.

Ich liebe dich. I love you. No sentence from a judge could be more threatening. It means that I am giving you a gift you may not want. I am making it very easy for you to injure me—if I am not making it inevitable—and in that way controlling your behavior. It means I want you as an adjunct to my life, or it means that I can survive like mistletoe or moss: only on the side of someone. It means that one way or other I intend to own you.

Will you be mine? Don't we ask that? Don't we desire that? Demand that? This breast, this thigh, this bankbook, this fine house, this princely carriage, this improved place in society. Don't we wait impatiently for the loved one's answer: I am yours? In *The Book of Hours* Rilke writes his first poem of possession, as reiterative as Pound's canto on usury and as fiercely full of invective. Mine, the verses chant. Mine: this land, this life, this wife, the stars. My dog? Mine, yes. My child? Mine, of course. Both the prince and the peasant are mine, as well as the flag of my country. What next? *Mein Gott.* From now on Rilke will wonder, when it comes to love, what it means, not to give, but to receive it—this onslaught; what it means to be hunted by loneliness and pursued by all the passions of possession.

Ownership is as awful as enslavement, for you shall see the marks of your fingers about wrists and ankles, the bruises of your angry eyes on cheeks and arms, the constriction of the chest, the terrible narrowing of a life to a whistle, to a whisper.

To take hold of someone is to be taken hold of. Isn't the hug a gesture of mutual envelopment? And so he tries to persuade his female admirers of the virtue of distance, and he sings to them through the safety of the posted page about the beauty of their adjacent solitudes and encourages them to stand on tiptoe (right where they are), the better to breathe the scent of their own society. When we hold on to one another, we do so only to go under together; we impoverish ourselves because no one person can become a world; to love this way is to live a surrogate life. "Throw the emptiness out of your arms," he will write in *The First Elegy*, "to broaden the spaces we breathe—maybe the birds will feel the amplified air with an inner flight." Not holding on, then, but letting go, becomes, in love, its fullest expression.

Certainly there is sadness in change, but change is our condition. There is not a moment that isn't purely momentary. Arrival and departure share the same space, and have, in a sense, the same spelling.

How I have felt it, that nameless state called parting,
and how I feel it still: a dark, sharp, heartless
Something that displays, holds out with unapparent hands,
a perfect union to us, while tearing it in two.

With what wide-open eyes I've watched whatever
was, while calling to me, loosening its hold,
remaining in the road behind as though all womankind,
yet small and white and nothing more than this:

a waving which has blown the hair beyond its brow,
a slight, continuous flutter—scarcely now
explicable: perhaps the tremor of a plum-tree
and the bough a startled cuckoo has set free.

It is the poet's purpose to put the world in words, and, in that way, hold
it steady for us. The poet can write of love, too, in a similarly immortalizing
fashion. But love alters its lovers even as they love, so that their love is altered too, and the next kiss comes from a different mouth and is pressed to
a different breast.

> Lovers, satisfied by one another, I am asking you
> about us. You embrace, but where's your proof?
> Look, sometimes it happens that my hands grow to know
> one another, or that my heavy head seeks their shelter.
> That yields me a slender sensation. But who wants to live just for that?
> You though, who, in one another's passion,
> grow until, near bursting, plead: "No more . . ."
> you, who, beneath one another's groping, swell
> with juice like the grapes of a vintage year;
> you, who may go like a bud into another's blossoming:
> I am asking you about us. I know
> you touch so blissfully because your touch survives such bliss,
> because the flesh you caress so tenderly stays flesh;
> because just below your fingertip you feel the tip of pure duration.
> So you expect eternity to entwine itself in your embrace.
> And yet, when you have endured the fear of that first look,
> the longing, later, at the window, and your first turn
> about the garden together: lovers, are you any longer what you were?
> When you lift yourselves up to one another's lips,
> and slip wine into wine like an added flavor: oh, how strangely
> soon is each drinker's disappearance from the ceremony.

Rilke and his wife set one another free, freeing their infant at the same
time by leaving him, blanket and basket, in the rushes of a relative. In
Paris, where Rilke goes to write on Rodin, he learns about another kind of
love—that of the artist for his work; and about another kind of life—one in
which women are only a relaxation; he learns of an existence utterly devoted to things—things observed, things made, things preserved; but what
strikes him first are the streets and people of Paris itself, and his profound
sense of estrangement from them—of disgust, loneliness, fear, despair; so
that death is the topic which pursues his pen.

Love and death: a Germanic theme indeed. Just as going and coming
are one, just as beginnings and endings overlap, so are loving and ceasing

to love, living and ceasing to live, reciprocals, and as we mature our death matures too (for every teeter, there's a totter — that's the rule), the way one wave rolls up the beach while another wave recedes, and each roar of the surf is succeeded by a quiet hiss.

> O Lord, grant each of us our own ripe death,
> the dying fall that goes through life —
> its love, significance, and need — like breath.
>
> For we are nothing but the bark and burrs.
> The great death we bear within ourselves
> is the fruit which every growing serves.
>
> For its sake young girls grow their charms,
> as if a tree-like music issued from a lyre;
> for its sake small boys long to shoulder arms,
> and women lean on them to listen and inspire
> these not yet men to share their heart's alarms.
> For its sake all that's seen is seen sustained
> by change itself, as if the frozen were the fire;
> and the work of every artisan maintained
> this myth and made a world out of this fruit,
> brought frost to it, wind, sunlight, rain.
> And into it life's warmth has followed suit,
> heart's heat absorbed, the fever of the brain:
> Yet when the angels swoop to pick us clean,
> they shall find that all our fruits are green.

If the right kind of love releases all things to return to their natures, then dying is an equivalent letting go of life; it is a refusal, any longer, to possess it. This thought is old enough to have preceded Plato, but the renunciation involved here is only of ownership and assimilation, of conquest and compulsion, which is to be replaced by a respect for difference and an encouragement of freedom. Our obligation to life is to experience the qualities of things, to love otherness, and to stand guard over every solitude.

William James remarked that the greatest chasm we could encounter in nature was that between two minds, and it has always been the aim of romantic love to cross that abyss, to create a new creature made of mingled intimacies, to fill one soul with another, thus overcoming difference, which is always felt to be threatening, and replacing personal autonomy with the mutual dependencies of the loving couple. Rilke, one of the greatest and most extreme of romantic poets, does not subscribe to this Dionysian dream, however, but rather emphasizes the Apollonian denial of mergers and mixtures, and the superior functions of detachment. "A togetherness between two people is an impossibility," he writes; and when we realize that between one consciousness and another there is more distance than between the farthest stars, then a side-by-side life will become possible, like that of two monads whose worlds are distinct, complete, and unimpeachable, yet divinely harmonious.

I have thought it important to set down a few of the facts which can be lifted from Rilke's biography in order to insist (before being forced to admit) that his theory of love is an obvious rationalization and excuse for his own conduct. Rilke was unable to meet the demands of familial intimacy. He wanted to be, as a poet, always superior to the drudgeries of daily life; and if he encouraged us and himself to embrace the beauty and reality of all things, he was still not about to take hold of the household mop; nor could the spiritual self he aspired to survive being heard going to the bathroom, or observed picking its nose. This kind of quartered closeness—in which another person learns to accept us as we have learned to accept ourselves, thereby sanctioning that acceptance—was not possible for him. He was unable to forgive his stomach for growling, or lewdness for following him through his long bouts of solitude, or the moments, so untranscendental, when he allowed his longing to spring out of his pants.

Indeed, we never have enough of these petty, even puerile, details: precisely how he felt, as a child, hearing the conversations of visitors while screened by the simplest of thin partitions from the guests in the living room; or with what whitened face his first love, Valerie von David-Rhonfeld, read his practice letter of farewell: "Dear Vally, thank you for the gift of freedom . . . ," or the quality of his last visit to Lou's lips, or his reaction, each time, to Rodin's earthy pursuit of pleasure; because, of love, there is no *a priori* knowledge; because it is, I am convinced, only from the innumerable accumulations of these impressions that one's overall feeling about love arises: both one's understanding of what it is supposed to be (an overwhelming and permanent passion); one's perception of what it actually is (a whimsically exercised proprietory power); and one's picture of how it ought ideally to be (a devotion like that for painting and poetry); it is these leaves, little by little and layer after layer, which build up the floor of the forest, despite the occasional hard knocks and exceptional traumas, like storms, which disturb it, since even these primal scenes and secret shames are made of so many small discriminations—a leer, a wink, the flip of a skirt, an odor out of place, an overheard word, a sigh out of sight—which mysteriously play some part in the effect of the whole.

Rilke's intense feeling for the instability of things: of how many disappointments is that sense the sum? since it led him to protect himself by erasing relations as rapidly as they were inscribed; and into what unknown number of rented rooms did his need to justify the certainty that "all is fleeting" consequently drive him?

Caught in relationships which produced nothing but acute and constant embarrassment, it is not surprising that we find that word "freedom," in the form of a brutal cliché, in his first farewell, or that his model for a proper life was composed of Lou Salomé's struggle to achieve her independence (though tied to a husband who had snared her through an attempted suicide), as well as Auguste Rodin's success in creating freely despite the curse of custom; so it was freedom from family he sought, freedom from community, from country, from the local language, from the military and a militarized education, from the inanities of courtship, the mock-heroics of the husband and the manliness of the male, from the details of a daily life determined by the economic exercycle or measured in amounts of cash, from sentimental celebrations of all kinds and those lies which become the blackmail and the bribes we pay to existence; because we ordinarily cannot escape it: the fact that our feelings are so rarely really ours and spring from us as simply and directly as grass, for even the grass is mowed and fertilized and seeded, so our comparison has to be with the free, unwanted weed; in that guise the genuine appears—out of place, improper, gauche—because our feelings have been institutionalized like someone sick or mad, or they've been the "up" in our upbringing, what we've been taught to believe we can manage if we can earn enough to pay their price—so shall our tastes and temperament change through a successful life from tin lizzie to limousine, from canned peas to caviar and snails, from "wham bam, thank you, ma'am" to muff dives done according to Olympic regs and textbook standards.

We think we go to bed with our eager groom, our blushing bride, when we go to bed with the principles of the Republic and in the best interests of Chambers of Commerce and Bureaus of Better Business.

We are not only victims of our love and work life, we also need to defend our flights and seeming failures, to justify ourselves before our inner bench. We can do that by finding reasons for what we may have done dumbbellishly and in the dark, as if wisdom would have chosen the same path, gone for the same goals, served and celebrated the same ideals.

If love is the proper feeling to have for whatever is best, then we merely have to find whatever is best. If love is truly good for both lover and beloved, then acts of love ought to be honest acts of aid and comfort. Love ought to be an improvement and not an indulgence. Love ought to be given freely to any excellence and not mocked by being lavished on the unworthy. There is no higher service we can render our fellows than to increase their freedom; therefore our declarations of love ought also to be declarations of our loved one's independence. Weak as we are, we may not be able to be moral toward all men, but at least we ought to be able to treat those we claim we love as autonomous souls and ends-in-themselves.

But love says gimme; love says, "you play the slave and I'll play the master"; love says comfort me, flatter me, complete me, forgive me; love says reflect my weakness as a show of strength; so it seems notably hard-boiled to insist that love ought to seek out value and serve it, whether in others or in one's self, whether in persons or in things. But if I love the good in you, do I love you or just the good? And if I love your beauty, is it you or beauty I adore?

Rilke is too complete a poet to chase the philosopher's wisps. It is not the beauty of the landscape but the landscape that is real, just as the character you or I presumably have cannot be removed like an appendix or pulled out like a tooth but suffuses itself through the soul the way tea leaves steep in tea water.

It is true that I may be more devoted to a principle than to my spouse, motor car, or dog, but if I am treating you as an end rather than as a mere means out of obedience to a rule rather than from affection, the word that describes the case should rather be "justice" than "love."

If our reward for being loved is solitude preserved and freedom encouraged, we may pass right through it, like the tail of a distant comet, and never feel the wash, thus avoiding indebtedness and gratitude as well as love; but love, as we say, is strong stuff in any version of its nature and affects its object willy nilly. Perhaps, when we declare ourselves: "I love you!" it is best if we are never believed, because who knows what damage the knowledge of our love may do; how it may be taken; what weaknesses it may threaten with exposure; what acceptance it may encounter; what revulsion it may cause?

Under the circumstances (and following the advice of Spinoza), it is safer to love objects which can more easily withstand affection than we can; from whom no grateful response can be demanded; and whose freedom is not likely to tax our own generosity. That is, such a love as a musician has for music is normally purer than a spouse's for a spouse, or a daddy for his Sugar, and is probably not going to demean or enslave the soul of a single song. On the other hand, this displacement of love from person to thing is not in the spirit of Spinoza after all, since Spinoza recommended loving thingless objects, objects of intellect, objects of thought, acts of intelligence; whereas the poet wants his human consciousness (in which Spinoza's objects also, if not exclusively, exist) first of all improved past understanding into wonderment and then lodged intrinsically within the net and measure of the thing itself—how strongly? as strongly as a molecule holds its elements in thrall.

Freedom scarcely needs a poet's endorsement; but why is solitude its equal? Because freedom finally means the opportunity to pursue ourselves, not in the supermarket sense or in terms of stocks and bonds, but in terms of the great vast theater of our head, the space of our imagination, the place where, if we can, we create. What better thing can we do for this momentary and material world than bring it within and set it up in an inner and immaterial and invisible world where consciousness is king and queen, the whole court and the castle?

> Are we, perhaps, here just to utter: house,
> bridge, fountain, gate, jug, fruit tree, window—
> at most: column, tower . . . but to utter them, remember,
> to speak in a way which the named never dreamed
> they could be. Isn't it the hidden purpose
> of this cunning earth, in urging on lovers
> to remake itself in the forms of their feeling?

In innerworld space the wide-open world can rest in peace.

> These things whose life
> is a constant leaving, they know when you praise them.
> Transient, they trust us, the most unremaining, to come
> to their rescue; they wish us to alter them utterly,
> whatever's without our invisible hearts, into—so endlessly—us!
> Whoever we are.

There is one characteristic that is curiously absent from most philosophical accounts of virtue or the higher feelings—a characteristic I have already briefly touched on—and it concerns the way these qualities appear

in the people who are supposed to have them, so that we are ready to say
that they *are* theirs (whatever accounts for "the interesting man" in Ortega
y Gasset's essay *On Love* or comprises "the great-souled one" in Aristotle);
for there are some women, for instance, who seem to wear their beauty like
a mask; there is no articulation of the spirit in their otherwise perfect faces;
and other sorts in whom honesty resides like a guest who has come for a
weekend visit, or what about that erotic passion which seems to have seized
a soul as suddenly as a hiccup? A few people are so up-front about their virtues, they might be bearing sandwich boards, while others are discreet or
even timid. There exist those who are scrupulous about money but careless
with the truth. Some thieves will steal your change, others your time, others
again will only Robin Hood, while still others have to filch knickknacks out
of dime stores or swipe stamps from the office postage. Some are brazen,
some are subtle, some are steady, others intermittent, and so on. In short,
every vice and every virtue, every feeling, every gesture of the mind, has a
manner, a style; and it is the style of many an errant knave which makes
him charming to us, and the style of some saints which makes us wish they
would go to the devil.

I suppose the popular word for this is "personality." Popular or not,
one's personal style is real enough, and may be, after all—as in the case of
the poet—what we fall in love with: a way of Being, a manner of moving,
thinking, feeling: our presence (our *Dasein*) in the world.

We should speak more often of *how* one loves or is loved, when we speak
of its nature, since it is there—in a style—that its nature really lies. Of
course, we do talk of lovers making love well or badly, but in a technical
sense more appropriate to putting up ladders or cleaning Venetian blinds;
yet we rarely comment on how a person's manner of loving makes that love
so elevating and vast, or how, in a different instance, it pains and poisons.
Then such skills as are essential to the poet will come importantly into play:
one's powers of observation, for instance, one's responsiveness, one's empa-
thy and imagination, scrupulosity and care and respect for nuance, one's
generosity and openness to experience, in short, one's general level of civilization: depth of desire, breadth of attention, degree of sensuality, sharp-
ness of sight and range of feeling, an adventurous fancy and a noble high-
mindedness of mind.

Are we surprised that the many women who loved the poet Rainer Maria Rilke loved first his lines and saw in them everywhere, like the breath
you would need to pronounce them, these very deep and enduring qualities
of spirit—not merely (to paraphrase Pope) the passion which lay behind

466   them, but the art and character which shaped its expression (as in these
words written by Rilke for his friend and lover, Lou Salomé):

> Put my eyes out: I can still see;
> slam my ears shut: I can still hear,
> walk without feet to where you were,
> and, tongueless, speak you into being.
> Snap off my arms: I'll hold you hard
> in my heart's longing like a fist;
> halt that, my brain will do its beating,
> and if you set this mind of mine aflame,
> then on my blood I'll carry you away.

Laurence Thomas

Reasons for Loving

Laurence Thomas is professor of philosophy at Syracuse University. He is the author of Living Morally *and articles on ethics, social practices, racism, slavery, and the holocaust.*[1]

The distinction between explanation and justification is a very important one. One readily appreciates its importance in a court of law. A plea of insanity for a person's killing versus one of self-defense draws mightily upon just this distinction. But with regard to our understanding of romantic love, this distinction is not among the many things that readily come to mind. I believe, however, that it is very relevant, and that when love is properly explicated with this distinction in mind, many of our intuitions about romantic love are spoken to. I mean if the saying "Love is never having to say you are sorry" is all that silly, why did it strike such a response chord in some or get such a negative reaction out of others? In what follows, I hope to speak to these things, albeit in a somewhat discursive way.

Before getting under way, though, a caveat is in order. It is one thing to have feelings of romantic love for an individual and yet another thing to act on those feelings. It can be quite morally wrong or irrational to act on one's feelings of romantic love. Most obviously, one morally should not act on them when this would ruin a clearly flourishing romantic relationship or when the object of those feelings is a child. And it is certainly irrational to pursue an individual who, with great resolve, has systematically spurned one's romantic overtures because, as it happens, the individual is unshakably gay and one is simply of the wrong gender. This essay is not much about the morality or rationality of acting on one's feeling of love.

Many aspects of romantic love are clearly a matter of choice, or at least they can be. We choose to date, to become sexually involved, to live together, to get married, and so on — though not *necessarily* in that order. We

---

[1]This essay was inspired by, and in a somewhat general way is a response to, some of the views of Robert C. Solomon, *Love: Emotion, Myth, and Metaphor* (Buffalo: Prometheus Books, 1990). I have also drawn upon the account of love which I put forth in *Living Morally: A Psychology of Moral Character* (Philadelphia: Temple University Press, 1989).

choose to do these things although sometimes we do them spontaneously. But ironically love itself or, at any rate, feelings of romantic attraction for another are not so clearly a matter of choice. If indeed we choose to have romantic feelings for another, we most certainly do not do this in any direct way: "Lo, let me have romantic feelings for so-and-so." The same holds for ceasing to have romantic feelings. Similarly, one does not stop loving someone by setting a deadline, in the way that one might give up cigarettes, say: after 10 October, I will no longer love so-and-so. Rather, one comes to the realization that one is no longer in love with so-and-so.

The language of romantic love tends to support this line of thought. We speak of falling in or out of love with someone. We speak of being smitten. And, of course, there is Cupid's arrow: a way of conquering the particularly resistant to love, I suppose. In any case, these metaphorical ways of talking about love would suggest that having feelings of love is much more a matter of something that happens to us rather than something that we choose to have.

I think that this is absolutely right, though I do not wish to deny that we can do things which are likely to promote the acquisition of feelings of love on our part or to extinguish them; for we do talk about giving love a chance. But even here, it seems that feelings of love are supposed to take off on their own—something like the romantic analogue to Pascal's Wager. And the thought seems to be that whether or not, in the end, feelings of love take off is not entirely a matter of what one does: one can do all the right things and not experience the "magic." Likewise, common wisdom has it that lovers are courting romantic disaster if they systematically set their career ambitions above their romantic interactions.

Our understanding of romantic love can be facilitated by looking at the sentiment or emotion of anger. We readily distinguish between rationally justified (that is, rationally correct) and unjustified anger or, in other words, irrational anger. If Jones says to Sanchez, "I am angry at you," then he needs to tell a story which rationally justifies his anger—if at least he is to be seen as a reasonable individual. The story could be factually incorrect (Sanchez did not make the disclosure, Jones did); or it could be one about which reasonable people can differ over whether or not anger is warranted (true, Sanchez drank too much, but he had no idea that he would be receiving an award that required an acceptance speech). Just so, a story is needed nonetheless.

Of course, anger can be inappropriate without being irrational. It can be excessive ("The children merely soiled the suit; you are acting as if they ruined it completely") or mean-spirited ("While you were rightly angry at Lee for what she did, you did not have to humiliate her so. That was mean!"). But excessive or mean-spirited anger is anger that is anchored in rationally justified considerations which then becomes untoward in some way or other. It is not anger that is out of order entirely—anger that is completely without rational justification. Simply to be angry at someone—at a perfect stranger, for instance, whom one believes has not adversely affected one in any way—is not to be angry in excess or to be mean-spirited; it is to be without any sort of rational justification for one's anger and thus to be irrational in one's anger. It cannot be rationally correct to be angry at a perfect stranger if one has this belief.

Paradigmatically, anger is conceptually tied to a belief the content of which is an assessment that one (or a loved one) has been made worse off in some way by an event or action: one (or the loved one) has been wronged or harmed or, at the very least, the realization of a desire has been frustrated. And when the cause of one's being worse off is another individual's action (as opposed to one's own), then anger is also tied to an assessment of the intentions and competencies, as well as the general state of mind, of the individual in question. It is one thing for a six-year-old to throw a piece of one's fine china on the floor intentionally and quite another for an adult to do so. And it is one thing for an adult to do so out of spite and quite another for an adult to do so because, having been raped only moments earlier, he has just suffered a deep emotional scar. Anger toward the six-year-old, and undoubtedly greater anger toward the adult acting out of spite, because greater competency is assumed here, is perhaps rationally justified in both instances. Anger toward the adult who has just been raped is surely not, because rape is such a deep, psychologically scarring harm, the immediate occurrence of which may undermine a person's self-control. It is because anger is conceptually tied to the belief-assessments mentioned here that it is subject to rational justification and so can be irrational.

Indeed, a person can have good reason to be angry: "They deliberately and knowingly destroyed your house because they did not want a Vietnamese living in the neighborhood. What do you mean you are not angry? You certainly ought to be!" Although it is true enough that we are reluctant to say that a person is irrational for not becoming angry while having a very good reason to be, it is worth noticing that we do offer explanations here: the person is too numbed or is in a state of extreme shock. In fact, if a person experiences no anger upon being the object of an egregious wrong and none of the foregoing explanations applies, we do wonder about the sound-

470   ness of the person's mental health. For the absence of anger, in the face of egregious wrong, suggests a psychologically unhealthy indifference to one's well-being. Against this point, the ideal of the Stoic life comes quickly to mind, according to which a form of self-discipline consists in being the kind of person who is not at all emotionally affected by any of the vicissitudes of life. Without attempting an assessment of the plausibility of Stoicism, let me just note that the doctrine need not be construed as denying that persons can have good reasons for being angry. Rather, it can be seen as insisting that through self-discipline such reasons need not give rise to anger.

Now, with romantic love things are quite different. We do not so much justify it as explain it: "Cohen loves Romero because . . . ," where the "because" is providing an explanation rather than a justification for Cohen's love for Romero. While Cohen's reason for loving Romero no doubt tells us something about Cohen's psychology, the reason is not really a matter of rational correctness. Cohen is not being rationally correct in loving Romero for his character any more than if Cohen were to love Romero for his beautiful eyes.

To be sure, we do think that romantic love can have inappropriate objects. The inappropriateness here, however, is of a moral rather than a rational nature. For instance, we generally think that it is inappropriate for an adult to have romantic love for a ten-year-old or for a parent to have romantic love for an adult child. Clearly, though, the heart of the incorrectness here is moral rather than rational.

What accounts for this difference between love and anger? The answer quite simply is that anger toward a person is conceptually tied to the belief that one has been made worse off by the individual. Without this belief at all or without sufficient warrant for the belief, the anger is utterly irrational. One cannot believe that so-and-so made one worse off *because* so-and-so looked up at the sky. By contrast, love is tied not so much to a belief about a person as it is to a desirous feeling to interact with a person in a certain way. Roughly (very roughly), love is feeling anchored in an intense and nonfleeting (but not necessarily permanent) desire to engage in mutual caring, sharing, and physical expression with the individual in question or, in any case, some idealized version of her or him. And there are simply no constraints whatsoever on the type of person who can be the object of this desire. This might seem false because of the truth that for any given person it is obvious that the desire of romantic love generally revolves around various types of individuals and thus involves beliefs about whether an individual is of a certain type or not. But the point here is that this restriction is owing to a person's own subjective, individual tastes and preferences. The desirous feelings of romantic love, itself, place no restrictions whatsoever on the type of person that may be the object of an individual's love. Hence, romantic love is not a matter of rational justification.

That is, no matter how wonderful and lovely an individual might be, on any and all accounts, it is simply false that a romantically unencumbered person must love that individual on pain of being irrational. It is simply false that a romantically unencumbered person thereby has a rationally compelling reason to love the individual. Or, there is no irrationality involved in ceasing to love a person whom one once loved immensely, although the person has not changed. By the same token, it cannot be shown that a person is rationally mistaken in loving another just because there is someone better in some important way, or whatever. Thus, being romantically attracted to the very individual who oppresses one is not ruled out on conceptual grounds. I realize that it is sometimes said, "You have every reason in the world to stop loving so-and-so." I suggest, however, that this is just colloquial for "You have every reason in the world to break off your relationship with so-and-so." It can be reasonable to do this even if one still loves the person. Similarly, we are sometimes surprised that a person's love for another has continued, and we ask, "Why do you still love so-and-so?" I take it to be evident, though, that this is a request for an explanation and not for a rational justification.

The nature of desire generally is such that there are very few rational constraints on what a person can desire. Aristotle, for instance, held only that it is irrational to desire the impossible, which on his view is the domain of wishes. This constraint rules out things like a person's desiring to be made of green cheese or to breathe without air. Presumably, it rules out males' desiring to bear children and the desire of foreign-born scholars of the U.S. Constitution (as now written) to be president of the United States, since they know that only native-born citizens can hold this office. However, the constraint does not rule out the highly improbable — say, the desire of a woman or a member of a visible ethnic minority (Hispanic, or Jew, or black) to be president of the United States. Nor does it rule out a desire for global peace or a desire for the United States to become a part of Canada — or conversely. So, it is patently obvious that in the realm of romantic love Aristotle's constraint leaves things pretty much unrestricted. There is nothing impossible about loving an evil person, or a very unintelligent person, or a very aesthetically unpleasing person, or a very self-

472 centered and arrogant person. And so on. Indeed, there is hardly anything impossible about loving the already romantically involved. Recall that Christianity admonishes its adherents to love their enemies. No one seems to think that the suggestion is ruled out of court on conceptual grounds.

Now, at the outset I indicated that it is enormously important to distinguish between having feelings of love and acting on them—in particular, nurturing or continuing to act on them. That a person has romantic feelings for someone can be perfectly understandable, and yet it can be quite foolish—downright imprudent—for the person to act on them, just as it can be quite foolish for a person to act on anger which the individual understandably has. After all, we sometimes admonish people to get over romantic feelings even though we regard having the feelings as perfectly understandable.

Of course, there can be all sorts of explanatory reasons for a person's having romantic love for another. However, offering an explanation here is no more to justify it than is offering an explanation for tidal waves or the greenhouse effect or the migration of various animals to justify any of these occurrences.

Explanatory reasons for a person's behavior or sentiments or desires can range over countless aspects of a person's life: upbringing, examples set by parents, a salient experience (romantic or otherwise), and so on. Moreover, while we are certainly conscious of some of the explanatory reasons in our lives and have some sense of their potency, it seems rather unlikely that we are conscious of all of them and that we properly appreciate the potency of all those of which we are conscious. Finally, even with those explanatory reasons which we have correctly identified and whose potency we properly appreciate, it seems most unlikely that we have all of them before us all of the time.

Together these considerations surely constitute one very important explanation for why feelings of romantic love are generally viewed as something which befalls us rather than something which we choose to experience, something which we choose to happen to us. For the upshot of these remarks just is that there are factors which dispose us to be romantically inclined or receptive to this or that kind of person: These factors are often owing to things that happened to us rather than to things that we chose to do, and we are not always aware of or mindful of these factors; nor are we always fully appreciative of the potency of those factors of which we are aware.

There can be no doubt that we make moral evaluations of the explanatory reasons why a person is romantically inclined towards an individual, some being considered more morally acceptable than others. I have surely said nothing to deny this. Thus, the remarks offered are quite compatible with Solomon's observation (p. xxxiv) that people love for a multitude of reasons, including money and sexual performance, as well as high quality of character. People generally think that the third is a morally better reason for loving a person than the second and the second better than the first.

I should like to conclude by considering one of the most interesting issues surrounding the nature of love, namely, the idea that it is or should be a kind of unconditional acceptance. Perhaps the most popular expression of this view was "love means never having to say you are sorry." Regarding love so conceived Solomon writes:

> I want to argue that the idea of the unqualified, unspecified, open-ended and totally tolerant love of "individual human being" is just another part of the love myth, derived, perhaps, from the Christian concept of the "soul"—that essential spiritual pit that lies at the core of each of us, beneath our clothes and our manners and our bodies and our genitals and our intelligence and accomplishments. But this is motivated, as usual, by our childish desire for a guarantee, as if hard-earned love, once "won," will not be so easily lost. (p. xxxiii)

I think that both sides — Solomon and the masses — have a point. Now, the idea that love means never having to say that one is sorry is surely mistaken. In fact, it seems most natural to think just the opposite. People who love one another are very much inclined to say that they are sorry when they hurt one another — or, at any rate, we think that they should be or that they would be in the absence of other factors. On the other hand, there is often a kernel of insight to many adages. I believe that seeing reasons for loving as explanatory rather than justificatory gives us some insight into what is behind the idea that love is some form of unconditional acceptance.

It is obvious that on my view a justificatory model of love would mean that loving someone should be a matter of rational argument — a weighing of reasons for and against doing so, in precisely the way that one might make a choice. What is not so obvious, perhaps, is that on this model it would seem that a person could have a claim to another's love. For if it is possible to give sufficient reasons why one person should love another, then presumably anyone can marshal those reasons, including the person desiring to be loved by the other. But offering sufficient reasons why one should

474 be provided with something is simply a way of laying claim to it. Although an appeal to rights is no doubt the customary way of laying claim to something, I take it to be obvious that invoking a right as a justification for being given something is simply a shorthand way of invoking a set of reasons. And I take it to be equally obvious that if there is anything anyone does not have a claim to, by way of rational considerations, it is another's romantic love. The very idea is repulsive. To be sure, one might on the basis of a romantic relationship have a claim to another's fidelity. All the same, having a claim to something given the assumption of romantic love should not be confused with having a claim to the romantic love itself.

When understood in the usual way, then, the idea that romantic love is unconditional is thus somewhat subverted on the explanatory model of love. For on that model, the idea does not mean that it is rational or proper for a person to love another under all circumstances no matter what, as the explanatory model does not in any way deny that the factors which incline a person to love another may, but need not, change over time. This model does not make the genuineness of love a function of either its longevity or its ability to persist in the face of radical change. On the explanatory model, love is unconditional in that there are no rational considerations whereby anyone can lay claim to another's love or insist that an individual's love for another is irrational. However much delight Lee may take in being the object of Sanchez's love, Lee has no claim to Sanchez's love on that account alone. *Love is not beholden, though everlasting it might be.* And if, by contrast, Lee should become a morally despicable human being, it is not on that account alone irrational for Sanchez to go on loving Lee. Of course, in most instances a person's behavior bears enormously upon the extent to which she or he is loved by another. But the point is, obviously, that there is no behavior such that if a person performs it, then someone has a claim to that individual's love or is thereby irrational to love that individual.

Now, I suggest that in general this is the way that we want love to be. That is, I suggest that few, if any, want to be loved by another only because the other feels beholden or obligated to do so, allowing that we can make sense of beholden or obligated love. After all, love is neither gratitude nor a place-holder for it. One can have debts of gratitude, these quite clearly admitting of rational justification (from which it hardly follows that there can be no disagreement). It is straightforwardly irrational to feel grateful to someone whom one believes has not helped one in any way whatsoever. Why should we embrace the explanatory model of love? The answer, quite simply, is that there is no deeper source of affirmation that that which is bestowed upon us, though we have no claim to it. This is true for the child and it is just as true for the adult. What is more, contrary to what Solomon seems to indicate in the passage quoted above, there is nothing foolish or self-centered about wanting to be thus affirmed. What is foolish is to expect the romantic love of anyone to abide by the asymmetry of parental love. For, although we surely suppose that children should be grateful to loving parents, it is not at all part of the ideal of the parent-child relationship that symmetry be obtained at some level. To expect gratitude on the part of one's child is not to expect, want, or wish for love-in-kind. A romantic lover is not and should not be thought of as a surrogate parent.

These remarks do not clash with what has been said concerning the explanatory model of love. The central claim made on behalf of the model is that romantic love is not based upon rationally compelling considerations. This claim differs entirely from the claim that there can be reasonable and unreasonable *expectations* concerning whether a person's love will endure. Talk about what a person must do on pain of being irrational is very different from talk about what others can reasonably expect a person to do. While, in general, one cannot reasonably expect a person to go on helping, though the much needed help is systematically unappreciated, it is not thereby irrational for a person to do so.

On the explanatory model of love as unconditional, it will certainly be true that a person can do things which will promote or frustrate the feelings of romantic love of another. This will be owing to facts about the psychology of the other. But to do what one has good reason to believe will promote another's love for one is not to have a claim to it; hence, it is not to ensure, by way of rational argument, that the other is beholden to love one. Although it is possible on this model that the psychology of some people will be such that they will love another no matter what the other does, this is not a constitutive feature of the explanatory model of love.

Solomon writes, "Every emotion may provide some meaning to life, but it is romantic love that provides the specific meaning we need the most: the meaningful relationship, that sense of belonging, in a world that has made belonging an achievement rather than a presupposition" (p. 139). In the end, Solomon and I both agree on the importance of romantic love in our lives: Romantic love fills a void in a society which makes belonging so very much a matter of achievement. But, alas, I want to say that love can fill that void only if it is unconditional. I have offered the explanatory model of romantic love as a way of rescuing the idea of unconditional romantic

476 love from the vulgar notion of unrestricted tolerance of another, which Solomon rightly detests. When one considers the explanatory model of unconditional love, the thought is very humbling, indeed: For love (whether
romantic or parental), albeit absolutely indispensable to our flourishing, is
that to which we cannot lay rational claim.

Ronald de Sousa
Love as Theater

Ronald de Sousa is professor of philosophy at the University of Toronto and the author of The Rationality of Emotions.

> When my love swears that she is made of truth
> I do believe her, though I know she lies.
> *William Shakespeare*

> O sweet Fancy! let her loose;
> Every thing is spoilt by use.
> *John Keats*

> Children of a future age
> Reading this indignant page
> Know that in a former time
> Love, sweet love, was thought a crime.
> *William Blake*

It is a commonplace that love motivates some of our worst behavior, ranging from dishonesty to murder. We should be more shocked by this than we are. Love is supposed to include a desire for the loved one's happiness; yet a dose of jealousy is considered standard equipment in any love affair, and typically the lover desires the loved one's happiness only insofar as the lover has caused it. Love, then, as it is daily celebrated in our plays, our novels, and our songs, is little more than an acute fit of narcissism.[1] What is astonishing is not that this occurs; we are jaded enough, by now, to accept many unsavory truths about human nature. Moreover, thanks to sociobiology, we are now possessed of a whole new range of explanations that can serve us as scientific warrant for many forms of bad behavior. But what is most astonishing is that we regard love as a *justification* for treating people far worse than we would ever condone treating a stranger. We accept this as casually as people used to accept that suspected criminals were to be tortured to extract their confessions, and the utopian idealist in some of us may surmise that sometime, perhaps, we shall be equally revolted by both these ancient barbarities. One might be excused, then, for searching for some alternative, however utopian.

On the other hand, Blake's apostrophe in my epigraph has not altogether lost its point: Sex is among those crimes that only love can excuse. Sexuality is widely held to need some sort of disinfection, if no longer by marriage at least by "commitment" or True Love. Prostitution is regarded as at worst a moral evil and at best an embarrassment—the only point of disagreement having to do with whether it is more degrading to the professional or to the customer. "Casual" sex and one-night stands are often thought to deserve scarcely less opprobrium. In this paper I want to argue for the rehabilitation of certain forms of imaginative rehearsals for love in "casual," "uncommitted," or even commercial sex. I base this plea on certain fairly commonplace observations about the nature of romantic love, our attitudes to love and sex, and the metaphysics that these attitudes presuppose.

Four problematic features of romantic love make literally impossible demands, which must drive us either to simple self-deception or to some other, more sophisticated response. Although we cannot, by definition, live the impossible, we can sometimes represent it—as witnessed by art as diverse as the poems of Homer and the drawings of Escher. In that vein, the alternative I suggest is that we attempt to apprehend the unattainable realizations symbolized by the impossible demands of romantic love by *playing at love*—by conscious, mutually consenting representations or simulations of love. I argue that a certain sort of sexual encounter, self-consciously limited to the present moment and without commitment to any subsequent relationship of any particular form, is a civilized successor to the old notion of romantic love. I shall call this the *theater of love*.

But first, a caveat. It is often said that attitudes to love and sex are largely determined by material conditions. Perhaps it is unreasonable to apply to past ages the standards—of feminism, of egalitarianism, or of sexual morality—that seem appropriate to our own. The cult of chastity and the peculiarities of chivalric love are explained and justified in terms of the realities of pregnancy and disease briefly alleviated in part of the twentieth century. In this vein, many think that AIDS has changed once again the face of what it is possible or desirable to advocate in matters of sex and its relation to love, at least for this century. This may be right; however, I ignore all such considerations in this essay. The mores of an age are defined not only by what can and does happen, but also by the utopias in terms of

which what can and does happen is evaluated. I speak in terms not of current social, demographic, or even medical realities, but for utopia. A disease, even unconquered, falls short of a philosophical argument. At the
very least, one should be able to take stock of what one has *lost*, of what one
might now be missing. In any case, I don't wish to speak of promiscuous sex
as such, but of promiscuous love. It will turn out, however, for reasons that
I will explain, that a certain measure of sexual promiscuity is entailed by
the relevant conception of promiscuous or "theatrical" love.

No argument about love can proceed without narrowing the topic. C.
S. Lewis[2] distinguishes among Affection, Friendship, Eros, and Charity, in
addition to what he calls "Liking and loves for the sub-human." All these
are important and valuable, and in some ineffable utopia perhaps all could
be felt for the same object at once; but in our world they are separable.
Our lives are not infrequently complicated by the hope that all might be
elicited by a single privileged object. But in fact they are—all too
notoriously—mutually detachable, if not positively independent. I wish
here to speak only of eros, and perhaps only of a very specific type of eros.
In the present argument I will take for granted that eros is indeed something that can be distinguished from the other kinds of love, and that other
types of love do not in general necessarily suffer from the absence of eros.
In our culture, eros is thought of as a prelude to marriage; but in marriage
affection and companionship are supposed to supplement it or replace it.
Here I will have nothing to say about that transition, except that, as will be
clear, it is necessarily a transition *out of* romantic love.

In the kind of eros I am talking about, the dominant feeling is precisely
that there is no possibility of real consummation. Of course, there may be
sexual intercourse of various sorts or degrees. There may be orgasm, which
may lead to the cessation of physical desire. But the experience I am trying
to isolate—that form of eros which I call *Romantic Love*—is characterized
by the feeling that nothing would actually constitute a consummation. The
phenomenological mark of love is this: *Love is the acute consciousness of
the impossibility of possession.*

This impossibility of possession or consummation is central to the classic conception of romantic love that we find in the troubadour tradition, as
well as in other writers from Sappho through Stendhal. Although an argument is frequently made that romantic love is specific to certain times and
places,[3] it is in fact exemplified by several literatures quite outside the period generally assigned to romantic love. Sappho's poetry bears witness to
its possibility in Greece; and Romeo and Juliet have distant Chinese cousins

in the legends of Yang Guifei (Tang dynasty, seventh to eight century) and of Liang Shanbo and Zhu Yingtai (Song dynasty, tenth to fourteenth century). What all these legends and stories have in common is the connection of romantic love and death, irrevocable separation, or some other insuperable obstacle. In the troubadour tradition there is also the practice of the "Asag" or test of love in which the lover was expected to spend the night in his mistress's arms without any sexual consummation.[4] But the "Ur-legend" of romantic love is that of Tristan and Iseult.[5] These classic stories of romantic love present four problematic features, each of which either consists in self-deception or offers an almost irresistible temptation to self-deception: *crystallization*, the *Platonic ideal*, the *anti-Platonic ideal*, and the problem of *repetition and transference*. I shall now explain these.

Crystallization: Stendhal, in his analysis of *amour passion*, accords a central place to a process which essentially consists in the concealment of the bare reality of the loved object. The name of this process is inspired by Stendhal's observation that if you deposited a twig for a few days in the Salzburg salt mines, it would acquire beautiful accretions of salt crystals: "I call 'crystallization' that operation of the mind which turns whatever presents itself into a discovery of new perfections in the object of love. . . . Here is the reason that love is the most powerful of all passions. In the case of other passions, desire must come to an accommodation with cold reality; in love alone, reality is keen to model itself on desire."[6] This view implies that romantic love is particularly resistant to the encroachment of the real. Whatever dissolves the shining crystals will reveal only a common twig, which seems doomed to banality. Crystallization consists essentially in self-deception, or at least in *bootstrapping*, that is, in the process of constituting certain features of the love object into virtues simply by the very fact that they come to be seen as such.

Whether this is a pessimistic assessment depends on your view of the desirability of self-deception. Bootstrapping seems appropriate when there is no issue about the reality of the object of concern: My enjoyment of a certain food or hobby, say, may be quite independent of any claim that the food has an objective virtue. But if there is an implicit claim of independent objectivity about the quality imputed to the object, then bootstrapping is self-deception. If realism is resolutely subordinated to the quality of feeling, one may find nothing wrong with self-deception. Otherwise, one may find the process disreputable.[7] In any case, self-deception finds itself at the heart of at least one conception of romantic love. The mechanism of self-deception here is *idealization*: the pretense that the object of love is an incarnation of the ideal. In this respect, crystallization is akin to the Platonic requirement, which is the second problematic feature of romantic love.

The Platonic requirement is the idealization of the object, which goes with the fact that consummation is always impossible or delayed. As Rougemont points out, for Tristan to marry Iseult would be an absurdity: "But let her get a divorce, and she shall be his! Together they shall experience 'real life'. . . . But . . . will the lover with all his desires gratified continue to be in love with his Iseult *once she has been wed*? For Iseult is ever a stranger. . . . She is the woman-from-whom-one-is-parted; to possess her is to lose her" (p. 284). I call this a *Platonic* condition, because it expresses the duality of desire and the conditions of its satisfaction, which lie at the heart of the Platonic conception of desire.[8] Since the true object of desire is something literally out of this world, it can never be possessed in this life. But the temptation exists to deny this impossibility, perhaps by believing that the loved object *is* the ideal or provides some sort of mystical path to the ideal. The Platonic condition encourages the self-deceptive process of crystallization.

The *anti-Platonic requirement*, however, is perhaps even more important to romantic love. It is the requirement that romantic love be essentially focused on a singular, particular *individual*. This is anti-Platonic not merely in the sense of going against the Platonist preoccupation with ideal types as opposed to concrete individuals. More interestingly, it gives rise to a kind of mirror-image paradox. The Platonic lover can never, in this world, find love's true object. But the lover whose love is focused essentially on an individual is condemned to an equal and opposite metaphysical frustration. If I love you, I must love you as you uniquely are; I must love you for being who you are and no other. But *being yourself and no other* is not enough to distinguish anyone, since it is a property shared by every particular. Thus I must *know* what properties distinguish you from others. But properties as such are general. If, therefore, knowledge involves more than mere acquaintance, considered as a purely causal relation devoid of conceptual content, it must have conceptual content. So knowledge itself is *intrinsically general*. I must always love my lover *for* some qualities, however inarticulate, which severally or together make him lovable for me. So although it is a love *of* an individual, my love is always motivated by some general characteristics. Singular love can no more be achieved than Platonic love, its equal and opposite chimera.

Actually there are two aspects to the anti-Platonic intuition. One con-

cerns time, the other uniqueness. The essential unrepeatability of any moment is something we must be human to experience:

> We alone can see death. When a beast is free
> its downfall is ever behind it; before it
> there is God. And when it walks, it walks
> inside Eternity, like a running brook.[9]

This may be a romantic view of animals, but it implies that animals cannot
feel romantic love. They may well feel other forms of love: attachment,
tenderness, companionship. But romantic love, in the full sense, requires
language, art, the conception of time as passing and the consciousness of
the inevitability of my own death—not just a sense of danger or loss, or
some instinctual cringing in front of something terrifying, but the actual
articulate knowledge of my own death.

To say that the experience of romantic love requires a linguistic apparatus of temporal notions doesn't mean that we need to *experience* it as depending on the linguistic apparatus in question. On the contrary, we feel
the need to experience time directly—or rather, since that is no more possible than any other form of direct perception, we need to feel *as if* we were
experiencing it directly. Again, a kind of self-deception is built into the
very heart of the experience.

The second aspect of the intuition of particularity has to do more directly with the *singularity* of persons. The person I love is just *this* and no
other; it would not even be her identical twin, if she had one. Yet how does
this cash out? To direct one's attention onto a particular person or a particular moment is certainly possible in *fact*, but I don't see how it can be possible even in principle to *know* that one is doing it. I have argued that we can
have knowledge only of the general. The general can be as specific as you
like but can never guarantee that it is not taking one singular object for another of the same kind. Here too, then, is an opportunity for self-
deception: The self-deception consists in believing that the contingent
uniqueness of the properties collected in the one loved object is identical
with the necessary uniqueness that pertains to any particular just as a matter of logic. "I love you only and could love no other," masks the fact that I
might become attracted by anyone having just your qualities.

This brings me to the fourth problematic feature of romantic love: *repetition and transference.* In scientific and more generally in all intellectual
matters one can hope to find novelty forever.[10] By contrast, our emotional

life is, I suspect, ineluctably repetitive. Our deepest emotional patterns are probably set in early years and generally prove desperately difficult to change. When two individuals meet, one might ideally expect their interaction to generate a novel and unique emotional pattern; but in practice we are seldom made as new by a new lover as we would like to think. Our emotional reactions to new people and situations tend to be based on coarse categorizations; our "new" emotions slot into old paradigm scenarios: In some measure, they are likely to consist in what psychoanalysts call *transference*. (Is that why there are so few love plots or does the causation run the other way?)[11] That too constitutes a fertile ground for self-deception: One wishes to see every encounter as a renewal, when in point of fact it is most often little more than a reenactment.

Any qualitative experience is in principle repeatable. But what one is purportedly experiencing in romantic love, I have argued, is something in principle unrepeatable. The temptation is to repeat, in a kind of emotional superstition, the gestures associated with the unrepeatable experience. But actual repetition of the same gestures with a different person necessarily fail of their impossible metaphysical goal, while repetition with the same *person* will transform the experience. It will turn into affection, perhaps, or sometimes into indifference, but in any case into *something else*. At best, we say, the illusions of early love lead to the reality of marriage, companionship, constant affection. These are indeed goods, perhaps among the highest goods to which the human condition is capable of attaining. But they are not the same good as was promised by the experience of romantic love.

All this suggests that the project of romantic love is in essence incoherent or impossible. (And also, in a certain sense, merely silly: For everything and every moment is unique in the metaphysical sense, and yet we don't care equally for everything.) Now in the face of heroic or impossible — not to say contradictory — tasks,[12] there are two common human reactions: religion and art. Disappointment is the motor of all art and religion. The deepest art and the most desperate religious belief is generated by those immovable disappointments that are metaphysically necessary. If my argument so far has been right, the disappointments of romantic love are of just that kind. I want to suggest that apart from the more conventional consolations of religion, and apart from the representation of love in art, there is a place for the idea that the experience of love itself can be, by mutual consent, consciously *simulated* or *played*. That is the *theater of love*.

But first, I offer two speculations about the motivations behind the self-deception (and deception) that is so rife in matters of love and sex. One comes from the assumption that there is a *natural teleology of love and sex*. The second stems from a defensiveness about self-deception which I label the *religious attitude*.

Teleology: Those people who would describe themselves as committed to strict monogamy do not generally claim to be immune from the experience of sexual *temptations*; and that term is applicable, of course, whenever someone thinks in terms of *resistance*. But why would one want to resist temptation? Partly because one assigns a teleology to sexual emotions: They are *supposed* to be *exclusive* and *overwhelming*. The relative impersonality of sexual desire[13] is therefore denied or relegated to an inferior role as some sort of immature and merely preliminary play. "When you encounter *real* love, you'll see that what you are experiencing *now* wasn't the *Real Thing*." If we drop the teleological prejudice, this maneuver no longer makes sense. It becomes reminiscent of the argument produced by the airline passenger refusing a drink in the *New Yorker* cartoon: "No thank you, I don't think Nature intended us to drink while flying."

The religious attitude: All art, as well as all religion, appeals to the willing suspension of commonsense belief—the "suspension of disbelief." The difference between the suspension of disbelief required by religion and that required by art is that religion is *deceptive* whereas art is merely *illusory*. That is, you're supposed to believe in the propositions advanced by the religion you espouse, but you are not expected to believe that the play you have gone to watch was anything but a simulation.

This, then, is my second diagnosis of the prevalence of self-deception in love and sex: It is because people will not accept the possibility that there can be nondeceptive, *honest simulations* in the area of romantic love. People are thus, in effect, condemned either to abstain from the exploration, in imaginative play, of the emotions typical of romantic love or else to treat it like religion—that is, to consider themselves in bad faith unless they actually believe in the simulation in which they are taking part. Self-deception becomes a *sine qua non* of love. In art, the avowed justification of all activity is typically, perhaps even by definition, aesthetic. In religion, on the contrary, aesthetic concerns are usually heretical. *Aesthetes of love* are everywhere condemned in much the way that aesthetes *tout court* are condemned by the religious. Aestheticism is the ultimate sacrilege—as in religion, so in love.

This isn't universally the case, since there is a whole tradition of art in the service of religion. There is, in a sense, a whole tradition of theater in the service of romantic love: I mean marriage ceremonies and their pageantry. But that pageantry actually has little to do with erotic or romantic love. It seems designed instead to emphasize the social aspects of marriage, its implication for family alliances, property, and procreation—all of which have traditionally been set in opposition to the erotic and to romantic love.

The theatrical ceremonies I have in mind, by contrast, consist in *staging the erotic gestures of love* with a view to pleasure and an *aesthetic* creation, or re-creation, of the poignancy of love, of the consciousness of the impossibility of possession, of individuality, and of the irreplaceability of time. Such ceremonies require some of the same qualities of art and of the best kinds of nonerotic love—integrity, honesty, intense attention, generosity, imagination, and a capacity to take pleasure in the pleasure of the other. It can therefore be demanding in the sense in which all aesthetic experiences can be demanding. Nevertheless it can remain primarily an aesthetic experience, a piece of theater, a form of play, because both parties agree to keep the experience of romantic love confined inside a kind of frame isolated from the rest of their lives and expectations. Indeed, when we remember the essential ingredients of the phenomenology of love—the intensification of the consciousness of temporality and particularity—we can see that the temporary character of such an encounter is not merely an accident: It is of the essence of the experience.

Unlike philosophical doubt, which is better termed *suspension of belief*, the *suspension of disbelief* required by art or religion is not easily effected merely by reflection. Art and religion typically enlist the sensual in the enterprise (though some religions, such as certain brands of Protestants, regard as suspect that enlistment of the sensuous). This is why sexual caresses can contribute essentially to the theater of love. When sex is involved, the power of theater enlists the power of biology in its aid. The theater of love presents a consensual simulation of love, rooted in the awareness of its own ephemeral character and heightened by sensual pleasure, in which the unrepeatability of the episode stands for the irreplaceability of the historical individual.

The power of sex has so frightened most cultures that they have surrounded it with elaborate myths and barriers. There is a long tradition of regarding sex as incompatible with love, as killing respect, an "expense of spirit in a waste of shame." There is also a long tradition of people killing one another for religion; could these two things be connected? In both cases, I surmise, what is at work is the defense of self-deception stemming from what I have pejoratively termed the religious attitude.

According to the religious attitude, if religion is treated as mere art, or if love is allowed to be, in Yeats's words, "a game that follows when I let the kerchief fall," then it threatens the process by which religion, including the social religion of sacred marriage and other institutions, is held up. It allows art to be mixed with life. But of course art—imagination, fantasy, play—is already mixed with life and love. The traditional views of romantic love, including Stendhal's crystallization, are nothing more than the careful cultivation of illusion. They differ from the proposal I am making mainly in that the illusions in question are, in the traditional perspectives, supposed to be cogent: They are supposed to be akin to the illusions of religion rather than to the illusions of art, in that they are supposed to be believed at every level rather than subject to a suspension of disbelief.

The issue, then, is not whether we should countenance self-deception, but whether we should countenance the self-conscious *playing out* of an emotion relatively insulated from the rest of reality. The view that we should not calls to mind Oscar Wilde's uncharacteristically moralistic definition of sentimentality: "A sentimentalist is one who desires to have the luxury of an emotion without paying for it."[14] But if one countenances any aesthetic experience beyond the painful and *costly* process of the creation of a work of art, why shouldn't we indulge in emotions without paying their full price in reality? For what is the desire for the contemplation of art, if not the desire to do just that?

There are disanalogies, of course. Theatrical performances are generally scripted and rehearsed; those of the theater of love are not obviously so. And yet to acknowledge the role of transference is to recognize that they have been scripted by our past and have been rehearsed before in earlier "performances." Aesthetic delight, here as elsewhere, lies in the small variations.

There is another interesting analogy, one that plays on a paradox about the conditions most conducive to the apprehension and telling of truths. We expect that in the theater, as in other literary arts, we will see our own lives delineated with more clarity and force than we can give them ourselves. Inside the context of a self-conscious pretense, or simulation, we can apprehend certain truths more freely and more clearly. Similarly, in the relative anonymity of an encounter with a stranger, certain truths may be realized, certain patterns of emotion or response revealed, which in the routine of our ordinary life are hidden or repressed. It is a platitude that intimacy requires old acquaintance; equally, it is a platitude that old acquaintance sometimes makes certain kinds of intimacy impossible. People tell all their secrets to strangers on planes, precisely because they are strangers. With those who know us, there is often too much at stake to tell the truth. With a stranger, like a priest, you have nothing to lose. With strangers, masks can be dropped which are desperately important to keep with one's intimates.

Needless to say, these virtues do not invariably bless any self-conscious attempt to play at love. Nor, for that matter, is every work of art a good one. But they are possible, and that, in the absence of countervailing dangers, would seem justification enough for pursuing the genre.

The power of biology and the power of theater are arguably those that hold the human mind in the tightest of all grips. So it is easy to see why the sorts of ceremonies I have in mind are generally considered *dangerous*. And indeed they are dangerous, just as art and religion are dangerous. Among its dangers are the obvious ones, of actually finding one has deceived oneself or the other, if only unintentionally. But there are also more straightforwardly aesthetic dangers. What, for example, is the difference between playing at attention to the particular and being enmired in the merest generality? Henri Bergson thought only comedy was general, while tragedy was particular.[15] In fact all art *aspires* to the particular, but with respect to its *subject matter* it can achieve only the general. It achieves the particular only in its *medium* — which is of course the fact exploited by abstract art. The one-night stand is the abstract art of love.

Another objection comes from the opposite direction: one that is implicit in Rougemont's analysis and is also illustrated in Huxley's *Brave New World*. The objection is that by playing at sexual love one will be trivializing its beauty and blunting its power. *We must hem sex in to keep it exciting.* This objection is interesting in that it involves exactly the kind of studied self-deception that I am in different terms myself advocating. Thus it can claim no moral high ground over the defense of promiscuity. But if taming the power of eros means inoculating it against its ancient association with death, as illustrated in the classic myths of romantic love, then perhaps that is an outcome that a civilized sensibility can welcome.

Another form of this objection is that far from "making the best" of the repetitiousness of our emotional life, the theater of love just guarantees that we shall sink into jaded insensibility.[16] How does the theater of love deal with the problem of the blunting of sensibility by repetition? The answer is that it does so in two ways: by using the power of sensuality to enhance our consciousness of time, and by relegating repetition to the frame rather than the content of the representation.

Habituation blunts the intensity of experience, but our senses have a remarkable capacity to regenerate, providing we give them time and opportunity. That is why the theater of love requires, in order to sustain our excitement, the enlistment of the biological power of sex as well as the psychological power of theater. Sensuality serves to intensify our consciousness of time, just as the rhetoric of art, appealing to our sensual and emotional responses in the evocation of ideas and images, serves to intensify our capacity to take a fresh view at familiar situations of life.

The second way that the theater of love deals with the problem of repetition brings out an unexpected analogy with real theater. The trick here is that wherever there is play or representation, not everything that is part of the representing medium need be part of what is represented. The actor's collapse on being shot belongs to the character, but the fact that the actor later gets up and takes a bow does not. Thus it is a normal if not universal fact about theatrical performances that they take place again and again. But that repetition, including the nightly resuscitation of the hero, is not part of the action represented: It is only an accident of the representing medium. It is an attribute of the frame, not of the represented story itself.

Different aspects of the representing medium can be shifted out or into the picture, in or out of the frame. The way that the theater of love deals with repetition, then, stems from its power to relegate the repetitious elements to the frame rather than to the content. And no wonder that some elements of the representation must fail to correspond to the thing represented, since what is represented or played at is, ex hypothesi, *impossible*.

So far I have been concerned with the mutual simulation of love between two people whose interest in the matter is the same. But my argument has obvious application to the aesthetics and ethics of prostitution. If the conscious simulation of love bolstered by the power of sex is a valuable form of theater, why should some people not make a profession of it? Unless we condemn theater in all its forms, there can't be anything wrong with the mere fact that we are being invited to experience emotions that don't correspond to anything that is immediately real. Why isn't prostitution regarded as just another form of theater?

One prima facie disanalogy is that theatrical performances aren't usually *mutual*: In prostitution, the audience is usually more active than the average theatergoer. Yet actors do get a kick out of their power to move an audience. Often, indeed, it is part of the professional actor's pride that audiences *love me enough to pay me*. Why might this not apply to the prostitute? (As has frequently been pointed out, it applies well enough to the wife.) Indeed, the analogy may be stronger here than the disanalogy. Some performers typically feel contempt for the audience, and vice versa. The prostitute feels contempt for the john, who reciprocates. But the carnie also feels contempt for the *rube*, who also reciprocates. And don't waiters in expensive restaurants feel much the same? The "legitimate" theater seems to escape this cycle of contempt. But perhaps this is not because of any intrinsic difference. More likely it varies according to the measure in which the audience esteems the actor. Mutual esteem is a mutual salve; perhaps much of what impedes mutual esteem has nothing intrinsically to do with the nature of the transaction, but rather with the level of social approbation generally accorded the transaction in question.

Probably a career in prostitution is one we should not wish upon our loved ones, even if we were happy for them to enter the closely similar professions of therapist, actor, or even traditional wife. But it remains to be shown that this is not merely a consequence of the social and ethical attitudes I have been questioning. One wouldn't have wished it on one's loved ones to be an actress in the eighteenth century, or for that matter, a Jew under the Nazis. But that was no reflection on the intrinsic dignity of actors or of Jews.

In this paper, I have attempted a rehabilitation of certain forms of sexual/emotional play as theater of love. My argument has been that the metaphysical impulses behind romantic love—the dilemmas created by emotional repetition and by the coexistence of the Platonic and the anti-Platonic requirements—might be served in a mode that mixes real sex and aesthetic imagination. I might in conclusion take my claim one step further. The theater of love is, in relation to traditional conceptions of romantic love, actually more civilized, at least in respect of two attributes of civilization. Call these attributes imagination and irony. To be civilized is, in part, to know how to substitute the activity of the imagination for the grosser propensities which evolution has bequeathed us. Thus the Greeks in the heyday of Athens were notoriously more civilized than the Romans in the heyday of Rome: The games of the Roman circuses involved ever increasing savagery; their stakes were real life and death, real freedom and riches, leaving nothing to the imagination. By contrast, the games of the Greeks were sports, in which no one had to die; human capacities were tested in an artistic, abstract context, and their reward was a few bay leaves. The superior civilization of the Greeks lay in their capacity to transpose the sociobiological reality of human aggression onto the plane of the imagination.[17] But another, perhaps more advanced characteristic of civilization is irony. Richard Rorty has defined the ironist as "the sort of person who faces up to the contingency of his or her own most central beliefs and desires"[18] — in particular, this means being self-conscious about the role of fantasy and imagination: to see art as art, and not as religion or as magic. The unattainability of so many of our aspirations drives us to take refuge in imagination at all stages of civilization; but in its primitive avatar this response is religion, in its civilized avatar it is the self-conscious pretending of art. I have argued that romantic love is analogous to religion in taking its illusions seriously. The theater of love may sometimes represent a form of *play*, in both senses of the word, which reflect a more advanced stage of civilization than romantic love itself.

Notes

[1] Or some other pathology of the self. See selection by Kathryn Pauly Morgan in this volume.

[2] C. S. Lewis, *The Four Loves* (Glasgow: Fontana, 1963).

[3] According to Niklas Luhmann, for example, love requires a certain "code" of communication, which needs to be set up in some sort of social context. Luhmann claims that the question of romantic love concerns the "genesis of a generalized symbolic communicative medium assigned specifically to facilitating, cultivating and promoting the communicative treatment of individuality." See Luhmann, *Love as Passion* (Cambridge, Mass.: Harvard University Press, 1986), esp. p. 14.

[4] See René Nelli, "Love's Rewards," in *Fragments for a History of the Human Body*, ed. Michel Feher with Ramona Naddaff and Nadia Tazi (New York: Zone, 1989), vol. 2.

[5] See Denis de Rougemont, *L'Amour et l'occident*, trans. into English as *Love and the Western World* (New York: Pantheon Books, 1956).

[6] Stendhal, *De l'Amour* (Paris: Cluny, 1938), pp. 43, 62.

[7] In *Madness and Reason* (London: George, Allen, Unwin, 1985) Jennifer Radden points out that several states, including religious or more broadly "symbolic" states and "aesthetic" ones, involve the sort of paradoxical conflict of belief traditionally associated with self-deception (p. 109). It is important to sort out the variety of states that can legitimately involve this kind of "duality" from those that cannot. My plea in this paper is that some of the ones that we generally disparage in the context of sex and love are in fact more worthy of respect, once hedged in the right ways, than some of those hallowed by tax deductions in our culture.

[8] (At least in those middle dialogues which have given their significance to the label "Platonic".) The notion of a necessarily unattainable otherworldly target of desire is developed in the *Symposium*, *Republic*, and *Phaedrus*. It is not plausibly attributed to the (late period) *Philebus*, but is prefigured in the (early) *Lysis* and *Meno*. Or so it has seemed to most readers. For a contrary view of the *Symposium* and the *Phaedrus*, in which the individual is seen as playing a far more genuine role, see Martha Nussbaum, *The Fragility of Goodness* (Cambridge and New York: Cambridge University Press, 1986).

⁹   *Ihn sehen wir allein: das freie Tier*
    hat seinen Untergang stets hinter sich
    und vor sich Gott: und wenn es geht, so gehts
    in Ewigkeit, so wie die Brunnen gehen (R. M. Rilke, Duino Elegy VIII)

[10]The reason for this has to do with the shape of intellectual progress: whenever we solve a problem or arrive at a theory, we generate new questions, questions which could not have been formulated before. The Greek atomists could not have asked, let alone answered, questions now asked about the structure of the atom. So in a clear sense, if we allow that *ignorance* may be defined as relating to *questions to which we have no answers*, our ignorance is far greater than that of the Greeks. Indeed, since every answer generates more than one question, ignorance grows faster than knowledge. And so, if ignorance be the food of intellectual curiosity, we may reasonably hope that the excitement of intellectual novelty will prove inexhaustible.

[11]On the finitude of stories, see Peter Brook, *Reading for the Plot* (New York: Random House, 1984). I explore the theme of the repetitiveness of emotions a little more in "Educating the Emotions," forthcoming in a special issue of *Inquiry* edited by Sophie Haratounian-Gordon.

[12]There cannot actually be any ontological contradictions, but there can be what I call ontological *tragedies*: Tragedies are sometimes called "contradictions," as in "the contradictions of capitalism," but they only involve self-undermining, not literal self-contradiction. See my *Rationality of Emotion* (Cambridge, Mass.: MIT Press, 1987), chap. 12.

[13]Cf. George Bernard Shaw: "Love . . . is the greatest of all human relations, far too great to be a personal matter. Could [a general] serve his country if he . . . refused to kill any enemy . . . unless he personally hated him?" (*Man and Superman*).

[14]Quoted in Michael Tanner, "Sentimentality," *Proceedings of the Aristotelian Society*, New Series (1976), 77:127.

[15]See Henri Bergson, *Le Rire: Essai sur la Signification du Comique* (Paris: Presses Universitaires de France, 1940).

[16]Is this what Blake meant when he said that "the road of excess leads to the palace of wisdom"? It depends which side you think he was on.

[17]I think I learned to think of Greece and Rome in these terms from William B. Macomber, in some lectures at the University of California, Santa Barbara, in 1971.

[18]Richard Rorty, *Contingency, Irony, and Solidarity* (Cambridge: Cambridge University Press, 1989), p. xv.

Robert C. Solomon

The Virtue of (Erotic) Love

Robert C. Solomon is Quincy Lee Centennial Professor of Philosophy at the University of Texas and the author of Love: Emotion, Myth and Metaphor *and* About Love.

In a famous—or infamous—passage, Kant off-handedly dismisses one of the most essential elements in ethics:

> Love out of inclination cannot be commanded; but kindness done from duty—although no inclination impels us, and even although natural and unconquerable disinclination stands in our way—is *Practical*, and not *Pathological* love, residing in the will and not of melting compassion.[1]

In the *Symposium*, on the other hand, Phaedrus offers us one of many contrasting comments by Plato in honor of erōs:

> That is why I say Love is the eldest of the gods and most honored and the most powerful for acquiring virtue and blessedness, for men both living and dead.[2]

This paper has two aims: to understand erotic (romantic, "pathological") love as itself a virtue, and to broaden our view of ethics.

Erōs and Ethics

> It (love) does not hesitate to intrude with its trash. . . . It knows how to slip its love-notes and ringlets even into ministerial portfolios and philosophical manuscripts. Every day it brews and hatches the worst and most perplexing quarrels and disputes, destroys the most valuable relationships and breaks the strongest bonds. . . . Why all this noise and fuss? . . . It is merely a question of every Jack finding his Jill. (The gracious reader should translate this phrase into precise Aristophanic language.) Why should such a trifle play so important a role?[3]
>
> *Arthur Schopenhauer*

Love as a virtue? Well, hardly. Motherly love, certainly; patriotism, perhaps. The love of humanity, to be sure, but romantic love? Erotic love? The passion that makes fools of us all and has led to the demise of Anthony, Cleopatra, young Romeo, Juliet, and King Kong? Love is nice, but it is not a virtue. Maybe it is not even nice. Hesiod in the *Theogony* warned against *erōs* as a force contrary and antagonistic to reason. Sophocles and Euripides both denounced *erōs*, in *Antigone* and *Hippolytus* respectively, and even Virgil had his doubts. Schopenhauer, much more recently, thought all love to be sexual and damnable, and today we are much more likely to invoke the cynical wit of Oscar Wilde or Kingsley Amis than the saccharine pronouncements of our latter-day love pundits. Indeed, running through the history of ideas in the West one cannot but be struck by the ambivalence surrounding this central and celebrated concept. It is cursed as irrational and destructive and praised as the origin of everything. *Erōs* is famous for its foolishness and at the same time elevated and venerated as a god, albeit at first a rather minor one, but by the time of early Christianity, nothing less than God as such.

Today, we find ourselves torn between such mundane considerations as dependency and autonomy, security and the dubious freedom to remain "uncommitted." It is hard to remind ourselves, therefore, that the history of love is intellectual warfare between bestiality on one side and divinity on the other. The word "love" has so often functioned as a synonym for lust that it is hard to take it seriously as a virtue. It has just as long been raised to cosmological status, by Parmenides, Empedocles, and Plotinus, for example, and it therefore seems somewhat small-minded to reduce it to a mere source of human relationships. Most modern philosophers have, accordingly, ignored it, Schopenhauer here as elsewhere being a bit eccentric, while moralists have had a field day playing the one side (lust) against the other (divine grace, piety, and contempt for all bodily functions, but particularly those that are best when shared).

In any discussion of love as a virtue, it is necessary, if by now routine, to mention some different "kinds" of love. (The notion of "kinds" may already be question begging here, for the more difficult issue may be what links, rather than distinguishes, e.g., friendship, sexual love, and parental affection.) In particular, it is essential that we distinguish *erōs* and *agapé*, the former usually translated as sexual love, the latter as selfless and certainly sexless love for humanity. The distinction is often drawn crudely. For instance, *erōs* is taken to be purely erotic and reduced to sexual desire, which it surely is not. Or *agapé* is characterized as selfless giving, opposed by *erōs* which thus becomes selfish taking (or at least craving). *Agapé* is idealized to the point where it becomes an attitude possible only to God, thus rendering it virtually inapplicable to common human fellow-feelings. *Erōs* by contrast is degraded to the profanely secular and denied any hint of spirituality. To think of love as a virtue, therefore, is first of all to expand (once again) the domain of *erōs*. (Romantic love, I am presuming, is one historical variant of *erōs*.) One need not deny the desirability (or the possibility) of altruistic *agapé* to insist that erotic *erōs* shares at least some of its virtues.

Eros, and what we now call "romantic love," should also be distinguished (carefully) from other forms of particular affection—for example, motherly, fatherly, brotherly, or sisterly love and friendship. I think that Schopenhauer was partly right when he suggested (with Freud following him) that all love is to some extent sexual. But to make this point one obviously needs a generously enlarged conception of sex and sexual desire, and I often fear that this insight is motivated as much by its titillating implications as by the impulse to clarify the nature of human bonding. A more modest thesis is that *erōs* (not sex) encompasses almost all intimate, personal affections. What characterizes *erōs* in general, we might then suggest, is an intense quasi-physical, even "grasping," affection for a particular person, a Buscaglian "urge to hug" if you will. (Plato often uses such desire-defined language in talking about *erōs*, even when he is reaching for the Forms.) In romantic love, sexual desire is undeniably a part of this affection, though it is not at all clear whether this is the source of the affection or rather its vehicle. *Erōs* differs from *agapé* in the prevalence of self-interested desire, but it is not thereby selfish and the desire is not just sexual. It also includes a much more general physical desire to "be with," such personal desires as "to be appreciated" and "to be happy together," such inspirational desires as "to be the best for you," and such "altruistic" desires as "to do anything I can for you." As laRochefoucauld once put it, "in the soul . . . a thirst for mastery; in the mind sympathy; in the body, nothing but a delicately hidden desire to possess, after many mysteries."[4]

It is a common mistake to think of the other person in sex as a mere "object" of desire, which leads to the idea that *erōs* too is degrading and seeks only its own satisfaction. Consider Kant on the matter:

> Because sexuality is not an inclination which one human being has for another as such, but is an inclination for the sex of another, it is a principle of the degradation of human nature, in that it gives rise to the

preference of one sex to the other, and to the dishonoring of that sex   495
through the satisfaction of desire.[5]

But surely the question (as Plato raised it 2300 years earlier) is *what* one desires when one sexually desires another person. In the *Symposium*, Aristophanes suggested that one desires not sex but permanent (re-)unification with the other; Socrates insisted that one really wants the Forms. Even if we consider such goals too fantastic for *erōs*, it is clear that the Greeks — as opposed to Kant and many moderns — saw that sexual desire was much, much more than desire for sex and not at all opposed to virtuous desire. At the very least, it is clear that sexual desire is some sort of powerful desire *for* the other person *through* sex. The question is: a desire *for what?* And by no means should we assume from the outset that the answer to this question has anything to do with sexual *objects*. Indeed, taking our clue from Hegel and Sartre, we might suggest rather that it has everything to do with sexual *subject*, and subjects by their very nature cannot be wholly sexual.

The most obvious difference between erotic (romantic) and other particular forms of love is the centrality of sexual (do not read "genital") desire, but there are two other differences that, philosophically, are much more illuminating. The first, though quite controversial, is the prerequisite of *equality* between lovers. This may seem odd in the light of modern accusations against love as a vehicle for the degradation and oppression of women (Shulamith Firestone, Marilyn French), but in historical perspective it becomes clear that — however far we may be from real equality — romantic love emerges only with the relative liberation of women from traditional subservient social and economic roles. Romantic love emerges only when women begin to have more of a choice about their lives — and about their lovers and husbands in particular. One thinks of John Milton's Adam, created early in the era of romantic love, who specifically requested from God not a mere playmate or companion or a mirror image of himself but an *equal*, for "among unequals what society/Can sort, what harmony or true delight?"[6] Or, paraphrasing Stendhal, we might say that love tends to create equals even where it does not find them, for equality is as essential to romantic love as authority is to parenthood — whether or not this is adequately acknowledged or acted upon.

One other difference between *erōs* and other loves is that romantic love, unlike familial love, for example, is unprescribed and often spontaneous. ("Romantic friendships" are especially worth noting in this context.) Critical to erotic, romantic love is the sense of *choice*. Family love, in this sense, is always prescribed. The love between husband and wife, or what such authors as de Rougemont call "conjugal love," might be considered prescribed in this sense too, including its sexuality. This is emphatically not to say that married love cannot be romantic, or that romantic love is characterized only by its novelty or by the excitement and anxiety consequent to that novelty. It is a common mistake to take the exhilaration of love as love—without asking what that exhilaration is *about*. Love and marriage often begin together even if they do not always remain together, and to separate them is just to say that love can be unhitched just as horses can, while carriages sit unmoving.

What could be virtuous about *erōs*? One might rationalize sexual love as the slippery slope to marriage, but this faint praise only reinforces our image of romantic love as something in itself childish, foolish, and a kind of conspiracy of nature and society to trick self-consciously rebellious adolescents into maturity. One might celebrate *erōs* as the often unrecognized source of many of our most beautiful creations, from Dante's poetry to the Taj Mahal, but this too is to demean love as a virtue and see it merely as a means, as Freud once saw anal retention as a means to great art. But it seems to me that *erōs* is not considered a virtue for three general sorts of reasons:

(1) *Erōs* is reduced to mere sexuality, and philosophers, insofar as they deign to dirty their minds with sex at all (*qua* philosophers, of course), tend to see sexuality as vulgar and not even a candidate for virtue. Part of this is the common perception of sex as either a form of recreation or a means to procreation, but in any case a set of desires constrained by ethics but hardly of ethical value in themselves.

(2) Love is an emotion and emotions are thought to be irrational, beyond our control, merely episodic instead of an essential aspect of character, products of "instinct" and intractable in the face of all evidence and objective consideration. Even Aristotle, one of the few friends of the passions in the history of philosophy, insisted that only states of character, not passions, can count as virtues.

(3) *Erōs* even insofar as it is not just sexual is self-love and the self-indulgence of desire, while an essential characteristic of the virtues is, in Hume's phrase, their utility, their being pleasing to others and based on such sentiments as compassion and sympathy. Romantic love, far from being "pleasing to others," tends to be embarrassing and sometimes harmful to others and self-destructive. It tends to be possessive, jealous, obsessive,

antisocial, even "mad." Such drama is not the stuff of which virtue is made.

I obviously believe that each of these objections to erotic love as a virtue is just plain wrong, but it will take most of this paper to spell out an alternative view. Simply, for now, let me state that these objections demean and misunderstand the nature of sexuality, the nature of emotions, and the nature of love in particular. So that I do not appear overly irrationalist and romantic here, let me draw Plato to my side. He clearly saw *erōs* as a virtue, and every one of the speakers in the *Symposium* agrees with this. Even Socrates, by far the most effete of the speakers, celebrates *erōs* not as the disinterested appreciation of beauty and wisdom (as many Oxford commentaries would make it seem) but rather as a "grasping" sensuality, perhaps of the mind rather than the body, but erotic none the less for that. (Why did he so distrust beauty in art but yet celebrate it in *erōs*?) In Plato's thinking, *erōs* was a virtue just because it was (in part) a passion, filled with desire and — in that peculiarly noble Socratic sense — self-obsessed as well.

Ethics and Subjectivity

One more word against Kant as a *moralist*. A virtue must be *our own* invention, *our* most necessary self-expression and self-defense; any other kind of virtue is a danger . . . "Virtue," "duty," the "good in itself," the good which is impersonal and universally valid — chimeras and expressions of decline, of the final exhaustion of life. . . . The fundamental laws of self-preservation and growth demand the opposite — that everyone invent *his own* virtue, his *own* categorical imperative.[7]
Friedrich Nietzsche

A single paradigm of rationality has retained hegemony in ethics since the Enlightenment. In the shadow of this paradigm, there is less difference than similarity between Kant and the utilitarians: moral philosophy is nothing if not objective, rational, based on principles, and exclusive of particular self-reference and mere personal perspectives. What is shocking is what the paradigm leaves out: most emotions and love in particular (except insofar as these might motivate duty or serve "the greatest good for the greatest number"). The persistence of this paradigm (which I will call "Kantian") has turned the most exciting subject in philosophy — or so it would seem from novels, the newspapers, soap operas, and ordinary gossip—into the dry quasi-legal tedium that we find in some philosophy journals. And worse, it has proved to many people—including many philosophers—that ethics has little to do with the intricate realities of human behavior. The elegant observations of Hume are shunted aside in favor of *policy* decisions. The neglect of personal inclinations in favor of legalistic universal principles leaves out the substance of the ethical, which is not principles but feelings. Bernard Williams points out that it would be "insane" to prefer an act of kindness born of principle rather than personal affection, as Kant recommends.[8] When one thinks of the myriad delights, affections, and felt obligations in love, one cannot help but decide that, given a choice between insisting that love is amoral (at best) and retaining the Kantian paradigm, one's preference is quite clear. Kant's line that we quoted from the *Groundwork* about "pathological love," even on the most generous interpretation (as "pathos" rather than "diseased"), dismisses romantic affection as wholly irrelevant to moral worth, and with this eliminates most of what we—and most of Kant's more romantic colleagues—take to be the very heart of morality.

Richard Taylor once wrote that he found Kantian ethics basically offensive, so much so that he insisted that he would have the same attitude toward a true Kantian that he would toward a person who "regularly drowned children just to see them squirm."[9] This is extreme, and it ignores many recent attempts to "humanize" Kant,[10] but the Kantian position is offensive, and one of the reasons for this is its resistance, if not rejection, of any inclusion of personal, particular feelings in moral evaluation. We find similar resistance in many modern Kantians, for instance, in Bernard Gert's *The Moral Rules* where he dismisses feelings as morally worthless and insists instead that "feelings are morally important only insofar as they lead to morally good actions."[11] It seems to me, on the contrary, that nothing is more important to our evaluation of a person's moral character than feelings, and not just because of our reasonable expectation that actions generally follow feelings. The worth of our feelings is not parasitic on the desirability of our actions. In love, the worthiness of our actions depends on the feelings they express. Generous and even heroic actions may follow from love, but the virtue of love stands quite on its own, even without such consequences (Socrates' criticism of Phaedrus in the *Symposium*). We may think Othello foolish and tragic but we still admire the motive, while Victorian literature is filled with Kantian gentlemen acting on their principles who are utterly repulsive (for instance, Mr. Collins in Jane Austen's *Pride and Prejudice*). Not only is it desirable to love, but those who have not loved (if not lost), or fear they cannot, rightly worry not only about their character but about their completeness as human beings—quite apart from any questions about action or performance. Love itself is admirable, quite apart from its effects and consequences.

Why is the tradition so opposed to love and other feelings as essential, even primary ingredients, in morality? The opposition is all the more surprising given the heavy emphasis on love (though as *agapé*) as the supreme virtue in the New Testament—and it is just this oddity that Kant is trying to explain away in the passage quoted. There seem to be several reasons for Kant's antagonism to feelings in moral evaluation. First and foremost, he seems to believe that only that which can be "commanded" is morally obligatory, and love as a passion cannot be commanded. This particular claim has been admirably disputed in Ed Sankowski's 1978 paper on "Love and Moral Obligation," where, in particular, he argues that we at least hold people responsible for fostering or evading the conditions that breed love.[12] One might challenge as well the claim that only that which can be commanded is moral; much of what goes into "good character," while it can be cultivated, cannot be commanded. One might also argue—as I have often—that the emotions are far more voluntaristic and under our control than we normally believe, and not just in the sense that we can foster or avoid the conditions in which they typically emerge. This is not to say that an emotion such as love can simply be produced, by an act of will or volition, as one might now produce a thought or a movement of one's finger. There may be, in Danto-esque phrase, no "basic action" where love is concerned. But there are lots of intentional actions of both mind and body that are not basic, and to insist that love can be produced *de nihilo* by a volition is surely to place an unreasonable demand on its moral virtue.

Second, on the Kantian paradigm, it is always the universal that is in question, never the particular. Here Kant is once again in agreement with New Testament ethics, for *agapé* could be argued to be universal (or, one might also say, indiscriminate) love, and not love for any particular person. (It is worth noting that Christian psychology did hold people responsible for their feelings, did believe that love could be commanded, and, in just the phrase disputed by Kant, demanded it.) But on many interpretations Christian love, as love, is emphatically the love of particulars—even if of every particular and not just of the universal (God, humanity) as such. Love—especially erotic or romantic love—is wholly particular. It is the elevation of one otherwise ordinary person to extraordinary heights with extraordinary privileges. The idea of a categorical imperative in such instances is laughable. On the Kantian model, the particularity of love would seem to be a form of irrationality—comparable to our tendency to make "exceptions" of ourselves, in this case, making exceptions of persons close to us. In love the particular is everything. The virtue of love is and ought to be entirely preferential and personal. The lover who gives special preference to his love (though not, of course, in a bureaucratic or departmental position) is virtuous. A lover who insisted on treating everyone including his or her lover the same would strike us as utterly repulsive.

Third, because morality is a matter of reason, the irrationality of the emotions (in general) is good enough reason not to make them central to ethics. The alleged irrationality of emotions is something more than their supposed involuntariness and particularity. Kant thinks that emotions are irrational, Bernard Williams suggests, because they are capricious. One might add that they also seem to be intrusive, disruptive, stubborn, stupid, and pointless. These are very different accusations, but they are often levied together against emotions in general and love in particular. As "feelings," it is often said that emotions are *non*rational (not even smart enough to be *ir*rational.) Or, granting emotions a modicum of aims and intelligence, it is insisted that emotions (*sui generis*) have limited ends and (at best) inefficient means. Against the "disruptive" view of emotions it should be argued that they do not always intrude or disrupt life but often (always?) define it and define the ultimate ends of rationality as well. Against the view that emotions are stupid, one could argue at length how emotional "intuition" is often more insightful and certainly more strategic than many of the ratiocinations of abstract moralizing, and against the view that emotions are aimless it should be said that all emotions have their aims, even if rather odd and sometimes limited. On the other hand, it should be commented that some emotions—among them love—have the most grandiose aims, far grander than the surely limited desire to be "reasonable." Consider Hegel:

> Love neither restricts nor is restricted; it is not finite at all . . . love completely destroys objectivity and thereby annuls and transcends reflection, deprives man's opposite of all foreign character, and discovers life itself without any further defect.[13]

The most common accusation against the emotions, and love in particular, is that they confuse or distort our experience (Leibniz called them "confused perceptions"). What is in question here is the infamous resistance of emotions to canons of consistency and evident facts, their alleged lack of "common sense" and tendency to bias perception and judgment, their apparent tolerance of contradiction (which Freud made one of the hallmarks of "the Unconscious"), their refusal to conform to obvious considerations of objectivity. In love, this is embarrassingly obvious. A homely lover looks longingly at his equally plain love and declares, "you are the most beautiful woman in the world." How are we to understand this? Self-deception? Insanity? Surely not "blindness" (which would be plain ignorance), for the problem is not that he cannot see. Indeed, he might well claim to see much *more* than we do, or more deeply. Impolitely pressed, our enraptured lover may resentfully concede the point, perhaps doing a phenomenological retreat to, "Well, she's the most beautiful woman in the world *to me!*" but we know how such qualifications are treated in philosophy—with proper epistemological disdain. In love one makes a claim, and it is a claim that is demonstrably false. Beauty is not in the eye of the beholder, perhaps, but is this an argument against love?

Consider in the same light the accusation of "intractability" that is thrown at the emotions as a charge, supposedly separating them from reason and rationality. (Amelie Rorty, for example, develops this charge at length in her "Explaining Emotions."[14]) It is worth noting that Kant rejected the emotions not because they were stubborn but because they were capricious, even though such a suggestion goes against the obvious—that emotions can be durable and devoted, even stubborn and intractable. In love, in particular, it is notoriously difficult, when one has been in love, to purge that emotion, even though it now has become an intolerable source of pain and not at all a source of pleasure. But is this an accusation against the emotions, or is it rather part of their virtue? It is passing fancy that we criticize, not unmovable devotion. It is sudden anger that we call irrational, not long-motivated and well-reasoned animosity (which is not to say, of course, that sudden anger is always improper or inappropriate, or that long-term outrage is not sometimes irrational and even insane). It is true that the emotions are stubborn and intractable, but this—as opposed to much less dependable action in accordance with principle—is what makes them so essential to ethics. Principles can be easily rationalized and reinterpreted. One trusts a person fighting in accordance with his passions far more than one fighting for abstract principles. (It is remarkable how principles can always admit convenient exceptions and emendations.) Intractability is a virtue of the emotions as rationalization is to reason a vice. In-

502 deed we might even say that the "truth" of emotions is their intractability, their resistance to every attempt to change them.

Objectively, what love sees and thinks is mostly nonsense, and what it values is quite contrary to everything that philosophical ethics likes to emphasize — objectivity, impersonality, disinterestedness, universality, respect for evidence and arguments, and so on. And yet, it seems to me that such irrationality is among our most important and charming features. We care about each other prior to any evidence or arguments that we ought to. We find each other beautiful, charming, and desirable, seemingly without reference to common standards. We think less of a lover if his or her love alters when it alteration finds, or if one bends to the opinions of friends. Love *ought* to be intractable, we believe, even if this same stubbornness causes considerable pain once the love is over. We are thoroughly prejudiced, to use a jaundiced word, thoroughly unreasonable. "Why do you love *her*?!" is a question that need not be answered or even acknowledged. Indeed, we even think it admirable, if also foolish, to love someone totally undeserving (from someone else's point of view). Love itself is the virtue, a virtue so important that rationality itself pales in importance.

Ultimately, the charge against the emotions — and against love in particular — is that of "subjectivity." Subjectivity is a notoriously slippery notion in philosophy which is often opposed to contrastingly tidy concepts of rationality and objectivity. The charge of "subjectivity" typically turns into an accusation of bias and unreasonableness. But, on the other hand, there is a complementary charge against objectivity, against impersonal, merely abstract ratiocination. There is that sense of "objectivity" — pursued by Camus and Thomas Nagel, for example — in which we are all infinitesimal specks in the galaxy, our lives no more significant than the lives of trees or sea polyps, our bodies nothing but the stuff of physiology, our sex a dubious advancement of the reproduction of bacteria, our speech nothing but noise, our lives meaningless. It is what Nagel calls "the view from nowhere," and in its extreme forms it is as undesirable as it is impossible. But such a viewpoint tends to dominate ethics and value theory as well, if in a more humane or anthropocentric scope. Most of contemporary ethics is still framed not as personal but as policy — to be applied, one suspects, by some imagined philosopher-king. The emphasis is not on being a "good person" but rather a just and fair administrator (being a good person is presumably the same). The model, thinly disguised by the evasive logic of "universalizability," is the bureaucrat, who treats everyone the same and has no

relevant personality of his or her own. Love is thus unethical, for against all
principles of ethics it has the audacity to view one other person as someone
very special and does not, as Mill insisted, count "everyone as one and only
one" at all.

On Love's Virtues: Plato's *Symposium* Revisited

> It is, in fact, just a love story. . . . Alcibiades, asked to speak about erōs,
> cannot describe the passion or its object in general terms, because his
> experience of love is an experience that happened to him only once,
> and in connection with an individual who is seen by him to be like no-
> body else in the world.[15]
> *Martha Nussbaum*

The classical text on the virtue(s) of erotic love is, of course, Plato's *Symposium,* and Plato (not Socrates) provides us with a portrait of *erōs* as a virtue
which is quite appropriate to our modern concept of romantic love. Let us
begin by saying very quickly that the concept of *erōs* there discussed is not
the same as our concept of romantic love, that Greek love is asymmetrical
love between man and youth rather than our symmetrical romance between man and woman, that Plato is doing much in that dialogue which is
by no means evident or easily comprehensible to the modern nonclassicist
reader. That said, we can remind ourselves that the subject of the dialogue
is the nature and the virtues of love. Each of the various speeches can be interpreted as a substantial theory. It is worth noting that Socrates objects to
Phaedrus' speech, in particular, because he stresses only the virtues of
love — we might say love's good social consequences — instead of the emotion
itself, while Aristophanes would give us an account of the nature of love
without giving us an adequate account of its virtues. I think that Socrates is
right on both counts: virtues are not virtues by virtue of their consequences
(against Hume, for example), and an analysis of love that does not tell us
how important it is — not just why we are obsessed with it — is inadequate.
But we might also note that the usual characterization of the dialogue is extremely misleading, that is, as a ladder of relatively forgettable speeches
leading up to a culmination — the speech by Socrates that tells us exactly
what love is. The usual assumption that Socrates acts here as the spokesman for Plato's own view seems utterly unsupportable. In this dialogue,
even the minor speeches portray essential aspects of love. For example, the
banal speech of Eryximachus the physician clumsily captures today's obses-

504   sion with love as a physiological phenomenon with health as its virtue. Most important, however, is the fact that in this dialogue, Socrates does not have the last or the best word. Martha Nussbaum, Michael Gagarin, and others have shown, convincingly, I believe, that Alcibiades' tragi-comic description of Socrates at the end of the dialogue is essential, if not the key, to the *Symposium*.[16] Indeed, one might even make the case that Plato is partially opposed to Socrates and uses Alcibiades as his argument. Socrates' speech makes love virtuous but only by ignoring or denying most of its essential features—its sexual passion, its interpersonality, its particularity, and its apparent irrationality. *Erōs*, in short, becomes excitement about philosophy. It is impersonal, indifferent to any particular person, "above" bodily desire. In contrast, Alcibiades emphasizes the very personal, passionate, irrational, physical aspect of love, the love for a particular, incomparable human being, not a desexed universal. A similar foil for Socrates is the delightful story by Aristophanes, once he has gotten over his hiccups, in which we are all imagined to be the offspring of perfect (spherical) ancestral beings, split in two by Zeus, twisted around and now desperately looking for our other halves. This explains the "infinite longing" that every lover knows, which includes the longing for sexual union but by no means can be satisfied just with that. Aristophanes is about to continue his story near the end of the dialogue—perhaps completing the account by telling us about virtue—when he is interrupted by Alcibiades, wholly drunk, who launches into his paean for Socrates, contradicting everything Socrates has just been arguing. Socrates is sandwiched between Aristophanes and Alcibiades and it must be said that the conclusion of the debate is that Socrates is weird. Here, I think, is Plato's own voice, not as Socrates *via* Diotima, but as Alcibiades, presenting love as it is against the perhaps admirable but admittedly inhuman efforts of Socrates to say what it should be ideally. I think that this is important for our concern here, because the problem with understanding love as a virtue is not just its undervaluation as sex and emotion: it is also its excessive idealization as something more—or completely different from—sexuality and personal passion. If we think that the virtue of love is nothing less than the virtues of divinity itself, then love may be virtuous but it will have little to do with us and our petty particular affections. If love is a virtue in the sense that I want to defend here, it must apply to Alcibiades as well as Socrates. Socrates gives us a noble sense of the idealization that is part and parcel of *erōs* but I think that we can safely say that he goes too far in abandoning the eroticism of the particular.

The History of Love

Having said all this, we may now agree that the Western concept of love (in its heterosexual and humanistic aspects) was—if not "invented" or "discovered"—at least developed in the twelfth century as never before. Only at that late date was man able to begin thinking consecutively about ways of harmonizing sexual impulses with idealistic motives, of justifying amorous intimacy not as a means of preserving the race, or glorifying God, or attaining some ulterior metaphysical object but rather as an end in itself that made life worth living.[17]

Irving Singer

The virtues, according to Alasdair MacIntyre, are historical. They perform different functions in different societies, and one would not expect the virtues of a warrior in Homeric Greece to be similar to those of a gentleman in Jane Austen's England. Love as a virtue is also functional and historical. Sexuality "fits" into different societies in different ways, and conceptions of love and marriage vary accordingly. However "obvious" the universal function of uninterrupted and unhampered heterosexual intercourse may be in the preservation of every society, sexual desire is virtually never limited to this end, and the myriad courtship rituals, mores, and emotions invented by human cultures attest to the variety of ends to which this basic *ur-lust* can be employed. The virtues of love, accordingly, are the intrinsic ends which *erōs* serves, one of which may be, as Stendhal used to argue, its existence for its own sake.

Sexual desire may seem like something of a constant through history, but the objects of desire (obviously) and the source, nature, and vicissitudes of that desire vary as much as societies and their philosophies. Love is defined not primarily by sex or the libido but by ideas, and romantic love, which is a very modern (eighteenth century) concept, involves certain specific ideas about sex, gender, marriage, and the meaning of life as well as the perennial promptings of biology. Strictly speaking, there is nothing in the *Symposium* (or anywhere else before the seventeenth century) about romantic love. Romantic love is part and parcel of Romanticism, a distinctively modern movement. It presupposes an unusually strong conception of privacy and individual autonomy, a relatively novel celebration of the emotions for their own sake, and a dramatic metaphysics of unity—of which sexual unity in love is a particularly exciting and tangible example. (Compare Hegel, "In love the separate does still remain, but as something united and no longer as something separate," or Shelley, "one soul of interwoven flame.") The speakers in Plato's *Symposium* praised courage, education, and wisdom as the virtues of love, but they had little to say of the virtues of heterosexuality (apart, of course, from its function of producing more Athenians). Charity, devotion, and chastity were praised as virtues of Christian love, but there was too little to say about the joys of sexuality. (Consider the classic seventeenth-century preface: "Let virtue be rewarded, vice be punished, and chastity treated as it deserves.") Romantic love has among its virtues the metaphysical legitimization of sexual desire, the motivation for marriage, and the equalization of the sexes, surely no part of Greek love and doubtful in traditional Christian love. (Contemporary Christian concepts of love, of course, have adopted and incorporated much of the romantic ideology.) Romantic love has as its virtue the expansion of the self to include another, hardly necessary in societies in which citizenship and other memberships provided all of the shared identity one could possibly imagine. Romantic love has as a virtue the expression of what we opaquely call "the inner self," again not a virtue that would have been understood in less psychological and more socially minded societies. To put the matter bluntly (and without argument), romantic love came of age only when newly industrialized and increasingly anonymous societies fostered the economically independent and socially shrunken ("nuclear") family, when women as well as men were permitted considerable personal *choice* in their marriage partners, when romantic love novels spread the gospel to the multitude of women of the middle class (whereas courtly love had been the privilege of a few aristocratic heroines), and, philosophically most important, when the now many centuries old contrast between sacred and profane love had broken down and been synthesized in a secular mode (like so many ideas in the Enlightenment). Romantic love depended on what Robert Stone has called "affective individualism," an attitude to the individual and the importance of his or her emotions that did not and could not have arisen until modern times.

It is essential that we keep the historical character of love in mind so that we do not get seduced by an idea that might well be prompted by the seeming timelessness of the *Symposium* or the always familiar (and cynical) view that love is nothing but hormonal agitation coupled with the uncertainties and frustrations of courtship—or as Freud put it, "lust plus the ordeal of civility." This idea is that love is itself something timeless and universal, a singular phenomenon which varies only in its culturization and interpretation but is otherwise universally the same. In fact, even the *Symposium* provides us with no fewer than half-a-dozen conceptions of love, and it is not clear to what extent these are disagreements about the true nature of *erōs* or different kinds of *erōs*. Socrates, in particular, is certainly giving us a new conception, a "persuasive definition." Historically, we find these variations played out on a grand scale, with Socrates setting the stage for an ethereal concept of love that comes of age with Christian theology, Alcibiades displaying the "languor" and its imagery that would come to characterize late medieval courtly love, and Aristophanes anticipating modern romantic love. But paganism, even in Plato, cannot begin to capture the range and complexity of romantic conceptions of love in modern times. To understand erotic love as we know it, it is necessary to appreciate the power of the long, if often antagonistic, history of Christian conceptions of love.

The history of erotic love has been determined not only by the fact that Christian thought demeaned sexual love as such but also by the Christian emphasis on the "inner" individual soul and the importance of such emotions as faith and devotion. The genius of Christianity was that it coopted erotic love and turned it into something else, still the love of one's fellow man and even perhaps the love of one's wife or husband, but no longer particularly sexual, no longer personal, no longer merely human. In its positive presentation, love became a form of idealization, even worship, an attempt to transcend not only oneself and one's own self-interests but also the limited self-interests of an *égoisme-à-deux*. It did not have to deny the sexual or the personal so much as the Christian conception of love aimed always "higher," toward not just virtue or happiness but perfection itself. On the negative side, it must be said (and often has been) that the Christian conception of love was also brutal and inhuman, denying not only our "natural" impulses but even the conception of a loving marriage as such. Saint Paul's advice, "better to marry than to burn," was one of the more generous sentiments governing this revised concept of love. Tertullian was not alone in insisting that even to look on one's wife with lust was a sin. Aristophanes' thesis that lovers experience that "infinite longing" which manifests and only momentarily satisfies itself in sex would be lost here. Indeed all such desires become antithetical to love, not an expression of it. To Nietzsche's observation that Christianity is Platonism for the masses we might add that because of Christian psychology, we now have psychoanalysis.

Christian theology may have encouraged and revered love above all else, but it was not erotic love that flourished. Alternative names for love—"*caritas*" and "*agapé*"—may have clarified the scholarship but not the phenomenology of the emotion. When one looked lovingly at another, who could say whether the feeling was divine *caritas* or nasty *erōs*, except that one knew that one *should* feel the former. An entire literature grew up, from which some of our favorite first-date dialogues are derived, distinguishing loving from sexual desire as if these were not only always distinguishable but even opposed. By the fourteenth century, this confusion had become canonized as Platonic love, for which Plato (or at least Socrates) is indeed to blame. Platonic love dispensed with Agathon, Aristophanes, and the others, took Diotima (whose name means "honor the god") at her word, and substituted Christian faith for pagan wisdom. Love had become even more idealized than Socrates had urged, but what had been gained in spirituality was more than lost in the denial of the erotic passions and the importance of happy human relationships for their own sake.

It was in reaction to this insensitivity to human desires and affections that courtly love was directed in the twelfth century. Romantic love is often identified historically with courtly love—which is rightly recognized as its significant late medieval predecessor. But the two are quite distinct, as Irving Singer has argued in his *Nature of Love*.[18] The two are often conflated (e.g., by Denis de Rougemont, in his much celebrated but dubious study of the subject),[19] and courtly love, in particular, is often reduced to the ridiculous image of the horny troubadour singing pathetically before the (very tall) tower of some inevitably fair but also unavailable lady. The name "courtly love," it should be noted, was not employed by the participants themselves but rather was applied much later—in the romantic period—by Gaston Paris, who used it to refer to the hardly frustrated or separated couple of Lancelot and Guinevere. Indeed, the paradigm of courtly love began not as chaste and frustrated (if poetic) desire but as secret, adulterous, and all-embracing illicit love. (C. S. Lewis continues this paradigm well into this century.)

Socially, courtly love was a plaything of the upper class. It was as much talk (and crooning) as action, and, perhaps most important, it was wholly distinct from, even opposed to, marriage. (It is not surprising that the texts and theories of the male troubadours—Andreas Capellanus, especially—were typically drawn from the adulterous advice of Ovid. But their female counterparts—Eleanor of Aquitaine, for example—did not take love and marriage any more seriously, in part because they were almost always already married.) What is often said of courtly love—that it rarely resulted in

consummation—is not true. Indeed, if anything, one might say that courtly love was *more* obsessed with sex than contemporary romantic love. The
fact that consummation came slowly and after considerable effort does not
eclipse the fact that consummation was the explicit and sometimes single
end of the endeavor.

Much of the history of our changing conceptions of love has to do with
the effort to bring together and synthesize the idealization suggested by
Plato and Christian love with the very real demands and desires of a couple
in love. The virtue of "courtly love" was its effort to carry out this synthesis
and at the same time introduce some sexual and aesthetic satisfaction into
a world of arranged marriages based wholly on social, political, and economic considerations (thus the separation—if not opposition—between
courtly love and marriage). It is courtly love that also introduces the essential romantic conception of erotic love as good in itself, a conception that
one does not find in the teleology of the *Symposium* and certainly does not
find in Christian concepts of love. In his study, Singer formulates five general features of love that characterize the courtly: (1) that sexual love between men and women is *itself* an ideal worth striving for, (2) that love en-
nobles both lover and beloved, (3) that sexual love cannot be reduced to
mere libidinal impulse, (4) that love has to do with courtship but not (necessarily) with marriage, and (5) that love involves a "holy oneness" between
man and woman.[20] It should be clear, as Singer goes on to argue in great
detail, how courtly love constituted an attempt to synthesize both pagan
and Christian conceptions of love, incorporating both ethical ideals and
sexual desire. The first feature signals a radical challenge to the traditional
Christian view of love, while the third is a rebuke of the vulgar view that
love is nothing but sexual desire. It is worth noting that the last feature
listed is very much in tune with much of Christian theology, and indeed,
the Aristophanic notion of love as a "union" would continue to be one of
the central but most difficult (and therefore often "magical" or "mystical")
themes of love through the romantic period. I shall try to develop this idea
more literally in the following section.

The distinction between love and marriage is of particular interest in
the history of love, and it is worth noting that these have not always been
linked so essentially as "horse and carriage," as one popular song would
have it. In Plato, for obvious reasons, the question of marriage did not even
arise in considerations of *erōs* (at least, for that form of *erōs* that was worthy of philosophical consideration). Ovid considered love and marriage as
opposites, although the marriage of one's intended did provide a challeng-

ing obstacle and thereby an additional source of excitement. The long history of marriage as a sacrament has little to say about sexual love and sometimes has much to say against it, and by the time of courtly love, courtship typically provided an alternative to loveless marriage rather than a prelude to marriage or — almost unheard of — the content of marriage itself. Gaston Paris and C. S. Lewis's paradigm of Lancelot and Guinevere may have represented excessive antagonism between love and all social and religious institutions and obligations, especially marriage, but courtly love cannot be conceived — whatever else it may have been — as a prelude to or a legitimate reason for marriage. Indeed, the idea that marriage is the culmination of love becomes popular only in the seventeenth century or so, as exemplified in Shakespeare's plays, especially in the comedies. And compared to the rigid ethos of Jane Austen's novels, for example, it must be said that our current understanding of love and marriage is quite in flux and confused.

Romantic love, we may now say, is the historical result of a long and painful synthesis between erotic pagan love and idealistic Christian love or, ahistorically, between Aristophanes and Alcibiades on the one hand and Socrates on the other. It is not just sexual, or even primarily sexual, but an idealistic up-dating of the pagan virtues of cultivation and sensuousness and Christian devotion and fidelity in the modern context of individual privacy, autonomy, and affectivity. To think that romantic love is without virtue is to grossly mistake romance with sexual recreation or unrealistic idealization and ignore the whole historical development that lies behind even the most ordinary love affair. But it is time to say something more about the nature of romantic love as such.

What is Romantic Love?

Love is the expression of an ancient need, that human desire was originally one and we were whole, and the desire and the pursuit of the whole is called love.[21]

Aristophanes

Romantic love, we may need to remind ourselves, is an emotion — an ordinary and very common emotion, even if it is experienced by most of us but once or twice in a lifetime. It is not a "force" or a "mystery." Like all emotions, it is largely learned, typically obsessive, peculiar to certain kinds of cultures with certain brands of philosophy. I will not here rehearse once again my usual analysis of emotion as a complex of judgments, desires, and values. Let me just claim, without argument, the weaker thesis that every emotion presupposes, if it is not composed of, a set of specifiable concepts (e.g., anger as offense, sadness as loss, jealousy as the threat of loss) and more or less specific desires and values, such as revenge in anger, care in sadness, possessiveness in jealousy. Love, accordingly, can and must be ana-lyzed in terms of such a set of concepts and desires, some of which are obvi-ous, the more interesting perhaps not so. It is evident enough that one set of desires in romantic love is the desire to be with, the desire to touch, the desire to caress, and here we are immediately reminded of Aristophanes' lesson: that which manifests itself as a sexual urge in love is actually some-thing much more, a desire to be reunited with, to be one with, one's love. From this, I want to suggest what I take to be the dominant conceptual in-gredient in romantic love, which is just this urge for *shared identity*, a kind of *ontological dependency*. The challenge, however, is to get beyond this familiar idea (and its kindred characterizations as a "union," "a merger of souls," etc.) and explain exactly what "identity" could possibly mean in this context. Aristophanes' wonderful metaphor is still a metaphor, and whether or not we would want Hephaestus to weld the two of us together, body and soul, the image does not do our understanding much good. Aris-tophanes claims that we want the impossible, indeed the unimaginable; he does not give us any indication of how we might in fact share an identity, over and above brief and not always well-coordinated unifications of the flesh.

More to the point, one might well quote Cathy's climactic revelation in *Wuthering Heights*: "I *am* Heathcliff—he's always, always in my mind— not as a pleasure, anymore than I am always a pleasure to myself—but as my own being." Here we have more than a hint of what is involved in shared identity, not a mystical union nor a frustrated physicality but a sense of presence, always "in mind," defining one's sense of self to one's self. Love is just this shared identity, and the desires of love—including especially the strong nonphysiological desire for sexual intercourse—can best be under-stood with reference to this strange but not at all unfamiliar concept. I can-not do justice to this challenge here, but let me at least present the thesis: Shared identity is the intention of love, and the virtues of love are essen-tially the virtues of this intended identity. This is not to deny or neglect sex but to give it a context. Nor does this give away too much to marriage (which is a legal identity) but it does explain how romantic love and mar-

riage have come so close together, the latter now considered to be the culmination of the former.

Before we say any more, however, let me express a Socratic caveat: I
think that it is necessary to display love as it is by itself, without confusing it
with all of the other Good Things we would like and expect to go with it—
companionship, great sex, friendship, someone to travel with, someone
who really cares, and, ultimately, marriage. Of course we want these
things, and preferably all in the same package, but love can and must be
understood apart from all of them. Without being depressing, let us remind ourselves that love often goes wrong, that love can be unrequited,
that love can interfere with or at least it does not assure satisfying sex, that
love and friendship are sometimes opposed, that love can be very lonely,
that love can be not only obsessive but insane. Not that love must be or often is all of these, but it can be, and so let us look at the virtues of love itself,
as Socrates insisted, not in terms of its consequences or its most desirable
embellishments.

The nature of identity in love, briefly described, is this. (You will note,
no doubt, a certain debt to Hegel and Sartre in what follows.) We define
ourselves, not just in our own terms (as adolescent existentialists and pop-
psychologists may argue) but in terms of each other. The virtues, in a society such as Aristotle's, are defined and assigned communally; the idea of
"private" virtues would be incomprehensible. But we distinguish public
and private with a vengeance, and we typically value our private, personal character more highly than our public persona, which is sometimes
thought to be superficial, impersonal, "plastic," and merely manipulative,
instrumental. A person's character is best determined by those who "really
know him," and it is not odd to us that a person generally known as a bastard might be thought to be a good person just on the testimony of a wife, a
husband, or a close friend. ("But if you knew Johnny as I do, you would see
that. . . .") In a fragmented world so built on intimate privacies, love even
more than family and friendship determines selfhood. Love is just this determining of selfhood. When we talk about "the real self" or "being true to
ourselves," what we often mean is being true to the image of ourselves that
we share with those we love most. We say, and are expected to say, that the
self we display in public performance, the self we present on the job, the
self we show to acquaintances, is not real. We sometimes take great pains to
prove that the self we share with our family (a historical kind of love) is no
longer the self that we consider real. Nor is it any surprise that the self we
would like to think of as most real is the self that emerges in intimacy, and

its virtues are the typically private virtues of honesty in feeling and expression, interpersonal passion, tenderness, and sensitivity.

The idea of an Aristophanic union—the reunification of two halves that already belong together—is charming and suggestive, but it is only half of the story. The other half starts with the fact of our differences and our stubbornness, and how we may ill fit together even after years of compromise and cohabitation. The freedom of choice that allows us virtually unrestricted range for our romantic intentions also raises the possibility—which was one of the suppositions of courtly love as well—that our choice will often be difficult, if not socially prohibited. (Who was the one girl in Verona that young Romeo should not have chosen? And the one woman wholly forbidden to Lancelot?) The process of mutual self-identification runs into conflict with one of its own presuppositions—the ideal of autonomous individualism. The selves that are to merge do not have the advantage of having adjusted to and complemented each other when the self was still flexible and only partially formed—as in societies where families arrange marriages between children who have grown up together. And whatever the nostalgic popularity of "first love" and the Romeo and Juliet paradigm, the truth is that most of us fall in love well advanced in our development, even into old age, when the self is full-formed and complementarity is more often an exercise in compromise. The development of love is consequently defined by a *dialectic*, often tender but sometimes ontologically vicious, in which each lover struggles for control over shared and reciprocal self-images, resists them, revises them, rejects them. For this reason, love—unlike many other emotions—takes time. It does not make sense to say of love, as it does of anger, that one was in love for fifteen minutes but then calmed down. But neither is this to say that there is no such thing as unrequited love, or that unrequited love is not love, for the dialectic, complete with resistance and conflict, can go on just as well in one soul as in two. Granted that the drama may be a bit impoverished, but as Stendhal often argued, the imagination may be enriched thereby. Or as Goethe once said, "If I love you, what business is that of yours?"

In Pursuit of a Passion (Conclusion)

True love, whatever is said of it, will always be honored by men; for although its transports lead us astray, although it does not exclude odious qualities from the heart that feels it—and even produces them—it nev-

ertheless always presupposes estimable qualities without which one
would not be in a condition to feel it.[22]
Jean-Jacques Rousseau

Love, briefly summarized, is a dialectical process of (mutually) reconceived
selfhood with a long and varied history. As such, it is much more than a
feeling and it need not be at all capricious or unintelligent or disruptive.
But the idea that love is concerned with selfhood might suggest that love is
essentially self-love, casting love in the role of a vice rather than a virtue.
And the suggestion that love is essentially the reconception and determination of oneself through another looks dangerously similar to some familiar
definitions of narcissism. But self-reference entails neither cynicism nor
narcissism. Although one does see oneself through the other on this analysis, and although as in narcissism the idea of "separation of subject and object" is greatly obscured, love as mutual self-defining reflection does not
encourage either vicious or clinical conclusions. Unlike narcissism, love
takes the other as its standard, not just as its mirror, which is why the
courtly lovers called it "devotion" (as in devoting oneself to God) and why
Stendhal—himself an accomplished narcissist—called "passion-love" the
one wholly unselfish experience. Love is not selfless but it is nevertheless the
antithesis of selfishness. It embodies an expansion of self, modest, perhaps,
but what it lacks in scope it more than makes up for in motivation.

The virtues of love can be understood in terms of this sense of this limited but passionate self-expansion. In a fragmented and mobile society, romantic love allows us to forge intensive ties to others, even to strangers.
There is much talk in ethics today of "communitarian" as opposed to indi-
vidualistic frameworks, but the fact is that passionately united community
larger than a small circle of carefully chosen friends strikes most of us as
oppressive if not dangerous. One may well lament the lack of public virtues
or the priority of private virtues, but the fact is that the primacy of privacy
is where we must now begin. Nor should one in Kantian enthusiasm for the
universal ignore the dramatic importance of the modest move from caring
only about oneself to caring about someone else. The expansion of selfhood
in love may be modest but, in today's climate of personal greed and "self-
fulfillment," it is for many successful citizens today one of the last virtues
left standing.

Romantic love is a powerful emotional ally—far better than communal
indignation and shared resentment—in breaking down the isolating individualism that has become the dubious heir of some of our favorite tradi-

tional values. But we remain staunch individualists, and the extent to which we will allow our virtues to be publicly determined remains limited indeed. But too many authors in recent years have simply dismissed such intimacies as love as not virtuous at all, when a more just judgment would seem to be that love is a particularly appropriate virtue in a society such as ours. With this it is essential to revise our concept of virtue. Some important virtues are not public, so we can no longer use Aristotle, nor even Hume, as our guide. Being virtuous does not mean for us "fitting into" the community; good character is rather privately determined by loving and being loved. This may make (some) virtues subjective, but subjectivity here does not mean capricious, incommensurable, eccentric, or "merely emotional"; it rather means private and personal. Our presumption is that a good person is not a public figure but a private one. Perhaps the accompanying assumption, no doubt false, is that a person who is loving in private will be a good person in public too.

There are other virtues of love, beyond this minimal self-expansion. We might, for instance, mention the sense of self-awareness that goes along with this dramatization of self and the often described sense of self-improvement that is its consequence, something argued by the early speakers in the *Symposium* and often propounded by some of the courtly troubadours. To love is to be intensely conscious of one's own "worth" and greatly concerned with one's virtues (not only charms) where being in love is already considered the first great step in the teleology of self-realization. ("Love me as I am" is not an expression or an instruction of love but rather a defensive reaction.) We might mention, too, the healthy and positive outlook on the world that often accompanies love, a form of generalized idealization that—while it might not take on the cosmic form suggested by Hegel in his early writings—nonetheless counters the cynicism and suspicion that have become the marks of wisdom in our society.

So too we might mention the fact that love is a remarkably inspirational and creative emotion—though one might somewhat cynically speculate that envy and resentment may be its betters in this regard. (It was not just Iago's intelligence that made him more than a match for Othello; he had his envy to motivate him.) The inspirational qualities of love and its impulse to creativity do not just refer, of course, to those who are particularly gifted, for we find at least attempts at poetic self-expression in even the most philistine lovers. Indeed, regardless of the quality of the products of such inspiration, one might argue—following Stendhal—that the exhilaration and inspiration of love is itself its greatest virtue, a virtue that is often ignored in the age-old over-appreciation for philosophical *apatheia*. I too would want to argue that romantic love is a virtue just because it is exciting. One rarely finds philosophers taking excitement as a virtue (Nietzsche being the most obvious exception), but I think many of us do in fact take energy, vitality, being "turned on" as virtuous, whatever might result and however exhausting. I think we ought to wonder about the frequent if implicit emphasis on dullness as a prominent feature of the virtues.

So too we might note the low esteem of sexuality in discussions of virtue. Romantic love is sexual love, and here too we can appreciate the resistance of traditionally modest moral philosophers. Sex, in the history of ethics, has been treated as a biological urge, a force (often an inhuman force) to be controlled. So treated, it is hard to see any virtue in it. Ethical questions about sex tend to focus on its restriction, and sexual love is offered at best as a legitimization of sex but still hardly a virtue. So too we should vehemently reject that picture of sex, evidently held by chaste Kant, which takes intercourse to be either a biological function (reproduction or, sanctioned by God, "procreation") or mere recreation—what Kant considered mutual masturbation. Either way, sex loses any status in ethics and, more mysteriously, loses its immediate connection with love (the conceptual problem that faced courtly love). But sex, I would argue, ought to be viewed not as an urge and neither as procreation nor recreation but rather as expression, defined neither by physiology nor by pleasure but rather circumscribed by ideas and what is expressed. In particular, sex is (or can be) an expression of love, though this is just part of the story (as Sartre in particular has gruesomely argued). But the point that should be made here is that love is a virtue in part because of and not despite its sexuality. My Nietzschean premise (though one can find a sublimated version of it in Spinoza) is that the virtues can be exhilarating, and this is (in part) what makes them virtues.

The foregoing points would be greatly misunderstood if they were taken to suggest that erotic love is some sort of "trump" virtue, more important than any others. Virtues can conflict, and any one virtue may be but a negligible exception in an otherwise wholly flawed or pathological character. To pretend that the private joys and obsessions of love raise no questions in terms of public engagement, to move from the objection that love has been neglected in ethics to the insistence that such personal emotions take the place of policy decisions in the public sphere, would be irresponsible. But the example of love makes it evident that the traditional objections to subjectivity in ethics, that appeal to emotions is whimsical, not serious and not subject to criticism, will not bear scrutiny. And against much of recent "virtue ethics," love seems to show that virtues should not be understood as traits (for no matter how "loving" one may be, the only virtue in love is actually loving), nor are all virtues instantiations of universal principles, as Frankena, for example, has argued.[23] It has too long been claimed without argument that subjectivity and emotion in ethics inevitably mean selfishness, prejudice, chaos, violence, and destruction, but the truth is that the nature of love, at least, is quite the opposite, not at all selfish, often tender, and creative. Indeed, against the obsessive emphasis on objectivity and impersonal equality in ethics, the aim of love is to *make* a single person extraordinary and to reconceptualize oneself in his or her terms, to *create* an escape from the anonymity of the Kantian moral world and thrive in a world *à deux* of one's own. Of course, to deny that love can go wrong — against the cumulative evidence of ten thousand romantic novels — would be absurd. It can destroy as well as conjoin relationships, and it can ruin as well as enhance a life. Yes, love can be dangerous, but why have we so long accepted the idea that the virtuous life is simple and uncomplicated rather than, as Nietzsche used to say, a work of romantic art? For love is a virtue as much of the imagination as of morals.

Notes

[1]I. Kant, *The Groundwork of the Metaphysics of Morals*, trans. H. J. Paton (New York: Harper & Row, 1964), p. 67 (p. 13 of the standard German edition).

[2]Plato, *The Symposium*, trans. W. Hamilton (London: Penguin Classics, 1951), p. 43.

[3]A. Schopenhauer, *The World as Will and Representation*, trans. E. Payne (New York, 1958), quoted in *Sexual Love and Western Morality*, ed. D. Verene (New York: Harper & Row, 1972), p. 175.

[4]La Rochefoucauld, *Maxims*, trans. J. Heayd (Boston and New York: Houghton Mifflin, 1917), no. 68.

[5]I. Kant, *Lectures on Ethics*, trans. L. Infield (Indianapolis, 1963), p. 164.

[6]J. Milton, *Paradise Lost* (New York: Random House, 1969), bk. 8, lines 383-85.

[7]F. Nietzsche, *The Antichrist*, trans. H. Kaufmann (New York, 1954), sect. 11.

[8]Bernard Williams, "Morality and the Emotions," in *Problems of the Self* (Cambridge: Cambridge University Press, 1973).

[9]Richard Taylor, *Good and Evil* (New York: Macmillan, 1970), p. xii.

[10]Barbara Herman, "The Practice of Moral Judgment," *Journal of Philosophy* 82, no. 8 (1985).

[11]Bernard Gert, *The Moral Rules* (New York: Harper & Row, 1973), p. 143.

[12]Edward Sankowski, "Love and Moral Obligation" and "Responsibility of Persons for their Emotions," in *Canadian Journal of Philosophy* 7 (1977): 829-40.

[13]G. W. F. Hegel, *Early Theological Manuscripts*, trans. T. Knox (Philadelphia: University of Pennsylvania Press, 1971), p. 305.

518   ¹⁴Amelie Rorty, "Explaining Emotions," in *Explaining Emotions* (Berkeley: University of California Press, 1980).

¹⁵M. Nussbaum, "The Speech of Alcibiades," *Philosophy and Literature* 3, no. 2 (1979).

¹⁶Ibid., and Michael Gagarin, "Socrates' Hubris and Alcibiades' Failure," *Phoenix* 31 (1977).

¹⁷I. Singer, *The Nature of Love*, vol. 2 (Chicago: University of Chicago Press, 1986), pp. 35–36.

¹⁸Ibid.

¹⁹Denis de Rougemont, *Love in the Western World* (New York: Harper & Row, 1974).

²⁰Singer, *Nature of Love*, pp. 22–23.

²¹*Symposium*, 64.

²²J. J. Rousseau, *Emile*, trans. A. Bloom (New York: Basic Books, 1979), p. 214.

²³William Frankena, *Ethics* (Englewood Cliffs, N. J.: Prentice-Hall, 1973), and in a recent newsletter to University of Michigan Philosophy Department alumni.

Source Notes and Acknowledgments

Plato: From *Symposium*, translated by A. Nehamas and P. Woodruff, copyright 1989. Reprinted with permission of Hackett Publishing Company, Inc., Indianapolis, Ind., and Cambridge, Mass.

Sappho: Poems translated by Jon Solomon, University of Arizona Classics Department, especially for this volume.

Theano: From *A History of Women Philosophers*, vol. 1, edited by Mary Ellen Waithe, translated by Vicki Lynn Harper (Dordrecht: Martinus Nijhoff, 1987), pp. 46–48. Reprinted by permission of Kluwer Academic Publishers.

Ovid: From *The Art of Love*, translated by Rolfe Humphries, copyright 1957. Reprinted by permission of Indiana University Press.

Augustine: From *The City of God*, reprinted by permission of the publishers and the Loeb Classical Library from Augustine, *The City of God*, translated by Philip Levine, Cambridge, Mass.: Harvard University Press, 1966.

Heloise and Abelard: From *Letters of Abelard and Heloise* (New York: J. Hardcastle, 1808).

Andreas Capellanus: From *On Love*, translated by John Jay Parry, copyright 1941 by Columbia University Press. Reprinted by permission of Columbia University Press.

John Milton: From "The Doctrine and Discipline of Divorce," in *Complete Poetry and Selected Prose of Milton* (New York: Modern Library, 1950), pp. 615–662.

Baruch Spinoza: From *Ethics*, in *The Rationalists*, translated by R. H. M. Elwes (New York: Doubleday/Dolphin, 1960).

520   Jean-Jacques Rousseau: From *Emile*: Introduction, translation, and notes by Allan Bloom. Foreword, introduction, English translation, and notes copyright 1979 by Basic Books, Inc. Reprinted by permission of Basic Books, Inc., Publishers, New York. From *New Heloise*: translated and abridged by Judith H. McDowell, University Park and London: The Pennsylvania State University Press, pp. 67–69, 95–97, and 114–116. Copyright 1968. Reproduced by permission of the publisher. From the *Second Discourse*: edited by Roger D. Masters, translated by Judith R. Masters and Roger D. Masters, St. Martin's Press, 1964.

G. W. F. Hegel: From *Early Theological Writings*, translated by T. M. Knox. Copyright 1948 by the University of Chicago, 1961 by Harper Torchbooks. Reprinted by permission of Harper and Row, Publishers, Inc.

Arthur Schopenhauer: From *World as Will and Idea*, from "The Metaphysics of the Love of the Sexes," in *The Works of Schopenhauer*, abridged ed., edited by Will Durant (New York: Frederick Ungar, 1928), pp. 330–363.

Stendhal: From *On Love*, translated by H. B. V. Scott-Moncrieff and C. K. Scott-Moncrieff (New York: Grosset and Dunlap, 1967).

Friedrich Nietzsche: From *Daybreak: Thoughts on the Prejudices of Morality*, translated by R. J. Hollingdale. Copyright 1982 by Cambridge University Press. Reprinted by permission of Cambridge University Press. From *The Joyful Wisdom*, translated by Thomas Common, in *The Complete Works of Friedrich Nietzsche*, edited by Oscar Levy (Edinburgh: T. N. Foulis, 1910), pp. 51–323. From *Beyond Good and Evil*, translated by Helen Zimmern (New York: Boni and Liveright, 1907). Selections from *Thus Spake Zarathustra* and *Twilight of the Idols* from *The Portable Nietzsche*, translated by Walter Kaufmann, copyright 1968. Reprinted by permission of Penguin Books USA, Inc. From *Ecce Homo*, translated by Walter Kaufmann (together with *On the Genealogy of Morals*, translated by Walter Kaufmann and R. J. Hollingdale), edited by Walter Kaufmann (New York: Random House, 1967).

Sigmund Freud: "On the Universal Tendency to Debasement in the Sphere of Love," "On Narcissism: An Introduction," and " 'Civilized' Sexual Morality and Modern Nervous Illness," from *The Standard Edition of the*

Complete Psychological Works of Sigmund Freud, translated and edited by
James Strachey (1953–1974). Reprinted by permission of Sigmund Freud
copyrights, the Institute of Psycho-Analysis, and Hogarth Press.

Carl Jung: "Marriage as a Psychological Relationship," from *The Collected
Works of C. G. Jung*, translated by R. F. C. Hull, Bollingen Series 20, vol.
17: *The Development of Personality*. Copyright 1954. Copyright renewed
1982 by Princeton University Press.

Karen Horney: From "The Overvaluation of Love: A Study of a Common
Present-Day Type," *Psychoanalytic Quarterly* 3 (1934): 605–638. Copyright
Association for the Advancement of Psychoanalysis of the Karen Horney
Psychoanalytic Institute and Center.

Rainer Maria Rilke: Poems from *Duino Elegies* and *New Poems* (1907);
translations are by William Gass and are reprinted with his permission.

Emma Goldman: "On the Tragedy of Women's Emancipation" and "Marriage and Love," from *Red Emma Speaks*, edited by Alix Kates Shulman
(New York: Random House, 1972).

Denis de Rougemont: From *Love in the Western World*, copyright 1940,
1956 by Pantheon Books, Inc. Reprinted by permission of Pantheon Books,
a division of Random House, Inc.

D. H. Lawrence: "The Mess of Love," from *Complete Poems of D. H. Lawrence*. Collected and edited by Vivian de Sola Pinto and F. Warren Roberts. Copyright 1964, 1971 by Angelo Ravagli and C. M. Weekley, execu-
tors of the Estate of Frieda Lawrence Ravagli. Reprinted by permission of
Viking Penguin, a division of Penguin Books USA, Inc. From *Women in
Love* by D. H. Lawrence. Copyright 1920, 1922 by D. H. Lawrence. Copyright renewed 1948, 1950 by Frieda Lawrence. Reprinted by permission of
Viking Penguin, a division of Penguin Books USA, Inc.

Jean-Paul Sartre: From *Being and Nothingness*, translated by Hazel E.
Barnes, 1956, Philosophical Library. Reprinted by permission of Philosophical Library.

Simone de Beauvoir: From *The Second Sex*, translated and edited by H.
M. Parshley. Copyright 1952 by Alfred A. Knopf Inc. Reprinted by permission of the publisher.

522   Philip Slater: From *The Pursuit of Loneliness*, copyright 1970, 1976 by Philip E. Slater. Reprinted by permission of Beacon Press.

Shulamith Firestone: From *The Dialectic of Sex*, copyright 1970. Reprinted by permission of William Morrow and Co., Inc.

Irving Singer: From the introduction to volume 1 of *The Nature of Love*, 2d edition, copyright 1966, 1984 by Irving Singer. Reprinted by permission of the University of Chicago Press.

Martha Nussbaum: "The Speech of Alcibiades: A Reading of Plato's *Symposium*," *Philosophy and Literature* 3, 2(1979):131–69. Reprinted by permission of the Johns Hopkins University Press.

Elizabeth Rapaport: "On the Future of Love: Rousseau and the Radical Feminists," first published in *Philosophical Forum* 5:1-2 (Fall-Winter) 1973. Reprinted with permission of *Philosophical Forum*.

Robert Nozick: "Love's Bond," from *The Examined Life*, copyright 1989 by Robert Nozick. Reprinted by permission of Simon & Schuster, Inc.

Robert C. Solomon: "The Virtue of (Erotic) Love," from *Ethical Theory: Character and Virtue, Midwest Studies in Philosophy* 13, pp. 12-31. Reprinted by permission of the publisher.